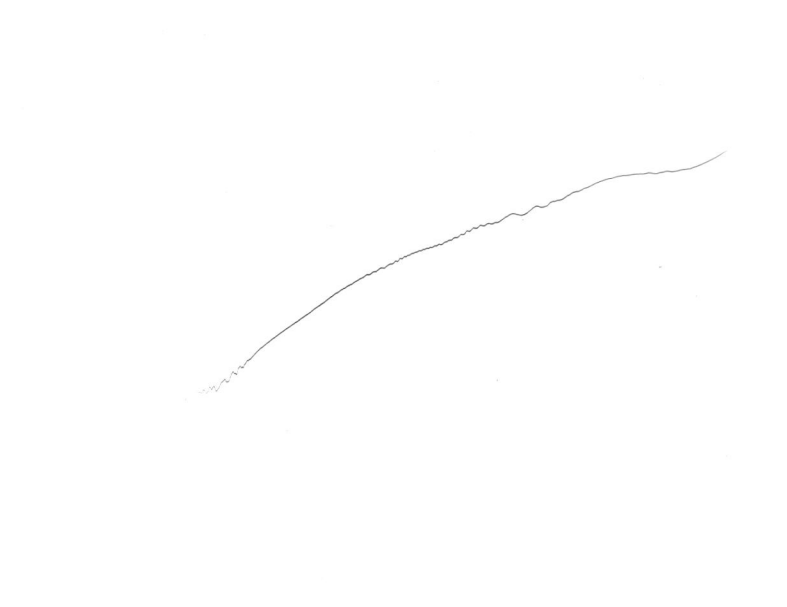

Patent Settlements in the Pharmaceutical Industry under US Antitrust and EU Competition Law

International Competition Law Series

VOLUME 75

Editor

In its series editor, Alastair Sutton, Kluwer is fortunate to engage and benefit from the experience and expertise of one of the world's outstanding authorities on European Union and international economic law.

Introduction

In their efforts to regulate competition in an increasingly complex business environment, competition authorities face a daunting task. The European Commission and Courts, as well as national courts and legislatures, policymakers, and regulators, are constantly proposing, enacting, reviewing, and enforcing new legal measures, often addressing novel situations. Every industry and service is affected.

Contents/Subjects

With many titles currently available and new ones appearing regularly, the series' coverage includes detailed analyses of relevant legislation and case law in major global trading jurisdictions, defences used in cases involving the digital network economy, state aid cases, enforcement methodologies and a great deal more.

Objective & Readership

The purpose of Kluwer's International Competition Law Series is to follow the ever-changing contours of this dynamic area of the law, keeping the practice in sharp focus so that practising lawyers (including in-house counsel) and academics can be assured of the most up-to-date guidance and sources, in the widest possible range of applications.

The titles published in this series are listed at the end of this volume.

Patent Settlements in the Pharmaceutical Industry under US Antitrust and EU Competition Law

Amalia Athanasiadou

Published by:
Kluwer Law International B.V.
PO Box 316
2400 AH Alphen aan den Rijn
The Netherlands
E-mail: international-sales@wolterskluwer.com
Website: lrus.wolterskluwer.com

Sold and distributed in North, Central and South America by:
Wolters Kluwer Legal & Regulatory U.S.
7201 McKinney Circle
Frederick, MD 21704
United States of America
Email: customer.service@wolterskluwer.com

Sold and distributed in all other countries by:
Air Business Subscriptions
Rockwood House
Haywards Heath
West Sussex
RH16 3DH
United Kingdom
Email: international-customerservice@wolterskluwer.com

Printed on acid-free paper.

ISBN 978-94-035-0113-0

e-Book: ISBN 978-94-035-0114-7
web-PDF: ISBN 978-94-035-0115-4

© 2018 Amalia Athanasiadou

All rights reserved. No part of this publication may be reproduced, stored in a retrieval system, or transmitted in any form or by any means, electronic, mechanical, photocopying, recording, or otherwise, without written permission from the publisher.

Permission to use this content must be obtained from the copyright owner. More information can be found at: lrus.wolterskluwer.com/policies/permissions-reprints-and-licensing

Printed in the United Kingdom.

To my parents Foteini & Sotiris,
To my brother Theo,
To Renato

Table of Contents

Preface	xxiii
List of Abbreviations	xxv
Acknowledgements	xxxi

Introduction			1
I	Patent Settlements Involving Reverse Payments		1
	A	Defining Reverse Payment Patent Settlements	1
	B	Problems and Challenges Raised by Reverse Payment Settlements	2
II	Background		3
	A	The Split of US Circuit Courts and the Resulting Uncertainty	3
	B	The Lack of EU Jurisprudence on Pharma Patent Settlements	4
III	Research Objectives		5
	A	Legitimate Versus Anticompetitive Settlements and Strategies	5
	B	Balancing Patent Law and Antitrust in the Applicable Tests	5
	C	Practical Guidance for the Pharmaceutical Industry	6
IV	Methodology		6
V	Outline		7

Part I
Pharma Innovation and Settlements — 9

Chapter 1
Pharma R&D and Settlements — 11

Introduction			11
Part 1	Risks and Costs in the Pharma Industry		11
	I	Challenges Faced by Drug Originators	11
		A The Immense Costs of Pharma Innovation	12

Table of Contents

			1	Research and Development Costs Globally	13
			2	Debating the Cost of Drug Development	14
			3	The Contribution of Government-Funded Investment in Pharma R&D	15
		B		The Decline in the R&D Performance of the Pharma Industry	16
			1	The Difficulties in Evaluating Pharma's Innovative Performance	17
			2	The Patent Cliff and Patenting Strategies	18
		C		Does the Patent System Incentivise Innovation?	19
			1	The Difference Between Pharma and Other Industries	20
			2	The Impact of the Breadth and Duration of Patent Protection on Innovation	22
			3	Antitrust Law Scrutiny and Its Role in Incentivising Innovation	24
	II			Generic Drug Manufacturers and Generic Entry	25
		A		The Extent and Timing of Generic Entry	25
		B		The Effects of Generic Entry	26
			1	Generic Penetration to the Market and Its Effects on Drug Prices	26
			2	Effects of Generic Entry on Sales' Volumes and Healthcare Spendings	28
			3	Incentivising Innovation on the Brand-Name and Generic Drug Markets	29
		C		Risks and Costs Related to Generic Entry	29
Part 2				The Benefits of Settlements	30
	I			Are Trials Vanished by Settlements?	31
	II			Costs and Risks of Patent Infringement Litigation	33
		A		Estimated Costs and Duration of Patent Infringement Litigation	34
		B		The Uncertainty Regarding the Litigation's Outcome	35
			1	US Jury Trials on Patent Infringement	35
			2	The Lack of Procedural Uniformity in Europe and the Unified Patent Court	35
			3	Patent Invalidation and Patent Infringement Rates	36
		C		The Impact of Settlements on Innovation Incentives	38
	III			The Social Cost of Settlements	38
Conclusions					40

Table of Contents

PART II
Pharma Settlements in the US ... 41

CHAPTER 2
The US Regulatory Framework ... 43
Introduction ... 43
Part 1   The US Agencies ... 45
    I   The United States Food & Drug Administration ... 46
    II   The United States Patent and Trademark Office ... 47
    III   The United States Federal Trade Commission ... 48
    IV   The United States Department of Justice ... 50
Part 2   Drug Market Entry in the US ... 51
    I   New Drug Entry to the US Market ... 51
    II   Generic Drug Entry under the Hatch-Waxman Act ... 52
         A   Section 505(b)(2) Applications ... 54
         B   The ANDA Mechanism ... 55
             1   Requirements of ANDA Submission ... 55
             2   Four Different ANDA Certifications ... 56
             3   Section viii "Carve-Out" Statements ... 57
         C   Paragraph IV ANDA ... 58
             1   FDA's Approval Triggers the 180-Day Exclusivity Period ... 59
             2   The 30-Month Stay to the ANDA's Approval ... 61
                 2.1   Multiple 30-Month Stays ... 61
                 2.2   Evergreening Strategies and "Sham" Patents ... 62
             3   The 180-Day Generic Exclusivity Period ... 63
                 3.1   FDA's Successful Defence Requirement ... 64
                 3.2   Exclusivity Only for the First Paragraph IV ANDA Filer ... 65
    III   Restoring Patent Protection for Innovators ... 66
         A   Patent Term Extension to Compensate FDA Review ... 66
         B   Non-patent Kinds of Exclusivity ... 67
             1   The 5-Year NCE Exclusivity ... 67
             2   The 3-Year NCS Exclusivity ... 68
             3   Orphan Drug Exclusivity ... 69
             4   Paediatric Exclusivity ... 70
    IV   Problems Faced and Amendments ... 71
         A   The Medicare Modernization Act ... 71
             1   Forfeiture of the 180-Day Exclusivity Period ... 72
             2   Other Amendments of the MMA ... 73
                 2.1   Civil Action to Obtain Patent Certainty ... 73
                 2.2   Counterclaim to Delist Patent from the Orange Book ... 74

Table of Contents

			2.3	Product-by-Product Exclusivity	75
		B	The Elimination of Parties' Adversity		75
			1	The Alignment of Parties' Interests and Retained Exclusivity	75
			2	Gaming the 180-Day Exclusivity Period	77
			3	Circumventing the Goals of the Hatch-Waxman Act	77
		C	Preserve Access to Affordable Generics Act		78
Conclusions					79

CHAPTER 3
The US Circuits' Split on Reverse Payment Settlements   81
Introduction   81

Part 1	Reverse Payment Settlements as Per Se Illegal				82
	I	Per Se Unlawful Restraints			82
		A	Per Se Illegality for Naked Restraints		82
		B	Restricting the Application of Per Se Illegality		84
	II	Reverse Payment Settlements as Per Se Illegal			86
		A	The Facts		87
			1	The Settlement Between HMR and Andrx	88
			2	How the Settlement Prevented Biovail's Generic Entry	89
		B	The DC Circuit Finds a Prima Facie Restraint of Trade		90
			1	The Hatch-Waxman Act Does Not Legitimise Delaying Generic Entry	90
			2	Market Share Allocation and Preservation of Monopoly	91
		C	The 6th Circuit Rules That the Restraints Are Per Se Illegal		92
			1	Novel Areas of Law Do Not Preclude Per Se Treatment	93
			2	Naked Horizontal Market Allocation Extending to Non-infringing Drugs	93
			3	Bolstering Patent Effectiveness Through Reverse Payments	94
	III	Criticising the Per Se Illegality of Reverse Payments			95
		A	The Elimination of Procompetitive Settlements		96
		B	Decreasing Patent Challenges and Innovation Incentives		97
Part 2	The Scope of the Patent Test				99
	I	The Scope of the Patent Test and Reverse Payments			100
		A	The Three-Step Inquiry of the Scope of the Patent Test		101

		B	Not Exceeding the Scope of the Patent	101
			1 The Duration of Delay to Generic Entry	102
			2 The Scope of the Products Delayed by the Agreement	102
			3 No Manipulation of the 180-Day Exclusivity Period	103
		C	The Sham or Baseless Litigation Standard	104
	II		How Patents Immunised Settlements from Antitrust	105
	III		Main Problems of the Scope of the Patent Test	107
		A	The Presumption of Patent Validity	107
			1 Section 282 of the Patent Act	108
			2 Refusing to Examine the Validity of the Underlying Patent	109
		B	Antitrust Immunity Granted by Weak or Invalid Patents	110
			1 The High Rates of Patent Invalidation	110
			2 The Patent Right Does Not Legitimise an Exclusion Payment	113
			3 Patent Validity as a Criterion for the Legality of Settlements	114
			4 The Probabilistic Nature of the Patent Right	116
			5 Invalid Patents Offering Antitrust Immunity	116
		C	Ignoring the Issue of Patent Infringement	118
			1 The Burden to Prove Patent Infringement Is on the Patent Holder	118
			2 The Size of the Payment Indicates Patent Invalidity or Non-infringement	119
	IV		The Judicial Preference for Settlements	121
		A	Reverse Payments as a Natural Consequence of Hatch-Waxman	121
		B	Subsequent Patent Challenges Eliminating Weak Patents	123
		C	Settlement Incentives Versus the Elimination of Invalid Patents	124
			1 Favourising the Settlement of Disputes at All Costs	124
			2 The Public Interest in Eliminating Unwarranted Monopolies	126
		D	The Impairment of Innovation	127
Part 3			Reverse Payments as Presumptively Illegal	128
	I		Proposals on a Truncated Rule of Reason Analysis	129
		A	The Proposed Tests by the FTC and the DOJ	130
			1 FTC's Proposal for the Presumptive Illegality of Unjustified Payments	130

Table of Contents

			2	The Shift of the DoJ Towards a Truncated Rule of Reason	132
	II		The "Quick-Look" Rule of Reason in the *K-Dur* Decision		134
		A	Facts		135
		B	The FTC's Antitrust Complaint Against the Settlements		135
			1	Horizontal Market Division Agreements	135
			2	Licensing Agreements as an Alibi for Payment	136
			3	The Antitrust Injury Suffered	137
		C	The 3rd Circuit Finds Payments Prima Facie Illegal		137
		D	Reception of the *K-Dur* Test		138
Conclusions					140

CHAPTER 4
FTC v. Actavis   141
Introduction   141

Part 1	*FTC v. Actavis*				142
	I	Facts and Procedural History			142
		A	The Generic Challenges and the Settlement Agreements		142
		B	The District Court and the Appellate Court Decisions		143
			1	The District Court Decision	143
			2	The Appellate Court Decision	144
	II	The Supreme Court Decision in *FTC v. Actavis*			145
		A	Rejecting the Scope of the Patent Test		145
			1	Reverse Payment Settlements Are Not Antitrust Immune	146
			2	Five Considerations to Reject the Scope of the Patent Test	147
			3	The Hatch-Waxman Act's Role in Reverse Payment Settlements	148
			4	The Public Interest Justifications	149
		B	Patent Settlements Are Not Per Se or Presumptively Illegal		150
			1	Rejecting the Per Se Illegality of Reverse Payment Settlements	150
			2	Rejecting the Presumptive Illegality of Reverse Payment Settlements	151
		C	The Rule of Reason for Reverse Payment Settlements		152

			1	Analysis of Ambiguous Practices under the Rule of Reason	152
			2	The Rule of Reason in *FTC v. Actavis*	153
			3	The Steps of the Rule of Reason Analysis for Reverse Payments	155
		D	\	The Questions of the Relevant Market and Market Power	155
			1	Reverse Payment Settlements under Sections 1 & 2 of the Sherman Act	155
			2	The Definition of the Relevant Market	156
			3	The Question of Showing Market Power	157
			4	Ways to Define the Relevant Market in Reverse Payment Cases	158
			5	Relevant Market Definition *Post Actavis*	161
	III	\	Applicable Test and Possible Justifications		163
		A	Anticompetitive Versus Permissible Settlements		163
			1	Agreements Splitting the Patent Term Without a Payment	164
			2	The Size of the Payment	164
			3	Evaluating the Value Conferred to Generics by Side-Deals	166
				3.1 Payments Disconnected from Deal's Impact	167
				3.2 The Complexity of Evaluating Side Deals	167
		B	Justifications for Settlements under *FTC v. Actavis*		168
			1	Patent Validity Cannot Serve as a Justification	168
			2	Earlier Generic Entry Is Not a Valid Justification	169
			3	Business Reasons and Risk Aversion Are Not Valid Justifications	170
	IV	\	The Dissenting Opinion in *FTC v. Actavis*		170
		A	Acting Within the Scope of the Patent		171
		B	Discouraging the Settlement of Disputes		172
	V	\	The Importance of *FTC v. Actavis*		173
		A	The Consumer Welfare Approach		173
		B	The Impact of Antitrust Scrutiny on Reverse Payments		174
Part 2	\	Non-cash Payments after *FTC v. Actavis*			175
	I	\	No-AG Commitments		176
		A	Defining Authorised Generic Drugs		176
		B	Economic Effects of Authorised Generics' Launch		177
		C	The Value and Frequency of No-AG Commitments		178

		D	No-AG Commitments as Part of Settlements	179
	II		Uncertainty Concerning No-AG Commitments	182
		A	Debating Whether *Actavis* Applies to No-AG Settlements	183
			1 The Difficulty of Providing a Reliable Estimate of Monetary Value	183
			2 Refusing to Apply Antitrust Scrutiny to No-AG Commitments	184
		B	*Actavis* Applies to No-AG Commitments	185
			1 The District Court Decision *In Re Lamictal*	186
			2 The 3rd Circuit Confirms That *Actavis* Cannot Be Limited to Cash Payments	188
			2.1 A No-AG Commitment Can Amount to Payment	189
			2.2 Estimating Generic Challengers' Profits from a No-AG Commitment	191
			2.3 No-AG Commitments Are Not Exclusive Licences	192
Part 3		Other Anticompetitive Strategies		194
	I	"Poison-Pill" or "Acceleration" Clauses		195
	II	Forgiveness of Damages		196
		A	The Potential Liability of Generic Entrants for Damages	196
		B	Forgiveness of Damages as a Concealed Payment	197
	III	Abuse of Restricted Drug Distribution		199
		A	Risk Evaluation and Mitigation Strategies	200
		B	Preventing Generics from Buying Samples of the Branded Drug	201
			1 *Actelion Pharms Ltd. v. Apotex Inc.*	201
			2 *Mylan Pharms v. Celgene Corp.*	201
	IV	Product Reformulations and Product-Hopping		202
		A	Defining Product-Hopping	202
		B	Generic Substitution	203
			1 The Mechanism of Generic Substitution	203
			2 Biosimilar or Interchangeable Drugs and Generic Substitution	204
		C	Anticompetitive Product-Hopping Strategies	205
			1 The Timing of Drug Product Reformulation	205
			2 Product-Hopping Effects to Generic Substitution	206
			3 Hard and Soft Product Switches as Monopolisation Strategies	207
			3.1 Hard Product Switch and Coercion of Patients	208

			3.2	Multiple Product Reformulations and Aggressive Marketing	210

			3.3	Product-Hopping Combined with No-AG Commitment	213
Conclusions					214

PART III
Pharma Settlements in the EU — 217

CHAPTER 5
The European Regulatory Framework — 219

Part 1	The European Pharma Regulatory Framework	220
I	Patent System and Patent Grants in Europe	220
A	The European Patent Convention and EPO	221
1	The European Patent with Unitary Effect	221
2	The Increasing Number of Patent Applications and Patentability Criteria	222
3	Patent Opposition Before the EPO and National Patent Authorities	223
II	The Entry of Pharmaceuticals to the European Market	224
A	Marketing Authorisation of Medicinal Products	225
1	Three Types of Marketing Authorisations in the European Union	225
2	Duration of Marketing Authorisation and Exclusivities	227
3	The EU Bolar Exemption and the Abridged Marketing Authorisation	228
B	Pricing and Reimbursement of Pharmaceuticals in the EU	229
C	Extending the Market Exclusivity of Medicinal Products	231
1	Supplementary Protection Certificates	231
2	Orphan Drug Market Exclusivity in the European Union	232
3	Paediatric Exclusivity in the European Union	233
D	Differences Between the EU and US Regulatory Frameworks	233
Part 2	Fundamentals of European Competition Law	234
I	Competition Enforcement and Procedural Aspects	235
A	National Competition Enforcement Authorities	235
B	Procedural Issues and Regulation 1/2003	237
1	The Convergence Rule	237
2	Avoiding Conflicting Decisions	238
3	Burden and Standard of Proof	239

II		Article 101 TFEU		240
	A	Defining the Concept of Undertakings		241
		1	Economic Activity and Definition of Undertaking	242
		2	Associations of Undertakings	244
	B	Agreements and Concerted Practices under Article 101(1) TFEU		245
		1	The Definition of Agreement under Article 101(1) TFEU	245
		2	Potential Competition	246
		3	Eliminating or Reducing Market Uncertainty	247
		4	Article 101(1) TFEU and the "Single Economic Entity" Doctrine	248
	C	Anticompetitive Object or Effect of the Agreement		249
		1	Restrictions by Object	249
			1.1 Expanding the Group of Restrictions by Object	251
			1.2 The Judgment of CJEU in *Cartes Bancaires*	252
		2	Restrictions by Effect	254
		3	A European Rule of Reason Analysis?	255
	D	Affecting Trade Between Member States		256
		1	An Appreciable Effect on Interstate Trade as a Jurisdictional Criterion	257
		2	Agreements of Minor Importance and the Notion of Appreciability	258
			2.1 *De Minimis*: The Lack of Appreciable Impact on Interstate Trade	258
			2.2 The EU Commission's *De Minimis* Notices	259
	E	Exceptions under Article 101(3) TFEU		260
		1	Four Cumulative Conditions for an Exemption under Article 101(3) TFEU	261
		2	From Individual Exemptions to Self-Assessment	261
		3	Restrictions by Object Can Also Fall under Article 101(3) TFEU	262
	F	Block Exemption Regulations and Guidelines		263
		1	Guidelines on Horizontal Cooperation Agreements	266
		2	The Research and Development Block Exemption Regulation	267
		3	The Block Exemption Regulation on Specialisation Agreements	269

			4	The Technology Transfer Block Exemption Regulation	270
				4.1 The 2014 Technology Transfer Block Exemption Regulation	270
				4.2 The 2014 TTBER Guidelines	274
III		Article 102 TFEU			275
	A	Introduction to Article 102 TFEU			276
	B	Defining and Detecting Dominance in the Internal Market			278
			1	Product Market Definition	279
				1.1 Qualitative Versus Quantitative Criteria and the SSNIP Test	279
				1.2 Product Market Definition in the Pharmaceutical Sector	280
			2	Geographic Market Definition	284
				2.1 General Criteria of Geographic Market Definition	284
				2.2 Geographic Market Definition in the Pharmaceutical Sector	285
			3	Defining the Temporal Market	286
	C	Assessing Market Power and Dominance			286
			1	Market Shares	287
			2	Other Factors Indicating Dominance and Barriers to Entry	288
			3	Countervailing Buyer Power	289
	D	The Concept of Abuse of Dominance			290
	E	Abuse of Dominance and the Exercise of IP-Related Rights			292
			1	TetraPak and the Acquisition of Exclusive Licences	292
			2	Standard-Essential Patents and Refusals to License	293
				2.1 The Commission's Investigations in the *Samsung* and *Motorola* Cases	294
				2.2 The CJEU Rules on SEP-Related Abuses of Dominance in *Huawei*	295
			3	The Manipulation of IP Rights in the *AstraZeneca* Case	296
				3.1 AstraZeneca's Product-Hopping Strategy	297
				3.2 Providing Misleading Information and Eliminating Competition	297
				3.3 The CJEU Affirms the Abuse of Dominant Position	299

Table of Contents

		F	Objective Justifications under Article 102 TFEU	299
Conclusions				300

CHAPTER 6
Delaying Generic Entry in the EU — 303
Introduction — 303
    I   The EU Commission Pharma Sector Inquiry — 303
    II   Health Expenditures in European Member States — 307
        A   The Importance of Generic Entry in the European Union — 308
        B   The Elimination of Adversity Between Competitors in the EU — 310

Part 1   The EU Commission Enforcement Cases — 311
    Introduction — 311
    I   *The Fentanyl and the Modafinil* Cases — 312
        A   Delaying the Entry of Generic Fentanyl in the Dutch Market — 312
        B   The Settlement Between Teva and Cephalon on Modafinil — 313
    II   *Lundbeck v. Commission* — 314
        A   The Role of the Patent in the Antitrust Analysis — 315
            1   The Presumption of Patent Validity in the Commission's Decision — 315
            2   Potential Competition and the Presumption of Patent Validity — 317
            3   The Rejection of the Scope of the Patent Test — 318
                3.1   The EU Commission's Rationale for Rejecting the Scope of the Patent Test — 318
                3.2   The General Court Rejects the Scope of the Patent Test — 320
        B   Lawful Patent Settlements — 322
            1   Settlements Falling Outside the Scope of Article 101(1) TFEU — 322
            2   The Legitimate Settlement Between Neolab and Lundbeck — 323
        C   Restriction of Competition by Object — 324
            1   The Commission's Criteria for Determining a Restriction by Object — 324
            2   The General Court Confirms the Restriction of Competition by Object — 325
                2.1   The Size and the Disproportionate Nature of the Reverse Payments — 326
                2.2   Exchanging Uncertainty for Certainty Through a Value Transfer — 327

			2.3	Reverse Payments and the *Cartes Bancaires* Decision	328
			2.4	Patent Settlements and the *Beef Industry* Agreements	330
	D	Justifications in the General Court's Decision			331
		1	Justifications for the Value Transfers as Part of the Settlements		331
			1.1	The Risk Asymmetry Between Originators and Generic Manufacturers	332
			1.2	The Irreparable Harm Caused by Generic Entry	332
		2	Justifications under Article 101(3) TFEU		333
			2.1	The Avoidance of Litigation Costs	334
			2.2	Preserving the Incentives to Innovate and Benefits to Consumers	335
	E	The Importance of Lundbeck and Its Comparison with *Actavis*			335
		1	How Does the *Lundbeck* Ruling Affect the Decision to Settle?		336
		2	Comparing the Tests in *Lundbeck* and *FTC v. Actavis*		337
		3	Lundbeck's Appeal Before the CJEU		338
III	*Commission v. Servier*				342
	A	The Facts			342
		1	Servier's Settlements and Technology Acquisitions		342
		2	Servier's Hard Product Switch to Second Generation Perindopril		344
	B	Settlements Violating Article 101(1) TFEU			344
	C	Side-Deals as Value Transfers in the Servier Settlements			345
		1	Servier's Acquisition of Lupin's Generic Patent Applications		346
		2	Servier's Acquisition and Licence Agreement with Krka		347
		3	Side-Deals on the Distribution of Authorised Generics		348
	D	The Analysis of the Anticompetitive Effects of the Settlements			349
		1	The Relevant Market and Servier's Position Within It		350
		2	The Non-challenge and the Non-compete Clauses of the Settlements		351

Table of Contents

			2.1	The Non-challenge Clauses and Their Effects	352
			2.2	The Non-compete Clauses	353
		3	Assessment of the Value Transfers in the Settlements		355
	E	Justifications under Article 101(3) TFEU			356
		1	Avoided Litigation Costs and the Acquired Technologies		357
		2	Outside the Scope of the Technology Transfer Block Exemption		358
	F	Servier's Abuse of Dominance under Article 102 TFEU			358
		1	Defining the Relevant Market and Servier's Market Position		359
		2	Servier's Continuous Exclusionary Strategy		360
			2.1	Servier's Acquisition of Azad's Non-infringing Production Process	360
			2.2	Servier's Settlements as Abuses of Dominance under Article 102 TFEU	362
		3	The Effects of Servier's Abuse of Dominance		364
	G	Servier's Action for Annulment Before the EU General Court			364
Part 2		National Competition Authorities' Decisions			365
	I	Preventing Substitution and Disparaging Generic Drugs			366
		A	Hard Product Switch as an Infringement of Article 102 TFEU		366
		B	Disparaging Generic Drugs on the Prescription Level		367
		C	Unwarranted Discounts and Naming and Shaming		368
	II	Divisional Patents as an Abuse of Dominance			369
	III	Preventing Off-Label Drug Use: The *Roche/Novartis* Case			372
		A	The Artificial Differentiation of Avastin and Lucentis		372
		B	The CJEU Upholds the Finding of a Restriction by Object		374
Conclusions					375

Conclusion				377
Part 1		Applicable Tests in the US and the EU		377
	I	The Scope of the Patent Test Is Rejected		378
		A	Reverse Payments Do Not Fall Within the Scope of Patents	378
		B	Restoring Uncertainty and the Balance Between IP and Antitrust	379
Part 2		Guidance for the Pharma Industry		380
	I	Patent Settlements Which Are Likely Illegitimate		380

II	Legitimate Patent Settlements		380
	A	Patent Settlements Without a Reverse Value Transfer	380
	B	Settlements Allowing Generic Entry Prior to Patent Expiration	381
	C	Legitimate and Justified Value Transfers	381
III	Grey Areas and Questionable Strategies		382
	A	The Broad Definition of Payment in Settlements	382
		1 Side-Deals	383
		2 Licensing Agreements	383
		3 Authorised Generic Distribution Agreements and No-Launch Commitments	384
	B	Other Types of Potentially Anticompetitive Strategies	385
		1 Product Switches and the Prevention of Generic Substitution	385
		2 The Acquisition of Competing Pharmaceutical Technologies	386
IV	Practical Advice for the Pharma Industry		387
	A	Settling Without an Exclusionary Value Transfer	387
	B	The Need for Close Monitoring and Compliance Training	387
	C	Foreseeing Risks and Avoiding Problematic Strategies	388

Closing Remarks	389
Bibliography	391
Table of Cases	427
Tables of Statutes & Legislation	465
Index	473

Preface

This book examines patent settlements between originators and generic pharmaceutical manufacturers under United States (US) antitrust and European Union (EU) competition law. The main focus of analysis is on patent settlements involving reverse payments, commonly known as "pay-for-delay" settlements. Reverse payments are big value transfers from originators to generic manufacturers as part of patent settlements, arguably aiming to delay generic entry to the market. These payments are referred to as "reverse" since in this context it is the patent holder that transfers value to the alleged patent infringer as part of the settlement; thus, the typical direction of the value transfer (from the infringer to the right holder) is reversed.

The principal goal of this book is to critically and comparatively analyse how such patent settlements are scrutinised by US and European courts and enforcement authorities and to discuss the applicable legal tests and the main criteria used for their assessment. To this effect, an elaborate analysis of the relevant jurisprudence is employed, starting from the split between US Circuit Courts and the application of the scope of the patent test and extending beyond the *FTC v. Actavis* decision of the US Supreme Court, to subsequent jurisprudence and to the evolution of patent settlement forms. In the EU, the first ruling of the General Court of the European Union in *Lundbeck v. Commission* is exhaustively analysed, along with the enforcement decisions of the EU Commission in *Servier* and other cases, but also selected decisions of National Competition Authorities of EU Member States.

Another important aim is to present the evolution in the form of patent settlements throughout the years and the constant sophistication of other types of strategies allegedly aiming to delay generic entry to the market. Cases involving various types of value transfers, product reformulations, product-hopping, no-AG commitments, licensing agreements, side-deals and other types of conduct are analysed, while the focus remains on the criteria and applicable tests used by courts and enforcement authorities when applying antitrust scrutiny.

The ultimate objective of this book is to provide guidance to the pharmaceutical industry regarding the types of patent settlements, strategies and conduct which may

Preface

be problematic from a US antitrust and EU competition law perspective and to assist it in structuring settlements which are both efficient and compliant with antitrust laws. The conclusion of this book provides concrete examples of illegitimate and legitimate settlements and conduct, putting the emphasis on conduct that falls within a grey zone and on the circumstances under which it could be problematic from an antitrust perspective.

List of Abbreviations

AAI	American Antitrust Institute
AAM	Association for Accessible Medicines
ABA	American Bar Association
Abbott	Abbott Laboratories
aff'd	Affirmed
AG	Authorised Generic Drug
AIPLA	American Intellectual Property Law Association
ALA	Acquisition and Licence Agreement (between Servier and Krka)
Alb. L.J. Sci. & Tech.	Albany Law Journal of Science and Technology
ALJ	Administrative Law Judge
ALS	Lou Gehrig's disease
Am. J.L. & Med.	American Journal of Law & Medicine
ANDA	Abbreviated New Drug Application
Andrx	Andrx Pharmaceuticals Inc.
Apr.	April
ASPE	Office for the Assistant Secretary for Planning and Evaluation
Ass'n	Association
Assocs.	Associates
ATR	Antitrust Division of the US Department of Justice
Aug.	August
Biotech. L. Rep.	Biotechnology Law Report
Biovail	Biovail Corporation
BLA	Biological License Application
BLEU	Belgium–Luxembourg Economic Union

List of Abbreviations

BMJ	formerly the British Medical Journal
C.C.D. Mass.	Circuit Court District of Massachusetts
C.C.S.D.N.Y.	Circuit Court Southern District of New York
C.F.R.	Code of Federal Regulations
Cal. Ct. App.	California Court of Appeals
Can. J. L. & Tech.	Canadian Journal of Law & Technology
Cath. U. L. Rev.	Catholic University Law Review
CBER	Center for Biologics Evaluation and Research
CBO	Congressional Budget Office
CDER	Center for Drug Evaluation and Research
CEE	Central and Eastern European Countries
cert.	*Certiorari*
Chem.	Chemical
CHMP	Committee for Medicinal Products for Human Use
Cipro I	*In re Ciprofloxacin Hydrochloride Antitrust Litigation*, 261 F. Supp. 2d 188 (E.D.N.Y. 2003)
Cipro II	*In re Ciprofloxacin Hydrochloride Antitrust Litig.*, 363 F. Supp. 2d 514 (E.D.N.Y. 2005)
Cir.	Circuit
CML Rev.	Common Market Law Review
CMS	Centers for Medicare & Medicaid Services
Co.	Company
Colum. L. Rev.	Columbia Law Review
Comm'n	Commission
Commc'ns	Communications
Corp.	Corporation
CPI	Competition Policy International
D. Conn.	US District Court for the District of Connecticut
D. Del.	US District Court for the District of Delaware
D.C.Cir.	US Court of Appeals for the District of Columbia
D.D.C.	US District Court for the District of Columbia
D.Mass.	District of *Massachusetts*
D.N.J.	US District Court for the District of New Jersey
D.R.I.	US District Court for the District of Rhode Island
Dec.	December
DoJ	US Department of Justice
E.C.L.R	European Competition Law Review
E.D. Mich.	US District Court for the Eastern District of Michigan

List of Abbreviations

E.D.N.Y.	US District Court for the Eastern District of New York
E.D.Pa	US District Court for the Eastern District of Pennsylvania
e.g.	*exempli gratia*
E.I.P.R.	European Intellectual Property Review
ECHR	European Court of Human Rights
ECN	European Competition Network
ed.	Edition
eds.	Editors
EFPIA	European Federation of Pharmaceutical Industries and Associations
EMA	European Medicines Agency
Ent. and Tech. Law	Entertainment and Technology Law
EphMRA	European Pharmaceutical Marketing Research Association
EPR	External Price Referencing
ESI	ESI Lederle, Inc.
et al.	*et alii*
etc.	*et cetera*
EUCERD	European Union Committee of Experts for Rare Diseases
FDA	Food and Drug Administration
FDAAA	Food and Drug Administration Amendments Act of 2007
Feb.	February
Fed.	Federal
Fla. L. Rev.	Florida Law Review
fn.	Footnote
Food & Drug L.J.	Food & Drug Law Journal
FTC Act	Federal Trade Commission Act (15 U.S.C §§ 41-58, as amended)
FTC	Federal Trade Commission
FY	Financial Year
GDP	Gross Domestic Product
Geneva	Geneva Pharmaceuticals
GmbH	Gesellschaft mit beschränkter Haftung (company with limited liability)
GSK	GlaxoSmithKline
Harv. J.L. & Tech.	Harvard Journal of Law & Technology
Hatch-Waxman Act	Drug Price Competition and Patent Term Restoration Act (Pub. L. No. 98-417, 98 Stat. 1585 (1984))
Health Law	Health Lawyer

List of Abbreviations

Heumann	Heumann Pharma GmbH & Co.
HMR /HMRI	Hoescht Marion Roussel, Inc.
HPM	Hyman, Phelps & McNamara
i.e.	*id est*
I.P.J.	Intellectual Property Journal
ICA	Italian Competition Authority
ICI	Imperial Chemical Industries, PLC
id.	*Idem*
IIC	International Review of Intellectual Property and Competition Law
IMI JU	Innovative Medicines Initiative Joint Undertaking
Inc.	Incorporated
Ind.	Industry
INN	International Nonproprietary Name
Int'l	International
Intell. Prop.	Intellectual Property
Iowa L. Rev.	Iowa Law Review
J. Marshall Rev.	John Marshall Review
J.	Journal
Jan.	January
L.J.	Law Journal
Labs.	Laboratories
Litig.	Litigation
Loy. U. Chi. L.J.	Loyola University Chicago Law Journal
Ltd.	Limited
Manag. Decis. Econ.	Managerial Decision Economics
Mar.	March
Marq. IP L. Rev.	Marquette Intellectual Property Law Review
Md. L. Rev.	Maryland Law Review
Media & Entert.	Media & Entertainment
Mfg	Manufacturing
Mich. L. Rev.	Michigan Law Review
Minn. L. Rev.	Minnesota Law Review
Mo. L. Rev.	Missouri Law Review
N.D. Ill.	US District Court for the Northern District of Illinois
N.D. W. Va.	US District Court for the Northern District of West Virginia
NCE	New Chemical Entity
NCS	New Clinical Studies

New. Eng. J. Med.	New England Journal of Medicine
NIH	National Institutes of Health (US)
NMEs	New Molecular Entities
No.	Number
Nos.	Numbers
Nov.	November
Nw. U. L. Rev.	Northwestern University Law Review
NYULR	New York University Law Review
Oct.	October
OECD	Organisation for Economic Co-operation and Development
Ohio St. L.J.	Ohio State Law Journal
Okla. L. Rev.	Oklahoma Law Review
OTC	Over-the-Counter Drug
p.	Page
para.	Paragraph
paras	Paragraphs
Pharms.	Pharmaceuticals
PhRMA	Pharmaceutical Research and Manufacturers of America
PLC	Public Limited Company
Pol'y, L. & Ethics	Policy Law & Ethics
pp.	Pages
PPACA	Patient Protection and Affordable Care Act
PTMT	USPTO-Patent Technology Monitoring Team
Q. J.	Quarterly Journal
R&D	Research and Development
RBC	Royal Bank of Canada
REdI	Regulatory Education For Industry
REMS	Risk Evaluation and Mitigation Strategies
S. Ct.	US Supreme Court
S.D. Fla.	US District Court for the Southern District of Florida
S.D.N.Y.	US District Court for the Southern District of New York
Sci. & Tech. L.	Science and Technology Law
Seattle U. L. Rev.	Seattle University Law Review
SEPs	Standard-Essential Patents
Sept.	September
Sherman Act	26 Stat. 209, 15 U.S.C. §§ 1-7
SKKU J.	SungKyunKwan Journal

List of Abbreviations

Soc.	Society
Stan. Tech. L. Rev.	Stanford Technology Law Review
Stat.	Statute
Tech.	Technology
TRIPS	Agreement on Trade Related Aspects of Intellectual Property Rights, Including Trade in Counterfeit Goods
U.S.C.	United States Code
U.S.F.L.	University of San Francisco Law Review
Univ.	University
UPC	Unified Patent Court
Upsher	Upsher-Smith Labotatories
US	United States
USPTO	United States Patent and Trademark Office
v.	Versus
Vol.	Volume
W.D. Pa.	US District Court for the Western District of Pennsylvania
Wash. U. L. Rev.	Washington University Law Review
Zenith	Zenith Goldline Pharmaceuticals

Acknowledgements

This book is an updated and extended version of my PhD thesis on "Patent Settlements in the Pharmaceutical Industry under US Antitrust and EU Competition Law" that was defended at the University of Neuchâtel Switzerland in September 2017.

I would like to thank Prof. Petros C. Mavroidis for his priceless comments, feedback, advice and support, from the very first moment I have started writing this book. I would also like to thank Prof. William E. Kovacic for his invaluable and elaborate comments, insights, encouragement and advice.

I would further like to thank the University of Neuchâtel and Prof. Evelyne Clerc for giving me the opportunity to work as a teaching and research assistant at the chair of Competition law and European law, allowing me to finance the research and writing of this book. My gratitude goes to Prof. Daniel Kraus for his feedback on my work and for his support and encouragement. I also take the opportunity to thank the Swiss Competition Commission (WEKO) and INGRES (Institut für den gewerblichen Rechtsschutz) for inviting me to present the subject of patent settlements in the pharmaceutical industry and for the very interesting discussions we have had. A special thanks to the editing team of Wolters Kluwer International and to Simon Bellamy for their excellent collaboration and hard work for the publication of this volume.

Writing this book would not have been possible without the love, support and help of my family: my partner Renato, my parents Foteini and Sotiris, my brother Theo, Romy, Erwin and Sandro. A big thank you to all of my friends for making life in Neuchâtel beautiful.

Introduction

I PATENT SETTLEMENTS INVOLVING REVERSE PAYMENTS

A Defining Reverse Payment Patent Settlements

The focus of this book is on patent settlements between brand-name drug manufacturers (originators) and generic drug manufacturers wishing to enter the market with their generic drug version. These patent settlements are commercial agreements to settle patent disputes between originators and generic manufacturers, concerning the issues of: (1) the validity of the patent(s) covering the relevant drug, and; (2) the infringement of the relevant patent(s) by the generic drug version at issue. The specific kind of settlements that are examined in this book are typically structured according to the following pattern. The brand-name manufacturer **A** holds one or more patents covering its brand-name drug product **X**. The generic drug manufacturer **B** wishes to enter the market with its generic drug version of product **X** and takes steps towards this direction, arguing that the brand-name manufacturer's patents are invalid and/or not infringed by its generic drug version. The brand-name manufacturer **A** sues the generic drug manufacturer **B** for patent infringement. Before there is any final decision on the matters of patent validity or of patent infringement, **A** and **B** settle. As part of the patent settlement, the brand-name drug manufacturer **A** makes a large value transfer to the generic drug manufacturer and alleged patent infringer **B**. In return, the generic manufacturer **B** commits to delay its generic entry to the market until an agreed date.

This type of patent settlements are commonly known as *pay-for-delay settlements*. They are also called *reverse payment settlements*, since they involve payments which flow in a reverse direction: while it is normally the alleged patent infringer that pays the patent holder damages and/or litigation costs, etc. in order to settle the patent dispute, in this type of settlements value flows the other way around: from the patent holder to the alleged infringer. The first question that comes to mind when first encountering such a reverse payment settlement is *why*? Why would a patentee *pay* an alleged infringer to respect its patent right and to refrain from entering the market, instead of merely enforcing its right? The answer to this question is anything but simple and depends on a number of factors such as the parties' stakes in the patent infringement litigation, their risk adversity, the economic consequences of generic entry but also on the regulatory framework on the entry of generic drug products to the market.

Reverse payment settlements primarily concern pharmaceutical products whose active ingredient is no longer protected by a patent, but which are still protected through one or more patents which are often mentioned in literature and practice as "secondary" patents. The more successful a pharmaceutical product is from a commercial perspective, the more likely it is that it is protected by a number of different patents, in an effort to protect the brand-name manufacturer's monopoly against generic entry for the longest period possible. "Blockbuster" pharmaceuticals are often protected by a net of different patents, not only covering the drug's active ingredient but also patents that are commonly referred to as "secondary" and which cover for example the process or the production method of a pharmaceutical's active ingredient. These "secondary" patents typically offer more narrow protection against generic entry than compound patents, since generic manufacturers may patent around them and find non-infringing ways of producing a generic drug version.

Notwithstanding that settlements are generally a legitimate and efficient way to end litigation and lighten the workload of courts and administrative authorities, patent settlements in the pharmaceutical sector which involve reverse payments to delay generic entry are likely to be found problematic under United States (US) antitrust and (European Union) EU competition law. The US part of this book focuses on reverse payment settlements concluded between brand-name drug manufacturers and generic drug manufacturers in the context of Hatch-Waxman Act patent infringement litigation and on the analysis of these settlements under US antitrust law. The EU part of this book examines similar types of reverse payment settlements in the pharmaceutical sector concluded in the European Union and discusses the legal problems they may give rise to under EU competition law.

B Problems and Challenges Raised by Reverse Payment Settlements

The most important problem raised by reverse payment settlements is that they are liable to delay generic drug entry to the market. One of the core regulatory objectives in both the US and the European Union is to encourage early generic entry to the market, since such entry is used as a mechanism to constrain healthcare expenditures. In a reverse payment settlement, the generic manufacturer commits to defer its generic entry to the market until an agreed date pursuant to a large value transfer. Absent the settlement, generic entry would have ordinarily occurred provided that the generic drug version would not infringe the relevant patent or that the relevant patent was invalid. A second major problem is that these settlements may shield from patent invalidation potentially weak patents, which could have been invalidated had the patent infringement litigation continued. As is examined in this book, one of the principal goals of enacting the Hatch-Waxman Act in the US was to encourage patent challenges aiming to eliminate from the market weak and potentially invalid patents,

Introduction

so as to put an end to unjustified monopolies and expedite generic entry. Nevertheless, a reverse payment settlement may be used in order to shield a patent from a finding of patent invalidity and to preserve the patentee's monopoly in the market until the agreed date of generic entry. A third problem raised by reverse payment settlements is that they may be employed in order to keep off the market generic drug versions which are not infringing the relevant patents. Due to the settlement between the litigating parties, the issue of patent infringement remains unresolved, leading to a situation whereby potentially non-infringing competition may be eliminated from the market pursuant to the settlement.

Because of the anticompetitive potential of reverse payment settlements and the impact they may have on generic entry and thus on pharmaceuticals' prices, US antitrust and EU competition law have been vigorously applied to such agreements. Due to the existence of the patent at the heart of the underlying dispute, the US antitrust/ EU competition law analysis of reverse payment settlements is very challenging and gives rise to multiple debates on the sensitive balance between intellectual property law and antitrust law. The highly specialised and complicated regulatory framework on pharmaceuticals and generic drug entry in both the US and the EU does not facilitate the analysis of reverse payment settlements and may also provide chances to "game" the market. For example, due to the particularities of the US regulatory framework of the Hatch-Waxman Act, brand-name manufacturers may temporarily achieve the parallel exclusion of all generic challengers from the market, merely by paying the first generic challenger to delay its market entry.

Last but not least, the constant evolution and sophistication of the form of reverse payment settlements further complicate their detection and antitrust analysis. While early reverse payment settlements involved large cash payments from brand-name manufacturers to generic challengers, the form of value transfers evolved throughout the years and nowadays includes but is not limited to side-deals, licensing and co-promotion agreements, no-AG commitments and other types of value transfers which are analysed in this book. In parallel, a number of brand-name manufacturers engaged in a great variety of elaborate strategies, aiming to protect their monopoly against generic competition: product reformulations and product switches, acquisitions of competing technologies and abuses of restricted drug distribution schemes are among the most interesting ones. The analysis of these strategies and of their potential impact on competition in the market is necessary in order to provide a bigger picture to the reader and to avoid a fragmented and incomplete analysis.

II BACKGROUND

A The Split of US Circuit Courts and the Resulting Uncertainty

When this research project started in May 2013, the split between US Circuit Courts was at its peak. Three diametrically different tests were applied for the adjudication of reverse payment settlement agreements between patent holders and generic manufacturers, concluded in the context of Hatch-Waxman litigation: the per se illegality approach, the scope of the patent test and the "quick-look" rule of reason. The scope of the patent test was the most prevalent test and was applied in numerous court decisions, rendering in essence patent settlements untouchable from antitrust scrutiny by finding that the potential exclusionary effects of reverse payment settlements fell within the exclusionary scope of the patent. Despite the harsh and constant criticism of this test by an overwhelming number of antitrust scholars, there was a considerable risk that the scope of the patent test would become the mainstream test for the adjudication of patent settlements, rendering in essence antitrust law inapplicable to such agreements due to the existence of the underlying patent.

Initially, this book aimed to analyse the split between US Circuit Courts, to criticise the application of the scope of the patent test to reverse payment settlements and to propose an alternative and more balanced analysis instead. However, in June 2013 the US Supreme Court resolved the split between Circuit Courts by opting for a rule of reason analysis of reverse payments and by explicitly rejecting the scope of the patent test. The weight of this book's analysis thus shifted towards the interpretation of the US Supreme Court's decision in *FTC v. Actavis* and on the impact it has had on patent settlements in the pharmaceutical industry. Even though the *Actavis* decision provided general guidelines and guidance to lower courts adjudicating reverse payments, it also created considerable uncertainty. The rapid evolution of the settlement mechanisms employed by pharmaceutical companies and the plurality of strategies potentially delaying generic entry create new questions and challenges, as extensively analysed in Chapter 4 of this book.

B   The Lack of EU Jurisprudence on Pharma Patent Settlements

Whereas the US Circuit Courts started ruling on reverse payment settlements roughly around 2001, the very first decision of the European General Court on pharmaceutical patent settlements was issued in September 2016. Up to that point, the only legal guidance available were the reports published by the European Commission in the context of its inquiry on competition in the pharmaceutical industry and the decisions of National Competition Authorities and national courts of EU Member States on a limited number of cases. Therefore, there was considerable uncertainty regarding the test that the European Union courts would adopt for the adjudication of patent settlements, the role that the patent would play in the competition law analysis, etc. It is noteworthy that when the settling pharmaceutical companies were in the position of competition law defendants in the EU, they raised virtually identical arguments to those that antitrust defendants have been advancing in the US under the scope of the patent test. Despite the huge differences between the legal, regulatory and economic realities of the US and the EU, this book highlights the great influence that the US has on the EU, also when it comes to the analysis of patent settlements in the pharmaceutical sector. As evidenced throughout the chapters of this book, there are great similarities in the legal standards and the criteria that were adopted in both jurisdictions for the antitrust/competition law analysis of patent settlements and other types of strategies in the pharmaceutical industry.

III RESEARCH OBJECTIVES

The main objective of this book is to provide the overview of the patent settlements and other types of strategies which are lawful or problematic under antitrust, focusing also on types of conduct that fall within "grey areas." Another objective is to examine the sensitive balance between patent law and antitrust, by analysing the applicable legal tests for the adjudication of reverse payment settlements under US antitrust and EU competition law. The ultimate goal is to provide guidance to the pharmaceutical industry and to assist it in structuring settlements and strategies which are compliant with US antitrust and EU competition law.

A Legitimate Versus Anticompetitive Settlements and Strategies

The core research objective of this book is to examine which types of patent settlements and other types of conduct are lawful and which ones have the potential to be problematic under US antitrust and EU competition law. In order to determine this, it is essential to examine how reverse payment settlements are discussed in the case law of the US and the EU, what is their economic *rationale* and also which types of antitrust concerns they may give rise to. Even though a strict, dogmatic categorisation of different types of patent settlements or other types of conduct as lawful or problematic is nearly impossible, US and European courts have provided guidance in their case law on the types of conduct that do not ordinarily raise antitrust concerns and on the ones that have a strong anticompetitive potential. This book aims to provide concrete examples of settlements that were found to be unproblematic from an antitrust/competition law perspective. Naturally, the analysis heavily focuses on settlements and other types of strategies which were found to violate US antitrust and EU competition law and on the specific criteria that were used for condemning them. One of the most interesting subjects of this book is the novel types of settlements and strategies which fall within grey areas and which cannot be unequivocally classified as legitimate or problematic. This book argues that even though patent settlements and other types of potentially exclusionary and abusive conduct change form rapidly, the main criteria for their assessment remain broadly the same.

B Balancing Patent Law and Antitrust in the Applicable Tests

The second goal of this book is to examine the sensitive balance between patent law and competition law by analysing the applicable tests for the adjudication of reverse payment settlements under US antitrust and EU competition law. Reverse payment settlements in the pharma industry are at the heart of the intersection between intellectual property law and antitrust law. The choice of the applicable test for the adjudication of reverse payment settlements directly reflects the effort to attain a balance between these two fields of law. The debate that led to the split of the US Circuit Courts mainly focused on whether such settlements fall within the exclusionary scope of the patent and are thus immune from the application of antitrust law. Chapter

3 discusses in detail this split and provides a detailed overview of the arguments and considerations in favour and against the application of antitrust scrutiny to reverse payment settlements, focusing on the need to preserve innovation incentives for brand-name drug manufacturers while ensuring access to affordable pharmaceuticals for consumers and decreasing healthcare costs. Another major issue is whether and to what extent courts and enforcement authorities shall examine the validity of the relevant patent(s) in order to conclude whether the patent settlements at issue violate antitrust law provisions. This book analyses the role that patents play in the antitrust analysis of settlements and other types of strategies in the pharmaceutical sector, on the basis of US and European case law. The ultimate objective is to highlight the main criteria used by courts and enforcement authorities in assessing the legitimacy of patent settlements and other types of strategies. These criteria shall also serve as guidance for the pharmaceutical industry, providing the standards that settlements and other types of conduct shall comply with in order to minimise the risk of infringing US antitrust and EU competition law.

C Practical Guidance for the Pharmaceutical Industry

The ultimate goal of this book is to provide practical guidance to the pharmaceutical industry and to assist its efforts to structure patent settlements and other types of strategies which are lawful under US antitrust and EU competition law. One major step towards achieving this goal is the detailed analysis of the criteria which are used by courts and enforcement authorities in order to examine the legality of such conduct. This book acknowledges the difficulty of settling a patent infringement dispute while complying with the standards of US antitrust and EU competition law but argues that it is still possible for the pharmaceutical industry to conclude settlements which are both efficient and legitimate. Even though there is a large variety of settlements and strategies analysed in the chapters of this book and the specificities of each case substantially differ, there are some fundamental principles that remain identical in the majority of decisions and which shall be respected when engaging in new types of settlements and strategies. Through these general guidelines, this book also aims to assist the pharmaceutical industry in the self-assessment of novel types of conduct so as to decrease the chances of violating US antitrust and EU competition law.

IV METHODOLOGY

The methodology chosen for this book is that of comparative legal analysis between the US and the European Union, examining how both jurisdictions have treated reverse payment settlements and other types of conduct in the pharmaceutical sector under antitrust law. The long and turbulent US experience, jurisprudence and doctrine on reverse payment settlements were used as the starting point of analysis in order to understand the mechanism of patent settlements, their impact on generic entry and on competition in the drug markets and the legal problems they may give rise to. The extensive study and analysis of the US Circuit Courts split on the applicable test for the

Introduction

adjudication of reverse payment settlements and of the relevant commentaries were indispensable in order to realise that reverse payment settlements are a three-fold exercise of balance: (1) balancing patent law and antitrust; (2) balancing innovation incentives with the need to spur generic competition; and (3) balancing the benefits of settlements and the need to prevent abuses and unjustified monopolies. Since the US Circuit Court split extended through a considerable time-period, it also provided reliable evidence on the influence of each applicable test not only on the number and form of patent settlements but also on the effects of applying antitrust scrutiny on the level of competition in the market. The ultimate goal is to benefit from the US experience on reverse payment settlements in order to save European courts, enforcement agencies, but also pharmaceutical companies considerable time and resources. The focus then turns to the European Union and on the similarities and the differences in the legal treatment of reverse payment settlements between these two different jurisdictions, in an attempt to increase legal security regarding the current standards applied in both the US and the EU.

Throughout the chapters of this book, the focus of analysis remains on jurisprudence and on real cases of patent settlements and other types of potentially anticompetitive conduct in the US and in the EU. Apart from the relevant case law, this book discusses a great variety of academic articles, written by prominent scholars and experts, specialised not only in US antitrust or EU competition law but also in intellectual property law and economics. The approach followed is not a strictly "black letter" approach: a variety of empirical studies is used in order to show the effects that the different applicable tests and the variable levels of antitrust scrutiny have had on the number and content of pharmaceutical patent settlements in both the US and the EU. Finally, some limited elements of law and economics are integrated in the analysis.

V OUTLINE

Before analysing reverse payment settlements in the pharmaceutical sector under antitrust law, it is indispensable to understand the economics of pharmaceutical entry to the market and to weigh the benefits of settlements against their social costs. In this regard, Chapter 1 (which also constitutes Part I of this book) focuses on the risks and costs of R&D in the pharmaceutical industry and the impact that generic entry has on the pharmaceutical market. It also discusses the benefits of settlements and their potential impact on innovation incentives.

Part II of this book is the US part and comprises of three chapters, starting from Chapter 2 and ending at Chapter 4. The first step for the analysis of reverse payment settlements and other types of strategies in the pharmaceutical sector is the examination of the applicable regulatory framework on pharmaceutical products. Chapter 2 provides the overview of the US agencies that are competent in the fields of pharmaceutical products, patent protection and antitrust enforcement, while it also analyses drug market entry in the US, focusing on the highly complicated provisions of the Hatch-Waxman Act. Chapter 3 analyses the split among US Circuit Courts regarding reverse payment settlements, critically discussing the three different tests that were used for their analysis: the per se illegality approach, the scope of the patent test and the "quick-look" rule of reason. Last but not least, Chapter 4 analyses the landmark decision of the US Supreme Court on *FTC v. Actavis* and the questions it gave rise to, while it also discusses subsequent jurisprudence of lower courts on other types of anticompetitive strategies. The research is not only limited to appellate court decisions but also extends to the previous stages of each case, starting from the relevant decisions of the enforcement authorities and following the evolution of each case through the briefs of the parties, describing a number of disparities between the decisions of different instances. The amicus curiae briefs of third parties were indispensable for the in-depth understanding of the legal problems that may arise from patent settlements and other types of conduct in the pharmaceutical industry. The enforcement decisions of the US Federal Trade Commission (FTC) were also essential in fully understanding the specificities of each case and the impact that seemingly minor differences may have on the legal analysis.

Finally, Part III of this book is the EU part which consists of two chapters: Chapter 5 and Chapter 6. Chapter 5 describes the EU regulatory framework, extensively analysing the patent system and the provisions regulating the market entry of pharmaceutical products in the EU. Further, it analyses the core provisions of EU competition law and the most relevant case law on the intersection of intellectual property law and competition law. The main goal of this chapter is to familiarise readers without a concrete EU competition law background with the most important notions of EU competition law, focusing on the ones that are of utmost importance for the analysis of reverse payment settlements. Chapter 6 discusses the most important case law on patent settlements and other types of strategies in the pharmaceutical sector which arguably delay generic entry in the EU market. It also compares and contrasts the applicable legal tests for the adjudication of patent settlements in the US and the EU. As in the US part, the analysis extends to the previous instances of each case, starting from the decisions of the enforcement authorities and following the evolution of each case. The EU part of this book also extends beyond the decision of the EU General Court in *Lundbeck v. Commission*: the lengthy decisions of the European Commission and the decisions of National Competition Authorities and national courts of EU Member States are vital parts of the analysis. The main points of this comparison between the US and the EU are presented in the conclusion of this book, which focuses on the applicable legal tests for the adjudication of pharmaceutical patent settlements and provides guidance on which types of conduct are legitimate, illegitimate or fall within grey areas. Finally, some practical guidance for the pharmaceutical industry is provided, with the aim to minimise the risk of engaging in conduct that could potentially infringe US antitrust and EU competition law.

PART I Pharma Innovation and Settlements

Part I of this book outlines the risks and costs of innovation for both brand-name drug manufacturers and generic drug manufacturers. Understanding the immense costs of pharma innovation and the need to spur innovation incentives is fundamental before analysing patent settlements in the pharmaceutical industry under US antitrust and EU competition law in Part II and Part III of this book respectively. Additionally, Part I discusses the benefits of settlements vis-à-vis patent litigation, aiming to highlight the importance of settlements for both the parties and for judicial systems but also to balance these benefits with the social costs such settlements may give rise to.

CHAPTER 1
Pharma R&D and Settlements

INTRODUCTION

The first chapter of this book is divided in two parts. The first part focuses on the risks and costs that pharma originators and generic manufacturers face and the impact of generic entry on the drug market. The challenges faced by drug originators come first in the order of analysis: the high costs and risks of pharma research and development (R&D), the massive expiration of patents covering blockbuster drugs – commonly known as the patent cliff – and the decline of pharma R&D performance shall be discussed before proceeding to the analysis of patent settlements in the pharma industry. The adequacy of innovation incentives provided by the pharma system is also debated. Further, the extent of generic entry and its effects on drug prices, healthcare costs and innovation incentives are presented, along with the costs and risks generic manufacturers face when they enter the market. The second part of this chapter focuses on the benefits of settlements and on how they allow parties to avoid lengthy and costly litigation, with an uncertain outcome. Courts themselves encourage parties to settle, in an effort to decrease litigation costs and inefficiencies, arguably leading to the vanishing of court trials. In an effort to provide a balanced overview, the impact of settlements on the innovation incentives of the parties is discussed, along with the social costs settlements may create.

PART 1 RISKS AND COSTS IN THE PHARMA INDUSTRY

I Challenges Faced by Drug Originators

One of the most important challenges faced by originators of brand-name drugs is refilling the product pipeline with new innovative drug products containing new molecules. Not only do R&D costs grow constantly but also increasingly stricter regulatory requirements on the safety and efficacy of pharmaceutical products burden even more originators. Regulatory control over drug prices and reimbursement levels and a wide range of statutory measures directly affect the prescribing practices of doctors and consequently have a major impact on the turnover of originators.[1] Finally, the much-dreaded patent cliff has become a reality, since a great number of blockbuster brand-name drugs have reached the end of patent protection.[2] The following sections focus on the analysis of the patent system and the debatable incentives for innovation it provides. The challenges faced by the decline in the productivity of pharma R&D, combined with the effects of the patent cliff on the brand-name drug market are also analysed.

A The Immense Costs of Pharma Innovation

The *rationale* behind patent protection is the need to reward successful innovation and to incentivise further R&D, with the ultimate goal of increasing social welfare. In the pharma industry, the high but also short-term monopoly profits that can be generated throughout the patent protection period of a successful blockbuster drug are the main incentive for originators to engage in costly R&D investments. The industry of pharmaceuticals has one of the highest ratios of R&D expenditures to sales, known as "R&D intensity."[3] In 2015, R&D expenditures in pharmaceuticals and biotechnology amounted to 15% of net sales, whereas R&D expenditures in software and computer services amounted to 10.5% of net sales.[4] There seems to be a correlation between drug prices and the amounts invested in R&D: if drug prices increase and the difference between the drug sales' revenues and the production costs increases, R&D investment also seems to rise; on the contrary when drug prices fall, R&D investment decreases.[5]

Pharma R&D activities are often presented as comprised of two distinct categories: (i) fundamental innovation aiming to develop new innovative medicines containing new compounds, which requires significant economic investment without any guarantee on its returns, and; (ii) incremental innovation focusing on the development of already existing drug products.[6] However, the above-mentioned distinction may not always be as clear-cut as it seems at first sight; it would be unfair to bulk-categorise as

---

1. European Commission, *Pharmaceutical Sector Inquiry Final Report*, July 8, 2009 [cited as: EU Commission, *Pharma Sector Inquiry*, 2009], points 145-147. *See* further *infra* Chapter 5, Part 1, Section II.B on drug pricing and reimbursement in the European Union.
2. EU Commission, *Pharma Sector Inquiry*, 2009, point 79.
3. *See* for instance WOLFE, R&D, 2014, pp. 2-4, stating that pharmaceuticals and medicines had the highest level of R&D intensity (13.4%), followed by computer and electronic products (10.2%).
4. EFPIA, *The Pharmaceutical Industry in Figures – Key Data 2017*, p. 10. Available at: https://www.efpia.eu/media/219735/efpia-pharmafigures2017_statisticbroch_v04-final.pdf. (last accessed on March 31, 2018) [cited as: EFPIA, *Pharma Key Data*, 2017].
5. *See* for instance GIACCOTTO, SANTERRE, VERNON, R&D Growth Rates, 2003, pp. 1-21, arguing that R&D increases with real drug prices; SCHERER, R&D Spending, 2001, pp. 216-220, analysing the link between profitability and R&D investments.
6. EU Commission, *Pharma Sector Inquiry*, 2009, point 132. *See also* GRABOWSKI ET AL., Consumer Welfare, 2012, pp. 367-368, noting that the pattern of incremental innovation is a characteristic of major therapeutic classes and has resulted in important economic and medical benefits.

incremental *any* innovation that is related to existing drug products, especially if such categorisation is done by legal experts who generally lack the scientific expertise to evaluate the results of pharma R&D.

1 Research and Development Costs Globally

According to European Federation of Pharmaceutical Industries and Associations (EFPIA), the pharma industry invested an estimated €35,000 million in R&D in Europe in 2016, rising from €33,500 million that was invested in 2015.[7] However, this data is not only limited to the European Member States but also extends to Switzerland, Norway, Serbia, Russia and Turkey.[8] In 2015, the estimated amount of pharma R&D expenditure in the US was $47,051 million.[9] Originator pharmaceutical companies are investing a big part of their revenues in R&D. The Swiss Novartis, one of the top originator drug manufacturers worldwide, reported that it invested $9 billion in R&D in 2017, amounting to 18.32% of its net sales.[10] In 2016, the American originator Pfizer reportedly invested $7,872 million in R&D, whereas it had invested $8,393 million in 2014.[11] Despite the high R&D costs, the pharma industry consistently ranks at the top of the most profitable industries worldwide.[12] The US is the world's largest pharmaceutical market and provides a good view of the economic proportions of the pharma industry. In 2015, the US pharma market reached $333 billion in sales – nearly triple the drug sales in China –[13] and accounted for 48.7% of world pharmaceutical sales.[14] In the same year, the European pharma industry accounted for 22.2% of world pharma sales.[15]

The R&D costs are used by the pharma industry as an argument that arguably justifies not only high drug prices but also patent protection prolongation strategies. As analysed in the following chapters of this book, the high costs of drug development, testing, marketing authorisation procedures, etc. are also invoked in an effort to justify

---

7. EFPIA, *Pharma Key Data*, 2017, pp. 4-9.
8. EFPIA, *Pharma Key Data*, 2017, p. 4.
9. EFPIA, *The Pharmaceutical Industry in Figures – Key Data 2016*, pp. 1-15. Available at: https://www.efpia.eu/media/25055/the-pharmaceutical-industry-in-figures-june-2016.pdf. (last accessed on March 31, 2018) [cited as: EFPIA, *Pharma Key Data*, 2016], p. 5. *See also* WOLFE, R&D, 2014, p. 3, Table 2, stating that $56.6 million were spent for R&D in the industry of pharmaceuticals and medicines, $47.6 million of which was paid for by the relevant drug company. Available at: https://www.nsf.gov/statistics/2016/nsf16315/ (last accessed on March 31, 2018).
10. Novartis, *Annual Report 2017*, p. 10.
11. Pfizer, *Financial Report 2016*, p. 21.
12. *See* for instance the Forbes Website, CHEN, Most Profitable Industries, 2016, ranking the health technology sector as the most profitable sector; in 2016 the generic pharma industry had 30% net margin and the major pharma 25.5%.
13. U.S. Department of Commerce, International Trade Administration, *2016 Top Markets Report: Pharmaceuticals – A Market Assessment Tool for U.S. Exporters*, May 2016, pp. 1-41. Available at: http://www.trade.gov/topmarkets/pdf/Pharmaceuticals_Top_Markets_Reports.pdf (last accessed on March 31, 2018). [cited as: U.S. Department of Commerce, *2016 Top Markets*].
14. EFPIA, *Pharma Key Data*, 2016, p. 4.
15. *Idem*. *See also* EU Commission, *Pharma Sector Inquiry*, 2009, point 72, stating that between 2000 and 2007 originator companies spent an average 17% of their global turnover on R&D.

the conclusion of anticompetitive patent settlements with generic challengers. It should however be borne in mind that R&D expenditures should not be perceived as mere *costs* for the originator companies. Instead such R&D expenditures could also be seen as a long-term *investment* which generates profits years after it was conducted and could arguably be included in the assets of originator companies.[16]

2 Debating the Cost of Drug Development

It is generally accepted that the R&D costs of new pharmaceutical products are extraordinarily high;[17] however the average cost of pharma R&D is largely disputed.[18] The R&D costs vary widely from one drug to another and depend on the type of drug, the likelihood of R&D failure but also on whether the drug concerns a new molecule which has never been used in a pharmaceutical product before or a modification of an existing drug, that is likely to be seen as incremental.[19] Estimates of pharma R&D costs per drug also include the cost of the failed attempts,[20] an approach that is met by scepticism and arguably leads to a lack of transparency regarding the actual R&D costs pharma companies incur.[21] According to a 2016 survey, the average cost of developing a drug (including the cost of failures) is $2.6 billion for the period between the 2000s and the early 2010s, while it was $1 billion in the previous decade.[22] However, the said survey is limited to 10 pharmaceutical companies and concerns the R&D costs of 106 randomly selected new drugs.[23] Previous versions of the same survey have been contested by a number of commentators arguing that the actual pharma R&D costs are in fact much lower.[24] A 2017 study also claims that the median cost of developing a

---

16. *See* for instance SCHERER, Prices and Progress, 2004, p. 929.
17. U.S. Department of Health and Human Services Report to the Congress, *Prescription Drugs: Innovation, Spending, and Patient Access*, (December 7, 2016), pp. 25-36. Available at: http://apps.who.int/medicinedocs/en/d/Js23128en/ (last accessed on March 31, 2018), discussing the innovation costs and the time it takes for brand-name manufacturers to bring new drugs to the market.
18. *See* for instance LARRIMORE, Follow-on Patents, 2010, p. 302, contesting the accuracy of PhRMA's claim that the R&D cost per approved drug was $1.3 billion in 2005.
19. CBO, *Research and Development in the Pharmaceutical Industry*, (October 2006), pp. 1-2. Available at: https://www.cbo.gov/sites/default/files/109th-congress-2005-2006/reports/10-02-drugr-d.pdf (last accessed on March 31, 2018). [cited as: CBO, Pharma R&D, 2006]. *See also* LIGHT, Misleading Congress, 2007, pp. 895-913, arguing that the R&D costs per drug are much lower than $800 million that Di Masi, Grabowski and Hansen estimated, and criticising the CBO for featuring this estimate as the grand average cost.
20. CBO, Pharma R&D, 2006, p. 19.
21. *See* for instance REID, BALASEGARAM, R&D in the Dark, 2016, p. 655.
22. DIMASI ET AL., R&D Costs, 2016, p. 26, stating that the total cost estimate is $2,558 million; PhRMA, *2016 Profile: Biopharmaceutical Research Industry*, pp. 46-57. Available at: phrma.org/sites/default/files/pdf/biopharmaceutical-industry-profile.pdf (last accessed on March 31, 2018).
23. DIMASI ET AL., R&D Costs, 2016, p. 26. The same authors have conducted a similar survey in 2003; *see* DIMASI ET AL., New Estimates, 2003, pp. 151-185.
24. FRANK, New Estimates, 2003, p. 325, acknowledging the criticisms against a previous version of the study in 2001 that lead to "heated debate;" CBO, Pharma R&D, 2006, pp. 19-21, criticising the DiMasi, Grabowski & Hansen 2003 study for basing their cost estimate on types of drugs that have been the source of most pharmaceutical breakthroughs and for relying on data that was

single cancer drug in the US was $648 million.²⁵ Other specialists argue that the cost of developing a new drug may vary from $521 million to more than $2,100 million depending on the type of therapy and the developing company.²⁶ According to a study examining a sample of seventeen biopharmaceutical molecules, the total cost of discovering and developing a biopharmaceutical to the point of initial regulatory marketing approval was $1,241 million in 2005.²⁷ Apart from being expensive, pharma R&D is also time-consuming and risky: on average twelve to thirteen years are needed from the first synthesis of an active substance until the respective drug reaches the market. Further, on average, only 1 or 2 out of 10,000 synthesized substances will successfully pass all development stages required to become marketable,²⁸ while only 1 out of 6 drugs that entered the clinical testing phase between 1993 and 2004 obtained marketing approval in the US.²⁹

3 The Contribution of Government-Funded Investment in Pharma R&D

An aspect that is often neglected – at least in the court decisions on settlements concluded in the context of patent infringement litigation which are examined in this book – is the government-funded and non-profit expenditures on basic and clinical research, the cost of which is substantial. In the US, the National Institutes of Health (NIH) invest annually more than $32 billion in medical research via competitive grants to researchers and institutions.³⁰ The majority of the government's spending relates to basic research on the mechanisms of diseases, on which pharma companies do not generally engage, focusing instead on applied R&D and the development of new

---

proprietary and could not be independently verified; ANGELL, Drug Companies, 2004, arguing that R&D costs are a relatively small part of the budgets of the big pharma companies. *See* further DIMASI ET AL., R&D Costs, 2016, pp. 28-31, referring and replying to the critique.

25. PRASAD, MAILANKODY, R&D Spending, 2017, analysing ten companies and their costs of developing cancer drugs. *See* however, HERPER, 2017, criticising the authors' analysis and arguing that this figure merely represents the median R&D spending of these ten companies.
26. ADAMS, BRANTNER, Cost of New Drug Development, 2006, pp. 420, 427.
27. DIMASI, GRABOWSKI, Biopharmaceutical R&D, 2007, pp. 472-479.
28. EFPIA, *Pharma Key Data*, 2016, p. 6. *See also* PAUL ET AL., R&D Productivity, 2010, p. 205, stating that the process of discovering and developing a new molecular entity required on average 13.5 years between 2000 and 2007.
29. DIMASI ET AL., Success Rates, 2010, pp. 275-277.
30. US Department of Health and Human Services, National Institutes of Health (NIH), Budget. Available at: https://www.nih.gov/about-nih/what-we-do/budget (last accessed on March 31, 2018). *See also* U.S. Department of Health and Human Services, National Institutes of Health (NIH), *Estimates of Funding for Various Research, Condition and Disease Categories (RCDC)*, February 10, 2016. Available at: https://report.nih.gov/categorical_spending.aspx (last accessed on March 31, 2018). Available at: https://report.nih.gov/categorical_spending.aspx (last accessed on March 31, 2018); National Institutes of Health, *History of Congressional Appropriations*, Fiscal Years 2000-2016, pp. 1-3. Available at: https://officeofbudget.od.nih.gov/pdfs/FY16/Approp%20History%20by%20IC%20FY%202000%20-%20FY%202016.pdf (last accessed on March 31, 2018). The National Institutes of Health requested a budget of $33.136 billion for the FY 2017; *see* Collins Francis S., Director, National Institutes of Health, *Testimony on the Fiscal Year 2017 Budget Request before the Senate Committee*, April 6, 2016, p. 4. Available at: http://www.nih.gov/sites/default/files/about-nih/nih-director/testimonies/testimony-fiscal-year-2017-budget-request-before-senate-committee.pdf (last accessed on March 31, 2018).

pharmaceuticals. The Federal funding of basic research directly expands the industry's opportunities for R&D: since information generated by basic research can be replicated at low cost, many of the resulting benefits are enjoyed by pharmaceutical companies.[31] Additionally, private sector R&D is also indirectly stimulated: many of the graduate students and post-doctoral researchers who are trained through the support of Federal grants in conducting basic research are later on employed by the pharma industry, where their publicly funded training enhances the productivity and profitability of the industry's R&D investments.[32] According to a 2015 study, many drugs which are described by expert physicians as "transformative" were based on discoveries made by academic researchers or were jointly developed by publicly funded and commercial institutions.[33] In the European Union, the EFPIA is supporting European R&D and patients' access to innovative medicines through the Innovative Medicines Initiative Joint Undertaking (IMI JU), a public-private partnership.[34] For the period of 2014-2024, the programme has a budget of €3.3 billion, half of which is financed by the European Union's Horizon 2020 Framework Program.[35]

Given the contribution of public investment in pharma innovation and research and its impact on the development of innovative drugs, this public investment should also be reflected in the pricing of drug products. In order to recoup the public investment in the development of pharma products, some commentators have suggested recoupment provisions in the licensing agreements for publicly funded research that is transferred to the pharma industry.[36] The recoupment of public investment in pharma R&D development is an additional argument advocating in favour of timely generic drug entry and against strategies illegitimately extending patent protection and originators' monopolies.

B   The Decline in the R&D Performance of the Pharma Industry

Even though the total spending on R&D by the pharma industry and by the US Federal government has tripled in real terms from 1990 to 2006, the number of innovative new drugs approved by the Food and Drug Administration (FDA) has not shown a comparable parallel increase in the US.[37] The increase in R&D spending is not associated with a higher output: the number of approvals per billion of US $ spent on

---

31. CBO, Pharma R&D, 2006, pp. 2-3.
32. CBO, Pharma R&D, 2006, p. 3.
33. KESSELHEIM, TAN, AVORN, Transformative Drugs, 2015, pp. 286-293, examining a sample of twenty-six drugs or drug classes approved by the FDA between 1984 and 2009.
34. Innovative Medicines Initiative Website, *Introducing IMI*. Available at: http://www.imi.europa.eu/content/mission (last accessed on March 31, 2018). *See also* European Commission Website, *Research and Innovation Funding 2014-2020*. Available at: https://ec.europa.eu/research/fp7/index_en.cfm (last accessed on March 31, 2018).
35. Innovative Medicines Initiative Website, *Introducing IMI*. Available at: http://www.imi.europa.eu/content/mission (last accessed on March 31, 2018).
36. *See* for instance ORIOLA, Strong Medicine, 2009, pp. 72-78, discussing the extent of the publicly funded innovation and research in the US and arguing in favour of a drug pricing policy that reflects public investment.
37. See further SCANNELL ET AL., Diagnosing the Decline, 2012, pp. 193-197, discussing some of the primary causes of R&D decline in pharma.

Chapter 1: Pharma R&D and Settlements

R&D has been constantly decreasing from 1981.[38] In 2017, the FDA-approved forty-six Novel Drugs, while in 2016 it had only approved twenty-two; between 2011 and 2016 an average of approximately thirty-four Novel Drugs per year were approved by the FDA.[39] On the contrary, biological medicinal products, isolated from a variety of natural resources,[40] have been steadily increasing,[41] with the exception of 2016.[42] As far as the European Union is concerned, twenty-seven New Active Substances were recommended for approval in 2016 by the European Medicines Agency, the majority of which concerned cancer treatments.[43]

1   The Difficulties in Evaluating Pharma's Innovative Performance

It is extremely difficult to evaluate the innovative performance of R&D in the pharma industry. Even though it is undeniable that the number of New Molecular Entities (NMEs) approved per year has declined, this number solely constitutes a quantitative criterion that overlooks the qualitative aspect of innovation. If for instance the invented new drugs are of higher quality than the older ones, this improvement in quality could partly or wholly recompensate the quantitative decline of NMEs.[44] Nevertheless, drug quality is even more difficult to measure and it is nearly impossible to objectively determine the impact of change in quality in the overall R&D performance of the pharma industry.[45]

Another reason why the number of approved NMEs is not an optimal performance measure to evaluate the pharma industry's R&D output, is that it ignores the

---

38. OECD, *Health at a Glance 2015*, pp. 188-189, Figure 10.16.
39. FDA, *New Drug Therapy Approvals Report for 2017*, p. 9, (January 2018). Available at: https://www.fda.gov/downloads/AboutFDA/CentersOffices/OfficeofMedicalProductsandToba cco/CDER/ReportsBudgets/UCM591976.pdf (last accessed on March 31, 2018). The Report also contains the numbers of FDA-approved Novel Drugs between 2008 and 2017. Indicatively, forty-five New Drugs were approved in 2015; forty-one in 2014; twenty-seven in 2013; thirty-nine in 2012 and thirty in 2011.
40. See further FDA, *What Are Biologicals: Questions & Answers*. Available at: http://www.fda.gov/AboutFDA/CentersOffices/OfficeofMedicalProductsandTobacco/CBER/ucm133077.htm (last accessed on March 31, 2018).
41. *See* for instance EvaluatePharma, *World Preview 2016*, p. 29, showing the increase of biological drugs for the period between 2001 and 2015. Twenty-four out of the fifty-six NMEs were biologicals in 2015, while twenty out of fifty NMEs were biologicals in 2014.
42. FDA Website, *2016 Biological License Application Approvals*, listing fifteen biologicals approved in 2016. Available at: https://www.fda.gov/BiologicsBloodVaccines/DevelopmentApproval Process/BiologicalApprovalsbyYear/ucm482397.htm. *See* however FDA Website, *2017 Biological License Application Approvals*, listing twenty-two biologicals approved in 2017. Available at: https://www.fda.gov/BiologicsBloodVaccines/DevelopmentApprovalProcess/Biological ApprovalsbyYear/ucm547553.htm. *See* further EvaluatePharma, *World Preview 2017*, p. 21, providing the overview of the number of FDA-approved biologicals and NMEs between 2001 and 2016.
43. European Medicines Agency, *Human Medicines Highlights 2016*, p. 1. Available at: http://www.ema.europa.eu/ema/index.jsp?curl=pages/audience/alp_audiencetype_000004.jsp&mi d=.(last accessed on March 31, 2018), p. 1.
44. CBO, *Pharma R&D*, 2006, p. 3.
45. *Idem*.

growing share of incremental product changes and reformulations.[46] A constant criticism is that an increasing share of the industry's R&D output concerns incremental improvements to existing drugs rather than new molecules.[47] Nevertheless, incremental innovations may also be essential for advancing patients' treatment.[48] Even actual imitation may create consumer benefits: for instance "me-too drugs" – that is brand-name drugs subsequent to a first pioneer brand-name drug – may benefit patients by providing alternatives to people who do not respond in the same way to all medication.[49] On the flipside, as analysed in the following chapters of this book, incremental changes to drug products may also be employed as part of evergreening and alleged product-hopping strategies.[50] Determining whether an incremental innovation actually advances patients' treatment is a complicated task and should be examined on a case-by-case basis.[51]

2 The Patent Cliff and Patenting Strategies

It is often argued that even though the cost of R&D constantly increases, drug sales constantly decline. The phenomenon of the so-called "patent cliff" has a direct impact on the market situation and sales of originators.[52] In 2011 and 2012 several blockbuster drugs – with a value of more than $30 billion a year in US sales – lost patent protection.[53] Within 2018, a plethora of key-patents have expired or will expire, arguably jeopardizing $290 billion of drug sales and constituting the first "patent cliff era."[54] The "second patent cliff era" extends from 2018 to 2022, when $249 billion of sales are allegedly at risk due to patent expirations.[55] The loss of revenues for originators due to patent expirations of successful drug products and its impact on innovation investments are causing increasing concern.[56] However, there is evidence showing a rather steady increase in the worldwide sales of prescription drugs between 2008 and 2017, forecasting further impressive increases until 2020.[57] Despite the patent

---

46. CBO, Pharma R&D, 2006, pp. 3-4.
47. Idem.
48. U.S. Department of Commerce, *2016 Top Markets*, p. 11.
49. CBO, Pharma R&D, 2006, p. 13.
50. *See infra* Chapter 4 and Chapter 6, analysing also product-hopping strategies involving incremental innovation in the US and in the EU.
51. *See* further SHADOWEN, LEFFLER, LUKENS, Market Discipline, 2011, pp. 700-704, analysing the economics of drug product reformulations, some of which are legitimate efforts to improve the product, while others are designed to inhibit generic entry.
52. *See also* EU Commission, *Pharma Sector Inquiry*, 2009, paras 165-166.
53. BELLONI, MORGAN Pharma Expenditures, 2016, p. 27.
54. EvaluatePharma, *World Preview 2012*, p. 6.
55. EvaluatePharma, *World Preview 2016*, pp. 9-10; *see also* EvaluatePharma, *World Preview 2017*, p. 9, forecasting worldwide sales at risk due to patent expiration.
56. *See* for instance PAUL ET AL., R&D Productivity, 2010, pp. 203, 205-214, proposing a model to increase R&D productivity as a means to ensure the pharma industry's survival. *See also* SCHUHMACHER, GASSMANN, HINDER, Changing R&D, 2016.
57. EvaluatePharma, *World Preview 2017*, pp. 3, 9.

cliff, worldwide sales of prescription drugs are still forecasted to show annual growth of 6.5% until 2022 arguably reaching $1.06 trillion worldwide.[58]

Attempting to ensure their protection from competition, pharmaceutical products are on average covered by three different patents.[59] The higher the sale predictions for a pharmaceutical product, the more aggressive the patenting strategy of the originator is likely to be in order to decrease the chances of generic competition.[60] In anticipation of the declining turnover following the expiration of patents covering blockbuster drugs, originators may engage in product life-cycle management strategies with two main aims: (i) to extend their time of market exclusivity before generic entry occurs, and; (ii) to maintain or if possible expand the markets covered by the brand-name products during their exclusivity period.[61] Such life-cycle strategies are for instance: measures enhancing consumers' loyalty in the product (including the criticism of efficacy/quality of generic drug versions); product reformulations and launches of second-generation brand-name drugs as part of a product-hopping strategy;[62] creation of patent clusters and defensive patenting;[63] litigation and settlements against other originators and generic manufacturers; launch of authorised generic versions, etc.[64] The legal problems raised by the above-mentioned practices are discussed in detail in the following chapters of this book.

C Does the Patent System Incentivise Innovation?

One of the main aims of intellectual property law is to solve the problems that arise when the product of creative activity – which was developed by the innovator at a high cost – can be reproduced by others at a much lower cost or can be easily appropriated.[65] The patent system and the legally induced market exclusivities accorded to innovators aim to provide them with adequate incentives in order for them to engage in R&D investment, by protecting them from imitators. Nevertheless, there are many critics of the patent system who argue that it actually inhibits innovation,[66] at least as far as

---

58. EvaluatePharma, *World Preview 2017*, p. 3.
59. LARRIMORE, Follow-on Patents, 2010, pp. 314-317.
60. *Idem*.
61. Deloitte LLP, *R&D Returns*, 2015, pp. 3-4.
62. *See infra* Chapter 4, Part 3, Section IV; Chapter 5, Part 2, Section III; Chapter 6, Part 3, Section I, analysing product hopping strategies in the pharma industry. *See also* DOMEIJ, Pharmaceutical Switching, 2013, pp. 280-285, describing the period after the introduction of generic substitution in Sweden and how successful product switching strategies have increased the total public costs despite the expiration of patent exclusivity for several blockbuster drugs.
63. *See* for instance EU Commission, *Pharma Sector Inquiry*, 2009, paras 484-536, analysing how patent clusters and divisional patent applications may serve to prevent or delay generic entry. *See also* ULLRICH, Strategic Patenting, 2013, pp. 262-270, discussing aggressive patenting strategies under Article 102 TFEU, their effects on competition and possible remedies.
64. EU Commission, *Pharma Sector Inquiry*, 2009, paras 166-167.
65. BURK, LEMLEY, Technology-Specific, 2002, p. 1158.
66. *See* for instance KHOURY, Differential Patent Terms, 2010, pp. 385-388, arguing that the strength of patent protection indirectly creates a disincentive to innovate; CHENG, Developmental Approach, 2012, pp. 25-41, presenting an overview of theoretical and empirical arguments supporting that the necessity of the patent system in order to spur innovation has been overstated, in both developed and developing countries. *See also* OHLHAUSEN, IP Skepticism,

some industries are concerned.[67] A number of economists have argued in favour of abolishing the patent system, since innovation is "the fruit of a competitive environment" and would anyways occur in the absence of patents due to enhanced competition.[68] Another of the main criticisms against the patent system is that it accords inventors more insulation from competition than needed in order to incentivise innovation, resulting in increased market prices beyond efficient levels and causing distortions in the allocation of resources.[69] Making patentability standards stricter, increasing patent fees, reducing the duration of patent protection or even denying patentability to inventions in certain industries are seen as measures that could stimulate innovation instead of ending innovative activity, by reducing the costs and risks for invention.[70]

1 The Difference Between Pharma and Other Industries

Even the harshest scepticists of the ability of the patent system to incentivise innovation generally accept that the pharmaceutical industry seems to be the exception. Patent protection provides a powerful incentive for the pharma industry to engage in R&D investments and innovation.[71] Pharmaceuticals' patents are generally much more valuable than patents in other industries:[72] chemical and pharma patents arguably account for over three-fourths of *all* patent value.[73] The importance of patent protection for the pharma industry is linked to the dependence of the industry's profits on patents, since patent rents arguably account for over half of the industry's net

---

   2016, pp. 110-116 and cited articles, providing an elaborate overview of the critics of the patent system and its ability to incentivise innovation and explaining some of the reasons for such scepticism.
67. BESSEN, MASKIN, Sequential Innovation, 2009, pp. 611-614, arguing that in industries like software or computers, patents may reduce welfare by blocking imitation and thus result in reduced innovation.
68. *See* for instance BOLDRIN, LEVINE, Against Patents, 2013, pp. 4-7; *see also* BOLDRIN, LEVINE, *Against Intellectual Monopoly*, 2008, Chapter 3 and Chapter 4, examining innovation without patents and criticising the patent system.
69. POSNER, *Economic Analysis of Law*, 2014, p. 407.
70. *See* for instance POSNER, *Economic Analysis of Law*, 2014, pp. 403-409; BESSEN, LOVE, Patent Polluters, 2013, pp. 84-91, advocating in favour of establishing patent "maintenance fees" in order to restrain patent abuse.
71. BESSEN, MEURER, Patents and Property, 2008, p. 19 arguing that empirical evidence suggests that the patent system decreases innovation, with some exceptions such as pharmaceuticals. BESSEN, MEURER, *Patent Failure*, 2008, pp. 27-152. See also BRONWYN, 2007, pp. 574-576, discussing empirical studies showing that patents may increase innovation in the sectors of pharma, biotechnology, medical instruments and specialty chemicals; MCDONALD S., Reinvention of Innovation, 2013, pp. 8-9, arguing that the innovation model of the pharma industry is particular, despite the fact that the industry insists there is a direct relation between more IP protection, more R&D and innovation.
72. BESSEN, MEURER, *Patent Failure*, 2008, pp. 106-109. *See* further CHENG, Developmental Approach, 2012, pp. 33-37, for an overview of the findings of a number of empirical studies confirming that patent protection is by far an important incentive to innovate in the pharmaceutical industry, when compared to other industries.
73. BESSEN, MEURER, *Patent Failure*, 2008, pp. 106-109.

income.[74] Pharmaceuticals' patents protect valuable intangible information on drugs, such as their chemical structure, qualities, efficacy and possible side effects; however, pharma companies do not profit by selling this intangible information – which would be largely useless for patients – but by selling the tangible drugs which incorporate it.[75] The close link between the tangible drug and the intangible valuable information it incorporates, combined with the particularities of the institutional, technological and regulatory context related to pharmaceuticals, makes the commercialisation of this intangible information easier through the use of exclusion rights.[76]

The difference between the pharmaceutical industry and other industries lies primarily in the high regulatory burdens initial drug innovators face: originators are the ones to bear the high cost of R&D and clinical trials, while generic manufacturers do not have to cover such costs and are at a large cost advantage compared to originators.[77] The ratio of the cost of inventing a new drug to the cost of copying it is extremely high in the pharma industry, so that the inventor may not be capable to recoup its upfront costs without patent protection.[78] In most other industries "imitators" face higher market entry costs and enjoy a much smaller advantage; imitation cost and time are found to be approximately two-thirds of the original development cost and time.[79] Moreover, pharmaceuticals' patents cover well-defined molecules and are more effective and easily enforceable against infringers than patents of other industries.[80] Thus, pharma patents have a bigger impact on imitation costs, increasing by 30% the ratio of imitation cost to innovation cost.[81]

Even as far as the pharmaceutical industry is concerned, the incentive-based patent system is imperfect and widely criticised.[82] The patent system is often "gamed" by originators through evergreening: incremental improvements are patented at an increasing rate, with the main goal of keeping generic competitors off the market.[83] The overload of patent offices and their limited resources may lead to the grant of "weak" patents further deteriorating the problem of evergreening.[84] Further, patent exclusivity is arguably linked to excessive drug prices,[85] especially in countries with no strict

---

74. BESSEN, MEURER, *Patent Failure*, 2008, p. 114, arguing that patent rents amounted for 63% of the net income of large pharmaceutical companies, after comparing their patent rents to their net income for the period between 1990 and 1997.
75. KAPCZYNSKI, SYED, Continuum of Excludability, 2013, pp. 1921-1923.
76. KAPCZYNSKI, SYED, Continuum of Excludability, 2013, p. 1922.
77. BESSEN, MEURER, Patents and Property, 2008, pp. 23-24.
78. POSNER, *Economic Analysis of Law*, 2014, pp. 407-408.
79. BESSEN, MEURER, *Patent Failure*, 2008, pp. 88-89; MANSFIELD, SCHWARTZ, WAGNER, Imitation Costs, 1981, p. 910.
80. BESSEN, MEURER, Patents and Property, 2008, pp. 152-154; LEMLEY, Industry-Specific, 2010, pp. 6-7.
81. MANSFIELD, SCHWARTZ, WAGNER, Imitation Costs, 1981, pp. 913-914.
82. *See* for instance BASHEER, Alternative Incentives, 2014, pp. 13-63, addressing these three main problems of the current patent and exclusivities system and analysing possible alternatives to incentivise innovation.
83. *See infra* Chapter 2, Part 2, Section II.D.2.2. discussing evergreening in US in the context of the Hatch-Waxman Act.
84. *See infra* Chapter 3, Part 2, Section III.B, discussing the high rates of patent invalidation in the US.
85. BASHEER, Alternative Incentives, 2014, p. 14.

governmental price controls such as the US.[86] Finally, pharmaceutical companies tend to focus their R&D on diseases affecting the developed countries in which they enjoy patent protection, neglecting diseases affecting developing countries such as tuberculosis which causes an estimated 2 million deaths annually.[87] These imperfections of the patent system have led commentators propose other alternative models to incentivise and to fund drug innovation, such as investment protection regimes, "prize" regimes or public funding models.[88] Nevertheless, a detailed analysis of possible alternatives to remedy the imperfections of the patent system falls outside the scope of this book.[89]

2 The Impact of the Breadth and Duration of Patent Protection on Innovation

The breadth of the patent, the length of the patent (its duration) and the height of the patent are the three measures which define the degree of market power that a patent provides to the patent holder.[90] The height of the patent refers to the novelty requirement and concerns the patent holder's power to protect itself from trivial improvements or applications which are close to the patent.[91] All three measures are directly linked to the incentives to innovate and affect the efficiency of the patent system.[92] As shown in the following chapters of this book, especially the breadth and the length of patent protection are highly relevant to the subject of patent settlements in the pharma industry. Patent protection that is short or too narrow may lead to reduced R&D investment and innovation, while a patent that is too long or too broad is likely to generate excessive profit for the patent holder and to pose obstacles to further innovation.[93] The size of the scope of the protection accorded by property rights

---

86. SCHERER, Prices and Progress, 2004, p. 929.
87. OUTTERSON, Patent Buy-Outs, 2006, pp. 159-173, analysing how R&D focuses on diseases affecting high-income markets such as the US and the EU, neglecting health conditions that affect poor countries; WHO, Investing in Health, 2001, pp. 76-86, 198, analysing how R&D for poor country disease conditions such as malaria, tuberculosis and AIDS are neglected by the international pharmaceutical industry.
88. See further BASHEER, Alternative Incentives, 2014, pp. 22-63, analysing alternative systems of providing incentives for pharma innovation; HUBBARD, LOVE, Healthcare R&D, 2004, pp. 0148-0150, discussing various business models in order to incentivize R&D, such as direct funding of drug development, prize models and competitive financing schemes through R&D investment intermediaries; LOVE, HUBBARD, Prizes, 2007, pp. 1534-1543, analysing how a prize fund system should be designed in order to finance innovation and maximise access to new inventions; See also KIM, SCHWARZ, Economic Prizes, 2005, pp. 44-63, proposing an economic prize system to boost pharma innovation.
89. For an interesting approach on optimal innovation incentives and the use of potential penalties for failures to innovate see AYRES, KAPCZYNSKI, Innovation Sticks, 2015, pp. 1799-1811. See also COOTER, ULEN, Law and Economics, 2014, pp. 116-117, discussing examples of reward systems and their social costs and benefits; BRONWYN, 2007, pp. 573-576, discussing various empirical studies on the influence of the patent system to innovation activities and alternative means of incentivising innovation; POSNER, Intellectual Property, 2005, pp. 65-69, discussing other alternative solutions in order to cover the fixed costs of innovation.
90. LANGINIER, GIANCARLO, Economics of Patents, 2002, pp. 7-10.
91. See further VAN DIJK, Product Improvements, 1996, pp. 152-154 describing the concept of patent height and examining its effect on improvement choices.
92. COOTER, ULEN, Law and Economics, 2014, pp. 108-109.
93. LANGINIER, GIANCARLO, Economics of Patents, 2002, pp. 7-11.

influences the profits of the property right holder and the incentives to create information: the greater the scope of property rights' protection, the greater the profits of the property right holder and the incentives to innovate.[94] On the other hand, a wide scope of protection aggravates the problem of excessive prices and of inadequate use of information.[95]

The breadth and the length of patent protection are interrelated measures; by increasing either one, the profits of the right holder and the incentives to innovate are increased. It is difficult to determine the optimal duration of patent protection: such duration should strike a balance between incentivising innovation and creativity on the one hand and discouraging dissemination on the other hand.[96] COOTER & ULEN provide a solid economic analysis on the effects of patent duration on innovation.[97] The authors argue that the incentives to innovate increase when the duration of the patent increases and the society benefits from more inventions. Nevertheless, the rate of innovative inventions decreases.[98] Thus, as the duration of the patent increases, the marginal benefit from innovation decreases.[99] On the flipside, society incurs more costs due to decreased dissemination as the duration of the patent increases: there is a presumption that the rate at which the social costs of patents increase decreases with the duration of the patent.[100] The longer the patent protection, the more time society searches for substitutes of patented goods and the more substitutes are found. Therefore, as the duration of the patent increases, there is a presumption that the marginal cost from less dissemination decreases.[101]

Beyond the difficulty of determining the optimal patent duration, another problem is that patent duration is uniform for all inventions: every invention is granted twenty years of patent protection in both the US and the EU.[102] It is a constant criticism that in order to truly incentivise innovation, the duration of patent protection should not be uniform for all industries,[103] but vary according to the individual characteristics of each invention.[104] Nevertheless, opting for "individualised" patent terms would be impractical and highly complicated since it is difficult to determine whether an improvement is really innovative; developing objective criteria for assessing the extent and quality of innovation and creating clear rules for calculating the optimal duration of each patent in a fair and transparent manner seems extremely challenging, if not impossible. Another problematic aspect of this approach is the difficulty in predicting

---

94. SHAVELL, *Foundations of Economic Analysis*, 2004, pp. 146-147.
95. SHAVELL, *Foundations of Economic Analysis*, 2004, p. 147.
96. COOTER, ULEN, *Law and Economics*, 2014, p. 111; LANGINIER, GIANCARLO, Economics of Patents, 2002, pp. 9-10, discussing briefly different approaches of commentators on the optimal scope of the patent for incentivising innovation while increasing the social welfare.
97. COOTER, ULEN, *Law and Economics*, 2014, p. 111.
98. *Idem.*
99. *Idem.*
100. *Idem.*
101. *Idem.*
102. *See infra* Chapter 2, Part 1, Section I.B for the US and Chapter 5, Part 1, Section III.C.1 for the EU.
103. BURK, LEMLEY, Technology-Specific, 2002, pp. 1183-1206, arguing that patent law is becoming technology-specific and that different industries should be treated differently.
104. COOTER, ULEN, *Law and Economics*, 2014, p. 111.

the impact of each invention on consumer welfare, in order to calculate the optimal duration of patent protection that would adequately compensate the innovator's success.

3 Antitrust Law Scrutiny and Its Role in Incentivising Innovation

While the role of patent law in incentivising innovation is often accepted as a universal truth, the role of antitrust in incentivising innovation is rarely mentioned. On the contrary, applying antitrust scrutiny is frequently blamed for decreasing innovation incentives and consumer welfare. Nevertheless, antitrust law may be a more effective promoter of innovation than patent law, especially given the transformations it had undertaken throughout the years in order to focus on increasing consumer welfare by promoting competition.[105] Consumer welfare is increased when consumers obtain the same good at lower prices, higher quality goods at the same price or when consumer choice is broadened.[106] Even though antitrust law is most often linked to static efficiency – the allocation of goods and services in the short run – it also focuses on dynamic efficiency: that is the ability of a market to produce innovation.[107] The focus of antitrust laws on dynamic efficiency is not surprising, given that on the long term, new technology and new innovative products lead to a greater enhancement of consumer welfare than lower prices obtained through static competition.[108] Thus, the clash between the objectives of patent law and antitrust law has been criticised as exaggerated and oversimplified.[109]

Whereas patent law remains largely indifferent to the performance and diversity of markets, antitrust law is empirical, market-based and much more sensitive to the differences among markets.[110] This can be explained by the fact that the fundamental principles of antitrust law have been articulated by courts, which have focused on the economic characteristics of the industry at issue in each case.[111] As analysed in the following chapters of this book, in antitrust cases concerning pharmaceuticals, courts take into consideration the regulatory framework that is specific to the pharmaceutical market and the barriers to entry this framework creates, the issue of potential competition in the drug market, the impact of the applicable legal standard on innovation incentives and settlement rates, etc. Preserving the incentives to innovate in the pharmaceutical industry is a core concern in the vast majority of court decisions on patent settlements which are analysed in this book. In the same time, courts highlight

---

105. HOVENKAMP, Reexamination, 2015, pp. 473-474, stating that antitrust cases are nowadays more difficult to win, the per se illegality rule is less frequently used by courts and the requirements of allegation and economic proof have been substantially heightened.
106. CHENG T., Patent-Antitrust Interface, 2013, pp. 388-389.
107. Idem.
108. CHENG T., Patent-Antitrust Interface, 2013, p. 390.
109. See for instance, LEMLEY, Industry-Specific, 2010, pp. 2-3, arguing that the notion that IP law promotes dynamic efficiency while antitrust concentrates on static welfare is wrong, or at least oversimplified; HOVENKAMP, Restraints, 2007, pp. 247-248, noting that the conflict between patent law and antitrust is largely exaggerated and does not exist.
110. HOVENKAMP, Reexamination, 2015, p. 474.
111. LEMLEY, Industry-Specific, 2010, pp. 10-11.

the crucial importance of eliminating from the market invalid patents which offer unwarranted monopolies and make sincere attempts to strike an optimal balance in structuring rules that preserve innovation incentives while in parallel deter market abuses.

II Generic Drug Manufacturers and Generic Entry

The main goal of generic drug manufacturers is to develop identical or equivalent generic drug products of an economically successful brand-name drug and to market them as soon as the relevant drug no longer enjoys patent protection or market exclusivity.[112] Generic companies may also try to enter the market with their generic drug versions while the brand-name drug still enjoys patent protection, by challenging the validity of the originators' patent(s) or by inventing around the patent, e.g., by discovering a non-infringing process to produce the non-protected drug compound. Naturally, generic companies focus on blockbuster brand-name drugs, whose generic versions tend to be highly profitable.[113]

A *The Extent and Timing of Generic Entry*

The value of the relevant market at the end of exclusivity is one of the main drivers of generic entry, which concentrates on successful brand-name drugs with high sales volumes and is more likely to occur near the end of patent protection.[114] Naturally, the economic incentives for generics to enter the market are much stronger with regard to blockbuster drugs. Expedited generic entry, especially in drug markets with high sales, is also valuable from a consumer welfare perspective, since it results in lower drug prices and higher access rates to drug products.[115]

The extent of generic entry is defined by the number of generic manufacturers that enter the market. In the US, due to the Hatch-Waxman Act framework and the 180-day exclusivity that is granted to the first successful generic challenger, there is only one generic manufacturer in the market for the first 180 days of generic entry. After this exclusivity period is over, other generic manufacturers are free to enter the market, provided their generic drug versions are not infringing any existing patents.[116] In the European Union there are no similar regulatory obstacles to generic entry: within

---

112. EU Commission, *Pharma Sector Inquiry*, 2009, para. 89.
113. EU Commission, *Pharma Sector Inquiry*, 2009, paras 185, 193. See idem paras 172-179: to examine generic entry in the EU, the Commission examined a sample of seventy-five top selling molecules in France, Germany and the United Kingdom, that faced loss of patent protection between 2000 and 2007.
114. EU Commission, *Pharma Sector Inquiry*, 2009, para. 189; PANATONNI, Generic Entry, 2011, pp. 137-138.
115. EU Commission, *Pharma Sector Inquiry*, 2009, para. 185. See however GRABOWSKI ET AL., Consumer Welfare, 2012, pp. 383-385, arguing that generic competition does not necessarily increase consumer welfare: its effects on non-price competition, promotional efforts and innovation of originators should also be taken into account.
116. *See infra* Chapter 2, explaining in detail how generic drug entry works in the US under the Hatch-Waxman Act.

one year from the expiration of exclusivity, four to five generic drug manufacturers appear to be active in the market.[117] The higher the sales of the relevant branded drug in the year before the loss of exclusivity, the higher the number of generic entrants will be.[118]

In the EU, generic entry occurs on average thirteen months after the loss of exclusivity for the brand-name drug, while it is generally faster concerning successful brand-name drugs.[119] However, it is not equally pervasive in all EU Member States: between 2000 and 2006 the highest generic entry rates were observed in Germany, Denmark, Finland, the UK and the Netherlands.[120] The regulatory environment has a large impact on generic entry. For instance, generic entry is much more likely to occur within one year from the loss of exclusivity in Member States where generic substitution is compulsory.[121] Moreover, generic drugs seem to enter the market faster in Member States where doctors are encouraged to prescribe pharmaceutical substances instead of a specific brand-name drug.[122]

B The Effects of Generic Entry

Generic entry changes the drug market from a monopoly market into one where more and cheaper resources of drug supply become available. The most immediate effects of generic entry are seen on the average price levels of the concerned products and on the originators sales' volumes. As analysed in the following sections, regulatory policies regarding doctors' prescriptions and compulsory generic substitution have a direct effect on the timing, number and market shares of generic drug manufacturers.

1 Generic Penetration to the Market and Its Effects on Drug Prices

The average cost of a generic drug in the US is 80%-85% less than the cost of the respective brand-name drug, when multiple generic companies have entered the market.[123] Due to their lower prices, generic drug versions quickly penetrate the market, capturing a high market share. The combined market share of generic

---

117. EU Commission, *Pharma Sector Inquiry*, 2009, para. 201. Three years after the expiration of exclusivity, the ratio of originators to generics is 1:6.
118. EU Commission, *Pharma Sector Inquiry*, 2009, para. 202 and p. 75, Figure 5. *See also* OLSON, WENDLING, Effect of Entry, 2013, p. 16, finding that the two drugs with the highest sales in their sample faced at least seven generic competitors.
119. EU Commission, *Pharma Sector Inquiry*, 2009, paras 191-193. For the top-selling category of drugs in the year prior to exclusivity expiry, the Commission found that generic entry took on average four months.
120. EU Commission, *Pharma Sector Inquiry*, 2009, para. 186, reporting that in these countries generic entry shares were above 50%, both in number and value terms. *See also idem* p. 68, Figure 13.
121. EU Commission, *Pharma Sector Inquiry*, 2009, para. 190.
122. EU Commission, *Pharma Sector Inquiry*, 2009, para. 197.
123. FDA Website, *Facts about Generic Drugs*. Available at: http://www.fda.gov/drugs/resourcesforyou/consumers/buyingusingmedicinesafely/understandinggenericdrugs/ucm167991.htm (last accessed on March 31, 2018).

manufacturers is often referred to as the "generic penetration rate."[124] As a result of generic entry, originators are forced to lower the prices of their brand-name drugs, using these price reductions as a defensive measure in order to preserve at least part of their market share. Generally, the higher the generic penetration rate, the higher the potential savings for the health systems.[125] According to the FDA, approved generic drugs account for 89% of prescriptions dispensed in the US, while between 2007 and 2017 generic drugs saved consumers more than $1.67 trillion.[126]

The level of generic drug prices is lower in the European Union compared to the US. Between 2005 and 2007 the EU price index for generic pharmaceuticals was on average 15% lower than the US benchmark.[127] Generic drug prices also vary between European Member States,[128] ranging from the same price as the brand-name drug, down to 60% less.[129] Generic entry in the European Union may lead to average price decreases by 20% within the first year of generic entry and by 25%-50% two years after the generic entry; in extreme cases, for specific medicines and in some Member States, prices may decrease up to 80%-90%.[130] Interestingly, generic entry may have an impact not only on the sales of the relevant brand-name drug but also on the sales of other drugs with different active ingredients.[131] Most European Member States are actively promoting the use of generic drugs, especially through generic substitution schemes.[132] The level of generic penetration in the European Union differs from one Member State to another and is largely influenced by public policy choices. For example, generic penetration tends to be higher in EU Member States where doctors are encouraged to prescribe active substances to patients instead of brand-name drugs, or where compulsory generic substitution exists so that pharmacists are obliged to dispense the cheapest generic drug version of the prescribed drug.[133]

---

124. EU Commission, *Pharma Sector Inquiry*, 2009, para. 231.
125. *Idem*.
126. UHL, FDA Voice, 2018. Available at: https://blogs.fda.gov/fdavoice/index.php/2018/02/2017-was-another-record-setting-year-for-generic-drugs/ (last accessed on March 31, 2018). *See also* OSTROFF, Generic Drug Review, 2016, arguing that between 2005 and 2014 the estimated cost savings due to generic drugs in the US were $1.68 trillion.
127. EU Commission, *Pharma Sector Inquiry*, 2009, para. 103, pp. 40-41, Figure 7.
128. *See* further WOUTERS, KANAVOS, 2017, calculating all commonly used drug price indices in seven European countries, based on 2013 IMS Health Data.
129. URBINATI ET AL., EU Pharma Expenditure, 2014. *See also*, Executive Agency for Health and Consumers (EAHC), European Commission, *EU Pharmaceutical Expenditure Forecast*, Final Report, November 26, 2012, pp. 61-74. Available at: https://ec.europa.eu/health/systems_performance_assessment/docs/creativ_ceutical_eu_pharmaceutical_expenditure_forecast.pdf. (last accessed on March 31, 2018), analysing the pharmaceutical budgets, savings, costs and net budget impact per year and per therapeutic class in France, Germany, Hungary, Poland, the United Kingdom, Portugal and Greece.
130. EU Commission, *Pharma Sector Inquiry*, 2009, paras 212, 225.
131. EU Commission, *Pharma Sector Inquiry*, 2009, paras 239-242.
132. *See infra* Chapter 6, Introduction, Section II, on the health expenditures in the EU.
133. EU Commission, *Pharma Sector Inquiry*, 2009, paras 170-171, 233-238; *see also idem* p. 62, Figure 11, presenting the generic market shares in the EU Member States. *See also* URBINATI ET AL., EU Pharma Expenditure, 2014, examining penetration rates and finding that they were high in France, Germany, Hungary, Poland, the United Kingdom (80%-100%), with the exception of Portugal and Greece (25%). *See also* EU Commission, *Pharma Sector Inquiry*, 2009, para. 190.

2 Effects of Generic Entry on Sales' Volumes and Healthcare Spendings

Generic penetration to the market has an immediate and incontestable effect on healthcare spendings. Due to their low prices, generic drugs are considered to be one of the most important means of constraining national healthcare expenses. Generic entry to the market has a twofold effect: first, it decreases the price levels of existing drugs through price competition and second it increases the share of generic drugs consumed by patients.[134] The entry of generic drugs to the market and the subsequent reduction in prices may also lead to an increased consumption of the relevant drug product.[135]

In 2016 the loss of patent protection resulted in a decrease of $16.9 billion in brand-name drug spending in the US, while in 2012 it had reached the pick of decreasing costs by $29.8 billion.[136] In 2015, 88% of dispensed prescriptions in the US were for generic drugs; yet they accounted for only 28% of total drug spending.[137] The decrease in brand-name drug spending is expected to continue in the next five years at an increasing rate: the losses of brand-name exclusivities from 2017 until 2021 are expected to have a 58% larger impact on invoice spending compared to the period of 2012-2017.[138] Since several biologic agents are expected to go off patent protection until 2018, biosimilar products are also expected to contribute to the savings of healthcare systems over the coming years,[139] despite the fact that their development and production are much costlier and time-consuming than that of generic drugs.[140] Due to the high cost of developing and producing biosimilars, it is expected that their

---

134. BELLONI, MORGAN Pharma Expenditures, 2016, pp. 27-28.
135. EU Commission, *Pharma Sector Inquiry*, 2009, paras 237-239.
136. QuintilesIMS Institute, *Outlook for Global Medicines through 2021: Balancing Cost and Value*, December 2016, p. 34, Exhibit 16. Available at: http://www.imshealth.com/en/thought-leadership/quintilesims-institute/reports/outlook_for_global_medicines_through_2021 (last accessed on March 31, 2018). [cited as: QuintilesIMS, *Global Medicines through 2021*, 2016], Impact of U.S. Losses of Exclusivity on Brand Spending US$Bn, presenting the decline in brand spending from 2012 as projected until 2021. Available at: http://www.imshealth.com/en/thought-leadership/quintilesims-institute/reports/outlook_for_global_medicines_through_2021; *See* however the report of the previous year, IMS Institute for Healthcare Informatics, *Medicines Use and Spending in the US: a Review of 2015 and Outlook to 2020*, April 2016, p. 9, Chart 4. Available at: http://www.imshealth.com/en/thought-leadership/quintilesims-institute/reports/medicines-use-and-spending-in-the-us-a-review-of-2015-and-outlook-to-2020 Last accessed on March 31, 2018), *Decline in Brand Spending from Loss of Exclusivity US$ Bn*, mentioning that in 2012 a $32.6 billion reduction in spending occurred.
137. GPHA, *Generic Pharmaceutical Association Annual Report*, 2015, pp. 14. Available at: http://www.gphaonline.org/gpha-media/gpha-resources/2015-gpha-annual-report (last accessed on March 31, 2018). For a great overview of generic penetration in the US market, covering the period from 1984 until 2009, see BERNDT, AITKEN, Brand Loyalty, 2011, pp. 181-188.
138. QuintilesIMS, *Global Medicines through 2021*, 2016, p. 34.
139. QuintilesIMS, *Global Medicines through 2021*, 2016, pp. 35-36; EU Commission, *Pharma Sector Inquiry*, 2009, para. 104.
140. *See* for instance HIRSCH, BALU, Specialty Pharmaceuticals, 2014, pp. 1717-1718, stating that while generic drugs are estimated to cost $1-$5 million to develop and take three to five years to produce, biosimilars will cost $100-$200 million to develop and take eight to ten years to produce.

price will be 20% to 40% lower than that of the respective brand-name drug,[141] so that their overall contribution to reducing healthcare costs may be less significant than the one of generic drugs.[142]

The rate of generic penetration in the EU between 2000 and 2007 was 30% one year after the first generic entry occurred, going up to 45% two years after the first generic entry.[143] Generic penetration is not uniform in all EU Member States: Germany, the Czech Republic, Denmark and the UK are among the Member States with the highest generic penetration rates, exceeding 50% within the first year of generic entry.[144] According to the Organisation for Economic Co-operation and Development's (OECD's) 2013 data, generics accounted for more than three-fourths of the volume of pharmaceuticals covered by basic public health coverage in the UK and Germany, while they amounted for less than one-fourth of the market in Greece, Luxembourg and Italy.[145] The regulatory policies of EU Member States affect generic penetration rates that are higher in Member States which encourage generic substitution and the prescription of active substances by doctors, instead of a specific brand-name drug.[146]

3 Incentivising Innovation on the Brand-Name and Generic Drug Markets

Apart from its effects to drug prices, generic competition puts a limit on the period originators enjoy monopoly profits, increasing their incentives to innovate and to find the next blockbuster drug.[147] However, innovation is not the monopoly of brand-name drug manufacturers. Generic drug manufacturers often need to invent around the originators' patents in order to enter the generic drug market earlier, especially concerning successful blockbuster drugs, whose compound is no longer patent protected. Thus, generic manufacturers also engage in R&D, especially concerning new formulations, dosage forms, etc. and in patenting strategies, in an effort to differentiate their generic drug from the brand-name drug or from other generic drug versions and to achieve faster marketing approval or higher reimbursement rates.[148]

C   Risks and Costs Related to Generic Entry

In most cases, generic drug manufacturers are not required to repeat the lengthy and costly clinical trials of originators; as a result their R&D costs are much lower.[149]

---

141. HIRSCH, BALU, Specialty Pharmaceuticals, 2014, pp. 1717-1718.
142. *See* for instance ELMENDORF, 2010, p. 2, stating that biological drugs are expected to lead to a reduction of 2% on the average drug prices.
143. EU Commission, *Pharma Sector Inquiry*, 2009, p. 87, Table 13.
144. EU Commission, *Pharma Sector Inquiry*, 2009, para. 234.
145. BELLONI, MORGAN Pharma Expenditures, 2016, pp. 30-31. *See also* OECD.Stat Website, *Pharmaceutical Market: Generic Market*, 2016, providing elaborate statistics concerning the % share of generics per value and volume in the OECD Member Countries. Available at: http://stats.oecd.org/index.aspx?DataSetCode=HEALTH_STAT (last accessed on March 31, 2018).
146. EU Commission, *Pharma Sector Inquiry*, 2009, para. 235.
147. EU Commission, *Pharma Sector Inquiry*, 2009, para. 92.
148. EU Commission, *Pharma Sector Inquiry*, 2009, paras 93-94, 460.
149. EU Commission, *Pharma Sector Inquiry*, 2009, paras 91, 99-102.

However, this does not mean that generic manufacturers do not incur important costs. Setting aside the development costs of producing a generic drug version, generic manufacturers also need to cover the costs of obtaining marketing authorisations for their generic drug products. Before obtaining marketing approval, generic drug manufacturers must prove that their drug is bioequivalent to the brand-name drug and meets rigid standards regarding the identity, strength, quality, purity and potency of the generic drug.[150] Moreover, generic manufacturing, packaging and testing must meet the respective quality standards and the same specifications of brand-name drug products.[151] The cost structure of generic manufacturers is considerably different from the cost structure of originators: for instance in 2007, manufacturing and marketing costs amounted to almost two-thirds of the generic manufacturers' annual turnover, while R&D costs were limited to 7%.[152] This difference in the cost structures is one of the main reasons generic pharmaceuticals are sold at much lower prices than the prepatent expiry price of brand-name drugs.[153]

By entering the generic market, the generic manufacturer is likely to be the target of patent infringement litigation suits from the brand-name drug manufacturer and the patent holder. The costs of patent litigation, which are exceedingly high even for originators, are even more burdensome for generic manufacturers, sometimes leading them to the verge of bankruptcy. This should not come as a surprise, since originators and generic manufacturers are normally in different leagues of economic power. Indicatively in 2009, the ten largest originator companies in the EU spent more than €40 billion per year – more than double the global turnover of the ten largest European generic manufacturers – solely on global marketing and promotional activities.[154]

PART 2   THE BENEFITS OF SETTLEMENTS

The first part of this chapter focused on the high risks and costs faced by both originators and generic drug manufacturers. As discussed, generic entry has a huge and rather immediate impact on average drug price levels and on the sales' volumes of originators. The immense costs and the uncertain results of R&D investment, combined with the fact that the profits from one blockbuster drug may amount to the lion's share of an originator's turnover, explain why originators are so eager to protect their monopoly on a successful drug product against generic entry for the longest period possible. In order to achieve this goal, an originator may conclude one or more patent settlements with potential generic competitors, aiming to delay or to prevent generic

---

150. FDA Website, *Facts about Generic Drugs*. Available at: http://www.fda.gov/drugs/resourcesforyou/consumers/buyingusingmedicinesafely/understandinggenericdrugs/ucm167991.htm (last accessed on March 31, 2018); EU Commission, *Pharma Sector Inquiry*, 2009, para. 91.
151. A Website, *Facts about Generic Drugs*. Available at: http://www.fda.gov/drugs/resourcesforyou/consumers/buyingusingmedicinesafely/understandinggenericdrugs/ucm167991.htm (last accessed on March 31, 2018). *See also* DAVIT ET AL., Bioequivalence Data, 2009, pp. 1583-1584.
152. EU Commission, *Pharma Sector Inquiry*, 2009, pp. 39-40, Table 7.
153. EU Commission, *Pharma Sector Inquiry*, 2009, para. 103.
154. EU Commission, *Pharma Sector Inquiry*, 2009, para. 102.

Chapter 1: Pharma R&D and Settlements

entry. Despite the antitrust implications such settlements may give rise to, a common reflex of courts adjudicating them is to highlight the public interest served by the settlement of patent disputes. Part two of this chapter focuses on the importance of settlements as a remedy to the high costs, risks and uncertainty of patent infringement litigation in both the US and the European Union. The aim is to introduce the reader to the culture of favourising the settlement of disputes over litigation but also to its problematic aspects and to the potential social costs settlements may create.

I Are Trials Vanished by Settlements?

Settlements are in essence presented as the answer to the main weaknesses of judicial review. Litigating before courts, especially on highly complicated and technical issues such as patent validity or patent infringement, may be expensive, inefficient, error-prone and extremely slow, consuming valuable resources not only of the litigating parties but also of the judiciary and competent administrative bodies such as patent offices.[155] Especially in common law jurisdictions such as the US, court litigation is often seen as an *ultimum remedium* to which the parties shall only turn when all their efforts to reach an out-of-court private settlement have failed. Courts themselves promote the conclusion of settlements between the parties, in an effort to save on the expenses of lengthy litigation which are incurred by the society.[156] The firm belief that settlements are beneficial and should be encouraged and facilitated is deeply rooted in the US legal culture and extends also to settlements concluded in the context of Hatch-Waxman litigation,[157] as shown in the following chapters of this book.

The roots of the settlement culture of the US lie in the 1938 amendment of the Federal Rules of Civil Procedure and Rule 16, which vested discretion to US judges to confer with lawyers and amend pleadings, obtain admissions to avoid unnecessary proof, limit expert witnesses, etc.[158] The 1983 amendments of Rule 16 committed US judges to the managerial model and the pursuit of settlements,[159] while further amendments in 1993 stressed the authority of courts to facilitate settlement or provide

---

155. EU Commission, *8th Report on the Monitoring of Patent Settlements (period January – December 2016)*, published on March 9, 2018, p. 2. Available at: http://ec.europa.eu/competition/sectors/pharmaceuticals/inquiry/ (last accessed on March 31, 2018) [cited as: EU Commission, *8th Patent Settlements Report*, 2018].
156. *See* for instance GROSS, SYVERUD, Getting to No, 1991, p. 320, noting that lawyers, judges and commentators agree in their majority that settlements are better, cheaper and faster than trials; YEAZELL, What We Asked, 2004, pp. 947-948, noting that in common law jurisdictions trials are often seen as wasteful.
157. HASTINGS, Dynamic Innovative Efficiency, 2011, pp. 43-44; CRANE, Exit Payments, 2002, pp. 748-750, 757-765; SCHILDKRAUT, Reverse Payment Fallacy, 2004, p. 1049.
158. FED. R. CIV. P. 16 (1938); the Federal Rules of civil procedure of 1938 can be found at 308 U.S. 645 et seq. (1938).
159. *See* further RESNIK, Privatisation of Process, 2014, pp. 1803-1806, describing the evolution of Rule 16, from a rule that focused on trial to a rule that made "scheduling and case management an express goal of pretrial procedure;" FED. R. CIV. P. 16(a), Notes of the Advisory Committee on Rules – 1983 Amendment.

for an "efficient and economic trial."[160] The phenomenon of the "vanishing trial" is a reality in the US legal order, as the number of civil and criminal trials that are terminated before courts is constantly decreasing.[161]

Favouring settlements instead of litigation is not the exclusive privilege of common law jurisdictions. One rather extreme example of a civil law jurisdiction promoting settlements is that of Switzerland, where conciliation attempts are in principle mandatory before ordinary and simplified court proceedings can be initiated.[162] If an agreement is not reached, the conciliation authority then issues an "authorisation to proceed", allowing the plaintiff to file an action before the court.[163] There is not an obligation to conduct compulsory conciliation proceedings with regard to patent-related proceedings.[164] However, the Federal Patent Court, which has exclusive jurisdiction over patent disputes in Switzerland,[165] strongly encourages settlement. In 2015, only one out of nineteen ordinary proceedings before the Federal Patent Court was terminated by judgment while sixteen were settled;[166] in 2016, the number of ordinary proceedings terminated by judgment increased, but still eight out of the seventeen ordinary proceedings were settled.[167] Between 2012 – when the

---

160. FED. R. CIV. P. 16(a), Notes of the Advisory Committee on Rules – 1993 Amendment. A compilation of all Notes of the Advisory Committee on the amendments of the Federal Rules of Civil Procedure, from 1937 until 2015 is available at: https://www.law.cornell.edu/rules/frcp/rule_16 (last accessed on March 31, 2018).
161. GALANTER, World Without Trials, 2006, pp. 7-14, analysing the decline in the number of case terminations before US courts between 1962 and 2004; GALANTER, Vanishing Trial, 2004, pp. 460-476, presenting elaborate data on the decreasing number of trials before federal and state courts. See also RESNIK, Declining Trial Rates, 2004, pp. 783-841, analysing various explanations for the decrease in the number of trials in the U.S. Federal Courts. See also U.S. Courts Website, *Federal Judicial Caseload Statistics*, providing annual reports, analysis, charts and data on the workload of U.S. Courts from 2001. Available at: http://www.uscourts.gov/statistics-reports/analysis-reports/federal-judicial-caseload-statistics (last accessed on March 31, 2018).
162. Article 197, Swiss Civil Procedure Code of December 19, 2018, RO 2010 1739; see also idem Articles 198, 199, exempting different kinds of proceedings from the obligation of conciliation attempt. Available at: https://www.admin.ch/opc/en/classified-compilation/20061121/index.html (last accessed on March 31, 2018). Note that the English versions of all Swiss legislation are provided for information purposes only and have no legal force; for instance the English translation of the Swiss Civil Procedure Code concerns the Code's version of May 1, 2013, which has been amended.
163. Article 209, Swiss Civil Procedure Code.
164. Article 198(f) Swiss Civil Procedure Code. The obligation for a conciliation attempt does not apply where a sole cantonal instance has jurisdiction; by analogy this exception applies also to proceedings before the Federal Patent Court which has exclusive jurisdiction over patent validity and infringement disputes, actions to issue a patent licence, etc. See Article 26, Federal Act on the Federal Patent Court of March 20, 2009, RO 2010 513. Available at: https://www.admin.ch/opc/en/classified-compilation/20071763/index.html (last accessed on March 31, 2018).
165. See Article 26, Federal Act on the Federal Patent Court. See also Federal Patent Court Website, *About the Court*. Available at: https://www.bundespatentgericht.ch/en/das-gericht/aufgaben-zustaendigkeiten/ (last accessed on March 31, 2018).
166. See Federal Patent Court, *Annual Report 2015*, p. 6. Out of nineteen ordinary proceedings, sixteen were settled, only one was terminated by judgment while one was declared groundless.
167. See Federal Patent Court, *Annual Report 2016*, p. 7. Out of seventeen ordinary proceedings, eight were settled, seven were terminated by judgment and two were declared groundless.

Federal Patent Court was created – and 2017, the ratio of settlements was 75%.[168] As a result of this extremely high rate of settlements during the first five years of the Federal Patent Court's existence, there is a lack of case law which troubles Swiss legal practitioners and creates considerable legal uncertainty.

II Costs and Risks of Patent Infringement Litigation

From an economic perspective, the higher the parties' stakes are in a case, the higher is the probability that the case will be litigated.[169] The risk adversity of the parties has an impact on the likelihood of settlement: the more risk averse the parties are, the higher the probability of them settling, instead of litigating, even if this means accepting less favourable settlement terms.[170] Litigation costs and settlement costs are not fixed but normally vary according to multiple factors: the parties' stakes, the complexity of the case, the relevant jurisdiction, etc.; the comparison between these two measures is a factor that affects the decision to settle.[171] However, litigation is not only an expense but also *an investment*: the more parties have to gain from litigation, the more they will be willing to spend on it.[172] Another factor that may play a role in the decision to settle instead of litigating is secrecy: a monetary settlement does not normally require court approval, so that its terms remain confidential between the parties: avoiding the public eye and any further actions may be of great importance for the settling parties.[173]

Patent litigation involves high transaction costs: court rulings concerning patent invalidity or patent infringement suits and the available remedies in case of infringement, such as injunctive relief or damages, are rare and expensive. As a result, litigating parties seldom pursue patent infringement litigation until the end. Settlement is more likely to occur during the first months of patent infringement litigation, approximately twelve to fifteen months from the filing of the patent infringement suit, in order to decrease the considerable litigation costs.[174] As analysed in the following sections, the patents which are most likely to be found invalid are the ones that typically lead to a settlement of the patent infringement suit; on the flipside, if the parties are not confident on the issue of patent validity or of infringement, they are much more likely to continue litigating until there is a final court determination on the merits of the case.

---

168. *See* Federal Patent Court, *Annual Report 2016*, p. 7.
169. POSNER, *Economic Analysis of Law*, 2014, pp. 779-784.
170. POSNER, *Economic Analysis of Law*, 2014, p. 782.
171. *Idem.*
172. *Idem.*
173. POSNER, *Economic Analysis of Law*, 2014, p. 783. However, settling parties in a Hatch-Waxman patent infringement lawsuit are obliged to file their settlement agreement with the FTC and the DoJ within ten business days from the execution of the agreement. *See infra* Chapter 2, Part 2, Section III.A.
174. KESAN, BALL, Patent Disputes, 2006, pp. 281-284.

A Estimated Costs and Duration of Patent Infringement Litigation

Patent infringement litigation is exceptionally expensive. According to the 2015 report of the American Intellectual Property Law Association (AIPLA), patent litigation costs range from $600,000 to $5 million, depending on the value that is at risk.[175] The costs of Hatch-Waxman patent infringement litigation between brand-name drug originators and generic manufacturers are also extremely high and may vary from $350,000 to $3 million.[176]

In the European Union, patent litigation regimes vary greatly from one Member State to another, and so do the average costs and the duration of patent infringement litigation.[177] For instance, the United Kingdom (UK) has the highest costs for patent infringement litigation in the European Union, while much lower average legal fees apply in Germany and Austria;[178] still, patent litigation costs are much lower in the European Union than in the US.[179] Between 2000 and 2007 the total cost of patent litigation in the European Union exceeded €420 million, while the average cost of originators' patent infringement litigation against generics in a single Member State was €230,000 per case.[180] Setting aside the cost of patent litigation, the costs of detecting and preventing patent infringement and enforcing intellectual property rights considerably burden the private sector.[181] The average duration of patent litigation in the European Union between 2000 and 2007 was 2.8 years; the average duration of patent infringement litigation exceeded 6 years in Portugal and Italy, while in Denmark, Finland, the UK and France this average duration was less than 2 years.[182]

---

175. AIPLA, 2015 Report Summary, pp. 37-42.
176. AIPLA, 2015 Report Summary, pp. 37-38.
177. *See* for instance EPO, Patent Litigation Overview, 2016, pp. 1-138, describing the main administrative law and civil law procedures on oppositions, appeals, infringement, revocation, remedies etc. with regard to patents in the EPC Contracting States.
178. EU Commission, *Pharma Sector Inquiry*, 2009, para. 659, stating that patent infringement litigation in the UK costs on average €993,000, while Germany and Austria had the lowest legal fees: €76,000 and €47,000 respectively.
179. GRAHAM, VAN ZEEBROECK, Patent Litigation Across Europe, 2014, p. 667, Table 1, finding that the average costs of the patent litigation system in the US ranged from €1 to €10 million, while they were between €150,000 and €1,500,000 in the UK, the most expensive EU Member State as far as patent litigation costs are concerned.
180. EU Commission, *Pharma Sector Inquiry*, 2009, paras 659-660.
181. *See* for instance European Observatory on Infringements of Intellectual Property Rights, *Private Costs of Enforcement of IPRs*, March 2017, pp. 10-19. Available at: https://euipo.europa.eu/tunnel-web/secure/webdav/guest/document_library/observatory/documents/div/Private%20Costs%20of%20Enforcement%20of%20IPR%20-%20FORMATTED.pdf. (last accessed on March 31, 2018), analysing the overall estimate of IPRs enforcement costs in the markets of fourteen different Member States.
182. EU Commission, *Pharma Sector Inquiry*, 2009, paras 635-638, and p. 228, Figure 8. *See also* the more recent study by GRAHAM, VAN ZEEBROECK, Patent Litigation Across Europe, 2014, p. 668, stating that patent litigation lasts on average one year in the Netherlands and in between twenty-four and thirty-six months in Belgium and Italy.

B The Uncertainty Regarding the Litigation's Outcome

1 US Jury Trials on Patent Infringement

Patent infringement litigation is not only lengthy and extremely expensive: it is also highly technical and likely to require scientific expertise. There is evidence that specialised intellectual property right courts resolve cases of intellectual property more efficiently and effectively, increasing the consistency and the predictability of case law.[183] However, to the criticism of many, non-specialised courts or sometimes a jury are called to examine and decide the highly technical and specialised issues of patent infringement or patent (in)validity in the US.[184] Courts and juries often feel uneasy and hesitant to examine patent validity issues, recognising their understandable lack of expertise in the fields of chemistry, physics and natural sciences. Acknowledging their limited scientific knowledge, juries are highly unlikely to question and invalidate the decision of the United States Patent and Trademark Office (USPTO) to grant a patent; there is evidence showing that compared to judges, juries are much more likely to uphold the validity of patents.[185] However, this discussion falls outside the scope of this book, since pharmaceutical patent litigation cases and Hatch-Waxman litigation virtually never trigger a jury trial.[186]

2 The Lack of Procedural Uniformity in Europe and the Unified Patent Court

Each European Member State has in place different procedural rules regarding patent infringement litigation.[187] These divergences in procedural rules not only have an impact on the duration of patent infringement litigation but may also create

---

183. International Intellectual Property Institute (IIPI), USPTO, *Study on Specialized Intellectual Property Courts*, January 25, 2012, pp. 4-6. Available at: iipi.org/wp-content/uploads/2012/05/Study-on-Specialized-IPR-Courts.pdf (last accessed on March 31, 2018), summarising the key-findings of the study.
184. *See* for example RAI, Specialised Trial Courts, 2002, pp. 889-897, arguing in favour of a specialised patent court or alternatively for the possibility for judges to appoint expert consultants on complicated findings of scientific facts. *See* however HAN M., Jury Right in Patent Litigation, 2014, pp. 676-683, arguing in favour of the right to a jury trial in patent cases.
185. LEMLEY, KENDALL, MARTIN, Rush to Judgment, 2013, p. 175, finding that 51.3% of the 158 bench trials ruled in favour of the patentee, while 62.9% of the 466 jury trials ruled for the patentee; ALLISON, LEMLEY, Empirical Evidence, 1998, p. 212, finding that juries hold valid more than two-third of patents, while just one-fourth of the cases decided on pretrial motion were decided in favour of the patentee. *See also* LEMLEY, Juries, 2013, pp. 1727-1733, discussing the subject of removing juries from the process of deciding patent validity and examining what this would change in patent litigation.
186. Pharmaceutical patent cases are almost never tried by juries, since they rarely involve damages claims. *See* further LEMLEY, KENDALL, MARTIN, Rush to Judgment, 2013, p. 176; COGGIO, DEMASI, Jury Trial, 2002, pp. 213-214, noting that the lack of damages in Hatch-Waxman Act actions negates the possibility of a jury trial. HAN M., Jury Right in Patent Litigation, 2014, pp. 670-672; LEMLEY, Juries, 2013, p. 1717.
187. For a detailed comparative analysis of some of the most distinctive systems of patent litigation in the European Union *see* GRAHAM, VAN ZEEBROECK, Patent Litigation Across Europe, 2014, pp. 669-680, analysing the patent litigation systems of France, Germany, the UK, the Netherlands, Italy, Spain and Belgium.

considerable uncertainty to litigating parties. For example, in case of conflicting outcomes by different Member States' courts on the matter of patent validity or patent infringement by a generic drug version, the generic manufacturer will be facing considerable legal uncertainty on whether it can legitimately enter the market or not.[188] Brand-name manufacturers are also in a highly uncertain position, since they may become involved in patent litigation in different Member States regarding the same patent dispute, incurring high costs in order to protect their patents.[189] Recognising the problem, the European Union created the Unified Patent Court (UPC), a specialised patent court with the aim to boost innovation and increase the efficiency and legal certainty on patent infringement litigation, while decreasing its costs and duration.[190] The UPC was expected to become operational by December 2017;[191] however this did not happen, and no new deadline has been announced to the date of this writing.[192] This court is destined to be a part of the legal system of the contracting Member States of the UPC Agreement, and it will in principle have exclusive competence in respect of European patents and European patents with unitary effect.[193]

3 Patent Invalidation and Patent Infringement Rates

Litigation rates are often used as a proxy for patent value: the more valuable a patent is, the more likely it is to be the object of patent litigation.[194] Unsurprisingly, the highest

---

188. EU Commission, *Pharma Sector Inquiry*, 2009, para. 638.
189. EU Commission, Press Release, *Justice for Growth: Commission fills legal gaps for Unitary Patent Protection*, IP/13/750, Brussels, July 29, 2013. Available at: http://europa.eu/rapid/press-release_IP-13-750_en.htm (last accessed on March 31, 2018) [cited as: EU Commission Press Release, *Unitary Patent Protection*, 2013].
190. Agreement on a Unified Patent Court, OJ C 175, 20.6.2013, p. 1-40; Council Regulation (EU) No. 1260/2012 of 17 December 2012 implementing enhanced cooperation in the area of the creation of unitary patent protection with regard to the applicable translation arrangements, OJ L 361, 31.12.2012, p. 89-92; Regulation (EU) No. 1257/2012 of the European Parliament and of the Council of 17 December 2012 implementing enhanced cooperation in the area of the creation of unitary patent protection, OJ L 361, 31.12.2012, p. 1-8. *See also* EU Commission Press Release, *Unitary Patent Protection*, 2013.
191. The UPC Agreement's provisional application phase started in late spring 2017. *See* further UPC Website, *Provisional Application*. Available at: https://www.unified-patent-court.org/news/upc-provisional-application (last accessed on March 31, 2018). *See also infra* Chapter 5, Part 1, Section I.A.1, describing the European èatent with a unitary effect.
192. *See* UPC Website, *Summing Up and Looking Forward to 2018*, available at: https://www.unified-patent-court.org/news/summing-and-looking-forward-2018 (last accessed on March 31, 2018).
193. Articles 1, 32, UPC Agreement; Unified Patent Court Website, *About the UPC*. Available at: https://www.unified-patent-court.org/ (last accessed on March 31, 2018). Any Member State of the EU can become member of the UPC Agreement, unlike states outside the European Union; apart from Spain and Portugal all twenty-five current Member States of the EU have signed the UPC Agreement on February 19, 2013. *See also* PINCKNEY, 2015, pp. 270-272, discussing the transitional provisions of Article 83 of the UPC Agreement which allow contracting Member States to opt-out of the exclusive competence of the UPC and suggesting possible interpretations.
194. *See* for instance ALLISON, LEMLEY, MOORE, Valuable Patents, 2003, pp. 439-443. *See* however, ALLISON, LEMLEY, WALKER, Trolls on Top, 2009, pp. 19-20, noting that the most litigated patents are IT software patents and their astonishment that the pharma industry had a less significant share of most litigated patents than expected.

patent litigation intensity occurs in the pharmaceutical and biotechnology sectors in both the European Union and the US.[195] The largest share of litigation extending to multiple EU Member States is observed in the pharmaceutical sector, a phenomenon that may be linked to repeated invalidity actions by competitors of the patent holder: when more than one European Member State markets are at issue, a finding of invalidity produces legal effects only within the national territory of the relevant Member State. Another reason may be the tactic of defensive litigation by the alleged infringer that is likely to seek a declaratory judgment of non-infringement in multiple jurisdictions.[196]

The outcomes of infringement and invalidity actions differ among the different jurisdictions of European Member States, so that it is rather difficult to draw general conclusions. The heterogeneity of patent validity litigation in different EU Member States is nicely illustrated in a 2017 paper, examining patent litigation cases and their outcomes in Germany, the UK, the Netherlands and France between 2000 and 2008.[197] However, an earlier paper extending to seven EU Member States argues that about 45% of European court decisions find that the patent rights at issue were infringed, while 49% find no patent infringement.[198] The statistics on patent invalidity litigation were similar: arguably half of the court decisions upheld the validity of the relevant patents, while the other half was found to be invalid.[199]

As far as the US are concerned, the results of the empirical studies concerning the rates of patent invalidation in the US territory vary largely ranging from 33% to 60%; what is however undisputed is that a big number of the patents that are litigated are found to be invalid by courts.[200] From an economic perspective, if the probability of patent invalidation is high, it is in the best interest of the patent holder to grant a cheap

---

195. GRAHAM, VAN ZEEBROECK, Patent Litigation Across Europe, 2014, p. 697, reporting that in the six EU Member States studied (Belgium, Germany, Spain, France, Greece and the Netherlands), in the pharmaceuticals and biotechnology sector there were on average three litigation cases per 1,000 patents. ALLISON, LEMLEY, MOORE, Valuable Patents, 2003, pp. 471-476, finding in the basis of a large population study that drugs, medicine, computer and communications patents are far more likely to be litigated; the results of the authors' sample study on pharmaceutical patents varied significantly from the large population study, but were not necessarily representative of the litigation patterns in the examined industries. For an older study covering the period between 1980 and 1984 in the US. see LANJOUW, SCHANKERMAN, Characteristics of Patent Litigation, 2001, pp. 135-136, Table 1, finding that there were 20.1 patent litigation filed cases per 1,000 patents in the sector of drugs and health.
196. GRAHAM, VAN ZEEBROECK, Patent Litigation Across Europe, 2014, pp. 705-706, Table 9, finding that 11.1% of pharma patent litigation occurs in two EU Member States, 5.2% in three EU Member States and 0.6% in more than five EU Member States.
197. See further CREMERS ET AL., EU Patent Litigation, 2017.
198. GRAHAM, VAN ZEEBROECK, Patent Litigation Across Europe, 2014, pp. 694-696. This paper examined patent litigation data in France, Germany, the UK, the Netherlands, Italy, Spain and Belgium.
199. GRAHAM, VAN ZEEBROECK, Patent Litigation Across Europe, 2014, p. 696.
200. See for instance LEMLEY, SHAPIRO, Probabilistic Patents, 2005, p. 76, arguing that 50% of litigated patents are found to be invalid; MANN, UNDERWEISER, Patent Quality, 2012, pp. 6-7, finding that 59.8% of litigated patents were found to be invalid by final ruling of the Court of Appeals for the Federal Circuit, examining all 266 cases decided from January 1, 2003 until December 31, 2009, concerning the validity of 366 patents; MOORE, Empirical Peek, 2000, p. 390, finding an invalidity rate of 33% for patent cases between 1983 and 1999.

patent licence and to preserve its patent; it is also in the best interest of the other party to accept such a licence which will allow it to enter the market and not to be economically burdened by the high costs continuing patent infringement litigation entails.[201] With regard to Hatch-Waxman litigation, the FTC found in 2002 that generic challengers won 73% of the cases in which a court has solved the patent dispute.[202] Other studies argue that brand-name drug manufacturers lose roughly half of their patent infringement litigation cases against generic drug manufacturers in the context of Hatch-Waxman litigation.[203]

C The Impact of Settlements on Innovation Incentives

For all the above-mentioned reasons, patentees may be particularly risk-averse, especially in the pharmaceutical sector where the economic stakes of patent litigation are immense. There is a link between the incentives to innovate and the possibility to settle patent litigation: risk-averse inventors may be more willing to engage into patentable R&D projects if they have the right to settle patent litigation disputes and to avoid the risks and costs involved in patent infringement litigation.[204] Therefore, a rule that would exclude the possibility to settle patent infringement litigation would indeed have a negative impact on the originators' incentives to innovate. However, the possibility of a court finding of invalidity or of non-infringement by a competing product is also necessary to stimulate the optimal amount of R&D.[205] Thus, giving a *carte blanche* to all types of patent settlements and legitimising patentees to shield their patents from judicial review on patent validity and to exclude non-infringing competition from the market would also have a negative effect on the innovation incentives.

III The Social Cost of Settlements

Even though the benefits of settlements and especially their role in avoiding costly, lengthy and inefficient litigation are constantly stressed, their disadvantages are often overlooked. The high costs of litigation are constantly and vividly underlined, while its benefits are often taken for granted. However, there have been strong voices advocating against settlements and highlighting their downsides for many years now.[206] Some of the weak points of settlements are for instance that the parties' consent to settle may

---

201. KESAN, BALL, Patent Disputes, 2006, p. 243; YEAZELL, What We Asked, 2004, pp. 950-954, explaining how the information produced during the discovery phase of trials is likely to have an impact on the parties' decision to settle.
202. FTC, *Generic Drug Entry Prior to Patent Expiration: An FTC study*, (2002), pp. 13-15. Available at: http://www.ftc.gov/sites/default/files/documents/reports/generic-drug-entry-prior-patent-expiration-ftc-study/genericdrugstudy_0.pdf. (last accessed on 31 March 2018) [cited as: FTC, *Generic Drug Entry*, 2002]. According to the FTC's study brand-name manufacturers won eight out of thirty cases that were litigated until a court judgment.
203. See PANATONNI, Generic Entry, 2011, p. 138, finding that brand-name manufacturers in her sample had a 50% chance of winning Hatch-Waxman patent infringement litigation.
204. CRANE, Exit Payments, 2002, pp. 759-762.
205. *Idem.*
206. *See* for instance the celebrated article of FISS, Against Settlement, 1984, pp. 1073-1090.

be coerced; the bargain between the parties may be conducted by someone without authority; or that important information and case law which would serve as a guide for the resolution of subsequent disputes of a similar nature will never become public.[207] The information produced by litigation may be important and useful for other parties beyond the given dispute; not only court decisions but also the pleadings, the records of hearings, the submissions, etc. may all contain valuable information and facts, affording the public an important opportunity to directly participate in the adjudicatory process.[208] Settlements deprive the public not only from such information on the resolution of the disputes at issue, but also on the patterns of such resolution.[209] On the flipside, the mandatory sharing of trade secrets, marketing studies, pricing information, etc. during the discovery process of litigation may also impose social costs. For instance, the alleged infringer might be able to free-ride on the patentee's trade secrets, reducing the latter's incentives to engage in innovation and R&D; while such free-riding may initially be beneficial for society, rules that do not protect incentives are costly on the long-term.[210]

Patent litigation is unique because it has the potential to put an end to undeserved monopolies and to open the relevant market to competition, not only to the benefit of the prevailing litigating party but also to the benefit of other competitors and ultimately to the benefit of consumers.[211] This is the reason why the invalidation of weak patents is seen by some commentators as a public good.[212] The importance of patent litigation to the public aggravates the problematic aspects of patent settlements. The legal problems raised by certain types of pharma patent settlements between originators and generic manufacturers, along with their social cost and their effects on consumer welfare are extensively discussed in the following chapters of this book. The main notion is that settlements which aim to render ironclad patents that were likely to be found invalid or non-infringed are problematic, since they prolong an unjustified monopoly to the detriment of competitors but also to the detriment of consumers who continue to pay supracompetitive monopoly prices. Typically, in such a problematic settlement, the cost of the settlement for the originator will largely exceed the projected cost of litigation for the parties; the difference between the projected litigation costs and the actual cost of settlement will likely represent the value transfer in return for the delay in generic entry.

---

207. Fiss, Against Settlement, 1984, pp. 1075-1084.
208. *See also* YELDERMAN, Patent Challenges, 2016, pp. 1950-1951, discussing how pleadings and trials may bring important information to the public.
209. YEAZELL, What We Asked, 2004, pp. 970-971, suggesting as a solution to this problem the imposition of an obligation to report settlement terms.
210. CRANE, Exit Payments, 2002, pp. 757-758. *See also* LYNDON, Secrecy and Innovation, 1993, pp. 10-12, discussing how patent and trade secret law provide rewards for innovative research.
211. YELDERMAN, Patent Challenges, 2016, pp. 1954-1958, discussing the distributional effects of patent challenges. *See also idem* pp. 1959-1995, discussing the conditions under which patent challenges increase competition.
212. LEMLEY, SHAPIRO, Probabilistic Patents, 2005, pp. 88-90.

CONCLUSIONS

The R&D costs pharma industry originators face are constantly increasing, while pharma R&D productivity has been decreasing at a global level as far as new molecules are concerned. Given the high costs and risks entailed in pharma R&D, preserving innovation incentives for originators is of crucial importance for the public interest. Unlike in other sectors, patent protection and the financial returns it ensures do provide adequate innovation incentives for pharma originators. The possibility to settle patent infringement suits seems to have a positive impact in increasing innovation incentives. However, the probability of patent invalidation and of facing competition in the market also increases innovation incentives for originators.

Settlements do save money, resources and valuable time for the parties and for the judicial systems and may be an efficient or even an optimal solution to some disputes. Nevertheless, settlements also produce important social costs. The benefits of litigation to the public should not be understated, especially when it comes to patent litigation. Litigation may lead to the elimination of invalid patents from the market and to expedited generic entry, benefiting consumers and public health schemes. On the flipside, a settlement may be used as a mechanism to artificially prolong patent monopoly, or to keep off the market non-infringing competing products.

The author of this book is not against *all* patent settlements among originators and generic manufacturers in the pharmaceutical industry. However, settlements should not be seen as a Holy Grail that shall remain at all instances untouchable from judicial and antitrust review. Parties are not to be given a *carte blanche* to settle, irrespective of the means and content of settlement, and the issues of patent validity and patent infringement. As is extensively discussed in the following chapters, some settlements with specific characteristics are illegal under US antitrust and European competition law, since they have the potential for destructive effects on competition, innovation incentives and on consumer welfare.

PART II Pharma Settlements in the US

Part II of this book provides a thorough analysis of reverse payment settlements between originators and generic manufacturers in the US, concluded in the context of Hatch-Waxman Act patent litigation. Chapter 2 analyses the legislative framework regulating the entry of brand-name drugs and generic drugs in the US market, focusing on the complicated provisions of the Hatch-Waxman Act. Chapter 3 provides a critical analysis of the three different applicable tests that were used by US Circuit Courts for the adjudication of reverse payment settlements: the scope of the patent test, the per se illegality approach and the "quick-look" rule of reason, discussing also the resulting split and the arguments in favour and against of each test. Finally, Chapter 4 discusses the *FTC v. Actavis* decision, the cornerstone of the rule of reason antitrust analysis of reverse payment settlements that resolved this split. Chapter 4 also discusses subsequent challenges arising from the adjudication of other settlement types in the pharmaceutical sector and of various strategies employed by brand-name manufacturers in an effort to shield their respective rights and market shares.

CHAPTER 2
The US Regulatory Framework

INTRODUCTION

Health expenditures are increasingly growing on a worldwide level and the US does not constitute an exception to this trend. The US national health expenditures are projected to grow at a rate of 5.5% per year between 2017 and 2026, while the healthcare share of the Gross Domestic Product (GDP) is expected to rise from 17.9% in 2016 to 19.7% in 2026.[213] In 1980, just four years before the enactment of the Hatch-Waxman Act, national health expenditures represented only 8.9% of the US GDP,[214] whereas by 2026, Federal, State and local US governments are expected to be funding 47% of national healthcare spending.[215]

The entry of the new brand-name drugs in the market has been relatively slow, as can be seen in Figure 2.1. From 2007 through 2015, the average of New Molecular Entity (NME) and new Biological License Application (BLA) approvals per year were thirty, with the exception of the calendar year of 2014 during which there were

---

213. CMS, *National Health Care Expenditures Projections 2017-2026, Forecast Summary*, pp. 1-3. Available at: https://www.cms.gov/Research-Statistics-Data-and-Systems/Statistics-Trends-and-Reports/NationalHealthExpendData/NationalHealthAccountsProjected.html (last accessed on March 31, 2018). [cited as: CMS, Expenditures Projections, 2018].
214. *See* further CATLIN, COWAN, U.S. Health Spending, 2015, p. 32, Exhibit 1.
215. CMS, Expenditures Projections, 2018.

forty-one approvals.[216] In 2017, a total of forty-six novel drugs were approved, eighteen of which were orphan drugs aiming to the treatment of rare diseases.[217]

Figure 2.1 FDA, New Drug Approvals, 2007-2017

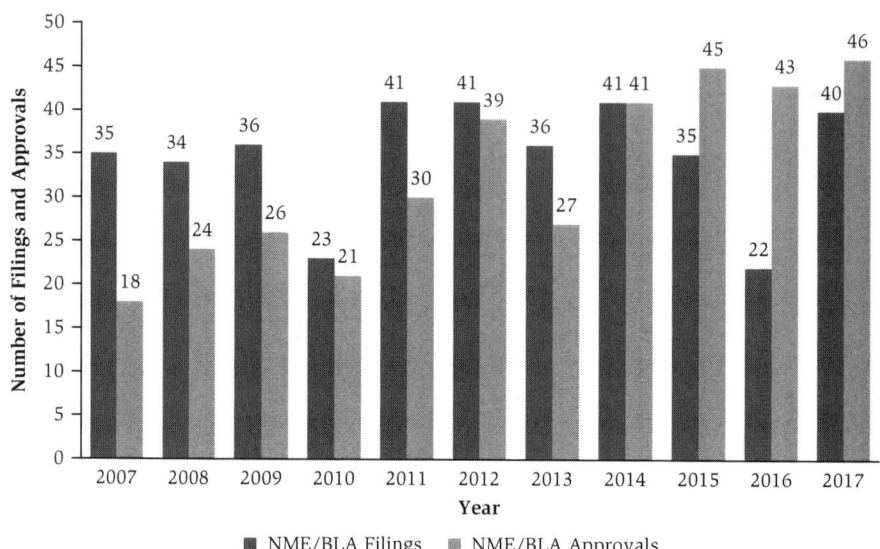

On the contrary, there has been a steady increase in the share of prescriptions for which a generic drug version is available, from 74% in 2007 to 84% in 2010, partly due to the fact that during that period several brand-name drugs lost their patent protection.[218]

---

216. Graph created with data presented in FDA, CDER, *2016 Novel New Drugs Summary*, pp. 1-17. Available at: https://www.fda.gov/drugs/developmentapprovalprocess/druginnovation/ucm 534863.htm (last accessed on March 31, 2018) and FDA, CDER, New Drugs, 2017 annual reports and publicly available data on FDA's official website https://www.fda.gov (last accessed on March 31, 2018). The number of NME/BLA Filings for 2017 is not clear in the FDA, CDER, *Novel Drug Approvals for 2017*. Available at: https://www.fda.gov/Drugs/Development ApprovalProcess/DrugInnovation/ucm537040.htm (last accessed on March 31, 2018) report, that only mentions that forty-six novel drugs were approved. According to FDA, CDER, *CDER New Drugs Program: 2017 Update*. Available at: https://www.fda.gov/downloads/AboutFDA/ CentersOffices/OfficeofMedicalProductsandTobacco/CDER/UCM587690.pdf (last accessed on March 31, 2018), p. 7, there were 43 filings until November 30, 2017, while the FDA, Office of Pharmaceutical Quality, *2017 Annual Report – One Quality Voice*, February 2018. Available at: https://www.fda.gov/downloads/AboutFDA/CentersOffices/OfficeofMedicalProductsand Tobacco/CDER/UCM598727.pdf (last accessed on March 31, 2018), p. 3, states that in 2017 there were 132 New Drug Applications.
217. FDA, *New Drug Therapy Approvals Report for 2017*, (January 2018), pp. 9-10. Available at: https://www.fda.gov/downloads/AboutFDA/CentersOffices/OfficeofMedicalProductsand Tobacco/CDER/ReportsBudgets/UCM591976.pdf (last accessed on March 31, 2018).
218. CBO, *Competition and the Cost of Medicare's Prescription Drug Program*, (July 2014), pp. 1-48. Available at: https://www.cbo.gov/publication/45552. (last accessed on March 31, 2018), p. 8.

The Hatch-Waxman Act also shares credit for this sharp increase in generic drug use, since in 1984, the year of its enactment, generic drug use accounted for 18.6% of drug prescriptions.[219] In 2013, generic drugs in the US amounted for 85% of all drug prescriptions dispensed, allegedly saving costumers and the healthcare system approximately $4 billion per week.[220] According to the FDA, nine out of ten prescriptions filled in the US are for generic drugs.[221] A mature generic market, where there is high penetration of generic products arguably amounts to a 77% increase of average savings for consumers.[222] Generics that have entered the US market between 2002 and 2014 reduced the prices of respective drugs in the US by 51% in their first year of entry and by 57% in the second year of generic entry to the market.[223]

Before analysing in detail the legislative framework of the Hatch-Waxman Act on the mechanisms for generic drug entry to the market, it is useful to briefly introduce the US agencies that are primarily involved in the entry of pharmaceutical products into the US market but also in antitrust scrutiny and enforcement in the US market. The following section introduces the US FDA, the US Patent and Trademark Office, the US FTC and the US Department of Justice (DoJ). Finally, this chapter introduces the function of a New Drug Application and explains how new drug products obtain market approval in the US.

PART 1   THE US AGENCIES

The following sections provide a brief overview of four US agencies that are competent in the fields of pharmaceutical products, patent protection and the enforcement of antitrust laws. The aim is to provide a reader with no background on US law, US agencies and enforcement authorities with the broad overview, before analysing in detail the US regulatory framework on pharmaceutical products.

---

219. FRANK, 2007, p. 1993.
220. IMS Institute, *Impact of Patent Settlements on Drug Costs: Estimation of Savings*, (June 2013), p. 2. Available at: https://www.imshealth.com/files/web/IMSH%20Institute/Healthcare%20Briefs/Impact_of_Patent_Settlements_on%20Drug_Costs.pdf. (last accessed on March 31, 2018) [cited as: IMS, Savings Estimation, 2013].
221. FDA Website, *Generic Drugs*. Available at: https://www.fda.gov/Drugs/ResourcesForYou/Consumers/BuyingUsingMedicineSafely/GenericDrugs/default.htm (last accessed on March 31, 2018).
222. FTC Staff Study, *Pay-for-Delay: How Drug Company Pay-Offs Cost Consumers Billions*, (January 2010), p. 8. Available at: http://www.ftc.gov/reports/pay-delay-how-drug-company-pay-offs-cost-consumers-billions-federal-trade-commission-staff. (last accessed on March 31, 2018). [cited as: FTC, *Pay-for-Delay*, 2010]. *See also* CBO, *Effects of Using Generic Drugs on Medicare's Prescription Drug Spending*, (September 2010), pp. 8-9. Available at: http://www.cbo.gov/sites/default/files/cbofiles/ftpdocs/118xx/doc11838/09-15-prescriptiondrugs.pdf. (last accessed on March 31, 2018), stating that retail prices of generics are on average 75% cheaper than the prices of branded pharmaceuticals.
223. IMS Institute, *Price Declines after Branded Medicines Lose Exclusivity in the U.S.*, January 2016, pp. 1-4. Available at: https://www.imshealth.com/files/web/IMSH%20Institute/Healthcare%20Briefs/PhRMA%20Generic%20Price%20Brief%20January%202016.pdf (last accessed on March 31, 2018).

I The United States Food & Drug Administration

The US FDA is an agency within the US Department of Health and Human Services which oversees medical products and tobacco, foods and veterinary medicine, global regulatory operations and policy.[224] One of the core missions of the agency is to protect public health and to ensure that human and veterinary drugs, vaccines and other biological products are safe and effective. The FDA is composed by a number of Centers and Offices: one of them is the Center for Drug Evaluation and Research (CDER) and is responsible for approving the marketing of new drugs and generic drugs, but also for overseeing the manufacturing, labelling and advertising of prescription drugs.[225]

The "Approved Drug Products with Therapeutic Equivalence Evaluations," commonly known as "Orange Book" is a publication of the FDA that first appeared in 1980 and is renewed on a monthly basis.[226] The Orange Book identifies all drug products which were approved by the FDA on the basis of safety and effectiveness under the Federal Food Drug and Cosmetic Act through New Drug Applications (NDAs) and Abbreviated New Drug Applications (ANDAs). The publication also contains all product changes received, patent information and exclusivity information on each drug product.[227] The inclusion of drug products in the list is independent of any judicial or administrative action against the respective drug.[228] Importantly, the Orange Book also includes therapeutic equivalence evaluations for approved multisource prescription drug products, which serve as a guide for subsequent generic substitution of the patented drugs by their corresponding generic versions.[229] The FDA is a valuable source of information, resources, reports and statistics regarding the US drug market, while it also provides valuable assistance to the pharmaceutical industry, including guidance and clarifications on the applicable regulatory and legal standards.[230] Additionally, the agency has taken active steps in facilitating and expediting the entry of low-cost generic drugs to the US market. For instance, in 2017 the FDA implemented a

---

224. *See* further FDA's official website: http://www.fda.gov/ (last accessed on March 31, 2018).
225. *See* further FDA Website, CDER History. Available at: https://www.fda.gov/AboutFDA/WhatWeDo/History/FOrgsHistory/HistoryofFDAsCentersandOffices/ucm2006090.htm (last accessed on March 31, 2018). Other Centers and Offices of the FDA are the Center for Biologics Evaluation and Research, the Office of Regulatory Affairs, the National Center for Toxicological Research, etc.
226. FDA, "Approved Drug Products with Therapeutic Equivalence Evaluations," Available at: http://www.fda.gov/Drugs/InformationOnDrugs/ucm129662.htm (last accessed on March 31, 2018). Since 2005, the Orange Book is publicly available on line: http://www.accessdata.fda.gov/scripts/cder/ob/default.cfm (last accessed on March 31, 2018).
227. FDA, "Frequently Asked Questions on the Orange Book." Available at: http://www.fda.gov/Drugs/InformationOnDrugs/ucm114166.htm (last accessed on March 31, 2018).
228. FDA Website, "Orange Book Preface," 38th edition. Available at: http://www.fda.gov/Drugs/DevelopmentApprovalProcess/ucm079068.htm (last accessed on March 31, 2018).
229. *See infra* Chapter 4, Part 3, Section IV.B on generic substitution in the US.
230. *See* for instance FDA Website, Resources for You (Drugs). Available at: https://www.fda.gov/Drugs/ResourcesForYou/default.htm (last accessed on March 31, 2018).

new policy aiming to speed up the review of generic drug applications,[231] while it also published a list of off-patent and off-exclusivity brand-name drugs, for which there are currently no available generics in the market.[232]

II The United States Patent and Trademark Office

The USPTO is the federal agency of the US Department of Commerce for granting patents and registering trademarks in the US, which dates from 1802.[233] The mandate of the USPTO is to serve the interests of inventors and businesses with respect to their inventions, corporate products and service identifications, and to administer patent laws since they relate to the granting of patents for inventions.[234] The USPTO also provides advice to the president of the US, the Secretary of Commerce and the US government on intellectual property, policy and protection while it promotes stronger and more effective IP protection around the world.[235] Apart from registering and granting patents and trademarks, the USPTO publishes and disseminates patent information, records assignments of patents, provides training to practitioners, protects intellectual endeavours and encourages technological progress so as "to preserve the United States' technological edge, which is the key to [...] current and future competitiveness."[236]

A patent for an invention is a property right "to exclude others from making, using, offering for sale, or selling the invention throughout the United States," from importing the invention, or in case the invention is a process, to exclude others from making/using/offering for sale or selling products made by that process.[237] If the two main criteria of novelty and non-obviousness are met, the USPTO grants a patent to the inventor. The legal standard applied by the USPTO assumes an application is patentable, so that the burden of proof lies with the patent examiner to present a prima facie case of patent invalidity.[238] The agency has been criticised numerous times for the limited time and resources devoted to the examination of patent applications, allegedly

---

231. CDER, MAPP 5240. Rev. 4, *Prioritization of the Review of Original ANDAs, Amendments and Supplements*, (September 11, 2017). Available at: https://www.fda.gov/downloads/AboutFDA/CentersOffices/OfficeofMedicalProductsandTobacco/CDER/ManualofPoliciesProcedures/UCM407849.pdf (last accessed on March 31, 2018).
232. FDA, *List of Off-Patent, Off-Exclusivity Drugs Without an Approved Generic*, 2017. Available at: https://www.fda.gov/downloads/Drugs/ResourcesForYou/Consumers/BuyingUsingMediciineSafely/GenericDrugs/UCM564441.pdf (Last accessed on March 31, 2018).
233. USPTO's official website, *General Information Concerning Patents*. Available at: http://www.uspto.gov/patents-getting-started/general-information-concerning-patents#heading-1 (last accessed on March 31, 2018).
234. Idem.
235. USPTO's official website, at: http://www.uspto.gov/about-us (last accessed on March 31, 2018).
236. USPTO's official website, at: http://www.uspto.gov/patents-getting-started/general-information-concerning-patents#heading-1 (last accessed on March 31, 2018).
237. 35 U.S.C. § 154 (a)(1).
238. In re Werner Kotzab, 217 F.3d 1365, 1371-1372 (Fed. Cir. 2000).

allowing bad quality patents to be granted.[239] The increase in the number of patents granted by the USPTO is impressive; from a total of 113,834 in 1995 and 157,718 in 2005, patent grants were more than double in 2014, reaching 326,033.[240] The number of patent applications is even more overwhelming: only in 2017, the USPTO received 647,388 patent filings: 373,093 of them were granted.[241]

Once the patent is issued, the patentee shall enforce it without aid of the USPTO.[242] The term of a patent is normally twenty years from the date in which the patent application was filed in the US, or exceptionally from the date another earlier related application was filed.[243] A patent grant is only effective in the US, US territories and US possessions.[244] Three different types of patents exist: (1) utility patents, granted for a useful process, machine, article of manufacture or composition of matter and new and useful improvements thereof;[245] (2) design patents, granted for "new, original and ornamental design for an article of manufacture;" and (3) plant patents, granted for inventions or discoveries and asexual reproduction of district and new varieties of plants.[246] Once a patent is issued by the USPTO, it enjoys a presumption of validity and the burden of establishing patent invalidity rests on the party asserting such invalidity.[247]

III The United States Federal Trade Commission

The FTC was created in 1914 and is the only federal agency with consumer protection and competition law jurisdiction in broad sectors of the economy.[248] The strategic goals of the FTC are to protect consumers, maintain competition and advance organisational performance.[249] The FTC is composed by five Commissioners who are appointed by the US President and approved by the Senate.[250] The agency is independent and insulated

---

239. *See* for instance LEMLEY, Rational Ignorance, 2001, pp. 1497-1508, 1523-1524, arguing also in favour of reversing the burden of proof to the patent applicant.
240. USPTO, PPTMT, *U.S. Patent Statistic Chart, Calendar years 1963-2015*. Available at: https://www.uspto.gov/web/offices/ac/ido/oeip/taf/us_stat.htm. (last accessed on March 31, 2018) [cited as: PTMT, *Patent Statistic*, 1963-2015].
241. USPTO, *Performance and Accountability Report FY 2017*, pp. 27. Available at: https://www.uspto.gov/sites/default/files/documents/USPTOFY17PAR.pdf (last accessed on March 31, 2018). [cited as: USPTO, *2017 Performance and Accountability Report*]. Note that the 2017 data is preliminary and will be finalised within FYI 2018.
242. USPTO's official website, at: http://www.uspto.gov/patents-getting-started/general-information-concerning-patents#heading-1 (last accessed on March 31, 2018).
243. *Idem*.
244. 35 U.S.C. § 154 (a)(2).
245. According to the USPTO, the term "composition of matter" refers to chemical compositions and may include mixtures of ingredients as well as new chemical compounds. *See* US PTO's official website, at: http://www.uspto.gov/patents-getting-started/general-information-concerning-patents#heading-1 (last accessed on March 31, 2018).
246. *Idem*.
247. 35 U.S.C. 282 (a).
248. 15 U.S.C. §§ 41-58. *See also* FTC's official website, at: https://www.ftc.gov/about-ftc (last accessed on March 31, 2018).
249. FTC, *One Page FTC Performance Snapshot*, February 2015. Available at: https://www.ftc.gov/about-ftc/performance. (last accessed on 31 March 2018).
250. 15 U.S.C. § 41. The Statute further clarifies that "[n]ot more than three of the Commissioners shall be members of the same political party."

from direct political control.[251] Apart from pursuing vigorous law enforcement against illegal and anticompetitive practices, the FTC advances customers' interests and collaborates with federal legislatures and international government agencies, while it also develops policy, research tools and educational programmes.[252] The FTC has three distinct Bureaus: the Bureau of Competition which is responsible for investigating and preventing anticompetitive mergers and business practices; the Bureau of Consumer Protection with the mandate to protect consumers from unfair, deceptive or fraudulent practices, and; the Bureau of Economics, evaluating the economic impact of FTC's actions.[253]

The legal basis used by the FTC to pursue anticompetitive conduct is Section 5 of the FTC Act, banning "unfair methods of competition" and "unfair or deceptive acts or practices."[254] The FTC has been rather hostile towards patent settlement agreements involving large transfers of value from brand-name drug manufacturers and patentees towards generic challengers in the context of Hatch-Waxman patent infringement litigation, arguing that pay-for-delay settlements effectively block all generic drug competition for an increasing number of branded drugs.[255] As analysed in Chapter 3 of this book, the agency was the antitrust plaintiff in prominent reverse payment settlement antitrust litigation cases, such as *FTC v. Actavis* and *FTC v. Schering-Plough*.[256] It is worth noting that the Agency has the possibility to launch administrative adjudication before an FTC Administrative Law Judge (ALJ) in the first instance; any appeals to such decisions are directly adjudicated before US federal courts of appeal. Additionally, the FTC has the possibility to seek preliminary or permanent injunctions in federal district courts in cases of (suspected) violation of any provision of law enforced by the FTC.[257] Apart from initiating antitrust lawsuits and advocating against reverse payment settlements,[258] the FTC has conducted several important empirical studies on several different aspects of pharmaceutical patent settlements,[259] which are extensively used in this book since they provide valuable insights.

---

251. *See* further KOVACIC, WINERMAN, *FTC*, 2015, examining FTC's political independence.
252. FTC's official website, at: https://www.ftc.gov/about-ftc (last accessed on March 31, 2018).
253. FTC's official website, at: https://www.ftc.gov/about-ftc/bureaus-offices (last accessed on March 31, 2018).
254. 15 U.S.C. § 45 (a).
255. FTC, *Pay-for-delay: When Drug Companies Agree Not to Compete*, Compilation of Press Releases. Available at: https://www.ftc.gov/news-events/media-resources/mergers-competition/pay-delay. (last accessed on March 31, 2018). [cited as: FTC, Press Releases List].
256. *FTC v. Actavis*, 133 S. Ct. 2223 (2013); *FTC v. Schering-Plough Corp. et al.*, 126 S. Ct. 2929 (2006).
257. *See* further 15 U.S.C. §§ 53(b).
258. For a useful overview of the FTC actions *see* further FTC, *Overview of FTC Actions in Pharmaceutical Products and Distribution*, April 2017. Available at: https://www.ftc.gov/system/files/attachments/competition-policy-guidance/overview_pharma_april_2017.pdf (last accessed on 31 March 2018). *See* further 15 U.S.C. § 46, the legal basis according FTC the power to investigate and publicly report.
259. *See* for instance FTC, Press Releases List, including a list of relevant FTC's press releases, studies and reports.

IV The United States Department of Justice

The DoJ is the federal executive department of the US government and has a broad array of responsibilities in the enforcement of law, national security and the criminal justice system.[260] The Judiciary Act of 1789 initially created the Office of the Attorney General as a one-person part-time position. Due to the increased workload, in 1870 the Congress passed the Act to Establish the Department of Justice and created DoJ, with the Attorney General as its head and the chief law enforcement officer of the Federal Government, assisted by the Office of the Solicitor General.[261] The DoJ prosecutes offenders of federal law and represents the US government in court, representing also the interests of Americans, and enforces federal civil and criminal laws, including environmental, civil rights, antitrust and tax laws.[262]

Among its several other divisions,[263] the DoJ's Antitrust Division has the mission to promote economic competition through enforcing and providing guidance on antitrust laws and principles. From 2009 until 2013, the Antitrust Division obtained more than $4.2 billion in criminal fines against antitrust violators.[264] Apart from being active in the enforcement of antitrust laws in the healthcare and pharmaceutical sector,[265] the Antitrust Division has also issued a number of publications, reports and studies – some of them in collaboration with the FTC.[266]

---

260. *See* 28 C.F.R., Chapter I, *Department of Justice* (2015).
261. Act to Establish the Department of Justice, ch. 150, 16 Stat. 162 (1870). *See also* US Department of Justice Overview, 2015, p. 1. Available at: http://www.justice.gov/about/fy15-budget-and-performance (last accessed on March 31, 2018).
262. US Department of Justice Overview, 2015, p. 1.
263. US Department of Justice Overview, 2015, p. 3. The DoJ comprises of the following divisions: the Antitrust Law Division, the Tax Division, the Civil Division, the Civil Rights Division, the Criminal Division, the Environmental and Natural Resources Division, the National Security Division and the Justice Management Division.
264. US Department of Justice, Antitrust Division (ATR), p. 2. Available at: http://www.justice.gov/about/fy15-budget-and-performance (last accessed on March 31, 2018).
265. For a summary of the DoJ Antitrust Division healthcare cases from 1983 to 2017 *see* DOJ, *Summary of Antitrust Division Health Care Cases*, (2017). Available at: https://www.justice.gov/atr/file/783756/download. (last accessed on 31 March 2018) [cited as: DoJ, *Health Care Cases*, 2017].
266. *See* for example FTC, U.S. Department of Justice, *Antitrust Guidelines for the Licensing of Intellectual Property*, (January 12, 2017), pp. 1-36. Available at: https://www.justice.gov/atr/IPguidelines/download (last accessed on March 31, 2018); FTC, U.S. Department of Justice, *Horizontal Merger Guidelines*, (August 19, 2010), pp. 1-34. Available at: https://www.ftc.gov/sites/default/files/attachments/mergers/100819hmg.pdf (last accessed on March 31, 2018). [cited as: FTC, DoJ, *Horizontal Merger Guidelines*, 2010]; FTC, U.S. Department of Justice, *Antitrust Guidelines for Collaborations between Competitors*, (April 2000), pp. 1-35. Available at: https://www.ftc.gov/sites/default/files/documents/public_events/joint-venture-hearings-antitrust-guidelines-collaboration-among-competitors/ftcdojguidelines-2.pdf. (last accessed on March 31, 2018). [cited as: FTC, DoJ, *Antitrust Guidelines*, 2000]. *See* further DoJ website, *Guidelines and Policy Statements*, available at: https://www.justice.gov/atr/guidelines-and-policy-statements-0 (last accessed on March 31, 2018).

PART 2   DRUG MARKET ENTRY IN THE US

I   New Drug Entry to the US Market

Since 1938, a brand-name drug manufacturer wishing to market and sell a new drug in the US shall seek FDA approval by submitting a New Drug Application (NDA).[267] Even before submitting a NDA, the first step in the process of marketing a new drug is to conduct studies *in vitro* (bench studies) and *in vivo* (animal studies) in order to determine the drug's toxicity levels, how it is metabolised, etc. If the results are promising, the sponsor of the drug will normally file an Investigational New Drug Application (IND) to the FDA so as to administer the investigational drug to humans and test the drug's diagnostic and therapeutic potential in clinical trials.[268] The data gathered throughout these trials of the IND will later become part of the NDA. The NDA shall contain information showing that the new drug is safe and effective, while other regulatory requirements shall be met, concerning the drug's proposed labelling and manufacturing methods.[269] According to the FDA, documentation included in the NDA shall comprise the ingredients of the drug, clinical trial results, results of animal studies and information on how the drug is manufactured, processed and packaged.[270]

The clinical trials normally comprise of three phases. Phase 1 of the clinical trials aims to determine "the metabolism and pharmacologic actions of the drug in humans, the side effects associated with increasing doses, and, if possible, to gain early evidence of effectiveness."[271] Phase 2 is designed to evaluate the drug's effectiveness for a particular indication in patients with the condition under study and to determine short-term side effects and risks associated with the drug.[272] Finally, during Phase 3 additional information about the effectiveness and safety of the drug is gathered, so as to evaluate the benefit-risk relationship of the drug and to provide a basis for labelling.[273] After the Phase 3 of the clinical trials, the originator shall file an NDA with the FDA, including among other information detailed reports of all animal studies and clinical testing, a full statement of the composition of the drug, any adverse reactions and other pertinent scientific literature information.[274] The sponsor of a New Drug Application must submit the patents for listing to the FDA within thirty days of the

---

267. NDA application on the basis of FD & C Act, Section 505(b)(2). *See also* FDA Website, *New Drug Application*. Available at: http://www.fda.gov/Drugs/DevelopmentApprovalProcess/HowDrugsareDevelopedandApproved/ApprovalApplications/NewDrugApplicationNDA/ (last accessed on March 31, 2018).
268. FDA Website, *Information for Sponsor-Investigators Submitting Investigational New Drug Applications (INDs)*. Available at: http://www.fda.gov/Drugs/DevelopmentApprovalProcess/HowDrugsareDevelopedandApproved/ApprovalApplications/InvestigationalNewDrugINDApplication/ucm071098.htm (last accessed on March 31, 2018).
269. 21 U.S.C. § 355(b); FD&C Act, Section 505(b)(2).
270. FDA Website, *New Drug Application*.
271. 21 C.F.R. § 312.21(a)(2015).
272. 21 C.F.R. § 312.21(b)(2015).
273. 21 C.F.R. § 312.21(c)(2015).
274. 21 U.S.C. §355(b)(1).

approval of the NDA. If the relevant patents are submitted after this 30-day period, these "late listed" patents will not block the approval of any pending paragraph IV ANDAs.[275]

As discussed in Chapter 1, due to the rigorous scientific demands to prove safety and effectiveness, a new drug may take from ten to fifteen years to develop, while the cost of bringing a new drug to the market can exceed 2 billion dollars.[276] On the contrary, the cost of R&D for a generic drug does not arguably surpass 1 or 2 million dollars.[277] The relatively low costs to entry for generic drugs result to increased competition since as above-analysed generic drug prices may be up to 80%-90% lower than the price of the respective reference brand-name drug.[278]

II Generic Drug Entry under the Hatch-Waxman Act

On September 2, 1984, the Drug Price Competition and Patent Term Restoration Act of 1984 was signed into law, amending with its Title 1 the Federal Food, Drug, and Cosmetic Act (FD&C Act).[279] Commonly known as the "Hatch-Waxman Act" from the last names of its two main sponsors, this act was enacted as a means for the Congress to strike a balance between: (1) inducing pioneering R&D of new drugs, and; (2) enabling competitors to bring low cost, generic copies of those drugs to market.[280] Representative Waxman, one of the main sponsors of the Act, stated "in passing the Hatch-Waxman Act, Congress drew a careful line between patent protection and the need to provide incentives for competition in the pharmaceutical industry."[281] The Hatch-Waxman Act was an attempt of the US Congress to attain the optimum balance between innovation and competition, a "deliberate effort to promote consumer access through litigated challenges."[282]

Before the enactment of the Hatch-Waxman Act in 1984, generic drug manufacturers did not have the possibility to rely on the innovator's clinical results that have established the safety and efficacy of the reference brand-name drug. Until then,

---

275. FDA, REdI, *Hatch-Waxman 101*, Generic Drugs Forum, Sheraton, (April 23-25, 2015), p. 11. Available at: http://www.fda.gov/downloads/Drugs/DevelopmentApprovalProcess/Small BusinessAssistance/UCM445610.pdf. (last accessed on March 31, 2018). [cited as: FDA, *Hatch-Waxman 101*, 2015].
276. *See supra* Chapter 1, Part 1, Section I.A, discussing the R&D costs, risks and duration.
277. ASPE Issue Brief, Expanding the Use of Generic Drugs, December 1, 2010, pp. 3-4. Available at: http://aspe.hhs.gov/basic-report/expanding-use-generic-drugs (last accessed on March 31, 2018). The estimations for R&D costs vary widely; *see* for instance Roth, 2013, pp. 259-264, arguing that for the same drug an innovator would have to spend $12.6 million for clinical trials, whereas the generic competitor would have to spend $2.6 million to demonstrate bioequivalence.
278. *See supra* Chapter 1, Part 1, Section II.B.1.
279. Drug Price Competition and Patent Term Restoration Act, Pub. L. No. 98-417, 98 Stat. 1585 (1984).
280. *Andrx Pharms., Inc. v. Biovail Corp.*, 276 F.3d 1368, 1371 (Fed. Cir. 2002); *Teva Pharms. USA, Inc. v. Pfizer, Inc.*, 395 F.3d 1324, 1327 (Fed. Cir., 2005); *Caraco Pharm. Labs., Ltd. v. Forest Labs., Inc.*, 527 F.3d 1278, 1283-1284 (Fed. Cir. 2008).
281. Representative Waxman, 130 Cong. Rec. 24425, (September 6, 1984), underscoring the "fundamental balance of the bill."
282. Hemphill, Paying for Delay, 2006, p. 1614.

generic manufacturers were obliged to repeat those high-cost clinical tests – an obligation which was a powerful deterrent to generic entry according to the FTC.[283] As a result, brand-name drug manufacturers barely faced any generic competition and their monopoly could last several years after the expiration of their patents.[284] Another problem further delaying generic entry was that a generic manufacturer wishing to conduct the above-mentioned clinical trials and to begin the FDA approval process was obliged to wait until the patents relevant to the drug expired,[285] since clinical trials were considered to be a "use" prohibited under the Patent Act.[286] A provision of the Hatch-Waxman Act, commonly known as the "Bolar amendment" changed that, stating that it is not an act of infringement to make use of the patented invention solely for uses that are reasonably related to the development and submission of information for receiving FDA approval.[287] Before the Hatch-Waxman amendments, patent law and the FDA drug approval process extended the term of the brand-name drug's patent and delayed the introduction of generic drugs.[288]

The Hatch-Waxman Act solved this problem by providing for a statutory experimental use exception.[289] Before this explicit statutory provision, the experimental use defence was merely used as a defence to liability for infringement generally. Nevertheless, this was a much narrower exception, since it only covered experiments with the patented article "for the sole purpose of gratifying a philosophical taste, or curiosity or for mere amusement."[290] Thus, this exception did not allow the use of a patented invention for promoting definite commercial purposes and the business interests of the infringer.[291] As analysed in the following sections, under the Hatch-Waxman Act, generic drug manufacturers who wish to enter the market and compete with a brand-name drug manufacturer have two main options: to file either a Section

---

283. FTC, *Generic Drug Entry*, 2002, pp. 3-4.
284. WANSHENG, 2008, pp. 455-456.
285. FTC, *Generic Drug Entry*, 2002, pp. 3-4.
286. *Roche Products, Inc. v. Bolar Pharmaceutical Co.*, 733 F.2d 858, 863 (Fed. Cir. 1984), "[U]nlicensed experiments conducted with a view to the adaption of the patented invention to the experimentor's business is a violation of the rights of the patentee to exclude others from using his patented invention."
287. 35 U.S.C. § 271(e)(1). This provision of the Hatch-Waxman is known as the "Bolar amendment" because it overruled *Roche Products, Inc. v. Bolar Pharmaceutical Co.*, 733 F.2d 858 (Fed. Cir. 1984), cert. denied, 469 U.S. 856 (1984), in which the Federal Court has held that it is an act of patent infringement to use a patented drug to perform tests in order to develop a generic drug.
288. FTC, *Generic Drug Entry*, 2002, pp. 3-4.
289. 35 U.S.C. § 271(e)(1) (2015). For further discussion of this provision *see Merck KGaA v. Integra Lifesciences I, Ltd.*, 125 S. Ct. 2372, 2376-2377, 2380 (2005), "[T]he statutory text makes clear that it provides a wide berth for the use of patented drugs in activities related to the federal regulatory process."
290. *Poppenhusen v. Falke*, 19 F. Cas. 1048, 1049 (C.C.S.D.N.Y. 1861) (No. 11,279). The experimental use doctrine as a defence to patent infringement originated in an opinion written by Supreme Court's Justice Story while sitting on circuit in Massachusetts: *Whittemore v. Cutter*, 29 F. Cas. 1120 (C.C.D. Mass. 1813) (No. 17,600).
291. *Roche Products, Inc. v. Bolar Pharmaceutical Co.*, 733 F.2d 858, 863 (Fed. Cir. 1984), "[w]e cannot construe the experimental use rule so broadly as to allow a violation of the patent laws in the guise of 'scientific inquiry', when that inquiry has definite, cognizable, and not insubstantial commercial purposes."

505(b)(2) application or an ANDA. A generic manufacturer may also file an ANDA with a Section viii "carve-out" Statement, arguing that the listed patent of the brand-name drug does not claim a use for which the generic applicant is seeking approval.[292] On October 2016, the FDA has published a Final Rule on ANDAs and Section 505(b)(2) applications, aiming to revise and clarify the respective FDA regulations.[293]

A Section 505(b)(2) Applications

Section 505(b)(2) was introduced to the Federal Food Drug and Cosmetic Act through the 1984 Hatch-Waxman amendments. A 505(b)(2) application is a new drug application submitted under Section 505(b)(1) that contains full reports of safety and effectiveness which rely – at least partly – on investigations which were not conducted by or for the applicant or for which the applicant has not obtained the right of reference or use. If a generic drug differs significantly from the brand-name drug, e.g., provides for a different route of administration of the active ingredient or another dosage form, has different strength or includes a substitution of the active ingredient of the brand-name drug (salt, ester or chelate) etc., this generic drug must be approved through Section 505(b)(2).[294] Applications on the basis of Section 505(b)(2) can also be submitted for drugs containing a New Chemical Entity (NCE) or a New Molecular Entity (NME), when the data necessary for the approval of the drug is derived from studies not conducted by or for the applicant.[295] Such studies may be published literature or a previous finding of the FDA on the safety and efficacy of already approved drugs,[296] while the applicant shall establish a "bridge" between the proposed drug product and each listed drug product that is relied upon, demonstrating that such reliance is scientifically justified.[297]

This process is commonly known as a "paper NDA application" and could be seen as a hybrid of a full NDA and an ANDA, requiring less data than the former and more than the latter. Unlike a full NDA, the filing and approval of a Section 505(b)(2) application may be delayed by patent or exclusivity protections of an approved drug product.[298] However, a Section 505(b)(2) application may be granted a 3-year New

---

292. 21 U.S.C. §§ 355(b)(2)(B), (j)(2)(A)(viii).
293. FDA, Department of Health and Human Services, *Abbreviated New Drug Applications and 505(b)(2) Applications*, 21 CFR Parts 314 and 320, Final Rule, 81 Federal Register 194, pp. 69580-69658 (October 2016). Available at: https://www.gpo.gov/fdsys/pkg/FR-2016-10-06/pdf/2016-22690.pdf (last accessed on March 31, 2018).
294. *See* further FDA, CDER, *Draft Guidance for Industry, Applications Covered by Section 505(b)(2)*, (October 1999), pp. 3-4. Available at: http://www.fda.gov/downloads/Drugs/Guidances/ucm 079345.pdf. (last accessed on March 31, 2018). [cited as: FDA, Section 505(b)(2) Applications, 1999]; note that the above-mentionned examples of generic drugs differing significantly from the respective brand-name drug are indicative and not exhaustive.
295. FDA, *Determining whether to Submit an ANDA or a 505(b)(2) Application – Draft Guidance for Industry*, (October 2017). Available at: https://www.fda.gov/downloads/Drugs/Guidance ComplianceRegulatoryInformation/Guidances/UCM579751.pdf. (last accessed on March 31, 2018). [cited as: FDA, *Draft Guidance for Industry*, 2017], pp. 3-4; FDA, Section 505(b)(2) Applications, 1999, pp. 3-4.
296. FDA, Section 505(b)(2) Applications, 1999, pp. 3-4.
297. FDA, *Draft Guidance for Industry*, 2017, p. 5.
298. FDA, Section 505(b)(2) Applications, 1999, p. 6.

Clinical Studies (NCS) exclusivity or a 5-year NCE exclusivity, while it may also be eligible for orphan drug or paediatric exclusivity.[299]

B The ANDA Mechanism

1 Requirements of ANDA Submission

The Hatch-Waxman Act regulates the requirements for the ANDA process, a process significantly reducing the costs of gaining generic marketing approval.[300] An ANDA is in essence an application which contains information showing that the proposed generic product "is identical in active ingredient, dosage form, strength, route of administration, labelling, quality, performance characteristics and intended use" to the previously approved NDA application of the respective brand-name drug.[301] The generic ANDA filer must prove that its generic drug and the relevant listed brand-name drug are bioequivalent and share the same active ingredients.[302] In principle, the generic drug shall also have the same labelling as the brand-name drug.[303] Nevertheless, specific changes from the reference listed product to the inactive ingredients of the generic drug are allowed by the FDA.[304] Moreover, limited changes in the route of administration, dosage form and strength but also the substitution of one of the reference drug's active ingredients for another may be allowed by the FDA, provided that these changes have been the subject of a suitability petition approved by the FDA and no further investigations are necessary in order to establish the safety and efficacy of the respective generic drug version.[305] This type of ANDA is referred to by the FDA as the "petitioned ANDA."[306] The submission of an ANDA triggers an initial review by the FDA, which is usually completed within sixty days and aims to confirm if the ANDA is sufficiently complete to permit substantive review.[307]

Notably, generic ANDA filers can rely on the clinical trial evidence provided in the brand-name holders' New Drug Application (NDA) and ANDAs do not contain

---

299. FDA, Section 505(b)(2) Applications, 1999, p. 7. *See infra* Chapter 2, Section II.B., analysing the different kinds of exclusivities in the US.
300. 21 U.S.C. §§ 355(j)(1), (j)(2)(A). *See also* FD&C Act, Section 505(j).
301. 21 U.S.C. §§ 355(j)(2)(A). *See further*, FDA, Small Business Assistance, "Frequently Asked Questions for New Drug Product Exclusivity," Q4. Available at: http://www.fda.gov/drugs/developmentapprovalprocess/smallbusinessassistance/ucm069962.htm (last accessed on March 31, 2018). The respective brand-name drug is also mentioned as the "reference listed drug (RLD)."
302. 21 U.S.C. §§ 355(j)(2)(A)(ii), 355(j)(2)(A)(iv).
303. 21 U.S.C. § 355(j)(2)(A)(v).
304. FDA, CDER, *Guidance for Industry, ANDA Submissions – Refuse to Receive Standards*, (May 2015), p. 9. Available at: http://www.fda.gov/downloads/Drugs/GuidanceComplianceRegulatoryInformation/Guidances/UCM370352.pdf. (last accessed on March 31, 2018).
305. *See* 21 CFR 314.93; FD&C Act, Section 505(j)(2)(C). In case such a petitioned ANDA, the labelling of the generic drug will of course not be identical to the reference brand-name drug.
306. FDA, *Draft Guidance for Industry*, 2017.
307. 21 C.F.R. § 314.101 (b)(1). Even though the provision does not contain a deadline for the FDA to complete this review, as a matter of policy the FDA respects the same 60-day requirement for the review of NDAs, provided at 21 C.F.R. § 314.101 (a)(1). *See* Hemphill, Paying for Delay, 2006, p. 1608, fn. 205.

clinical studies; as above-mentioned, they do however need to provide information establishing bioequivalence to the brand-name drug.[308] This is the main reason why generic companies can market their drugs at lower cost, since they do not face the high drug development costs brand-name manufacturers do.[309] As mentioned above, before the enactment of the Hatch-Waxman Act, generic filers were obliged to conduct their own clinical trials and bare their high cost, a cost which was a serious deterrent to generic entry.

2 Four Different ANDA Certifications

Generic ANDA applicants must also submit one of the following four certifications, addressing each patent covering the listed drug and listed in FDA's "Approved Drug Products with Therapeutic Equivalence Evaluations," commonly known as the *Orange Book*.[310] These certifications shall be made regarding each patent that the NDA holder associates with the concerned drug, extending to formulations and methods of use.[311]

More specifically, the generic ANDA filer is required to certify either:

I) that [the required] patent information was not been filed [with the FDA],[312] or;
II) that [the relevant] patent has expired,[313] or;
III) the day on which [the relevant] patent will expire,[314] or;
IV) that [the relevant] patent is invalid or will not be infringed by the manufacture, use, or sale of the new drug for which the application is submitted.[315]

This certification is significant since it determines the day on which the approval of the ANDA will be made effective by the FDA.[316] If the generic filer opts for a paragraph I or a paragraph II certification, FDA approval may be made effective immediately.[317] In case the generic filer makes paragraph III certification, the approval of the application by the FDA will be made effective the date when the patent expires.[318] Things are more complicated with regard to paragraph IV certifications, where the effective date of FDA approval depends on the outcome of further events

---

308. 21 U.S.C. § 355(j)(2)(A). In general, a generic drug is bioequivalent to the brand-name drug when it delivers the same amount of active ingredient in a patient's bloodstream, over the same amount of time as the brand-name drug.
309. 21 U.S.C. § 355(b)(1). Brand-name manufacturers shall conduct extensive animal and human studies of safety and effectiveness, which must accompany their NDAs.
310. A digital publication of the latest edition of the Orange Book is available at: http://www.accessdata.fda.gov/scripts/cder/ob/default.cfm (last accessed on March 31, 2018).
311. 21 U.S.C. § 355(b)(1).
312. 21 U.S.C. § 355(j)(2)(A)(ii)(vi)(I).
313. 21 U.S.C. § 355(j)(2)(A)(ii)(vi)(II).
314. 21 U.S.C. § 355(j)(2)(A)(ii)(vi)(III).
315. 21 U.S.C. § 355(j)(2)(A)(ii)(vi)(IV).
316. *Eli Lilly and Company v. Medtronic Inc.*, 110 S. Ct. 2683, 2692 (1990).
317. 21 U.S.C. §§ 355(c)(3)(A), (j)(5)(B)(i).
318. 21 U.S.C. §§ 355(c)(3)(B), (j)(5)(B)(ii).

triggered by the Hatch-Waxman Act and is linked with the beginning of the 180-day exclusivity period, as explained in the following section.[319]

3 Section viii "Carve-Out" Statements

If a patent only covers a method of use, a generic manufacturer may file a Section viii Statement instead of paragraph III or paragraph IV certification, certifying that it does not seek approval for the method of use that is claimed in the patent.[320] In such a case, the generic applicant shall also provide a proposed label "carving out" the proposed method of use. Section viii Statements do not ordinarily trigger patent litigation and do not entail certification or notice requirements to the patent holder or the possibility for a 30-month stay of FDA approval, since the generic applicant "carves out" from the generic drug's label anything related to the patented method in the brand-name drug's label.[321] This procedure can also be used by generic challengers wishing to circumvent the 3-year NCS exclusivity by "carving out" the information on the clinical trials and the relevant approval.[322] As long as this so-called "skinny label" does not make the generic drug less safe or effective for the remaining non-protected conditions of use, it will be approved by the FDA.[323]

Brand-name drug manufacturers have tried to prevent generics' Section viii Statements, arguing that even though the generic drugs concerned were not directly infringing the relevant patents, they should be prohibited since their marketing would inevitably "induce" infringement.[324] This claim was rejected by the Court of Appeals for the Federal Circuit in *Warner-Lambert v. Apotex*, which found that inducement required more than mere knowledge that infringement would occur – generic companies could not be held liable unless they specifically promoted the generic drug for the carved-out use.[325]

In another attempt to limit the use of carved-outs, certain brand-name drug manufacturers have tried to list use codes substantially exceeding the scope of the use patent, since representations of patent information in use codes are not evaluated by the FDA.[326] A patent use code is a "[c]ode to designate a use patent that covers the approved indication or use of a drug product" which may be repeated for multiple

---

319. 21 U.S.C. §§ 355(c)(3)(C), (j)(5)(B)(iii).
320. 21 U.S.C. § 355(j)(2)(B); 21 CFR 314.92(a)(1), 314.94(a)(12)(iii).
321. FDA, Department of Health and Human Services, *Applications for FDA Approval to Market a New Drug*, Final Rule, 68 Federal Register 117, pp. 36682, No. 117, (June 18, 2003). Available at: http://www.fda.gov/OHRMS/DOCKETS/98fr/061803a.pdf. (last accessed on March 31, 2018). [cited as: FDA, NDA Final Rule, 2003].
322. Once the relevant method patent or exclusivity expire, generic challengers often try to amend their generic drugs' labels and add back any previously carved-out uses.
323. 21 C.F.R. § 314.127(a)(7). See further KARST, 2014.
324. RAI, 2012, p. 491. As RAI explains, due to the generic substitution practices, carved-out generic drugs will inevitably be prescribed also for patented uses.
325. *Warner-Lambert Co. v. Apotex*, 316 F.3d 1348, 1364-1365 (Fed. Cir. 2003).
326. RAI 2012, pp. 491-492. See also FDA, NDA Final Rule, 2003, at 36683.

applications, products and patents.³²⁷ The Supreme Court recognised in its ruling in *Caraco* that generic companies which are sued for patent infringement can file a counterclaim challenging the submission of overly broad listings of use codes by the patent holder.³²⁸ Nevertheless, this claim to correct over-breadth can only be filed by a generic company in the context of paragraph IV infringement litigation and cannot be initiated by generic challengers outside this context.³²⁹

C Paragraph IV ANDA

The paragraph IV ANDA is a mechanism introduced by the Hatch-Waxman Act which aims to the challenge and elimination of weak or invalid patents blocking the entry of lower-cost generic drugs. Generic manufacturers wishing to enter the market before the expiration of the brand-name manufacturer's patents listed in the Orange Book, shall file a paragraph IV certification, arguing either patent invalidity or non-infringement of the brand-name drug by their generic drug. The filing of a paragraph IV ANDA constitutes an act of *artificial* patent infringement according to 35 U.S.C. § 271(e)(2).³³⁰ This provision was designed to create an artificial act of infringement so as to establish the jurisdiction of federal courts and enable the early judicial resolution of the arising patent dispute between the patent holder and the generic filer.³³¹ If the generic paragraph IV ANDA filer loses in the patent infringement litigation trial, it is obliged to withdraw its paragraph IV ANDA and substitute it with a paragraph III ANDA, committing not to enter the market until the patent expires.³³² Litigation was the instrument chosen by the regulator in order to accelerate generic entry through the Hatch-Waxman Act; however the involuntary consequence was a number of

---

327. FDA, *Orange Book Data Files*, Data Descriptions. Available at: http://www.fda.gov/Drugs/InformationOnDrugs/ucm129689.htm (last accessed on March 31, 2018).
328. *Caraco Pharmaceutical Laboratories, Ltd., et al., v. Novo Nordisk A/S et al.*, 132 S. Ct. 1670, 1687-1688 (2012).
329. *See infra*, Chapter 2, Part 2, Section III.A.2.2, on the possibility for the generic challenger to assert a counterclaim to correct or delete a patent improperly listed to the Orange Book.
330. 35 U.S.C. § 271(e)(2), "It shall be an act of infringement to submit [...] an application under section 505(j) of the Federal Food, Drug, and Cosmetic Act or described in section 505(b)(2) of such Act for a drug claimed in a patent or the use of which is claimed in a patent." *See also Glaxo, Inc. v. Novopharm, Ltd.*, 110 F.3d 1562, 1569-1570 (Fed. Cir. 1997), discussing the filing of a paragraph IV ANDA as an artificial act of patent infringement which is sufficient to create controversy and enable a court to promptly resolve any dispute concerning patent infringement, but which does not meet the patentee's burden of proving ultimate patent infringement.
331. *Caraco Pharm. Labs., Ltd. v. Forest Labs., Inc.*, 527 F.3d 1278, 1283 (Fed. Cir. 2008), referring to *Glaxo Group Ltd. v. Apotex, Inc.*, 376 F.3d 1339, 1351 (Fed. Cir. 2004) and *Eli Lilly and Company v. Medtronic Inc.*, 110 S. Ct. 2683, 2693 (1990), "Quite obviously, the purpose of (e)(2) [...] is to enable the judicial adjudication upon which the ANDA and paper NDA schemes depend."
332. 21 C.F.R. § 314.94(a), "An applicant who [...] is sued for patent infringement [...] shall amend the certification if a final judgment in the action against the applicant is entered finding the patent to be infringed. In the amended certification, the applicant shall certify under paragraph (a)(12)(i)(A)(3) of this section that the patent will expire on a specific date."

settlement agreements between competitors including large payments and value transfers aiming to delay generic entry, virtually cancelling the aim of the Hatch-Waxman Act as analysed in Chapter 3.

1 FDA's Approval Triggers the 180-Day Exclusivity Period

The date on which FDA approval is made effective for the first paragraph IV ANDA, is also the date on which the 180-day generic exclusivity is triggered. This date triggering exclusivity is crucial for NDA holders and subsequent paragraph IV ANDA filers, since the FDA cannot approve subsequent paragraph IV ANDAs until the first ANDA filer's 180-day exclusivity expires.[333] Before this "full" approval, the FDA may issue a tentative approval of the ANDA application, notifying the applicant that its ANDA meets the requirements for approval but is blocked by a patent, an exclusivity period or a statutory stay.[334] This tentative approval of the ANDA does not render the drug approved and "full" FDA approval is not automatic after the tentative approval: the generic challenger must show that its ANDA still meets the FDA approval requirements at the time of "full" approval.[335]

When the initial ANDA review is completed by the FDA, the paragraph IV generic filer shall provide notice of its paragraph IV certification to the patent holder and the NDA owner within twenty days,[336] including "a detailed statement of the factual and legal basis of the opinion of the applicant that the patent is invalid or will not be infringed."[337] This certification requirement imposes a duty of care on the generic challenger to provide a well-based notice letter.[338] The patent holder then has forty-five days from the day it received notice of the paragraph IV certification to sue the generic

---

333. *Caraco Pharm. Labs., Ltd. v. Forest Labs., Inc.*, 527 F.3d 1278, 1284 (Fed. Cir. 2008). As explained in *Caraco*, NDA holders and subsequent paragraph IV ANDA filers have conflicting interests with regard to triggering the exclusivity period. NDA holders have strong incentives to prevent the triggering effect – in other words to avoid patent infringement litigation – since subsequent paragraph IV ANDAs cannot be approved until the exclusivity period expires. On the contrary, subsequent paragraph IV ANDA filers have strong incentives to generate a triggering effect. Note however that in both the *Caraco* and the *Pfizer* cases, MMA amendments did not apply due to MMA's "grandfather provision," specifying that MMA's amendments do not apply for paragraph IV ANDAs made before the enactment of MMA on December 8, 2003. *See* further Medicare Prescription Drug, Improvement and Modernization Act of 2003, Public Law 108-173, 108th Congress, 117 Stat. 2460, Section 1102(b) and *Teva Pharms. USA, Inc. v. Pfizer, Inc.*, 395 F.3d 1324, 1328-29 (Fed. Cir. 2005).
334. 21 U.S.C. § 355(j)(5)(B)(iv)(II)(dd)(AA).
335. 21 U.S.C. § 355(j)(5)(B)(iv)(II)(dd)(BB).
336. 21 U.S.C. § 355(b)(3)(B) (2015); FD&C Act, Section 505(j)(2)(B)(iv), 21 C.F.R. § 314.95(b) (2015), "The applicant shall send the notice ... when it receives from FDA an acknowledgement letter stating that its abbreviated new drug application is sufficiently complete to permit a substantive review." *See also* 21 U.S.C. § 355(j)(2)(B).
337. 21 U.S.C. § 355(b)(3)(D)(ii). *See also* 21 U.S.C. § 355(j)(2)(B)(iv)(II).
338. *Yamanouchi Pharm. Co., Ltd. et al., v. Danburry Pharmacal, Inc., et al.*, 231 F.3d 1339, 1347 (Fed. Cir. 2000), "The joint operation of 271(e) and 285 require the paragraph (2) infringer to display care and regard for the strict standards of the Hatch-Waxman Act when challenging patent validity. As already noted, the Hatch-Waxman Act authorizes challenges to the validity of patents in accordance with strict statutory requirements."

filer for patent infringement.[339] If the patent holder refrains from filing a patent infringement suit, FDA approval of the paragraph IV ANDA will be made effective immediately after this 45-day term has elapsed.[340] If the patent holder does sue the generic filer for patent infringement, the paragraph IV ANDA will be approved either when there is a court judgment trigger (a judicial determination of non-infringement of the relevant patent by the court adjudicating the patent infringement suit) or alternatively upon the expiration of the 30-month stay of FDA approval, a stay that begins on the day of receipt of notice of the paragraph IV filing.[341]

If the district court adjudicating the patent infringement suit decides that the patent at issue is invalid or is not infringed by the generic drug, FDA approval of the paragraph IV ANDA shall be made effective from the date of the court's judgment or the date of the settlement order or consent decree which states that the relevant patent is invalid or not infringed.[342] On the contrary, if the district court finds that the patent has been infringed and the generic filer appeals against it, FDA approval will be made effective upon the date on which the Court of Appeals reverses the district court decision and finds that the patent at issue is invalid or not infringed, or the date of a settlement agreement or consent decree reaching the same conclusion.[343] The district court may also grant a preliminary injunction prohibiting the generic challenger from commercially manufacturing or selling its generic drug. In that case, the date when FDA approval is made effective similarly depends on the subsequent finding of (in)validity or (non) infringement.[344]

Table 2.1 may facilitate the comprehension of this complicated scheme:[345]

Table 2.1 FDA Approval of Paragraph IV ANDAs

1.	Patent infringement lawsuit pending before 30-month stay expires	→	FDA can only tentatively approve paragraph IV ANDA
2.	Lawsuit still pending for thirty months	→	FDA can approve paragraph IV ANDA
3.	Generic challenger wins infringement lawsuit	→	FDA can approve paragraph IV ANDA
4.	Dismissal/settlement of lawsuit	→	FDA can usually approve paragraph IV ANDA on agreed date

---

339. 21 U.S.C. § 355(j)(5)(B)(iii).
340. *Idem.*
341. *Idem.*
342. 21 U.S.C. § 355(j)(5)(B)(iii)(I).
343. 21 U.S.C. § 355(j)(5)(B)(iii)(II).
344. 21 U.S.C. §§ 355(j)(5)(B)(iii)(III), (j)(5)(B)(iii)(IV). In case the patent is subsequently found to be invalid or not infringed, FDA approval of the paragraph IV ANDA shall be made effective as provided in 21 U.S.C. § 355(j)(5)(B)(iii)(I), that is from the date of the court's judgment or the date of the settlement order or consent decree which states that the relevant patent is invalid or not infringed. On the contrary, if the patent is found to be valid or infringed, FDA approval of the paragraph IV ANDA shall be made effective as provided in 21 U.S.C. § 355(j)(5)(B)(iii)(II).
345. Table created on the basis of FDA, *Hatch-Waxman 101*, 2015, p. 11.

5.	Brand-name manufacturer wins →	FDA can only tentatively approve paragraph IV until patent expires

2   The 30-Month Stay to the ANDA's Approval

As mentioned in the previous section, if the patent holder files a patent infringement suit against the paragraph IV filer within forty-five days from receiving notification of the filing, there will be a 30-month stay of FDA approval of the generic product, beginning on the day of receipt of notice of the paragraph IV filing.[346] The patent holder can also file an infringement lawsuit prior to the tentative ANDA approval and the marketing of the generic drug. However, the patent holder normally has a greater interest in filing an infringement lawsuit after receiving the notification by the generic, so as to delay the approval of the generic drug for a longer time-period. Even a single 30-month stay can last for more than three years.[347] The 30-month stay superficially resembles the preliminary injunction, which is often available to patent holders, but is much less costly than a typical injunction, on top of being automatic.[348] The patent holder is not required to show irreparable harm or likelihood of success on the merits or to post a bond in order to pay the alleged generic infringer's damages if the infringement suit is decided in the generic manufacturer's favour.[349]

2.1   Multiple 30-Month Stays

According to FDA's interpretation of the Hatch-Waxman amendments, multiple 30-month stays to an ANDA application are possible and have happened on a number of instances.[350] Also after a generic challenger has filed a paragraph IV ANDA, originators have the possibility to list additional patents in the Orange Book covering the reference brand-name drug. As the FDA does not regulate the listing of patents – assuming that patent holders will list patents in good faith – the FDA does not review the patents to determine whether they claim indeed the drug product described in the NDA.[351] If the

---

346. 21 U.S.C. § 355(j)(5)(B)(iii).
347. HEMPHILL, Paying For Delay, 2006, pp. 1566-1567.
348. HEMPHILL, Paying For Delay, 2006, p. 1608.
349. *Idem*.
350. TROY Daniel E., Chief Counsel, U.S. FDA, *Drug Price Competition and Patent Term Restoration Act of 1984 (Hatch-Waxman Amendments)*, before the Senate Committee and the Judiciary, August 1, 2003. Available at: http://www.fda.gov/newsevents/testimony/ucm115033.htm. (last accessed on March 31, 2018), "[T]here have been a number of instances where there has been more than a single 30-month stay. These include paroxetine hydrochloride (Paxil) and gabapentin (Neurontin). [...] of the 442 active ANDAs that contained paragraph IV certifications, only 17 have had multiple 30-month stays, representing 3.8 percent of all applications with patent challenges. However, we note that a significant number of these products have high dollar value annual sales, and we are aware of some instances where multiple stays have resulted in the delay of a generic drug approval for a number of years."
351. FTC, *Comment of the Federal Trade Commission, In the Matter of Applications for FDA Approval to Market a New Drug; Patent Listing Requirements and Application of 30-Month Stays on Approval of Abbreviated New Drug Applications Certifying that a Patent Claiming a Drug is*

patent holder submits newly issued patents to the FDA, after the filing of an ANDA application, the generic paragraph IV filer is required to provide paragraph IV certifications and the corresponding notices for the later-issued patents as well; in case there will be subsequent infringement lawsuits from the patent holder, new 30-month stays will arise.

The Medicare Prescription Drug, Improvement and Modernization Act of 2003 (MMA), amending the Hatch-Waxman Act, attempted to put an end to multiple 30-month stays by precluding such stays for patents submitted to the FDA by the patent holder subsequently to the submission of an ANDA or a 505(d)(2) application by generic challengers.[352] Nevertheless, even *post* MMA, multiple 30-month stays are still possible in limited cases: if for instance an ANDA contains a paragraph IV and a paragraph III certification, and the generic challenger subsequently converts the latter to a paragraph IV certification, a second 30-month stay will still be possible.[353] According to the FDA, the removal of multiple 30-month stays removes the incentive for the brand-name drug manufacturer to obtain additional patents later on in the patent life of the product described by the NDA.[354] In the absence of multiple 30-month stays, subsequently submitted "secondary" patents are less likely to serve as a basis of preliminary injunction of the brand-name drug manufacturer precluding generic drug entry.[355]

2.2 Evergreening Strategies and "Sham" Patents

One of the ways to abuse the provisions of the Hatch-Waxman Act was to obtain multiple 30-month FDA stays through the use of the so-called "sham" or "secondary" patents. These are patents which typically claim features which are peripherally related to the branded drug, such as intermediates, metabolites, etc., or which claim products closely related but not identical to a patented drug.[356] Such patents are normally "weaker" than compound patents since they are easier to prove invalid or to patent around for generic drug manufacturers. These patents have typically little value even if valid, because they add little to the patentees' technology or because other alternative patents or technological solutions which serve the same purpose are available.[357] Despite their relatively low power, such "secondary" patents can be used to keep

---

      Invalid or Will Not Be Infringed, Docket No. 02N-0417, December 23, 2002, pp. 8-10. Available at: https://www.ftc.gov/policy/policy-actions/advocacy-filings/2002/12/ftc-comment-food-and-drug-administration-concerning. (last accessed on March 31, 2018).

352. MMA, Title XI, Section 1101(a)(2)(A)(ii)(I), 1101(b)(2)(B)(i), amending FD&C Act, Sections 505(j)(5)(B)(iii), 505(c)(3)(C) respectively. *See infra* Chapter 2, Part 2, Section IV.A. analysing the MMA amendments.
353. FDA, CDER, *Draft Guidance for Industry, Listed Drugs, 30-month Stays and Approval of ANDAs under MMA of 2003, Q&As*, 69 Federal Register 213, 64314-64315, (November 4, 2004). Available at: http://www.fda.gov/OHRMS/DOCKETS/98fr/04-24675.pdf. (last accessed on March 31, 2018).
354. FDA, NDA Final Rule, 2003, at 36676.
355. *Idem.*
356. *See* further SOEHNGE, 2003, pp. 71-73.
357. HOVENKAMP, Scope of the Patent, 2015, p. 543.

generic competitors off the market. Between 2001 and 2010, more than 80% of the patents challenged in the US through paragraph IV ANDA certifications were not compound patents.[358] Originator drug companies wishing to create a protective cluster around big-earning, blockbuster drugs usually apply for several patents per drug and list additional patents even after a paragraph IV ANDA was filed, a strategy commonly known as "evergreening."[359] For example, in *Andrx Pharmaceuticals v. Biovail Corp.* – a pay-for-delay case that is analysed in Chapter 3 – the brand-name manufacturer Biovail had triggered a second 30-month stay of the FDA approval of the ANDA filed by the generic manufacturer Andrx, by acquiring an exclusive licence for a patent covering the extended release formulation of the active ingredient of the branded drug.[360]

3 The 180-Day Generic Exclusivity Period

In an attempt to incentivise generic filers to challenge weak or invalid patents, the first paragraph IV ANDA filer who submits a "substantially complete application" is automatically eligible for the bounty of 180-day generic exclusivity.[361] The economic importance of this exclusivity period is vast. Generic manufacturers often make over half their profits on a drug during these six months of exclusivity; once other generic drug versions are in the market, profits fall sharply.[362] According to the FDA, *all* generic manufacturers who file paragraph IV ANDAs on the same first day are considered to be first filers and share the exclusivity period.[363] Shared 180-day exclusivity period can also occur when multiple generic challengers file paragraph IV ANDAs for different

---

358. HEMPHILL, SAMPAT, Evergreening, 2012, p. 334, Table 4: out of the 190 patents challenged, only 31 were compound patents.
359. HEMPHILL, SAMPAT, Evergreening, 2012, pp. 327-328; HERMANN, 2011, p. 1799.
360. *Andrx Pharm., Inc. v. Biovail Corp.*, 276 F.3d 1368, 1372-1373, (Fed. Cir. 2002). As explained in the Court of Appeals for the Federal Circuit's decision, due to the second "extended release" patent, the FDA refused to approve Andrx's paragraph. IV ANDA upon the expiry of the 30-month stay. See also *Andrx Pharm., Inc. v. Biovail Corp.*, 175 F. Supp. 2d 1362, 1375 (S.D. Fla. 2001); the district court had shortened the second 30-month stay, finding that the second patent was a "sham" listing, aiming to delay Andrx's generic entry to the market, but the Federal Circuit disagreed and reversed this decision.
361. 21 U.S.C. § 355(j)(5)(B)(iv).
362. HEMPHILL, LEMLEY, Earning Exclusivity, 2011, p. 948; COUGHLIN, DEDE, Game-Playing, 2006, pp. 525-526, stating that most generic companies estimate making 60%-80% of their potential profits on the generic product during the exclusivity period.
363. FDA, CDER, *Guidance for Industry: 180-day Exclusivity When Multiple ANDAs Are Submitted on the Same Day*, (July, 2003), p. 5. Available at: http://www.fda.gov/downloads/drugs/guidancecomplianceregulatoryinformation/guidances/ucm072851.pdf. (last accessed on March 31, 2018). See also *FTC v. Actavis*, 133 S. Ct. 2223, 2246 (2013) (Chief Justice Roberts dissenting), "[t]hus if ten generics file an application to market a generic drug on the first day, all will be considered first applicants" [internal quotation marks omitted]. See further FDA, CDER, CBER, *Guidance for Industry: 180-day Exclusivity: Questions and Answers* (January 2017), pp. 4, 9. Available at: https://www.fda.gov/downloads/Drugs/GuidanceComplianceRegulatoryInformation/Guidances/UCM536725.pdf. (last accessed on March 31, 2018) clarifying that there is one 180-day exclusivity for each drug product but separate 180-day exclusivities for each strength of the same drug product.

dosage forms/strengths of the same reference patented drug.³⁶⁴ Rather than monopoly followed by general generic entry, the 180-day exclusivity period creates an intermediate stage of duopoly between the brand-name manufacturer and the first generic paragraph IV filer.³⁶⁵ This exclusivity is rightly characterised as a "subtype of market exclusivity" since it tends to create *a duopolistic market of the brand-name drug manufacturer and the first generic entrant*, both of which typically have market power.³⁶⁶

3.1 FDA's Successful Defence Requirement

During the exclusivity period, the FDA is estopped from approving a subsequent paragraph IV ANDA of another generic filer.³⁶⁷ The first paragraph IV ANDA filer is entitled to the exclusivity period whether or not it establishes that the relevant patents are invalid or not infringed by its generic drug.³⁶⁸ This point has been criticised by several prominent academics, arguing that the bounty of exclusivity should be awarded instead only to a paragraph IV ANDA filer that has *successfully defended* its ANDA and proved the invalidity or non-infringement of the relevant patent.³⁶⁹ Indeed, for a certain period, the FDA applied a "successful defence requirement:" in order to receive the 180-day exclusivity period, the first generic paragraph IV filer had to: (1) be sued for patent infringement by the patent holder, and; (2) prevail in the subsequent patent infringement litigation.³⁷⁰

However, in the *Mova* decision this requirement was found to be inconsistent with the plain language of the Hatch-Waxman Act and unenforceable,³⁷¹ thus was declared invalid and removed by the FDA in 1998.³⁷² After the 2003 MMA amendments, FDA approval of later filed ANDAs cannot be delayed on account of a settlement between innovator and the first-filing generic firm.³⁷³ Even though there is no longer a

---

364. KORN ET AL., 2009, pp. 342-343.
365. HEMPHILL, Paying For Delay, 2006, pp. 1559-1560.
366. HELED, 2015, pp. 317-318.
367. 21 U.S.C. § 355(j).
368. *Caraco Pharm. Labs., Ltd. v. Forest Labs., Inc.*, 527 F.3d 1278, 1283 (Fed. Cir. 2008).
369. *See* for instance HEMPHILL, LEMLEY, Earning Exclusivity, 2011, pp. 948, 969-984.
370. *Mova Pharm. Corp. v. Shalala*, 955 F. Supp. 128, 130-131 (D.D.C. 1997). *See also In re Tamoxifen Citrate Antitrust Litigation*, 466 F.3d 187, 218 (2nd Cir. 2006), noting that at the time of the settlements in question, "the established law was that a generic manufacturer must successfully defend a patent infringement lawsuit in order to obtain exclusivity" [internal quotation marks omitted]. The court made a distinction between the case at issue and *Andrx Pharmaceuticals., Inc. v. Biovail Corp. Int'l*, 256 F.3d 799, 810 (D.C. Cir. 2001), where the settlement agreement was signed after the "successful defense" requirement has been struck down. *See* further *infra* Chapter 3, Part 1, on the analysis of the *Andrx Pharmaceuticals* case.
371. *Andrx Pharmaceuticals., Inc. v. Biovail Corp. Int'l*, 256 F.3d 799, 810 (D.C. Cir. 2001). The court referred to *Mova Pharm. Corp. v. Shalala*, 955 F. Supp. 128, 130-131 (D.D.C. 1997).
372. *In re Tamoxifen Citrate Antitrust Litigation*, 466 F.3d 187, 195 (2nd Cir. 2006). *See also* FDA, 180-day Exclusivity Guidance, 2017, pp. 11-13, providing examples where the 180-day exclusivity period of the first paragraph IV ANDA filer does not block the approval of subsequent ANDAs.
373. 21 U.S.C. § 355(j)(5)(D), providing for forfeiture of entitlement to 180-day exclusivity period if the litigating parties settle.

successful defence requirement, if the first paragraph IV ANDA filer loses in the patent infringement litigation with the patent holder or if it converts its ANDA to a paragraph III ANDA, it is no longer eligible for the 180-day exclusivity period.[374]

3.2   Exclusivity Only for the First Paragraph IV ANDA Filer

The 180-day exclusivity period is strictly reserved only for the first generic ANDA filer: a subsequent generic challenger will not be eligible for the exclusivity bounty, even if the first challenger forfeits its exclusivity.[375] Its purpose is to encourage paragraph IV challenges of invalid or weak patents by rewarding the first generic challenger for undertaking the costs and risks of patent litigation. The first generic challenger is in a duopoly situation with the brand-name drug manufacturer during the exclusivity period,[376] so that it can sell its generic drug version at a substantially higher price than when other generics enter the market.[377] Paragraph IV challenges have become the rule rather than the exception due to the 180-day exclusivity period; "[w]ith very little downside and huge upside, exclusivity is the driving force to the huge increase in first-to-file paragraph IV filings."[378] The high complexity of the Hatch-Waxman regulatory framework has created confusion not only to the industry but also to the US courts. For instance, in *Tamoxifen*, the 2nd Circuit claimed that subsequent ANDA filers were also eligible for the statutory 180-day exclusivity period and that the settlement of the patent holder with the first ANDA filer opened the way for immediate challenges to the patent, by subsequent generic challengers.[379] On its subsequent decision in *Arkansas Carpenters*, the panel acknowledged that the *Tamoxifen* decision had erred and relied on an "unambiguous mischaracterization of the Hatch-Waxman Act."[380]

---

374. Examples of conversion of a paragraph IV ANDA to a paragraph III ANDA were examined in *In re Ciprofloxacin Hydrochloride Antitrust Litig.*, 544 F. 3d 1323, 1339 (Fed. Cir. 2008); *In re Tamoxifen Citrate Antitrust Litigation*, 466 F.3d 187, 212-218 (2nd Cir. 2006).
375. 21 U.S.C. § 355(j)(5)(D)(iii).
376. The brand-name patent holder can however launch its own "authorized generic version" of the drug during the 180-exclusivity period, on the basis of its initial NDA application, and compete with the paragraph IV challenger on the generic market. See further *infra*, Chapter 4, Part 2, Section I.A, analysing authorised generic drugs and their role in pharmaceutical patent settlements.
377. See for instance DRUSS ET AL., Prozac, 2004, p. 214, showing that the price of generic Fluoxetine (generic version of Prozac) fell from $1.13 per tablet to $0.32 per tablet, after Barr Laboratories 180-day exclusivity period expired.
378. RBC Capital Markets, "Pharmaceuticals: Analyzing Litigation Success Rates," (January 15, 2010), p. 3. Available at http://www.amlawdaily.typepad.com/pharmareport.pdf (last accessed on March 31, 2018).
379. *In re Tamoxifen Citrate Antitrust Litigation*, 466 F.3d 187, 214-215 (2nd Cir. 2006), arguing that reverse exclusionary payments "opened [...] the patent to immediate challenge by other generic manufacturers [...] spurred by the additional incentive [...] of potentially securing the 180-day exclusivity period available upon a victory in a subsequent infringement lawsuit."
380. *Arkansas Carpenters Health & Welfare Fund v. Bayer AG*, 604 F.3d 98, 109-110 (2nd Cir. 2010), referring to *In re Tamoxifen Citrate Antitrust Litigation*, 466 F.3d 187, 214 (2nd Cir. 2006).

III Restoring Patent Protection for Innovators

Patent protection is in essence a mechanism to spur the investment in R&D, enabling innovators to regain part of their investment and to exclude others from making/using/selling their invention for a certain time-period. As analysed in Chapter 1, brand-name drug manufacturers face problems in the R&D of new drugs, which is time-consuming and also entails high costs. According to Pharmaceutical Research and Manufacturers of America (PhRMA), only two out of ten marketed drugs generate revenues that match or exceed their R&D costs.[381] Due to the time gap between the grant of a patent and the FDA approval of the NDA – an approval which requires safety and efficacy testing of the drug – the effective term of many patents is significantly shorter.[382] The Hatch-Waxman Act attempted to preserve adequate incentives for brand-name drug manufacturers to invest in the development of new drugs; in order to restore patent protection for the innovators, it extended the patent's term in specific circumstances.[383]

A Patent Term Extension to Compensate FDA Review

According to FDA, the effective patent term of new drugs is frequently less than twenty years, since patents are obtained before the drug products are marketed.[384] The length of the effective patent term is influenced by the requirements of the FD&C Act and the Public Health Service Act which provide for extensive animal and human testing of drug products, so as to prove their safety and efficacy.[385] In order to compensate patent holders for the marketing time they have lost while developing the drug and while waiting for the review and approval of the FDA, there was a patent term extension provision in the Hatch-Waxman Act.[386] 35 U.S.C. § 156 restores the patent term that was effectively lost due to the premarket approval requirements before a regulating agency.[387] The statutory requirements for the patent term extension of a patent claiming the product or a method of using or manufacturing the product are the following:[388] (1) the term of the patent has not expired before the respective application

---

381. PhRMA, "2015 Biopharmaceutical Research Industry Profile," Washington DC, April 2015, p. 1. Available at: http://www.phrma.org/sites/default/files/pdf/2015_phrma_profile.pdf. (last accessed on March 31, 2018).
382. FTC, *Generic Drug Entry*, 2002, p. 4.
383. *See* further FD&C Act, Section 505(j)(5)(F).
384. FDA Website, *Small Business Assistance: Frequently Asked Questions on the Patent Term Restoration Program*. Available at: http://www.fda.gov/Drugs/DevelopmentApprovalProcess/SmallBusinessAssistance/ucm069959.htm (last accessed on March 31, 2018).
385. Public Health Service Act, 58 Stat. 682, Chapter 373; 42 U.S.C., Chapter 6A. *See also* FDA Website, *Small Business Assistance: Frequently Asked Questions on the Patent Term Restoration Program*.
386. 35 U.S.C. § 156.
387. *See also* the presentation by TILL Mary C., Legal advisor of the USPTO, "Hatch-Waxman Bootcamp," Presentation, July 2010, pp. 1-23. Available at: http://www.uspto.gov/patents/law/exam/presentation/hatch_waxman_20jul1020.ppt. (last accessed on March 31, 2018).
388. 35 U.S.C. § 156(a).

for the patent term extension;[389] (2) the patent term has never been extended before;[390] (3) an application for patent term extension is submitted by the patent holder;[391] and (4) the product was subject to a regulatory review period prior to its commercial marketing.[392] A maximum of five years patent term extension can be restored to a patent,[393] but the patent life – meaning the potential marketing time of the product – cannot exceed fourteen years.[394] In the European Union, Supplementary Protection Certificates play the same role in compensating innovators for the time-period between the filing of an application for a new drug product and the granting of the authorisation to place that product on the market.[395]

B Non-patent Kinds of Exclusivity

Market exclusivity and data exclusivity are two distinct types of exclusivities. Market exclusivity in essence imposes a prohibition on the FDA to accept or approve applications for comparable or identical products for a certain exclusivity period. Market exclusivity is a "strong" kind of exclusivity since it confers the beneficiary the possibility to sell a product at a high profit margin, without however guaranteeing market power.[396] On the contrary, data exclusivity prevents generic applicants from relying on information the beneficiary has submitted in support of the marketing approval of the relevant product and maintains in this way a barrier to market entry. Data exclusivity does not preclude subsequent applicants from submitting their approval applications and from entering the market upon the administrative approval of their product, provided that the latter rely on their own data.[397]

1 The 5-Year NCE Exclusivity

If a drug's NDA contains a new chemical entity – that is a chemical entity which was never previously approved by the FDA either alone or in combination in another NDA – a 5-year marketing exclusivity is granted to the drug's NDA.[398] The Hatch-Waxman Act establishes an extended filing prohibition with regard to new chemical entity drugs; potential generic challengers are prohibited from submitting a paragraph IV ANDA

---

389. 35 U.S.C. § 156(a)(1).
390. 35 U.S.C. § 156(a)(2).
391. 35 U.S.C. § 156(a)(3).
392. 35 U.S.C. § 156(a)(4).
393. 35 U.S.C. § 156(g)(6).
394. 35 U.S.C. § 156(c)(3). *See also* FDA Website, *Small Business Assistance: Frequently Asked Questions on the Patent Term Restoration Program*.
395. *See infra* Chapter 5, Part 1, Section II.C.1.
396. HELED, 2015, pp. 315-316.
397. HELED, 2015, pp. 316-317.
398. 21 C.F.R. § 314.108(a), (b)(2) (2012). *See also* FD&C Act, Section 505(j)(5)(F)(ii), explaining NCE exclusivity with regard to ANDA submissions; FD&C Act, Section 505(c)(3)(E)(ii), explaining NCE exclusivity with regard to a 505(b)(2) application for a drug containing an active moiety protected by NCE exclusivity.

application for a drug containing the same active moiety[399] as the new chemical entity the first four years after the introduction of the new chemical entity brand-name drug.[400] Further, the FDA cannot accept paragraph I, II and III ANDAs in the first five years after NDA approval.[401] This type of exclusivity applies even if the relevant product containing the new chemical entity is unpatented, off-patent or the patent covering it is invalid.[402] Thus, even if the innovator's drug includes a new active ingredient but is not protected by a patent, generic manufacturers cannot file a paragraph IV ANDA in the absence of a patent to challenge; instead, generics must wait for five years before their paragraph IV ANDA can be filed with the FDA.[403]

2   The 3-Year NCS Exclusivity

A 3-year data exclusivity can be granted for drug products which contain an active moiety that has been already approved by the FDA, if the submitted NDA contains reports of new clinical investigations (bioequivalent studies excepted) which were conducted by the sponsor and were essential to the approval of the NDA. This 3-year exclusivity will be granted if these new clinical studies have led to the development of new or changed formulations in an already approved drug product, which affect for example its active ingredients, dosage form, conditions of use or route of administration.[404] If a drug product is granted this type of exclusivity, a generic drug application cannot be approved for this new or changed formulation or use for a period of three years from the FDA approval of the relevant NDA.[405] However, generic manufacturers can still obtain FDA approval to sell their generic drugs for previously approved uses of the relevant drug, which are not covered by this 3-year data exclusivity. Once these generic drugs are available at the market, doctors and pharmacists cannot be prohibited from substituting the generic off-label version for the branded version. Off-label

---

399. An active moiety is defined as "the molecule or ion, excluding those appended portions of the molecule that cause the drug to be an ester, salt [...] or other noncovalent derivative [...] of the molecule, responsible for the physiological or pharmacological action of the drug substance." See further, FDA Website, *Small Business Assistance – Frequently Asked Questions for New Drug Product Exclusivity*, Q9. Available at: http://www.fda.gov/drugs/developmentapprovalprocess/smallbusinessassistance/ucm069962.htm (last accessed on March 31, 2018).
400. See further KARST, 2013. KARST explains that an NDA sponsor with a single questionable new chemical entity patent listed in the Orange Book might request the FDA to delist this patent prior to the expiration of four years following the new chemical entity NDA approval: "[i]f there is not a reasonable basis to assert a patent against the sponsor of an ANDA, then the listing of that patent could actually trigger ANDA approval much earlier than expected. Alternatively, if there is not a patent, then the ANDA cannot even be submitted until the 5-year NCE exclusivity period expires."
401. 21 U.S.C. §§ 355(j)(5)(F)(ii), (c)(3)(E)(ii) (2010); 21 C.F.R. § 314.108(b).
402. 21 U.S.C. §§ 355(c)(3)(E)(ii), (j)(5)(F)(ii). See also WHEATON, 1986, pp. 464-465; BAKER, Drug Apartheid, 2008, pp. 306-307.
403. See further HEMPHILL, Paying For Delay, 2006, p. 1610, arguing that FDA approval likely takes an additional year, providing the innovator with six years of exclusivity.
404. 21 C.F.R. § 314.108(b). See further, FDA Website, *Small Business Assistance – Frequently Asked Questions for New Drug Product Exclusivity*, Q6.
405. 21 U.S.C. §§ 355(c)(3)(E)(iii), (j)(5)(F)(iii)-(iv). However, the FDA can tentatively approve such applications on the basis of 21 U.S.C. § 355(c)(3)(E)(iii).

use is legal in the US and may be an important source of innovation; however it may also raise questions of safety and efficacy.[406] Off-label use is the reason why the NCS exclusivity has arguably only a limited effect in increasing the incentives to conduct clinical trials on new uses of previously approved drugs.[407]

3   Orphan Drug Exclusivity

There are a number of rare diseases and conditions, either affecting less than 200,000 people in the US or affecting more people, but for which the costs of R&D development of a pertinent drug cannot be reasonably expected to be recouped by its sales.[408] Due to the high cost of R&D and their limited margin for profit generation, drugs for these diseases have not been developed and are commonly known as *orphan* drugs. Since there is a public interest in the development of orphan drugs, the US has passed already in 1983 the Orphan Drug Act, aiming to encourage the development of orphan drugs, by providing financial incentives and reducing their development costs.[409] A 7-year exclusivity is accorded to the manufacturers of orphan drugs, during which the FDA cannot approve another application or issue another licence for the same drug.[410] This is a statutory exclusivity and not merely a data exclusivity.[411] Moreover, the FDA may make grants and enter into contracts to assist the orphan drug manufacturer in bearing the costs of clinical testing, of developing medical devices or medical foods.[412] Multiple orphan drug exclusivity is also possible, when an orphan drug meets the applicable criteria for orphan drug designations for multiple diseases or conditions.[413] Even though one might have expected that the relevant markets for these drugs would be too small to be lucrative, several products enjoying Orphan Drug Exclusivity have had big

---

406. STAFFORD, 2012, pp. 920-922. *See also* RADLEY, FINKELSTEIN, STAFFORD, 2006, pp. 1023-1025, examining the proportion and frequency of off-label drug use and finding that it substantially varies across functional classes.
407. EISENBERG, 2005, p. 730.
408. 21 C.F.R. § 316.20 (b)(8), defining as a "rare disease or condition" any disease or condition that affects fewer than 200,000 persons in the US. Such diseases are for instance ALS (Lou Gehrig's disease), muscular dystrophy, myoclonus or Huntington's disease.
409. Orphan Drug Act, Public Law 97-414, 96 Stat. 2049, "An Act to amend the Federal Food, Drug, and Cosmetic Act to facilitate the development of drugs for rare diseases and conditions, and for other purposes," January 4, 1983, amending 21 U.S.C. Chapter 9 §§ 301 et seq., 360aa.
410. 21 C.F.R. 316.31. *See also* FD&C Act, Section 527; 21 U.S.C. §§ 360aa-360ee. However, the FDA can approve such applications exceptionally, if for instance the manufacturer of the orphan drug cannot assure the availability of sufficient quantities of the drug to meet patients' demand or if the manufacturer consents to the approval of other applications.
411. 21 U.S.C. § 360cc(a). Statutory exclusivity prohibits the approval of "such drug for such disease or condition for a person who is not the holder of such approved application" whereas data exclusivity (such as the NCE and the NCS exclusivity) prevents the FDA from allowing generic competitors to file an ANDA instead of submitting an NDA.
412. 21 U.S.C. 360ee.
413. *See further*, FDA, Orphan Drug Regulations, 21 C.F.R. Part 316, Final Rule, 78 Federal Register 113, p. 35121, June 12, 2013. Available at: http://www.gpo.gov/fdsys/pkg/FR-2013-06-12/pdf/2013-13930.pdf (last accessed on March 31, 2018).

and profitable markets for off-label use,[414] while worldwide orphan drug sales are forecasted to total $209 billion from 2017 to 2022.[415]

4 Paediatric Exclusivity

Children suffer not only from typical "childhood diseases" but also from diseases that occur in adult populations; in the latter case, they are typically treated by the same drugs as those used to treat adults. However, only a small fraction of drugs used as therapies for children in the US has been studied in paediatric patients or is properly labelled for use in paediatric patients.[416] This absence of paediatric testing and labelling poses significant risks for children who undergo physiologic and developmental changes: some of these risks are inadequate dosing, inability to benefit from therapeutic advances due to insufficient information, or failure to produce dosage forms that can be used by young children (e.g., chewable tablets or liquids).[417]

In an effort to remedy this problem, the Congress enacted in November 1997 the Food and Drug Administration Modernization Act of 1997 (FDAMA),[418] amending the FD&C Act and establishing economic incentives for pharmaceutical companies to conduct paediatric studies.[419] On the basis of Section 505(A) of FD&C Act, the FDA is able to issue Written Requests for paediatric studies prior to the approval of a new drug application (NDA),[420] if it determines that information on the use of a specific drug in the paediatric population may produce health benefits.[421] The FDA can further issue Written Requests for paediatric studies to holders of already approved NDAs.[422] In order to incentivise the pharmaceutical industry to conduct these paediatric studies requested by the FDA, Section 505(A) provides for a 6-month period of marketing exclusivity (paediatric exclusivity).[423] This paediatric exclusivity is attached to any

---

414. EISENBERG, 2005, pp. 726-727, referring to Taxol and AZL as successful examples.
415. EvaluatePharma, *Orphan Drug Report*, 2017, p. 8.
416. See further, WOODCOCK Janet, Director of CDER, Department of Health and Human Services, FDA, *Implementation of the Pediatric Exclusivity Provisions*, May 8, 2001. Available at: http://www.fda.gov/newsevents/testimony/ucm115220.htm. (last accessed on March 31, 2018). [cited as: WOODCOCK, Pediatric Exclusivity, 2001].
417. *Idem*.
418. Food and Drug Administration Modernization Act, Public Law 105-115, 111 U.S. 2296, amending the Federal Food, Drug and Cosmetic Act, Title 21 U.S.C. 301: Food and Drugs. See further FDA Website, *FDA Backgrounder on FDAMA*. Available at: https://www.fda.gov/RegulatoryInformation/LawsEnforcedbyFDA/SignificantAmendmentstotheFDCAct/FDAMA/ucm089179.htm (last accessed on March 31, 2018).
419. Already in early 1990s the FDA had implemented a number of voluntary measures to encourage the industry to submit paediatric labeling information. See WOODCOCK, Pediatric Exclusivity, 2001.
420. It should be noted that FDA's Written Requests create no obligation for the manufacturer to conduct the requested study.
421. Notably, the FDA can require paediatric studies of a new drug or biological product if the product is likely to be used in "a substantial number of paediatric patients" or to provide a "meaningful therapeutic benefit" to paediatric patients." See further WOODCOCK, Pediatric Exclusivity, 2001.
422. The FDA can require paediatric studies for already approved and marketed drugs if either of the above-mentioned conditions applies and inadequate labelling poses significant risks.
423. 21 U.S.C. § 355a (2010).

existing exclusivity or patent protection on a drug for which the FDA has requested paediatric studies, when a drug manufacturer has conducted such studies.[424]

Paediatric exclusivity is the only kind of exclusivity which starts running from the end of any other exclusivity protection (e.g., New Drug Product Exclusivity and Orphan Drug Exclusivity) or from the end of patent protection.[425] Additionally, paediatric exclusivity is not limited to the product for which paediatric studies have been conducted by the manufacturer, but it attaches to *all* the manufacturer's formulations, dosage forms and indications for products which contain the same active moiety, provided these have remaining marketing exclusivity or patent life.[426] This mechanism employed to incentivise paediatric testing has been quite successful: from 1998 until April 2016, paediatric exclusivity was granted to 214 manufacturers, awarding their paediatric studies in response to FDA's requests.[427]

IV Problems Faced and Amendments

A *The Medicare Modernization Act*

The Medicare Prescription Drug, Improvement and Modernization Act of 2003 (MMA Act) was designed to "close the legal loopholes" of the Hatch-Waxman Act which delayed generic drug approval.[428] The MMA includes provisions of the Greater Access to Affordable Pharmaceuticals Act of 2002 (GAAP);[429] the GAAP passed the Senate but the House of Representatives refused to act on the bill.[430] As above-analysed, the MMA put an end to multiple 30-month stays of FDA approval. Another core amendment of the MMA was the introduction of the requirement for the settling parties in a Hatch-Waxman patent infringement lawsuit to file their settlement agreement with the FTC and the Assistant Attorney General of the DoJ's Antitrust Division within ten

---

424. 21 U.S.C. § 355a (b)(1) (2010).
425. See further FDA, "Qualifying for Pediatric Exclusivity Under Section 505A of the Federal Food, Drug, and Cosmetic Act: Frequently Asked Questions on Pediatric Exclusivity (505A), The Pediatric Rule, and their Interaction," [internal quotation marks omitted]. Available at: http://www.fda.gov/drugs/developmentapprovalprocess/developmentresources/ucm077915.htm (last accessed on March 31, 2018).
426. See further FDA, "Qualifying for Pediatric Exclusivity Under Section 505A of the Federal Food, Drug, and Cosmetic Act: Frequently Asked Questions on Pediatric Exclusivity (505A), The Pediatric Rule, and their Interaction," Q.9. It should also be noted that paediatric exclusivity is not conditioned upon the approval of labelling containing information on paediatric use based on studies conducted.
427. FDA, *Pediatric Exclusivity Determinations List*, April 2016, pp. 1-11. Available at: https://www.fda.gov/downloads/Drugs/DevelopmentApprovalProcess/DevelopmentResources/UCM223058.pdf (last accessed on March 31, 2018).
428. Medicare Prescription Drug, Improvement, and Modernization Act of 2003, Pub. L. No. 108-173, 117 Stat. 2066, 108th Congress, (2003), codified at 21 U.S.C. § 355(j)(5)(D). *See also* MEADOWS, 2003.
429. S.812 – Greater Access to Affordable Pharmaceuticals Act of 2002, 107th Congress (2001-2002).
430. SENATOR METZENBAUM Howard M. (Ret.), Chairman of the Consumer Federation of America, *Testimony before the Senate Judiciary Committee, regarding Legislative and Regulatory Responses to the FTC Study on Barriers to Entry in the Pharmaceutical Marketplace*, (June 17, 2003), pp. 1-5. Available at: http://www.consumerfed.org/pdfs/61803Testimony.pdf. (last accessed on March 31, 2018), pp. 2-3.

business days from the execution of the agreement.[431] The following sections analyse the provisions of the MMA concerning the forfeiture of the 180-day exclusivity period of the first generic paragraph IV ANDA filer and the rest of the amendments aiming to expedited generic entry.

Despite the best intentions, the MMA did not succeed to eliminate reverse payment settlements, since its provisions concerning the forfeiture of the exclusivity period were circumvented by settling parties.[432] In a number of instances, the parties abused the litigation process to limit competition, by introducing for instance to their settlement agreements covenants not to sue subsequent ANDA filers, since such infringement lawsuits could have led to the invalidation of the patent at issue and generic entry of a later ANDA filer.[433]

1 Forfeiture of the 180-Day Exclusivity Period

The main changes brought by the MMA are the provisions concerning the forfeiture of the 180-day exclusivity period of the first paragraph IV generic challenger.[434] More specifically, forfeiture of the exclusivity period will occur:

(i) if the paragraph IV filer fails to market its generic drug either within seventy-five days after the FDA approval of its application has been made effective or within thirty months after the date of its ANDA submission;[435]

(ii) if the paragraph IV ANDA filer withdraws the paragraph IV application or if the Secretariat finds that the application does not meet the requirements for approval;[436]

(iii) if the paragraph IV ANDA filer amends or withdraws the paragraph IV certifications;[437]

(iv) if the paragraph IV ANDA filer fails to obtain a tentative FDA approval within thirty days after the application is filed;[438]

(v) if the paragraph IV ANDA filer enters into an agreement with another applicant, the listed drug application holder or the patent owner;[439]

(vi) if all of the patents for which the generic challenger submitted a paragraph IV ANDA application have expired.[440]

---

431. MMA, Section 1112, (a), (c).
432. The MMA Act did not confer new enforcement authorities to the FTC or the DoJ. *See further* Sandoval, Covenants Not to Sue, 2009-2010, pp. 170-178.
433. *See further* Sandoval, Covenants Not to Sue, 2009-2010, pp. 170-178, discussing different circumvention mechanisms employed by the parties to limit competition *post* MMA.
434. *See further* FDA, 180-day Exclusivity Guidance, 2017, pp. 14-26, providing a great overview of all the cases where the 180-day exclusivity period may be forfeited.
435. 21 U.S.C. § 355(j)(5)(D)(i)(I). The provision clarifies that forfeiture will occur on the earlier of this two dates.
436. 21 U.S.C. § 355(j)(5)(D)(i)(II). The requirements of ANDA approval are listed in 21 U.S.C. § 355(j)(4).
437. 21 U.S.C. § 355(j)(5)(D)(i)(III).
438. 21 U.S.C. § 355(j)(5)(D)(i)(IV).
439. 21 U.S.C. § 355(j)(5)(D)(i)(V).
440. 21 U.S.C. § 355(j)(5)(D)(i)(VI).

In order to trigger the forfeiture provision (v) – commonly mentioned as the "collusive agreement forfeiture provision" – a final decision from the FTC or a court finding that the settlement violates antitrust law is required, which cannot or has not been appealed.[441] Having such a final judgment is however difficult and time-consuming, so that this forfeiture provision is unlikely to be triggered and has "no teeth."[442] Appellate court decisions typically take years to be issued after the lawsuit challenging a settlement is filed, ranging for instance from six to thirteen years after the settlement was concluded, rendering the forfeiture provisions practically ornamental.[443]

Before the introduction of these forfeiture provisions, settlement agreements between the brand-name manufacturer and the first generic paragraph IV filer created the infamous "approval bottleneck" effect, blocking the triggering of the exclusivity period.[444] When the first generic challenger neither marketed commercially its generic drug nor secured a judicial determination of patent invalidity or non-infringement, the FDA was unable to approve the paragraph IV ANDAs of subsequent generic filers.[445] Not all settlements took advantage of the bottleneck effect: some generic firms altered their ANDA filing from a paragraph IV to a paragraph III certification, removing the block of subsequent filers.[446] However, a few settlements also included a provision allowing the generic filer to revert its paragraph III to a paragraph IV certification, if another generic challenger managed to invalidate the patent, a tactic which was allegedly used to manipulate the exclusivity period and delay the market entry of subsequent generic challengers.[447] After the MMA, the first commercial marketing by any first applicant eligible for exclusivity triggers the exclusivity period.[448]

2 Other Amendments of the MMA

2.1 Civil Action to Obtain Patent Certainty

Another novelty introduced by the MMA was the possibility to file a "civil action to obtain patent certainty" in order to prevent patent holders from forestalling the

---

441. FDA, 180-day Exclusivity Guidance, 2017, p. 25.
442. HEMPHILL, LEMLEY, Earning Exclusivity, 2011, pp. 971-972.
443. CARRIER, Payment After Actavis, 2014, p. 15, illustrating with concrete examples of reverse payment settlement cases and calculating the years from the time the settlements were concluded until the relevant appellate decisions were published.
444. PATEL, 2009, pp. 1085-1109, analysing the "approval bottleneck" pre-MMA and post-MMA.
445. See further HEMPHILL, Paying for Delay, 2006, pp. 1586-1588. Note that the *Ciprofloxacin* and the *Tamoxifen* settlement agreements discussed *infra* were concluded before the adoption of the MMA Act-under the MMA Act, the generic challengers would have forfeited their respective exclusivity periods.
446. See for instance *In re Ciprofloxacin Hydrochloride Antitrust Litig.*, 544 F. 3d 1323, 1339-1340 (Fed. Cir. 2008); *In re Tamoxifen Citrate Antitrust Litigation*, 466 F.3d 187, 193-194 (2nd Cir. 2006).
447. See for instance *In re Tamoxifen Citrate Antitrust Litigation*, 466 F.3d 187, 221-222, 224 (2nd Cir. 2006). In the *Tamoxifen* settlements, Barr had the right to revert its pargraph III to a paragraph IV certification, if another generic challenger managed to invalidate the patent, a tactic which – according to the plaintiffs was used to manipulate the exclusivity period and delay generic entry.
448. 21 U.S.C. § 355(j)(5)(B)(iv).

resolution of paragraph IV disputes. Before the introduction of the MMA amendments, an innovator could refuse to file an infringement suit within the 45-day period, give up its right to the 30-month stay and wait to initiate patent infringement litigation once the generic product had already received FDA approval and was put on the market – in the latter case, the damages awarded would be much higher.[449] This civil action provision was designed to the benefit of generic challengers, giving them some control over the risk of potential infringement litigation.[450] After the MMA amendments, in case the patent holder does not file an infringement lawsuit within forty-five days, the generic ANDA filer can sue the patent holder to obtain a declaratory judgment that the relevant patents listed at the Orange Book are either invalid or not infringed.[451] In such a case, the paragraph IV filer shall provide to the patentee confidential access to its ANDA for infringement evaluation.[452]

2.2 Counterclaim to Delist Patent from the Orange Book

After the MMA amendments, if the patent holder sues the generic challenger for patent infringement, the generic challenger may assert a counterclaim seeking an order requiring the patent holder to correct or delete patent information which was improperly listed to the Orange Book.[453] Such a counterclaim may be based "on the ground that the patent does not claim either (aa) the drug for which the [generic challenger's] ANDA application was approved; or (bb) an approved method for using the drug."[454] The FDA has a purely ministerial duty in listing patents in the Orange Book and does not review the patents submitted by the NDA holder while it does not assess whether the claims in these patents cover the approved drug.[455] The generic challenger cannot

---

449. PINCUS, 1991, pp. 95-99, discussing the jurisprudence and practice of computing damages in patent infringement actions. *See also* COURY, Saisie, 2003, pp. 1113-1115.
450. UNDERSTAHL, 2005, p. 370.
451. 21 U.S.C. § 355(j)(5)(C). *See* 35 U.S.C. § 271(e)(5), where the Congress extended federal jurisdiction over civil actions to obtain patent certainty. *See* further *Teva Pharms. USA, Inc. v. Pfizer, Inc.*, 395 F.3d 1324, 1329 (Fed. Cir. 2005), *Teva Pharm. USA, Inc. v. Novartis Pharm. Corp.*, 482 F.3d 1330, 1342-1343 (Fed. Cir. 2007), *Caraco Pharm. Labs., Ltd. v. Forest Labs., Inc.*, 527 F.3d 1278, 1285-1286 (Fed. Cir. 2008), discussing the civil actions to obtain patent certainty after MMA.
452. 21 U.S.C. § 355(j)(5)(C)(i)(III).
453. 21 U.S.C. § 355(c)(3)(D)(ii)(I).
454. 21 U.S.C. §§ 355(c)(3)(D)(ii)(I)(aa), 355(c)(3)(D)(ii)(I) (bb).
455. *Apotex, Inc. v. Thomson*, 347 F.3d 1335, 1347-49 (Fed. Cir. 2003), "[b]ecause we find nothing in the Hatch-Waxman Act that supports Apotex's argument that the FDA has a duty to screen Orange Book submissions by NDA applicants and to refuse to list those that do not satisfy the statutory for listing, we conclude that [FDA]'s interpretation of the Act set forth in 21 C.F.R. § 314.53(f) is a reasonable one: that the Act does not require it to police the listing process by analyzing whether the patents listed by NDA applicants actually claim the subject drugs or applicable methods of using those drugs." *See also* 21 C.F.R. § 314.53(f), "[i]f any person disputes the accuracy or relevance of patent information submitted to the agency under this section and published by FDA in the list, or believes that an applicant has failed to submit required patent information, that person must first notify the agency in writing stating the grounds for disagreement."

recover damages from succeeding in such a delisting counterclaim but this mechanism facilitates an early resolution of the ANDA patent infringement suits.[456]

2.3 Product-by-Product Exclusivity

The main purpose of the MMA was to enhance the effectiveness and efficiency of the enforcement of the antitrust laws.[457] To that effect, the MMA adopted the "product-by-product" exclusivity policy that replaced the "patent-by-patent" exclusivity. Before the enactment of the MMA, separate exclusivity periods were accorded for each patent challenged successfully by a paragraph IV certification, creating a complicated landscape since the FDA would award a 180-day exclusivity period to each first paragraph IV ANDA filer for a different patent on the same drug. This created overlapping, mutually blocking exclusivity periods and the absurd result that no generic filer could launch its drug product until *all* the overlapping exclusivities expired, further delaying generic entry.[458] Post MMA, there can only be one exclusivity period per drug product, which can however be shared by more than one applicants.

B The Elimination of Parties' Adversity

The Hatch-Waxman Act was criticised for affecting the "bargaining dynamic" between patent holders and potential generic entrants and for offering opportunities for both unilateral anticompetitive behaviour and collusion of the patent holder and the generic challenger through anticompetitive settlements.[459] The Act interfered with the incentives of the parties to litigate and involuntarily limited their adversity by aligning their interests, providing them with an incentive to settle or even collude instead of litigating.[460]

1 The Alignment of Parties' Interests and Retained Exclusivity

Despite the best of intentions, the 180-day exclusivity period was abused by the brand-name and generic pharmaceutical companies and did not fully serve its purpose to incentivise the elimination of weak patents. Even though the number of paragraph IV ANDAs and of patent challenges increased, a great number of these challenges resulted in reverse payment settlement agreements between the generic challengers

---

456. UNDERSTAHL, 2005, p. 371.
457. S. 754 – Drug Competition Act of 2002, 107th Congress, Section 3, (2001-2002).
458. Such an overlapping exclusivity periods' case reached the courts in *Apotex, Inc. v. Food & Drug Admin.*, 393 F.3d 210, 211 (D.C. Cir. 2004). *See also* KORN ET AL., 2009, pp. 340-343.
459. HOVENKAMP, JANIS, LEMLEY, Anticompetitive Settlements, 2003, p. 1752.
460. HOVENKAMP, Actavis, 2014, p. 26, "[b]y contrast, the pay-for-delay settlements permit the parties to share the full monopoly overcharge, giving each of them an expected value greater than the probable value of the patent in question;" HEMPHILL, LEMLEY, Earning Exclusivity, 2011, pp. 962-965, noting 180-day bounty "set[s] the stage for a peculiar form of non-aggression pact;" HOVENKAMP, JANIS, LEMLEY, Anticompetitive Settlements, 2003, p. 1752.

and the respective patent holders.[461] Patent holders facing even a small risk of patent invalidation by the generic challenger, have huge economic incentives to settle with their perspective competitor. Their monopoly over the drug is at stake, a monopoly which can translate into hundreds of millions of dollars of profits per year.[462] Instead of dragging themselves into the long and insecure process of patent litigation, a risk-benefit analysis – setting aside any antitrust considerations – leads to the conclusion that sharing the monopoly profits with the generic challenger for a certain period of time is far more "reasonable" than suffering even a 10% chance of losing their patent protection, earlier than expected. Moreover, in case of a settlement agreement, patent holders are able to negotiate the exact time of generic entry, securing their patent monopoly until nearly the official expiration of their patent protection.

From the generic challengers' perspective, a settlement with the patent holder normally means a big value transfer, but also the certainty of entering the market with its generic drug first at an agreed time – usually shortly before the official patent expiry – and the certainty of enjoying the 180-day exclusivity period, which will not be forfeited despite the settlement agreement. The time point just before the patent expiration is the equilibrium entry point for the generic drug product. This point maximises the monopoly's returns and the pie of profits to share between the parties: the longer possible the monopoly, the bigger the payoff.[463]

Further, through a settlement, the generic challenger will avoid the high costs of patent litigation, which raise the total cost of a paragraph IV ANDA challenge to more than $10 million.[464] Economically, settling the infringement lawsuit and splitting the monopoly profits for a certain period is the most beneficial option for both the generic manufacturer and the patent holder, especially since the anticipated profits of the patent holder in the absence of generic competition are higher than the combined profits of the parties when they compete.[465] Thus, both parties have a substantial incentive to settle at the latest generic market entry date possible and to maximise the monopoly profits of the brand manufacturer, part of which will be paid to the generic challenger as compensation for refraining from an early generic entry.[466]

---

461. HEMPHILL, LEMLEY, Earning Exclusivity, 2011, pp. 948-949.
462. *See FTC v. Watson Pharmaceuticals et al.*, 677 F.3d. 1298, 1313-1314 (11th Cir. 2012); *Valley Drug Co. v. Geneva Pharms, Inc.*, 344 F.3d 1294, 1310 (11th Cir. 2003); *In re Ciprofloxacin Hydrochloride Antitrust Litigation*, 261 F. Supp. 2d 188, 208 (E.D.N.Y. 2003).
463. HOVENKAMP, Scope of the Patent, 2015, pp. 545-546.
464. HEMPHILL, LEMLEY, Earning Exclusivity, 2011, p. 948; HERMANN, 2011, p. 1795, both citing GOODMAN ET AL., 2004.
465. *In re Tamoxifen Citrate Antitrust Litigation*, 466 F.3d 187, 209 (2nd Cir. 2006); *In re Schering-Plough Corp.*, 136 F.T.C. 956, 989 (2003), vacated, *Schering-Plough Corp. v. FTC*, 402 F.3d 1056 (11th Cir. 2005). *See also* HOVENKAMP, Scope of the Patent, 2015, pp. 545-548. *See also* EDLIN, HEMPHILL, HOVENKAMP, SHAPIRO, Actavis Inference, 2015, p. 587.
466. *In Re Cipro Cases I & II*, 348 P.3d 845, 867-868 (Cal., May 7, 2015). *See* further SHAPIRO, Antitrust Limits, 2003, pp. 394-395; BULOW, Gaming of Patents, 2004, p. 166; ELHAUGE, KRUEGER, Patent Settlement Puzzle, 2012, pp. 289-290; MUNGAN, Perverse Incentives, 2013, pp. 27, 34; HOVENKAMP, Actavis, 2014, pp. 8-13, discussing the incentives of the parties to settle a Hatch-Waxman patent infringement suit.

2   Gaming the 180-Day Exclusivity Period

In order to ensure that the settling generic challenger retained its 180-day exclusivity period and that the introduction of other generics to the market was stalled for as long as possible, many settlement agreements included a clause automatically resiliating the agreement in case another generic company managed to invalidate the relevant patent.[467] Another popular mechanism of retaining the 180-day exclusivity was a clause under which the generic challenger agreed to convert its paragraph IV ANDA to a paragraph III ANDA. In case other generic companies would later file paragraph IV ANDAs, the settling generic retained the right to convert its ANDA back to a paragraph IV ANDA and to claim its alleged entitlement to the 180-day exclusivity period. The ultimate – and blatantly anticompetitive – goal of such clauses was to block and further delay the introduction of other competing generic products to the market.[468] Ironically, the Hatch-Waxman Act provided the regulatory entry barrier of the 180-day exclusivity period, a barrier that guaranteed the success of the cartels between patent holders and generic challengers.[469]

Another version of this strategy is "poison-pill clauses." Poison-pill clauses in a reverse payment settlement setting are clauses which permit the settling generic to accelerate its entry when a non-settling subsequent generic challenger enters the market. A typical poison-pill clause will provide that the settling generic will refrain from entering the market until a predefined agreed date *unless* another generic company is successful in challenging the relevant patent.[470] In the latter case, the generic is free to immediately launch its generic drug and rip the benefits of the 180-day exclusivity period, a risk-free strategy that ensures the first challenger's exclusivity.[471]

3   Circumventing the Goals of the Hatch-Waxman Act

This alignment of the parties' interests had distractive effects on competition. A settlement between the patent holder and the first generic challenger meant that the patent infringement court could not rule: (1) on whether the patent was infringed by the generic drug or not, and; (2) on whether the patent was valid or not. In the absence of a court determination on the issue of patent validity, the Hatch-Waxman Act's goal to eliminate invalid patents blocking generic entry was not reached. It would be implausible to attribute to the Hatch-Waxman regime an inherent tolerance for settlements aiming to secure additional profits such as illegitimate reverse payment settlements.[472] The goal of expediting generic entry to the market was circumvented, since the introduction of the first generic challengers' product to the market was

---

467. In re Ciprofloxacin Hydrochloride Antitrust Litig., 544 F. 3d 1323, 1328-1329 (Fed. Cir. 2008); In re Tamoxifen Citrate Antitrust Litigation, 466 F.3d 187, 193-194 (2nd Cir. 2006).
468. See In re Ciprofloxacin Hydrochloride Antitrust Litig., 544 F. 3d 1323, 1339 (Fed. Cir. 2008); In re Tamoxifen Citrate Antitrust Litigation, 466 F.3d 187, 212-218 (2nd Cir. 2006).
469. HOVENKAMP, Scope of the Patent, 2015, pp. 524-525.
470. CARRIER, Payment After Actavis, 2014, pp. 37-40.
471. CARRIER, Payment After Actavis, 2014, p. 40.
472. See further HEMPHILL, Paying For Delay, 2006, pp. 1613-1614.

postponed until nearly the expiration of the relevant patent(s). As above-analysed, the introduction of other generic drug versions by subsequent generic challengers was withheld through the 180-day exclusivity period manipulations and eventual multiple 30-month stays to FDA approval.

In the absence of a decision on the issue of patent infringement, even if a generic drug product did not infringe the originator's patent and could thus have been marketed with no further delay, it was not until the expiration of the relevant settlement agreement. Possibly invalid patents were made ironclad through such settlements and served as a pretext to delay competition and to prolong unjustified drug monopolies. The settling parties, patent holders and generic challengers gained from such anticompetitive settlement agreements, to the detriment of consumers, national health schemes and other generic drug manufacturers. Pharma patent settlements with the above-mentioned characteristics were vigorously scrutinised by the FTC and led to a major split between US Circuit courts, which is extensively analysed in Chapter 3 of this book.

C Preserve Access to Affordable Generics Act

The Preserve Access to Affordable Generic Act (PAAG) was first championed in 2007 by Senators Kohl and Grassley but has been re-introduced another four times to the day of this writing.[473] The bill aims to prevent pay-for-delay settlements by establishing a presumption of illegality for agreements where the generic manufacturer receives *anything of value* – including an exclusive licence – or where the generic manufacturer agrees to limit or forgo R&D, manufacturing, marketing or sales of the ANDA product for any period of time.[474] The 2013 version of the bill further aimed to amend the Federal Trade Commission Act (FTC Act)[475] by creating a new section which allows the FTC to bring lawsuits against the parties to a reverse payment settlement agreement under the presumption of illegality.[476] After the decision of the US Supreme Court in *FTC v. Actavis, Inc.*, 133 S. Ct. 2223 (2013), the approach of presumptive illegality for pay-for-delay settlements was abandoned in favour of the application of the rule of reason, so that the standard of presumptive illegality does not longer appear in the 2017 version of the PAAG; the exceptions with regard to legitimate transfers of value outlined in the *Actavis* decision are also reflected therein.[477]

---

473. Preserve Access to Affordable Generics Act, S. 316, 110th Cong. (2007); Preserve Access to Affordable Generics Act, S. 369, 111th Cong. (2009); Preserve Access to Affordable Generics Act, S. 27, 112th Cong. (2011); Preserve Access to Affordable Generics Act, S. 214, 113th Cong. (2013); Preserve Access to Affordable Generics Act, S. 124 115th Cong. (2017). *See* further the website of U.S. Congress on the PAAG, available at: https://www.congress.gov/bill/115th-congress/senate-bill/124 (last accessed on March 31, 2018).
474. Section 3,Preserve Access to Affordable Generics Act, S. 124 115th Cong. (2017).
475. 15 U.S.C. §§ 41-58; PAAG in particular aims to amend 15 U.S.C. 44 et seq.
476. Preserve Access to Affordable Generics Act, S. 214, 113th Cong. § 3 (2) (2013).
477. Section 3, Preserve Access to Affordable Generics Act, S. 124 115th Cong. (2017). *See* further *infra*, Chapter 4, analysing in detail the landmark decision of *FTC v. Actavis, Inc.*, 133 S. Ct. 2223 (2013).

The 2017 PAAG allows some kinds of consideration in settlements between brand-name manufacturers and generic challengers: (1) the right to market the ANDA product in the US before the expiration of any patent that is the basis of the patent infringement claim; (2) a payment for litigation expenses not exceeding $7.5 million, or; (3) "a covenant not to sue on any claim that the ANDA product infringes a US patent."[478] The bill further aims to increase transparency in the pharmaceutical sector by amending the MMA and requiring brand-name and generic manufacturers to submit to the FTC *any* agreement they enter into relating to the manufacturing, sale or marketing of a drug or relating to the exclusivity period, within thirty days of entering such agreement,[479] broadening the already existing requirement of settlements' notification. Additionally, the CEO or the company official negotiating such a settlement agreement shall file a certification that the materials filed with the agreement are complete, final and exclusive.[480]

Some commentators supported that this bill arguably balances the interests of pharmaceutical manufacturers and could be a possible response of the Congress to the remaining uncertainty on reverse payment settlements, even *post FTC v. Actavis*.[481] The prohibition of large value transfers in settlement agreements could restore the settling parties' adversity, especially concerning the questions of patent validity and infringement, an adversity much needed to avoid anticompetitive settlements.[482] However, other specialists considered that the proposed amendments would neither enhance competition nor benefit the public since the PAAG provides few incentives to generic challengers to challenge patents and would accord too much power to the FTC.[483]

CONCLUSIONS

The Hatch-Waxman Act amendments were highly ambitious and have dramatically changed both generic entry mechanisms but also innovation incentives for patent holders in the US Two of the most fundamental changes brought by the Hatch-Waxman Act were the introduction of the ANDAs and of the Bolar exemption, which admittedly facilitated generic entry to the market. Despite these major steps forward and the considerable regulatory efforts in balancing patent protection and competition in the pharmaceutical markets, the Hatch-Waxman Act backfired in many ways. The 180-day exclusivity period which was initially destined to serve as an incentive to challenge weak patents, was in some cases imaginatively abused by settling competitors. The

---

478. Section 3, Preserve Access to Affordable Generics Act, S. 124 115th Cong. (2017).
479. Section 5, Preserve Access to Affordable Generics Act, S. 124 115th Cong. (2017) proposes the amendment of Section 1112(c)(2) of the Medicare Prescription Drug, Improvement, and Modernization Act of 2003 (21 U.S.C. 355 note).
480. Section 4, Preserve Access to Affordable Generics Act, S. 124 115th Cong. (2017).
481. *See* for instance, Quinn, 2014, pp. 11-12.
482. Hovenkamp, Scope of the Patent, 2015, pp. 522-525.
483. Bagherian, Congress's response, 2007, pp. 166-170, arguing also that the Supreme Court "should establish the rule of reason as the sole standard of analysis" for reverse payment settlements. Han, Circuit-Splitting Headache, 2013, pp. 930-931.

30-month stay of FDA approval for the respective generic product also proved to be problematic, especially since multiple 30-month stays were possible and the duration of such stays was occasionally longer, largely delaying generic entry to the market. All in all, the Hatch-Waxman Act is a highly technical and complicated piece of legislation: its weaknesses now known after years of analysis by courts and commentators, they should be diminished by the Congress through proper amendments. The European Union has one less reason of concern in the adjudication of potentially problematic reverse payment settlements: thankfully, on this side of the ocean the Hatch-Waxman Act does not apply.

CHAPTER 3
The US Circuits' Split on Reverse Payment Settlements

INTRODUCTION

Patent settlements between originators of brand-name drugs and generic drug manufacturers in the context of Hatch-Waxman litigation have led to one of the most controversial splits between US Circuit Courts, which is presented in this chapter. The first decision of a Circuit Court adjudicating a reverse payment settlement found it to be prima facie illegal; later on, the same settlement was declared per se illegal by another Circuit Court.[484] However, a number of Circuit Courts rejected these strict approaches and applied the scope of the patent test, finding that a patent settlement agreement that falls within the scope of the patent shall not be subject to antitrust scrutiny. In 2012, the 3rd Circuit rejected the application of the scope of the patent test in its decision *In re K-Dur Antitrust Litigation* and found that reverse payment settlements between originators and generic challengers should be treated as presumptively unlawful.[485] This decision stressed further the split between Circuit Courts on the applicable legal standard for the adjudication of reverse payments. In 2013, the Supreme Court of the US granted *certiorari* to a reverse payment settlement case and resolved the Circuit split through its decision in *FTC v. Actavis*, ruling that such settlements should be analysed under the rule of reason. Following the *FTC v. Actavis* decision, one could argue that looking back at the split between the Circuit Courts is of little interest; however, this is not the case. The issues that are discussed in these Circuit decisions remain highly

---

484. *See infra* Chapter 3, Part 1, analysing the decisions of *Andrx Pharmaceuticals., Inc. v. Biovail Corp. Int'l*, 256 F.3d 799, 806 (D.C. Cir. 2001), finding a reverse payment settlement to be prima facie illegal, and; *In re Cardizem CD Antitrust Litig.*, 332 F.3d 896,908 (6th Cir. 2003), finding the same and a subsequent reverse payment settlements to be per se illegal.
485. *In Re: K-Dur Antitrust Litigation*, 686 F.3d 197 (3rd Cir. 2012).

relevant and continue to cause debates, so that it is useful to have a thorough understanding of them before analysing the *FTC v. Actavis* decision in Chapter 4 of this book.

This chapter analyses the *rationale* of the Circuit Courts in applying the per se illegality approach, the "quick-look" rule of reason and the scope of the patent test to reverse payment settlements, along with the criticisms that each approach gave rise to. Part 1 presents the shift from a finding of a prima facie illegal restraint by the D.C. Circuit to a finding of per se illegality of the same reverse payment settlements by the 6th Circuit. It also discusses the possible adverse effects of the application of the per se illegality standard to reverse payment settlements, focusing on the elimination of procompetitive settlements, patent challenges and innovation. Part 2 focuses on the scope of the patent test and its evolution through time. It also discusses in detail the problematic aspects of this test, which granted antitrust immunity to reverse payment settlements while overlooking the crucial issues of patent infringement and patent validity. Finally, Part 3 of this chapter presents the presumptive illegality approach that was advocated by the FTC and the DoJ for settlement agreements involving unjustified value transfers and the decision of the 3rd Circuit in *In re K-Dur Antitrust Litigation*, finding that the reverse payment settlement at issue was prima facie illegal.[486]

PART 1   REVERSE PAYMENT SETTLEMENTS AS PER SE ILLEGAL

I   Per Se Unlawful Restraints

A   *Per Se Illegality for Naked Restraints*

Section 1 of the Sherman Act prohibits every contract, combination in the form of trust or otherwise, or conspiracy in restraint of trade or commerce.[487] The Sherman Act's prohibition of *every* agreement in restraint of trade has been interpreted by the US Supreme Court as a prohibition limited to agreements which *unreasonably* restrain trade.[488] Nevertheless, certain kinds of agreements will so often prove to be harmful to competition and so rarely prove to be justified, that antitrust laws do not require proof that they are in fact anticompetitive in the particular circumstances at issue; instead such agreements will be found to be illegal per se.[489] Generally, a restraint is classified as per se illegal when it appears to be on its face a restraint which would always or almost always tend to restrict competition or decrease output.[490]

---

486. *In Re: K-Dur Antitrust Litigation*, 686 F.3d 197 (3rd Cir. 2012).
487. 15 U.S.C. § 1.
488. *NYNEX Corp. v. Discon, Inc.*, 119 S. Ct. 493, 497 (1998); *Business Electronics Corp. v. Sharp Electronics Corp.*, 108 S. Ct. 1515, 1518 (1988); *National College Athletic Ass'n ("NCAA") v. Board of Regents*, 104 S. Ct. 2948, 2959 (1984); *Arizona v. Maricopa County. Medical Soc.*, 102 S. Ct. 2466, 2472 (1982).
489. *NYNEX Corp. v. Discon, Inc.*, 119 S. Ct. 493, 497 (1998).
490. *Broadcast Music, Inc., et al., v. CBS, Inc. et al.*, 99 S. Ct. 1551, 1562-1563 (1979).

Chapter 3: The US Circuits' Split on Reverse Payment Settlements

The predictable pernicious effects of per se unlawful restrains on competition and their limited potential for precompetitive benefits,[491] render unnecessary costly proof requirements such as proof of market power or the analysis of the intent behind the restraint, of any claimed procompetitive justifications and of the restraint's actual effect on competition.[492] An act which falls within the per se illegal category of restraints will be condemned whenever it occurs, without further inquiry into the circumstances.[493] The per se rule may be seen as a rule of judicial economy, since it renders a thorough economic investigation of the industries involved unnecessary: courts applying it are not required to determine on a case-by-case basis whether a particular restraint was unreasonable.[494] As HOVENKAMP explains, the rule of per se illegality is a generalised application of the rule of reason; "in fullest flower, a *per se* rule condemns conduct without proof of power, effect, or purpose and without hearing claims of legitimate objectives."[495] The harshness of the per se rule is the reason that this standard is restrictively applied only once a court, based on previous experience, can confidently predict that the restraint would be condemned under a rule of reason analysis.[496]

There is also a statutory distinction which seems to directly affect the choice between the rule of reason and per se illegality. Section 1 of the Sherman Act arguably applies a harsh standard on concerted conduct, while Section 2 of the Sherman Act reserves a more favourable treatment to unilateral actions.[497] Cases concerning unilateral actions falling under Section 2 are normally evaluated under the rule of

---

491. *Northern Pacific Ry. Co. v. United States*, 78 S. Ct. 514, 518 (1958). *See also Continental T.V., Inc. v. GTE Sylvania, Inc.*, 97 S. Ct. 2549, 2557 (1977), quoting *Northern Pacific Ry. Co. v. United States*, 78 S. Ct. 514, 518.
492. *Arizona v. Maricopa County. Medical Soc.*, 102 S. Ct. 2466, 2473 (1982).; *National College Athletic Ass'n ("NCAA") v. Board of Regents*, 104 S. Ct. 2948, 2959 (1984); *Eastman Kodak Co. v. Image Technical Services, Inc.*, 112 S. Ct. 2072, 2091-2092 (1992) (Judge Scalia, dissenting), "[p]er se rules of antitrust illegality are reserved for those situations where logic and experience show that the risk of injury to competition [...] is so pronounced that it is needless and wasteful to conduct the usual judicial inquiry into the balance between the behavior's procompetitive benefits and its anticompetitive costs;" HOVENKAMP, AREEDA, *Fundamentals of Antitrust*, 2014, p. 15-43.
493. *FTC v. Superior Court Trial Lawyers Ass'n*, 110 S. Ct. 768, 780 (1990), quoting *Arizona v. Maricopa County. Medical Soc.*, 102 S. Ct. 2466, 2473 (1982), "[o]nce experience with a particular kind of restraint enables the Court to predict with confidence that the rule of reason will condemn it, it has applied a conclusive presumption that the restraint is unreasonable." *See also* HOVENKAMP, AREEDA, *Fundamentals of Antitrust*, 2014, p. 15-44.
494. *Northern Pacific Railway Company v. United States*, 78 S. Ct. 514, 518 (1958); *See also National Soc. of Professional Engineers v. United States*, 98 S. Ct. 1355, 1365 (1978), noting that the per se approach is reserved for agreements "so plainly anticompetitive that no elaborate study of the industry is needed to establish their illegality."
495. HOVENKAMP, AREEDA, *Fundamentals of Antitrust*, 2014, p. 15-36.
496. *Arizona v. Maricopa County. Medical Soc.*, 102 S. Ct. 2466, 2473 (1982); *Broadcast Music, Inc., et al., v. CBS, Inc. et al.*, 99 S. Ct. 1551, 1553 (1979), quoting *United States v. Topco Assocs., Inc.*, 92 S. Ct. 1126, 1133-1134 (1972), "It is only after considerable experience with certain business relationships that courts classify them as per se violations of the Sherman Act." *See however*, GRAGLIA, Leegin Creative, 2007, p. 831. GRAGLIA argues that "considerable experience" is not indispensable, since horizontal price-fixing and horizontal market division were declared illegal per se already the first time they reached the Supreme Court in *Trans-Missouri Freight Ass'n v. United States*, 17 S. Ct. 540, 559 (1897) and *United States v. Addyston Pipe & Steel Co. et al.*, 85 F. 271, 294, 295-296 (6th Cir. 1898), aff'd 20 S. Ct. 96 (1899), respectively.
497. 15 U.S.C. §§ 1-2; LEMLEY, LESLIE, Categorical Analysis, 2008, p. 1223.

reason, whereas a significant number of concerted practices allegedly violating Section 1 is examined under the per se rule.[498] For example, horizontal agreements which always or almost always tend to raise prices or reduce output are considered to be per se illegal.[499] Such conduct includes bid-rigging and market division agreements,[500] tying,[501] group boycotts,[502] allocating customers, suppliers, territories or lines of commerce.[503] Agreements which are reasonably necessary and related to achieving procompetitive benefits from an efficiency-enhancing integration of economic activity shall be analysed under the rule of reason, even if they generally fall under the per se illegal category.[504] Therefore, naked restraints which are not accompanied by any joint production or distribution activity are likely to be found per se illegal,[505] while ancillary restraints, which are collateral to a main legitimate transaction that promises to increase output or productivity will normally be scrutinised under the rule of reason.[506]

B *Restricting the Application of Per Se Illegality*

US courts have been gradually abandoning the application of the per se illegality rule in favour of a rule of reason analysis. An example of the increasingly restrictive application of the per se illegal approach are vertical price-fixing agreements. Horizontal agreements fixing prices have been per se illegal for decades, irrespectively of whether they concern the fixing of maximum or minimum prices.[507] Even though price-fixing cartels are tempting to business persons, they are very dangerous to society; their conceivable social effects are small, speculative and premised on the

---

498. LEMLEY, LESLIE, Categorical Analysis, 2008, p. 1223.
499. FTC, DoJ, *Antitrust Guidelines*, 2000, pp. 8-9. *See* further *United States v. Trenton Potteries Co.*, 47 S. Ct. 377 (1927) (on price fixing); *United States v. Socony-Vacuum Oil Co.*, 60 S. Ct. 811, 839-840 (1940); *National College Athletic Ass'n ("NCAA") v. Board of Regents*, 104 S. Ct. 2948, 2595 (1984), "[h]orizontal price fixing and output limitation are ordinarily condemned as a matter of law under an illegal per se approach because the probability that these practices are anticompetitive is so high" [internal quotation marks omitted]; *Catalano, Inc., v. Target Sales, Inc.*, 100 S. Ct. 1925, 1927-1928 (1980).
500. *Palmer v. BRG of Georgia*, 111 S. Ct. 401 (1990); *United States v. Addyston Pipe & Steel Co. et al.*, 85 F. 271 (6th Cir. 1898).
501. *Northern Pacific Ry. Co. v. United States*, 78 S. Ct. 514, 518-520 (1958). *See also Standard Oil Co. of California and Standard Stations v. United States*, 69 S. Ct. 1051, 1058 (1949) and *International Salt Co. v. United States*, 332 U.S. 392, 68 S. Ct. 12, 15 (1947), ruling that foreclosing competitors from any substantial market through tying agreements was per se unreasonable.
502. *Fashion Originators' Guild of America, Inc., et al. v. FTC*, 61 S. Ct. 703, 707-708 (1941).
503. FTC, DoJ, *Antitrust Guidelines*, 2000, pp. 8-9.
504. FTC, DoJ, *Antitrust Guidelines*, 2000, p. 4. *See* further LEMLEY, LESLIE, Categorical Analysis, 2008, pp. 1207-1270, discussing and criticising the categorisation of restraints in antitrust.
505. HOVENKAMP, AREEDA, *Fundamentals of Antitrust*, 2014, p. 15-42.
506. *Rothery Storage & Van Co. v. Atlas Van Lines, Inc.*, 792 F. 2d 210, 224 (D.C. Cir. 1986); *Polk Bros., Inc. v. Forest City Enters., Inc.*, 776 F.2d 185, 189-190 (7th Cir. 1985).
507. *United States v. Trenton Potteries Co.*, 47 S. Ct. 377 (on price fixing); *United States v. Socony-Vacuum Oil Co.*, 60 S. Ct. 811, 839-840 (1940); *Catalano, Inc., v. Target Sales, Inc.*, 100 S. Ct. 1925, 1927-1928 (1980). *See also Texaco Inc., v. Dagher*, 126 S. Ct. 1276, 1279-1280 (2006), confirming that horizontal price fixing agreements between competitors fall under the per se unlawful category but refraining from applying the per se illegality rule to the pricing policy of a joint venture formed by two competitors.

existence of price-fixing power.[508] On the contrary, the distinction between minimum and maximum price fixing used to be important for the analysis of vertical price-fixing agreements. In 1911, the Supreme Court ruled that vertical agreements fixing minimum prices were per se illegal in the decision of *Dr Miles Medical Co. v. John D. Park & Sons Co.*,[509] while in 1951 the decision of *Kiefer-Stewart Co. v. Joseph E. Seagram* expanded the per se illegal approach to vertical agreements fixing maximum prices.[510] It was not until 1997 that the Supreme Court held in *State Oil Co. v. Khan* that vertical agreements fixing maximum prices should be evaluated under the rule of reason.[511] Thus, for the 10-year period until *Leegin Creative Leather Prods Inc. v. PSKS, Inc.* was decided in 2007, the distinction between vertical agreements setting minimum or maximum prices was crucial and determined the applicable standard of analysis.[512]

In 2007, the Supreme Court's historical decision of *Leegin*, explicitly reversed *Dr. Miles* and thereafter rendered *all* vertical agreements on prices subject to a rule of reason analysis,[513] irrespectively of whether they fix minimum or maximum prices, an evolution which arguably reinforced the distinction between vertical and horizontal restraints.[514] The rule of reason analysis adopted in *Leegin* has two main consequences. First, suppliers attempt to make their resale price maintenance agreements more explicit and make clear that an agreement exists; second, once an agreement exists, the rule of reason standard applies and the liability standard required may be similar to the standard imposed to monopolisation cases under Section 2 of the Sherman Act.[515]

---

508. HOVENKAMP, AREEDA, *Fundamentals of Antitrust*, 2014, p. 15-40.
509. *Dr. Miles Medical Co. v. John D. Park & Sons Co.*, 31 S. Ct. 376, 379, 384-385 (1911), "[b]ut agreements or combinations between dealers, having for their sole purpose the destruction of competition and the fixing or prices, are injurious to the public interest and void. They are not saved by the advantages which the participants expect to derive from the enhanced price to the consumer."
510. *Kiefer-Stewart Co. v. Joseph E. Seagram & Sons, Inc.*, 71 S. Ct. 259, 260 (1951) holding that maximum resale price fixing is illegal per se. See also *Albrecht v. Herald Co.*, 88 S. Ct. 869, 873-874 (1968), adhering to *Kiefer-Steward* decision on the per se illegality of maximum price fixing.
511. *State Oil Co. v. Khan*, 118 S. Ct. 275, 282-284 (1997), overruling the decision of *Albrecht v. Herald Co.*, 88 S. Ct. 869, 873-874 (1968) and ruling that vertical agreements fixing maximum prices should be analysed under the rule of reason.
512. See also LEMLEY, LESLIE, Categorical Analysis, 2008, pp. 1224-1225.
513. *Leegin Creative Leather Prods Inc. v. PSKS, Inc.*, 127 S. Ct. 2705, 2725 (2007). See however, GRAGLIA, Leegin Creative, 2007, pp. 812-819. GRAGLIA argues that *Dr. Miles* was partly overruled by *United States v. Colgate & Co.*, 39 S. Ct. 465 (1919), despite *United States v. A. Schrader's Son, Inc.*, 252 U.S. 85, 99 (1920), where the Supreme Court expressly denied such overruling. According to GRAGLIA the two other means of "escaping" *Dr. Miles* were *United States v. General Electric Co.*, 47 S. Ct. 192 (1926) and the Miller-Tydings Act, 50 Stat. 693 (1937) (repealed in 1975, when Congress enacted the Consumer Goods Pricing Act, 89 Stat. 801, amending 15 U.S.C. § 1, 45(a)).
514. LEMLEY, LESLIE, Categorical Analysis, 2008, p. 1224.
515. HOVENKAMP, Leegin, 2010, p. 11. HOVENKAMP stresses that the principal difference in the analysis will be that under Section 1 of the Sherman Act, the main inquiry will focus on whether an agreement "restraints trade", normally requiring a showing of reduction in output. On the other hand, the inquiry under Section 2 of the Sherman Act will focus on whether the challenged practice is undertaken by a firm which is dominant and on whether competitors are unreasonably excluded.

Another example of the shift towards the rule of reason analysis are non-price vertical restraints. Typical non-price vertical restraints concern restrictions imposed on costumers, location or territory. For example, a territorial vertical restraint exists when sellers are assigned exclusive territories in which competition has been limited. Horizontal market division agreements, by means of which competitors allocate exclusive geographic markets to each other, are per se illegal.[516] Vertical market division agreements were also found to be illegal per se in the *United States v. Arnold, Schwinn & Co.* decision of 1967.[517] However, the Supreme Court overruled *Arnold, Schwinn & Co* in 1977 by its decision in *Continental T.V. Inc. v. GTE Sylvania Inc.* and ever since non-price vertical restraints are scrutinised under the rule of reason.[518] Before the decision of *Leegin* there was a sharp differentiation in the treatment of price and non-price vertical restraints, since the former were considered per se illegal while the latter were analysed under the rule of reason.[519] The court in *Leegin* stressed that there was little economic justification for the applying differential treatment to vertical price and to non-price restraints and that both should be analysed under the rule of reason.[520]

II Reverse Payment Settlements as Per Se Illegal

In 2003, the 6th Court found that reverse payment settlements were per se illegal in its decision in *In re Cardizem CD Antitrust Litig.*[521] The decision concerned a set of settlements between the brand-name manufacturer Hoescht Marion Roussel and two

---

516. *United States v. Topco Assocs., Inc.*, 92 S. Ct. 1126, 1133-1134 (1972), finding that the territorial restrictions *in casu* were a horizontal restraint and thus a per se violation of Section 1 of the Sherman Act; *Continental T.V., Inc. et al. v. GTE Sylvania Inc.*, 97 S. Ct. 2549, 2561-2562 (1977), fn. 28, reaffirmed the per se illegality rule for similar horizontal territorial restraints as applied in *United States v. Topco Assocs., Inc.*, 92 S. Ct. 1126 and *United States v. General Motors Corp.*, 86 S. Ct. 1321 (1966). See also *Palmer v. BRG of Georgia*, 111 S. Ct. 401, 403, ruling that the horizontal agreement to divide geographic markets was "unlawful at its face."
517. *United States v. Arnold, Schwinn & Co.*, 87 S. Ct. 1856, 1867 (1967). See however the earlier decision of the Supreme Court in *White Motor Co. v. United States*, 83 S. Ct. 696, 702 (1963), ruling that very little was known for vertical territorial limitations, excluding the application of per se illegality.
518. *Continental T.V., Inc. et al. v. GTE Sylvania Inc.*, 97 S. Ct. 2549, 2561-2562 (1977), ruling that "departure from the rule-of-reason standard must be based upon demonstrable economic effect rather than – as in *Schwinn* – upon formalistic line drawing."
519. *Monsanto Co. v. Spray-Rite Service Corp.*, 104 S. Ct. 1464, 1470 (1984), "[n]evertheless, it is of considerable importance that independent action by the manufacturer, and concerted action on nonprice restrictions, be distinguished from price-fixing agreements, since under present law the latter are subject to *per se* treatment and treble damages."
520. *Leegin Creative Leather Products, Inc. v. PSKS, Inc.*, 127 S. Ct. 2705, 2723 (2007).
521. *In re Cardizem CD Antitrust Litig.*, 332 F.3d 896,908 (6th Cir. 2003), "[t]here is simply no escaping the conclusion that the Agreement, all of its other conditions and provisions notwithstanding, was, at its core, a horizontal agreement to eliminate competition in the market for Cardizem CD throughout the entire United States, a classic example of a *per se* illegal restraint of trade." The second decision applying the per se illegality rule to a reverse payment settlement was the decision of district court of South Florida *In re Terazosin Hydrochloride Antitrust Litig.*, 352 F. Supp. 2d 1279 (S.D. Fla. 2005), which was subsequently reversed by *Valley Drug Co. v. Geneva Pharms, Inc.*, 344 F.3d 1294 (11th Cir. 2003), applying the scope of the patent test.

generic ANDA challengers. Hoescht Marion Roussel, Inc. (HMR) and Andrx Pharmaceuticals Inc. (Andrx) – which was the first paragraph IV ANDA filer – concluded a settlement agreement in the context of Hatch-Waxman litigation. This settlement was attacked by Biovail Corporation (Biovail), a subsequent generic manufacturer which wished to enter the market with its generic version of Cardizem CD but was blocked from doing so because of the HMR/Andrx settlement.[522] Biovail's suit led to the decision of the D.C. Circuit Court in *Andrx Pharmaceuticals., Inc. v. Biovail Corp* in 2001.[523] The D.C. Circuit Court had found that the settlement agreement between the parties was similar to a final private settlement which resolved the underlying patent infringement litigation by substituting it with a market allocation agreement; therefore, it could be reasonably seen as an attempt to allocate market share and to preserve monopolistic conditions.[524] Several antitrust suits followed by direct and indirect purchasers of Cardizem CD, which were adjudicated in the *In Re Cardizem* decision of the 6th Circuit Court. While the D.C. Circuit had found in *Andrx Pharmaceuticals., Inc. v. Biovail Corp* that the restraints imposed by the reverse payment settlements at issue were prima facie illegal, the 6th Circuit took a stricter approach and found in *In re Cardizem CD Antitrust Litig* that they were per se illegal. In order to provide the reader with a detailed view of a typical reverse payment settlement before *FTC v. Actavis*, the facts of this settlement and the arguments of the D.C. Circuit in finding a prima facie illegal restraint are first discussed, followed by the analysis of the *In re Cardizem CD Antitrust Litig* decision of the 6th Circuit.

A   The Facts

It should be stressed that the HMR/Andrx agreement was concluded before the 2003 Hatch-Waxman amendments and the introduction of the provisions on the forfeiture of the 180-day exclusivity period.[525] At this time, an agreement of the patent holder with the first paragraph IV ANDA filer could result in an eternal statutory bottleneck. Before 2003, the FDA could not approve the paragraph IV ANDAs of subsequent filers until the first filer marketed its generic drug version or until there was a judicial determination of either patent invalidity or patent infringement.[526]

---

522. *Andrx Pharmaceuticals., Inc. v. Biovail Corp. Int'l*, 256 F.3d 799, 806 (D.C. Cir. 2001).
523. *Andrx Pharmaceuticals., Inc. v. Biovail Corp. Int'l*, 256 F.3d 799 (D.C. Cir. 2001).
524. *Andrx Pharmaceuticals., Inc. v. Biovail Corp. Int'l*, 256 F.3d 799, 811,819. *See also idem* at 815, "[a]s Biovail has pleaded the facts, HMRI and Andrx combined to achieve an unlawful objective, namely, the extension of the exclusivity period granted under the Hatch-Waxman Amendments. Accordingly, we conclude that Biovail can allege an antitrust injury, that is, one the antitrust laws were designed to prevent and that flows from that which makes the defendant's conduct unlawful."
525. Medicare Prescription Drug, Improvement, and Modernization Act of 2003, Pub. L. No. 108-173, § 1102(a) (1), 117 Stat. 2066, 2457-58 (2003). 21 U.S.C. § 355(j) (5) (D) (i) (III) provides for forfeiture of the 180-day exclusivity period if the ANDA filer withdraws its paragraph IV ANDA; 21 U.S.C. § 355(j)(5)(D)(i)(V) provides for forfeiture when an ANDA filer enters into an agreement related to the ANDA filing which is subsequently adjudicated to be a violation of antitrust laws. See further *supra* Chapter 2, Part 2, Section IV.A.
526. *See supra* Chapter 2, Part 2, Section IV.A, on the amendment of the Hatch-Waxman Act by the Medicare Prescription Drug, Improvement and Modernization Act in 2003. *See also* HEMPHILL, Paying for Delay, 2006, pp. 1586-1588.

1 The Settlement Between HMR and Andrx

HMR manufactured and marketed Cardizem CD, a brand-name prescription drug for the treatment of angina and hypertension and for the prevention of heart attacks and strokes. HMR's patent on Cardizem CD's active ingredient (diltiazem hydrochloride) expired in November 1992. On September 22, 1995, Andrx filed an ANDA with the FDA, seeking approval to manufacture and sell its generic version of Cardizem CD. Some months later, on December 1995, Andrx was the first generic manufacturer to file a paragraph IV ANDA to the FDA, stating that its generic product did not infringe any of the listed patents covering Cardizem CD.[527] Subsequent to Andrx's paragraph IV ANDA, the US Patent Office issued to Carderm Capital, L.P. (Carderm) US Patent No. 5,470,584 ('584 patent) for Cardizem CD's dissolution profile, which Carderm licensed to HMR.[528]

In January 1996, HMR filed a patent infringement suit against Andrx, alleging that the latter's generic version of Cardizem CD would infringe the '584 patent and triggered the 30-month period during which the FDA could not approve Andrx's ANDA. However, in September 1997, the FDA issued a tentative approval of Andrx's generic drug, indicating that it would be finally approved either upon the expiration of the 30-month stay in July 1998 or upon the court's determination that it did not infringe the '584 patent.[529] On September 24, 1997, Andrx and HMR entered into an interim settlement agreement.[530] It is noteworthy that in the year of their settlement, the US sales of Cardizem CD raised up to $692 million.[531]

Under the settlement terms, Andrx committed not to market a bioequivalent or a generic version of Cardizem CD until either: (1) Andrx obtained a favourable, final and unappealable determination of the patent infringement case; (2) HMR and Andrx entered into a licence agreement, or; (3) HMR entered into a licence agreement with a third party. Importantly, Andrx further agreed to diligently prosecute its ANDA and not to relinquish or compromise any of the rights deriving from it, its 180-day exclusivity period included. HMR from its part agreed to make interim payments of $40 million per year to Andrx, payable quarterly, beginning on the date Andrx received final FDA approval and ending on the date that Andrx marketed its generic drug version or was found adjudged liable for patent infringement.[532] Moreover, HMR agreed to pay Andrx $100 million yearly once: (1) there was a final and unappealable determination that

---

527. Later on in 1996, Faulding Inc. also filed a paragraph IV ANDA for its generic version of Cardizem CD and was sued for patent infringement by HMR in January 1997. *See Andrx Pharmaceuticals., Inc. v. Biovail Corp. Int'l*, 256 F.3d 799, 803 (D.C. Cir. 2001), fn. 4.
528. *In re Cardizem CD Antitrust Litig.*, 332 F.3d 896, 902, stating that the dissolution profile claimed by the '584 patent was for 0%-45% of the total dialtizem to be released within eighteen hours. In April 1996, Andrx amended its ANDA and specified that the dissolution profile of its generic product was not less than 55% of the total dialtizem to be released within eighteen hours.
529. *Andrx Pharmaceuticals., Inc. v. Biovail Corp. Int'l*, 256 F.3d 799, 803 (D.C. Cir. 2001), fn. 5. As the court clarifies, FDA issued a tentative approval of Andrx's ANDA instead of a final approval because of the pending infringement suit and the 30-month statutory stay of FDA approval.
530. The settlement agreement between HMR and Andrx was not a final settlement agreement, but an interim one and did not end the patent infringement litigation between the parties.
531. HEMPHILL, Drug Patent Settlements, 2007, p. 32, referring to HELLER, Pivotal Year, 1999.
532. *Andrx Pharmaceuticals., Inc. v. Biovail Corp. Int'l*, 256 F.3d 799, 803-804 (D.C. Cir. 2001).

Chapter 3: The US Circuits' Split on Reverse Payment Settlements

'584 patent was not infringed; (2) HMR dismissed the patent infringement case, or; (3) there was a final and unappealable determination that did not determine the issues of patent's validity, enforcement, or infringement, and HMR failed to refile its patent infringement action.

Once the 30-month statutory period expired in July 1998, FDA issued its final approval of Andrx's ANDA. Complying with the above-analysed agreement, HMR began making quarterly payments to Andrx, while Andrx refrained from bringing its generic drug to the market. Nevertheless, in September 1998, Andrx sought FDA approval for a reformulated generic version of Cardizem CD and certified to HMR that this reformulated product did not infringe the '584 patent. In June 1999, FDA approved Andrx's reformulated generic drug, while HMR and Andrx settled the patent infringement case and terminated their agreement. Upon the termination of the agreement, HMR paid Andrx a final sum of $50.7 million, increasing the total amount of its payments to Andrx to $89.83 million. On June 23, 1999 Andrx began marketing its generic product, Cartia XT, for a substantially lower price than Cardizem CD, capturing a substantial share of the market.

2 How the Settlement Prevented Biovail's Generic Entry

In June 1997, Biovail filed its paragraph IV certification for a generic version of Cardizem CD. HMR did not file a patent infringement suit against it. In 1998 Andrx filed suit against the FDA, Biovail and other generic ANDA applicants, aiming to clarify its status and rights as the first ANDA filer for Cadrizem CD. Andrx sought injunctive relief, requiring the FDA to provide it with the 180-day exclusivity period for its generic version of Cardizem CD.[533] Further, Andrx sought injunctive relief prohibiting the FDA from approving any paragraph IV ANDA for a generic of Cardizem CD submitted by Biovail, before the expiration of Andrx's 180-day exclusivity period or a court decision on the HMR patent infringement suit against Andrx. Biovail counterclaimed and sustained that Andrx had violated Sections 1 and 2 of Sherman Act.

Final FDA approval of Andrx's ANDA was granted on July 3, 1998. Even though the 30-month statutory stay period had expired and Andrx was free to market and sell its generic drug, it refrained from doing so, pursuant to its agreement with HMR. Since Andrx did not market its generic version of Cardizem CD, its 180-day exclusivity period was not triggered; as a result, the FDA was estopped from giving final approval to subsequent applications by other generic drug manufacturers wishing to market competing generic versions of Cardizem CD. In June 1999, when HMR and Andrx terminated their agreement, Andrx began marketing its generic version of Cardizem CD and activated the 180-day exclusivity period. Upon the expiration of Andrx's exclusivity period, the FDA-approved Biovail's ANDA on December 23, 1999.

---

533. *Andrx Pharmaceuticals., Inc. v. Biovail Corp. Int'l*, 256 F.3d 799, 803-804 (D.C. Cir. 2001). Andrx required FDA to accord it a 180-day exclusivity period for its generic versions of Cardizem CD and Dilacor XR.

B The DC Circuit Finds a Prima Facie Restraint of Trade

The district court for the District of Columbia found that Biovail could not plead an antitrust injury causally linked to Andrx's alleged anticompetitive behaviour.[534] Even absent the HMR/Andrx agreement, Biovail would not have been able to market its generic version; any delay to the marketing of subsequent generic versions was caused by the statutory scheme of the Hatch-Waxman Act and not by the parties' settlement.[535] The district court noted that even if it would invalidate the HMR/Andrx settlement, it could not force Andrx to enter the market before the conclusion of HMR's patent infringement suit litigation.[536] As analysed in the following section, on appeal the D.C. Circuit disagreed with the district court. On the basis of their agreement, HMR had paid Andrx $10 million dollars quarterly in order for the generic challenger not to enter the market; such a payment from the patent holder to the generic challenger could strongly suggest the anticompetitive intent of the parties in concluding the agreement.[537]

1 The Hatch-Waxman Act Does Not Legitimise Delaying Generic Entry

Andrx argued that it was acting in accordance with the rights granted to it by the Hatch-Waxman Act and that such an exercise of statutory rights could not support an antitrust claim against it.[538] The court rejected the allegation that the parties' conduct was not only permitted but also contemplated by the Hatch-Waxman Act.[539] The Congress's aim in passing the Hatch-Waxman amendments of 1984,[540] was to provide patients faster with generic, reasonably priced, drugs.[541] The Hatch-Waxman Act did

---

534. *Andrx Pharm., Inc. v. Friedman*, 83 F. Supp. 2d 179, 185-187 (D.D.C. 2000).
535. *Andrx Pharm., Inc. v. Friedman*, 83 F. Supp. 2d 179, 184 (D.D.C. 2000), "any loss in potential sales of Biovails' product, therefore is only marginally, if at all, related to the agreement."
536. *Andrx Pharm., Inc. v. Friedman*, 83 F. Supp. 2d 179, 184 (D.D.C. 2000). The district court noted that "no generic Cardizem manufacturer could market its product until 180 days from the conclusion of the litigation, an eventuality perfectly within the scheme set forth by the Hatch-Waxman Amendments."
537. *Andrx Pharmaceuticals., Inc. v. Biovail Corp. Int'l*, 256 F.3d 799, 809 (D.C. Cir. 2001), citing BALTO, Antitrust Risks, 2000, p. 335, "[a] payment flowing from the innovator to the challenging generic firm may suggest strongly the anticompetitive intent of the parties in entering the agreement and the rent-preserving effect of that agreement."
538. *Andrx Pharmaceuticals., Inc. v. Biovail Corp. Int'l*, 256 F.3d 799, 809 (D.C. Cir. 2001), citing the Consolidated Answering Brief for Defendant-Appellee Andrx Pharmaceuticals, Inc., *Biovail Corporation v. Andrx Pharmaceuticals*, (Nos. 00-5050, 00-5396) (December 28, 2000), point 31 [cited as: Andrx, Answering Brief, *Biovail v. Andrx*], "[a] plaintiff cannot be injured in fact by private conduct excluding him from the market when a statute prevents him from entering that market in any event," citing *City of Pittsburgh v. West Penn Power Co.*, 147 F. 3d 256, 268 (3rd Cir.1998)."
539. Andrx, Answering Brief, *Biovail v. Andrx*, point 32.
540. The Hatch-Waxman amendments of 1984 simplified the FDA approval procedure for generic manufacturers introducing the ANDA system; to be distinguished from the 2003 Hatch-Waxman amendments which were subsequent to the *Andrx* case. *See* further *supra* Chapter 2, Part 2, on the analysis of the Hatch-Waxman framework.
541. *Andrx Pharmaceuticals., Inc. v. Biovail Corp. Int'l*, 256 F.3d 799, 809 (D.C. Cir. 2001). The court cited *In re Barr Lab., Inc.*, 930 F. 2d 72, 76 (D.C. Cir. 1991), "Congress sought to get generic drugs into the hands of patients at reasonable prices-fast."

not envision in any way the agreement of the first paragraph IV ANDA filer and the patent holder aiming to delay the start of the 180-day exclusivity period.[542] The appellate court noted that by virtue of its agreement with HMR, Andrx not only received HMR's quarterly payments but also retained the benefit of the 180-day exclusivity period "without starting the clock."[543] Moreover, Andrx's commitment not to trigger its exclusivity period denied Biovail the possibility to market its own generic drug version and was liable to cause Biovail's injury. Thus, even though the Hatch-Waxman amendments legally barred Biovail from marketing its generic product, Andrx had extended this legal bar by manipulating the start of its exclusivity period.[544]

2 Market Share Allocation and Preservation of Monopoly

The D.C. Circuit court stressed that the restraints imposed by the HMR/Andrx agreement could be reasonably seen as attempts of market share allocation and of preservation of monopolistic conditions.[545] The generic manufacturer's alleged injury – Andrx stalling Biovail's entry to the generic market – was the type of injury antitrust law meant to prevent. If Biovail's allegations were correct, the HMR/Andrx agreement had not enhanced competition or benefited consumers; on the contrary it had preserved HMR's monopoly.[546] Entry into the market is one of antitrust law's mechanisms to deter the exploitation of market power.[547] Although Andrx and HMR had argued that their settlement agreement did not settle the litigation,[548] Andrx's commitment to continue the prosecution of its ANDA and to shield its 180-day exclusivity period went beyond a mere wish to maintain the *status quo*.[549] On the basis of Biovail's arguments, Andrx and HMR aimed to achieve the unlawful objective of extending the exclusivity period granted by Hatch-Waxman.[550] Therefore, Biovail could allege an antitrust injury.[551] Biovail's injury was "the result of foregone profits, i.e., the

---

542. *Andrx Pharmaceuticals., Inc. v. Biovail Corp. Int'l*, 256 F.3d 799, 809 (D.C. Cir. 2001).
543. *Andrx Pharmaceuticals., Inc. v. Biovail Corp. Int'l*, 256 F.3d 799, 810 (D.C. Cir. 2001).
544. Idem.
545. *Andrx Pharmaceuticals., Inc. v. Biovail Corp. Int'l*, 256 F.3d 799, 811 (D.C. Cir. 2001).
546. *Andrx Pharmaceuticals., Inc. v. Biovail Corp. Int'l*, 256 F.3d 799, 813 (D.C. Cir. 2001).
547. *Andrx Pharmaceuticals., Inc. v. Biovail Corp. Int'l*, 256 F.3d 799, 814 (D.C. Cir. 2001).
548. *Andrx Pharmaceuticals., Inc. v. Biovail Corp. Int'l*, 256 F.3d 799, 803 (D.C. Cir. 2001), "HMRI and Andrx entered into an agreement [...] purporting to maintain the *status quo* pending the outcome of HMRI's patent infringement suit against Andrx."
549. *Andrx Pharmaceuticals., Inc. v. Biovail Corp. Int'l*, 256 F.3d 799, 813 (D.C. Cir. 2001), quoting *Rothery Storage & Van Co. v. Atlas Van Lines, Inc.*, 729 F. 2d 210, 224 (D.C. Cir. 1986), "[t]o be ancillary, and hence exempt from the *per se* rule, an agreement eliminating competition must be subordinate and collateral to a separate, legitimate transaction [...]. If [the restraint] is so broad that part of the restraint suppresses competition without creating efficiency, the restraint is, to that extent, not ancillary."
550. *Andrx Pharmaceuticals., Inc. v. Biovail Corp. Int'l*, 256 F.3d 799, 812 (D.C. Cir. 2001). "[l]ikewise, as long as Andrx was pursuing FDA approval, Biovail could not use 21 C.F.R. § 314.107 (c)(3) to revoke the 180-day exclusivity period. Indeed, according to the HMRI-Andrx Agreement, Andrx was to continue to pursue approval, which prevented the FDA from denying it with the 180-day exclusivity period."
551. *Andrx Pharmaceuticals., Inc. v. Biovail Corp. Int'l*, 256 F.3d 799, 815 (D.C. Cir. 2001).

difference between the competitive market price [Biovail] would have charged had it been in the market and its total costs."[552] After the decision of the D.C. Circuit, Biovail and Andrx settled.[553]

C The 6th Circuit Rules That the Restraints Are Per Se Illegal

Direct and indirect purchasers of the drug Cardizem CD attacked the HMR/Andrx settlement and argued that absent the payments of $40 million per year, Andrx would have marketed its generic drug right after receiving FDA approval. They argued that the settlement violated Section 1 of the Sherman Act, shielding from competition both parties, postponing the start of the 180-day exclusivity period and subsequently the entry of other generic competitors to the market. The district court of the Eastern District of Michigan concluded that the plaintiffs had adequately alleged an antitrust injury, noting that their claim consisted of higher prices paid for drugs resulting from the agreement diminishing competition between HMR and Andrx, while it also alleged a causal connection between the agreement and the decreased generic competition.[554] The plaintiffs requested a partial summary judgment on whether the HMR/Andrx agreement was a per se illegal restraint of trade. The district court concluded that the payment of $40 million to Andrx in order not to enter the market was a naked, horizontal restraint of trade and thus per se illegal.[555]

The 6th Circuit upheld the District Court's decision and confirmed that direct and indirect purchasers of Cardizem CD were forced to pay higher prices for the branded drug as they were deprived of its generic versions due to a per se illegal horizontal market restraint.[556] The alleged injury of paying higher prices for a product due to the lack of competition in the market, was an injury that could derive from the anticompetitive effects of the HMR/Andrx agreement and the reverse payment. After the decision of the 6th Circuit, several large settlements followed, yielding $110 million to direct purchasers of Cardizem CD.[557] Moreover, indirect purchasers and State Attorneys General received upon settlement $80 million.[558]

---

552. *Andrx Pharmaceuticals., Inc. v. Biovail Corp. Int'l*, 256 F.3d 799, 817 (D.C. Cir. 2001).
553. Andrx Corp., *Annual Report Pursuant to Section 13 or 15(d) of the Securities Exchange Act*, for the fiscal year ended on December 31, 2002. Available at: http://www.getfilings.com/o00009 50144-03-004118.html (last accessed on March 31, 2018), at 4, "[i]n July 2002, Andrx and Biovail Corporation entered into a settlement agreement resolving with prejudice all pending litigation and disputes between the two companies relating to Biovail's Cardizem CD."
554. *In re Cardizem CD Antitrust Litig.*, 105 F. Supp. 2d 618, 645-658 (E.D. Mich. 2000).
555. *In re Cardizem CD Antitrust Litig.*, 105 F. Supp. 2d 618, 705-706 (E.D. Mich. 2000).
556. *In re Cardizem CD Antitrust Litig.*, 332 F.3d 896, 910 (6th Cir. 2003).
557. Andrx Corp., Report (Form 8-K), Exhibit 99.1, *Andrx Corporation Reports Financial Results For the Third Quarter of 2002*, Press Release dated October 31, 2002, p. 4. Available at: http://www.sec.gov/Archives/edgar/data/1123337/000095014402010970/g78973exv99w 1.htm. (last accessed on March 31, 2018), "[d]uring 2002, Aventis Pharmaceuticals, Inc. [...] and Andrx entered into a binding settlement with the direct purchaser class of plaintiffs in the Cardizem CD antitrust litigation [...]. The settlement requires a total payment of $110 million by Aventis and Andrx to this class."
558. Press Release, Office of the Attorney General of the State of California, *Attorney General Lockyer Announces $80 Million Settlement of Antitrust Case Against Drug Makers For Limiting Access to*

1 Novel Areas of Law Do Not Preclude Per Se Treatment

Similarly to the DC Circuit Court, the appellate court for the 6th Circuit found that HMR and Andrx had committed a per se violation of antitrust laws. Even though Hatch-Waxman settlements were at that time a novel area of law, per se treatment was not precluded for that reason alone.[559] The allegations of the defendants on the precompetitive benefits of their agreements were simply irrelevant, given that the per se rule allows courts to presume that certain behaviours are anticompetitive as a class, without the need of wasting judicial resources in evaluating the actual anticompetitive effects and procompetitive justifications of each individual case.[560] The FTC also highlighted that the effects of horizontal agreements allocating territories are well-understood so that it is not necessary for either the agency or courts to have first-hand experience with the practice in a specific industry context.[561] In any case, antitrust rules are not market specific but apply to classes of agreements: naked horizontal restraints have been per se illegal for decades,[562] while some naked restraints included in patent settlement agreements have also been found to be illegal per se.[563]

2 Naked Horizontal Market Allocation Extending to Non-infringing Drugs

Like the DC Circuit, the 6th Circuit also found that the HMR/Andrx agreement safeguarded HMR's exclusive access to the market of Cardizem CD. In return for a payment of $40 million annually Andrx, the only potential generic competitor at the time, agreed to refrain from entering the market even after obtaining FDA approval of its ANDA.[564] The HMR/Andrx agreement also restrained Andrx from marketing other bioequivalent or generic versions of Cardizem CD, that were not at issue at the pending litigation since the agreement's restrictions extended to non-infringing and potentially non-infringing versions of generic Cardizem.[565] In spite of the presence of a patent dispute, this part of the agreement amounted to naked horizontal market allocation and

---

Generic Heart Medication, (January 27, 2003). Available at: http://oag.ca.gov/news/press-releases/attorney-general-lockyer-announces-80-million-settlement-antitrust-case-against (last accessed on March 31, 2018), stating that $21 million would be accorded as compensation to individual consumers, $4.5 million would reimburse the expenses of state-government agencies, and the remaining amount would be distributed to health plans and other third parties.

559. *In re Cardizem CD Antitrust Litig.*, 332 F.3d 896, 908 (6th Cir. 2003). The court relied on *Arizona v. Maricopa County. Medical Soc.*, 102 S. Ct. 2466, 2476 (1982).
560. *In re Cardizem CD Antitrust Litig.*, 332 F.3d 896, 908 (6th Cir. 2003).
561. *In re Schering-Plough Corp.*, Final FTC Order, 136 F.T.C. 956 (FTC 2003), pp. 22-23. *See also idem*, p. 23, fn. 25, referring to the decision of *Arizona v. Maricopa County. Medical Soc.*, 102 S. Ct. 2466 (1982).
562. HOVENKAMP, Sensible Antitrust Rules, 2004, p. 27, mentioning *United States v. Trans-Missouri Freight Ass'n*, 17 S. Ct. 540, 547-548 (1897); *United States v. Addyston Pipe & Steel Co. et al.*, 85 F. 271, 278-279 (6th Cir. 1898).
563. *See United States v. Singer Mfg. Co.*, 83 S. Ct. 1773 (1963); *Hartford-Empire Co. v. United States*, 65 S. Ct. 373 (1945). *See also* HOVENKAMP, Sensible Antitrust Rules, 2004, p. 27.
564. *In re Cardizem CD Antitrust Litig.*, 332 F.3d 896, 907 (6th Cir. 2003).
565. *In re Cardizem CD Antitrust Litig.*, 332 F.3d 896, 908 (6th Cir. 2003), fn. 13.

could only be justified as part of a patent licence.[566] The agreement had the effect of delaying the entry of subsequent generic competitors who were unable to enter the market before the expiration of Andrx's 180-day exclusivity period, which Andrx had explicitly committed not to relinquish or transfer.[567] Therefore, there was no doubt the HMR/Andrx agreement was a horizontal agreement to eliminate competition in the market for Cardizem CD throughout the US, "a classic example of a *per se* illegal restraint of trade."[568]

3 Bolstering Patent Effectiveness Through Reverse Payments

The settling parties unsuccessfully argued that the settlement was a mere attempt to enforce patent rights or an interim settlement of the patent infringement suit.[569] The 6th Circuit stressed that "it is one thing to take advantage of a monopoly that naturally arises from a patent, but another thing altogether to bolster the patent's effectiveness [...] by paying the only potential competitor $40 million per year to stay out of the market."[570] The defendants contended that Andrx would have stayed out of the market even in the absence of the settlement agreement and the payments of $40 million per year, because of the risk of incurring damages in the pending patent infringement litigation.[571] However, a patentee confident of the durability of its patent and the validity of its infringement claim against a generic challenger would not have paid millions of dollars to accomplish the same effect that its patent and its patent infringement suit could have accomplished.[572] Given HMR's big payment to Andrx the 6th Circuit found it probable that HMR's patent infringement suit against Andrx was a "paper tiger" which could not have deterred Andrx from marketing its generic product once approved by the FDA.[573] In other words, the court found that the big reverse payment from the patent holder to the alleged generic infringer was an indicator of the weakness of HMR's patent rights and indicated the low probability to achieve the same exclusionary effect through a patent infringement suit.

---

566. HOVENKAMP, JANIS, LEMLEY, Anticompetitive Settlements, 2003, p. 1765, "The agreement was a naked horizontal market division agreement, and the only justification for such agreements is that market divisions such as territorial and field-of-use restrictions are lawful when they are contained in patent licenses."
567. *In re Cardizem CD Antitrust Litig.*, 332 F.3d 896, 907 (6th Cir. 2003).
568. *In re Cardizem CD Antitrust Litig.*, 332 F.3d 896, 908 (6th Cir. 2003). *See also idem* at 914: "[t]he complaints allege a plain vanilla horizontal agreement to restrain trade in the form of a multimillion dollar cash payment in consideration for forbearance by Andrx from selling on the market a product that it was ready and able to sell at a price lower than that charged by HMR for the patented product."
569. *In re Cardizem CD Antitrust Litig.*, 332 F.3d 896, 908 (6th Cir. 2003).
570. *Idem.*
571. *In re Cardizem CD Antitrust Litig.*, 332 F.3d 896, 915 (6th Cir. 2003).
572. *Idem. See also* WILLIG, BIGELOW, Toward Agreements, 2004, pp. 668-669, acknowledging that a patent holder who knows that the economic value of its market is of long duration, will be less likely to prefer settlement to litigation.
573. *In re Cardizem CD Antitrust Litig.*, 332 F.3d 896, 915 (6th Cir. 2003).

III Criticising the Per Se Illegality of Reverse Payments

The Supreme Court adopts a rather conservative approach vis-à-vis per se rules, which also extends to the application of the per se illegality rule in antitrust law cases. The per se illegality rule should not be adopted for administrative convenience, since it can be counterproductive and increase the total cost of the antitrust system, by prohibiting procompetitive conduct that should be encouraged.[574] Even though per se rules may decrease administrative costs,[575] they may in parallel increase litigation costs by indirectly encouraging frivolous suits against legitimate practices.[576]

Despite an initial clash between the positions of the DoJ and the FTC until 2008,[577] neither of them supported the application of the per se illegality rule to Hatch-Waxman patent settlements. The DoJ advocated in favour of the application of the rule of reason, recognising the efficiency-enhancing objectives of settlements in conserving judicial resources and allowing parties to save litigation costs. Further, the likelihood of anticompetitive effects of patent settlements was not so great so as to render unnecessary a further examination of the challenged conduct.[578] The FTC did not support the application of the per se illegality for the totality of reverse payments either. Instead, the agency was in favour of a more extensive analysis of any procompetitive effects of such settlements, without however foreclosing the possibility of a more truncated approach in specific cases.[579] The initial openness of the FTC towards the per se illegality approach was criticised by courts and academia and gradually evolved into a presumptive illegality approach that the agency supported in *FTC v. Actavis*.[580] The following sections present the debate on the possible adverse effects that the application of a per se illegality rule could have by eliminating settlements and originators' innovation incentives.

---

574. *Leegin Creative Leather Products, Inc. v. PSKS, Inc.*, 127 S. Ct. 2705, 2709 (2007). *See idem* at 2718, "[w]ere the Court now to conclude that vertical price restraints should be *per se* illegal based on administrative costs, we would undermine, if not overrule, the traditional 'demanding standards' for adopting *per se* rules. [...] Any possible reduction in administrative costs cannot alone justify the *Dr. Miles* rule."
575. *Continental T.V., Inc. et al. v. GTE Sylvania Inc.*, 97 S. Ct. 2549, 2557 (1977), fn. 16, stating that "*per se* rules tend to provide guidance to the business community and to minimize the burdens on litigants and the judicial system of the more complex rule-of-reason trials, [...] but those advantages are not sufficient in themselves to justify the creation of per se rules."
576. *Leegin Creative Leather Products, Inc. v. PSKS, Inc.*, 127 S. Ct. 2705, 2718 (2007).
577. The FTC consistently supported the application of the rule of reason, with a presumption of illegality for large unjustified payments, while until 2008 the DoJ held a friendly stance towards reverse payments. *See* further *infra*, Chapter 3, Part 3, Section I.
578. Brief for the United States as Amicus Curiae Supporting Plaintiffs-Appellants, *In re K-Dur Antitrust Litigation*, (Nos. 10-2077, 10-2078, 10-2079) (May 18, 2011), pp. 20-22 [cited as: U.S., *Amicus* Brief, *In re K-Dur*], citing *National College Athletic Ass'n ("NCAA") v. Board of Regents*, 104 S. Ct. 2948, 2961-2962 (1984).
579. *See* FTC, Final Order, *Schering-Plough*, 2003, p. 58, "[w]e are not prepared to say that all such payments should be seen as per se illegal or inherently suspect [...] This particular case warrants a more extensive analysis of competitive effects, without foreclosing the possibility that a more truncated process will be appropriate is some future case."
580. FTC Brief on Writ of *Certiorari* to the United States Court of Appeals for the Eleventh Circuit, *FTC v. Watson Pharmaceuticals Inc. et al.*, (No. 12-416) (January 22, 2013), pp. 33-40 [cited as: FTC, *Certiorari* Brief, *FTC v. Watson Pharmaceuticals*].

A The Elimination of Procompetitive Settlements

The importance of settlements in the US legal order is huge; there is a firm belief that settlements should be encouraged and facilitated, while costly, lengthy and inefficient litigation should be avoided.[581] This stance in favour of settlements extends to settlements concluded in the context of Hatch-Waxman litigation. One of the constant criticisms against the application of antitrust scrutiny to Hatch-Waxman settlements is that such scrutiny will lead to the elimination of procompetitive settlements between the parties, to the detriment of consumers and innovation incentives.[582] The adversaries of the application of the per se rule for the adjudication of Hatch-Waxman patent settlements have argued that it failed to consider the nuances of the patent system and banned settlements that would have been efficiency-creating and procompetitive.[583] The adoption of per se illegality for reverse payment settlements would allegedly be "socially counterproductive" and would instigate unnecessary litigation,[584] while it would also have adverse effects on consumer welfare by prohibiting potentially procompetitive settlements, leading to higher drug costs because of delayed competition.[585]

It is not disputed that the per se rule produces certain false positives. However, the social cost of these false positives is small if the application of the per se rule is limited only to naked restraints which lack redeeming social benefits.[586] The 6th Circuit acknowledged in *In Re Cardizem CD* that the application of a per se rule may lead to the condemnation of a settlement agreement that could have been permitted under a rule of reason analysis, but noted that this risk has been tolerated as a necessary cost of this approach.[587] Reverse payment settlements in which the patent infringement plaintiff pays the infringement defendant to stay out of the plaintiff's market, would be per se unlawful under antitrust if such an agreement would not be part of a patent settlement.[588] In such cases, the holder of a patent that makes a large exclusion payment most probably seeks a "guaranteed insulation from competition" without risking that its patent will be held invalid.[589]

Even the partisans of applying antitrust scrutiny to reverse payment settlements agreed that the rule of per se illegality of reverse payment settlements could be too extreme and could have resulted in forbidding settlements whose anticompetitive effect was subtle, such as those not including a large payment or creating an approval

---

581. *See also supra* Chapter 1, Part 2, on the importance of settlements to the US legal order.
582. The same concern is repeatedly expressed in the European Union reverse payment settlement cases. *See infra* Chapter 6, Part 1, on the analysis of the *Lundbeck v. Commission* decision of the European General Court.
583. *See* for instance KURLANDER, Rebalancing Pay-For-Delay, 2015, pp. 699-700.
584. WILLIG, BIGELOW, Toward Agreements, 2004, pp. 677-678.
585. BUTLER, JAROSCH, Policy Reversal, 2010, p. 121.
586. HOVENKAMP, AREEDA, *Fundamentals of Antitrust*, 2014, p. 15-43.
587. *In re Cardizem CD Antitrust Litig.*, 332 F.3d 896, 907 (6th Cir. 2003). The court cited *Arizona v. Maricopa County. Medical Soc.*, 102 S. Ct. 2466, 2743 (1982), "[f]or the sake of business certainty and litigation efficiency, we have tolerated the invalidation of some agreements that a full-blown inquiry might have proved to be reasonable."
588. HOVENKAMP, *Federal Antitrust Policy*, 2011, pp. 269-270.
589. HOVENKAMP, JANIS, LEMLEY, Anticompetitive Settlements, 2003, pp. 1761-1762.

bottleneck.[590] The likelihood to commit false positives could be avoided by considering reverse payment settlements presumptively illegal instead of per se illegal: under a truncated rule of reason analysis, the settling parties would at least be offered the opportunity to present their procompetitive justifications for the settlement.[591] Applying a harsh yet not a per se illegal standard would not impede settlements; the *ex ante* effect of a harsh rule would be that settlements would take a different form.[592] For instance, parties could agree to a delayed entry for the generic, at a date before the expiration of a patent, which would be determined according to the parties' estimation on the likely outcome of the patent infringement litigation.[593]

The proponents of the per se illegality standard for reverse payment settlements argued that any settlement which requires a payment is most likely anticompetitive so that the general ban of reverse payment settlements could have been the most efficient solution.[594] Despite the broad disapproval of the application of the per se rule to reverse payment settlements,[595] its application could be desirable in limited cases, e.g., when a patent holder attempts to increase the level of patent protection beyond the optimal level, by shielding from competition a knowingly invalid patent.[596] Nothing in the Patent Act contemplates that a patent holder can pay its competitor to stay out of the market.[597] If the patent at issue was valid and infringed, the patent holder would be in the position to eliminate competition by enforcing its patent rights, without the need for a large payment. When a patent holder attempts to eliminate competition through collusion, antitrust law should weigh in.[598]

B *Decreasing Patent Challenges and Innovation Incentives*

The impact a per se illegality rule could have on patent challenges by generic manufacturers was also a cause for concern. It was argued that banning reverse payment settlements could reduce the incentives for generic filers to challenge patents, by reducing their settlement options if they were sued for patent infringement, a result

---

590. *See* for instance HEMPHILL, Paying for Delay, 2006, p. 1596.
591. *Idem.*
592. HOVENKAMP, JANIS, LEMLEY, Anticompetitive Settlements, 2003, pp. 1760-1761.
593. HOVENKAMP, JANIS, LEMLEY, Anticompetitive Settlements, 2003, p. 1762, arguing that courts should not object to a delayed-entry settlement which represents the parties' estimate of the expected litigation outcome, provided that such delay is not combined with an exclusion payment or a concealed exclusion agreement e.g., a cartelisation agreement.
594. DAVIS, Per Se Illegal, 2009, pp. 287-301; CHAVES MOSIER, RITCHESON, Faultline, 2003, p. 511, arguing in favour of per se illegality where the payment exceeds litigation costs and the exclusion agreement facially exceeds the patent grant; *See also* OWENS, Per Se Prohibition, 2013, pp. 1382-1399.
595. DICKEY, ORSZAG, TYSON, Economic Assessment, 2010, pp. 385-390, 399, arguing against the per se illegality of reverse payment settlements which can have procompetitive effects. Interestingly, the authors also suggest that prohibiting cash payments could lead to settlements involving other business arrangements, more complicated and difficult to evaluate. *See also* DICKEY, RUBINFELD, Generic Drug Investment, 2012, pp. 622-624.
596. LANGENFELD, WENQING, Settlement Agreements With Payments, 2003, pp. 789-790.
597. HOVENKAMP, *Federal Antitrust Policy*, 2011, p. 271.
598. HOVENKAMP, JANIS, LEMLEY, Anticompetitive Settlements, 2003, pp. 1761-1762.

which could be deemed anticompetitive.[599] However, the statutory 180-day exclusivity period granted by the Hatch-Waxman Act to the first generic challenger and the profits it accrues should be sufficient to incentivise generic challenges.[600] If the main incentive of a generic challenger is the possibility to receive a big exclusion payment instead of entering the generic market, such a challenge is likely to result in an unjustified foreclosure effect on the market by blocking the entry of subsequent generic challengers, causing consumer harm. Even though incentivising the challenge of possibly invalid patents is one of the core aims of the Hatch-Waxman Act, not all generic challenges are desirable; the ones that are abusive and aim to market partitioning arrangements should be deterred.

The possible negative impact antitrust scrutiny could have on the originators' innovation incentives is a recurring discussion even after the resolution of the Circuits' split.[601] Especially with regard to per se illegality, it was argued that such a strict rule would allegedly limit the patent holder's ability to protect its intellectual property rights, reduce innovation and the consumer surplus generated by these innovations.[602] However, legitimising pay-for-delay settlements is an unorthodox way to spur innovation. These settlements cannot be justified under the Patent Act's general policy of protecting innovation.[603] In any case, immunising reverse payment settlements from antitrust scrutiny is more likely to incentivise R&D investment on incremental innovation instead of revolutionary projects, actually hindering technological progress.[604] Applying antitrust scrutiny to reverse payments could foster technological progress and strong R&D.[605] On the contrary, insufficient scrutiny for reverse payment settlements has the potential to backfire and to hamper innovation, by elevating weak patents to the same level of exclusionary potential and monopoly possibilities as the strong patents, steering the incentives of innovators from genuine – and costly – innovation to cheaper pseudo-innovation which is much less valuable socially.[606]

---

599. See *Asahi Glass Co., Ltd. v. Pentech Pharmaceuticals, Inc.*, 289 F. Supp. 2d 986, 992 (N.D. Ill. 2003).
600. Davis, Per Se Illegal, 2009, pp. 297-298. Davis proposed that if the exclusivity period profits were not deemed sufficient, Congress could consider extending the duration of the 180-day exclusivity period.
601. See supra Chapter 1, Part 1, on the costs of pharma R&D and innovation incentives. See also infra Chapter 4, Part 1, Section VI, analysing the dissenting opinion in *FTC v. Actavis* and the Dissenting Justices' concerns that antitrust scrutiny would have an adverse effect to the settlement incentives.
602. Langenfeld, Wenqing, Settlement Agreements With Payments, 2003, pp. 797-807, advocating in favour of a rule of reason approach as the general test for the adjudication of reverse payment settlements. See also Crane, Exit Payments, 2002, p.760, "[a] rule prohibiting exit payments may have the unintended effect of increasing the risks of engaging in inventive activity, and therefore lead to a sub-optimal amount of innovation."
603. Hemphill, Paying for Delay, 2006, p. 1613.
604. Mungan, Perverse Incentives, 2013, pp. 37-46.
605. See also *Idem*, arguing that reverse payments should be condemned as illegal in order to foster R&D and technological progress.
606. *In Re Cipro Cases I & II*, 348 P.3d 845, 868 (Cal., May 7, 2015); Mungan, Perverse Incentives, 2013, pp. 42-44; Elhauge, Krueger, Patent Settlement Puzzle, 2012, pp. 294-295.

Chapter 3: The US Circuits' Split on Reverse Payment Settlements

PART 2   THE SCOPE OF THE PATENT TEST

US courts first used the scope of the patent formulation in order to restrict conduct which reached beyond the statutory authorisation granted to the patentee,[607] since patent abuse has been perceived by the Supreme Court as conduct which reaches beyond the scope of the patent.[608] In the first half of the twentieth century, the scope of the patent formulation was introduced from patent law into antitrust law and was extensively used in order to assess tying arrangements, licence agreements, or other contracts involving patents and settlements of patent infringement lawsuits.[609] Later on, the scope of the patent doctrine was used defensively, with parties arguing that as long as an agreement did not extend the patent monopoly beyond its lawful scope, the relevant conduct would be lawful even if it was prima facie anticompetitive.[610] The scope of the patent standard is not always a helpful tool for antitrust analysis and can have harmful effects on competition.[611]

The foundations of the scope of the patent test for the assessment of reverse payment settlements in the context of Hatch-Waxman litigation can be traced in the *in Re Cardizem CD Antitrust Litigation* decision of the 6th Circuit that was analysed in part 1 of this chapter.[612] In *in Re Cardizem CD*, the 6th Circuit found that the settlement at issue prevented not only the marketing of generic versions of the branded drug, but also of drugs beyond the framework of the pending patent infringement litigation.[613] Even though the 6th Circuit condemned the agreement as a per se illegal restraint of trade,[614] the court's punishment of conduct outside the patent's scope was adopted by later courts which used the scope of the patent test for quite different purposes, shifting its meaning.[615]

The following sections analyse the application of the scope of the patent test in a series of reverse payment settlement cases. The evolution of the test from the three-step inquiry of *Valley Drug* to the sham or baseless litigation standard applied in the *Tamoxifen* decision is discussed. The problems created by the application of the scope

---

607. HOVENKAMP, Scope of the Patent, 2015, pp. 515-516, 525-526.
608. *Carbice Corp. of Am. v. Am. Patents Dev. Corp.*, 51 S. Ct. 334, 336 (1931), "[c]ontrol over the supply of such unpatented material is beyond the scope of the patentee's monopoly;" *Mercoid Corp. v. Mid-Continent Inv. Co.*, 64 S. Ct. 268, 271 (1944), stating that the ability to "acquire a monopoly which is not plainly within the terms of the grant." See further HOVENKAMP, Scope of the Patent, 2015, pp. 515-516.
609. HOVENKAMP, Reexamination, 2015, pp. 476-477.
610. HOVENKAMP, Scope of the Patent, 2015, pp. 526-528. *See* for instance *Bement v. National Harrow Company*, 22 S. Ct. 747, 755, arguing that the very object of patent laws is monopoly and as a rule any conditions which are not in their very nature illegal and are agreed between the patentee and the licensee will be upheld by courts; even conditions which keep up the monopoly or fix prices should not be seen as automatically illegal.
611. HOVENKAMP, Scope of the Patent, 2015, pp. 515-516.
612. *In re Cardizem CD Antitrust Litig.*, 332 F.3d 896 (6th Cir. 2003).
613. *See supra*, Chapter 3, Part 1, Section II.C for the analysis of the *In Re Cardizem* decision. CARRIER, Scope of the Patent Test, 2012, p. 2, referring to *In re Cardizem CD Antitrust Litig.*, 332 F.3d 896, 908 (6th Cir. 2003), fn. 13.
614. *See supra*, Chapter 3, Part 1, Section II.C for the analysis of *In re Cardizem CD Antitrust Litig.*, 332 F.3d 896 (6th Cir. 2003).
615. CARRIER, Scope of the Patent Test, 2012, pp. 2-5.

of the patent test are presented in detail, focusing on the antitrust immunity the test granted to obviously anticompetitive settlements by virtually ignoring the issues of patent validity and patent infringement. Due to the number of decisions that applied the scope of the patent test and for the sake of brevity, the facts of each reverse payment settlement case are not discussed in detail. Suffice to say that most of the below-analysed cases concerned settlements involving big value transfers from the brand-name manufacturer to the first (and sometimes to subsequent) generic ANDA IV filers, in return for delaying generic entry until the expiration of the relevant patent, or until a finding of patent invalidity or unenforceability. These settlements concerned highly profitable blockbuster drugs; in the majority of cases, the patents covering the active ingredient had already expired and the relevant patents which were the object of the underlying patent infringement dispute were secondary patents, covering for example manufacturing processes or release methods.

I The Scope of the Patent Test and Reverse Payments

Several Circuit Courts rejected both the per se illegality approach and the application of the rule of reason to reverse payment settlements.[616] Applying the notorious scope of the patent test, these courts found that reverse payments settlements were *immune* from antitrust scrutiny, so long as their anticompetitive effects fell "within the scope of the exclusionary potential of the patent."[617] Courts applying the scope of the patent test did not clearly and uniformly outline how this test should be applied or how the exclusionary scope of a patent should be defined. Instead of looking into the issues of patent validity and patent infringement, courts applying the scope of the patent test took for granted that the patent holder was entitled to exclude *all* competition from the market. These court decisions seemed also indifferent concerning the type of the underlying patent: under the scope of the patent test, the exclusionary potential of secondary formulation patents was equated with that of patents covering the active ingredient of the respective brand-name drug.[618] Even the invalidation of the underlying patent subsequent to the reverse payment settlement agreement did not alter this status of antitrust immunity granted under the scope of the patent test. All the settlements that were accorded a *carte blanche* under the scope of the patent test

---

616. *See* for instance *Valley Drug Co. v. Geneva Pharms, Inc.*, 344 F.3d 1294, 1311 (11th Cir. 2003).
617. *FTC v. Watson Pharmaceuticals*, 677 F.3d 1298, 1312 (11th Cir. 2012).
618. *See* for instance *In re Ciprofloxacin Hydrochloride Antitrust Litig.*, 544 F. 3d 1323 (Fed. Cir. 2008), where the underlying patent covered the active ingredient of Bayer's brand-name drug Cipro R.; in contrast to *Valley Drug Co. v. Geneva Pharms, Inc.*, 344 F.3d 1294 (11th Cir. 2003), in which Abbott's compound patent on the drug Hytrin had expired and Abbott held other patents relating to various crystalline forms of the compound and various methods of use and preparation of the compound, and; *Schering-Plough Corp. v. FTC*, 402 F.3d 1056 (11th Cir. 2005), where Schering held only a formulation patent on the extended-release coating surrounding the active ingredient, since the active ingredient of the drug K-Dur 20 was commonly used and unpatentable.

involved huge value transfers from the patent holders to the generic challengers and ensured the insulation of the market from generic competition until the nominal expiration of the underlying patent.[619]

A The Three-Step Inquiry of the Scope of the Patent Test

The 11th Circuit formulated in its decision in *Valley Drug* a concrete three-step analysis of reverse payment settlements under the scope of the patent test.[620] This analysis included: (1) the consideration of the scope of the exclusionary potential of the patent; (2) the determination of whether the settlement agreements at issue exceeded this scope; and (3) the examination of the anticompetitive effects thereof.[621] Under the scope of the patent test, the patent constituted an exception to antitrust liability, an exception which was however limited by the terms of the patent and the statutory rights granted to the patentee.[622] Thus, settlement provisions going *beyond* the exclusionary power of the patent at issue should be subject to traditional antitrust analysis in order to assess their potential anticompetitive effects and determine whether they violate Section 1 of the Sherman Act.[623] This three-step test of the *Valley Drug* decision was also applied by the 11th Circuit in the *Schering-Plough Corp. v. FTC* and the *Andrx Pharmaceuticals v. Elan Corporation* decisions.[624] The scope of the patent test was extended by the 2nd Circuit which applied the "sham litigation" standard at the *In re Tamoxifen Citrate Antitrust Litigation* decision,[625] going beyond this three-step inquiry.

B Not Exceeding the Scope of the Patent

Despite the number of decisions applying the scope of the patent test, Circuit Courts did not provide a uniform definition of when the scope of the patent *was* exceeded. Some decisions focused on the temporal element of the duration of delay to generic entry,

---

619. For example, in *Valley Drug Co. v. Geneva Pharms, Inc.*, 344 F.3d 1294 (11th Cir. 2003), the patent holder Abbott agreed to pay the first generic challenger Geneva $4.5 million per month until either another generic manufacture brought a respective generic drug in the market or Abbott won a favourable judgment on its patent infringement claim. Abbott also concluded a reverse payment settlement with the second generic challenger, Zenith, and committed to a payment schedule, agreeing to pay Zenith a $3 million advance, $3 million after three months and $6 million every three months thereafter until the agreement was terminated. In *Schering-Plough Corp. v. FTC*, 402 F.3d 1056 (11th Cir. 2005), the patent holder Schering undertook the obligation to pay the first generic challenger ESI: (1) a $5 million non-contingent payment representing legal fees, and; (2) an additional $10 million contingent on FDA's approval, while on the basis of a side licensing agreement between the parties, Schering agreed to pay ESI an additional $15 million.
620. *Valley Drug Co. v. Geneva Pharms, Inc.*, 344 F.3d 1294 (11th Cir. 2003).
621. *Valley Drug Co. v. Geneva Pharms, Inc.*, 344 F.3d 1294, 1312 (11th Cir. 2003).
622. Idem.
623. *Valley Drug Co. v. Geneva Pharms, Inc.*, 344 F.3d 1294, 1312-1313 (11th Cir. 2003).
624. *Schering-Plough Corp. v. FTC*, 402 F.3d 1056, 1065-1066 (11th Cir. 2005), referring to *Valley Drug Co. v. Geneva Pharms, Inc.*, 344 F.3d 1294, 1312 (11th Cir. 2003); *Andrx Pharmaceuticals Inc. v. Elan Corporation*, 421 F.3d 1227 (11th Cir. 2005).
625. *In re Tamoxifen Citrate Antitrust Litigation*, 466 F.3d 187 (2nd Cir. 2006).

whereas other focused on the scope of the products concerned by the settlement or the potential competitors whose entry was barred from the settlement agreement.

1   The Duration of Delay to Generic Entry

In *Valley Drug*, the 11th Circuit focused on the *duration of the delay* and ruled that a reverse payment settlement allowing generic entry before the expiration of the patent had a narrower exclusionary effect than the patent itself.[626] Under this standard, virtually any settlement agreement allowing for generic entry before the expiration of the patent would be immunised from antitrust scrutiny, irrespectively of the size of the payment from the originator to the generic challenger or of whether the patent at issue was invalid or not infringed. In its subsequent decision in *Andrx Pharmaceuticals v. Elan Corporation*, the 11th Circuit focused again on the temporal element of exclusion: a licensing agreement, coupled with a promise by the first generic challenger to refrain from *ever* marketing its generic drug, would exceed the scope of exclusion intended by the patent.[627] The court also accepted that the scope of the patent at issue could have been exceeded, if it was proven that the settlement agreement effectively barred *any* generic competitors from entering the market.[628]

2   The Scope of the Products Delayed by the Agreement

In *Schering-Plough*, the 11th Circuit focused on the *scope of the products* which were delayed by the agreement and found that it was sufficiently narrow: no other products were delayed by the settlements apart from the generic version of the relevant brand-name drug, as the language of the settlement agreement covered the identical reach of the patent.[629] The 2nd Circuit used a similar standard in *Tamoxifen*: the relevant patent covered the *compound* of the drug and thus excluded by its nature *all* generic versions, unlike a formulation patent which could only exclude specific infringing formulations or delivery methods.[630] A settlement agreement which did not

---

626. *Valley Drug Co. v. Geneva Pharms, Inc.*, 344 F.3d 1294, 1305 (11th Cir. 2003).
627. *Andrx Pharmaceuticals Inc. v. Elan Corporation*, 421 F.3d 1227, 1235 (11th Cir. 2005), "Andrx alleged that the Elan-SkyePharma licensing agreement, coupled with SkyePharma's putative agreement to refrain from ever marketing a generic controlled release naproxen medication, 'effectively barred any generic competitors from entering the market' [...] If true, this dynamic would exceed the scope of exclusion intended by the '320 patent."
628. *Andrx Pharmaceuticals Inc. v. Elan Corporation*, 421 F.3d 1227, 1235 (11th Cir. 2005).
629. *Schering-Plough Corp. v. FTC*, 402 F.3d 1056, 1073 (11th Cir. 2005). *See also FTC v. Watson Pharmaceuticals*, 677 F.3d 1298, 1306-1312 (11th Cir. 2012), reiterating the previous rulings of the 11th Circuit applying the scope of the patent test. It should be noted that in *FTC v. Watson Pharmaceuticals*, 677 F.3d 1298, the 11th Circuit found that the FTC had not sufficiently pleaded an antitrust claim; therefore, the court did not analyse the alleged antitrust violation in detail.
630. *In re Tamoxifen Citrate Antitrust Litigation*, 466 F.3d 187, 214 (2nd Cir. 2006). The court pointed out that in the *In re Ciprofloxacin* cases the patent similarly covered the active ingredient of the drug; unlike the patents in *Valley Drug* and *In re Cardizem* which were formulation patents. See further *In re Ciprofloxacin Hydrochloride Antitrust Litig.*, 544 F. 3d 1323 (Fed. Cir. 2008).

restrain the entry and marketing of non-infringing products did not unlawfully extend the scope of the patent.[631] The 2nd Circuit applied this standard also in its *Arkansas Carpenters Health & Welfare Fund v. Bayer AG* decision, finding that the patent at issue covered the compound of the drug and thus *any* generic version would necessarily infringe the scope of the patent.[632] All of the above-mentioned decisions did not examine whether the relevant compound patents were valid or not, taking their exclusionary effect as granted.

3   No Manipulation of the 180-Day Exclusivity Period

In re Ciprofloxacin the generic manufacturers agreed not to market their generic versions until the expiration of the relevant patent and not to challenge the validity of the patent, in return of the patent holder's payments to that end. The Court of Appeals for the Federal Circuit found in that this settlement was "well within Bayer's rights as a patentee."[633] The criterion that the court used was that the *180-day period has not been manipulated* by the settling parties; the generic manufacturer was not entitled to the exclusivity period and thus there was no bottleneck effect for subsequent challengers; therefore, the agreement did not extend outside the scope of the patent.[634] Relying on *Standard Oil Co. v. United States*, the Court of Appeals for the Federal Circuit noted that the settlement of patent claims and the exchange of consideration between the parties are not excluded by the Sherman Act, despite the possibility of having adverse effects on competition.[635] A similar standard was applied by the 2nd Circuit in the *Arkansas Carpenters* decision which found that in the absence of manipulation of the exclusivity period or of prohibition of marketing of non-infringing products, the scope of the patent was not exceeded by the settlement agreement including a large reverse payment from the originator to the generic challenger.[636]

---

631. *In re Tamoxifen Citrate Antitrust Litigation*, 466 F.3d 187, 214 (2nd Cir. 2006). The 2nd Circuit noted that this element differentiated the Zeneca/Barr agreement from the *In re Cardizem* agreement which extended to the prohibition of marketing of non-infringing products, leading the 6th Circuit to the decision that the agreement was per se illegal; further, the agreements adjudicated in *Valley Drug* and in *K-Dur Antitrust Litigation* also extended to non-infringing products.
632. *Arkansas Carpenters Health & Welfare Fund v. Bayer AG*, 604 F.3d 98, 106 (2nd Cir. 2010).
633. *In re Ciprofloxacin Hydrochloride Antitrust Litig.*, 544 F. 3d 1323, 1333 (Fed. Cir. 2008).
634. *In re Ciprofloxacin Hydrochloride Antitrust Litig.*, 544 F. 3d 1323, 1339 (Fed. Cir. 2008). The *Ciprofloxacin* settlement was concluded while FDA's successful defence requirement was still in place and Barr was ineligible for the 180-exclusivity period since it had already acknowledged its infringement and the validity of the '444 patent in the consent judgment; Barr had also converted its paragraph IV into a paragraph III certification.
635. *In re Ciprofloxacin Hydrochloride Antitrust Litig.*, 544 F. 3d 1323, 1333 (Fed. Cir. 2008). The court relied on *Standard Oil Co. v. United States*, 51 S. Ct. 421, 424, fn. 5 (1931).
636. *Arkansas Carpenters Health & Welfare Fund v. Bayer AG*, 604 F.3d 98, 106 (2nd Cir. 2010). The *Arkansas Carpenters* decision concerned the part of the *Ciprofloxacin* case that remained with the 2nd Circuit.

C The Sham or Baseless Litigation Standard

The common idea behind the application of the scope of the patent test is that a patent holder should not incur antitrust liability when it chooses to exclude others from producing its patented work.[637] However, patent law does not extend a patentees' monopoly beyond its statutory right to exclude: "[t]he possession of a valid patent or patents does not give the patentee any exemption from the provisions of the Sherman Act beyond the limits of the patent monopoly."[638] As above-analysed, courts applying the scope of the patent test found that the scope of this statutory right to exclude also encompassed reverse payments from the originator to the generic challenger, aiming to the exclusion of the latter from the market; such payments fell within the exclusionary scope of the patent and were thus immunised by antitrust scrutiny. An additional requirement, the so-called "sham or baseless litigation standard" was gradually integrated in the scope of the patent test jurisprudence. An indicative decision is that of the 11th Circuit in *Schering-Plough*. The FTC was the antitrust plaintiff in *Schering-Plough*, but had not alleged that patent holder's patent was *invalid* or that the two infringement suits against the generic challengers were *shams*.[639] Based on the lack of these allegations, the 11th Circuit found that there was a presumption of patent validity, which entitled Schering to exclude from the market alleged patent infringers.[640]

The 2nd Circuit in *Tamoxifen* confirmed that a payment from a patent holder to a generic competitor was not violating antitrust laws, unless the exclusionary effects of the settlement agreement exceeded the scope of the patent at issue. The court found that the damage to competition by the settlement was the result of the monopoly granted to the patent holder by patent law,[641] while even excessive payments to settle a dispute were not necessarily unlawful.[642] The 2nd Circuit pushed the scope of the patent test a step further by finding that *absent fraud* or extension of this monopoly beyond the patent's scope, the remaining question was whether the underlying infringement suits were *objectively baseless*.[643] The validity of the underlying patent in *Tamoxifen* had been upheld by court decisions and this was enough for the 2nd Circuit to conclude that the underlying infringement suits at issue were not objectively baseless.[644]

This sham or baseless litigation standard was criticised for immunising reverse payments from antitrust liability even more than the scope of the patent test as applied by the 11th Circuit, since the latter did not go as far as to consider sham or objectively

---

637. *Schering-Plough Corp. v. FTC*, 402 F.3d 1056, 1067 (11th Cir. 2005).
638. *Idem*, citing *United States v. Singer Mfg. Co.*, 83 S. Ct. 1773, 1785 (1963).
639. *Schering-Plough Corp. v. FTC*, 402 F.3d 1056, 1068 (11th Cir. 2005).
640. *Schering-Plough Corp. v. FTC*, 402 F.3d 1056, 1067-1068 (11th Cir. 2005).
641. *In re Tamoxifen Citrate Antitrust Litigation*, 466 F.3d 187, 210 (2nd Cir. 2006).
642. *In re Tamoxifen Citrate Antitrust Litigation*, 466 F.3d 187, 213 (2nd Cir. 2006).
643. *Idem*.
644. *Zeneca Ltd. v. Novopharm Ltd.*, No. 96-1364, (Fed. Cir. 1997) (unpublished opinion); *Zeneca Ltd. v. Pharmachemie B.V.*, No. 96-12413, (D. Mass. 2000); *AstraZeneca UK Ltd. v. Mylan Pharms., Inc.*, No. 00-2239 (W.D. Pa. 2000).

baseless litigation to be a prerequisite for antitrust liability.[645] The sham or baseless litigation standard in essence amounted to per se legality of reverse payment settlements aiming to the exclusion of generic drugs from the market, given that it was virtually impossible for parties to prove that the underlying patent infringement suit is a sham.[646] The effects of the sham or baseless litigation standard were immediate: the number of Hatch-Waxman settlements after the *Tamoxifen* decision reached an "all-time high" of fifty-four settlements in 2009,[647] while in the four years following the decision, the FTC identified fifty-three pharmaceutical patent settlements involving exclusion payments,[648] making the 2nd Circuit itself realise that there were imperative reasons to revisit the decision.[649] The standard applied in *Tamoxifen* was criticised for inappropriately permitting patent holders to contract out of the statutorily imposed risk of patent invalidation and for according them antitrust immunity by barring *any* antitrust scrutiny; as a result it did not protect the public interest in the elimination of undeserved patents.[650]

Nevertheless, the 11th Circuit's take on the scope of the patent test also evolved and embraced the sham or baseless litigation standard of the 2nd Circuit. In *FTC v. Watson Pharmaceuticals*, the court stated that "[o]ur *Valley Drug, Schering-Plough* and *Andrx* decisions establish the rule that absent sham litigation or fraud in obtaining a patent, a reverse payment settlement is *immune* from antitrust attack, so long as its anticompetitive effects fall within the exclusionary potential of the patent."[651] The 11th Circuit argued that the sole reason it did not explicitly apply the sham or baseless litigation standard in its previous decisions was the absence of allegations – in those cases – that the patents at issue were fraudulently obtained or that the patent infringement litigation at issue was a sham.[652]

II How Patents Immunised Settlements from Antitrust

Even courts applying the scope of the patent test agreed that reverse payment settlements would have amounted to per se antitrust violations if they merely involved

---

645. See further Brief for the United States as *Amicus Curiae, Joblove v. Barr Labs., Inc.,* (No. 06-830) (May 23, 2007), p. 16, fn. 15, "application of the Second Circuit's standard would largely immunize such agreements from Antitrust scrutiny."
646. HOVENKAMP, JANIS, LEMLEY, LESLIE, *IP And Antitrust*, 2015, pp. 15-34, 15-35.
647. RBC Capital Markets, Pharmaceuticals: *Analyzing Litigation Success Rates*, (January 15, 2010), p. 8. Available at http://www.amlawdaily.typepad.com/pharmareport.pdf. (last accessed on March 31, 2018). [cited as: RBC, Litigation Success Rates, 2010], "The number of settlements in 2009 reached an all-time high of 54, up from 45 in the prior year;" it should also be noted that there was a jump in the number of settlements from 21 in 2007 to 45 in 2008.
648. FTC, *Pay-for-Delay*, 2010, p. 4.
649. *Arkansas Carpenters Health & Welfare Fund v. Bayer AG*, 604 F.3d 98, 109 (2nd Cir. 2010), noting that after *Tamoxifen*, twenty out of twenty-seven Hatch-Waxman settlements involved reverse payments.
650. Brief for the United States in Response to the Court's Invitation, *Arkansas Carpenters Health & Welfare Fund v. Bayer AG*, (Nos. 05-2851-cv(L), 05-2852-cv (CON), 05-2863-cv (CON), on appeal from the United States District Court for the Eastern District of New York, (July 7, 2009), at 14-15. [cited as: U.S., Response Brief, *Arkansas Carpenters v. Bayer*].
651. *FTC v. Watson Pharmaceuticals*, 677 F.3d 1298, 1312 (11th Cir. 2012).
652. *FTC v. Watson Pharmaceuticals*, 677 F.3d 1298, 1312 (11th Cir. 2012), fn. 10.

a firm making monthly payments to its competitors in order for them to refrain from entering the market.[653] However, it was argued that the element differentiating the Hatch-Waxman settlements from such anticompetitive agreements was the fact that one of the parties held a patent.[654] Courts applying the scope of the patent test insisted that "a patent by its very nature is anticompetitive" and constitutes "an exemption to the general rule against monopolies and to the right of access to a free and open market."[655] The exclusionary effects of reverse payment settlement agreements were equated to the exclusionary effects "that are at the heart of the patent right," which could not trigger a per se condemnation.[656] The courts applying the scope of the patent test argued that the outcome of a rule of reason antitrust analysis would be the same as under a patent law analysis examining the rights of exclusion accorded by the patent, at least for settlements whose anticompetitive effects did not exceed the scope of the patent.[657] Therefore, the scope of the patent analysis was "completely consistent with the Supreme Court's precedent"[658] and duly appreciated the underlying tension between antitrust and patent laws.[659] Interestingly, the 11th Circuit acknowledged that there are kinds of agreements such as tying or price fixing which are per se illegal irrespectively of whether one of the parties holds a patent.[660]

Courts applying the scope of the patent test also found that the allocation of territories by a patentee did not always constitute territorial market allocation triggering antitrust liability. In *Valley Drug*, the 11th Circuit found that the district court erred in characterising the two reverse payment settlement agreements at issue as territorial market allocation agreements, by failing to consider that the '207 patent gave the patent holder (Abbott) the right to exclude others from making, using or selling anhydrous terazosin hydrochloride until the patent's expiration.[661] The key element differentiating similar patent settlement agreements from clearly anticompetitive agreements allocating markets was the existence of the patent; absent the patent, such a market allocation agreement would be clearly anticompetitive since it resulted in

---

653. *Valley Drug Co. v. Geneva Pharms, Inc.*, 344 F.3d 1294, 1304 (11th Cir. 2003).
654. *Idem.*
655. *In re Ciprofloxacin Hydrochloride Antitrust Litig.*, 544 F. 3d 1323, 1333 (Fed. Cir. 2008). The court cited *Dawson Chem. Co. v. Rohm & Haas Co.*, 100 S. Ct. 2601, 2622-2623, (1980); *Precision Instrument Manufacturing Co. et al., v. Automotive Maintenance Machinery Co.*, 65 S. Ct. 993, 998 (1945).
656. *Valley Drug Co. v. Geneva Pharms, Inc.*, 344 F.3d 1294, 1306 (11th Cir. 2003).
657. *In re Ciprofloxacin Hydrochloride Antitrust Litig.*, 544 F. 3d 1323, 1336 (Fed. Cir. 2008).
658. *Idem.* The Court of Appeals for the Federal Circuit relied on *Walker Process Equip., Inc. v. Food Mach & Chem. Corp.*, 86 S. Ct. 347, 349-351, (1965), where the Supreme Court held that there may be a violation of the Sherman Act in cases a patent is procured by fraud but recognised that a patent is an exception to the general rule against monopolies.
659. *In re Ciprofloxacin Hydrochloride Antitrust Litig.*, 544 F. 3d 1323, 1333 (Fed. Cir. 2008). The court referred to *In re Tamoxifen Citrate Antitrust Litigation*, 466 F.3d 187, 201-202 (2nd Cir. 2006); *Andrx Pharmaceuticals Inc. v. Elan Corporation*, 421 F.3d 1227, 1235 (11th Cir. 2005); *Schering-Plough Corp. v. FTC*, 402 F.3d 1056, 1066 (11th Cir. 2005); *Valley Drug Co. v. Geneva Pharms, Inc.*, 344 F.3d 1294, 1312 (11th Cir. 2003).
660. *Valley Drug Co. v. Geneva Pharms, Inc.*, 344 F.3d 1294, 1306 (11th Cir. 2003).
661. *Valley Drug Co. v. Geneva Pharms, Inc.*, 344 F.3d 1294, 1305 (11th Cir. 2003).

reduced competition, increased prices and diminished output.[662] Courts insisted that patents create by their very nature an environment of exclusion and cripple competition; the patent holder had the legal right to exclude potential generic entrants from the generic market until either the patent's invalidation or proof that the respective generic products did not infringe it.[663] The power of patentees to exclude infringing competition from the market was seen as the essence of a patent grant[664] and served as an incentive to innovation and the public disclosure of inventions.[665] Under the scope of the patent test, courts never examined the issue of patent validity or of patent infringement by the relevant generic drug version; instead they took for granted that the patentees at issue had a lawful right to exclude the relevant generics from the market, upgrading the possibility that the relevant patent was infringed by the generic drug versions into a certainty. The problems caused by this approach are discussed in detail in the following sections.

III Main Problems of the Scope of the Patent Test

The scope of the patent test was criticised as one of the most unhelpful patent and competition law rules, since it suggests that a patent practice should only be evaluated under antitrust rules if it reaches "beyond the scope of the patent."[666] This formulation suggests that a patent is seen as a fortress whose insides cannot be touched by antitrust scrutiny and are not harmful while everything outside its walls may be challenged and is competitively harmful.[667] The following sections describe in detail the most important problems created by the application of the scope of the patent test: (1) the elevation of the presumption of patent validity from a procedural presumption into a substantive right granting automatic legality to patent settlements; (2) the antitrust immunity granted to settlements concerning potentially weak or invalid patents; and (3) the problems raised by ignoring the issue of patent infringement by the relevant generic drug version and by legitimising the exclusion of potentially non-infringing competition from the market.[668]

A *The Presumption of Patent Validity*

The presumption of patent validity – as employed by the courts applying the scope of the patent test – was criticised as inappropriate, since it led to a number of decisions

---

662. *Schering-Plough Corp. v. FTC*, 402 F.3d 1056, 1064 (11th Cir. 2005), "[a]lthough we recognised in *Valley Drug* that an agreement to allocate market is clearly anticompetitive, resulting in reduced competition, increased prices and diminished output, we nonetheless reversed for a simple reason: one of the parties held a patent" [internal quotation marks omitted].
663. *Schering-Plough Corp. v. FTC*, 402 F.3d 1056, 1065-1066 (11th Cir. 2005).
664. *Valley Drug Co. v. Geneva Pharms, Inc.*, 344 F.3d 1294, 1306 (11th Cir. 2003).
665. *Valley Drug Co. v. Geneva Pharms, Inc.*, 344 F.3d 1294, 1305-1306 (11th Cir. 2003).
666. HOVENKAMP, Reexamination, 2015, pp. 476-477.
667. *Idem*.
668. See also CARRIER, Scope of the Patent Test, 2012, pp. 5-8, analysing these problems raised by the application of the scope of the patent test.

which automatically permitted reverse payment settlements, without subjecting them to any antitrust scrutiny.[669] The distortion of the presumption of patent validity from a procedural presumption into a substantive right of the patentee to exclude all generic competition from the market and the legal problems it gave rise to are extensively discussed in the following sections.

1 Section 282 of the Patent Act

According to Section 282 of the Patent Act, patents shall be presumed valid and any party asserting the invalidity of a patent shall carry the burden of establishing it.[670] This presumption of patent validity is a procedural presumption for the allocation of the burden of proof and has no separate evidentiary value in patent litigation.[671] Further, it does not require courts to adopt a decisional approach which accepts patent claims as valid[672] and "does not entitle a patentee to evade the test of patent litigation any more than a criminal defendant's presumption of innocence entitles him to avoid trial."[673] In the context of Hatch-Waxman settlements, generic challengers have to carry the burden of defeating the presumption of patent validity; however this presumption is a procedural device and not a substantive right of the patent holder.[674]

Courts applying the scope of the patent test to reverse payment settlements took for granted the validity of the underlying patent and transformed the procedural presumption of Section 282 of the Patent Act into substantive evidence of patent validity.[675] Presuming that the patent at issue was 100% valid, this approach equated the term of the reverse payment settlement with the remaining life of the patent.[676] By ruling that a reverse payment agreement was within the "scope of the patent," courts automatically accepted that the patent at issue was valid and had been infringed, rendering the rebuttable presumption of patent validity into an irrebuttable presumption of infringement.[677] It was thus presumed that the exclusion of the generic

---

669. KUTCHER, Waiting Is the Hardest Part, 2013, pp. 1128-1129. See also U.S., Amicus Brief, In re K-Dur, p. 15, "The standard adopted below inappropriately permits patent holders to contract their way out of the statutorily imposed litigation risks of invalidation [...] while in effect claiming antitrust immunity for that private contract."
670. 35 U.S.C. § 282(a).
671. See for instance W.L. Gore & Assocs., Inc. v. Garlock, Inc., 721 F.2d 1540, 1553 (Fed. Cir. 1983), "[t]he presumption has no separate evidentiary value. It cautions the decisionmaker against a rush to conclude invalidity."
672. Stratoflex, Inc. v. Aeroquip Corp., 713 F.2d 1530, 1534 (Fed. Cir. 1983), "[t]he presumption, like all legal presumptions, is a procedural device, not substantive law. It does require the decisionmaker to employ a decisional approach that starts with acceptance of the patent claims as valid and that looks to the challenger for proof of the contrary."
673. Corrected Brief for 28 Professors of Law, Business and Economics as *Amici Curiae* Supporting Appellants *In re Ciprofloxacin Hydrochloride Antitrust Litig.*, (No. 2008-1097) (February 8, 2008), p. 12.
674. *In Re: K-Dur Antitrust Litigation*, 686 F.3d 197, 214, citing *Stratoflex, Inc. v. Aeroquip Corp.*, 713 F. 2d 1530, 1534 (Fed. Cir. 1983).
675. CARRIER, Scope of the Patent Test, 2012, pp. 6-7.
676. HOVENKAMP, Scope of the Patent, 2015, pp. 532-533.
677. 118 Professors Amici Brief, pp. 21-22. See also HOVENKAMP, Reverse Payment, 2011, pp. 16-17, arguing that courts putting emphasis on the presumption of patent validity seem to ignore the

manufacturer from the market would ultimately occur, regardless of whether the parties would litigate or settle.[678] Additionally, by extending the presumption of patent validity to the substance of the patent, these decisions in essence rendered every decision of the US Patent and Trademark Office (USPTO) into a final decision,[679] despite the fact that patents simply represent a legal conclusion reached by the USPTO.[680] There are objective reasons for which patents should not be treated as ironclad, linked to the challenges faced by the USPTO in terms of both time and resources. As FARRELL and SHAPIRO noted, in 2008 the USPTO issued per month about 15,000 patents; a patent examiner normally devoted about fifteen to twenty hours for every patent application, while a substantial percentage of the patents that were subsequently evaluated at trial were found to be invalid.[681] The number of patent grants seems to be skyrocketing year by year: in 2015 the USPTO issued 325,979 patents,[682] while 373,093 patents were issued in 2017.[683]

2 *Refusing to Examine the Validity of the Underlying Patent*

Courts applying the scope of the patent test to reverse payment settlements did not consider that the analysis of the validity of the underlying patents was either necessary or appropriate in the absence of fraud or sham litigation.[684] On the basis of the presumption of patent validity, settlements were not unlawful if they served to protect that to which the patent holder is legally entitled to: the monopoly over the manufacture and distribution of the patented invention.[685] The law was interpreted so as to allow the settlement of patent infringement suits even if they involved weak patents: such settlements were merely an *extension* of a valid patent monopoly.[686]

These courts acknowledged the risk of protecting undeserved patent monopolies which rested on patents of dubious quality; the less sound the patent was and the less certain its infringement by a generic drug, the more the scope of the patent test benefited the patent holder by allowing it to exclude generic competition on the basis of a weak or even invalid patent.[687] Nevertheless, encouraging the settlement of

---

question of whether the patent at issue is infringed by the generic manufacturer's product; if it is not, the agreement resembles a naked market division agreement.
678. KUTCHER, Waiting is the Hardest Part, 2013, p. 1131, fn. 238.
679. KUTCHER, Waiting is the Hardest Part, 2013, p. 1128.
680. *In Re: K-Dur Antitrust Litigation,* 686 F.3d 197, 214-215 (3rd Cir. 2012), citing *Lear, Inc. v. Adkins,* 89 S. Ct. 1902, 1911(1969).
681. FARRELL, SHAPIRO, Weak Patents, 2008, p. 1347, fn. 1, noting that in fiscal year 2006, the PTO issued 183,000 patents, while from 1998 until 2008, it issued 1.7 million patents; in contrast, the European Patent Office issued 63,000 patents in 2006.
682. PTMT, *Patent Statistic,* 1963-2015. It should also be noted that in 2015, the PTO received 629,647 patent applications, whereas in 2010 it had received 520,277 patent applications.
683. USPTO, *2017 Performance and Accountability Report,* p. 27.
684. *In re Ciprofloxacin Hydrochloride Antitrust Litig.,* 544 F. 3d 1323, 1336-1337 (Fed. Cir. 2008).
685. *In re Ciprofloxacin Hydrochloride Antitrust Litig.,* 544 F. 3d 1323, 1337 (Fed. Cir. 2008). The court referred to *In re Tamoxifen Citrate Antitrust Litigation,* 466 F.3d 187, 208-209 (2nd Cir. 2006).
686. *In re Tamoxifen Citrate Antitrust Litigation,* 466 F.3d 187, 211 (2nd Cir. 2006).
687. *In re Tamoxifen Citrate Antitrust Litigation,* 466 F.3d 187, 210-211 (2nd Cir. 2006).

disputes was considered to be more important that putting an end to settlements protecting undeserved patent monopolies.[688] Even though large reverse payments indicated the patent holder's doubts on the patent's strength or breadth, courts deemed it unwise to consider the patent at issue invalid on the basis of the patent holder's fear of losing it.[689] Courts applying the scope of the patent test considered it was "too late in the journey" to adopt the alternative rule of allowing only settlements concerning valid patents that were lawfully conferring monopoly power to their holders.[690] Nevertheless, the Supreme Court did not share this view and rejected the application of the scope of the patent test for reverse payment settlements, as is extensively analysed in Chapter 4 of this book.

B Antitrust Immunity Granted by Weak or Invalid Patents

Patent exceptionalism is the view that antitrust law should yield in the presence of a patent, since patents carve out an exception to the applicability of antitrust laws.[691] The roots of patent exceptionalism are located in the decision of the Supreme Court in *United States v. General Electric*, which allowed a patentee to conclude a licensing agreement fixing the sale price with its competitor.[692] This decision was widely criticised by the US government of that time and by antitrust specialists for providing antitrust immunity to naked price fixing, hidden under the guise of an intellectual property licensing agreement.[693] The Supreme Court later on explained that ruling, stating that patent laws which accord a monopoly on an invention are *"in pari materia* with the antitrust laws and modify them *pro tanto.*"[694] Patent exceptionalism was a core notion in the analysis of reverse payment settlements under the scope of the patent test, whereby the existence of a patent in essence sanctified the restrictions imposed by these settlements, rendering them untouchable to antitrust scrutiny.

1 The High Rates of Patent Invalidation

One of the main criticisms against the scope of the patent test is that it failed to take into consideration the high invalidation rates of patents which have been the object of

---

688. *In re Tamoxifen Citrate Antitrust Litigation*, 466 F.3d 187, 211 (2nd Cir. 2006), "[s]o long as the law encourages settlement, weak patent cases will likely be settled even though such settlements will inevitably protect patent monopolies that are, perhaps, undeserved."
689. *In re Tamoxifen Citrate Antitrust Litigation*, 466 F.3d 187, 210 (2nd Cir. 2006).
690. *In re Tamoxifen Citrate Antitrust Litigation*, 466 F.3d 187, 212 (2nd Cir. 2006).
691. *See* for instance *Schering-Plough*, 402 F.3d 1056, 1065-1066, arguing that by their nature patents create an environment of exclusion and thus cripple competition. *See* further, FELDMAN, Patent Exceptionalism, 2014, pp. 66-72, discussing the origins of patent exceptionalism and the influence that the *FTC v. Actavis* decision had in arguably putting an end to it.
692. *See* HEMPHILL, Paying for Delay, 2006, pp. 1600-1601; *United States v. General Electric*, 47 S. Ct. 192, 196 (1926), ruling that a licensor patent holder may impose the condition that sales by the licensee should be at prices fixed by the licensor and subject to change at his discretion.
693. HOVENKAMP, JANIS, LEMLEY, Anticompetitive Settlements, 2003, p. 1747.
694. *Simpson v. Union Oil Co.*, 84 S. Ct. 1051, 1058 (1964), concerning a consignment lease programme achieving a resale price maintenance.

reverse payment settlements. According to a relevant FTC study, generics prevailed in 73% of Hatch-Waxman patent infringement suits that were litigated between 1992 and 2002.[695] The Royal Bank of Canada (RBC) Capital Markets report concluded that from 2000 to 2009, generic challengers have prevailed in 48% of the cases that have gone to trial;[696] however, when one takes into consideration patent settlements and the cases that were dropped, the success rate of generic challengers climbs up to 76%.[697]

Other statistical studies relating to patent invalidation in the litigation of patent infringement suits – not exclusively in the Hatch-Waxman context – confirm that there is reason for concern. According to an empirical study by ALLISON and LEMLEY, 46% of the patents challenged in patent litigation before the US Court of Appeal for the Federal Circuit were found to be invalid between 1989 and 1996.[698] The statistics of the University of Houston Law Center demonstrate that the percentages of patent invalidation through litigation remained relatively stable throughout the years: in 2013, accused patent infringers prevailed in 42% of litigated cases concerning patent validity.[699] Between 2000 and 2009, the most litigated patents – the patents that received the most challenges – fared quite bad in patent litigation: patentees won in only 10.7% of the cases.[700] The parties settled in 90.5% of the patent litigation cases concerning the most litigated patents.[701] There were far more findings of invalidity than findings of non-infringement: the relevant patents were found to be invalid in 69.7% of the cases.[702] According to a 2015 study, approximately one-third of patents that are litigated to final judgment are found to be invalid. Out of the remaining two-thirds of patents that are found to be valid, almost one-fourth are found not infringed.[703]

The USPTO's process of patent approval could provide a possible explanation for the high percentage of subsequent patent invalidation. The total average time a patent examiner spends on a patent application is a maximum of eighteen hours. During that time, the examiner must read the patent application, search and identify relevant prior art, decide whether the patent application should be allowed by comparing the patent

---

695. FTC, *Generic Drug Entry*, 2002, p. 13, demonstrating that generic challengers prevailed in 73% of paragraph IV challenges that were litigated before courts between 1992 and 2002; *In Re: K-Dur Antitrust Litigation*, 686 F.3d 197, 215.
696. RBC, Litigation Success Rates, 2010, p. 4. According to RBC's report, from 2000 to 2009, generic challengers prevailed in 82 of the rulings and lost in 89 of them.
697. RBC, Litigation Success Rates, 2010, p. 4.
698. ALLISON, LEMLEY, Empirical Evidence, 1998, pp. 187, 205. *See also idem* p. 209, Table 2, "Success of Particular Grounds of Invalidity:" interestingly, the most frequent grounds on which courts invalidated the patents concerned were: (1) obviousness of the patent (58 out of 300 cases); (2) Section 102 Non-Prior Art (43 out of 300 cases), and; (3) Section 102 Prior-Art (37 out of 300 cases).
699. UNIVERSITY OF HOUSTON LAW CENTER, PATSTATS: U.S. Patent Litigation Statistics, *Rulings in 2013*, Validity Decisions, 01-16. Available at: http://www.patstats.org/2013_Full_Year_Posting.html. (last accessed on March 31, 2018). According to the statistics accused patent infringers prevailed in 133 out of 316 validity decisions (42%), while patent owners prevailed in 183 out of 316 validity decisions (approximately 58%).
700. ALLISON, LEMLEY, WALKER, Patent Quality, 2011, pp. 687-689.
701. ALLISON, LEMLEY, WALKER, Patent Quality, 2011, p. 689.
702. ALLISON, LEMLEY, WALKER, Patent Quality, 2011, pp. 706-707, stating that in 60 out of 86 cases involved findings of patent invalidity.
703. TU, Invalidated Patents, 2015, pp. 151-152.

claims to the prior art and write an office action explaining why any patent claims were rejected.[704] The USPTO was criticised numerous times for the poor quality of the examination of patent applications. Indicatively, the above-mentioned 2015 study argues that in the sample of patents analysed approximately 77 % of prior art references – the most common basis used to invalidate patents in subsequent litigation – were not found by the USPTO during the examination of the respective patent applications.[705] A possible solution in order to increase the quality of patent grants would be to increase the time spent on the examination of patent applications,[706] even though the efficiency of such a solution is debatable.[707] Another proposal would be to change the legal standards applied by the USPTO in the examination of patent applications, instead of amending its level of effort.[708] Currently, the USPTO must carry the burden to provide a reason *not* to issue the patent sought;[709] reversing this burden and requiring patent applicants to carry the burden of proving their invention is patentable could be a possible solution.[710]

The effect of patent litigation on stock market evaluations is enormous: companies may lose up to 0.85 % of their value subsequent to a court decision invalidating a patent, but only gain 0.7 % after a "valid and infringed" finding.[711] It is thus unsurprising that patent holders do not only focus on keeping competitors outside the market but also on keeping their patents *in* the market.[712] For a patentee, the value of resolving the legal uncertainty over the validity or infringement of a patent is arguably equal to the value of the initial patent grant, a paradigm that indicates the size of illegal uncertainty on the issue of patent validity.[713] Given the high rates of patent invalidation or non-infringement findings and the extremely high financial stakes of brand-name drug manufacturers, especially on patents of blockbuster drugs – reverse payment settlements were a means for the holder of a weak patent to buy its way out of both immediate generic competition and the possibility of patent invalidation.[714]

---

704. Lemley, Rational Ignorance, 2001, p. 1500; Thomas J.R., Patent Bounties, 2001, p. 314, estimating that time to sixteen to seventeen hours per patent application.
705. Tu, Invalidated Patents, 2015, pp. 159-163. See 35 U.S.C. §§ 102, 103 on the requirements of novelty, prior art and non-obviousness.
706. Lemley, Rational Ignorance, 2001, pp. 1508-1509, proposing that the average time of eighteen hours a patent examiner spends on average per patent application should be doubled.
707. Moore, Worthless Patents, 2005, pp. 1551-1552, noting that it would be inefficient to spend more time evaluating worthless patent applications.
708. Lemley, Rational Ignorance, 2001, p. 1524.
709. See for example *In re Werner Kotzab*, 217 F.3d 1365, 1371 (Fed. Cir. 2000).
710. Lemley, Rational Ignorance, 2001, p. 1524.
711. Henry, Market Effects, 2013, pp. 57, 63-64.
712. Marco, Vishnubhakat, Certain Patents, 2013, pp. 119-120, 130-132.
713. Marco, Vishnubhakat, Certain Patents, 2013, pp. 104-105, 132-133.
714. *In Re: K-Dur Antitrust Litigation*, 686 F.3d 197, 215. The 3rd Circuit also referred to *In re Tamoxifen Citrate Antitrust Litigation*, 466 F.3d 187, 211 (2nd Cir. 2006), which recognised that risk, despite applying the scope of the patent test.

2 The Patent Right Does Not Legitimise an Exclusion Payment

The Patent Act was used as a standard argument by the patent holders that insisted on an innovation-protective antitrust policy, seeking an exception to the ordinary function of antitrust laws.[715] On the flipside, plaintiffs in reverse payment settlement cases repeatedly argued that the Patent Act does not shield private settlement agreements from the possibility of antitrust liability.[716] The patent right itself does not legitimise a payment from the patentee to the alleged generic infringers in order for the latter to stay out of the market; any exclusion from the market achieved through a payment and not through judicial enforcement should not be shielded from antitrust liability.[717]

On the basis of the Supreme Court's jurisprudence, the existence of a patent does not exempt agreements between competitors from antitrust scrutiny under the Sherman Act.[718] Reverse payment settlements between originators and generics are excluding competition irrespectively of the weakness or the narrowness of the patent claim, offering an opportunity that is *not* provided by the patent system itself. Quite the contrary: it is possible that weak patents are invalidated through patent litigation. Moreover, it should be stressed that narrow patents cannot legitimately block the entry of non-infringing generic drugs to the market.[719] The *source of exclusion* in reverse payment settlements is the payment and not the patent, so that any underlying patent rights cannot justify the exclusion of the generic filer from the market.[720] Patent policy awards exclusion only on the basis of the patent's power while it is clear that an exclusion payment is not included on the patentee's right to exclude.[721] This power to

---

715. HEMPHILL, Paying for Delay, 2006, pp. 1600-1601.
716. U.S., *Amicus* Brief, *In re K-Dur*, p. 15, "[t]he Patent Act does not, however, shield such private agreements from the possibility of antitrust liability."
717. *Valley Drug Co. v. Geneva Pharms, Inc.*, 344 F.3d 1294, 1309 (11th Cir. 2003).
718. Brief for the FTC as *Amicus Curiae* Supporting Appellants and Urging Reversal, *In re K-Dur Antitrust Litigation*, (Nos. 10-2078, 10-2077, 10-2079) (May 18, 2011), p. 20 [cited as: FTC, *Amicus* Brief, *In re K-Dur*]. The FTC referred to *United States v. Masonite Corp.*, 62 S. Ct. 1070, 1077 (1942), "[t]he owner of a patent cannot extend his statutory grant by contract or agreement. A patent affords no immunity for a monopoly not fairly or plainly within the grant;" *United States v. Line Material Co.*, 68 S. Ct. 550, 561 (1948), "[i]t is equally well settled that the possession of a valid patent or patents does not give the patentee any exemption from the provisions of the Sherman Act beyond the limits of the patent monopoly. By aggregating patents in one control, the holder of the patents cannot escape the prohibitions of the Sherman Act;" *United States v. Singer Mfg. Co.*, 83 S. Ct. 1773, 1785-1787 (1963) (Justice White concurring), "[t]he patent laws do not authorize, and the Sherman Act does not permit, such agreements between business rivals to encroach upon the public domain and usurp it to themselves."
719. FTC, *Amicus* Brief, *In re K-Dur*, p. 21.
720. ABBOTT, MICHEL, Right Balance, 2005, pp. 12-13. *See also idem* p. 18: "[t]he scope of the patent grant does not include the right to pay potential competitors to stay off the market, because the source of the exclusion is the payment, not the exclusionary power of the patent. Because the payment falls outside the scope of the patent grant, antitrust law must judge its legality."
721. ABBOTT, MICHEL, Right Balance, 2005, p. 19, "[T]he presumption of validity does not alter the fundamental nature of an exclusion payment as the purchase of exclusion that could not have been obtained through the power of the patent. Nor does it alter the patent policy that awards exclusion based only on the power of the patent."

exclude alleged infringers is neither absolute nor defined by the patentee's unilateral views on the coverage of its patent, until there is a final court ruling on patent validity and infringement.[722]

The size and the scope of patent protection are directly linked to the profits of the patent holder and its incentives to engage in R&D; the greater that scope is, the greater the patent holder's profits and incentives to innovate will be.[723] However, there is also an economic *rationale* against extending the scope of patent protection so as to include the right to pay a competitor to stay out of the market and opting instead for "adjusting" the scope of patent protection so as to treat some conduct of the patent holder as infringing and other as legitimate. It would be rational to treat as legitimate conduct that is profitable at a comparatively low social cost and to consider as infringing behaviours which result in high total costs per dollar of profit.[724] Extending the scope of patent protection so as to include payments to generic entrants in order for them to refrain from entering the market would amount to legitimising a behaviour which results in extremely high social costs per dollar of profit. Not only would such a legitimisation make no legal sense from a patent law perspective – since the scope of patent protection in no way covers exclusion payments and the cartelisation of markets – but also from a consumer welfare perspective.

3   Patent Validity as a Criterion for the Legality of Settlements

Another point of debate was whether courts adjudicating reverse payment settlements should examine the validity of the underlying patent or the merits of the patent infringement suit. Some antitrust experts argued that a reverse payment settlement could be legal if the patent at issue was valid and the agreement did not extend the patent holder's monopoly beyond the patent's scope.[725] There were voices advocating in favour of a "trial within a trial," permitting courts at least a limited inquiry into patent validity before examining the antitrust claims at issue.[726] A more radical view was that considering the merits of the patent infringement suit should be seen as inappropriate since the question of whether a settlement is illegal under antitrust law should not depend on the strength of the underlying patent. A patent holder and a generic challenger that settled using a reverse payment to share the resulting monopoly rents should be found to violate antitrust law, even if the underlying patent was indeed valid.[727] In case the underlying patent was valid, a patent holder should be sufficiently

---

722. ABBOTT, MICHEL, Right Balance, 2005, p. 12.
723. SHAVELL, *Foundations of Economic Analysis*, 2004, pp. 146-147.
724. SHAVELL, *Foundations of Economic Analysis*, 2004, p. 147.
725. HOVENKAMP, JANIS, LEMLEY, Anticompetitive Settlements, 2003, p. 1735.
726. HOVENKAMP, JANIS, LEMLEY, Anticompetitive Settlements, 2003, pp. 1734-1735; COTTER, Refining Presumptive Illegality, 2003, pp. 1811-1812; GRAHAM, Terazosin Test, 2006, pp. 443-446. See however O'ROURKE, BRODLEY, Preliminary Views, 2002, p. 53, "any precise identification of the antitrust risk would require assessment of patent validity and scope. But these issues can only be fully resolved through patent litigation, and settlement precludes litigation. The alternative of assessing probable validity and infringement in an antitrust proceeding fails to provide a tractable or predictive legal standard."
727. *See* for instance OKADA, Beyond the Scope, 2012, p. 330.

protected simply by relying *on the patent itself* in order to exclude competitors from the market before the end of the patent's term.[728]

As CARRIER stressed already in 2012, the fact that a settlement extending beyond the scope of the patent violates antitrust laws does not suggest that a settlement *within* the facial patent scope is automatically valid; such settlements could also violate antitrust laws, depending on whether the patent at issue is valid or not.[729] It was argued that if the patent at issue was valid, then an agreement under which a patent holder pays the generic to drop its challenge and to postpone its entry to the market could fall within the patent's scope and would not pose antitrust concerns.[730] Nevertheless, one should bear in mind that if the source of exclusion of generic competition from the market is a value transfer from the patent holder to the generic manufacturer, such an agreement would still be problematic from an antitrust law perspective. On the contrary, if a patent is not valid, it does not have *any* exclusionary scope and the patent holder is not entitled to pay the generic challenger in order to delay its entry to the market, since such an agreement would be similar to a market allocation agreement.[731] DOLIN agreed that in order to determine whether a reverse settlement was pro or anticompetitive, one should examine the strength of the patent and what the likely conclusion of the parties' litigation would be.[732] Following a similar line of reasoning, SHAPIRO argued that a patent holder's assertion that its patent was valid and infringed by a rival did not entitle it to "negotiate a monopoly outcome;" rather, the patent holders' rights should be measured according to the probability for it to win the infringement lawsuit, in conjunction with the breadth of exclusion that such a victory would allow.[733] It was also sustained that in order to evaluate the legitimacy of a settlement agreement, the court assessing the antitrust suit needed to determine both the objective odds for each party to prevail in the patent infringement litigation suit, but also of the likely dates of generic entry under alternative litigation outcomes.[734] However, it is difficult to imagine how such determinations could be made by courts in practice and on the basis of which criteria, allowing the verification of their objectivity.

---

728. CARRIER, Scope of the Patent Test, 2012, p. 6.
729. CARRIER, Scope of the Patent Test, 2012, p. 5.
730. CARRIER, Scope of the Patent Test, 2012, p. 6.
731. *Idem. See also* CRANE, Exit Payments, 2002, p. 761, stressing the social cost in permitting to the patentee to enjoy monopoly rents in case a patent is invalid or the generic product is not infringing it.
732. DOLIN, Patent Invalidity Signals, 2011, p. 282, also arguing that what is missing from the antitrust analysis is that settlements are detrimental to consumers only in case the generic challenger would have prevailed in the litigation. DOLIN proposes a patent law solution to the problem of reverse settlements through patent reexamination.
733. SHAPIRO, Antitrust Limits, 2003, p. 395.
734. ADDANKI, DASKIN, Patent Settlement Agreements, 2008, pp. 2136-2138. *See idem* at pp. 2138-2139, ADDANKI and DASKIN arguing that there is no substitute for a fact-specific analysis of reverse payment agreements agreement and their context.

4 The Probabilistic Nature of the Patent Right

The high rates of patent invalidation led some experts argue that a patent should be perceived as granting a "probabilistic" and not an actual property right.[735] The advocates of the probabilistic nature of patents argued that the majority of patents represented highly uncertain or "probabilistic" property rights, being in essence "lottery tickets."[736] In any case, the patent grant only entitles the patent holder to sue and try to prevent others from infringing its patent, but does not guarantee that the patent shall be declared valid or that the defendant in the patent infringement suit has indeed infringed it. Put plainly, a patent does not provide "the right to exclude" but rather the "right to *try* to exclude."[737]

Not everybody agreed that patent rights are merely probabilistic; the adversaries of this theory argued that there was no reason to treat patents as more probabilistic than any other kind of property.[738] The US legal system does not recognise the notion that "property is not property until a court says so," whereas plaintiffs cannot substitute the *possibility* of harm for *actual* harm in no area of law.[739] The theory of probabilistic patent rights was seen as a mere evasion of the presumption of patent validity, which could never replace the application of a rule of reason analysis to patent settlements, combined with the examination of patent validity.[740] Rather than going as far as to consider patents as probabilistic property rights, antitrust courts and enforcement authorities could instead examine the specificities of each patent settlement and focus their inquiry on the *source* of any exclusion or limitation of generic competition in the market: the exclusionary power of the patent or an anticompetitive collusive agreement?

5 Invalid Patents Offering Antitrust Immunity

Courts applying the scope of the patent test did not consider that the subsequent invalidation of the patent at issue was a sufficient reason to apply antitrust scrutiny to reverse payment settlements. In *Valley Drug* the relevant patent was found invalid after the conclusion of the settlement agreements.[741] Even though the plaintiffs argued that

---

735. AYRES, KLEMPERER, Perverse Benefits, 1999, pp. 985-1033; SHAPIRO, Antitrust Limits, 2003, p. 395.
736. LEMLEY, SHAPIRO, Probabilistic Patents, 2005, pp. 80-83.
737. SHAPIRO, Antitrust Limits, 2003, p. 395. *See also* LEFFLER & LEFFLER, Pay a Competitor, 2002, on the probabilistic nature of patent rights.
738. MCDONALD, False Positives, 2003, pp. 68-69; DOLIN, Patent Invalidity Signals, 2011, p. 317.
739. MCDONALD, False Positives, 2003, pp. 71-72.
740. MCDONALD, False Positives, 2003, p. 75. *See also* SHAPIRO, Settlements Between Rivals, 2003, pp. 73-76, and LEFFLER & LEFFLER, Response to Kevin McDonald, 2003, pp. 77-82, rebutting the criticisms expressed in MCDONALD's article.
741. The patent was declared invalid on September 1, 1998, and the invalidity judgment was confirmed on January 10, 2000. *See Abbott Labs. v. Geneva Pharms., Inc., et al.*, 1998 U.S. Dist. Nos. 96-C-3331, 96-C-5868, & 97-C-7587, (N.D. Ill. September 1, 1998), pp. 6-7. Claim 4 of the '207 patent was held invalid on the basis of 35 U.S.C. § 102(b), because the crystalline form of terazosin hydrochloride claimed in the patent was sold in the US more than one year before Abbott applied for the patent. Abbott appealed to the Court of Appeals for the Federal Circuit,

an invalidated patent was not relevant to the court's antitrust analysis, the 11th Circuit found that the reasonableness of agreements with regard to antitrust law was to be judged at the time these agreements were entered into.[742] Since at the time of the settlements the patent was still valid and the applicants had not alleged neither that it was procured by fraud nor that the settling parties knew it was invalid, the subsequent invalidity of the patent did not render it irrelevant to the antitrust analysis.[743] The court held that it would be undermining the incentives offered by patent law if it were to expose the settling parties to antitrust liability merely because the patent was subsequently declared invalid.[744] Taking into consideration the invalidation of the patent would give rise to considerable uncertainty and could potentially discourage the settlement of patent validity challenges; the settlement options would be restricted, the cost of patent enforcement would be augmented and the incentives for disclosure and innovation would be impaired.[745]

Valley Drug was not the only reverse payment settlement case where the relevant patent was found to be invalid. In *Tamoxifen*, Zeneca's patent covering the drug Tamoxifen was found to be invalid by the district court.[746] While Zeneca's appeal against the district court's invalidation decision was pending, Zeneca and Barr entered into a confidential settlement agreement.[747] The 2nd Circuit took into consideration subsequent court decisions on patent infringement suits of Zeneca against other generic challengers, which upheld the validity of Zeneca's patent.[748] The court insisted that absent fraud or extension of the patentee's monopoly beyond the patent's scope, the remaining question was whether the underlying infringement suits were objectively baseless. The 2nd Circuit concluded that the payments to settle the dispute, even if excessive, were not necessarily unlawful despite the subsequent patent invalidation.[749] In her dissenting opinion in *Tamoxifen*, Judge Pooler criticised the majority's finding that a patent must be presumed valid on appeal and argued that it was

---

which affirmed the lower court's summary judgment in *Abbott Labs. v. Geneva Pharms., Inc.*, 182 F.3d 1315, 1318-1319 (Fed. Cir. 1999). Abbott's petition for *certiorari* was denied in *Abbott Lab. v. Geneva Pharms., Inc.*, 120 S. Ct. 796 (2000).
742. *Valley Drug Co. v. Geneva Pharms, Inc.*, 344 F.3d 1294, 1306 (11th Cir. 2003).
743. *Valley Drug Co. v. Geneva Pharms, Inc.*, 344 F.3d 1294, 1306-1307 (11th Cir. 2003).
744. *Valley Drug Co. v. Geneva Pharms, Inc.*, 344 F.3d 1294, 1308 (11th Cir. 2003).
745. *Valley Drug Co. v. Geneva Pharms*, Inc., 344 F.3d 1294, 1308-1309 (11th Cir. 2003). However, the court accepted an exception to this rule in cases where antitrust liability would not undermine the encouragement of genuine invention and disclosure.
746. *Imperial Chem. Indus., PLC v. Barr Labs., Inc.*, 795 F. Supp. 619, 626-627, 629 (S.D.N.Y. 1992), "U.S. Patent 4,536,516 (PEX 200) covering tamoxifen is invalid and is unenforceable by the plaintiff ICI because ICI deliberately, knowingly and fraudulently with purpose to deceive and mislead with respect to material matters: a) withheld from the PTO information material to its evaluation of the patent application [...]; b) withheld the same information in the specifications of the patent." The decision of the district court was vacated by *Imperial Chem. Indus., PLC v. Heumann Pharma GmbH & Co.*, 991 F.2d 811, (Fed. Cir. 1993) (unpublished opinion).
747. *In re Tamoxifen Citrate Antitrust Litigation*, 466 F.3d 187, 193-194 (2nd Cir. 2006).
748. *Zeneca Ltd. v. Novopharm Ltd.*, No. 96-1364; *Zeneca Ltd. v. Pharmachemie B.V.*, No. 96-12413 (D. Mass. 2000); *AstraZeneca UK Ltd. v. Mylan Pharms., Inc.*, No. 00-2239 (W.D. Pa. November 30, 2000).
749. *In re Tamoxifen Citrate Antitrust Litigation*, 466 F.3d 187, 213 (2nd Cir. 2006).

impossible to consider Zeneca's patent as presumptively valid; such a ruling virtually implied that the district court's finding that Zeneca's patent was invalid was entitled to no deference.[750]

C Ignoring the Issue of Patent Infringement

One of the major problems in the application of the scope of the patent test to reverse payment settlements was that it virtually ignored the issue of patent infringement. In a patent infringement suit against a generic paragraph IV filer, a patent holder should normally prove: (1) that the relevant patent is valid, and; (2) that the generic filer's drug infringes the patent.[751] Under the scope of the patent test the question of whether the patent at issue was indeed infringed by the generic drug was never examined. It should be highlighted that even if a patent is indeed valid, this does not automatically mean that it is infringed by the relevant generic drug. Notably, 23.7% of patents that are found to be valid in a final judgment on patent litigation are also found not to be infringed.[752] When it comes to pharmaceuticals, different kinds of patents have different exclusionary potential: while patents covering the compound of a drug will normally be infringed by *all* generic drug versions, secondary patents – covering for instance the process for the production of the compound – cannot exclude from the market generic drug products that use other processes. In any case, a patent does not provide to the patent holder the right to exclude rivals *allegedly* infringing it, absent a court order confirming such infringement.[753] A payment to an *alleged* infringer to stay out of the market, which aims to exclude *allegedly* infringing competition goes beyond the patent grant and damages consumers.[754]

1 The Burden to Prove Patent Infringement Is on the Patent Holder

Under the scope of the patent test, the litigated issue in the underlying patent infringement suits of patentees against the generic challengers was largely ignored. Courts not only accepted that the relevant patents were valid but also presumed that patent holders would have prevailed in the underlying patent infringement litigation.[755] By granting antitrust immunity to reverse payment settlements on the basis of the presumption of patent validity, courts in essence presumed that patentees could exclude *all* generic competitors from entering the market for the entire duration of the

---

750. *In re Tamoxifen Citrate Antitrust Litigation*, 466 F.3d 187, 230 (2nd Cir. 2006), (Judge Pooler dissenting).
751. CARRIER, Scope of the Patent Test, 2012, p. 7. *See also SmithKline Diagnostics, Inc. v. Helena Labs. Corp.*, 859 F. 2d 878, 889 (Fed. Cir. 1988), placing the burden of proving patent infringement on the patent owner.
752. TU, Invalidated Patents, 2015, pp. 151-152.
753. LEMLEY, SHAPIRO, Probabilistic Patents, 2005, pp. 93-94.
754. *See* further, SHAPIRO, Settlements Between Rivals, 2003, pp. 71-73.
755. *See* for instance *In Re: K-Dur Antitrust Litigation*, 686 F.3d 197, 214, criticising the application of the scope of the patent test to reverse payment settlements.

patent term. This simplistic scope of the patent test allowed courts to dispose of the issue of infringement merely by observing the existence of the patent.[756]

There is a major difference between patent validity and infringement: in patent validity cases, the patentee can rely on the initial presumption that its patent is valid; on the contrary, in patent infringement cases, the burden of demonstrating infringement lies on the patent holder.[757] As above-analysed, a generic challenger filing a paragraph IV ANDA may either certify that the relevant patent(s) covering the brand-name drug is invalid or that it will not be infringed by the manufacture, use and sale of the generic drug.[758] When a generic challenger files a paragraph IV ANDA stating that its generic drug does not infringe the relevant patent, the patent holder shall carry the burden of proving the infringement of its patent.[759]

Courts should differentiate between the cases in which a paragraph IV challenger certified that the patent was invalid and the cases in which the generic challenger certified that the patent was not infringed by the generic drug version.[760] Notably, when a generic challenger certifies non-infringement, patent validity may be irrelevant, since the patent holder is not accorded the right to exclude non-infringing products.[761] In such cases, it would be sufficient for courts to assess the grounds of patent infringement, while the burden of proof should be carried by the patent holder. A settlement excluding from the market generic versions which are not infringing the patent is likely to be a per se violation of antitrust laws even in the absence of a reverse payment.[762]

2 The Size of the Payment Indicates Patent Invalidity or Non-infringement

Courts applying the scope of the patent test recognised that the magnitude of a reverse payment may raise suspicions on the parties' conviction regarding the validity of the relevant patent.[763] Nevertheless, they denied that it could be inferred by the size of the payment alone that the patent infringement suit lacked merit,[764] since even a patentee confident on the validity of its patent was likely to pay an alleged infringer a large

---

756. CARRIER, Scope of the Patent Test, 2012, p. 8.
757. CARRIER, Scope of the Patent Test, 2012, p. 7. CARRIER also referred to *Egyptian Goddess, Inc. v. Swisa, Inc.*, 543 F.3d 665, 679 (Fed. Cir. 2008), where the court stated that "[t]he patentee bears the ultimate burden of proof to demonstrate infringement by a preponderance of the evidence." See also *Under Sea Indus., Inc. v. Dacor Corp.*, 833 F.2d 1551, 1557 (Fed. Cir. 1987), citing *Envirotech Corp. v. Al George, Inc.*, 730 F.2d 753, 758 (Fed. Cir. 1984), "[t]he burden always is on the patentee to show infringement."
758. 21 U.S.C. § 355(j)(2)(A)(ii)(vi)(IV); see further *supra* Chapter 2, Part 2, Section II.D.
759. In Re: *K-Dur Antitrust Litigation*, 686 F.3d 197, 214. The court referred to *Egyptian Goddess, Inc. v. Swisa, Inc.*, 543 F. 3d 665, 679 (Fed. Cir. 2008). See also ABBOTT, MICHEL, Right Balance, 2005, p. 11; SANDOVAL, Covenants Not to Sue, 2009-2010, pp. 163-170, stressing that the presumption of patent validity does not apply to patent infringement cases and that the patent holder still needs to carry the burden of making a prima facie case of infringement.
760. THOMAS, Lawful Reverse Payments, 2007, p. 37.
761. Idem.
762. Idem.
763. *Valley Drug Co. v. Geneva Pharms, Inc.*, 344 F.3d 1294, 1310 (11th Cir. 2003); *In re Tamoxifen Citrate Antitrust Litigation*, 466 F.3d 187, 208-209 (2nd Cir. 2006).
764. *Valley Drug Co. v. Geneva Pharms, Inc.*, 344 F.3d 1294, 1310 (11th Cir. 2003).

amount in order to conclude a settlement.[765] Moreover, it was difficult to determine how much of the payment amounted to reimbursement for provisions other that acknowledgement of patent invalidity.[766] On the basis of the *Tamoxifen* decision, as long as the patent litigation at issue was neither a sham nor otherwise baseless, the patent holder making a large reverse payment was aiming to protect its lawful monopoly – a monopoly to which it was presumably entitled to.[767] Courts concluded that it made "economic sense" for a patent holder to pay part of its monopoly profits to the generic challenger, so as to maintain its market for itself; if the amount paid to the generic challenger exceeded the latter's potential profits in case of market entry, it also made "economic sense" for the challenger to settle.[768] A point that did not seem to preoccupy courts applying the scope of the patent test to reverse payments is that conduct which makes economic sense for the colluding parties is not automatically legal under antitrust laws.

Courts applying the scope of the patent test argued that the size of a payment should not affect the availability of the settlement remedy for the parties, since safeguarding the settlement incentives for the litigating parties was of major importance.[769] There were also a number of commentators maintaining that reverse cash payments were not necessarily unlawful and that other factors such as risk aversion or asymmetric information should be assessed in order to provide a definite answer to whether such settlements violate antitrust laws.[770] However, the FTC manifestly disagreed with the view that monetary payments were an indispensable prerequisite for the settlement of Hatch-Waxman litigation; in the absence of payments, parties would have concluded different settlements with possibly earlier generic entry dates.[771] Courts applying the scope of the patent test rejected this position as "myopic," arguing that it ignored the nature of patent litigation and the role reverse payments held in settlements.[772] Interestingly, courts argued that generic challengers could have gained more by entering the generic market, in the absence of the settlements.[773] Nevertheless, there is evidence that the generic challengers' profits by reverse payment

---

765. *Valley Drug Co. v. Geneva Pharms, Inc.*, 344 F.3d 1294, 1310 (11th Cir. 2003). The court cited *Ciprofloxacin Hydrochloride*, 261 F. Supp. 2d 196, 234 (E.D.N.Y. 2003).
766. *Valley Drug Co. v. Geneva Pharms, Inc.*, 344 F.3d 1294, 1310 (11th Cir. 2003).
767. *In re Tamoxifen Citrate Antitrust Litigation*, 466 F.3d 187, 208-209 (2nd Cir. 2006).
768. *In re Tamoxifen Citrate Antitrust Litigation*, 466 F.3d 187, 209-210 (2nd Cir. 2006). Interestingly, the 2nd Circuit acknowledged that in case the generic challenger would win the patent litigation, "the total profits of the patent holder and the generic manufacturer on the drug in the competitive market will be lower than the total profits of the patent holder alone under a patent-conferred monopoly."
769. *Schering-Plough Corp. v. FTC*, 402 F.3d 1056, 1075 (11th Cir. 2005).
770. SHAPIRO, Antitrust Limits, 2003, p. 408. *See also* SCHILDKRAUT, Reverse Payment Fallacy, 2004, pp. 1059-1065, discussing certain commentators' views on risk aversion and arguing that when there is a gap in the litigants' views on the date of generic entry, reverse payment settlements may be the only way to achieve settlement; COTTER, Refining Presumptive Illegality, 2003, pp. 1811-1815, disagreeing with the condemnation of all settlements whose reverse payment exceeded the plaintiff's avoided litigation costs, but inviting courts to remain sceptical of such agreements.
771. *Schering-Plough Corp. v. FTC*, 402 F.3d 1056, 1073 (11th Cir. 2005).
772. *Idem.*
773. *Schering-Plough Corp. v. FTC*, 402 F.3d 1056, 1075 (11th Cir. 2005).

settlements are considerably higher than the profits they would have made by marketing their generic versions of the drug.[774]

A large number of antitrust specialists disagreed with this approach and stressed the importance of the size of reverse payments for the antitrust analysis. HOVENKAMP suggested that a high exit payment should be considered as strong evidence of patent invalidity or of lack of patent infringement by the generic challenger.[775] Other commentators also agreed that the size of an exclusion payment was inversely related to the likelihood for a patentee to prevail in its patent infringement suit.[776] A naked cash payment from the patent holder to the generic manufacturer, which exceeded the avoided litigation costs, should be seen as clear sign that the settlement may be anticompetitive, since a patent holder would only pay the alleged infringer an amount higher than the litigation costs if it believed it was buying later entry than a court would allow, had the litigation continued.[777] As extensively analysed in Chapter 4 of this book, a very similar approach was subsequently adopted by the US Supreme Court. However, the practical difficulty of applying this rule is to determine the accurate value of the avoided litigation costs, since such determination presupposes having access to private information and remains a subjective estimation which cannot be objectively verified.[778] In any case, a high payment from the patent holder to the generic challenger should normally suggest that the former has market power on the relevant market.[779]

IV The Judicial Preference for Settlements

A *Reverse Payments as a Natural Consequence of Hatch-Waxman*

For courts applying the scope of the patent test, reverse payment settlements were "a natural by-product" of the Hatch-Waxman Act and were encouraged by it.[780] Courts made a distinction between ordinary patent infringement cases and patent infringement cases in the context of Hatch-Waxman litigation. Whereas in typical patent infringement cases it was logical for the alleged infringer to pay the patent holder a

---

774. HEMPHILL, Paying for Delay, 2006, pp. 1581-1582, arguing that the first generic filer's profits from settlement are higher than its expected gains had it won the patent infringement suit, since enjoying the exclusivity period with certainty is preferable to an earlier market entry.
775. HOVENKAMP, *Federal Antitrust Policy*, 2011, p. 271, "[s]omeone with good title to a property right does not generally have to pay others not to trespass."
776. HOVENKAMP, JANIS, LEMLEY, Anticompetitive Settlements, 2003, p. 1758. See also JACOBO-RUBIO, TURNER, WILLIAMS, 2016, pp. 31-32, finding that brand-name firms value deterring generic entry much more than generic manufacturers value the right to enter the market.
777. SHAPIRO, Antitrust Limits, 2003, p. 408.
778. *See also infra* Chapter 4, Part 1, Section III.A.2, discussing the difficulty of estimating the expected litigation costs even after the decision of *FTC v. Actavis, Inc.*, 133 S. Ct. 2223 (2013).
779. HOVENKAMP, JANIS, LEMLEY, Anticompetitive Settlements, 2003, p. 1757.
780. *Schering-Plough Corp. v. FTC*, 402 F.3d 1056, 1075 (11th Cir. 2005), "Hatch Waxman Act essentially redistributes the relative risk assessments and explains the flow of settlement funds and their magnitude;" *In re Tamoxifen Citrate Antitrust Litigation*, 466 F.3d 187, 205-206 (2nd Cir. 2006), noting that reverse payment settlements were "to be expected in the drug-patent context because the Hatch-Waxman Act created an environment that encourages them;" *In re Ciprofloxacin Hydrochloride Antitrust Litigation*, 544 F.3d 1323, 1333, fn. 11 (Fed. Cir. 2008), arguing that an exclusion payment "is not unexpected under the Hatch-Waxman Act."

significant amount in order to settle, this was not the case in Hatch-Waxman patent infringement litigation.[781] Under the Hatch-Waxman Act, a generic manufacturer had huge incentives to file a paragraph IV ANDA: if successful, it would benefit from the highly profitable 180-day exclusivity period during which it would be the sole generic seller in the market.[782] On the contrary, the patent holder's risk in losing its infringement suit was huge, amounting to a loss of its patent monopoly.[783] Under the Hatch-Waxman Act, litigation risks were "redistributed" and big exclusion payments from a patentee to a generic challenger were not unexpected.[784] This logic went so far as to not find problematic from an antitrust perspective a settlement clause prohibiting also *future challenges* to the validity of the patent.[785] In *Ciprofloxacin*, the Court of Appeals for the Federal Circuit noted that such a clause was common in patent settlements and concluded that "the mere fact that the Agreements insulated Bayer from patent validity challenges by the generic defendants was not in itself an antitrust violation," especially since the agreements did not seem to impede other generic manufacturers from challenging the validity of the patent.[786]

The two main sponsors of the Hatch-Waxman Act, Senator Hatch and Representative Waxman, did not share the view that reverse payment settlements were a natural consequence of the Act. Senator Hatch characterised reverse payment settlements as "appalling,"[787] whereas Representative Waxman argued that the scope of the patent test "turned on its head" the legislative policy of lowering pharmaceutical prices by enhancing competition.[788] Representative Waxman stressed that the object of the Congress in passing the Hatch-Waxman Act was to draw a line between patent protection and the need to provide incentives for competition in the pharmaceutical industry.[789] The object of the Act was a deliberate effort to promote consumer access to

---

781. In re Tamoxifen Citrate Antitrust Litigation, 466 F.3d 187, 206-207 (2nd Cir. 2006).
782. In re Tamoxifen Citrate Antitrust Litigation, 466 F.3d 187, 207 (2nd Cir. 2006).
783. In re Tamoxifen Citrate Antitrust Litigation, 466 F.3d 187, 206-207 (2nd Cir. 2006). See also, McDonald, Wrong Way, 2002, pp. 9-11, arguing that the Hatch Waxman Act: (1) "dictates" payments from the patent holder to the generic challenger who has a much smaller stake in the pending patent infringement suit, and; (2) increases the possibility of settlement by providing a broad range of settlements that are "rational."
784. In re Ciprofloxacin Hydrochloride Antitrust Litig., 544 F. 3d 1323, 1333 (Fed. Cir. 2008). The court referred to *Schering-Plough Corp. v. FTC*, 402 F.3d 1056, 1074 (11th Cir. 2005).
785. In re Ciprofloxacin Hydrochloride Antitrust Litig., 544 F. 3d 1323, 1333-1334 (Fed. Cir. 2008).
786. Idem. The Court of Appeals for the Federal Circuit referred to the subsequent challenges of the '444 patent by Ranbaxy, Mylan, Schein and Carlsbad to support its position.
787. Senator Hatch Orrin, *On Greater Access to Pharmaceuticals Act*, 148 Cong. Rec. S7565 (July 30, 2002). Available at: http://www.gpo.gov/fdsys/pkg/CREC-2002-07-30/pdf/CREC-2002-07-30-pt1-PgS7565.pdf. (last accessed on March 31, 2018), "[a]s a coauthor of the Drug Price Competition and Patent Term Restoration Act, I can tell you that I find these type of reverse payment collusive arrangements appalling."
788. Representative Henry A. Waxman Brief as *Amicus Curiae* in support of Petitioner for a Writ of Certiorari in *FTC v. Watson Pharmaceuticals, Inc., et al.*, (No. 12-416) (January 29, 2013), p. 25. [cited as: Waxman, *Amicus* Brief, *FTC v. Watson Pharmaceuticals*], "[t]he policy chosen by the Eleventh Circuit, however much it may benefit brand-name manufacturers who wish to preserve their monopoly profits is a bad policy from the perspective of the consumer, precisely the constituency Congress was seeking to protect," quoting *K-Dur Antitrust Litigation*, 686 F.3d 197, 217 [internal quotation marks omitted].
789. Representative Waxman, 130 Cong. Rec. 24425, (September 6, 1984).

affordable drugs through litigated patent challenges.[790] In other words, the fundamental purpose of the Hatch-Waxman Act was "to promote *patent challenges*, not agreements *not to challenge patents.*"[791]

B Subsequent Patent Challenges Eliminating Weak Patents

The provisions of the Hatch-Waxman Act proved to be highly complicated and difficult to apply even for US courts.[792] An example of the confusion around the Hatch-Waxman Act provisions is the decision of the 2nd Circuit Court in *Tamoxifen*, where the court erroneously considered that the settlement of the patent holder with the first ANDA filer *opened the way* for immediate challenges to the patent, by subsequent generic challengers that were also incentivised to file an ANDA application by the 180-day exclusivity period.[793] As already analysed, the 180-day exclusivity period is accorded only to the first generic filer of a paragraph IV ANDA.[794]

Courts applying the scope of the patent test argued that even though patents of the most questionable validity were the most likely to be the subject of exclusion payments, a patent holder could not afford paying subsequent ANDA filers to stay off the market *ad infinitum*, since every settlement would reduce the profitability of patent monopoly.[795] For instance, in the *Tamoxifen* case the patent holder had concluded a reverse payment settlement only with the first generic challenger and not with the three subsequent generic ANDA filers.[796] A weak patent and a big payment to the first generic would have the same result as "blood in the water;" they would presumptively attract many subsequent generic challengers, restoring competition to the market sooner or later.[797] Even if the patent holder could escape competition once and share its monopoly profits with the first challenger, these profits would be eventually spent to subsequent generic challengers.[798] Nevertheless, later cases proved that it is not precluded for a patent holder to pay several generic challengers to stay off the market. In the *King Drug Co. of Florence, Inc. v. Cephalon, Inc.* case, the patent holder paid *four* generic manufacturers in order to delay their entry to the market;[799] however, the

---

790. HEMPHILL, Paying for Delay, 2006, p. 1614.
791. CARRIER, Unleashed, 2010, p. 4.
792. *See supra* Chapter 2, Part 2, on a detailed analysis of the Hatch-Waxman Act provisions.
793. *In re Tamoxifen Citrate Antitrust Litigation*, 466 F.3d 187, 214-215 (2nd Cir. 2006), "the Settlement Agreement ended all litigation between Zeneca and Barr and thereby opened the tamoxifen patent to immediate challenge by other potential generic manufacturers, which did indeed follow – spurred by the additional incentive (at the time) of potentially securing the 180-day exclusivity period." This misinterpretation of the Hatch-Waxman Act was also criticised by the 3rd Circuit in *In Re: K-Dur Antitrust Litigation*, 686 F.3d 197, 215.
794. 21 U.S.C. § 355 (j)(5)(B)(iv); *see* further *supra* Chapter 2, Part 2, Section II.D.
795. *In re Tamoxifen Citrate Antitrust Litigation*, 466 F.3d 187, 211-212 (2nd Cir. 2006); *In re Ciprofloxacin Hydrochloride Antitrust Litig.*, 363 F. Supp. 2d 514, 534 (E.D.N.Y. 2005), "[I]t is unlikely that the holder of a weak patent could stave off all possible challengers with exclusion payments because the economics simply would not justify it."
796. *In re Tamoxifen Citrate Antitrust Litigation*, 466 F.3d 187, 212 (2nd Cir. 2006).
797. *FTC v. Watson Pharmaceuticals*, 677 F.3d 1298, 1315 (11th Cir. 2012).
798. *Idem.*
799. *King Drug Co. of Florence, Inc. v. Cephalon, Inc.*, 702 F. Supp. 2d 514, 521-522. (E.D. PA. 2010).

district court adjudicating these reverse payment settlements applied the scope of the patent test and found no antitrust violation.[800]

In reality, a settlement with the first paragraph IV ANDA filer removes from the market the most motivated competitor of the brand-name manufacturer.[801] Even if subsequent generic challenges will follow, previous jurisprudence demonstrated that the monopoly profits of a patent holder are high enough to pay several generic challengers in order for them to stay off the market and to diminish the risk of a possible patent invalidation.[802] As analysed in Chapter 4 of this book, in *FTC v. Actavis* the Supreme Court rejected the view that a first settlement would necessarily provoke a series of challenges, since subsequent generic challengers would not enjoy the incentive of the 180-day exclusivity period, while they would have to stay out of the market for a 30-month stay period before their ANDA applications would be approved.[803]

C Settlement Incentives Versus the Elimination of Invalid Patents

1 Favouring the Settlement of Disputes at All Costs

As analysed in Chapter 1 of this book, the importance of settlements for the US legal order is huge. Litigation is generally seen as a last resort and courts themselves promote the conclusion of settlements instead of lengthy, inefficient and uncertain litigation.[804] The firm belief that settlements are beneficial and should be encouraged and facilitated at all costs is a recurring argument in the court decisions applying the scope of the patent test to reverse payment settlements.[805] Courts stressed the complexity and uncertainty of patent litigation and argued that applying harsh antitrust rules to reverse payments would chill settlements, increase patent enforcement costs and decrease the

---

800. *King Drug Co. of Florence, Inc. v. Cephalon, Inc.*, 702 F. Supp. 2d 514, 521-522. (E.D. PA. 2010).
801. HEMPHILL, Paying for Delay, 2006, pp. 1584-1586, supporting that the first paragraph IV ANDA filer is the most motivated due to the possibility of obtaining the180-day exclusivity period; HEMPHILL, Aggregate Approach, 2009, p. 674. *See* for instance, agreeing with HEMPHILL: CARRIER, Unsettling Settlements, 2009, pp. 56-57, 73, "[A]fter the brand firm settles with the first generic filer, subsequent generics would be less motivated to pursue a challenge since they would be further behind in the approval process, would not be entitled to the market exclusivity period, and would receive a return dependent on the outcome of the first filer's suit;" LEARY, Antitrust Issues, 2007, pp. 388-390; BACKUS, Reversing Course, 2007, p. 406.
802. *In Re: K-Dur Antitrust Litigation*, 686 F.3d 197, 215. The court cited *King Drug Co. of Florence, Inc., et al. v. Chephalon, Inc., et al.*, 702 F. Supp. 2d 514, 521-522 (E.D. PA. 2010), where the respective patent holder had settled infringement suits with four generic manufacturers which agreed to delay market entry in exchange for significant payments.
803. *FTC v. Actavis, Inc.*, 133 S. Ct. 2223, 2235 (2013). *See infra* Chapter 4, Part 1, providing a detailed analysis of the *FTC v. Actavis* decision.
804. *See* further *supra* Chapter 1, Part 2, on the benefits of settlements.
805. *Schering-Plough Corp. v. FTC*, 402 F.3d 1056, 1071-1075 (11th Cir. 2005); *In re Tamoxifen Citrate Antitrust Litigation*, 466 F.3d 187, 202 (2nd Cir. 2006); *In re Ciprofloxacin Hydrochloride Antitrust Litig.*, 544 F. 3d 1323, 1333 (Fed. Cir. 2008), where in order to establish that "the long-standing policy in the law in favour of settlements" extended to patent infringement litigation, the court relied on *Flex Foot, Inc. v. CRR, Inc.*, 238 F. 3d 1362, 1368 (Fed. Cir. 2001); *Foster v. Hallco Mfg. Co.*, 947 F. 2d 469, 477 (Fed. Cir. 1991), neither of which concerned reverse payment settlements concluded in the Hatch-Waxman context.

value of patent protection.[806] If transfers of value from the patent holder to the generic challenger would be forbidden, patent holders would be put in a detrimental position with regard to their right to negotiate and conclude settlements due to their patent rights.[807] Additionally, such a prohibition of value transfers could arguably have anticompetitive results by decreasing the incentives of generic manufacturers to challenge patents,[808] while it would also counter the goals of patent laws, leading to multiple continuing lawsuits, increasing legal uncertainty and delaying innovation.[809] Courts went as far as to argue that so long as the law encouraged settlements, infringement suits on weak patents could be settled, despite the fact that such settlements would protect undeserved patent monopolies,[810] manifestly ignoring that such a principle would lead to the survival of monopolies based on fatally weak or invalid patents.[811]

Hatch-Waxman patent litigation was seen as a game of Russian roulette, where even a party which was likely to win "may not want to take a turn."[812] Since hundreds of millions of dollars of lost profits were at stake[813] and patent litigation in the Hatch-Waxman context was an all or nothing affair, it made sense for a patent holder to settle the infringement action if it was not likely to prevail, even if it had a 49% chance of winning.[814] According to courts applying the scope of the patent test, it was thus *reasonable* for rational parties to settle in order to avoid the cost of litigation and the chance of losing, and such settlements were not violating antitrust laws.[815] Fortunately for consumers and public healthcare schemes, the Supreme Court did not agree with this line of argumentation.

---

806. *Valley Drug Co. v. Geneva Pharms, Inc.*, 344 F.3d 1294, 1309 (11th Cir. 2003).
807. *Schering-Plough Corp. v. FTC*, 402 F.3d 1056, 1072 (11th Cir. 2005). The FTC provided a safe harbour for payments less than $2 million as reimbursement of litigation costs. *See also* WILLIG, BIGELOW, Toward Agreements, 2004, pp. 669-673, arguing that cash payments could enable parties to reach an otherwise impossible settlement, which would be "socially superior" to litigation.
808. *Schering-Plough Corp. v. FTC*, 402 F.3d 1056, 1075 (11th Cir. 2005). The court cited *Asahi Glass Co., Ltd. v. Pentech Pharmaceuticals, Inc.*, 289 F. Supp. 2d 986, 994 (N.D. Ill. 2003). It should be noted that the *Asahi Glass* case concerned the antitrust treatment of a settlement between a brand manufacturer and a generic challenger, without a payment.
809. *In re Tamoxifen Citrate Antitrust Litigation*, 466 F.3d 187, 203 (2nd Cir. 2006).
810. *In re Tamoxifen Citrate Antitrust Litigation*, 466 F.3d 187, 211, 215 (2nd Cir. 2006), finding that there was no legal requirement for parties to litigate an issue fully "for the benefit of others."
811. *See further* US, *Amicus* Brief, *Joblove v. Barr*, p. 14, "While it is true that the law generally encourages settlements, the Patent Act does not embody a policy of promoting the interests of patent holders at all costs."
812. *FTC v. Watson Pharmaceuticals*, 677 F.3d 1298, 1313 (11th Cir. 2012).
813. *Idem. See also* JACOBO-RUBIO, TURNER, WILLIAMS, 2017, p. 3, arguing that the average stakes for brand-name firms in Hatch-Waxman litigation amount to $4.6 billion, while the average stakes for generic manufacturers are $236.8 million.
814. *FTC v. Watson Pharmaceuticals*, 677 F.3d 1298, 1313 (11th Cir. 2012).
815. *Idem.*

2 The Public Interest in Eliminating Unwarranted Monopolies

The DoJ criticised the application of the scope of the patent test which barred any consideration of whether Hatch-Waxman settlements violated antitrust laws, offering no protection to the vital public interest in eliminating unwarranted restraints on competition.[816] On the basis of the Supreme Court's jurisprudence, the public interest mandates the abolishment of trade restraints imposed by invalid or narrow patents: the right to challenge a patent is not only a private right accorded to individuals but is also founded on public policy.[817] This logic should also apply to reverse payment settlements which permitted the division of the monopoly rents between potential competitors, in the absence of any reassurance that the patent at issue was valid.[818] If potential competitors conclude agreements to remain in cartels instead of challenging the validity of the relevant patent or instead of inventing around the patent, such an agreement should be found to be anticompetitive.[819] The persistence of courts to champion the settlement of Hatch-Waxman infringement suits was criticised for favouring judicial efficiency over the promotion of competitive and fair drug markets.[820] HEMPHILL argued that the underlying reason for the judicial preference for Hatch-Waxman settlements was the unwillingness of judges to address highly technical pharmaceutical patent cases and to examine the merits of the relevant patent infringement suits.[821]

In her dissenting opinion in *Tamoxifen*, Judge Pooler also stressed that litigation was "critically important to the general well-being in light of the recent trend towards capping the maximum amounts insurers and public benefit plans will spend on medication."[822] While a Hatch-Waxman settlement protected the interests of the settling parties, it did not necessarily promote public interest; whether it did or not should be judged on the basis of the facts of each case. More particularly, the public interest in the invalidation of weak patents was not sufficiently protected by subsequent generic challenges to the patent, for the simple reason that there was a significant time gap between the first-filer litigation and subsequent challenges; during this time gap, consumers did not have access to low-cost generics.[823] In the *Tamoxifen* case, the

---

816. U.S., *Amicus* Brief, *In re K-Dur*, p. 16. *See also In re Ciprofloxacin Hydrochloride Antitrust Litig.*, 544 F. 3d 1323, 1334 (Fed. Cir. 2008), describing the similar position of the antitrust plaintiffs in that case.
817. *Edward Katzinger Co. v. Chicago Metallic Manufacturing Co.*, 67 S. Ct. 416, 419-420 (1947); *In Re: K-Dur Antitrust Litigation*, 686 F.3d 197, 216.
818. *In Re: K-Dur Antitrust Litigation*, 686 F.3d 197, 216.
819. *United States v. Studiengesellschaft Kohle, m.b.H.*, 670 F.2d 1122, 1136 (D.C.Cir. 1981); *In Re: K-Dur Antitrust Litigation*, 686 F.3d 197, 216.
820. KUTCHER, Waiting Is the Hardest Part, 2013, p. 1111.
821. HEMPHILL, Paying for Delay, 2006, p. 1547, arguing that judges have developed a "judicial reflex in favor of settlement." The Supreme Court in *FTC v. Actavis* provided a similar explanation about the hesitance of courts to examine the merits of infringement suits. *See* further *infra* Chapter 4, Part 1.
822. *In re Tamoxifen Citrate Antitrust Litigation*, 466 F.3d 187, 226 (2nd Cir. 2006), (Judge Pooler dissenting).
823. *Idem*.

patent was shown to be vulnerable to attack and the generic manufacturer had been paid to keep its generic product of the market; it was thus unlikely that such a settlement benefited the public.[824]

Courts applying the scope of the patent test insisted on the high costs of patent litigation which would be avoided though settlement, but failed to consider the much more important cost of reverse payment settlements to the public. As the DoJ noted, "[a]llowing the patent holder to claim antitrust immunity for its private contracts as if they were litigated injunctions, while evading the risks of litigation, deprives consumers of significant benefits from price competition in the pharmaceutical industry."[825] According to a 2010 FTC study, the annual drug purchaser savings to be gained by eliminating pay-for-delay agreements raised up to $3.5 billion per year.[826] A 1-year delay in the generic entry of a drug arguably represented a transfer of $12 million from consumers to drug producers.[827] The high cost of reverse settlements for the public led SHAPIRO argue that consumers had a property right to the level of competition they would have enjoyed if the parties would have litigated the patent infringement suit instead of settling.[828] This argument was rejected in *Cipro II* by the district court, which found that there was no legal basis for restricting the rights of patentees to choose between settling and litigating.[829]

D The Impairment of Innovation

Courts applying the scope of the patent test not only stressed the multiple private and social benefits of settlements vis-à-vis "the caustic environment of patent litigation,"[830] but also argued that litigation could have detrimental effects on innovation, reducing the R&D and marketing incentives.[831] Imposing antitrust scrutiny to patent settlements would be distorting the balance between antitrust and patent law and could hinder

---

824. *In re Tamoxifen Citrate Antitrust Litigation*, 466 F.3d 187, 226 (2nd Cir. 2006), (Judge Pooler dissenting). *See also idem* at 228, Judge Pooler argued that the proper antitrust standard would be that of reasonableness considering the individual circumstances of each agreement, relying primarily on the strength of the patent as it appeared at the time of settlement and secondarily: (1) on the amount of payment to defer generic entry; (2) the amount the generic manufacturer would earn during its exclusivity period, and; (3) any ancillary anticompetitive effects of the agreement.
825. U.S., *Amicus* Brief, *In re K-Dur*, pp. 17-18.
826. FTC, *Pay-for-Delay*, 2010, p. 10, estimating the annual purchaser savings to be gained by the elimination of pay-for-delay agreements to $3.5 billion per year.
827. HEMPHILL, Aggregate Approach, 2009, p. 650.
828. SHAPIRO, Antitrust Limits, 2003, p. 396.
829. *In re Ciprofloxacin Hydrochloride Antitrust Litig.*, 363 F. Supp. 2d 514, 531-532 (E.D.N.Y. 2005), (cited as *Cipro II*), "[t]his concept of a public property right in the outcome of private lawsuits does not translate well into the realities of litigation, and there is no support in the law for such a right. There is simply no legal basis for restricting the rights of patentees to choose their enforcement vehicle (*i.e.*, settlement versus litigation)."
830. *Schering-Plough Corp. v. FTC*, 402 F.3d 1056, 1075 (11th Cir. 2005).
831. *Valley Drug Co. v. Geneva Pharms, Inc.*, 344 F.3d 1294, 1308 (11th Cir. 2003); *Schering-Plough Corp. v. FTC*, 402 F.3d 1056, 1075 (11th Cir. 2005); *In re Tamoxifen Citrate Antitrust Litigation*, 466 F.3d 187, 203 (2nd Cir. 2006).

patent innovation.[832] Additionally, not all settlements excluded competition from the market; for example settlements containing licences could be beneficial to the public by introducing new rivals to the market,[833] enabling competitive production and further innovation.[834] There was a general tendency of demonising the function of antitrust laws and of largely ignoring the contribution of antitrust scrutiny in increasing the consumer welfare and incentivising innovation.[835]

However, the incentive structure of the patent system was in reality distorted by reverse payment settlements that excluded generic competition from the market, and by courts applying the scope of the patent test and granting to patentees rights that the Congress had not accorded.[836] The exclusionary power of a patent, its exclusionary scope and strength, should be proportionate to the contribution of the inventor in order for technological innovation to be incentivised.[837] This was certainly not the case when it came to settlements regarding weak or even invalid patents, which were immunised from antitrust scrutiny under the scope of the patent test. This legitimisation of exclusion payments allowed patentees to enhance the exclusionary power of their patent and to obtain a degree of market control that would not have been provided by their patent, distorting the statutory incentive structure of the patent system.[838]

PART 3 REVERSE PAYMENTS AS PRESUMPTIVELY ILLEGAL

The "truncated" or "quick-look" rule of reason arguably constitutes a sort of intermediate category between the rule of reason analysis and the per se rule. This "quick-look" rule of reason is limited to cases in which an observer with even a basic understanding of economics could conclude that the arrangements in question would have an anticompetitive effect on costumers and on markets.[839] This standard of analysis applies in cases where per se condemnation is inappropriate, but "no elaborate industry analysis is required to demonstrate the anticompetitive character of an inherently suspect restraint."[840] A restraint falls within this category and is

---

832. *Schering-Plough Corp. v. FTC*, 402 F.3d 1056, 1075 (11th Cir. 2005); *Valley Drug Co. v. Geneva Pharms, Inc.*, 344 F.3d 1294, 1308 (11th Cir. 2003); *In re Tamoxifen Citrate Antitrust Litigation*, 466 F.3d 187, 203 (2nd Cir. 2006).
833. *Schering-Plough Corp. v. FTC*, 402 F.3d 1056, 1075 (11th Cir. 2005); *In re Tamoxifen Citrate Antitrust Litigation*, 466 F.3d 187, 215 (2nd Cir. 2006), arguing that Zeneca's licence to Barr reduced the value of the reverse payment since "money also flowed from Barr to Zeneca" while it also added a competitor to the market and thus increased competition.
834. *Schering-Plough Corp. v. FTC*, 402 F.3d 1056, 1075 (11th Cir. 2005).
835. See supra Chapter 1, Part 1, Section I.C.3 on the role of antitrust scrutiny in incentivising innovation.
836. ABBOTT, MICHEL, Right Balance, 2005, pp. 20-21.
837. ABBOTT, MICHEL, Right Balance, 2005, p. 21.
838. *Idem*, arguing further that in enacting patent laws, Congress had implicitly balanced "the static efficiency of competition and the low prices against the dynamic efficiency of increased incentives to seek patentable inventions."
839. *FTC v. Actavis, Inc.*, 133 S. Ct. 2223, 2237 (2013); *California Dental Ass'n v. Fed. Trade Comm'n*, 119 S. Ct. 1604, 1612 (1999).
840. *Nat'l Collegiate Athletic Ass'n ("NCAA") v. Bd. of Regents of Univ. of Okla.*, 104 S. Ct. 2948, 2964; *United States v. Brown Univ.*, 5 F.3d 658, 669 (3d Cir. 1993); *FTC v. Indiana Federation of Dentists*, 106 S. Ct. 2009, 2018 (1986).

Chapter 3: The US Circuits' Split on Reverse Payment Settlements

considered as presumptively illegal if it is highly suspicious, "nearly naked" or "facially unreasonable," nearly to the point of deserving per se condemnation.[841] However, the lack of judicial experience with a particular restraint may cause doubts, making it necessary to assess any justifications invoked by the defendants.[842] In case these justifications suggest that the restraint is naked, the per se rule should be applied.[843]

The application of the scope of the patent test to reverse payment settlements did not only cause the reaction of the FTC and the DOJ but also of a number of judges and courts. The 3rd Circuit rejected the scope of the patent test and stressed further the split between Circuit Courts by considering the reverse payment settlements at issue in the *In re K-Dur* decision as presumptively illegal. The decision concerned the same settlement as the *In re Schering-Plough* decision of the 11th Circuit. While the 11th Circuit had previously found that the settlement was immune from antitrust scrutiny by applying the scope of the patent test, the 3rd Circuit disagreed and found that it presumptively violated antitrust laws. This part describes the truncated rule of reason standards proposed by the FTC and the DOJ, while it also analyses the *In re K-Dur* decision of the 3rd Circuit and the criticisms it gave rise to.

I Proposals on a Truncated Rule of Reason Analysis

The application of the scope of the patent test to reverse payment settlements did not only lead to heavy criticism and polemic debates; it also spurred the need to propose an alternative legal rule for the adjudication of reverse payments. The analysis of these payments under a truncated rule of reason attempted to strike a balance between the per se illegality – which forbade all settlements involving reverse payments – and the scope of the patent test which immunised these payments from antitrust analysis.

HOVENKAMP, JANIS and LEMLEY proposed a complete rule for reverse payments: a payment from the patent holder to a generic challenger aiming to the latter's exit from the market should be presumptively unlawful and shift the burden of proof to the patent holder alleging its patent's infringement.[844] The patent holder would then have to defend by cumulatively showing: (1) *ex ante* that its chances in prevailing in the patent infringement suit against the generic were significant,[845] and; (2) that the size of the payment did not exceed the expected value of litigation and any collateral costs

---

841. HOVENKAMP, *Federal Antitrust Policy*, 2011, p. 285.
842. Idem. As HOVENKAMP explains, if the invoked justifications seem "plausible and sufficient to suggest that the restraint is profitable without regard to any power that the defendants might have, then a full rule of reason inquiry will be necessary."
843. HOVENKAMP, *Federal Antitrust Policy*, 2011, p. 285.
844. *See further* HOVENKAMP, JANIS, LEMLEY, Anticompetitive Settlements, 2003. *See also* HEMPHILL, Paying for Delay, 2006, pp. 1561-1562, arguing that patent settlements including a compensation from the patent holder to the generic challenger should be treated as presumptively illegal restraints of trade.
845. *See also* CRANE, Exit Payments, 2002, pp. 779-796. CRANE has linked the legitimacy of reverse payments to the *ex ante* estimation of the likelihood of success of the patent holder's infringement suit: if such likelihood was high, such payments should be allowed by antitrust, whereas if the likelihood of success was low the payment should be prohibited.

related to the lawsuit.[846] Stretching this standard further, it was argued that even settlements which did not raise a red flag and which used non-cash compensation should be presumptively illegal.[847] HEMPHILL looked into the future and argued already in 2006 that even settlement agreements including small cash payments could use other means to provide non-cash compensation, such as term-dividing agreements, securing the generic filer's 180-exclusivity period.[848] As the years passed and the threat of antitrust scrutiny became inevitable for settlements between brand-name patent holders and generic manufacturers, settlements including non-cash value transfers and side-deals became the mainstream and big cash payments gradually disappeared.[849]

A The Proposed Tests by the FTC and the DOJ

The application of the scope of the patent test was met with dismay by the FTC, which from the very beginning advocated in favour of applying antitrust scrutiny to reverse payment settlements. On the contrary, the DoJ was not initially so hostile to the presence of reverse payments in patent settlements between brand-name patent holders and generic challengers. The following sections outline the evolution in the official positions of the FTC and the DoJ during the Circuit split and before the decision of the US Supreme Court in *FTC v. Actavis*.

1 FTC's Proposal for the Presumptive Illegality of Unjustified Payments

From the very dawn of reverse payment settlements, the FTC took a stance against settlements in which a generic manufacturer received value in order to defer marketing its generic drug.[850] The existence of a reverse payment as part of a settlement raised a "red flag" and mandated further inquiry; however, the FTC was not prepared to argue that *all* such settlements were per se illegal or should be viewed as inherently suspect.[851] Instead, the FTC argued in favour of the application of the rule of reason to

---

846. HOVENKAMP, JANIS, LEMLEY, Anticompetitive Settlements, 2003, pp. 1759-1763. For a comparable "quick-look" approach *see also* BLAIR, COTTER, Illegal Per Se, 2002, pp. 534-538.
847. HEMPHILL, Paying for Delay, 2006, pp. 1561-1562.
848. *Idem*.
849. *See infra* Chapter 4, Parts 2 and 3 on non-cash payments and other anticompetitive strategies delaying generic entry.
850. FTC, Final Order, *Schering-Plough*, 2003, pp. 13-15. *See also* FTC, Final Order, *Schering-Plough*, 2003, p. 4, "It is further ordered that in connection with the Sale of Drug Products, each Respondent shall cease and desist, directly or indirectly, from being a party to any Agreement resolving or settling a Patent Infringement Claim in which: a. an ANDA Filer receives anything of value; and b. the ANDA Filer agrees not to research, develop, manufacture, market, or sell the ANDA Product for any period of time."
851. FTC, Final Order, *Schering-Plough*, 2003, pp. 57-58; *FTC, Certiorari Brief, FTC v. Watson Pharmaceuticals*, pp. 33-40, rejecting the per se illegality approach and arguing that unjustified payments from the patent holder to the generic challenger should be seen as presumptively illegal.

Chapter 3: The US Circuits' Split on Reverse Payment Settlements

reverse payment settlements, which would also allow the adoption of presumptive illegality for clearly anticompetitive agreements.[852]

The main task of such a rule of reason analysis should be to determine whether the source of exclusion was the strength of the patent or a payment.[853] Agreements which settled the patent dispute without a payment but with the parties' consensus on an early generic entry, prior to the patent's expiration, were unlikely to pose an anticompetitive problem; such settlements could be defended on the grounds that the resulting exclusion merely reflected the parties' estimations on the strength of the patent.[854] On the contrary, an unjustified payment would most probably indicate that the patent holder was buying a greater degree of exclusion and should be seen as a quid pro quo for a delay, resembling a market allocation agreement.[855] Therefore, settlement agreements involving any kind of payment and resulting in delay to generic entry should be treated as presumptively illegal since they were "inherently suspect."[856] The burden of proof would then shift to the settling parties and could be carried either by proving that the payment was for something other than delay or that their settlement achieved beneficial efficiencies.[857] The FTC clarified that its proposed analysis would not necessitate an inquiry into the merits of the patent infringement lawsuit, since a substantial unjustified payment paired with a commitment not to enter the market would clearly reflect an improper agreement to restrict market competition.[858]

The application of the scope of the patent test to the reverse payment settlements at issue in the *Schering-Plough* case by the 11th Circuit made the FTC file a petition for writ of *certiorari*, spurred by the necessity to seek the correction of a rule that conflicted with fundamental antitrust principles and jeopardised billions of dollars of consumer

---

852. FTC, *Amicus* Brief, *In re K-Dur*, p. 14, "Patent settlement agreements should be assessed under the antitrust rule of reason – a rule that, as recent Supreme Court teachings make clear, is flexible enough both to take into account the patent context and to recognize a presumption of illegality for types of agreements whose likely anticompetitive impact is clear."
853. FTC, *Amicus* Brief, *In re K-Dur*, p. 23.
854. *Idem*; FTC, Final Order, *Schering-Plough*, 2003, pp. 18-19, "[t]he order does not prohibit all settlement agreements that specify a generic entry date coupled with the payment of value to the generic, but excepts payments that are limited to litigation costs of up to $2 million if the Commission has been notified of the settlement" [internal quotation marks omitted]. *See also* DOLIN, Patent Invalidity Signals, 2011, p. 309 (describing FTC's proposed threshold of $2 million as "an approach that would have made all such settlements illegal per se in all but name"); HOVENKAMP, JANIS, LEMLEY, LESLIE, *IP And Antitrust*, 2006, § 7.4e, 7-39, arguing that payments should be permitted if they are no more than the expected value of litigation and collateral costs, provided that the *ex ante* likelihood for the patent holder to prevail in its infringement suit is significant. *See also* HOVENKAMP, JANIS, LEMLEY, Anticompetitive Settlements, 2003, pp. 1758-1759; SHAPIRO, Antitrust Limits, 2003, p. 76, fn. 10, "cash payments should be calculated net of the patent holder's avoided litigation costs."
855. FTC, *Amicus* Brief, *In re K-Dur*, p. 14.
856. FTC, *Amicus* Brief, *In re K-Dur*, p. 25. The FTC cited *N. Tex. Specialty Physicians v. FTC*, 528 F.3d 346, 361 (5th Cir. 2008), upholding the FTC's "inherently suspect" analysis as in line with the Supreme Court's decision in *California Dental*, while noting that courts should be attentive to the application of the burden shifting.
857. FTC, *Amicus* Brief, *In re K-Dur*, pp. 25-26.
858. FTC, *Amicus* Brief, *In re K-Dur*, pp. 26-27. The FTC had already followed this approach in 2003 as evidenced in FTC, Final Order, Schering-Plough, 2003, pp. 70, "it would not be necessary, practical, or particularly useful for the Commission to embark on an inquiry of the merits of the underlying patent dispute when resolving antitrust issues in patent settlements."

savings on prescription drugs.[859] A number of *amici* joined FTC's effort to convince the US Supreme Court to grant *certiorari*, among which were thirty-four US states with the District of Columbia[860] and Representative Henry A. Waxman.[861] Even though the Supreme Court refused to grant *certiorari*,[862] the same set of reverse payment settlements was revisited seven years later by the 3rd Circuit in the *In re K-Dur* decision which is analysed in the following sections.

2 The Shift of the DoJ Towards a Truncated Rule of Reason

The DoJ did not initially support FTC's presumptive illegality approach; on the contrary, it opposed the grant of *certiorari* by the Supreme Court at *Schering-Plough* and argued that the presence of a payment was not sufficient to renter a Hatch-Waxman settlement illegal. Instead, the likelihood of success of the parties' claims should be taken into consideration, examined *ex ante*.[863] Even though the DOJ recognised that reverse payment settlements could pose a risk of restricting competition, it denied that there was indeed a Circuit split on the appropriate legal standard mandating the Supreme Court's review.[864]

Subsequently the DoJ took a different approach and sided with the FTC as evidenced in its amicus curiae briefs in the cases of *Ciprofloxacin*[865] and *K-Dur*,[866] arguing that reverse payment settlements should be generally evaluated under the rule of reason and agreeing that payments in exchange for delaying generic entry should be treated as presumptively illegal under Section 1 of the Sherman Act.[867] The DoJ argued that the presumption of illegality could be rebutted by the defendants if they provided a "reasonable explanation for the payment" and showed that the degree of competition preserved by the settlement was consistent with the parties' contemporaneous

---

859. Brief for the FTC on Petition for a Writ of *Certiorari* to the United States Court of Appeals for the Eleventh Circuit, *FTC v. Schering-Plough Corp. et al.*, (No. 05-273) (August 29, 2005), p. 1, fn. 1.
860. Brief of States as *Amici Curiae* Supporting FTC on petition for a Writ of *certiorari*, *FTC v. Schering-Plough*, (No. 05-273) (September 30, 2005).
861. Brief for Representative Henry A. Waxman as *Amicus Curiae* Supporting Petitioner, *FTC v. Schering-Plough Corp.*, (No. 05-273) (September 30, 2005).
862. *FTC v. Schering-Plough Corp. et al.*, 126 S. Ct. 2929 (2006).
863. The DoJ through the Solicitor General opposed FTC's *certiorari* petition. *See* further Brief for the United States as *Amicus Curiae* on Petition for Writ of *Certiorari*, *FTC v. Schering-Plough Corp.*, (No. 05-273) (May 17, 2006), p. 11 [cited as: U.S., *Amicus* Brief, *FTC v. Schering-Plough*]. *See also* HEMPHILL, Paying for Delay, 2006, pp. 1557-1558.
864. U.S., *Amicus* Brief, *FTC v. Schering-Plough*, pp. 8, 16-17.
865. U.S., Response Brief, *Arkansas Carpenters v. Bayer*, pp. 10-11.
866. U.S., *Amicus* Brief, *In re K-Dur*.
867. POZEN Sharis A., Acting Assistant Attorney General, Antitrust Division, U.S. Department of Justice, *Promoting Competition and Innovation Through Vigorous Enforcement of the Antitrust Laws on Behalf of Consumers*, Washington D.C., April 23, 2012, p. 10. Available at: http://www.justice.gov/atr/public/speeches/282515.pdf. (last accessed on March 31, 2018), "We have called for a presumptive illegality standard – we declined to advocate a rule that all reverse payment settlements are *per se* illegal." *See also* U.S., *Amicus* Brief, *In re K-Dur*, p. 10.

estimation of success prospects in case of patent litigation,[868] a test quite similar to the proposal of HOVENKAMP, JANIS and LEMLEY in 2003.[869] This change in DoJ's view was arguably the result of the 2008 change of administration and the subsequent shift in the department's leadership.[870]

The amicus curiae brief of the DoJ submitted in the *K-Dur* case provides a detailed proposal for the application of the presumptive illegality approach to reverse payment settlements. First, the antitrust plaintiff should prove the existence of a reverse payment, in accordance to a three-fold test: (1) prove that the generic challenger withdrew its patent infringement or invalidity defence; (2) prove that money or other consideration serving the same purpose flowed from the patent holder to the generic challenger; and (3) prove that the payment went hand-in-hand with an agreement to withdraw the invalidity or the non-infringement defences.[871] Once this burden is satisfied, the plaintiff has established a prima facie case of unlawful restraint and the burden of proof shifts to the defendant, who must provide a legitimate justification for the agreement, proving that it did not impose an unreasonable restraint on competition.[872] The DoJ clarified that patent settlements are not ordinarily viewed as naked restraints, but stressed that payments seemingly in exchange for market exclusion require justification.[873] The defendants would be able to clearly rebut the presumption of unlawfulness by showing that the payment was equal to the patent holder's avoided litigation costs.[874] However, in case the avoided litigation costs would be exceeded, the nature and extent of the generic competition permitted by the agreement should be analysed.[875] If no generic competition was allowed until the expiration of the patent, the defendants would be unable to satisfy their burden, since such an agreement would be anticompetitive by its nature, eliminating even the *possibility* of generic competition.[876]

The DoJ stressed that if a settlement involved a payment in exchange for delay in generic entry and a withdrawal of the patent challenge, it was not necessary to examine

---

868. U.S., *Amicus Brief, In re K-Dur*, pp. 11-12. *See* however, BUTLER, JAROSCH, Policy Reversal, 2010, pp. 86-89, criticising the rule proposed by the DoJ in its *Arkansas Carpenters* brief for not being a rule of reason approach but a presumptive illegality standard.
869. HOVENKAMP, JANIS, LEMLEY, Anticompetitive Settlements, 2003, pp. 1759-1761, also suggesting that reverse payment settlements should be seen as presumptively unlawful, arguing that the antitrust defendants could rebut this presumption by proving both: (1) the significant likelihood to prevail in the patent infringement suit, and; (2) that the payment did not exceed litigation costs and costs collateral to the lawsuit. However, in contrast to the DoJ proposal, the authors requested at least a limited inquiry to the merits of the patent infringement suit.
870. HANKS, JACOBSON, MUSGROVE, SHEN, Proper Exercise, 2011, "[i]n the Schering-Plough case, the DoJ under Bush filed an amicus brief disagreeing with the FTC and encouraging the Supreme Court to deny review. Now, however, the DoJ has changed course to reflect the Obama administration's disfavor for reverse payment settlements." *See also* KENDALL, DoJ Shifts Policy, 2009.
871. U.S., *Amicus Brief, In re K-Dur*, pp. 24-25.
872. U.S., *Amicus Brief, In re K-Dur*, pp. 25-26, 28-29. The DoJ did not consider it necessary for the court to determine whether the patent holder would have prevailed at its patent infringement litigation.
873. U.S., *Amicus Brief, In re K-Dur*, p. 25.
874. U.S., *Amicus Brief, In re K-Dur*, p. 29.
875. *Idem*.
876. U.S., *Amicus Brief, In re K-Dur*, p. 30.

the patent's validity or non-infringement. Such a settlement would most likely disadvantage consumers, since the payment revealed the patent holder's uncertainty with regard to the outcome of the patent infringement litigation and its will to avoid the risk of competition.[877] Finally, the DoJ suggested that the defendants could not rebut the presumption of illegality if the settlement did not allow *any* generic competition until the expiration of the patent.[878] However, if generic entry was allowed before the patent expiration, the burden would be satisfied upon proof that the settlement preserved a degree of competition consistent with the expected outcome of the infringement litigation.[879]

II The "Quick-Look" Rule of Reason in the *K-Dur* Decision

The *K-Dur* decision of the 3rd Circuit analysed the exact same reverse settlement agreement as the prior *Schering-Plough* decision of the 11th Circuit Court. While in *Schering-Plough* it was the FTC that had submitted the antitrust suit, the *K-Dur* decision concerns private damages cases by private parties which were filed after the FTC filed its antitrust suit, arguing that the settlements at issue kept generic versions of the drug *K-Dur* 20 off the market.[880] The *K-Dur* decision is of major importance, since it stressed the split among the US Circuit Courts on the matter of Hatch-Waxman settlements by rejecting the scope of the patent test and concluding that the reverse payments at issue constituted a prima facie evidence of antitrust violation.[881] The Circuit Courts split was resolved only in 2013, when the Supreme Court granted *certiorari* and ruled for the first time on reverse payment settlements in the *FTC v. Actavis* decision, opting for a rule of reason analysis.[882] After *Actavis*, the Supreme Court granted the writ of *certiorari* for the *K-Dur* decision and vacated the judgment, remanding it to the 3rd Circuit for further consideration in light of *FTC v. Actavis*.[883] In its turn, the 3rd Circuit remanded the case to the US District Court for the District of New Jersey for further proceedings.[884]

---

877. U.S., *Amicus* Brief, *In re K-Dur*, pp. 27-28.
878. U.S., *Amicus* Brief, *In re K-Dur*, p. 30.
879. U.S., *Amicus* Brief, *In re K-Dur*, p. 31. *See* however Davis, Per Se Illegal, 2009, p. 302, criticising DoJ's proposed standard as vague, arguing instead that reverse payment settlements would be legal only "if they allow generic competition to occur at approximately the expected value entry date."
880. The plaintiffs in *K-Dur* were Louisiana Wholesale Drug Company Inc., on behalf of a class of wholesalers and retailers who purchased *K-Dur* directly from Schering, and nine individual plaintiffs, including pharmacies. *See further In Re: K-Dur Antitrust Litigation*, 686 F.3d 197, 202.
881. *See also* FTC, *Certiorari* Brief, *FTC v. Watson Pharmaceuticals*, pp. 10-15, describing the split between Circuit Courts in the matter of reverse payments and stressing that the contrast between the *K-Dur* and the *Schering-Plough* decisions vividly represents that conflict.
882. *FTC v. Actavis, Inc.*, 133 S. Ct. 2223 (2013).
883. *Merck & Co., Inc., Petitioner v. Louisiana Wholesale Drug Company Inc., et al.*, 133 S. Ct. 2849 (2013), and *Upsher-Smith Laboratories, Inc., Petitioner v. Louisiana Wholesale Drug Company Inc., et al.*, 133 S. Ct. 2849 (2013), vacating *In re K-Dur Antitrust Litig.*, 686 F. 3d 197.
884. *See In re K-Dur Antitrust Litig.*, Nos. 10-2077, 10-2078, 10-4571, (3rd Cir., 2013), remanding the case to the US District Court for the District of New Jersey for further proceedings. The latter decided on the case on February 2016; *see In re K-Dur Antitrust Litig.*, Civil Action No. 01-cv-1652 (SRC)(CLW),MDL Docket No. 1419, (D.N.J., February 25, 2016).

Chapter 3: The US Circuits' Split on Reverse Payment Settlements

A Facts

Schering-Plough manufactured and marketed *K-Dur 20*, a supplement taken in conjunction with prescription medicines for the treatment of high blood pressure or congestive heart disease. Schering-Plough held patent number 4,863,743 (the '743 patent), a formulation patent on the extended-release coating surrounding the active ingredient which was commonly used and unpatentable.[885] Two generic filers, Upsher-Smith Labotatories (Upsher) and ESI Lederle, Inc. (ESI) challenged the '743 patent and Schering-Plough sued them for patent infringement.[886]

Schering settled with both generic challengers. On the basis of the Schering-Upsher settlement, Upsher gained the right to enter the market with its generic version of *K-Dur 20* five years before the expiration of the Schering-Plough's secondary patent,[887] and granted Schering licences to market five of Upsher's products. In return, Schering undertook the obligation to pay Upsher: (1) $60 million in initial royalty fees; (2) $10 million in milestone royalty payments; and (3) 10% or 15% royalties on sales. As far as the Schering-ESI settlement is concerned, Schering allowed ESI to enter the market with its generic drug almost three years before the '743 patent's expiration day.[888] Further, Schering agreed to pay ESI up to $10 million if the FDA would approve the latter's generic drug by a certain date. The parties also concluded a side licensing agreement: in return for the right to license two of ESI's products, Schering agreed to pay ESI $15 million. In total, Schering undertook the obligation to pay ESI: (1) a $5 million non-contingent payment representing legal fees; (2) an additional $10 million contingent on FDA's approval; and (3) $15 million on the basis of the side licensing agreement.

B The FTC's Antitrust Complaint Against the Settlements

1 Horizontal Market Division Agreements

In 2001, in its initial administrative complaint in the case of *Schering-Plough*, the FTC concluded that the above-analysed settlements between Schering-Plough and the generic manufacturers constituted unreasonable restraints to commerce and unfair methods of competition; thus, they violated Section 5 of the FTC Act.[889] Schering had monopoly power in the manufacture and sale of potassium chloride supplements and engaged in conduct aiming to unlawfully preserve this monopoly, while it also conspired with the two generic manufacturers to monopolise the relevant markets in

---

885. Schering's patent number 4,863,743 (the '743 patent) was to expire on September 5, 2006.
886. *In Re: K-Dur Antitrust Litigation*, 686 F.3d 197, 205-206.
887. Schering and Upsher agreed to the date of September 1, 2001 as the earliest date Upsher could enter the market with its generic drug, five years before the expiration of the '743 patent.
888. On the basis of the settlement agreement, ESI could market its Micro-K 20 starting from January 1, 2004.
889. 15 U.S.C. §§ 41-58; FTC, Administrative Complaint, *In re Schering-Plough Corp., Upsher-Smith Laboratories, Inc., and American Home Products Corp.*, Docket No. 9297, points 68-69 (March 30, 2001) [cited as: FTC, Administrative Complaint, *Schering-Plough*, 2001].

violation of Section 5 of the FTC Act.[890] In its Full Commission decision in 2003, the FTC argued that these reverse payment settlements were naked horizontal agreements to allocate time between competitors; therefore they were analogous to horizontal agreements allocating geographic areas which are routinely condemned as per se violations.[891] Being mindful of the fact that some courts were opposed to the condemnation of reverse payments in settlements,[892] the FTC emphasised that it had not applied the per se standard in the *Schering-Plough* case and acknowledged that there could be possible justifications for such agreements.[893]

2 Licensing Agreements as an Alibi for Payment

The FTC found that Schering's payments to Upsher and ESI in the context of the relevant licensing agreements were not bona fide payments but aimed to delay generic entry.[894] The products that Schering licensed in from the generic manufacturers were evidently of little value, since Schering only marketed one out of five Upsher products – without making important sales – and one out of three ESI products.[895] The FTC's position was that the licence payments to the generic challengers were thus not based on the value of the licensed products, but on the amount that the generic filers demanded in order to settle the patent litigation.[896] According to the FTC, none of the payments represented legitimate consideration; their object was to shield Schering's branded drug from competition by Upsher until 2001 and by ESI until 2004.[897] The settlement agreement with Upsher, the first generic challenger, was concluded before the 2003 amendment of the Hatch-Waxman Act introducing the forfeiture provisions of the 180-day exclusivity,[898] so it blocked *all* generic companies from entering the market until the lapse or forfeiture of Upsher's 180-day exclusivity period.[899] Thus, the FTC concluded that these payments were a quid pro quo for an agreement to postpone the generic entry dates, which had the purpose and effect to unreasonably restrain and injure competition by preventing the entry of generic drugs competing with the

---

890. FTC, Administrative Complaint, *Schering-Plough*, 2001, points 70-71.
891. FTC, Final Order, *Schering-Plough*, 2003, pp. 22-23.
892. FTC, Final Order, *Schering-Plough*, 2003, p. 53, fn. 54, referring to *Asahi Glass Co., Ltd. v. Pentech Pharmaceuticals, Inc.*, 289 F. Supp. 2d 986, 994 (N.D. Ill. 2003). *See also* at 971-972, where the FTC referred to the *In Re Cardizem* decision applying the per se illegality approach, but recognised that the trend of courts was going towards the opposite direction of the scope of the patent test, as evidenced by the decisions of *Valley Drug*, *In re Ciprofloxacin* and *In Re Tamoxifen*.
893. FTC, Final Order, *Schering-Plough*, 2003, p. 53, fn. 54.
894. FTC, Administrative Complaint, *Schering-Plough*, 2001, points 44, 64-65 and 56-57.
895. FTC, Administrative Complaint, *Schering-Plough*, 2001, points 45-46 and 56.
896. FTC, Administrative Complaint, *Schering-Plough*, 2001, points 56-57.
897. FTC, Final Order, *Schering-Plough*, 2003, p. 18, "[w]e conclude [...] that the payments from the pioneer to the generics were, in whole or in substantial part, consideration for delay rather than for products licensed from the generic."
898. *See supra* Chapter 2, Part 2, Section IV.A, analysing the 2003 MMA Act amendments and the forfeiture provisions of the 180-day exclusivity period.
899. FTC, Administrative Complaint, *Schering-Plough*, 2001, points 65-66.

brand-name drug.[900] Even licensing agreements where money flowed "in the right direction" and which appeared perfectly normal, could potentially lead to market outcomes that were, from the standpoint of customers, inferior to the potential results of patent litigation.[901]

3 The Antitrust Injury Suffered

The FTC argued that as a result of these settlement agreements, consumers were deprived of the benefits of competition between the patent holder and Upsher, ESI and other potential generic competitors. In the absence of less expensive generic versions, consumers were forced to pay the higher price of Schering's brand-name drug.[902] The agreements not to compete and not to market generic versions of *K-Dur* 20 constituted unreasonable restraints to commerce and unfair methods of competition *ergo* violated Section 5 of the FTC Act.[903] Additionally, Schering had monopoly power in the manufacture and sale of potassium chloride supplements and engaged in conduct aiming to unlawfully preserve this monopoly power, while it also conspired with the two generic manufacturers to monopolise the relevant markets in violation of Section 5 of the FTC Act.[904] ESI agreed to a consent order based on its litigation settlement with Schering,[905] while Upsher decided to appeal.

C The 3rd Circuit Finds Payments Prima Facie Illegal

The appellate court for the 3rd Circuit rejected the scope of the patent test which did not subject reverse payment settlements to *any* antitrust scrutiny.[906] The court found that the test improperly restricted the application of antitrust law and was against the policies of the Hatch-Waxman Act and the Supreme Court's precedent on patent litigation and competition.[907] The 3rd Circuit disagreed with the virtually unrebuttable presumption of patent validity that was created by the scope of the patent test and questioned the assumption that subsequent generic challengers would eventually

---

900. FTC, Administrative Complaint, *Schering-Plough*, 2001, points 63-67. *See also* FTC, Final Order, Schering-Plough, 2003, p. 50, "We therefore conclude that there is substantive evidence to support Complaint Counsel's claim that delayed generic entry in this situation would harm consumers by depriving them of the choice of a lower-cost generic version of K-Dur 20."
901. *See* for instance ADDANKI, DASKIN, Patent Settlement Agreements, 2008, pp. 2128-2133, criticising FTC's proposed analysis as an unwarranted "blanket condemnation" by arguing that a reverse payment does not render a settlement anticompetitive, but also accepting that a settlement involving a licence agreement could have anticompetitive effects.
902. FTC, Administrative Complaint, *Schering-Plough*, 2001, point 67.
903. 15 U.S.C. §§ 41-58; FTC, Administrative Complaint, *Schering-Plough*, 2001, points 68-69.
904. FTC, Administrative Complaint, *Schering-Plough*, 2001, points 70-71.
905. FTC, Decision and Agreement Containing Consent Order, *In the matter of Schering-Plough Corporation, Upsher-Smith Laboratories and American Home Products*, Docket No. 9297 (April 2, 2002). Available at: http://www.ftc.gov/sites/default/files/documents/cases/2002/04/scheringplough_do.htm (last accessed on March 31, 2018).
906. *In Re: K-Dur Antitrust Litigation*, 686 F.3d 197, 215-218.
907. *In Re: K-Dur Antitrust Litigation*, 686 F.3d 197, 214, 217.

eliminate weak patents from the market.[908] Additionally, it stressed that valid patents should be seen as a limited exception to the free exploitation of ideas, while the judicial preference for settlement should not displace countervailing public policy objectives such as the protection of consumers from unjustified patent monopolies.[909]

Instead of the scope of the patent test, the 3rd Circuit opted for a "quick-look" rule of reason analysis on the basis of the economic realities of reverse payment settlements concluded in the Hatch-Waxman context.[910] The court treated *any* payment from the patent holder to a generic challenger agreeing to delay its entry to the market as prima facie evidence of an unreasonable restraint of trade. This prima facie evidence could be rebutted if the settling parties were able to show either that: (1) the payment was for a purpose other than delaying generic entry or; (2) the payment offered some procompetitive benefit, which could not have been achieved in the absence of a reverse payment.[911] With regard to the second defence, the 3rd Circuit clarified it was meant to cover the rare exceptions when a reverse payment could potentially increase competition, e.g., a moderate cash payment, enabling a generic manufacturer to avoid bankruptcy and begin marketing a generic drug, increasing the amount of competition in the market.[912]

The 3rd Circuit stressed that it supported the approach of the D.C. Circuit in *Andrx Pharmaceuticals v. Biovail*, concurring with the conclusion that a payment from the patent holder to the generic challenger may be a strong indicator of the anticompetitive intent of the settling parties.[913] It was unnecessary to examine the merits of the underlying patent infringement suit, since in the absence of proof of another offsetting consideration, the payment was evidently a quid pro quo for delaying generic entry.[914] As analysed in Chapter 4 of this book, the Supreme Court in *FTC v. Actavis*, albeit refusing to opt for a truncated rule of reason approach, has virtually accepted the same principles for assessing reverse payments as the 3rd Circuit in *K-Dur*.[915]

D Reception of the K-Dur Test

The test applied by the 3rd Circuit in *K-Dur* was criticised for failing to include any factors which could indicate the parties' assessment of patent validity.[916] Another criticism was that the "quick-look" rule of reason would improperly force the parties to

---

908. *In Re: K-Dur Antitrust Litigation*, 686 F.3d 197, 214-215.
909. *In Re: K-Dur Antitrust Litigation*, 686 F.3d 197, 215-218.
910. *In Re: K-Dur Antitrust Litigation*, 686 F.3d 197, 218.
911. *Idem*.
912. *Idem*.
913. *Idem*. The court cited *Andrx Pharmaceuticals., Inc. v. Biovail Corp. Int'l*, 256 F.3d 799, 809 (D.C. Cir. 2001), "[a] payment flowing from the innovator to the challenging generic firm may suggest strongly the anticompetitive intent of the parties entering the agreement."
914. *In Re: K-Dur Antitrust Litigation*, 686 F.3d 197, 218. The court cited *In re Schering-Plough Corp.*, Final Order, 136 F.T.C. 956, 988 (2003), "[a]bsent proof of other offsetting consideration, it is logical to conclude that the *quid pro quo* for the payment was an agreement by the generic to defer entry beyond the date that represents an otherwise reasonable litigation compromise."
915. *See infra* Chapter 4, Part 1, on the analysis of *FTC v. Actavis*.
916. KUTCHER, Waiting Is the Hardest Part, 2013, pp. 1139-1140, "[the court] failed to include any factors that would account for the parties' reasonable assessment of patent validity. Even

litigate the patent infringement suit or to settle without a reverse payment, despite the uncertainty of litigation and its potential adverse consequences.[917] The decision allegedly imposed too harsh antitrust scrutiny on parties settling with reverse payments, while it overlooked the monopolistic nature of patent law, burdening brand-name companies and discouraging innovation on the long-run.[918]

On the flipside, other commentators have seen in *K-Dur* the proper standard of analysis for reverse payment settlements, arguing that it balanced effectively the incentives to brand-name drug innovation against the need to spur both generic challenges targeting weak patents and the price competition of low-cost generic drugs.[919] The "quick-look" rule of reason was seen as the golden section between the per se rule, which could potentially "over-punish" the settling parties, and a "prohibitive" rule of reason analysis, under which courts would have to examine not only the merits of the patent infringement lawsuit but also all of the relevant circumstances of each settlement.[920] The "quick-look" rule of reason could arguably ease administrability for courts in contrast to the rule of reason standard applied in the *FTC v. Actavis* decision, making simpler the detection of anticompetitive agreements aiming to maintain an illegal market monopoly.[921] The constant sophistication of the settlement agreements which increasingly involve multiple licensing agreements (as was the case in *K-Dur*), side agreements (e.g., back-up manufacturing and promotion services as in *FTC v. Actavis* case) or no-AG commitments (as in the *Effexor XR* case) instead of big cash payments highlights this need for simplicity.[922] These evolved settlement mechanisms employed by the settling parties are likely to make the analysis of settlement agreements an increasingly burdensome and complicated task, both for the FTC or other antitrust plaintiffs but also for the adjudicating courts.[923]

---

though the Third Circuit focused on the scope of the patent's improper extension of the presumption of patent validity, the patent does convey a patentee some exclusionary rights within the scope of a valid patent."

917. KHATIBIFAR, Patent-Centric Standard, 2013, p.1392. KHATIBIFAR does not approve of the scope of the patent test adopted by the 2nd Circuit in *Tamoxifen* either, noting that "[t]he primary beneficiaries of this test are those who hold weak patents." Further, KHATIBIFAR advocates that any standard of review shall involve an evaluation of the patent's strength at the time of settlement and argues that the Court of Appeals for the Federal Circuit is the proper venue for such an evaluation. Note that the Federal Circuit is a specialist court with exclusive jurisdiction over patent disputes on the basis of 28 U.S.C. § 1295.
918. WANG, Patentee's Dilemma, 2014, pp. 1236-1237.
919. SCHIPPER, Bad Medicine, 2014, pp. 1261-1262; OKADA, Beyond the Scope, 2012, pp. 327-340. *See also* HAN, Circuit-Splitting Headache, 2013, p. 943, arguing in favour of a presumptive illegality approach when the value of payment exceeds litigation costs, and in favour of per se illegality when the settlement exceeds the scope of the patent.
920. OKADA, Beyond the Scope, 2012, pp. 328-329.
921. SCHIPPER, Bad Medicine, 2014, pp. 1261-1262. *See also* OKADA, Beyond the Scope, 2012, pp. 324-332, arguing in favour of the *K-Dur* decision's presumptive illegality analysis for reverse payment settlements.
922. *See infra* Chapter 4, Parts 2 and 3, analysing alternative settlement mechanisms.
923. *See also* OKADA, Beyond the Scope, 2012, p. 336, advocating in favour of the presumptive illegality approach and highlighting the increased complexity of settlements.

CONCLUSIONS

This chapter provided a detailed analysis of the split between US Circuit Courts on the applicable legal standard to analyse patent settlements involving reverse payments from the brand-name manufacturer to the generic challenger. Initially, the 6th Circuit concluded that Hatch-Waxman settlements involving big value transfers were horizontal agreements aiming to eliminate competition in the drug market and thus were a classic example of per se illegal restraints. Taking a diametrically different approach, the 11th Circuit, the 2nd Circuit and the Court of Appeals for the Federal Circuit applied the scope of the patent test, virtually immunising reverse payment settlements from *any* antitrust scrutiny, without looking into the issue of patent validity or patent infringement. Disagreeing with this position, the 3rd Circuit stressed that split by finding that *any* payment from the patent holder to the generic challenger in order to delay generic entry should be treated as a prima facie evidence of an unreasonable restraint of trade, allowing the settling parties to provide justifications and prove any procompetitive benefits of such a settlement.

The scope of the patent test was the most widely used standard before the decision of the US Supreme Court in *FTC v. Actavis*. The impact that the application of the scope of the patent test had was tremendous: encouraged by the lack of antitrust scrutiny, patent settlements involving reverse payments to delay generic entry increased dramatically. Had the scope of the patent test been confirmed by the Supreme Court, the realities of patent settlements would have changed once and for all, distorting the fragile balance between patent law and antitrust, to the detriment of consumers. Naked agreements aiming in the elimination of competition in the drug market would be sanctified due to the existence of the underlying patent, without examining if this patent conferred indeed the power to eliminate *all* generic competition from the market. The effects of the application of the scope of the patent test extended also to the European Union: it suffices to read the arguments of the settling parties in the case of *Lundbeck v. Commission*, advocating in favour of the application of the scope of the patent test as the applicable standard in the European Union and arguing that patent settlements do not fall within the scope of competition laws. Luckily for competition and for consumers, the Supreme Court rejected the application of the scope of the patent test and opted instead for a rule of reason analysis which is analysed in detail in the following Chapter.

CHAPTER 4

FTC v. Actavis

INTRODUCTION

The split between US Circuit Courts regarding the applicable legal standard for the adjudication or reverse payment settlements paved the road to *FTC v. Actavis*, the first decision of the US Supreme Court on that matter. The harsh criticism against the application of the scope of the patent test, not only by a great number of important commentators but also by the FTC, the DoJ, Senator Orrin Hatch and Representative Henry Waxman – the main sponsors of the Hatch-Waxman Act – were warning signs that the test was unlikely to survive the Supreme Court's review. The *FTC v. Actavis* decision of June 2013 rejected the scope of the patent test as the applicable test for reverse payment settlements, while it also refused to apply a "quick-look" rule of reason standard. Instead, the Supreme Court opted for a rule of reason analysis, making reference to the sliding scale of reasonableness in the antitrust analysis.

  This chapter presents a thorough analysis of the *FTC v. Actavis* decision of the Supreme Court. In Part 1, the *Actavis* settlement facts and the decisions of the district court and the appellate court are presented. Further, the main axons of the *FTC v. Actavis* ruling of the Supreme Court are analysed, outlining the *Actavis* rule of reason test for reverse payment settlements. A discussion on the application of the *Actavis* test follows, aiming to answer some of the most pressing questions the decision gave rise to. The dissenting opinion of Chief Justices Roberts, Scalia and Thomas in *FTC v. Actavis* is also critically analysed. Part 2 of this chapter addresses one of the most important questions *post Actavis*: does the ruling also apply to non-cash payments and notably to settlements involving no-AG commitments? After an analysis of the impact of no-AG commitments on the drug market, the debate among lower courts is presented, along with the position that prevailed.

  Part 3 of this chapter focuses on the analysis of other complex anticompetitive strategies employed to delay generic entry, which extend beyond the frame of reverse payment settlements. "Poison-pill" or "acceleration" clauses, forgiveness of damages, abuse of restricted drug distribution and product-hopping are outlined in detail on the basis of the relevant case law and are critically discussed. The purpose of this final part is to demonstrate how the challenges of regulators and antitrust enforcers increase and multiply over time, subsequent to *FTC v. Actavis*. Even though a great step forward, the decision of the Supreme Court is not a panacea to all the imaginative anticompetitive strategies which constantly evolve. Chapter 4 is the final chapter of the American Law part of this book, followed by the European law part which is comprised by Chapter 5 and Chapter 6.

PART 1 FTC V. ACTAVIS

I Facts and Procedural History

A *The Generic Challenges and the Settlement Agreements*

In 1999, Solvay Pharmaceuticals (Solvay) filed a New Drug Application (NDA) for the brand-name drug AndroGel, which was approved by the FDA a year later. The FDA also granted Solvay a 3-year NCS exclusivity for AndroGel.[924] In 2003, Solvay was granted patent 6,503,894 (the '894 patent) for the gel formulation used in AndroGel by the USPTO, since the patent covering the active ingredient of the drug (synthetic testosterone) had expired decades earlier.[925] Solvay began marketing and selling the drug with great success; from 2000 until 2007, the revenue from AndroGel's sales in the US exceeded $1.8 billion, a number much higher than the drug's development costs.[926]

Subsequently, in 2003, two generic companies, first Watson Pharmaceuticals (Watson) – which subsequently acquired Actavis, Inc. and adopted its name for its global operations – and then Paddock Laboratories (Paddock), filed an ANDA for their own generic versions of AndroGel with paragraph IV certifications based on both patent invalidity and non-infringement.[927] Paddock joined Par Pharmaceuticals (Par) in order to share the litigation's costs and risks, agreeing in return to share part of its potential profits with Par. Taking the paragraph IV route automatically amounts to an artificial act of patent infringement and in 2003, Solvay filed a patent infringement lawsuit against Watson and Paddock. In 2005, the generic manufacturers filed motions for a summary judgment on the validity of '894 patent. While the motions were pending, the 30-month automatic stay of FDA approval expired and Watsons' first-to-file generic drug was approved in January 2006.[928] Watson forecasted that its generic

---

924. *In re: AndroGel Antitrust Litigation (No. II)*, 687 F. Supp. 2d 1371, 1372-1375 (ND Ga. 2010). See *supra* Chapter 2, Part 2, Section III.B, on different kinds of non-patent exclusivities.
925. Besins Healthcare S.A. (the company that developed the drug and granted Solvay a licence to market AndroGel) and Solvay were granted the '894 patent which was to expire in August 2020.
926. *FTC v. Watson Pharmaceuticals et al.*, 677 F. 3d. 1298, 1304 (11th Cir. 2012).
927. Paragraph IV certification on the basis of 21 U.S.C § 355(j)(2)(A)(vii)(IV).
928. 21 U.S.C. § 355(j)(5)(B)(iii) provides for a 30-month automatic stay of FDA approval in case the patent holder files a patent infringement suit against the generic filer, within 45 days from the paragraph IV certification of the latter. See *supra* Chapter 2, Part 2, Section II.D on the paragraph IV mechanism.

drug version would be sold for only 25% of AndroGel's price and would decrease the brand-name drug's profits by 90%, decreasing Solvay's profits by $125 million per year.[929] However, before the court decided any motions of the patent infringement actions and before the generic drug products were put in the market, the litigating parties settled on September 2006.

As part of the settlement agreements, Solvay agreed to voluntarily dismiss the patent infringement actions and the generic companies agreed not to enter the market with their generic versions until August 31, 2015, unless another manufacturer launched a generic version of AndroGel before that date. Moreover, the settling parties entered into business promotion agreements, by means of which the generics undertook the obligation to promote Solvay's branded AndroGel, while Solvay committed to share its profits from AndroGel with Watson and Par.[930] The most striking elements of these agreements are the huge amounts Solvay paid the generic manufacturers in order to settle, even though the latter had no claim for damages against Solvay. Concretely, Solvay paid $60 million to Par and $12 million to Paddock while it agreed to share some of the AndroGel monopoly profits with Watson for nine years (through September 2015), estimating that those payments would be between $19 and $30 million per year.

In 2009, the FTC and direct and indirect purchasers of AndroGel filed an antitrust lawsuit against Solvay, Watson, Par and Paddock, alleging that the settlement agreements were unlawful agreements not to compete, in violation of the Sherman Act and of Section 5(a) of the FTC Act.[931] The plaintiffs contended that the aim of these settlements was to illegitimately maintain Solvay's monopoly by postponing generic entry and to share the profits between the parties at the expense of consumers.[932] With regard to the business promotion agreements, the plaintiffs alleged that they were merely a way for Solvay to pay the generic companies to stay out of the market until the expiration of the agreement.

B The District Court and the Appellate Court Decisions

1 The District Court Decision

In 2010, the District Court for the Northern District of Georgia applied the scope of the patent test and concluded that since the FTC did not allege that the scope of Solvay's patent was exceeded by the settlements, it was not material whether the defendants settled their disputes with reverse payments.[933] As above-analysed in Chapter 3, courts

---

929. *FTC v. Watson Pharmaceuticals, Inc.*, 677 F.3d 1298, 1305 (11th Cir. 2012).
930. *In re: AndroGel Antitrust Litigation (No. II)*, 687 F. Supp. 2d 1371, 1375 (ND Ga. 2010).
931. 15 U.S.C. §§ 1-2; 15 U.S.C. § 45(a)(1), banning "[u]nfair methods of competition in or affecting commerce, and unfair or deceptive acts or practices in or affecting commerce."
932. FTC, Second Amended Complaint for Injunctive and Other Equitable Relief, *FTC v. Watson Pharmaceuticals, Inc., et al.*, no. 1:09-CV-00955-TWT, (May 28, 2009). Available at: http://www.ftc.gov/sites/default/files/documents/cases/2009/05/090528androgelfinalcmpt.pdf (last accessed on March 31, 2018), analysing how these settlements harm competition and consumer welfare, pp. 35-38.
933. *In re: AndroGel Antitrust Litigation (No. II)*, 687 F. Supp. 2d 1371, 1377-1379 (ND Ga. 2010).

applying the scope of the patent test were required to examine the scope of the "exclusionary potential" of the patent – which was not uniformly defined by all Circuits – and to determine the extent to which the agreements at issue exceeded that scope.[934] When this scope was not exceeded, the agreement would not be considered problematic from an antitrust perspective. In the District Court's opinion, the settlements among Solvay and the generic manufacturers did not constitute an antitrust violation since they only: (1) excluded generic AndroGel from the market and not any other product; (2) provided for five years less exclusion than the patent term (AndroGel's gel formulation patent was to expire in August 2020); and (3) prevented the three settling generic companies from entering the market and did not prevent the generic entry of any other companies.[935] The FTC appealed the District Court's decision alleging that it had sufficiently pleaded an antitrust claim by asserting that the parties had entered into the reverse settlements even though Solvay was not likely to prevail in its patent infringement claim against the generic manufacturers.[936]

2 The Appellate Court Decision

The Court of Appeals for the 11th Circuit upheld the decision of the District Court and also applied the scope of the patent test, ruling that "absent sham litigation or fraud in obtaining a patent, a reverse payment settlement is immune from antitrust attack so long as its anticompetitive effects fall within the exclusionary scope of the patent."[937] What counted was the "potential exclusionary power" of the patent at the time of settlement. Even a subsequent court decision finding that the relevant patent was invalid would not alter this finding, if such invalidation would occur after the settlement.[938] The 11th Circuit reaffirmed its previous rulings that patent holders have a "lawful right to exclude others from the market," that "a patent confers the right to cripple competition" and finally emphasised that public policy favours the settlement of disputes and courts could not require parties to continue to litigate.[939]

---

934. *Valley Drug Co. v. Geneva Pharms, Inc.*, 344 F.3d 1294, 1312 (11th Cir. 2003), "[t]hese arguments require consideration of the scope of the exclusionary potential of the patent, the extent to which these provisions of the Agreements exceed that scope, and the anticompetitive effects thereof"). *See* further *supra* Chapter 3, Part 2, on the analysis of the scope of the patent test.
935. *In re: AndroGel Antitrust Litigation (No. II)*, 687 F. Supp. 2d 1371, 1377 (ND Ga. 2010).
936. FTC Brief as Plaintiff-Appellant in *FTC v. Watson Pharmaceuticals, Inc., et al.*, (No. 10-12729-DD), (June 26, 2010), pp. 22-32. Available at: http://www.ftc.gov/sites/default/files/documents/cases/2010/07/100726androgelbrief.pdf (last accessed on March 31, 2018).
937. *FTC v. Watson Pharmaceuticals, Inc.*, 677 F.3d 1298, 1312 (11th Cir. 2012). The 11th Circuit referred to its case law applying the "scope of the patent" test in: *Valley Drug Co. v. Geneva Pharms, Inc.*, 344 F.3d 1294, 1311 (11th Cir. 2003); *Schering-Plough Corp. v. FTC*, 402 F.3d 1056, 1076 (11th Cir. 2005); *Andrx Pharmaceuticals, Inc. v. Elan Corp.*, 421 F.3d 1227, 1235 (11th Cir. 2005).
938. *FTC v. Watson Pharmaceuticals, Inc.*, 677 F.3d 1298, 1308-1309 (11th Cir. 2012).
939. *FTC v. Watson Pharmaceuticals, Inc.*, 677 F.3d 1298, 1314 (11th Cir. 2012), supporting the argument that if the FTC's position were adopted, the benefit of settling litigation would be lost and settlements would be discouraged). The 11th Circuit referred to *Valley Drug*, 344 F.3d 1294, 1306, on the lawful right to exclude others from the market and to *Schering-Plough*, 402 F.3d 1056, 1065-1066, on the right to cripple competition.

Therefore, the 11th Circuit found that the FTC did not sufficiently state an antitrust claim since, in the court's opinion: (1) the FTC equated the likely failure of the infringement claim with an actual result; (2) the FTC's approach required a precarious after-the-fact calculation of the possibility for the patent holder to prevail in the lawsuit; (3) such an approach would impose heavy burdens on parties and courts, depriving them of the benefits of settlement; (4) non-specialised Circuit Courts were ill-equipped to adjudicate the merits of a patent infringement claim; and (5) it would be difficult for a patent holder to escape competition merely by paying the first generic challenger since many other challengers would follow.[940]

II The Supreme Court Decision in *FTC v. Actavis*

A *Rejecting the Scope of the Patent Test*

In June 2013, the Supreme Court found that the 11th Circuit erred in affirming dismissal of the FTC complaint and reversed this decision in *FTC v. Actavis*.[941] The Supreme Court emphasised that patent and antitrust policies are *both* relevant in determining the "scope of patent monopoly" and consequently the scope of antitrust law immunity conferred by a patent, since referring to what the holder of a valid patent would do does not provide a valid answer to the antitrust question.[942] The underlying patent "may or may not be valid, and may or may not be infringed;" even though a valid patent confers certain exclusionary rights to its holder, an *invalidated* patent carries no such rights.[943] The Supreme Court stressed that courts should be able to assess the likely anticompetitive effects of patent settlements *without* litigating the validity of the patent,[944] a stance that was saluted by some and criticised by others.[945]

Rather than measuring the length or amount of a restriction only against the length of a patent's term or its earning potential, the Supreme Court held that traditional antitrust factors, such as likely anticompetitive effects, redeeming virtues, market power and potentially offsetting legal considerations should be considered to determine whether the restraint at issue exceeded the limits of the patent monopoly.[946] The Supreme Court stressed that "patent-related settlement agreements can sometimes violate antitrust laws," while overly restrictive patent licensing agreements (e.g.,

---

940. *FTC v. Watson Pharmaceuticals, Inc.*, 677 F.3d 1298, 1312-1315 (11th Cir. 2012).
941. *FTC v. Actavis, Inc.*, 133 S. Ct. 2223 (2013).
942. *FTC v. Actavis, Inc.*, 133 S. Ct. 2223, 2230-2231 (2013).
943. *FTC v. Actavis, Inc.*, 133 S. Ct. 2223, 2231 (2013).
944. *FTC v. Actavis, Inc.*, 133 S. Ct. 2223, 2237 (2013), "a court, by examining the size of the payment, may well be able to assess its likely anticompetitive effects along with its potential justifications without litigating the validity of the patent."
945. For a criticism of the choice not to examining the validity of the patent as part of the analysis *see* for instance: KNUCKLES, Ongoing Dilemma, 2014, pp. 532-537, arguing that the Supreme Court went too far and supporting the need for the analysis of the underlying patent. *See* however EDLIN, HEMPHIL, HOVENKAMP, SHAPIRO, Activating Actavis, 2013, pp. 18-19, arguing that even if an antitrust court could reliably find that a patent was valid and "strong," such a finding would have limited utility in assessing the parties' antitrust liability.
946. *FTC v. Actavis, Inc.*, 133 S. Ct. 2223, 2231 (2013).

multiple patentee agreements fixing retail prices) have also been struck down under antitrust laws.[947] Despite the general policy of favouring the settlement of disputes, the true underlying concern of the 11th Circuit was that applying antitrust scrutiny to reverse payment settlements would result in lengthy, complex and expensive patent litigation.[948]

1 Reverse Payment Settlements Are Not Antitrust Immune

The scope of the patent test in essence granted antitrust immunity to reverse settlements, provided that the anticompetitive restraints imposed by a reverse settlement did not exceed the "potential exclusionary scope" of the patent. As extensively analysed in Chapter 3 of this book, this test was criticised by several commentators who disapproved of courts assuming patent validity and allowing the patent holder to pay huge amounts in order to shield its patent from being challenged and to keep generic competitors off the market.[949] Decisions applying the scope of the patent test[950] were criticised for misunderstanding patent policy and for avoiding the adjudication of the anticompetitive concerns created by the reverse payment at issue, conveniently "pushing them under the patent scope rug" with disastrous effects on competition.[951] Since the "scope of the patent" test was adopted for the adjudication of reverse payment settlements, there has been an increase of settlements which may have involved pay-for-delay payments from three (in 2005) to forty (in 2012).[952]

Rejecting the scope of the patent test, the Supreme Court ruled that even if it were to accept that the anticompetitive effects of a reverse payment settlement could fall within the exclusionary scope of the patent, such a characterisation would not immunise the agreement from antitrust attack: a traditional antitrust analysis should be

---

947. *FTC v. Actavis, Inc.*, 133 S. Ct. 2223, 2232 (2013). The Supreme Court referred to the following cases: *United States v. Singer Mfg. Co.*, 83 S. Ct.1773 (1963), where the agreements at issue violated antitrust laws, despite settling patent disputes; *United States v. Line Material Co.*, 68 S. Ct. 550 (1948), holding that antitrust laws forbid multiple cross-licensing agreements fixing retail prices; *United States v. New Wrinkle, Inc.*, 72 S. Ct. 350 (1952), refusing antitrust immunity on the basis of the existence of a patent; *Standard Oil Co. (Indiana) v. United States*, 51 S. Ct. 421 (1931), upholding the cross-licensing agreements at hand but stressing that such agreements would have violated the Sherman Act had the patent holders dominated the industry and limited the manufacture and supply of a patented product.
948. *FTC v. Actavis, Inc.*, 133 S. Ct. 2223, 2234 (2013).
949. *See* the 118 Law, Economics, and Business Professors and the American Antitrust Institute Brief as *Amici Curiae* in *FTC v. Watson Pharmaceuticals, Inc. et al.*, no. 12-416, pp. 30-31, (January 29, 2013), criticising the "scope of the patent" test. See HEMPHILL, Paying for Delay, 2006, pp. 1600-1604, and; COTTER, Antitrust Implications, 2004, pp. 1090-1093, advocating in favour of the presumptive illegality approach for reverse payment settlements.
950. *See* for instance *In re Tamoxifen Citrate Antitrust Litigation*, 466 F.3d 187, 212-213 (2nd Cir. 2006); *In re Ciprofloxacin Hydrochloride Antitrust Litig.*, 544 F.3d 1323, 1332-1337 (Fed. Cir. 2008). *See also King Drug Co. of Florence, Inc., et al. v. Cephalon, Inc., et al.*, 702 F. Supp. 2d 514, 528-29, 533 (E.D. Pa. 2010).
951. 118 Professors *Amici* Brief, pp. 13-14, 32.
952. FTC Report, *Agreements Filed with the Federal Trade Commission under the Medicare, Prescription Drug, Improvement and Modernization Act of 2003: Overview of Agreements Filed in FY 2012*. Available athttps://www.ftc.gov/tips-advice/competition-guidance/industry-guidance/health-care/pharmaceutical-agreement-filings (last accessed on March 31, 2018).

applied instead.⁹⁵³ As the Supreme Court noted, "[w]hether a particular restraint lies beyond the limits of patent monopoly, is a conclusion that flows from that analysis and not its starting point."⁹⁵⁴ The Supreme Court concluded that if a reverse payment is "large and unjustified" it could have significant anticompetitive effects which should be assessed by examining, on the one hand, the size of the payment and, on the other hand, the potential justifications invoked, without litigating the validity of the patent.⁹⁵⁵

2 Five Considerations to Reject the Scope of the Patent Test

In *FTC v. Actavis*, the Supreme Court employed five considerations against the application of the scope of the patent test in the case at hand. First, the restraint at issue had the potential for genuine effects on competition: the price of branded AndroGel was kept at patentee-set levels, the monopoly benefits were divided between the settling parties, while the first paragraph IV ANDA filer which would have introduced competition to the market quickly, was removed from consideration. The payment amounted to a *purchase* by the patentee of the exclusive right to sell its product, a right which would be lost if the patent litigation would have continued and in case the underlying patent was found to be invalid or not infringed by the generic product.⁹⁵⁶ Second, even though the Supreme Court accepted that a reverse payment "reflecting traditional settlement considerations" would not normally raise equal concerns that a patent holder was using its monopoly profits to avoid the risks of patent invalidation or of a finding of non-infringement, it affirmed that the anticompetitive consequences such payments give rise to would sometimes prove to be unjustified.⁹⁵⁷

Third, the *size* of the payment was acknowledged to be a strong indicator of the patentee's power to charge prices higher than the competitive level and to bring about anticompetitive harm in practice. A firm without such power is unlikely to make large payments to induce competitors to stay out of its market and reverse payment agreements are associated with higher-than-competitive profits, an indicator of market power.⁹⁵⁸ Fourth, the size of an unjustified reverse payment is also a strong indicator of the patent's weakness, so that it is normally not necessary for courts to litigate patent validity in order to answer the antitrust question. An unjustified large reverse payment normally suggests that the patentee has strong doubts about the patent's survival, so that the payment's objective is to maintain supracompetitive prices and to split the profits between the settling parties rather than face a competitive market.⁹⁵⁹ The

---

953. *FTC v. Actavis, Inc.*, 133 S. Ct. 2223, 2230-2231 (2013).
954. *FTC v. Actavis, Inc.*, 133 S. Ct. 2223, 2231-2232 (2013).
955. *FTC v. Actavis, Inc.*, 133 S. Ct. 2223, 2236-2237 (2013). The Supreme Court stressed that "the size of the unexplained payment can provide a workable surrogate for a patent's weakness, all without forcing a court to conduct a detailed exploration of the validity of the patent itself."
956. *FTC v. Actavis, Inc.*, 133 S. Ct. 2223, 2231-2234 (2013).
957. *FTC v. Actavis, Inc.*, 133 S. Ct. 2223, 2236 (2013).
958. *Idem.*
959. *Idem.*

prevention of even a small risk of competition through a payment constitutes the relevant anticompetitive consequence of such a settlement.[960]

Fifth, the Supreme Court considered that litigating parties would not be prevented from settling their lawsuits if large unjustified reverse payments were subject to antitrust scrutiny and liability. On the contrary, parties should seek other means of settlement that do not restrict competition, such as allowing the generic manufacturer to enter the market before the patent's expiration, without paying it to stay out of the market prior to that point.[961] Even though settling parties may prefer settlements including a reverse payment, when the reason for such a preference is the desire to create and to share monopoly profits, antitrust is likely to prohibit such an arrangement.[962]

The Supreme Court employed these five considerations in order to clarify the reasons for which it rejected the scope of the patent test and chose instead to subject reverse payment settlements to antitrust scrutiny. Ironically, some courts subsequent to *Actavis* misinterpreted these considerations as guidance from the Supreme Court, in "the inquiry as to whether a settlement payment satisfies the rule of reason."[963] Such misinterpretation of the *Actavis* decision would cause great confusion if widely adopted and could amount to challenging the Supreme Court's authority by allowing lower courts to revisit issues that were already resolved in *Actavis*.[964]

3 The Hatch-Waxman Act's Role in Reverse Payment Settlements

Representative Henry A. Waxman, one of the two principal sponsors of the Hatch-Waxman Act, filed a brief as amicus curiae in the *Actavis* case, arguing that the scope of the patent test immunised reverse payment settlements from antitrust scrutiny and "turned on its head" the legislative policy of lowering pharmaceutical prices by enhancing competition.[965] In its decision in *Actavis*, the Supreme Court made extensive reference to the provisions of the Hatch-Waxman Act and highlighted that reverse payment settlements delaying competition were condemned by the sponsors of the Act themselves.[966] The scope of the patent test finds no support in the Hatch-Waxman Act,

---

960. *FTC v. Actavis, Inc.*, 133 S. Ct. 2223, 2236 (2013).
961. *FTC v. Actavis, Inc.*, 133 S. Ct. 2223, 2237 (2013).
962. Idem.
963. *In re Loestrin 24 Fe Antitrust Litig.*, 45 F. Supp. 3d 180, 190 (D.R.I. September 4, 2014). See also *In re Lamictal Direct Purchaser Antitrust Litigation*, No. 12-cv-995 (WHW) (D. N.J. 2014), pp. 14-15, "[t]he *Actavis* opinion lays out five considerations to guide district courts in applying the rule of reason in this context" [internal quotation marks omitted].
964. DAVIS, MCEWAN, Deactivating Actavis, 2015, pp. 575-577.
965. WAXMAN, *Amicus Brief, FTC v. Watson Pharmaceuticals*, p. 25, "[t]he policy chosen by the Eleventh Circuit, however much it may benefit brand-name manufacturers who wish to preserve their monopoly profits is a bad policy from the perspective of the consumer, precisely the constituency Congress was seeking to protect," quoting *K-Dur Antitrust Litigation*, 686 F.3d 197, 217 [internal quotation marks omitted].
966. *FTC v. Actavis, Inc.*, 133 S. Ct. 2223, 2234 (2013). The Supreme Court cited Senator Orrin Hatch, 148 Cong. Rec. 14437 (2002), "it was and it is very clear that the [Hatch-Waxman Act] was not designed to allow deals between brand and generic companies to delay competition;" and Representative Henry A. Waxman 146 Cong. Rec. 18774 (2000), introducing the Drug

which is a statute of "general precompetitive thrust," aiming to facilitate generic challenges to weak patents and which requires parties to a Hatch-Waxman dispute to report the terms of their settlements to federal antitrust regulators.[967]

The Supreme Court examined the role the Hatch-Waxman Act in altering the reality of patent settlements in the context of patent litigation. Even though a big payment to a generic challenger would normally send the signal that the patentee lacked confidence in its patent, amounting to blood in the water and attracting a "feeding frenzy" of generic challenges as the 11th Circuit argued,[968] this would not necessarily be the case due to two unique features of the Hatch-Waxman Act. First, only the first paragraph IV ANDA filer is entitled to the valuable 180-day exclusivity period, during which it markets first the only generic drug which competes with the brand-name drug. Subsequent generic challengers thus stand to win a lot less by bringing a paragraph IV challenge after the first generic already entered the market, so that a payment to the first generic challenger will not necessarily provoke a wave of generic challenges.[969] Second, a later generic paragraph IV filer will need to wait not only for the 180-day period of the first generic entrant to be over before it enters the market, but also for the 30-month stay of the FDA approval of its own ANDA application, that will arise if the patent holder sues for patent infringement.[970] These two features combined mean that a reverse payment settlement between the first generic challenger and the patentee removes from consideration the most motivated and important challenger, who is also the one that is closest to introducing competition to the market.[971]

4 The Public Interest Justifications

The courts which applied the scope of the patent test to reverse payment settlements argued that the test served the public interest by encouraging the settlement of disputes instead of costly and complex litigation.[972] In response to this public interest consideration, certain scholars pointed out that settlements which have adverse effects on

---

Competition Act of 2000 with the aim of deterring companies from "strik[ing] collusive agreements to trade multimillion dollar pay-offs by the brand company for delays in the introduction of lower cost, generic alternatives."
967. *FTC v. Actavis, Inc.*, 133 S. Ct. 2223, 2234 (2013).
968. *FTC v. Watson Pharmaceuticals, Inc.*, 677 F.3d 1298, 1315 (11th Cir. 2012), "[i]f the patent actually is vulnerable, then presumably other generic companies [...] will attempt to enter the market and make their own challenges to the patent. Blood in the water can lead to a feeding frenzy. Although a patent holder may be able to escape the jaws of competition by sharing monopoly profits with the first one or two generic challengers, those profits will be eaten away as more and more generic companies enter the waters by filing their own paragraph IV certifications attacking the patent."
969. *FTC v. Actavis, Inc.*, 133 S. Ct. 2223, 2235 (2013).
970. See also supra, Chapter 2, Part 2, Section I.D. on the analysis of the 180-day exclusivity and the 30-month stay of FDA approval.
971. *FTC v. Actavis, Inc.*, 133 S. Ct. 2223, 2235 (2013).
972. *FTC v. Watson Pharmaceuticals, Inc.*, 677 F.3d 1298, 1314 (11th Cir. 2012); *Schering-Plough Corp. v. FTC*, 402 F.3d 1056, 1072 and 1075 (11th Cir. 2005). The 2nd Circuit also supported the view that courts should encourage settlements in its decision *In re Tamoxifen Citrate Antitrust Litig.*, 466 F.3d, 187, 202 (2nd Cir. 2006). See further supra Chapter 3, Part 2, Section III.C.

consumers are not desirable, while the settlement of patent infringement suits does not necessarily require a reverse payment settlement; other means could be employed, which do not limit competition.[973] The Supreme Court agreed with the latter position and stressed that the relevant antitrust question focuses on the reasons for which the parties prefer settlements including reverse payments: if the underlying reason for such a payment is the extension and sharing of patent monopoly profits, the settlement may be in breach of antitrust laws.[974] Fears concerning the chilling of legitimate settlements are widely overstated, since the imposition of antitrust scrutiny on patent settlements merely removes the incentive to settle so as to split the monopoly profits resulting from agreements restrictive of competition.[975]

B Patent Settlements Are Not Per Se or Presumptively Illegal

1 Rejecting the Per Se Illegality of Reverse Payment Settlements

As above-analysed in Chapter 3, three different Circuit Courts rejected the application of the scope of the patent test to reverse payment settlements: the D.C. Circuit, the 6th Circuit and the 3rd Circuit.[976] The most radical approach was that of the 6th Circuit, which found reverse payment settlements to be per se illegal restraints of trade.[977] The Supreme Court in *Actavis* did not discuss the possibility to adopt the per se illegal approach for the reverse payment settlements at issue, despite the fact that they were not ancillary to any kind of joint production activity, technology sharing or licensing. Therefore, it was argued that the Supreme Court's decision to apply a rule of reason analysis was driven by patent law considerations, since outside the context of patent law such an agreement would be per se unlawful and could even amount to a criminal violation.[978] Even *post Actavis*, the supporters of the per se illegality approach insisted that it is the most efficient liability rule, superior to a rule of reason approach, since it would minimise error costs.[979] However, the majority of the adversaries of the scope of the patent test supported the "quick-look" rule of reason approach, which was also rejected by the Supreme Court in *Actavis*, as analysed in the following section.

---

973. 118 Professors *Amici* Brief, pp. 26-30; CARRIER, Unsettling Settlements, 2009, pp. 60-61, arguing that the Hatch-Waxman Act's specific framework has displaced any general preference for settlements. *See also K-Dur Antitrust Litigation*, 686 F.3d 197, 217-218, noting the Congress's determination that patent challenges necessary for consumer protection should not be set aside in the name of judicial preference for settlement.
974. *FTC v. Actavis, Inc.*, 133 S. Ct. 2223, 2237 (2013).
975. *In Re Cipro Cases I & II*, 348 P.3d 845, 858 (Cal., May 7, 2015).
976. *See supra* Chapter 3, Part 1 and Part 3.
977. *In re: Cardizem CD Antitrust Litigation, et al.*, 332 F.3d 896, 908 (6th Cir. 2003), ruling that the agreement at issue was a per se illegal restraint of trade. *See supra* Chapter 3, Part 1.
978. HOVENKAMP, Scope of the Patent, 2015, p. 518.
979. OWENS, Per Se Prohibition, 2013, pp. 1397-1399.

2 Rejecting the Presumptive Illegality of Reverse Payment Settlements

Numerous scholars of antitrust law supported the adoption of a "quick-look" analysis arguing that reverse payment settlements should be deemed presumptively unlawful, unless parties could invoke procompetitive justifications and rebut this presumption.[980] The "quick-look" approach is reserved for highly suspicious restraints, almost to the point of deserving per se condemnation, but for which at least some consideration of defences or justifications is required due to the lack of judicial experience.[981] Under this approach, once the plaintiff shows that the restraint exists, the anticompetitive effect is presumptively established and the burden of proof shifts to the defendant; the latter must then provide procompetitive justifications for the restraint which outweigh its anticompetitive effects.[982] As above-analysed in Chapter 3, the 3rd Circuit court applied the "quick-look" rule of reason for the analysis of reverse payment settlements in its decision in *In re K-Dur*, opposing the application of the scope of the patent test.[983]

Thirty-one US States joined forces and filed a brief as *Amici curiae* in *FTC v. Actavis*, arguing that drug patents which are challenged under the Hatch-Waxman provisions are usually weak and thus represent "aggressive claims of rights to exclude competition that are legally tenuous."[984] It was also submitted that if the patent at issue is either invalid or not infringed, pay-for-delay agreements should be seen as a form of market division, whereby settling parties, rather than allocating geographic markets, allocate time in between them.[985] 118 Law, Economics, and Business Professors who filed a brief as *Amici curiae* in *FTC v. Actavis* argued that even if market division could ever be justified, it should never be tolerated when it concerns pay-for-delay agreements in the pharmaceutical industry, burdening patients with billions of extra dollars a year and resulting in limited access to prescription medications.[986]

---

980. *See* for instance KUTCHER, Waiting is the Hardest Part, 2013, pp. 1141-1145; ELHAUGE, KRUEGER, Patent Settlement Puzzle, 2012, pp. 323-329; HEMPHILL, Aggregate Approach, 2009, pp. 668-670; HOVENKAMP, JANIS, LEMLEY, Anticompetitive Settlements, 2003, pp. 1759-1766; 118 Professors *Amici* Brief, pp. 30-35.
981. HOVENKAMP, *Federal Antitrust Policy*, 2011, pp. 285-286, explaining that the only acceptable justifications in a "quick-look" inquiry are those showing that the restraint tends to increase output and therefore decrease price. *See supra*, Chapter 3, Part 3, on the application of the "quick-look" rule of reason to reverse payment settlements.
982. HOVENKAMP, *Federal Antitrust Policy*, 2011, pp. 287-289, arguing that the burden of proof should lie with the party whose claim is hardest to believe.
983. *In Re: K-Dur Antitrust Litigation*, 686 F.3d 197, 214 (3rd Cir. 2012), adopting the presumptive illegality approach. *See* further *supra* Chapter 3, Part 3.
984. The States of New York, Arizona, Arkansas et al. Brief as *Amici Curiae* in support of Petitioner for a Writ of *Certiorari*, *FTC v. Watson Pharmaceuticals, Inc., et al.*, no. 12-416, p. 21, (November 5, 2012). *See also* HEMPHILL, SAMPAT, Evergreening, 2012, pp. 327-339, demonstrating that weak patents are disproportionately targeted by paragraph IV challenges.
985. CARRIER, Unsettling Settlements, 2009, pp. 71-73.
986. 118 Professors *Amici* Brief, p. 32. *See idem* pp. 13, 23, arguing that reverse payment settlements pose dangers analogous to territorial market allocation and that paying the generic manufacturer to stay out of the market amounts to market division if the patent is invalid. *See also* FTC, *Pay-for-Delay*, 2010, p. 10, estimating the annual purchaser savings to be gained by the elimination of pay-for-delay agreements at $3.5 billion per year.

The Supreme Court rejected the view that reverse payment settlements are presumptively unlawful. Similarly to its *California Dental* decision – in which the application of a "quick-look" rule of reason was rejected in favour of a full rule of reason analysis –[987] the Supreme Court reaffirmed in *FTC v. Actavis* that the "quick-look" rule of reason is only appropriate in cases where "an observer with even a rudimentary understanding of economics could conclude that the arrangements in question would have an anticompetitive effect on customers and markets."[988] According to the Supreme Court, this criterion was not satisfied with regard to reverse payment settlements, whose likelihood of bringing about anticompetitive effects depended on a number of conditions.[989] The refusal of the Supreme Court to adopt the presumptive illegality approach is not astonishing given the great disparities in the jurisprudence of lower courts on reverse payment settlements. Nevertheless, some antitrust experts argued that the Supreme Court opted for a de facto rule of presumptive illegality "all but in name," due to political or prudential considerations.[990]

C The Rule of Reason for Reverse Payment Settlements

1 Analysis of Ambiguous Practices under the Rule of Reason

The focus on reasonableness began with the *Standard Oil* decision of 1911, in which the Supreme Court ruled that the standard of reason was the measure to be used for determining whether in a given case, a particular act had brought about the wrong which the Sherman Act had the purpose to prevent; ever since the rule of reason virtually dominated the antitrust analysis in the US.[991] The rule of reason analysis is reserved for categories of practices which are facially ambiguous: under some circumstances, a type of conduct may be anticompetitive while under other circumstances it may be lawful.[992] Courts applying the rule of reason are required to weigh a practice's anticompetitive consequences against its prospective procompetitive benefits, since the test is reserved for practices which have a certain potential for both competitive harm and possible social gains. The rule of reason analysis contains more presumptions than any alternative truncated approach; presumptions that are omnipresent and an essential part of the antitrust analysis.[993]

---

987. *California Dental Assn. v. Fed. Trade Comm'n*, 119 S. Ct. 1604, 1612 (1999), finding that an agreement among dentists which restricted prices and quality advertising required a full rule of reason analysis instead of a "quick-look" rule of reason. See also HOVENKAMP, California Dental, 2000, pp. 170-184, analysing the *California Dental* decision and its effect of narrowing the range of horizontal actions which can be subjected to a "quick-look" analysis.
988. *FTC v. Actavis, Inc.*, 133 S. Ct. 2223, 2237 (2013), citing *California Dental Assn. v. Fed. Trade Comm'n*, 119 S. Ct. 1604, 1612 (1999).
989. *FTC v. Actavis, Inc.*, 133 S. Ct. 2223, 2237-2238 (2013). See further *infra* Chapter 4, Part 1, Section II.C.2, analysing the criteria which are linked to the likelihood of a reverse payment settlement to bring about anticompetitive effects according to the Supreme Court.
990. See for instance COTTER, Not the Rule of Reason, 2014, pp. 43-48.
991. *Standard Oil Co. v. United States*, 31 S. Ct. 502, 515-516 (1911). See HOVENKAMP, AREEDA, Fundamentals of Antitrust, 2014, p. 15-3.
992. *California Dental Ass'n v. Fed. Trade Comm'n*, 119 S. Ct. 1604, 1617-1618 (1999).
993. AREEDA, Rule of Reason, 1981, pp. 36-40; HOVENKAMP, Scope of the Patent, 2015, pp. 32-33.

A practice having offsetting procompetitive benefits may be threatening only if the defendants concerned have significant market power. Even a prima facie anticompetitive practice may be justified by procompetitive explanations.[994] These practices will typically be assessed through an inquiry into the defendants' individual or collective market power and a determination of the practice's competitive effects.[995] The main goal of the inquiry is to determine the effect that the challenged practice will have on market output: increasing or decreasing it.[996] Courts have argued that a high market share creates a presumption of market power; however, this presumption can be rebutted by showing that the barriers to entry are low or that rivals can readily expand their output.[997] Moreover, in exclusive dealing cases analysed under the rule of reason, courts presume anticompetitive harm from long-duration contracts and a lack of anticompetitive harm in contracts of shorter duration.[998]

In a rule of reason case, the plaintiff bears the burden of proving that the challenged restraint is of "a type reasonably calculated to have anticompetitive effects" which can be measured by reduced output in a defined market; once this requirement is satisfied, the burden shifts to the defendant, who is then required to show that the restraint at issue serves a legitimate objective.[999] The analysis of a contractual restraint under the rule of reason normally requires demonstrating: (1) sufficient power to warrant a conclusion of plausible anticompetitive harm; (2) a restraint liable to reduce output or increase price; and (3) that the restraint cannot be justified by efficiencies or another redeeming virtue.[1000]

2 The Rule of Reason in FTC v. Actavis

Having rejected both the scope of the patent test and the presumptive illegality approach, the Supreme Court ruled that a rule of reason analysis should be adopted for scrutinising reverse payment settlements under antitrust law.[1001] The Supreme Court stressed in its decision in *Actavis* that the likelihood of a reverse settlement creating anticompetitive effects depends on: (1) the payment's size; (2) the payment's scale

---

994. HOVENKAMP, Sensible Antitrust Rules, 2004, p. 20.
995. HOVENKAMP, JANIS, LEMLEY, Anticompetitive Settlements, 2003, p. 1728.
996. Idem.
997. *Rebel Oil Co., Inc. v. Atlantic Richfield Co.*, 51 F.3d 1421, 1438 (9th Cir. 1995), "[a] market share of 44 percent is sufficient as a matter of law to support a finding of market power, if entry barriers are high and competitors are unable to expand their output in response to supracompetitive pricing;" *FTC et al. v. Promedica Health System Inc.*, No. 3:11 CV 47., at 20-22, 35-37 (N.D. Ohio. March 29, 2011); *Allen v. Dairy Farmers of America, Inc.*, 748 F. Supp. 2d 323, 340 (D. Vt. 2010), finding that market share's evidence is given weight but not conclusiveness by courts.
998. *Omega Environmental, Inc. v. Gilbarco Inc.*, 127 F.3d 1157, 1172 (9th Cir. 1997); *Roland Machinery Co. v. Dresser Industries Inc.*, 749 F.2d 380, 394-395 (7th Cir. 1984), "[e]xclusive-dealing contracts terminable in less than a year are presumptively lawful under section 3;" *Paddock Publications, Inc. v. Chicago Tribune Co. et al.*, 103 F.3d 42, 47 (7th Cir. 1996), cert. denied, 117 S. Ct. 2435 (1997); *Barry Wright Corp. v. ITT Grinnell Corp.*, 724 F.2d 227, 237 (1st Cir. 1983); *U.S. Healthcare, Inc. v. Healthsource, Inc.*, 986 F.2d 589, 596 (1st Cir. 1993).
999. HOVENKAMP, AREEDA, *Fundamentals of Antitrust*, 2014, p. 15-7.
1000. HOVENKAMP, Actavis, 2014, p. 22.
1001. *FTC v. Actavis, Inc.*, 133 S. Ct. 2223, 2236-2237 (2013).

vis-à-vis the anticipated litigation costs; (3) the payment's independence from other services provided to the patent holder; and (4) the lack of any other convincing justification.[1002] Even a payment which aims to prevent a small risk of patent invalidity in essence seeks to prevent the risk of competition and that consequence "constitutes the relevant anticompetitive harm."[1003]

Several prominent antitrust law experts have expressed their disapproval for the strict categorisation of antitrust analysis, arguing instead in favour of a "sliding scale" analysis composed of varying presumptions and proof requirements.[1004] The Supreme Court in *FTC v. Actavis* embraced this approach and confirmed that there is a "sliding-scale" in appraising reasonableness, stressed that "the quality of proof required should vary with the circumstances" and encouraged lower courts to structure their antitrust analysis of reverse payment settlements with regard to the individual circumstances of each case.[1005] The goal should be to find the golden section between using abbreviated antitrust theories which would not allow a proper analysis on the one hand and considering every potential fact of theory of minimal importance on the other hand.[1006] For these reasons, it was argued that the rule of reason analysis that the Supreme Court opted for in *Actavis* is not substantially different from the "quick-look" approach that the FTC supported.[1007] Beyond this debate, a more important question is whether lower courts are apt or willing to embrace the "sliding scale in appraising reasonableness" as the Supreme Court invited them to do.[1008] This seems rather improbable since historically, lower courts tend to recognise the rule of reason, the presumptive illegality and the per se illegality as three distinct tests; the antitrust continuum approach has not been widely embraced in practice.[1009] Unsurprisingly, one of the first district court decisions on reverse payment settlements *post Actavis* applying the rule of reason did not consider the possibility to apply a less rigid standard than the ordinary rule of reason analysis.[1010]

1002. *FTC v. Actavis, Inc.*, 133 S. Ct. 2223, 2237 (2013).
1003. *FTC v. Actavis, Inc.*, 133 S. Ct. 2223, 2236 (2013).
1004. HOVENKAMP, AREEDA, *Fundamentals of Antitrust*, 2014, p. 15-35, "There is always something of a sliding scale in appraising reasonableness, [...]. [T]he quality of proof required should vary with the circumstances." *See also* LEMLEY, LESLIE, Categorical Analysis, 2008, pp. 1256-1270, criticising the system of restraints' categorisation and advocating in favour of a more nuanced approach and greater reliance on empirical evidence.
1005. *FTC v. Actavis*, 133 S. Ct. 2223, 2237-2238 (2013).
1006. *FTC v. Actavis, Inc.*, 133 S. Ct. 2223, 2237-2238 (2013).
1007. COTTER, Not the Rule of Reason, 2014, arguing that the majority opinion in *Actavis* adopted a de facto presumptive illegality approach, even if it suggests that it did not, due to political reasons. *See also* TOKIC, Relevant Product Market, 2015, p. 293, "it is questionable whether reverse payment settlements could ever survive antitrust scrutiny under the current framework, even though the court has rejected the presumptively illegal approach in favor of the rule of reason standard" [internal quotation marks omitted]; KNUCKLES, Ongoing Dilemma, 2014, p. 533.
1008. *FTC v. Actavis, Inc.*, 133 S. Ct. 2223, 2237-2238 (2013).
1009. LEMLEY, LESLIE, Categorical Analysis, 2008, pp. 1218-1219, referring to the Supreme Court's failed attempt to encourage lower courts in appraising the sliding scale of reasonableness, reflected in *National College Athletic Ass'n ("NCAA") v. Board of Regents*, 104 S. Ct. 2948 (1984).
1010. *See* for instance *In re Lamictal Direct Purchaser Antitrust Litigation*, No. 12-cv-995 (WHW) (D. N.J. 2014). *See* however *King Drug Company of Florence, Inc., et al., v. Smithkline Beecham*

3   The Steps of the Rule of Reason Analysis for Reverse Payments

The decision of the Supreme Court of California in *Cipro I & II* provides a good example on how lower courts interpreted the *Actavis* rule of reason; according to the court, *Actavis* mandated four essential steps for a plaintiff to successfully challenge a reverse payment settlement.[1011] First, the antitrust plaintiff must show that the settlement includes a limitation on the generic challenger's entry to the market. Second, that the settlement includes cash or *equivalent financial consideration*. Third, that this consideration exceeds the value of any goods or services provided by the generic manufacturer to the brand – other than delay in generic entry – and fourth, that this consideration exceeds the brand-name manufacturer's expected litigation costs, had the settlement not been concluded.[1012] Once the antitrust plaintiff manages to show an agreement which involves a reverse payment settlement and delays generic entry, the burden of proof shifts to the defendants, who have to show evidence on litigation costs and the value of collateral products and services related to the settlement.[1013] If they fail to do so, the plaintiff has managed to satisfy its burden on these points; if the defendants succeed, the burden of proof then shifts back to the plaintiff who must show that any value transfer exceeds litigation costs or the value of other products or services.[1014] If this latter burden is satisfied, the plaintiff succeeds in making a prima facie case of anticompetitive settlement.[1015]

D   The Questions of the Relevant Market and Market Power

1   Reverse Payment Settlements under Sections 1 & 2 of the Sherman Act

Reverse payment settlements may trigger antitrust claims under both Section 1 of the Sherman Act, which prohibits agreements that unreasonably restrain trade or commerce, and Section 2 of the Sherman Act, prohibiting monopolisation and attempts to monopolise.[1016] As analysed *infra* in Chapter 6 of this book, this is also the case in the European Union, where reverse payment settlement cases may fall within the scope of both Article 101 and Article 102 TFEU, prohibiting anticompetitive agreements and abuses of dominant position respectively.[1017] An antitrust plaintiff alleging a violation

---

Corp., et al., 791 F.3d 388, 413 (3rd Cir. 2015), vacating the judgment of the district court in *In Re Lamictal*, "[o]n remand, we invite the District Court to proceed with the litigation under the traditional rule of reason, tailored, as necessary, to the circumstances of this case."

1011. *In Re Cipro Cases I & II*, 348 P.3d 845 (Cal., May 7, 2015). See also *infra* Chapter 4, Part 2, Section II.B.2., on a similar analysis of the *Actavis* rule of reason articulated in *King Drug Company of Florence, Inc., et al., v. Smithkline Beecham Corp., et al.*, 791 F.3d 388 (3rd Cir. 2015).
1012. *In Re Cipro Cases I & II*, 348 P.3d 845, 865 (Cal., May 7, 2015).
1013. *In Re Cipro Cases I & II*, 348 P.3d 845, 867 (Cal., May 7, 2015).
1014. *Idem*.
1015. *Idem*, noting that the larger the gap between the value paid and the actual litigation costs and the fair market value of any other products or services that are part of the agreement, the stronger the inference of an anticompetitive settlement.
1016. 26 Stat. 209, 15 U.S.C. §§ 1-2.
1017. See *infra* Chapter 6, Part 1, Section III, analysing the *Servier* case.

of Section 1 of the Sherman Act shall establish two main elements: first, that the defendant has market power in the relevant market and second, the defendant's specific intent to restrain competition.[1018] Similarly, a Section 2 plaintiff shall demonstrate the defendant's specific intent of monopolising the market and a "dangerous probability" of succeeding in doing so.[1019] The definition of the relevant market is an essential part of the antitrust analysis under both Section 1 and Section 2 of the Sherman Act; absent the definition of the relevant market, it is nearly impossible to measure the defendant's ability to limit or eliminate competition.[1020] Plaintiffs are requested to make allegations towards the aim of defining the relevant market also in antitrust cases concerning patented products.[1021]

2 The Definition of the Relevant Market

The relevant market comprises of two components: the relevant product market and the relevant geographical market.[1022] In patent law cases, the definition of the relevant product market is more important, considering that the patent functions as a legal barrier to enter into the market.[1023] A group of products constitutes a market if a hypothetical defendant controlling its output may maximise its profits by charging significantly higher than the competitive prices, for a significant time-period.[1024] In order to define the relevant product market, one shall examine the products that are interchangeable by consumers for the same purposes[1025] and are considered such close substitutes that a relatively slight price change will induce intolerable shifts of demand from one product to the other.[1026] Such products have a high degree of interchangeability for buyers and therefore also a high cross-elasticity of demand.[1027]

1018. *CVD, Inc. v. Raytheon Co.*, 769 F.2d 842, 851 (1st Cir., 1985).
1019. *Idem*; *Handgards, Inc. v. Ethicon, Inc.*, 743 F.2d 1282, 1293 (9th Cir.1984).
1020. *Walker Process Equip. Inc. v. Food Mach. & Chem. Corp.*, 86 S. Ct. 347, 350 (1965); *Berkey Photo, Inc. v. Eastman Kodak Co.*, 603 F.2d 263, 268 (2nd Cir., 1979), stressing that defining the relevant market is the first step in the court's analysis of a monopolisation claim; *Morgenstern v. Wilson*, 29 F.3d 1291, 1296 (8th Cir., 1994), "[a]n actual monopolization claim often succeeds or fails strictly on the definition of the product or geographic market."
1021. *Delano Farms Co. v. California Table Grape Comm'n*, 655 F.3d 1337, 1351-1352 (Fed. Cir., 2011).
1022. *Brown Shoe Co. v. United States*, 82 S. Ct. 1502, 1523 (1962); *United States v. E. I. du Pont de Nemours & Co.*, 77 S. Ct. 872, 877 (1957).
1023. *Avery Dennison Corp. v. Acco Brands, Inc.*, No. CV99-1877DT (MCX), *14, (C.D. Cal., 22 February 2000), "[c]ommon entry barriers include: patents or other legal licenses, control of essential or superior resources, entrenched buyer preferences, high capital entry costs and economies of scale."
1024. HOVENKAMP, AREEDA, *Fundamentals of Antitrust*, 2014, p. 5-59, explaining that prices are "significantly higher" in general when they are 5% above current price levels of 10% above the competitive level.
1025. *United States v. E. I. du Pont de Nemours & Co.*, 76 S. Ct. 994, 1005-1006 (1956).
1026. HOVENKAMP, AREEDA, *Fundamentals of Antitrust*, 2014, p. 5-73, 5-74; *Korkala v. Allpro Imaging, Inc.*, No. 08-2712, at *5-6 (D. N.J., August 10, 2009), "[d]ifferences in price, use, and quality of the product and substitutes proffered are factors taken into consideration when determining reasonable interchangeability" [internal quotation marks omitted]; *Tunis Brothers Co., Inc. v. Ford Motor Co.*, 952 F.2d 715, 722 (3rd Cir. 1991); *Queen City Pizza v. Dominos Pizza*, 124 F.3d 430, 437 (3rd Cir. 1997).
1027. HOVENKAMP, AREEDA, *Fundamentals of Antitrust*, 2014, p. 5-73, 5-74.

The concept of reasonable interchangeability is not limited to the functional interchangeability of products but also to the actual inclination of consumers to switch from one product to another as a response to price changes.[1028] Another key-concept for the definition of the relevant product market is that of economic substitutability.[1029] Two products are in the same relevant market if substitutability of either demand or supply is very high at a competitive price level.[1030] The examination of potential barriers to enter the relevant product market also plays an essential role.[1031] To define the product market with higher precision, courts evaluate the existence of potential sub-markets within the product market; such sub-markets may form a separate market for antitrust scrutiny purposes.[1032] Some of the main criteria for evaluating the existence of such sub-markets are cross-elasticity of demand, industry or public recognition of the sub-market as a separate economic entity, any peculiar characteristics and uses of the relevant product, distinct consumers or prices, sensitivity to price changes, specialised vendors, etc.[1033] All in all, the definition of the relevant product market is often a challenging and complicated endeavour.

3 The Question of Showing Market Power

Market power is a firm's ability to increase its profits by reducing its output and by charging more than a competitive price for its product(s), without losing so many sales that the price increase is at the end unprofitable.[1034] Market power is also expressed as "the ratio of a seller's marginal cost to its profit maximizing price;" it is in essence a function of three different values: the defendant's market share, the demand elasticity in the entire market and the cross-elasticity of supply of competitors or potential competitors.[1035] There is a correlation between market power and market shares: all other things equal, a firm with a large market share can increase prices profitably much easier than a firm with a small market share.[1036] A firm with a large market share of a defined relevant market is likely to have market power within that market, so that the computation of market shares is used as a proxy for the calculation of market power in

---

1028. *American Academic Suppliers, Inc. v. Beckley-Cardy, Inc.*, 922 F.2d 1317, 1320-1321 (7th Cir. 1991); *Brown Shoe Co. v. United States*, 82 S. Ct. 1502, 1523-1524 (1962), "[t]he outer boundaries of a product market are determined by the reasonable interchangeability of use or the cross-elasticity of demand between the product itself and substitutes for it;" *George R. Whitten, Jr., Inc. v. Paddock Pool Builders, Inc.*, 508 F.2d 547, 552 (1st Cir. 1974).
1029. *Matsushita Elec. Indus. Co. v. Zenith Radio Corp.*, 106 S. Ct. 1348, 1356-1357 (1986).
1030. Hovenkamp, Areeda, *Fundamentals of Antitrust*, 2014, p. 5-61, noting that if product A and product B do not belong in the same market, a significant price increase beyond competitive price levels in product A, will not induce consumers to buy instead product B, neither induce producers of product B to produce more product A.
1031. *American Academic Suppliers, Inc. v. Beckley-Cardy, Inc.*, 922 F.2d 1317, 1320-1321 (7th Cir. 1991).
1032. *Brown Shoe Co. v. United States*, 82 S. Ct. 1502, 1523-1524 (1962).
1033. Idem.
1034. Hovenkamp, *Federal Antitrust Policy*, 2011, pp. 88-89.
1035. Sullivan, Hovenkamp, Shelanski, Leslie, *Antitrust Law*, 2014, pp. 638-641.
1036. Hovenkamp, *Federal Antitrust Policy*, 2011, pp. 90-91.

antitrust cases.¹⁰³⁷ Alternative ways to establish market power include measuring residual demand directly, observing the existence of persistent price discrimination and persistent monopoly profits.¹⁰³⁸

Intellectual property rights do not confer *ipso facto* any market power; the great majority of patents do not confer substantial market power in a relevant market.¹⁰³⁹ IP rights are relatively easy to obtain, may have low to no market value and their holders usually face competition from a number of rivals.¹⁰⁴⁰ With regard to patents, the mere possession of a patent does not create a presumption of market power.¹⁰⁴¹ While the Supreme Court initially employed a presumption that patents confer substantial power in a line of cases concerning tying, subsequently this presumption was abandoned in favour of more vigorous market power requirements.¹⁰⁴² On the contrary, the Supreme Court's jurisprudence on Section 2 of the Sherman Act is consistent throughout the years: sufficient market power cannot be inferred from the existence of intellectual property rights.¹⁰⁴³

4   Ways to Define the Relevant Market in Reverse Payment Cases

As analysed in Chapter 3, before the *Actavis* decision of the Supreme Court, courts applied the scope of the patent test, the presumptive illegality and the per se illegality approach for the adjudication of reverse payment settlements. This is the reason why the definition of the relevant product market is nearly absent in *pre-Actavis*

1037. HOVENKAMP, AREEDA, *Fundamentals of Antitrust*, 2014, p. 5-18; HOVENKAMP, *Federal Antitrust Policy*, 2011, pp. 92-93.
1038. HOVENKAMP, *Federal Antitrust Policy*, 2011, pp. 146-155.
1039. SULLIVAN, HOVENKAMP, SHELANSKI, LESLIE, *Antitrust Law*, 2014, p. 706; HOVENKAMP, AREEDA, *Fundamentals of Antitrust*, 2014, pp. 5-107, 5-110.
1040. HOVENKAMP, AREEDA, *Fundamentals of Antitrust*, 2014, pp. 5-107, 5-110.
1041. *Jefferson Parish Hosp. Dist. No. 2 v. Hyde*, 104 S. Ct. 1551, 1571, fn. 7 (1984) (O'Connor, J., concurring), "[...] a patent holder has no market power in any relevant sense if there are close substitutes for the patented product."); *In re Indep. Serv. Orgs. Antitrust Litig.*, 203 F.3d 1322, 1325-1326 (Fed. Cir. 2000). "[a] patent alone does not demonstrate market power."); *Abbott Labs. v. Brennan*, 952 F.2d 1346, 1354-1355 (Fed. Cir. 1991), "[a] patent does not of itself establish a presumption of market power in the antitrust sense;" *CCPI, Inc. v. Am. Premier, Inc.*, 967 F. Supp. 813, 817-818 (D. Del. 1997), "[...] merely obtaining a patent for a product does not create a product market for antitrust purposes;" *C.R. Bard, Inc. v. M3 Systems, Inc.*, 157 F.3d 1340, 1368 (Fed. Cir. 1998), "[i]t is not presumed that the patent-based right to exclude necessarily establishes market power in antitrust terms."
1042. *Jefferson Parish Hosp. Dist. No. 2 v. Hyde*, 104 S. Ct. 1551, 1560-1561 (1984). See also *Motion Picture Parents Co. v. Universal Film Mfr. Co.*, 37 S. Ct. 416, 518-519 (1917); *Morton Salt Co. v. G.S. Suppiger Co.*, 62 S. Ct. 402, 404-406 (1942), condemning tying without any previous inquiry into market power. See further HOVENKAMP, AREEDA, *Fundamentals of Antitrust*, 2014, pp. 5-110, 5-112.
1043. *United States v. E. I. du Pont de Nemours & Co.*, 76 S. Ct. 994, 1011-1012 (1956), commonly known as the Cellophane case, finding that despite the fact that in general patents confer monopoly the antitrust defendant lacked market power; *Walker Process Equip., Inc. v. Food Mach & Chem. Corp.*, 86 S. Ct. 347, 350 (1965), finding that the definition of the relevant market is necessary to measure the defendant's ability to lessen or destroy competition; *Spectrum Sports, Inc., v. McQuillan*, 113 S. Ct. 884, 890-892, (1993) finding that the definition of a relevant market is necessary and that a patent does not presumptively define the relevant market.

jurisprudence on patent settlements concluded in the context of Hatch-Waxman litigation.[1044] For instance, in *Schering-Plough* the 11th Circuit rejected the application of the rule of reason by the FTC and the ALJ;[1045] the latter's analysis included the definition of the relevant geographic and product markets, calculating market shares, etc. but was found to be an "inappropriate way of analysing" the reverse payments at issue.[1046]

The adoption of the rule of reason for the antitrust analysis of reverse payment settlements is likely to change this in the long term: defining the relevant product market is likely to become increasingly important.[1047] Determining who creates the demand for the pharmaceutical product is not always easy, given the major role doctors, pharmacists and insurance companies play in choosing and prescribing a drug to a patient, who in most cases has little to no saying on the matter.[1048] Even if one accepts that common market definition principles established in the Supreme Court's jurisprudence shall apply also to the definition of pharmaceuticals' markets, the actions of physicians, pharmacists, patients and third-party payers shall also be considered in defining the relevant markets.[1049] Given the specificities and complexities of the highly regulated market of pharmaceuticals, determining the relevant

---

1044. *See* for instance *Valley Drug Co. v. Geneva Pharms, Inc.*, 344 F.3d 1294 (11th Cir. 2003); *In Re: K-Dur Antitrust Litigation*, 686 F.3d 197, 214 (3rd Cir. 2012); *FTC v. Watson Pharmaceuticals*, 677 F.3d 1298 (11th Cir. 2012), none of the decisions discussing the question of the relevant market. *See* however *In re Cardizem CD Antitrust Litig.*, 105 F. Supp. 2d 618, 680-681 (E.D. Mich. 2000), ruling that a brand-name drug and its generic versions formed the relevant market; *In re Terazosin Hydrochloride Antitrust Litig.*, 352 F. Supp. 2d 1279, 1319, fn. 40 (S.D. Fla. 2005), finding that even though the per se rule makes unnecessary the definition of relevant market and anticompetitive effects, the relevant market at issue was the brand-name drug and its generic equivalents.
1045. *Schering-Plough Corp. v. FTC*, 402 F.3d 1056, 1065 (11th Cir. 2005), rejecting the application of the rule of reason in *Schering-Plough Corp., Upsher-Smith Labs. & Am. Home Prods. Corp.*, Initial Decision, FTC Docket, No. 9297 (June 27, 2002), pp. 101-119.
1046. *Schering-Plough Corp. v. FTC*, 402 F.3d 1056, 1065 (11th Cir. 2005), rejecting the application of the rule of reason, including the definition of the relevant product and geographic markets, as inappropriate.
1047. TOKIC, Relevant Product Market, 2015, pp. 286-287. *See also Copperweld Corp. v. Independence Tube Corp.*, 104 S. Ct. 2731, 2740 (1984), stressing that a rule of reason analysis requires "an inquiry into market power and market structure;" *Continental T.V., Inc. v. GTE Sylvania Inc.*, 97 S. Ct. 2549, 2564-2566 (1977); *Tanaka v. Univ. of S. Cal.*, 252 F.3d 1059, 1063 (9th Cir. 2001), "[a] restraint violates the rule of reason if the restraint's harm to competition outweighs its procompetitive effects. The plaintiff bears the initial burden of showing that the restraint produces 'significant anticompetitive effects' within a relevant market" [internal quotation marks omitted]; *California Dental Ass'n v. Fed. Trade Comm'n*, 224 F.3d 942, 952 (9th Cir. 2000), "[p]roving injury to competition in a rule of reason case almost uniformly requires a claimant to prove the relevant market and to show the effects of competition within that market."
1048. DANZON, CHAO, Regulation, 2000, pp. 314-321; GUHA, LACY, WOODHOUSE, Competition, 2008, pp. 6-8.
1049. *See* for instance MORSE, Product Market Definition, 2003, pp. 659-662, arguing that common market definition principles shall apply also to pharmaceutical markets, but acknowledging the role of physicians, pharmacists, patients and third-party payers in defining the relevant market "in the future."

product market is not a simple task and raises doubts on whether the traditional empirical analysis of the relevant product market is going to suffice.[1050]

One option would be to define the relevant product market on the basis of therapeutically substitutable drugs available to a doctor,[1051] since evidence of competition has been detected between therapeutic substitutes.[1052] This method was already employed in reverse payment settlement cases *pre-Actavis*; for instance, in *Schering-Plough* the ALJ examined the functional interchangeability of potassium supplements; after finding that they were interchangeable with the *K-Dur* 20 drug, he ruled that they were the relevant product market.[1053] In order to determine therapeutic equivalence of drugs in reverse payment cases, the FTC relied *inter alia* on drugs' safety and efficacy, possible side effects, the drugs' chemical composition, the risks associated with switching patients from one drug to another, etc.[1054]

Quantifying the cross-price elasticity of demand for branded and generic drugs belonging to the same therapeutic class is also possible. There is a degree of interrelationship between branded drugs and their respective generics – evidenced also by the price decreases of the brand-name drug subsequent to generic entry – which led some courts define the relevant product market as the combined group of brand-name drugs and their respective generic versions.[1055] A study (limited however to only four drugs) found that there is quite high demand elasticity between generic substitutes, while the demand elasticity between therapeutic substitute drugs which are chemically distinct is

---

1050. TOKIC, Relevant Product Market, 2015, pp. 291-292. *See* SORENSEN, SHADOWEN, Model Jury Instructions, 2015, pp. 654-662, proposing direct and indirect ways for a jury in a reverse payment settlement case to define the relevant market and assess the brand-drug manufacturer's market power.
1051. MORSE, Product Market Definition, 2003, p. 676, arguing that product market analysis should focus on the drugs' therapeutic indications and consider whether drugs may be substitutes for the treatment of disease or condition at issue, on the basis of the drugs' mechanisms of action, therapeutic profiles, methods of administration and side effects. *See also Barr Laboratories Inc. v. Abbott Laboratories*, 978 F. 2d 98, 115-116 (3rd Cir. 1992), where the court instructed the jury to consider whether the products at issue are reasonably interchangeable from the point of view of doctors and pharmacists, the persons creating the demand for the products at issue.
1052. DANZON, CHAO, Regulation, 2000, pp. 341-345, noting that the number of therapeutically equivalent molecules does not seem to put competitive pressure on price, while lower prices is evidence of competition between therapeutic substitutes of successive entrants.
1053. *Schering-Plough Corp., Upsher-Smith Labs. & Am. Home Prods. Corp.*, Initial Decision, FTC Docket, No. 9297 (June 27, 2002), pp. 84-90, the Administrative Law Judge decision finding that the relevant product market are *all* potassium supplements, not only the extended release ones; *see* FTC, Administrative Complaint, *Schering-Plough*, 2001, p. 4, arguing that the relevant product markets were *all* potassium supplements, including the narrower market of 20-milliequivalent extended-release potassium supplements. *See also* FTC, Complaint, *Abbott Labs. & Geneva Pharm., Inc.*, FTC Docket Nos. C-3945, 3946 (May 22, 2000), paras 10-12 [cited as: FTC, Complaint, *Abbott Labs. & Geneva Pharm.*, 2000]; FTC, Complaint, *Hoechst Marion Roussel, Inc. & Andrx Corp.*, FTC Docket No. 9293 (March 16, 2000), para. 12 [cited as: FTC, Complaint, *Hoechst Marion Roussel, Inc. & Andrx Corp.*, 2000]. In both complaints the FTC found that the relevant product market at issue was the respective brand-name drug and its generic equivalents.
1054. *See also* FTC, Complaint, *Abbott Labs. & Geneva Pharm.*, 2000, paras 10-12; FTC, Complaint, *Hoechst Marion Roussel, Inc. & Andrx Corp.*, 2000, para. 12.
1055. *Geneva Pharms. Tech. Corp. v. Barr Labs., Inc.*, 201 F. Supp. 2d 236, 269-270 (S.D.N.Y. 2002).

smaller but sometimes significant.[1056] However, the role that pharmaceuticals' prices play in physicians' prescribing practices is neither clear nor stable.[1057]

5 *Relevant Market Definition* Post Actavis

The questions of whether market definition will play a meaningful role to the rule of reason analysis and of whether and to what extent the anticompetitive effects of patent settlements need to be demonstrated are two of the many questions that are considered to be still open after the *Actavis* decision.[1058] The Supreme Court's observation that the size of a payment is a strong indicator of market power[1059] has been interpreted by some of the leading commentators as implying that there is no need to define the relevant market and to compute the respective market share, if there is a large unjustified reverse payment.[1060] It was argued that market power can be measured even in the absence of a market definition, and *Actavis* was interpreted as ruling that market power can be inferred by a very large payment from a patentee to a rival so that the latter stays out of its market.[1061]

Other antitrust experts considered that showing that the brand-name firm had market power in the relevant product market was a prerequisite in order to establish that a reverse payment had anticompetitive effects.[1062] It was also sustained that even if a settlement involves a large payment, the size of the payment merely indicates the wealth of the antitrust defendant, since it could emanate from other patented or not patented products.[1063] However, the Supreme Court did create a presumption upon the finding of a large payment, by requiring the defendant to provide an explanation for a payment that exceeds the anticipated litigation costs.[1064] Case law subsequent to *Actavis* also found that a reverse payment, exceeding litigation costs and the value of collateral products and services, raises the presumption that the patent holder has sufficient market power to conclude a settlement generating significant anticompetitive effects.[1065]

1056. FISHER, COCKBURN, GRILICHES, HAUSMAN, Demand, 1997, p. 445.
1057. *See* for instance *SmithKline Corp. v. Eli Lilly & Co.*, 427 F. Supp. 1089, 1117 (E.D. Pa. 1976), where the court stressed that physicians do not employ a cost-benefit analysis in their daily prescribing practice; *Warner-Lambert Co.*, 87 F.T.C. 812, 877 (1976), where the FTC argued that physicians are not so fixed on their prescribing factors that they will always be indifferent to a substantial price increase and will not shift their prescriptions to lower-priced alternatives.
1058. *See* further, WRIGHT Joshua D., Commissioner, FTC, Remarks, *FTC v. Actavis and the Future of Reverse Payment Cases*, (September 26, 2013), p. 8. Available at: https://www.ftc.gov/sites/default/files/documents/public_statements/ftc-v.actavis-future-reverse-payment-cases/130926actavis.pdf. (last accessed on March 31, 2018).
1059. *FTC v. Actavis, Inc.*, 133 S. Ct. 2223, 2236 (2013).
1060. HOVENKAMP, *Innovation and Competition*, 2013, p. 100; HOVENKAMP, JANIS, LEMLEY, LESLIE, *IP And Antitrust*, 2015, p. 15-44.
1061. HOVENKAMP, AREEDA, *Fundamentals of Antitrust*, 2014, pp. 5-10 to 5-13.
1062. ADDANKI, BUTLER, Activating Actavis, 2014 pp. 86-89.
1063. TOKIC, Relevant Product Market, 2015, pp. 288-289.
1064. *See* HOVENKAMP, Scope of the Patent, 2015, pp. 33-34.
1065. *In Re Cipro Cases I & II*, 348 P.3d 845, 869 (Cal., May 7, 2015), "[l]ogically, a patentee would not pay others to stay out of the market unless it had sufficient market power to recoup its

A number of district court decisions subsequent to *Actavis* have discussed the matter of the relevant market.[1066] In the *post Actavis* decision of *Nexium*, the district court for the district of Massachusetts accepted the plaintiffs' allegation that the relevant market was the market for brand-name drug and its generic equivalents sharing the same active ingredient.[1067] The court noted that a jury would be better equipped for the factual determination of reasonable interchangeability between the brand-name drug and its generic versions.[1068] Even though other drugs could be used to treat related health conditions, this was immaterial with regard to the product market inquiry. Moreover, according to the Supreme Court's jurisprudence a market can be comprised by one single product.[1069] Plaintiffs did not even need to define the relevant market in order to state their antitrust claims in *Nexium*. Direct evidence of market power was available since the brand-name drug's price was maintained in supercompetitive levels, without losing substantial sales to other products prescribed for the same purposes.[1070] In *Aggrenox*, another reverse payment settlement case after *Actavis*, the plaintiffs alleged a narrower definition of the product market, limited to the generic version of a particular drug and excluding from its scope the chemically identical brand-name drug version.[1071] In *Aggrenox* too the court stressed that a "fact-intensive inquiry" was required to define the relevant market, but upheld as highly plausible the allegation that the brand-name manufacturer was able to charge supercompetitive prices in a market with no cross-elasticity of demand with other drugs.[1072]

---

payments through supercompetitive pricing;" *In Re Nexium (Esomeprazole) Antitrust Litig.*, 968 F. Supp. 2d 367, 385 (D. Mass. 2013) "[t]his Court need not engage in an extensive analysis of circumstantial evidence of market power because direct evidence of such power is available – the Direct Purchasers have thoroughly alleged that AstraZeneca, in its position as a monopolist, has been able to charge supercompetitive prices for brand Nexium."

1066. *In Re Nexium (Esomeprazole) Antitrust Litig.*, 968 F. Supp. 2d 367, 387-388 (D. Mass. 2013), affirmed by *In Re Nexium (Esomeprazole) Antitrust Litig.*, 842 F.3d 34, (1st Cir. 2016); *In re Aggrenox Antitrust Litig.*, 94 F. Supp. 3d 224, 245-247 (D. Conn. March 23, 2015).
1067. *In Re Nexium (Esomeprazole) Antitrust Litig.*, 968 F. Supp. 2d 367, 387-388 (D. Mass. 2013).
1068. *Idem*, "[a]lthough it may be beyond this Court's competence to confirm the accuracy of the Direct Purchasers' characterization of the reasonable interchangeability of brand Nexium with other drugs, such a factually intensive determination is better left for resolution by a jury."
1069. *In Re Nexium (Esomeprazole) Antitrust Litig.*, 968 F. Supp. 2d 367, 387-388 (D. Mass. 2013), noting that a brand-name drug and its generic versions can "fall within the bounds of a relevant market." The court referred to *Eastman Kodak Co. v. ImageTechnical Services, Inc.*, 112 S. Ct. 2072, 2089-2090 (1992).
1070. *In Re Nexium (Esomeprazole) Antitrust Litig.*, 968 F. Supp. 2d 367, 388-389, fn. 19, (D. Mass. 2013), "[t]his Court need not engage in an extensive analysis of circumstantial evidence of market power because direct evidence of such power is available – the Direct Purchasers have thoroughly alleged that AstraZeneca, in its position as a monopolist, has been able to charge supercompetitive prices for brand Nexium."
1071. *In re Aggrenox Antitrust Litig.*, 94 F. Supp. 3d 224, 245-247 (D. Conn. March 23,2015).
1072. *In re Aggrenox Antitrust Litig.*, 94 F. Supp. 3d 224, 247 (D. Conn. March 23, 2015).

III Applicable Test and Possible Justifications

A Anticompetitive Versus Permissible Settlements

The ruling of the Supreme Court in *FTC v. Actavis* does not provide a clear-cut, black-or-white answer on which settlements are unlawful from an antitrust perspective. Opting for a rule of reason analysis, the Supreme Court ruled that "large and unjustified payments" *may* have anticompetitive effects and that parties who make such payments *may* be unable to justify them.[1073] Nonetheless, the Supreme Court provided examples of lawful settlements, stating that it is normally permissible: (1) to make a payment which reflects traditional settlement considerations and does not exceed the litigation costs saved by means of the settlement, or to pay the fair value for services the generic has promised to perform,[1074] and; (2) to conclude a settlement that allows generic entry prior to the patent's expiration without any payment to the generic challenger.[1075]

On the contrary, an unexplained large reverse payment normally reflects the serious doubts the patent holder has concerning the validity of its patent and suggests that the objective of the payment is to prolong monopoly profits and to divide them among settling parties; the maintenance of prices at patentee-set levels and the exclusion of competition constitute the anticompetitive consequences of such a payment.[1076] If a settlement involves a large unexplained payment over a long period of time and that payment is subject to a number of contingencies which are related to the patent at issue, it is quite likely that the settling parties are sharing monopoly profits generated by avoiding competition.[1077]

Both of the proposed examples of the Supreme Court were criticised as problematic. With regard to the fair value of services, it is objectively difficult to determine the exact criteria on which such fair value could be calculated. On the other hand, even settlements allowing generic entry prior to the patent's expiration without any payment could prove to be problematic and merely be used to conceal other forms of anticompetitive agreement; *ergo* licensing agreements should not be credited "as a robustly procompetitive defence" and be granted categorical antitrust immunity.[1078] After all, when a patent is likely to be found invalid, licensing may amount to an excellent opportunity for the parties to collude under the guise of lawful patent licensing.[1079] Commentators urged lower courts and juries not to upgrade these two examples of justifications by the Supreme Court to categorical exceptions to the application of

---

1073. FTC v. Actavis, Inc., 133 S. Ct. 2223, 2237 (2013).
1074. FTC v. Actavis, Inc., 133 S. Ct. 2223, 2236 (2013).
1075. FTC v. Actavis, Inc., 133 S. Ct. 2223, 2234, 2237 (2013). The Court stated that such a settlement without payment "would also bring about competition, again to the consumer's benefit." The reasoning of the Court is supported by the relevant FTC study, demonstrating that agreements including payment on average prohibit generic entry for seventeen months longer than agreements without payments. See further, FTC, *Pay-for-Delay*, 2010, p. 4.
1076. FTC v. Actavis, Inc., 133 S. Ct. 2223, 2236-2237 (2013).
1077. TOKIC, Relevant Product Market, 2015, p. 294.
1078. CRANE, Reverse Payment Fallacy, 2014, pp. 57-58.
1079. POSNER, *Economic Analysis of Law*, 2014, pp. 420-421.

antitrust scrutiny. As far as litigation costs are concerned, it was argued that the Supreme Court did not create a safe harbour for reverse payments that do not exceed litigation costs.[1080] Along a similar line of reasoning, it was noted that even payments that represent a fair value of the provided services are not ironclad and should be subject to antitrust scrutiny if it is shown that the underlying agreements represented a payment to delay generic entry.[1081]

1 Agreements Splitting the Patent Term Without a Payment

Absent a payment, an agreement to postpone generic entry arguably represents a fair approximation of the expected level of competition, had the parties litigated the patent infringement suit.[1082] The compromise of the parties on the entry date is an indicator of the parties' joint assessment of the likely outcome of the patent infringement litigation lawsuit.[1083] Pure "patent-term split agreements" where the settling parties divide the remaining patent term and chose a time for generic entry before patent expiration do not violate antitrust laws; any delay in generic entry may be attributed to the effective strength of the challenged patent(s) and not to the settlement agreement.[1084] Nevertheless, certain caveats are still necessary; first, such a settlement should not include *any form* of exclusion payment. Naturally, there is always a risk that the parties will attempt or succeed to conceal a secret exclusion payment, e.g., by agreeing under the table to cartelise the industry after generic entry.[1085] Second, the settlement should not lead to a bottleneck effect for subsequent generic challengers, allowing the first paragraph IV ANDA filer to "park" its 180-day exclusivity period, since this would still distort competition even in the absence of a reverse payment.[1086]

2 The Size of the Payment

The size of the payment is a key element in determining whether an agreement between a patent holder and a generic challenger is a "pay-for-delay" agreement or a potentially justifiable settlement. The Supreme Court did not expressly quantify what should be considered as a large payment; it merely stated that the size of the payment should be examined vis-à-vis the following parameters: (1) the anticipated litigation costs, if the infringement lawsuit were litigated; (2) the independence of the payment

---

1080. EDLIN, HEMPHILL, HOVENKAMP, SHAPIRO, Actavis Inference, 2015, p. 592.
1081. SORENSEN, SHADOWEN, Model Jury Instructions, 2015, p. 670.
1082. *In Re Cipro Cases I & II*, 348 P.3d 845, 865 (Cal., May 7, 2015).
1083. HOVENKAMP, JANIS, LEMLEY, LESLIE, *IP And Antitrust*, 2015, pp. 15-48-15-50.
1084. CARRIER, Payment After Actavis, 2014, pp. 16-18.
1085. HOVENKAMP, JANIS, LEMLEY, LESLIE, *IP And Antitrust*, 2015, p. 15-50. See for instance *In Re Skelaxin (Metaxalone) Antitrust Litigation*, Case No. 1:12-md-2343, (E.D. Tenn. 2013), at 54-56; 104-106, finding evidence suggesting secret meetings and a secret payment associated with the settlement.
1086. JACOBO-RUBIO, TURNER, WILLIAMS, 2016, pp. 31-32, arguing that in settlements with retained exclusivity but no payments, courts should examine the strength of the relevant patents under hypothetical litigation, since the value of such retained exclusivity depends on the probability for the generic to win the Hatch-Waxman patent infringement litigation.

from other services provided to the patent holder by the generic challenger; and (3) the lack of any other "convincing justification."[1087] With regard to anticipated litigation costs, their estimation can be tricky especially since antitrust defendants have strong incentives to distort and inflate their predictions of expected litigation costs in an attempt to mask a potential payment for delay.[1088] It was maintained that a payment lower than $5 to $10 million could be considered to be a refund for the avoidance of litigation costs, whereas payments over these amounts should be justified.[1089] In cases before the decision of *FTC v. Actavis*, the FTC had accepted that a payment of up to $2 million could be considered as a payment for expected litigation costs and not as a payment to delay competition.[1090] However, in two stipulated orders for permanent injunction entered by the FTC in reverse payment settlement cases in 2016 and 2017, settlements restricting generic entry and including cash payments of up to $7 million as reimbursement for litigation fees were not prohibited.[1091] If the 2017 PAAG bill passes, a payment for litigation expenses not exceeding $7.5 million could be considered as permissible.[1092] In any event, courts should attempt to estimate the anticipated litigation costs on a case-by-case basis, instead of opting for a "one-number-fits-all" solution.[1093]

The lack of a concrete definition of what constitutes a "large payment" gave rise to a debate among academics, who failed to reach a common conclusion. It was argued that it is nearly impossible to determine the scale of a payment with respect to the gross revenues of the settling pharmaceutical companies, since products, sales and profit ratios of companies vary to such an extent that it is impossible to find an "one size fits all" solution.[1094] It was also suggested that the value of the uncertainty over the outcome of the infringement suit should be included to the litigation costs, while the brand-manufacturer's risk aversion should also be taken into account.[1095] Even if the

---

1087. *FTC v. Actavis, Inc.*, 133 S. Ct. 2223, 2237 (2013).
1088. KRUEGER, Implementing Actavis, 2014, p. 121.
1089. CARRIER, Unjustified Payments, 2013.
1090. *See* FTC, Decision, *In re Bristol-Myers Squibb Co.*, 135 F.T.C. 444, Docket No. C-4076 (April 14, 2003); *In re Schering-Plough Corp.*, 136 F.T.C. 956, 1062 (2003).
1091. FTC, *Stipulated Order for Permanent Injunction with Teikoku Seiyaku Co., Ltd., and Teikoku Pharma USA, Inc.*, Case No. 2:16-cv-01440-PD, (March 30, 2016), p. 6; FTC, *Stipulated Order for Permanent Injunction with Endo Pharmaceuticals Inc. and Endo International PLC*, Case No. 17-cv-00312, (January 23, 2017), p. 6.
1092. Section 3, Preserve Access to Affordable Generics Act, S. 124, 115th Cong. (2017). *See* further *supra* Chapter 2, Part 2, Section IV.C.
1093. *See also* KRUEGER, Implementing Actavis, 2014, pp. 120, proposing that courts should examine whether the reverse payment effectuated exceeds the upper bound of litigation costs in similar cases and call patent lawyers as expert witnesses to provide evidence on the estimated cost of litigation for the patent holder.
1094. MORRISON, Antitrust Scrutiny, 2013; *See also* BERNARD, Rewriting, 2013, p. 3, arguing that the payment of $1 million may or may not be large, depending on the product concerned. *See also* JACOBO-RUBIO, TURNER, WILLIAMS, 2017, pp. 34-35, noting that their estimates on generic firm stakes in paragraph IV litigation may help in the framing of the "large and unjustified" inquiry under *FTC v. Actavis*.
1095. HARRIS, MURPHY, WILLIG, WRIGHT, Activating Actavis, 2014, pp. 85-88. *See also* BIERI, Reasonable Approach, 2014, pp. 144-148, arguing that settlements involving a value transfer from the brand-name holder to the generic company could arguably have procompetitive effects by allowing generic entry earlier that it would otherwise have occurred absent the payment.

author of this book does not have the necessary background in economics to critically assess the merits of these positions, such an overbroad expansion of litigation costs seems impermissible from a legal point of view, since it adds to litigation expenses the value of certain exclusion based on a doubtful patent.[1096] According to the Supreme Court, the elimination of uncertainty is the main anticompetitive aspect of pay-for-delay settlements and it would be paradoxical to accept that the cost of buying such elimination of uncertainty can be considered as a "litigation cost." It should be noted that a court decision *post Actavis* argued that parties can still use financial considerations in order to bridge small gaps concerning their subjective perceptions of their potential of prevailing in the patent infringement litigation suit.[1097] However, the same decision noted that using value transfers in order to align the parties' previously conflicting perspectives on when generic entry is economically desirable shall not be tolerated under antitrust law scrutiny.[1098]

3 Evaluating the Value Conferred to Generics by Side-Deals

Side-deals between brand-name drug manufacturers and generic challengers are often part of settlement agreements and seem to occur much more often in a settlement context than outside it.[1099] Due to the increased antitrust scrutiny of reverse payment settlements, naked payments from the brand-name manufacturer to the alleged generic infringer are no longer the rule. Increasingly complicated and sophisticated value-transfer schemes reign, combining patent settlements with no-AG commitments (no-AG commitments), licences or deals concerning drug production, distribution, development and product promotion.[1100] Sometimes, these side agreements are expressly contingent on the generic challenger's commitment to delay its entry to the market.[1101] Settlements can also include overpayments by the brand-name manufacturers for generic manufacturers' products and services or alternatively underpayments by the generic firms for value provided by the brand-name firms.[1102] These

---

1096. *See* further HOVENKAMP, JANIS, LEMLEY, LESLIE, *IP And Antitrust*, 2015, pp. 15-46, 15-47; *See also* KRUEGER, Implementing Actavis, 2014, pp. 120, "reverse payments in excess of the patent holder's anticipated future litigation costs are never necessary to induce procompetitive settlements."
1097. *In Re Cipro Cases I & II*, 348 P.3d 845, 868-869 (Cal., May 7, 2015).
1098. *Idem.*
1099. HEMPHILL, Aggregate Approach, 2009, pp. 663-668.
1100. *See* for instance the settlement agreements in *In re Aggrenox Antitrust Litig.*, 94 F. Supp. 3d 224 (D. Conn. March 23, 2015); *In Re Niaspan Antitrust Litig.*, 42 F. Supp. 3d. 735 (E.D. Pa. September 5, 2014); *In re Loestrin 24 Fe Antitrust Litig.*, 45 F. Supp. 3d 180, 185-187 (D.R.I. September 4, 2014), all including co-promotion or back-up manufacturing side-deals. *See also In re Actos End Payor Antitrust Litigation*, No. 1:14-cv-02846 (S.D.N.Y.), at *5-10, discussing settlement agreements whereby the patentee granted the alleged generic infringers non-exclusive licenses containing "acceleration clauses."
1101. *In Re Niaspan Antitrust Litig.*, 42 F. Supp. 3d. 735, 753 (E.D. Pa. September 5, 2014), "[t]he plausibility of plaintiffs' allegations concerning the true nature and purpose of these payments is bolstered by the fact that these agreements were expressly contingent on Barr's promise to delay generic entry." Kos (the patentee) was only obligated to pay Barr (the generic challenger) royalties as long as the latter's generic drug was kept off the market.
1102. HEMPHILL, Aggregate Approach, 2009, pp. 663-664.

side-deals involving "difficult-to-value assets" call for considerable caution since they may be added to the settlement as a cover for purchasing additional freedom from competition.[1103] Side-deals used as "fig leaves" for agreements to eliminate competition have been condemned as illegal restraints of trade.[1104] Evaluating the exact value conferred by side-deals and their (in)dependence from a Hatch-Waxman settlement possibly delaying generic entry, is not going to be neither a simple nor an uncontroversial matter *post Actavis*.

3.1   Payments Disconnected from Deal's Impact

Typically, the payment to the generic challenger for such a side deal is disconnected from the deal's actual impact on the profits or sales of the brand-name manufacturer. For example, the *Aggrenox* settlement between the generic challenger Barr Pharmaceuticals Inc. (Barr) and the patent holder Boehringer Ingelheim Pharmaceuticals Inc. (Boehringer) included a co-promotion agreement, on the basis of which a subsidiary of Barr would educate doctors about Aggrenox. Barr was compensated *regardless* of whether this co-promotion agreement generated any additional sales of the drug for Boehringer.[1105] Similarly, *In Re Niaspan Antitrust Litig.*, there was a co-promotion agreement which was part of the settlement between the generic challenger Barr and the patent holder Kos Pharmaceuticals Inc. (Kos). Kos agreed to pay Barr a royalty which was based on the overall sales of the promoted drugs – Niaspan and Advicor – regardless of whether those sales were generated by the sales' force of Barr.[1106]

3.2   The Complexity of Evaluating Side Deals

The case of *FTC v. AbbVie* illustrates well the complexity of evaluating side-deals and the controversies they may give rise to. In its complaint against the brand-name drug manufacturer AbbVie Inc. (AbbVie) concerning the drug AndroGel, the FTC alleged that AbbVie engaged in baseless patent infringement lawsuits against potential generic entrants, motivated by anticompetitive purposes.[1107] The agency also alleged that AbbVie entered into anticompetitive settlement agreements with its potential generic competitors. AbbVie had entered into a side agreement with the generic challenger Teva Pharmaceuticals Inc. (Teva). On the basis of this side-deal, Abb Vie would supply an authorised generic version of the drug TriCor to Teva, at a reduced price. The FTC

1103. *In Re Cipro Cases I & II*, 348 P.3d 845, 866 (Cal., May 7, 2015). *See also* BULOW, Gaming of Patents, 2004, pp. 165-171, analysing examples of such side-deals. CARRIER, Unsettling Settlements, 2009, pp. 78-79, arguing that side payments exceed the fair market value and occur in most settlements that restraint generic entry.
1104. *In Re Cipro Cases I & II*, 348 P.3d 845, 866 (Cal., May 7, 2015), referring to *Getz Bros. & Co. v. Federal Salt Company*, 147 Cal. 115, 118 (Cal. June 10, 1905).
1105. *In re Aggrenox Antitrust Litig.*, 94 F. Supp. 3d 224, 236 (D. Conn. March 23, 2015).
1106. *In Re Niaspan Antitrust Litig.*, 42 F. Supp. 3d. 735, 743-745 (E.D. Pa. September 5, 2014).
1107. FTC, Complaint for Injunctive and other Equitable Relief, *FTC v. AbbVie et al.*, Case 2:14-cv-05151-HB, (September 8, 2014), pp. 20-26 [cited as: FTC, Complaint, *FTC v. AbbVie et al.*, 2014].

argued that this side-deal was used as a large reverse payment from Abb Vie to Teva in order for the latter to delay its entry to the AndroGel market.[1108] The District Court of Pennsylvania adjudicating FTC's complaint found that the settlement agreement between AbbVie and Teva on AndroGel did not contain itself any value transfer while it allowed Teva to enter the market before the expiration of the relevant patent; thus it was legal under *FTC v. Actavis*.[1109] The court also found that the side-deal concerning the authorised generic of the drug TriCor did not amount to a payment from AbbVie to Teva; nevertheless the court acknowledged that the FTC correctly alleged that something of value passed from AbbVie to Teva, insisting however that it did not amount to a reverse payment under the *Actavis* standard.[1110]

B Justifications for Settlements under FTC v. Actavis

A particularly thorny question arising from the Supreme Court's decision in *FTC v. Actavis* is what should be considered as a valid justification for a reverse payment settlement. The Court merely stated that "[t]here may be other justifications" for reverse payments, without however providing any examples of such justifications.[1111] Is common sense sufficient for fact-finders to determine if the aim of a value transfer is to delay generic entry or if the payment simply represents fair consideration for provided services, as one commentator argued?[1112] The following analysis shows that providing a valid justification for a large reverse payment, exceeding the anticipated litigation costs plus the value of any other services delivered to the patent holder, is not a simple task for the settling parties.[1113]

1 Patent Validity Cannot Serve as a Justification

Typical defences for reverse payment settlement agreements in the *pre-Actavis* era, such as patent strength or patent policy can no longer be used as justifications for reverse payments.[1114] The rejection of the "scope of the patent" test was interpreted by some scholars as implying that the Supreme Court did not acknowledge that the existence of a valid patent may serve as a valid defence for an unjustified large

---

1108. FTC, Complaint, *FTC v. AbbVie et al.*, 2014, pp. 26-33.
1109. *FTC v. AbbVie Inc. et al.*, 107 F.Supp.3d 428, 436 (E.D.Pa. May 6, 2015).
1110. Idem., 436-437. See however *FTC v. AbbVie Inc. et al.*, Civil Action No. 14-5151, (E.D. Pa. September 15, 2017), awarding partial summary judgment to the FTC and finding that AbbVie's and Besins' patent infringement suits against Teva and Perrigo Co. were objectively baseless.
1111. *FTC v. Actavis, Inc.*, 133 S. Ct. 2223, 2236 (2013).
1112. CARRIER, Unjustified Payments, 2013.
1113. EDLIN, HEMPHILL, HOVENKAMP, SHAPIRO, Activating Actavis, 2013, p. 19, arguing that in order to defend a payment to reduce competition, defendants in a reverse payment settlement case shall show that competition is enhanced or at least not delayed by the settlement.
1114. EDLIN, HEMPHILL, HOVENKAMP, SHAPIRO, Activating Actavis, 2013, pp. 19-20; SORENSEN, SHADOWEN, Model Jury Instructions, 2015, p. 670.

payment.[1115] Subsequent courts agreed with this position: even when the patent is likely valid, a payment seeking to prevent even a small risk of competition constitutes the relevant anticompetitive harm of the settlement.[1116] In any case, considering whether the agreement is justified as procompetitive should not focus on whether the patent concerned ultimately proves to be valid or invalid.[1117] The relevant time for assessing the anticompetitive effects of a settlement is the time when the settlement was concluded, at which point a patent's validity is "unknown and unknowable."[1118] Just as subsequent patent invalidation does not prove that an agreement was anticompetitive when it was concluded, later evidence showing patent validity will not automatically show that the settlement agreement was procompetitive.[1119] In any case, a large and otherwise unjustified reverse payment creates a strong inference that the settling parties believed *ex ante* that the relevant patent was invalid or not infringed.[1120]

2   Earlier Generic Entry Is Not a Valid Justification

In the *In Re Cipro Cases I & II* decision – one of the first higher court decisions after *Actavis* on a reverse payment case – the Supreme Court of California discussed the possible justifications for a payment exceeding litigation costs and the fair value of any collateral products or services.[1121] The court found that a settlement cannot be found procompetitive merely because it allows generic drug entry at an earlier time than if the patent holder would have prevailed in the patent infringement litigation.[1122] Since antitrust law condemns the purchase of freedom from competition, the relevant baseline should be whether generic entry is postponed beyond the time point when it would have occurred absent the settlement.[1123] However, a subsequent District Court's order concerning another set of reverse payment settlements argued that the resolution of the patentee's litigation uncertainty constitutes a procompetitive justification for reverse payment settlements.[1124]

1115. EDLIN, HEMPHILL, HOVENKAMP, SHAPIRO, Activating Actavis, 2013, p. 21, "[y]ou may not consider the validity of the patent as a defense"); HOVENKAMP J.H., *Innovation and Competition Policy*, Chapter 4, p. 101, "[n]ote that the one defense that the Court did not acknowledge was that the patent was valid."
1116. *In Re Cipro Cases I & II*, 348 P.3d 845, 863 (Cal., May 7, 2015).
1117. *In Re Cipro Cases I & II*, 348 P.3d 845, 870-871 (Cal., May 7, 2015).
1118. *In Re Cipro Cases I & II*, 348 P.3d 845, 870 (Cal., May 7, 2015).
1119. *Idem.*
1120. HOVENKAMP, JANIS, LEMLEY, LESLIE, *IP And Antitrust*, 2015, pp. 15-44, 15-45.
1121. *In Re Cipro Cases I & II*, 348 P.3d 845, 869-871 (Cal., May 7, 2015).
1122. *In Re Cipro Cases I & II*, 348 P.3d 845, 870 (Cal., May 7, 2015).
1123. *Idem. See also* SORENSEN, SHADOWEN, Model Jury Instructions, 2015, p. 679, noting that Jury cannot consider as defence that an agreement permitted generic entry before the expiration of the patent; the issue to decide is whether the agreement delayed generic entry.
1124. *King Drug Company of Florence, Inc., v. Cephalon Inc., et al.*, Order by Judge Mitchell S. Goldberg, (Civil Actions No. 2:06-cv-1797, No. 2:06-cv-1833, No. 2:06-cv-2768 (E.D. Pa. October 5, 2015), pp. 1-2. Judge Goldberg's initial grant of class certification was subsequently vacated; *see further In re Modafinil Antitrust Litig.*, 837 F.3d 238 (3rd Cir. 2016).

3 Business Reasons and Risk Aversion Are Not Valid Justifications

The allegations that the parties settled for "business reasons" or that the settlement agreement "made economic sense" are not admissible justifications under *Actavis*. The fact that the settlement agreements were profit-generating for both parties is irrelevant from an antitrust point of view. As two commentators put it "[b]reaking the antitrust laws may let a lawbreaker make more money; but that is no defense."[1125] Risk aversion of either the patent holder or the generic challenger is also an inadmissible justification. The fact that a patent holder may be willing to make a large payment to a generic challenger in order to avoid even a 5% chance of patent invalidation does not justify a reverse payment neither makes it ironclad to antitrust liability, as the dissenting judges suggested.[1126] As the majority opinion stressed in *Actavis*:

> [t]he owner of a particularly valuable patent might contend, of course, that even a small risk of invalidity justifies a large payment. But, be that as it may, the payment (if otherwise unexplained) likely seeks to prevent the risk of competition. And, as we have said, that consequence constitutes the relevant anticompetitive harm.[1127]

The alleged risk aversion of the generic challenger shall also be rejected if proposed as a justification for a reverse payment. Agreeing to receive a large payment from the patent holder and not to compete in the market for a certain time-period cannot be justified on the generic manufacturer's fear of losing in the patent infringement litigation suit or of being liable to pay damages to the patent holder.

IV The Dissenting Opinion in *FTC v. Actavis*

The *FTC v. Actavis* decision of the Supreme Court was not unanimous. Chief Justices Roberts, Scalia and Thomas chose to dissent and delivered an opinion heavily criticising the application of the rule of reason to reverse payment settlements, advocating instead in favour of the application of the scope of the patent test. The dissenting judges disagreed – among other points – with the majority's opinion that reverse payment settlements mainly arise in the context of pharmaceutical patent litigation and argued that settlements where a patentee pays the alleged infringer to drop its invalidity claim are common in intellectual property litigation in general.[1128] The points of the dissenting opinion which are discussed in the following sections are of particular interest.

1125. SORENSEN, SHADOWEN, Model Jury Instructions, 2015, p. 680.
1126. *FTC v. Actavis, Inc.*, 133 S. Ct. 2223, 2244-2245 (2013), Chief Justice Roberts dissenting. See *infra* Chapter 4, Part 1, VI, on the dissenting opinion in *FTC v. Actavis Inc.*
1127. *FTC v. Actavis, Inc.*, 133 S. Ct. 2223, 2236 (2013).
1128. *FTC v. Actavis, Inc.*, 133 S. Ct. 2223, 2242-2243 (2013), Chief Justice Roberts dissenting. See however HOVENKAMP, Actavis, 2014, pp. 13-16, arguing that pay-for-delay settlements are a predominant feature of the Hatch-Waxman Act.

A Acting Within the Scope of the Patent

Following a line of reasoning largely similar to that of Circuit Court decisions applying the scope of the patent test, the dissenting Justices in *FTC v. Actavis* argued that a patent "carves out an exception to the applicability of antitrust laws."[1129] The scope of the patent was defined as "the rights conferred to by the patent," forming a zone within which the patent holder can operate without facing antitrust liability; only if the actions of a patentee went *beyond* the scope of its patent, they would be subject to antitrust scrutiny.[1130] Actions falling within the scope of the patent can be subject to antitrust scrutiny only in exceptional cases, e.g., when parties settle sham litigation or where the patent has been obtained through fraud.[1131] In the case at hand, Solvay had paid a generic challenger and potential competitor to respect its patent, and the dissenting Justices deemed that this conduct was within the scope of its patent.

While it is true that exercising the rights conferred by the patent does not in principle give rise to antitrust violations, we first need to have a closer look on the nature of the rights that a patent confers. Is the right to make a big payment to a competitor aiming to delay its entry to the market included in the "scope of the patent"? Definitely not. A patent confers the right to prevent the manufacture, use and sale of a patented invention and a patentee can prevent potential patent infringers from entering the market *via* civil remedies, preliminary injunctions, interlocutory relief, actions before an industrial property office, civil court procedures and criminal law actions which defer from one jurisdiction to another.[1132] If the patent infringement has already occurred, the patentee is entitled to claim damages or account for profit. These enforcement mechanisms are the legitimate way of protecting the patent monopoly, whereas a payment to the alleged generic patent infringer in return for delaying to enter the market cannot possibly be considered to fall "within the scope of the patent."

Ironically, the dissenting Justices acknowledged that the scope of the patent should be determined by reference to patent law.[1133] However, no patent law grants the right *to pay* a competitor to stay out of the market, and the *means* used by the patentee to achieve the exclusion of competitors matter. Merely enforcing the patent through the mechanisms available under patent law – e.g., through a patent infringement lawsuit – would of course be legitimate. Nevertheless, an anticompetitive exclusionary payment should not be "sanctified" because of the existence of a patent. A naked market division agreement is not authorised by the Patent Act, irrespectively of whether it goes beyond the scope of the patent protection.[1134]

1129. *FTC v. Actavis, Inc.*, 133 S. Ct. 2223, 2228 (2013).
1130. *FTC v. Actavis, Inc.*, 133 S. Ct. 2223, 2239 (2013), Chief Justice Roberts dissenting, referring to *United States v. Singer Mfg. Co.*, 83 S. Ct. 1773, 1784-1785 (1963). *See also idem* at 2242 "[w]hen the [patent] holder steps outside the scope of the patent, he can no longer use the patent as his defense."
1131. *Professional Real Estate Investors, Inc. v. Columbia Pictures Industries, Inc.*, 113 S. Ct. 1920, 1928-1929 (1993), on sham litigation; *Walker Process Equipment Inc., supra*, at 177, 86 S. Ct. 347, 350 on fraud before the USPTO.
1132. WIPO, *IP Handbook*, 2004, Chapter 4, pp. 208-213, 228-230.
1133. *FTC v. Actavis, Inc.*, 133 S. Ct. 2223, 2240 (2013), Chief Justice Roberts dissenting.
1134. HOVENKAMP, Reexamination, 2015, pp. 477-478.

Additionally, the dissenting opinion largely avoided to consider the particularities of the Hatch-Waxman Act, even though it is common ground that courts cannot effectively evaluate reverse payment settlements without reference to its provisions.[1135] For instance, the dissenting Justices stressed that the Supreme Court has never held that it is an antitrust violation to refrain from challenging a patent. While true, this point seems out of context in Hatch-Waxman patent litigation. A generic paragraph IV ANDA filer *has* already challenged the patent, by filing its ANDA application, which constitutes an artificial act of patent infringement.[1136] The antitrust scrutiny imposed to unjustified large payments by the *Actavis* majority ruling does not amount to coercing generic drug manufacturers into challenging patents; it simply aims to discourage exclusionary conduct that violates antitrust laws.

B Discouraging the Settlement of Disputes

The dissenting Justices argued that risk-averse patent holders may be willing to make large payments in order to avoid even a 5% risk of finding patent invalidity, while they also maintained that the size of the payment is not indicative of patent invalidity chances.[1137] One of the main concerns of the dissenting Justices, voiced also in subsequent jurisprudence, was that imposing antitrust scrutiny under the rule of reason would discourage the settlement of patent disputes,[1138] a concern that was also shared by a number of antitrust specialists.[1139] However, as discussed in Chapter 3 of this book, settlements may also serve as a means to protect the precarious monopoly granted by particularly weak or even invalid patents.[1140] As one empirical study found, parties settled in 90.5% of the patent litigation cases between 2000 and 2009; however patentees prevailed only in 10.7% of the cases that were litigated to the end and not settled.[1141] It can thus be inferred that a great number of settlements covering invalid patents could have been concluded. Since the quality of the issued patents is rather precarious, discouraging the settlement of Hatch-Waxman patent litigation may not necessarily be as undesirable as the dissenting Justices deemed it to be.[1142] On the contrary, discouraging such problematic settlements could play a vital role in the elimination of invalid patents from the marketplace,[1143] helping to resolve a problematic reality that is stalling both innovation and competition.

1135. Carrier, Response to Roberts, 2014, pp. 38-40; Ghosh, Convergence, 2014, pp. 100-102.
1136. *See supra*, Chapter 2, Part 2, Section D, explaining that the mechanism of a paragraph IV ANDA.
1137. *FTC v. Actavis, Inc.*, 133 S. Ct. 2223, 2244-2245 (2013), Chief Justice Roberts dissenting.
1138. *FTC v. Actavis, Inc.*, 133 S. Ct. 2223, 2243-2244 (2013), Chief Justice Roberts dissenting. *See also In re Loestrin 24 Fe Antitrust Litig.*, 45 F. Supp. 3d 180, 192, "[w]hether one thinks that the majority got it right or not, there can be no dispute that the holding in Actavis and the abandonment of the scope-of-the-patent test will make it more difficult for patent litigants to settle."
1139. *See* for instance Knuckles, Ongoing Dilemma, 2014, pp. 533-534.
1140. *See supra* Chapter 3, Part 2, Section III.B, discussing the high rates of patent invalidation and why a patent does not legitimise an exclusion payment.
1141. Allison, Lemley, Walker, Patent Quality, 2011, pp. 687-689.
1142. Tokic, Relevant Product Market, 2015, pp. 280-281.
1143. Tokic, Relevant Product Market, 2015, p. 281.

Pharmaceutical companies have argued that harsh antitrust scrutiny of reverse payment settlements could result to less generic challenges, to the detriment of consumers. However, generic challenges that are concluded by the brand manufacturer paying the generic challenger not to compete, do not enhance but instead hamper competition; deterring this type of settlements does not amount to consumers' loss.[1144] The fact that settlements including a payment exceeding litigation costs or the fair value of any received goods or services will be deterred by the imposition of antitrust scrutiny should not be a cause of concern; those settlements would have simply facilitated the sharing of monopoly profits.[1145] Discouraging such unlawful settlements which result in consumer harm is one of the main objectives of the Supreme Court's decision in *Actavis*. If anything, antitrust scrutiny may chill generic challenges to strong and valid patents, increasing their value, while letting untouched the incentives to challenge weak patents.[1146]

V The Importance of *FTC v. Actavis*

A *The Consumer Welfare Approach*

The *Actavis* decision was perceived by the FTC as a "significant victory for American consumers, American tax-payers and competition."[1147] The Supreme Court made explicit in its decision that a payment in return for staying out of the market keeps prices at patentee-set levels and has as a result that "the patentee and the challenger gain; the consumer loses."[1148] In essence, the Supreme Court equated higher consumer prices with harm, making no reference to the producers' welfare.[1149] Even though the *Actavis* decision was not unanimous, both the majority and the dissenting judges agreed that consumer welfare is the ultimate objective of antitrust law.[1150] The Supreme Court's emphasis on consumer welfare rather than on total welfare was highlighted by one of the leading authorities on antitrust, who noted that consumer welfare generally focuses only on the welfare of consumers and does not offset producer benefits against consumer harms.[1151] On the contrary, total welfare "refers to the aggregate value an economy produces, without regard for the way that gains or

---

1144. *In Re Cipro Cases I & II*, 348 P.3d 845, 868 (Cal., May 7, 2015).
1145. *In Re Cipro Cases I & II*, 348 P.3d 845, 868-869 (Cal., May 7, 2015).
1146. MUNGAN, Perverse Incentives, 2013, p. 7, showing that a generic challenger is expected to lack the incentives to challenge a strong patent if reverse payment settlements are considered to be illegal.
1147. RAMIREZ Edith, *Statement of FTC's Chairwoman before the U.S. Senate*, Washington DC, of July 23, 2013, p. 2. Available at: http://www.ftc.gov/sites/default/files/documents/public_statements/statement-chairwoman-edith-ramirez-pay-delay-settlements/130923pfdopeningstatement_0.pdf. Last accessed on March 31, 2018).
1148. *FTC v. Actavis, Inc.*, 133 S. Ct. 2223, 2234-2235 (2013).
1149. HOVENKAMP, Actavis, 2014, pp. 7-8.
1150. *FTC v. Actavis, Inc.*, 133 S. Ct. 2223, 2238 (2013), Chief Justice Roberts dissenting, "[t]he point of antitrust law is to encourage competitive markets to promote consumer welfare."
1151. HOVENKAMP, Actavis, 2014, p. 7.

losses are distributed."[1152] For instance, if a practice harms consumers $X million in the form of higher prices while benefiting producers by $X + 1 million, then total welfare is larger despite consumers being worse of.[1153] The focus on consumer welfare is not novel, since horizontal agreements reducing market output, leading to price increases or reduced innovation have arguably never been approved by courts on the grounds that producers' surplus compensated consumer losses.[1154]

There were also criticisms concerning the effect of prohibiting reverse payment settlements under the *Actavis* rule on consumer welfare: limiting the possible payments strictly to the litigation costs could result in equilibrium settlements decreasing consumer welfare.[1155] It was alleged that consumer welfare might be enhanced by settlements involving payments which exceed litigation costs or the fair value of provided goods or services, since such settlements could also permit earlier generic entry.[1156] However, it was argued that if a rational patentee – confident on its patent's validity – would be asked to pay a generic challenger an amount higher than its litigation costs to bridge the gap between the parties' differing expectations, the patentee would ordinarily choose to litigate.[1157]

B The Impact of Antitrust Scrutiny on Reverse Payments

The *Actavis* decision has been described as a historic one. If the dissenting justices would have prevailed and upheld the scope of the patent test, this would be the end of antitrust scrutiny for the vast majority of reverse payment settlements,[1158] amounting to huge losses for consumers and public health schemes.[1159] What the Supreme Court made clear in *Actavis* is that unjustified reverse payments, aiming to keep competitors off the market, to preserve prices at patentee-set levels and to divide the benefit between the settling parties, are harmful to consumers and cannot be considered antitrust immune.[1160] After *Actavis*, patents are no longer to be treated as presumptively ironclad for antitrust purposes since purchasing freedom from the possibility of competition is illegal whether done by a patentee or by anyone else.[1161] The majority opinion was surprisingly general, starting with a paradigm of two companies litigating in a patent infringement suit, without any mention of a generic drug dispute or of the

---

1152. HOVENKAMP, Antitrust's Welfare Goals, 2013, p. 2471.
1153. HOVENKAMP, Actavis, 2014, pp. 7-8.
1154. EDLIN, HEMPHILL, HOVENKAMP, SHAPIRO, Activating Actavis, 2013, p. 17. *See also* HOVENKAMP, Antitrust's Welfare Goals, 2013, p. 2477, stressing that antitrust policy in the US. follows a consumer welfare approach and condemns restraints harming consumers, irrespectively of the existence of "offsetting efficiencies" and regardless their size.
1155. KOBAYASHI, WRIGHT, GINSBURG, TSAI, Multiple ANDA, 2015, p. 91.
1156. HARRIS, MURPHY, WILLIG, WRIGHT, Activating Actavis, 2014, pp. 86-88.
1157. *In Re Cipro Cases I & II*, 348 P.3d 845, 869 (Cal., May 7, 2015).
1158. CARRIER, Five Arguments, 2013, pp. 1-3.
1159. *See supra* Chapter 4, Part 1, Section VI, analysing the dissenting opinion in *FTC v. Actavis*.
1160. *FTC v. Actavis, Inc.*, 133 S. Ct. 2223, 2226 (2013), "Payment for staying out of the market keeps prices at patentee-set levels and divides the benefit between the patentee and the challenger, while the consumer loses."
1161. *In Re Cipro Cases I & II*, 348 P.3d 845, 864-865 (Cal., May 7, 2015), "Actavis makes clear that for antitrust purposes patents are no longer to be treated as presumptively ironclad."

Hatch-Waxman Act. The court subsequently stated that "most if not all settlements arise in the context of pharmaceutical drug regulation,"[1162] leading some commentators to argue that the *Actavis* scrutiny only applies to the context of Hatch-Waxman litigation.[1163] However, the opinion clearly adopted a general route in the antitrust analysis of reverse payment settlements, refusing to subordinate antitrust concerns to patent law concerns.[1164] The rather broad wording of the majority's holding could lead to more antitrust scrutiny in general, representing a major policy change and having an impact on the patent system.[1165]

As outlined in the following sections of this chapter, the effects of the Supreme Court's decision were immediate: the number of pharmaceutical settlements, potentially involving illegitimate payments for delay, decreased significantly after the *FTC v. Actavis* decision. From the historic high of 40 in FY 2012, the number went down to 21 settlements in FY 2014 and to only 14 out of a total of 170 settlements filed with the FTC in FY 2015.[1166] The number of potential pay-for-delay settlements with the first paragraph IV filer also fell down to 7 in FY 2015, from 23 in FY 2012.[1167] Despite speculations to the contrary and exaggerated concerns, the number of total pharmaceutical settlements did not decline after *FTC v. Actavis* and was not significantly different in 2014-2015 when compared to the number of settlements in years 2011-2013.[1168]

PART 2   NON-CASH PAYMENTS AFTER *FTC V. ACTAVIS*

Setting aside the big questions *post Actavis* on the size of the payment and the justifications invoked for showing the alleged procompetitive effects of an otherwise

---

1162. FTC v. Actavis, Inc., 133 S. Ct. 2223, 2227 (2013). *See also* HOVENKAMP, Actavis, 2014, pp. 13-16, arguing that pay-for-delay settlements are a predominant feature of the Hatch-Waxman Act.
1163. *See* for instance MCDONALD, I Said So, 2013, p. 42, "the *Actavis* analysis by its terms applies only to Hatch-Waxman patent cases" [internal quotation marks omitted].
1164. HOVENKAMP, Actavis, 2014, pp. 3-4.
1165. TOKIC, Relevant Product Market, 2015, pp. 277-278.
1166. FTC Report, *Agreements Filed with the Federal Trade Commission under the Medicare, Prescription Drug, Improvement and Modernization Act of 2003: Overview of Agreements Filed in FY 2014*. Available at: https://www.ftc.gov/tips-advice/competition-guidance/industry-guidance/health-care/pharmaceutical-agreement-filings (last accessed on March 31, 2018) [cited as: FTC, *Agreements Filed*, 2014]; FTC Report, *Agreements Filed with the Federal Trade Commission under the Medicare, Prescription Drug, Improvement and Modernization Act of 2003: Overview of Agreements Filed in FY 2015*. Available at: https://www.ftc.gov/system/files/documents/reports/agreements-filed-federal-trade-commission-under-medicare-prescription-drug-improvement-modernization/overview_of_fy_2015_mma_agreements_0.pdf (last accessed on March 31, 2018) [cited as: FTC, *Agreements Filed*, 2015]. Settlement agreements containing both explicit compensation from the brand manufacturer to the generic challenger and a restriction on the latter's ability to market its generic product competing with the branded product, are considered by the FTC as "settlements potentially involving pay-for-delay."
1167. *See infra* Chapter 4, Part 2, Section I.C, Table 4.0, presenting complete statistics on the number of total and potentially problematic settlements from 2007 until 2015.
1168. FTC, Agreements Filed, 2015, pp. 2-3.

unexplained value transfer, another fundamental question arises: *what falls under the definition of payment*? Should antitrust scrutiny be limited to big cash payments or do other forms of value transfers also qualify as payments? If one looks up the term of payment in *Black's Law Dictionary*, it is defined as "[t]he performance of an obligation by the delivery of *money* or some *other valuable thing* accepted in partial or full discharge of the obligation."[1169] Another definition of payment is a "sum of *money* or *equivalent* paid or payable, esp. in return for goods or services or in discharge for a debt."[1170] Both definitions recognise the substitutability of value, making no distinction between transfers of money and transfers of other type of consideration; historically US courts adopted this broad definition of payment.[1171] As analysed in the sections below, not all district courts agreed with this fundamental definition, making a distinction without difference between payments of money and other forms of value transfer for the application of *FTC v. Actavis*.

I No-AG Commitments

A *Defining Authorised Generic Drugs*

An authorised generic drug is a generic version of the brand-name drug that is authorised under the same FDA approval as the brand-name drug. Authorised generics do not bear the brand-name or the trademark of the brand-name manufacturer, but they are manufactured to the branded drug's specifications.[1172] Even though the brand-name drug manufacturer can market itself the authorised generic drug, it is more common to license it to a generic manufacturer. In 2017, the FDA listed 1031 different authorised generics in the US market.[1173]

Only ¼ of NDA holding companies do not launch an authorised generic drug; however, if generic drug entry has not occurred, a brand-name drug manufacturer is unlikely to launch an authorised generic.[1174] When faced with generic entry, innovators have the possibility to license the authorised generic out to a generic firm, in order for the latter to sell a no-branded generic version of the drug, under the innovator's own licence. The ultimate goal may be to stem the large losses brand-name

---

1169. *Black's Law Dictionary*, 2014, p. 1309; *In re Aggrenox Antitrust Litig.*, 94 F. Supp. 3d 224, 242 (D. Conn. March 23, 2015); *In Re Niaspan Antitrust Litig.*, 42 F. Supp. 3d. 735, 751 (E.D. Pa. September 5, 2014).
1170. *In re Aggrenox Antitrust Litig.*, 94 F. Supp. 3d 224, 242 (D. Conn. March 23, 2015). *See also In re Lipitor Antitrust Litig.*, 46 F. Supp. 3d 523, 542 (D.N.J. September 12, 2014).
1171. *Sousa v. First Cal. Co.*, 101 Cal. App. 2d 533, 540, (1950), "[payment] may take place by the delivery and acceptance of other things of value instead of money;" *Hill v. United States*, 263 F.2d 885, 886 (3rd Cir. 1959); *Dynair Electronics, Inc. v. Video Cable, Inc.*, 55 Cal. App. 3d 11, 16-18, (Cal. Ct. App. 1976); *Staff Builders of Philadelphia, Inc. et al. v. Koschitzki et al.*, 989 F.2d 692, 695 (3d Cir. 1993).
1172. *See* FTC, *Authorized Generic Drugs: Short-Term Effects and Long-Term Impact*, (August 2011), pp. i, 4. Available at: https://www.ftc.gov/reports/authorized-generic-drugs-short-term-effects-long-term-impact-report-federal-trade-commission. (last accessed on 31 March 2018) [cited as: FTC, *Authorized Generics*, 2011].
1173. FDA, *Listing of Authorized Generics as of March 30, 2017*. Available at: https://www.fda.gov/AboutFDA/CentersOffices/OfficeofMedicalProductsandTobacco/CDER/ucm126391.htm.
1174. FTC, *Authorized Generics*, 2011, pp. 16-17.

manufacturers incur from the fast switch of sales from the brand-name drug to the generic drug.[1175] It is not random that the introduction of authorised generics to the market is substantially more frequent regarding drug products with higher branded drug sales pre-generic entry.[1176] The relative prices of both authorised generics and first generic drugs are possibly correlated with market size: the products with lower relative prices and higher market size tend to be products for which both a generic version and an authorised generic are marketed.[1177]

B Economic Effects of Authorised Generics' Launch

Two are the main economic effects of launching an authorised generic drug. First, the authorised generic takes up a substantial share of the first generic challengers' sales: adding one authorised generic drug to a market with only one ANDA generic drug is likely to reduce the generic's revenues by 45% compared to what it would have earned absent the authorised generic drug competition.[1178] Second, the price competition between the generic drug and the authorised generic drug decreases the level of generic drug prices, a decrease that according to the FTC ranges from -6.9% to -13.5%.[1179] The competition created by authorised generics on the generic drug level made generic manufacturers complain that the launching of authorised generics reduced the generic manufacturers' profits during the 180-day exclusivity period and violated the Hatch-Waxman Act.[1180] Due to the decrease in their profits, generics argued that their incentives to challenge branded drugs were reduced, so that generic entry was deterred. It was sustained that the introduction of an authorised generic in the market might arguably be viewed as an unlawful exclusionary practice, since it reduces or even eliminates the incentive of generic challengers to enter the market by reducing the value of the first challenger's exclusivity period.[1181] The FTC recognised that launching an authorised generic reduces the incentives of independent generic firms to enter the market,[1182] but nevertheless refrained from recommending taking action against authorised generics.[1183] The launch of authorised generics by patent holders during the 180-day exclusivity period is not considered to raise antitrust concerns or to violate the

---

1175. FTC, *Authorized Generics*, 2011, pp. 12-14, 26-27.
1176. FTC, *Authorized Generics*, 2011, p. 41.
1177. FTC, *Authorized Generics*, 2011, pp. 41-42, 46-47.
1178. See FTC, *Authorized Generics*, 2011, pp. 57-59, finding also that the ANDA generic drug usually captures a greater market share when it does not face competition from an AG. See also RADER, Balancing Innovation, 2009, pp. 6-7.
1179. FTC, *Authorized Generics*, 2011, pp. 41-48.
1180. See for instance *Teva Pharm. Indus. Ltd. v. Crawford*, 410 F.3d 51, 52-53 (D.C. Cir. 2005); *Mylan Pharm., Inc. v. FDA*, 454 F. 3d 270, 273-274 (N.D. W. Va. September 29, 2005).
1181. HOVENKAMP, JANIS, LEMLEY, LESLIE, *IP And Antitrust*, 2015, p. 15-58.
1182. FTC, *Authorized Generics*, 2011, pp. 71-72; LEIBOWITZ Jon, Oral Statement of FTC Commissioner, Hearing of the Senate Special Committee on Aging, July 20, 2006, p. 3. Available at: https://www.ftc.gov/public-statements/2006/07/oral-statement-commissioner-jon-leibowitz-hearing-senate-special-committee (last accessed on March 31, 2018).
1183. FTC, *Authorized Generics*, 2011, pp. 113-119.

provisions of the Hatch-Waxman Act,[1184] as long as it is not predatory and does not entail pricing below cost or a pattern intended to deter generic manufacturers from challenging patents.[1185]

C The Value and Frequency of No-AG Commitments

Even though the launch of an authorised generic is not problematic from an antitrust perspective, a promise not to launch an authorised generic drug (a no-AG commitment) made by the originator as part of a settlement with a generic competitor can raise antitrust concerns.[1186] Already in 2009, the former FTC Chairman Jon Leibowitz stressed that no-AG commitments as part of patent settlements can be "a huge bargaining chip." The competition introduced by an authorised generic substantially shrinks the revenues of the first generic entrant during its 180-day exclusivity period and arguably amounts to 47%-51% revenue loss.[1187] The decision not to launch an authorised generic drug is non-random and reflects a deliberate choice of the brand-name drug manufacturer having a good understanding of the drug's product market.[1188] This decision often amounts to an appealing and convenient way to transfer value from the brand-name manufacturer to the generic challenger.[1189]

Patent settlements between brand-name drug and generic manufacturers included no-AG commitments, arguably using them as a means of value transfer from the innovator to the generic challenger, aiming to induce the latter to delay its entry to the market.[1190] In FY 2005, only three settlements included a no-AG commitment, while in FY 2010 such commitments were part of fifteen settlements amounting to nearly 60% of agreements containing a payment to the first generic challenger in return for restricting its entry to the market.[1191] However, as illustrated in Table 4.1, after *FTC v.*

1184. *Teva Pharm. Indus. Ltd. v. Crawford*, 410 F.3d 51, 53-55 (D.C. Cir. 2005), finding that the launch of an AG is not violating the provisions of the Hatch-Waxman Act; *Mylan Pharm., Inc. v. FDA*, 454 F. 3d 270, 276-277 (N.D. W. Va. September 29, 2005), finding that there is no legal basis for the FDA to prohibit the launch of authorised generics during the 180-day exclusivity period.
1185. HOVENKAMP, JANIS, LEMLEY, LESLIE, *IP And Antitrust*, 2015, pp. 15-59, 15-61.
1186. FTC, *Authorized Generics*, 2011, pp. 139-153.
1187. LEIBOWITZ Jon, Statement of former FTC Chairman, *On the release of the Commission's Interim Report on Authorized Generics*, June 2009, pp. 1-2. Available at: https://www.ftc.gov/sites/default/files/documents/reports/authorized-generics-interim-report-federal-trade-commission/p062105authgenstatementleibowitz.pdf. (last accessed on March 31, 2018). [cited as: LEIBOWITZ, Interim Report Statement, 2009]; FTC, *Authorized Generics*, 2011, p. 33, finding that the expenditures of the first challenger's generic drug – a proxy for its revenues – were 40% to 52% lower when an AG was present.
1188. FTC, *Authorized Generics*, 2011, p. 42.
1189. FTC, *Authorized Generics*, 2011, pp. 152-153.
1190. FTC, *Authorized Generics*, 2011, p. 141. *See* for instance *Sanofi-Aventis et al. v. Apotex Inc. et al.*, 659 F.3d 1171, 1174 (Fed. Cir. 2011); *In Re Nexium (Esomeprazole) Antitrust Litig.*, 968 F. Supp. 2d 367, 392 (D. Mass. 2013); *King Drug Company of Florence, Inc., et al., v. Smithkline Beecham Corp., et al.*, 791 F.3d 388 (3rd Cir. 2015).
1191. FTC, *Authorized Generics*, 2011, pp. 145-146.

Actavis, the number of no-AG commitments in pharmaceutical patent settlements has declined sharply, from nineteen in FY 2012, to four in FY 2013, five in FY 2014 and four in FY 2015.[1192]

Table 4.1   FTC, Agreements Filed under MMA, 2007-2015

	FY 2007	FY 2008	FY 2009	FY 2010	FY 2011	FY 2012	FY 2013	FY 2014	FY 2015
Final Settlements	33	66	68	113	156	140	145	160	170
Potential Pay-for-Delay	14	16	19	31	28	40	29	21	14
Potential Pay-for-Delay involving 1st filers	11	13	15	26	18	23	13	11	7
Potential Pay-for-Delay including no-AG commitment	11	6	4	3	10	19	4	5	4

D   No-AG Commitments as Part of Settlements

Settlements between the patent holder and the first generic paragraph IV ANDA filer evolved through time. As antitrust scrutiny rose into a concrete possibility, the settling parties frequently employed a "no-AG commitment" in their settlements, allegedly in the form of non-cash payment aiming to delay generic entry. Already from 2003 it was stressed that in case exclusion payments would be considered illegal, the parties would have an incentive to conceal those payments and resort to non-cash types of compensation.[1193] A way for the brand-name manufacturer to transfer value to the generic challenger is through a commitment not to launch an authorised generic drug version, agreeing in essence not to compete with the generic challenger in the generic drug market. Another form of essentially the same mechanism is a "no-licence commitment," through which a patentee commits not to license its patent(s) to another generic company, and not to allow another generic company to launch an authorised generic

---

1192. Table 4.0 was created on the basis of FTC's Annual Filings Reports from FY 2007 until FY 2015. See FTC Report, *Agreements Filed with the Federal Trade Commission under the Medicare, Prescription Drug, Improvement and Modernization Act of 2003: Overview of Agreements Filed in FY 2007*. Available at: https://www.ftc.gov/tips-advice/competition-guidance/industry-guidance/health-care/pharmaceutical-agreement-filings (last accessed on March 31, 2018) until FTC, Agreements Filed, 2015. All FTC's Annual Filings Reports from FY 2004 until FY 2015 are publically available on FTC's Website.
1193. HOVENKAMP, JANIS, LEMLEY, Anticompetitive Settlements, 2003, p. 1760, providing as an example of non-cash compensation the patentee's abstinence from price competition in another market.

drug and to compete with the first paragraph IV ANDA filer.[1194] This is a mechanism that was used in several patent settlement agreements, some of which are analysed in the following sections.[1195]

Even though the generic manufacturer will profit if it prevails in the Hatch-Waxman litigation and enters the market, its gains will be much lower compared to the losses of the brand-name manufacturer: competition will shrink the aggregate total profits of the two companies.[1196] No-AG commitments are profitable to both brand-name manufacturers and generic challengers: the former increase their revenues because of later generic entry as a return for the no-AG commitment, whereas the generic manufacturers' revenues during the 180-day exclusivity period are considerably higher in the absence of *any* competition in the generic drug market.[1197] When an authorised generic drug is marketed, generic wholesale prices average at 70% of the brand-name drug's market price (pre-generic entry). However, in the absence of an authorised generic drug, generic wholesale prices average at 80% of the brand-name drug price.[1198] Other things equal, using a no-AG commitment as a reverse payment can harm consumers in two ways; first, by delaying generic entry and keeping brand-name drug prices high during that delay period; second, by reducing competition on the generic drug market and keeping generic drug prices high.[1199] Therefore, settlements including a no-AG commitment may raise even higher antitrust concerns than settlements involving a monetary payment, since they embody a second agreement not to compete on the generic market, resulting in inflated generic drug prices after generic entry occurred, in the absence of an AG.[1200]

1194. *See* for instance *In re Loestrin 24 Fe Antitrust Litig.*, 45 F. Supp. 3d 180, 185 (D.R.I. September 4, 2014), a settlement where Warner Chilcott agreed not to launch an AG itself and not to license another generic manufacturer to market an AG during Watson's 180-day exclusivity period.
1195. FTC, *Authorized Generics*, 2011, p. 152.
1196. FTC Brief as *Amicus Curiae* in Support of Plaintiffs-Appellants, *In Re Lamictal Direct Purchaser Antitrust Litigation, King Drug Company of Florence, Inc., et al. v. SmithKlineBeecham Corp. et al.*, (No. 14-1243), pp. 9-10 (April 28, 2014). Available at: https://www.ftc.gov/system/files/documents/amicus_briefs/re-lamictal-direct-purchaser-antitrust-litigation/140428lamictalbrief.pdf. [cited as: FTC, *Amicus* Brief, *In Re Lamictal*].
1197. FTC, *Authorized Generics*, 2011, pp. 141-142.
1198. FTC, *Amicus* Brief, *In Re Lamictal*, p. 12; FTC, *Authorized Generics*, 2011, p. iii.
1199. Towey, Albert, FTC, Change Behavior, 2016. *See also* Hovenkamp, Scope of the Patent, 2015, pp. 24-25, arguing that with a no-AG settlements consumers still feel the full burden of a reverse payment settlement delaying generic entry, plus the additional burden of lessened generic competition throughout the exclusivity period; Kurlander, Rebalancing Pay-For-Delay, 2015, pp. 693-696.
1200. FTC, *Amicus* Brief, *In Re Lamictal*, pp. 28-30; Edlin, Hemphill, Hovenkamp, Shapiro, Actavis Inference, 2015, pp. 596-598; Carrier, Eight Reasons, 2015, pp. 716-717. According to the FTC, such no-AG settlements can be viewed not only as reverse payments but also as reciprocal agreements not to compete which are independently subject to rule of reason scrutiny. *See* further *Standard Oil Co. (Indiana) v. United States*, 51 S. Ct. 421, 422-427 (1931), analysing a patent settlement agreement under the rule of reason; *Palmer v. BRG of Georgia*, 111 S. Ct. 401, 402-403 (1990), finding an agreement of market allocation anticompetitive on its face, regardless of whether parties split a market within which both do business or merely reserving one market for each party.

Apart from explicit commitments not to compete with an authorised generic, the competitive dynamics of the market can also be affected if the brand-name drug manufacturer: (1) enters a settlement with the generic challenger that creates incentives for the brand-name manufacturer not to launch an authorised generic; (2) appoints a subsequent generic challenger to market the authorised generic version of the litigated product, after the end of the first generic's 180-day exclusivity period, or; (3) grants to the initial generic challenger the right to market the authorised generic version of another drug product.[1201] Further, agreements containing a declining royalty structure – a royalty structure in which the generic challenger's obligation to pay royalties is reduced or terminated if the brand-name manufacturer launches an authorised generic – are also categorised by the FTC as settlements containing "possible compensation," since they may achieve the same effect as an explicit no-AG commitment.[1202]

Another way to conceal the "stigma" of a reverse payment is to mask such a transaction through a licensing agreement, by means of which the first generic IV ANDA filer is authorised to distribute the branded drug or an authorised generic, transmitting some share of the proceeds to the originator in the form of royalties.[1203] Such settlements could prove to be even more detrimental to competition by preserving the monopoly price level until the termination of the settlement, depriving consumers of lower prices that would occur once other generic entrants would enter the market absent the settlement.[1204] This is not to say that all licensing agreements are anticompetitive.[1205] However, agreements serving as "concealed" payments of this kind could satisfy the *FTC v. Actavis*. The first generic product in the market is normally sold at a price which is on average 15% lower than the brand-name drug's price; much larger price decreases occur with the entry of the second and subsequent generic competitors in the market, ending up to an 85% discount.[1206] Previous estimations of the effect of generic entry to average drug prices also reach similar conclusions, showing that whereas the average market price of the first generic is 94% of the brand-name drug's price, the second generic version is normally marketed for 52% of the brand-name drug's price, as shown in Figure 4.1.[1207]

1201. FTC, *Authorized Generics*, 2011, pp. 149-153.
1202. FTC, *Agreements Filed*, 2014, p. 2.
1203. CRANE, Reverse Payment Fallacy, 2014, pp. 56-57.
1204. CRANE, Reverse Payment Fallacy, 2014, pp. 57-58.
1205. *See* for instance ROBERT, FALCONI, 2006, pp. 525-526, arguing that licence settlement agreements are by their nature procompetitive since they eliminate the costs, delays and uncertainties of patent litigation.
1206. FTC, *Pay-for-Delay*, 2010, p. 8.
1207. Chart created on the basis of data published on the website of FDA, *Generic Competition and Drug Prices*. Available at: http://www.fda.gov/AboutFDA/CentersOffices/OfficeofMedicalProductsandTobacco/CDER/ucm129385.htm (last accessed on March 31, 2018). *See also* OLSON, WENDLING, Effect of Entry, 2013, p. 17, fn. 24, stating that the second generic competitor is expected to lower the price by 10% compared to the first generic manufacturer.

Figure 4.1   FDA, IMS, Retail Sales, 2005

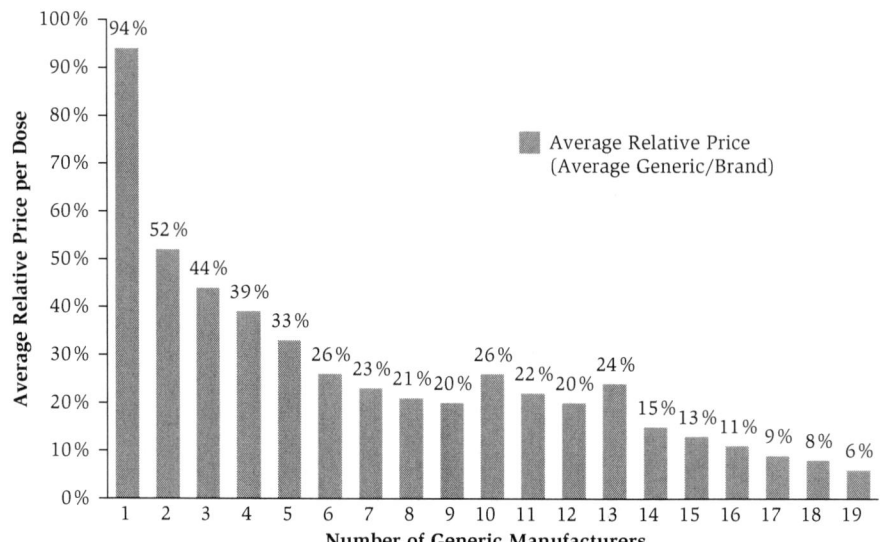

II Uncertainty Concerning No-AG Commitments

The form of reverse payment settlements evolved through time and explicit monetary payments were gradually eliminated from settlements. Alternative means of value transfers were used instead. Soon after the *Actavis* decision, a debate rose among lower courts on the question of whether the *Actavis* antitrust scrutiny should be applied to non-cash payments and notably to settlements including no-AG commitments. Initially, two district court decisions refused to apply antitrust scrutiny to non-monetary value transfers, arguing that *Actavis* is limited to cash payments; however, these decisions were subsequently overruled.[1208] The following sections present the different approaches of courts and commentators on the matter and the position that eventually prevailed.

1208. *See In re Loestrin 24 Fe Antitrust Litig.*, 45 F. Supp. 3d 180 (D.R.I. September 4, 2014), vacated by *In re Loestrin 24 Fe Antitrust Litig.*, 814 F.3d 538 (1st Cir. 2016), and; *In re Lamictal Direct Purchaser Antitrust Litigation*, No. 12-cv-995 (WHW) (D. N.J. 2014), pp. 19-26, vacated by *King Drug Company of Florence, Inc., et al., v. Smithkline Beecham Corp., et al.*, 791 F.3d 388 (3rd Cir. 2015).

Chapter 4: *FTC v. Actavis*

A Debating Whether Actavis Applies to No-AG Settlements

1 The Difficulty of Providing a Reliable Estimate of Monetary Value

The settlement in the *Effexor XR Antitrust Litigation* case is a typical example of a reverse payment that took the form of a no-AG commitment.[1209] The settlement in *Effexor* did not include an explicit transfer of value from Wyeth (the brand-name drug manufacturer) to Teva (the generic paragraph IV filer). Teva agreed to delay its generic entry into the market of "extended release" Effexor until July 2010 (more than two years after the patent covering the compound of the drug had expired); Wyeth in return committed not to launch its own authorised generic drug, providing Teva with eleven months of exclusivity on the generic market by means of an exclusive licence to sell a generic version of Effexor.[1210] The main argument of Teva and Wyeth as defendants in the antitrust lawsuit was that their settlement did not include a reverse monetary payment from Wyeth to Teva and therefore was not subject to antitrust scrutiny under *Actavis* as a matter of law.[1211] From the defendants' point of view, the settlement did not fall under the definition of reverse payment settlements and consequently did not risk antitrust liability, since the *Actavis* decision should be interpreted as suggesting that early-entry agreements do not need to be analysed under the rule of reason.[1212]

Ruling on the *Effexor* case, the district court for the district of New Jersey appeared somehow uncertain on whether antitrust scrutiny should be applied to settlements involving no-AG commitments instead of straightforward payments.[1213] It is worth noting that the 3rd Circuit subsequently reversed the district court's decision and held that no-AG commitments may also be considered as large value transfers to which antitrust scrutiny shall be applied.[1214]

Some district courts took the same route as the district court in *Effexor* and accepted that the Supreme Court did not indicate that reverse payments *had to be* cash

---

1209. *In re Effexor XR Antitrust Litig.*, No. 11-CV-5479, (D.N.J. October 6, 2014); FTC Brief as *Amicus Curiae*, *In re: Effexor XR Antitrust Litigation*, no. 11-5479 (PGS)(LHG), (August 14, 2013). [cited as: FTC, *Amicus* Brief, *In Re Effexor XR*]. *See also* ATHANASIADOU, FTC v. Actavis, 2015, pp. 264-266, briefly analysing the *Effexor* settlement.
1210. Indirect Purchaser Class Plaintiffs' Consolidated Class Action Complaint and Jury Demand, *In re: Effexor XR Antitrust Litigation*, (September 1, 2012), paras 276-294, alleging that Wyeth also agreed not to sell an authorised generic of the "instant release" Effexor XR and granted Teva an exclusive licence amounting to at least a year and a half of generic exclusivity before the compound's patent expired.
1211. Supplemental Memorandum in Support of Teva Defendants' Motions to Dismiss, *In re: Effexor XR Antitrust Litigation*, no. 11-5479 (PGS)(LHG), (August 7, 2013), pp. 3-6 [cited as: Teva Defendants' Support Memorandum, *In re: Effexor XR*, 2013]; Supplemental Memorandum in Further Support of Wyeth's Defendants' Motions to Dismiss All Complaints, *In re: Effexor XR Antitrust Litigation*, no. 11-05479, Doc. No. 231, (August 7, 2013), pp. 2-5.
1212. Teva Defendants' Support Memorandum, *In re: Effexor XR*, 2013, pp. 5, 8.
1213. *In re Effexor XR Antitrust Litig.*, No. 11-CV-5479, (D.N.J. October 6, 2014), at *62.
1214. *In re Lipitor Antitrust Litig.*, *In re Effexor XR Antitrust Litig.*, 868 F.3d 231, 258-266 (3rd Cir. 2017), reversing the district court's decision and finding that the complaints at issue plausibly alleged an actionable reverse payment settlement.

payments;[1215] however, in order to apply *Actavis* scrutiny, these courts demanded that the relevant non-cash payments are converted to a *reliable estimate of monetary value*. Only then could the alleged payment be analysed against the *Actavis* criteria so as to determine whether it was indeed large compared to legal fees and the value of other services provided from the generic challenger to the patent holder.[1216] These district courts further required the antitrust plaintiffs to provide "reliable foundation" showing that the parties concluded a reverse payment settlement and to how the alleged non-monetary payment was calculated.[1217] Ironically, these court decisions also acknowledged that it was extremely difficult for plaintiffs to plead a precise dollar value for a non-monetary value transfer.[1218]

2 Refusing to Apply Antitrust Scrutiny to No-AG Commitments

Other district courts straightforwardly denied applying antitrust scrutiny under *Actavis* to settlements including other forms of transfer of value,[1219] a denial that was greeted by a number of antitrust specialists.[1220] Adopting the "literal holding" of *Actavis*, these courts limited antitrust scrutiny exclusively to cash payments, albeit recognising that the settling parties were likely to evade antitrust scrutiny by opting for alternative forms of payment.[1221] Decisions taking such a stance and refusing to apply antitrust scrutiny to potentially costly non-cash payments were heavily criticised.[1222] In some of the decisions, district courts also required plaintiffs to discuss the saved litigation costs

---

1215. *In re Effexor XR Antitrust Litig.*, No. 11-CV-5479, (D.N.J. October 6, 2014), at *62; *In re Wellbutrin XL Antitrust Litig.*, No. 08-cv-2431, No. 08-cv-2433, (E.D. Pa. January 17, 2014), at *9, "[t]he Court is not prepared at this point to accept [...] that only a large cash payment from the patentee to the generic is subject to antitrust scrutiny under Actavis;" *In re Lipitor Antitrust Litig.*, 46 F. Supp. 3d 523, 542 (D.N.J. September 12, 2014), (not concerning a settlement involving a no-AG commitment, but a settlement allegedly including a forgiveness of damages), "*Actavis* does not define payment or provide any clarity as to whether a payment can be something other than a monetary payment."
1216. *In re Lipitor Antitrust Litig.*, 46 F. Supp. 3d 523, 542-543 (D.N.J. September 12, 2014); *In re Effexor XR Antitrust Litig.*, No. 11-CV-5479, (D.N.J. October 6, 2014), at *66.
1217. *In re Effexor XR Antitrust Litig.*, No. 11-CV-5479, (D.N.J. October 6, 2014), at *69-73, finding that the plaintiffs failed to provide evidence determining the value of the payment. See also CARRIER, Pleading Standards, 2016, pp. 34-37, criticising the *Effexor* and the *Lipitor* decisions for raising the pleading standards to unprecedented levels.
1218. *In re Loestrin 24 Fe Antitrust Litig.*, 45 F. Supp. 3d 180, 193 (D.R.I. September 4, 2014), "pleading facts sufficient to glean the monetary value of non-cash settlements is a tall task, one that would typically require considerable discovery to achieve."
1219. *See In re Loestrin 24 Fe Antitrust Litig.*, 45 F. Supp. 3d 180, 193-195 (D.R.I. September 4, 2014); *In re Lamictal Direct Purchaser Antitrust Litigation*, No. 12-cv-995 (WHW) (D. N.J. 2014), pp. 21-26, "[...] when the Supreme Court said payment it meant a payment of money" [internal quotation marks omitted].
1220. *See* for instance MCDONALD, I Said So, 2013, p. 42.
1221. *In re Loestrin 24 Fe Antitrust Litig.*, 45 F. Supp. 3d 180, 193-195 (D.R.I. September 4, 2014).
1222. HOVENKAMP, Scope of the Patent, 2015, p. 24, "[...] that is a little like saying that an incipient cartel or market division agreement cannot be regarded as socially costly simply because on cannot predict accurately how much harm it will do." *See also* CARRIER, Pleading Standards, 2016, pp. 34-41, criticising the *Effexor* and the *Lipitor* decisions for imposing unrealistic expectations under the guise of plausibility and for ignoring smoking guns in the examined settlements.

for the settling parties,[1223] despite the fact that on the basis of well-established jurisprudence, plaintiffs do not need to plead evidence that supports their allegations.[1224] Even though the Supreme Court required in *Twombly* that plaintiffs provide factual allegations rising above the speculative level and fulfil a "plausibility" requirement, the court allowed the complaint to proceed even if actual proof of the alleged facts was improbable.[1225]

Even district courts which denied applying antitrust scrutiny to settlements involving no-AG commitments recognised that their approach was problematic. In *Loestrin*, despite finding that *Actavis* only applies to cash payments, the district court for the District of Rhode Island conceded that the Supreme Court's decision can serve as a solution to anticompetitive pay-for-delay settlements *only* if it encompasses both cash and "increasingly prevalent" non-cash payments.[1226] The court recognised that the form of payment for delay is of no importance as long as value is exchanged for a brand manufacturer to continue its monopoly with fewer competitors.[1227] The rather absurd reasoning of the district court in *Loestrin* was found to be erroneous and various theories were proposed in an attempt to explain it, ranging from judicial error to ideological opposition to the *Actavis* ruling.[1228] Subsequently, the appellate court for the 1st Circuit vacated the district court's judgment and held that non-monetary payments *do* fall within the scope of *Actavis*, stressing that the settlements at issue in *Actavis* also involved multimillion dollar side deals which served as payments to delay the market entry of generic manufacturers.[1229]

B Actavis *Applies to No-AG Commitments*

The vast majority of courts eventually embraced a broad definition of payment and stressed that *Actavis* would be nothing but an arbitrary restriction on the form reverse payments take if it was only applied to cash payments.[1230] The term reverse payment

---

1223. In re Lipitor Antitrust Litig., 46 F. Supp. 3d 523, 546 (D.N.J. September 12, 2014).
1224. 48 Law, Economics and Business Professors and the American Antitrust Institute Brief as Amici Curiae in Support of Appellants, In Re Lipitor Antitrust Litigation, Nos. 14-4202, 14-4203, 14-4204, 14-4205, 14-4206, 14-6202, 14-4632, (December 28, 2015), pp. 5-6; In re Ins. Brokerage Antitrust Litig., 618 F.3d 300, 325, fn. 25 (3rd Cir. 2010); Bogosian v. Gulf Oil Corp., 561 F.2d 434, 446 (3rd Cir. 1977); W. Penn Allegheny Health Sys., Inc. v. UPMC, 627 F.3d 85, 98 (3rd Cir. 2010).
1225. Bell Atlantic Co. et al. v. Thomas Twombly et al., 127 S. Ct. 1955, 1964-1966 (S. Ct. 2007).
1226. In re Loestrin 24 Fe Antitrust Litig., 45 F. Supp. 3d 180, 194 (D.R.I. September 4, 2014).
1227. In re Loestrin 24 Fe Antitrust Litig., 45 F. Supp. 3d 180, 194 (D.R.I. September 4, 2014), "[...] it is of relatively little import whether a payment for delay is made in the form of cash or some other form of consideration. When a patent holder pays a would-be generic competitor to stay out of the market – regardless of the form of the payment – value is exchanged and the brand manufacturer is able to continue on with fewer competitors."
1228. DAVIS, McEWAN, Deactivating Actavis, 2015, pp. 558-563. The authors also noted that the Supreme Court should better take into account the institutional needs and limitations of lower courts, when establishing legal standards and be "a bit more practical."
1229. In re Loestrin 24 Fe Antitrust Litig., 814 F.3d 538, 549-552 (1st Cir. 2016), holding that Actavis applies also to settlements including non-monetary payments.
1230. King Drug Company of Florence, Inc., et al., v. Smithkline Beecham Corp., et al., 791 F.3d 388, 403-406 (3rd Cir. 2015); In re Opana ER Antitrust Litigation, 162 F. Supp. 3d 704, 716-717,

cannot be limited to cash payments since such a limited reading of the Supreme Court's case would be alien to the context of antitrust law, elevating a formalistic approach over economic realities.[1231] Nowhere in the *Actavis* decision did the court require an explicit sort of monetary transaction as a prerequisite; pursuant to the Supreme Court's decision reverse payments may take other forms than cash.[1232] Valuable no-AG commitments plausibly incentivise generic challengers to accept a later entry date than they would have in the absence of such a commitment and this is exactly the harm that the *Actavis* decision aimed to prevent.[1233] The *In Re Lamictal* decision which is analysed in the following sections concerned a reverse payment settlement including a no-AG commitment and was the first no-AG case to reach the appellate courts *post Actavis* in 2015. It is described as "the most important federal decision since *Actavis*,"[1234] since it is the first appellate decision resolving the above-mentioned split among district courts in favour of a broad definition of payment.

1 The District Court Decision In Re Lamictal

Lamictal is a drug available in the form of tablets and chewables, used to treat epilepsy and bipolar disorders and is highly profitable for GlaxoSmithKline (GSK).[1235] GSK and

---

(N.D. Ill. February 10, 2016); *In re Loestrin 24 Fe Antitrust Litig.*, 814 F.3d 538, 549-550 (1st Cir. 2016); *United Food & Commercial Workers Local 1776 v. Teikoku Pharma USA, Inc.*, 74 F. Supp. 3d 1052, 1069-1070 (N.D. Cal. November 17, 2014); *In re Lipitor Antitrust Litig.*, 46 F. Supp. 3d 523, 542 (D.N.J. September 12, 2014); *In re Aggrenox Antitrust Litig.*, 94 F. Supp. 3d 224, 242 (D. Conn. March 23, 2015), "if antitrust scrutiny can be avoided simply by making one's large and unjustifiable reverse-payment settlement in gold bullion rather than dollars, then *Actavis* stands for nothing but an arbitrary restriction on the form such payments can take."

1231. *In Re Niaspan Antitrust Litig.*, 42 F. Supp. 3d. 735, 751 (E.D. Pa. September 5, 2014), "the term reverse payment is not limited to a cash payment […] To read Actavis as so limited would be particularly anomalous in the context of antitrust law, in which economic realities rather than a formalistic approach must govern" [internal quotation marks omitted].

1232. *In Re Nexium (Esomeprazole) Antitrust Litig.*, 968 F. Supp. 2d 367, 392 (D. Mass. 2013), "[n]owhere in Actavis did the Supreme Court explicitly require some sort of monetary transaction to take place for an agreement between a brand and generic manufacturer to constitute a reverse payment;" *Time Ins. Co. v. AstraZeneca AB*, No. 14-4149, 52 F. Supp. 3d 705, 710 (E.D. Pa. October 1, 2014), "reverse payments deemed anti-competitive pursuant to Actavis may take forms other than cash payments;" *In re Aggrenox Antitrust Litig.*, 94 F. Supp. 3d 224, 242 (D. Conn. March 23, 2015), "payment is not limited to cash transfers" [internal quotation marks omitted]; *United Food & Commercial Workers Local 1776 v. Teikoku Pharma USA, Inc.*, 74 F. Supp. 3d 1052, 1069-1070 (N.D. Cal. November 17, 2014); *In re Actos End Payor Antitrust Litigation*, No. 1:14-cv-02846 (S.D.N.Y.), at *13 "[t]his Court shares the majority view that *Actavis's* holding is not limited to payments made in cash."

1233. *Food & Commercial Workers Local 1776 v. Teikoku Pharma USA, Inc.*, 74 F. Supp. 3d 1052, 1071 (N.D. Cal. November 17, 2014), "[i]f the no-authorized-generic term has any value – which defendants concede it does – then it plausibly incentivized Watson to accept an entry date later than it otherwise would have. This is precisely the harm that *Actavis* sought to prevent."

1234. Carrier, Non-cash Payments, 2015.

1235. *In re Lamictal Direct Purchaser Antitrust Litigation*, No. 12-cv-995 (WHW) (D. N.J. 2014), pp. 3-4. Indicatively, from March 2007 to March 2008, GSK's domestic sales of Lamictal tablets surpassed $2 billion and between 2004 and 2005 Lamictal chewable products' sales exceeded $50 million.

the generic challenger Teva Pharmaceutical Industries Ltd. (Teva) entered into a settlement agreement, agreeing to keep a generic version of Lamictal off the market. On the basis of their agreement, GSK allowed Teva to enter the market with certain generic versions of the drug, before all patent claims expired but at a later time than Teva proposed.[1236] GSK agreed to abstain from producing its own authorised generic version of Lamictal during Teva's 180-day exclusivity period.[1237] This no-AG commitment took the form of an exclusive licence.[1238] Taking into consideration the fact that Lamictal is a block-bluster drug, this no-AG commitment allegedly increased the revenues of Teva from its generic drug version by hundreds of millions of dollars.[1239] Teva itself acknowledged in its 2008 annual report that its revenues substantially increased with "major contributions" from products such as lamotrigine (Lamictal), sold with generic market exclusivity.[1240] Additionally, Teva noted that its revenues and profits from generic products decline as other competing generics enter the market, as it faces increasing competition from brand-name manufacturers launching authorised generics.[1241]

In February 2012, the direct purchasers of the drug Lamictal from GSK sued GSK and Teva, alleging that the parties have entered into a reverse payment settlement, conspired to delay generic competition for Lamictal tablets in violation of Section 1 of the Sherman Act and also conspired to monopolise the lamotrigine tablet market in violation of Section 2 of the Sherman Act.[1242] However, the district court in *Lamictal* affirmed the dismissal of the complaint on remand and interpreted *Actavis* as requiring a *monetary* payment to occur as part of the settlement, making a distinction between cash payments and other forms of value transfers that makes neither legal nor economic sense.[1243] Despite the long-standing insistence of the Supreme Court that antitrust analysis focuses on economic substance and not form,[1244] the district court

---

1236. *In re Lamictal Direct Purchaser Antitrust Litigation*, No. 12-cv-995 (WHW) (D. N.J. 2014), pp. 3-4. Teva was allowed to enter the market 37 months before the expiration of the relevant patent for the lamotrigine chewables, and lamotrigine tablets approximately 6 months before the expiration or the relevant patent.
1237. *In re Lamictal Direct Purchaser Antitrust Litigation*, No. 12-cv-995 (WHW) (D. N.J. 2014), pp. 5-6.
1238. *In re Lamictal Direct Purchaser Antitrust Litigation*, No. 12-cv-995 (WHW) (D. N.J. 2014, p. 5.
1239. FTC, *Amicus Brief, In Re Lamictal*, p. 13.
1240. TEVA PHARMACEUTICAL INDUSTRIES LTD., *Annual Report 2008*, Form 20-F, (February 27, 2009), p. 5. Available at: http://media.corporate-ir.net/media_files/IROL/73/73925/fr/2008/2008-ar-20f.pdf. (last accessed on March 31, 2018). [cited as: TEVA PHARMACEUTICAL INDUSTRIES LTD, *Annual Report 2008*, Form 20-F, (February 27, 2009)].
1241. *Idem*.
1242. *In re Lamictal Direct Purchaser Antitrust Litigation*, No. 12-cv-995 (WHW) (D. N.J. 2014), p. 6; *King Drug Company of Florence, Inc., et al., v. Smithkline Beecham Corp., et al.*, 791 F.3d 388, 398 (3rd Cir. 2015).
1243. *In re Lamictal Direct Purchaser Antitrust Litigation*, No. 12-cv-995 (WHW) (D. N.J. 2014), pp. 19-26. See FTC, *Amicus Brief, In Re Lamictal*, pp. 17, 22, "[t]he district court elevated form over substance when it concluded that such reverse payments trigger antitrust scrutiny only when they are made in cash rather than in kind."
1244. *American Needle, Inc. v. National Football League*, 130 S. Ct. 2201, 2211 (2010), quoting *Copperweld Corp. v. Independence Tube Corp.*, 104 S. Ct. 2731, 2742-2743, fn. 21 (1984) "substance, not form, should determine whether a[n] [...] entity is capable of conspiring;" *Eastman Kodak Co. v. Image Technical Services, Inc.* 112 S. Ct. 2072, 2082 (1992) "[l]egal

found in *Lamictal* that a no-AG commitment could not be considered as "payment" under *Actavis*.[1245] Based on the absence of a money payment, the fact that the no-AG commitment was chronically limited to Teva's 180-day exclusivity period and the "early" entry of Teva, the district court concluded that the settlement agreement was reasonable and not the sort which required the "*Actavis* scrutiny."[1246] The court went as far as to say that "other types of settlement are explicitly exempt" from antitrust scrutiny on the basis of *FTC v. Actavis*.[1247] Applying largely wrongly the five considerations of the Supreme Court and the rule of reason analysis,[1248] the court alleged that even if rule of reason could apply to no-AG settlements, the settlement between GKS and Teva would have survived antitrust scrutiny.[1249]

2 The 3rd Circuit Confirms That Actavis Cannot Be Limited to Cash Payments

The direct purchasers of Lamictal appealed before the 3rd Circuit against the district court's decision, insisting that the no-AG commitment at issue constituted a reverse payment from GSK to Teva and that *FTC v. Actavis* is not limited to reverse payments of cash.[1250] The 3rd Circuit agreed with the appellants and found that the district court erred in its judgment, since the *Actavis* ruling could not be limited to reverse payments of cash.[1251] On the contrary, a no-AG agreement representing an unexplained large transfer of value from the patent holder to the alleged generic infringer should be subject to antitrust scrutiny under the rule of reason.[1252] No-AG commitments are likely to present similar problems as reverse cash payments, since such a commitment transfers a great monetary value to the first generic filer.[1253] Limiting the holding of *Actavis* to cash payments would mean that all future parties seeking to conclude anticompetitive reverse payment settlements could evade antitrust scrutiny merely by

---

presumptions that rest on formalistic distinctions rather than actual market realities are generally disfavored by antitrust law," while "[i]n determining the existence of market power, [...] this Court has examined closely the economic reality of the market at issue."
1245. *In re Lamictal Direct Purchaser Antitrust Litigation*, No. 12-cv-995 (WHW) (D. N.J. 2014), pp. 19-26.
1246. *In re Lamictal Direct Purchaser Antitrust Litigation*, No. 12-cv-995 (WHW) (D. N.J. 2014), p. 25.
1247. *In re Lamictal Direct Purchaser Antitrust Litigation*, No. 12-cv-995 (WHW) (D. N.J. 2014), pp. 19-20.
1248. Davis, McEwan, Deactivating Actavis, 2015, pp. 574-575, noting that the court erroneously required the plaintiffs to prove the existence of a reverse payment and show that it was large and unjustified, whereas *Actavis* clearly places the burden of providing justifications for the payment upon antitrust defendants.
1249. *In re Lamictal Direct Purchaser Antitrust Litigation*, No. 12-cv-995 (WHW) (D. N.J. 2014), pp. 27-30.
1250. *King Drug Company of Florence, Inc., et al., v. Smithkline Beecham Corp., et al.*, 791 F.3d 388, 399 (3rd Cir. 2015).
1251. *King Drug Company of Florence, Inc., et al., v. Smithkline Beecham Corp., et al.*, 791 F.3d 388, 403 (3rd Cir. 2015).
1252. *Idem.*
1253. *King Drug Company of Florence, Inc., et al., v. Smithkline Beecham Corp., et al.*, 791 F.3d 388, 404 (3rd Cir. 2015). *See also* Davis, McEwan, Deactivating Actavis, 2015, pp. 567-573, noting that there is no economic reason why non-cash payments shall be exempted from *Actavis* scrutiny.

opting for alternative means of value transfer.[1254] A number of court decisions agreed with this position and adopted a broad definition of payment.[1255]

2.1 A No-AG Commitment Can Amount to Payment

By making a no-AG commitment, the patentee transfers the profit it would have made by marketing its authorised generic product to the generic challenger; plus more, in the form of higher generic drug prices since there is generic monopoly and not a duopoly between the first generic drug and the authorised generic.[1256] A no-AG commitment alters the nature of the settlement to *more* than an agreed-upon early generic entry and may "provide strong evidence that the patentee seeks to induce the generic challenger to abandon its claim with a share of its monopoly profits that would otherwise be lost in the competitive market."[1257] The main concern with combining the valuable no-AG commitment with an early-entry date provision is that the generic challenger may be willing to accept a later entry date without any corresponding benefit to consumers.[1258] Through a no-AG commitment, the generic challenger obtains something it would not

---

1254. FTC, *Amicus* Brief, *In Re Lamictal*, p. 23; FTC Brief as *Amicus Curiae*, *In re Wellbutrin XL Antitrust Litig.*, Case no.: 2:08-cv-2431, Case no.: 2:08-cv-2433, (September 26, 2013), pp. 8-13, 17 [cited as: FTC, *Amicus* Brief, *In Re Wellbutrin XL*]; FTC, *Amicus* Brief, *In Re Effexor XR*, pp. 9, 16.
1255. *In re Aggrenox Antitrust Litig.*, 94 F. Supp. 3d 224, 242 (D. Conn. March 23, 2015), "if antitrust scrutiny can be avoided simply by making one's large and unjustifiable reverse-payment settlement in gold bullion rather than dollars, then *Actavis* stands for nothing but an arbitrary restriction on the form such payments can take." *In Re Niaspan Antitrust Litig.*, 42 F. Supp. 3d. 735, 751 (E.D. Pa. September 5, 2014), "the term reverse payment is not limited to a cash payment [...] To read *Actavis* as so limited would be particularly anomalous in the context of antitrust law, in which economic realities rather than a formalistic approach must govern" [internal quotation marks omitted]; *In Re Nexium (Esomeprazole) Antitrust Litig.*, 968 F. Supp. 2d 367, 392 (D. Mass. 2013), "[n]owhere in *Actavis* did the Supreme Court explicitly require some sort of monetary transaction to take place for an agreement between a brand and generic manufacturer to constitute a reverse payment;" *Time Ins. Co. v. AstraZeneca AB*, No. 14-4149, 52 F. Supp. 3d 705, 710 (E.D. Pa. October 1, 2014), "reverse payments deemed anti-competitive pursuant to *Actavis* may take forms other than cash payments;" *United Food & Commercial Workers Local 1776 v. Teikoku Pharma USA, Inc.*, 74 F. Supp. 3d 1052, 1069-1070 (N.D. Cal. November 17, 2014); *In re Wellbutrin XL Antitrust Litig.*, 868 F.3d 132, 163 (3rd Cir. 2017), "because the agreements at issue here are such as to implicate the concerns identified in *Actavis*, they are not immune from antitrust scrutiny and must, to a degree, be evaluated under the rule of reason test."
1256. *King Drug Company of Florence, Inc., et al., v. Smithkline Beecham Corp., et al.*, 791 F.3d 388, 405 (3rd Cir. 2015).
1257. *Idem*, citing *FTC v. Actavis, Inc.*, 133 S. Ct. 2223, 2235 (2013).
1258. *King Drug Company of Florence, Inc., et al., v. Smithkline Beecham Corp., et al.*, 791 F.3d 388, 405, fn. 23 (3rd Cir. 2015). *See also In Re Niaspan Antitrust Litig.*, 42 F. Supp. 3d. 735, 752 (E.D. Pa. September 5, 2014), "[i]n this respect, a no-AG provision works exactly as would a payment of cash. One can logically infer that, all else equal, with a no-AG provision, a generic would be willing to agree to a later entry date than it would otherwise agree to in order to settle a patent-infringement case."

have otherwise obtained, had it prevailed in the patent infringement litigation: monopoly on the generic market for the 180-day exclusivity period in the absence of an authorised generic drug.[1259]

The 3rd Circuit rejected the view that the *Actavis* ruling should be limited only to cash payments and noted that it is problematic for a patentee to leverage some part of its patent power to cause anticompetitive harm.[1260] The anticompetitive consequences of a pay-for-delay agreement employing a no-AG commitment may be as harmful as settlements involving cash payments.[1261] As with cash payments, the chance of eliminating a questionable patent is vanished: through its no-AG commitment, the brand-name manufacturer avoids the risk of patent invalidation or of a finding of non-infringement.[1262] The prevention of the risk of competition beyond what the patent's strength would otherwise allow is the anticompetitive harm of such settlements, and the incurred consumer harm.[1263] As the FTC put it, whether the sharing of monopoly profits between the settling parties takes the form of gold bullions, stocks, free goods, real estate or no-AG commitments is of trivial importance: the potential for consumer harm is still present.[1264] Substituting one form of consideration for another should not alter the antitrust analysis employed since this substitution does not protect consumers from the harms of anticompetitive settlements.[1265] Even the dissenting opinion in *FTC v. Actavis* recognised that the majority's ruling could apply to non-cash transactions.[1266]

1259. *King Drug Company of Florence, Inc., et al., v. Smithkline Beecham Corp., et al.*, 791 F.3d 388, 407 (3rd Cir. 2015), "[w]hat GSK gave Teva was a 180-day monopoly over the generic market. The first-filing generic cannot capture this value by early entry alone. It can only hope to obtain this value with the brand's self-restraint, and here, without GSK's no-AG commitment, GSK allegedly would have introduced an AG;" FTC, *Amicus* Brief, *In Re Lamictal*, p. 16.
1260. *King Drug Company of Florence, Inc., et al., v. Smithkline Beecham Corp., et al.*, 791 F.3d 388, 406-407 (3rd Cir. 2015); *In re Wellbutrin XL Antitrust Litig.*, 868 F.3d 132, 160-163 (3rd Cir. 2017). *See also* CARRIER, Eight Reasons, 2015, pp. 706-720, explaining why *Actavis* also applies to reverse payments in the form of no-AG commitments, also criticising the decisions of the district court in *Lamictal* and *Loestrin* as erroneous.
1261. *King Drug Company of Florence, Inc., et al., v. Smithkline Beecham Corp., et al.*, 791 F.3d 388, 405 (3rd Cir. 2015).
1262. *Idem.*
1263. *King Drug Company of Florence, Inc., et al., v. Smithkline Beecham Corp., et al.*, 791 F.3d 388, 410 (3rd Cir. 2015). *See also In re Aggrenox Antitrust Litig.*, 94 F. Supp. 3d 224, 240-241 (D. Conn. March 23, 2015), "[a]ny settlement that takes the risk of patent invalidation into account will tacitly reflect the value of continuing the patent monopoly."
1264. FTC, *Amicus* Brief, *In Re Lamictal*, p. 17. *See also In re Aggrenox Antitrust Litig.*, 94 F. Supp. 3d 224, 242-243 (D. Conn. March 23, 2015), "large and unjustified reverse payments that can bring with [them] the risk of significant anticompetitive effects [...] can bring those effects regardless of the particular form the transfer of value takes and thus are not limited to cash payments" [internal quotation marks omitted].
1265. FTC, *Amicus* Brief, *In Re Lamictal*, p. 23.
1266. *FTC v. Actavis*, 133 S. Ct. 2223, 2239, 2245 (2013), "[The majority's] logic [...] cannot possibly be limited to reverse-payment agreements [...] The Government's brief acknowledges as much, suggesting that if antitrust scrutiny is invited for such cash payments, it may also be required for 'other consideration' and 'alternative arrangements'."); *King Drug Company of Florence, Inc., et al., v. Smithkline Beecham Corp., et al.*, 791 F.3d 388, 406, fn. 25 (3rd Cir. 2015), citing *FTC v. Actavis*, 133 S. Ct. 2223, 2239, 2245 (2013).

In a rule of reason analysis similar to the one articulated by California's Supreme Court in *Cipro I & II*,[1267] the 3rd Circuit Court found in *King Drug* that the application of the rule of reason analysis to reverse payment settlements has three steps. First, the plaintiff shall prove the existence of a payment for delay or put otherwise, of a payment to prevent the risk of competition.[1268] Second, if the existence of such a payment is proven, the burden of proof then shifts to the defendant to show any legitimate justifications so as to explain the presence of the challenged term and to prove the lawfulness of that term, under the rule of reason.[1269] Finally, the plaintiff has the chance to rebut the explanation given by the defendant.[1270] Lower courts should structure this rule of reason analysis depending on the specificities of each case, avoiding both too abbreviated antitrust theories that would not allow proper analysis and considering every fact and theory of minimal importance.[1271] The antitrust defendants subsequently filed a petition for a writ of *certiorari* challenging the 3rd Circuit's decision in *King Drug*, but the Supreme Court denied it.[1272]

2.2 Estimating Generic Challengers' Profits from a No-AG Commitment

The step of attempting to quantify the value of the alleged payment from the patent holder to the generic is missing from the *Lamictal* rule of reason steps, even though it is considered to be an essential step of the analysis of alleged non-cash reverse payments.[1273] Estimating the exact value of a no-AG provision is almost impossible; a rough value approximation on the basis of economic assumptions seems to be a more administrable strategy.[1274]

In a settlement including a no-AG commitment, the profits of the settling generic are not limited to the gains resulting from its early generic entry alone.[1275] The value transferred to the generic with a no-AG commitment is that of a 180-day monopoly on the generic market, whereas the Hatch-Waxman exclusivity period does not guarantee such a monopoly: the brand-name manufacturer can launch an authorised generic and

---

1267. See *supra* Chapter 4, Part 1, Section III.C.3, analysing the decision of *In Re Cipro Cases I & II*, 348 P.3d 845 (Cal., May 7, 2015).
1268. *King Drug Company of Florence, Inc., et al., v. Smithkline Beecham Corp., et al.*, 791 F.3d 388, 412 (3rd Cir. 2015).
1269. *Idem*, citing *FTC v. Actavis*, 133 S. Ct. 2223, 2231, 2235-2237 (2013). See also CARRIER, *King Drug*, 2016, pp. 2-7, applauding the 3rd Circuit's finding that *Actavis* also applies to non-cash payments and noting that its reasoning was consistent with antitrust law's emphasis on form over substance.
1270. *King Drug Company of Florence, Inc., et al., v. Smithkline Beecham Corp., et al.*, 791 F.3d 388, 412 (3rd Cir. 2015).
1271. *Idem*; citing *FTC v. Actavis Inc.*, 133 S. Ct. 2223, 2238 (2013).
1272. *SmithKline Beecham Corporation, et al. v. King Drug Company of Florence, Inc., et al.*, 137 S. Ct. 446, (S. Ct. 2016).
1273. See for instance, EDLIN, HEMPHILL, HOVENKAMP, SHAPIRO, Actavis Inference, 2015, pp. 592-594, "[...] for noncash reverse payments, the courts should seek to measure the dollar value sacrificed by the patent holder as a result of the agreement it reached with the alleged infringer."
1274. EDLIN, HEMPHILL, HOVENKAMP, SHAPIRO, Actavis Inference, 2015, p. 597.
1275. *King Drug Company of Florence, Inc., et al., v. Smithkline Beecham Corp., et al.*, 791 F.3d 388, 408 (3rd Cir. 2015).

compete on a generic level with the first filer, even during the 180-day exclusivity period. In the absence of the no-AG commitment, it would be economically rational for the brand-name manufacturer to launch an authorised generic. By refraining to do so, the brand-name manufacturer transfers substantial value to the generic challenger as an inducement to ensure a longer period of supracompetitive monopoly profits to be split between the settling parties, on the basis of a patent which is potentially invalid or not infringed.[1276] The value of that generic monopoly during the exclusivity period can be vast: the FTC argues that for a branded drug with annual sales of $1 billion, a no-AG commitment could increase the first generic entrant's revenue during the exclusivity period from $154 million to $255 million.[1277] The 3rd Circuit agreed that the no-AG commitment at issue may represent an unexplained large value transfer from the patent holder to the alleged generic infringer that cannot be adequately justified and is subject to a rule of reason analysis under *FTC v. Actavis*.[1278] It remains to be seen how other Circuit Courts will treat reverse payment settlements involving no-AG commitments.

2.3 No-AG Commitments Are Not Exclusive Licences

The settling parties in *Lamictal* argued that no-AG agreements are not reverse payments but exclusive licences that patent law expressly contemplates. Since the patent statute specifically authorises the right to restrain competition in the challenged manner, GSK's concession not to produce an authorised generic during Teva's 180-day exclusivity period was an exclusive licence and thus immune from antitrust scrutiny.[1279] The 3rd Circuit rejected the argument that the no-AG agreement was in fact an "exclusive licence." Some lower courts took a similar stance rejecting the argument that a no-AG commitment has the same economic effect as the grant of an exclusive licence to enter the market before the expiration of the patent.[1280] In exclusive licences no other than the licensee may practice the patent, excluding even the licensor/patentee from doing so.[1281] Nevertheless, the no-AG commitment in the *Lamictal* case allowed both the GSK and Teva to make bioequivalent drugs practicing the patent; this

---

1276. *King Drug Company of Florence, Inc., et al., v. Smithkline Beecham Corp., et al.*, 791 F.3d 388, 410 (3rd Cir. 2015); FTC, Amicus Brief, *In Re Lamictal*, pp. 26-27, "[i]n a no-AG deal, the branded company [...] transfers economic value to the generic as surely as if it had written a check."
1277. FTC, Amicus Brief, *In Re Lamictal*, pp. 24-27.
1278. *King Drug Company of Florence, Inc., et al., v. Smithkline Beecham Corp., et al.*, 791 F.3d 388, 409-410 (3rd Cir. 2015); *In re Wellbutrin XL Antitrust Litig.*, 868 F.3d 132, 160-163 (3rd Cir. 2017).
1279. *King Drug Company of Florence, Inc., et al., v. Smithkline Beecham Corp., et al.*, 791 F.3d 388, 406 (3rd Cir. 2015).
1280. *In Re Niaspan Antitrust Litig.*, 42 F. Supp. 3d. 735, 751-752 (E.D. Pa. September 5, 2014); *United Food & Commercial Workers Local 1776 v. Teikoku Pharma USA, Inc.*, 74 F. Supp. 3d 1052, 1070-1071 (N.D. Cal. November 17, 2014). *See also* EDLIN, HEMPHILL, HOVENKAMP, SHAPIRO, Actavis Inference, 2015, p. 598, noting that a no-AG provision cannot be defended on the grounds that it is an exclusive licence.
1281. *King Drug Company of Florence, Inc., et al., v. Smithkline Beecham Corp., et al.*, 791 F.3d 388, 407, fn. 27 (3rd Cir. 2015).

was not an exclusive licence granted to Teva but rather a restriction imposed on the patentee, preventing competition on the generic drug market.[1282]

Under *FTC v. Actavis*, it is problematic to leverage part of the patent power from the patentee in order to eliminate the risk of competition. Even though the payment of "hundreds of millions of dollars" in *Actavis* was combined with a licence allowing the generic challenger to enter the market sixty-five months before the expiration of the patent, this early-entry licence did not immunise the settlement from antitrust scrutiny.[1283] As with the settlement in *Actavis*, a no-AG commitment is not solely an early-entry agreement. Notwithstanding the "early entry," the antitrust problem is that in the absence of the no-AG commitment, generic entry could have occurred earlier and the risk of competition could have been preserved.[1284]

The patent holder is entitled to grant exclusive or other licences but such right does not extend to a promise not to compete by not launching an authorised generic, in an effort to induce the generic challenger to respect the patent and to quit its patent invalidity or non-infringement claim.[1285] As other courts noted, licences also worth money and granting them can be considered as transferring money: if such transfer is unlawful, its unlawfulness is not cured because of the *form* of the value transfer, irrespective of whether the grant of an exclusive licence would otherwise be valid.[1286] The issue in such settlements is not whether the *form* of the payment is legal but whether its *purpose* is legal.[1287] Exclusive licences are not ironclad from antitrust scrutiny when used in anticompetitive ways and antitrust law invalidates the improper use of patent monopoly.[1288] Despite not making a general statement about patent

---

1282. *King Drug Company of Florence, Inc., et al., v. Smithkline Beecham Corp., et al.*, 791 F.3d 388, 407, fn. 27 (3rd Cir. 2015). The 3rd Circuit cited also *Mannington Mills, Inc. v. Congoleum Industries, Inc.*, 610 F.2d 1059, 1071 (3rd Cir. 1979), "[w]here the license restriction results primarily in benefits for the licensees rather than the patentee, the anticompetitive restriction cannot be justified as a subsidy for the patentee's inventive activity;" *United States v. New Wrinkle, Inc.*, 72 S. Ct. 350, 354 (1952), "[p]atents give no protection from the prohibitions of the Sherman Act [...] when the licenses are used, as here, in the scheme to restrain;" *Moraine Prods. v. ICI America, Inc.*, 538 F.2d 134, 145 (7th Cir. 1976), "[w]here a patent license is used to protect the licensee in addition to the patentee or is used to allow the licensees to divide a market among themselves, thus enabling them jointly to regiment an industry under the guise of a patent license, there is good reason to declare such a restrictive scheme illegal."
1283. *King Drug Company of Florence, Inc., et al., v. Smithkline Beecham Corp., et al.*, 791 F.3d 388, 407 (3rd Cir. 2015).
1284. *King Drug Company of Florence, Inc., et al., v. Smithkline Beecham Corp., et al.*, 791 F.3d 388, 408 (3rd Cir. 2015).
1285. *King Drug Company of Florence, Inc., et al., v. Smithkline Beecham Corp., et al.*, 791 F.3d 388, 407 (3rd Cir. 2015).
1286. *In re Aggrenox Antitrust Litig.*, 94 F. Supp. 3d 224, 245 (D. Conn. March 23, 2015).
1287. *Idem*; *In re Lipitor Antitrust Litig.*, 46 F. Supp. 3d 523, 543 (D.N.J. September 12, 2014), "it is clear that the Supreme Court focuses on the antitrust intent of the settling parties rather than the manner of payment;" *In re Effexor XR Antitrust Litig.*, No. 11-CV-5479, (D.N.J. October 6, 2014), at *64.
1288. *King Drug Company of Florence, Inc., et al., v. Smithkline Beecham Corp., et al.*, 791 F.3d 388, 407 (3rd Cir. 2015), referring to *FTC v. Actavis, Inc.*, 133 S. Ct. 2223, 2227, 2231 (2013); *Palmer v. BRG of Georgia*, 111 S. Ct. 401, 403 (1990), finding unlawful at its face an agreement not to compete based on an exclusive copyright licence; *United States v. Line Material Co.*, 68 S. Ct. 550, 562 (1948), "[i]t is not the monopoly of the patent that is invalid. It is the improper use of that monopoly;" FTC, *Amicus* Brief, *In Re Wellbutrin XL*, p. 14, "neither does statutory

licences, the 3rd Circuit stated that the explicit authorisation of patent licensing in the Patent Act does not amount to an authorisation of reverse payments which prevent generic competition.[1289] Patent licensing agreements are dynamically coming under antitrust's spotlight: antitrust experts are increasingly preoccupied by licensing agreements which include no-challenge clauses that prohibit the patent licensee from challenging the validity of the licensed patent.[1290]

PART 3   OTHER ANTICOMPETITIVE STRATEGIES

Even before the antitrust condemnation of reverse payment settlements aiming to delay generic entry, a vast variety of strategies was employed aiming to preserve monopoly profits of successful drugs.[1291] On early stages of the pay-for-delay era, innovators filed new patents on the same drug product in an attempt to take advantage of the regulatory system before the amendments brought by the Medicare Prescription Drug, Improvement and Modernization Act of 2003.[1292] Before 2003, adding additional patents to a drug – subsequent to the filing of a paragraph IV ANDA by a generic manufacturer – forced the generic filer to amend its paragraph IV ANDA certification, triggering corresponding patent infringement suits by the innovator and resulting in additional 30-month automatic stays of FDA approval.[1293] As was analysed *supra* in Chapter 2, upon FTC's harsh criticism against this multiple stays practice, the MMA amendments of 2003 provided the solution by clarifying that there can only be one 30-month stay in the approval of each ANDA application.[1294]

---

permission to use exclusive patent licenses (which are often procompetitive) mean that patent holders are entitled to use such licenses to violate the antitrust laws."

1289. *King Drug Company of Florence, Inc., et al., v. Smithkline Beecham Corp., et al.*, 791 F.3d 388, 407 (3rd Cir. 2015).
1290. See for instance CHENG T., No Challenge Clause, 2016, pp. 469-498, analysing no-challenge clauses and the consumer harm they may give rise to; GAL, MILLER, Challenge Clauses, 2017, pp. 1491-1528, arguing that expanding antitrust scrutiny to no-challenge clauses is justified under *Actavis* and is also the socially optimal rule; HOVENKAMP E., Challenge Restraints, 2016, pp. 50-52, arguing that no-challenge restraints are the exact kind of conduct that antitrust law is intended to police.
1291. HEMPHILL, Paying for Delay, 2006, pp. 1619-1620.
1292. FTC, *Generic Drug Entry*, 2002, pp. 39-44, 55. FTC's analysis on multiple stays identified three categories of patents which raised questions as to whether they should be classified in the Orange Book: (1) patents which may not considered to claim the drug formulation or method of use approved through the NDA, such as metabolite patents, drug intermediate patents and polymorph patents; (2) product-by-process patents, claiming a drug product produced by a specified process, and; (3) patents constituting double patenting since their claimed subject matter is obvious due to the claims of another patent invented by the same person. *See also supra* Chapter 2, Part 2, Section IV.A, on the 2003 MMA amendments.
1293. The FDA was also mindful of the problem of multiple stays and issued a proposed rule with the objective to make the patent listing process more efficient and proposing only one opportunity for a 30-month stay in the approval day of each ANDA. *See* FDA, Department of Health and Human Services, *Applications for FDA Approval to Market a New Drug: Proposed Rule*, 21 CFR Part 314, [Docket No. 02N–0417] (September 12, 2002), pp. 29-37. Available at: http://www.fda.gov/OHRMS/DOCKETS/98fr/PATENT.pdf. (last accessed on March 31, 2018).
1294. *See supra*, Chapter 2, Part 2, Section I.D.2.

As the possibility of antitrust liability for payments to delay generic entry rose into a certainty, new distribution and trademark-backed branding strategies were increasingly employed. For instance, poison-pill or no-licence clauses were used in a multitude of settlement agreements, serving as a safeguard for the 180-day exclusivity period of the first generic challenger. Once it became evident that cash payments to delay generic entry were highly problematic from an antitrust perspective, clauses of "forgiveness of damages" became common in settlement agreements. The introduction of "new-but-related" drugs is another common strategy even *post Actavis*: once the patent protection of a drug is approaching its end, innovators create separately patentable alterations and attempt to convince doctors and patients to switch to the new version of the drug, engaging in the infamous tactic of product-hopping.[1295] These alternative anticompetitive strategies are presented in the following sections.

I "Poison-Pill" or "Acceleration" Clauses

The strategy of "poison-pill" or "acceleration" clauses in the reverse payment setting was discussed in Chapter 2 as one of the strategies which were used to "game" the 180-day exclusivity period.[1296] Briefly put, under a poison-pill clause the generic challenger commits not to enter the market with its generic version up to an agreed date, *unless* another generic challenger succeeds to enter the market before this date; in this case, the first challenger may enter the market and enjoy its 180-day exclusivity period.[1297] Thus, a poison-pill clause is a win-win provision for the generic challenger who enters into a reverse payment settlement with the patentee. Securing a later generic entry is very important to both the patentee, but also to the generic challenger, since it affects the monopoly profits the two parties can split.[1298]

By making the 180-day exclusivity period a certainty, rather than a probability, the patent holder confers value to the settling generic firm.[1299] Enjoying this exclusivity period with certainty is more important to the generic challenger than entering the market at an earlier date; if future demand for the drug at issue is expected to increase, the generic manufacturer may even prefer a later entry date, provided that the increase in projected profits exceeds the discount for the delay in their receipt.[1300] If the brand-name drug manufacturer and the generic challenger are splitting the profits of the prolonged monopoly, the longer this monopoly will last, the higher the payback to

---

1295. *See further* HEMPHILL, Paying for Delay, 2006, pp. 1619-1620, fn. 232, mentioning as one of the most famous transitions the one from the anti-heartburn drug Prilosec to Nexium.
1296. *See supra*, Chapter 2, Part 2, Section IV.B.2 on poison pill clauses in reverse payment settlement agreements.
1297. *See* for instance *In re Actos End Payor Antitrust Litigation*, No. 1:14-cv-02846 (S.D.N.Y.), at *5-10, discussing the terms of the settlement agreements whereby the patentee granted the alleged generic infringers non-exclusive licences containing "acceleration clauses." On the basis of these clauses, if another generic competitor would enter the market with its generic version of the branded drug, the settling generics would also be able to enter the market at the same date.
1298. HEMPHILL, Paying for Delay, 2006, pp. 1592-1593.
1299. HEMPHILL, Paying for Delay, 2006, p. 1590.
1300. *Idem*.

the generic challenger will be. As above-analysed in, delayed entry can align the incentives of the innovator and the generic challengers.[1301] Poison-pill clauses increase the complexity of adjudicating settlements and discourage subsequent generic challengers from filing patent challenges and trying to enter the market.[1302]

A poison-pill clause should also fall under the *Actavis* antitrust scrutiny, since it offers the settling generic challenger *more* that it could have won through litigation absent the settlement.[1303] Agreements containing such clauses provide significant value to the settling generic company; not only does the generic manufacturer hold on to its 180-day exclusivity period without risking forfeiting it by losing in the patent infringement litigation, but it is also guaranteed that it will be the first generic entrant to the market.[1304] Further, a poison-pill clause reduces the incentives of subsequent challengers to enter the market: later ANDA filers are "condemned" to wait through the end of this "unforfeitable" exclusivity period before marketing their generic drugs.[1305] A poison-pill clause may also be combined with a "no-licence" clause, by means of which the patentee commits not to licence its patent(s) to another generic company, preventing authorised generics' competition – the only possible form competition on generic level during the first IV ANDA filers' 180-day exclusivity period.[1306] The above-analysed characteristics of poison-pill clauses raise high concerns and led to initiatives calling for a legislative amendment banning the use of such clauses that seem to be a standard component of most Hatch-Waxman settlements.[1307]

II Forgiveness of Damages

A *The Potential Liability of Generic Entrants for Damages*

As analysed in Chapter 2, the filing of a paragraph IV ANDA amounts to an artificial act of patent infringement and legitimises the patent holder to file a patent infringement lawsuit against the generic paragraph IV ANDA filer, before the generic manufacturer enters the market.[1308] Most generic challengers wait for the patent infringement litigation to end and refrain from launching their generic drug and entering the market "at risk," before a court ruling that the patent is invalid or not infringed. One of the main reasons behind this tactic is that generic challengers are deterred by the high

---

1301. *See supra*, Chapter 2, Part 2, Section IV.B.1; HEMPHILL, Paying for Delay, 2006, p. 1590. *See also* HOVENKAMP, JANIS, LEMLEY, Anticompetitive Settlements, 2003, p. 1762, noting that in the absence of an exclusion payment, delayed entry does not align the incentives of the pioneer and the generic litigants: "[g]enerics will want the delay to be as short as possible, and patentees to make the delay as long as possible."
1302. *See* for instance CARRIER, Pharma Complexity, 2014, pp. 10-11.
1303. CARRIER, Payment After Actavis, 2014, p. 40.
1304. *Idem.*
1305. CARRIER, Payment After Actavis, 2014, pp. 37-41.
1306. *See supra*, Chapter 4, Part 2, on non-cash payments and the mechanism of no-AG commitments.
1307. Hearing, Protecting Consumer Access to Generics, 2009, pp. 214-215. *See also* Protecting Consumers Access to Generic Drugs Act of 2013, H.R. 3709, 113th Cong., (2013-2014).
1308. 35 U.S.C. § 271(e)(2). *See supra*, Chapter 2, Part 2, Section I.D, on the analysis of the paragraph IV ANDA.

liability they may incur in case of a launch "at risk," if the court subsequently finds the patent to be valid and/or infringed by their generic drug. From 2003 to 2009 there were only twenty-eight early generic launches at risk in the US.[1309]

In case of a launch at risk, if the court finds that the patent is valid and infringed by the generic drug, the generic company will be liable to pay up to treble damages or other monetary relief to the patentee.[1310] These damages rise up to at least a "reasonable royalty for the use made by the invention by the infringer" plus interest and other costs, as decided by the competent court.[1311] The brand-name manufacturer can claim lost profits if it carries the rather low burden of showing with reasonable probability that "but for" the infringement, it would have made the generic infringers' sales.[1312] This is not a difficult burden to carry, since generic sales originate directly at the expense of the branded drug's sales: a brand-name drug may lose up to 44% of its market share the first year a generic enters the market.[1313] Moreover, generic entrants can be held liable for the reduction in the brand-name drug's price, resulting from the entry of the generic drug. Due to the high stakes of a launch at risk, generic manufacturers attempting it are normally confident on their "footing."[1314] Preparations for a launch at risk may infer that the protection offered by the relevant patent is rather weak, since the generic manufacturer is not intimidated by the prospect of damages exceeding its profits or the prospect of a preliminary injunction which would spoil the expensive preparations made for the generic launch.[1315]

B   Forgiveness of Damages as a Concealed Payment

Risking great liability, a generic challenger may settle with the patentee in return for the "forgiveness" of all or part of the potential damages. Such forgiveness may concern a launch at risk or another litigation pending between the parties. This was for instance the case on the settlement concerning the drug Lipitor, "the largest selling drug of all time," grossing $1 billion per month.[1316] In the "sweetheart deal" concerning Lipitor, Pfizer – the patentee – agreed to dismiss damages claims against Ranbaxy – the generic challenger – related to *Accupril II* litigation, possibly worth hundreds of millions of

---

1309. RBC, Litigation Success Rates, 2010, p. 3.
1310. *See* 35 U.S.C. §§ 271(e)(4)(C), 284 (2016).
1311. 35 U.S.C. § 284.
1312. *Rite-Hite Corp. v. Kelley Co.*, 56 F.3d 1538, 1544-1545 (Fed. Cir. 1995), "[t]o recover lost profits damages, the patentee must show a reasonable probability that, but for the infringement, it would have made the sales that were made by the infringer" [internal quotation marks omitted]. *See also Crystal Semiconductor Corp. v. TriTech Microelectronics Int'l, Inc.*, 246 F.3d 1336, 1353 (Fed. Cir. 2001); *Water Tech. Corp. et al. v. Calco Ltd.*, 850 F.2d 660, 671, 7 U.S.P.Q.2D (BNA) 1097, 1106 (Fed. Cir.1988).
1313. CBO, *How Increased Competition From Generic Drug Has Affected Prices and Returns in the Pharmaceutical Industry*, (July 1998), pp. xii. Available at: https://www.cbo.gov/sites/default/files/105th-congress-1997-1998/reports/pharm.pdf. (last accessed on March 31, 2018). *See also* FTC, *Pay-for-Delay*, 2010, p. 8, finding that generics can substitute up to 90% of total prescriptions for a molecule.
1314. *In Re Niaspan Antitrust Litig.*, 42 F. Supp. 3d 735, 756 (E.D. Pa. September 5, 2014).
1315. HEMPHILL, Aggregate Approach, 2009, p. 650.
1316. *In re Lipitor Antitrust Litig.*, 46 F. Supp. 3d 523, 541 (D.N.J. September 12, 2014).

dollars.[1317] In exchange, Pfizer received an allegedly "pretextual" payment of $1 million and Ranbaxy's commitment to delay the entry of generic versions of Lipitor.[1318]

The district court adjudicating the *Lipitor* case required the antitrust plaintiffs to convert the effectuated non-cash payment to a "reliable estimate" of monetary value, in order to proceed to a rule of reason analysis as mandated by *Actavis*.[1319] Further complicating the position of the plaintiffs, the district court also required the plaintiffs to demonstrate the evidence upon which Pfizer would have relied to prove lost profits and to show: (1) the demand for the product; (2) the absence of non-infringing substitutes; (3) the manufacturing and marketing capacity; and (4) the amount of profit.[1320] The plaintiffs failed to meet the court's requirements and the defendants' motion to dismiss the Direct Purchasers' antitrust complaint was granted with prejudice.[1321] The decision was criticised since the antitrust plaintiffs could not have met the required evidence thresholds on a motion to dismiss,[1322] while the Supreme Court had made clear in *Actavis* that it is the antitrust defendants and not the plaintiffs who shall carry the burden of justifying a proven payment to the generic competitor.[1323]

The district court's decision in *Lipitor* was appealed and subsequently reversed by the 3rd Circuit.[1324] The 3rd Circuit stressed the large expected value of Pfizer's claims against Ranbaxy and the high likelihood of its success, agreeing with the plaintiffs that Ranbaxy's release from these claims as part of its settlement with Pfizer was unjustified and "far exceeded" any of Pfizer's saved litigation costs or any services provided by Ranbaxy.[1325] Further, the 3rd Circuit found that the heightened pleading standard that the district court required plaintiffs to meet was not required under *FTC v. Actavis*, the language of which was deliberately vague with regard to the parameters of antitrust claims against reverse payment settlements.[1326] By claiming that the alleged reverse payment was: (i) sufficiently large to permit a plausible deduction of Pfizer's power to bring about an anticompetitive harm and of its doubts on the ability of the underlying patents to lawfully prevent competition and; (ii) unjustified, the plaintiffs

---

1317. *In re Lipitor Antitrust Litig.*, 46 F. Supp. 3d 523, 541.
1318. *Idem*. The agreement between Pfizer and Ranbaxy also granted Ranbaxy the right to market Lipitor in at least eleven foreign markets, outside US.
1319. *In re Lipitor Antitrust Litig.*, 46 F. Supp. 3d 523, 542-543 (D.N.J. September 12, 2014).
1320. *In re Lipitor Antitrust Litig.*, 46 F. Supp. 3d 523, 544-545 (D.N.J. September 12, 2014).
1321. *In re Lipitor Antitrust Litig.*, 46 F. Supp. 3d 523, 544-550 (D.N.J. September 12, 2014).
1322. CARRIER, Pharma Complexity, 2014, pp. 11-12.
1323. *FTC v. Actavis, Inc.*, 133 S. Ct. 2223, 2236 (2013), "[a]n antitrust defendant may show in the antitrust proceeding that legitimate justifications are present, thereby explaining the presence of the challenged term and showing the lawfulness of that term under the rule of reason."
1324. See *In re Lipitor Antitrust Litig., In re Effexor XR Antitrust Litig.*, Nos. 14-4202, 14-4203, 14-4204, 14-4205, 14-4206, 14-4602 & 14-4632, Nos. 15-1184, 15-1185, 15-1186, 15-1187, 15-1274, 15-1323 & 15-1342, 855 F.3d 126, 151-152 (3rd Cir. 2017), concluding that the 3rd Circuit has jurisdiction to reach the merits of the appeals in the *Lipitor* and *Effexor XR* cases; *In re Lipitor Antitrust Litig., In re Effexor XR Antitrust Litig.*, 868 F.3d 231 (3rd Cir. 2017), reversing the district court's decision and finding that the complaints at issue plausibly alleged an actionable reverse payment settlement.
1325. *In re Lipitor Antitrust Litig., In re Effexor XR Antitrust Litig.*, 868 F.3d 231, 253-254 (3rd Cir. 2017).
1326. *In re Lipitor Antitrust Litig., In re Effexor XR Antitrust Litig.*, 868 F.3d 231, 254-257 (3rd Cir. 2017).

have sufficiently alleged an antitrust claim.[1327] The burden of justifying the rather large reverse payment in *Lipitor* was thus on the defendants, who failed to do so.[1328]

The disparities between the decisions of the district court and the 3rd Circuit in the *Lipitor* case illustrate that the "forgiveness" of potentially high damages by the brand-name manufacturer in the context of a Hatch-Waxman settlement is a complicated and controversial matter, which is neither easy for antitrust plaintiffs to show nor for courts to decide.[1329] Such a forgiveness amounts to a payment, but it is also possible that the source of the settlement's exclusionary power is the patent. A proposal for the antitrust analysis of such clauses is to compare the amount of the potential damages that were forgiven to the likelihood that the relevant patent was invalid or not infringed. Logically, the stronger the patent, the lower the amount of damages that the patentee would be willing to forgive.[1330] However, an *ex post* determination of the likelihood of patent invalidity or non-infringement remains a highly difficult endeavour and would burden excessively the litigating parties and the courts attempting to adjudicate such cases, both time-wise and cost-wise. Irrespectively of which method will be followed by courts in future cases, the complexity added by a second set of patents and the related potential damages calls for caution, especially when the brand-name manufacturer forgives a high amount of damages from an unrelated litigation.[1331]

III Abuse of Restricted Drug Distribution

Pharmaceuticals which are subject to limited distribution schemes are not available through standard retail pharmacies; instead, the drug manufacturer distributes them through selected specialty pharmacies, eliminating the wholesalers.[1332] Another way to prevent generic competition is through the abuse of such restricted drug distribution schemes. A blatant example of this strategy is Turing Pharmaceuticals' distribution system, which engineered and maintained a 5000% price increase for the drug Daraprim through the restrictions it imposed. In 2015, the price of the drug was raised from $13.50 to $750 per pill. In parallel, Turing switched to a "controlled distribution system" for the drug, under which both prescriptions and supplies of Daraprim could

---

1327. *In re Lipitor Antitrust Litig., In re Effexor XR Antitrust Litig.*, 868 F.3d 231, 255-256 (3rd Cir. 2017). *See also idem* 258-259, applying the same analysis to the consolidated appeals in the *Effexor* case and concluding that the antitrust plaintiffs in *Effexor* plausibly alleged a reverse payment settlement under *Actavis*.
1328. *In re Lipitor Antitrust Litig., In re Effexor XR Antitrust Litig.*, 868 F.3d 231, 256-258 (3rd Cir. 2017).
1329. *See* for instance 48 Professors, *Amici* Brief, *In Re Lipitor*, pp. 13-18, criticising the district court for the excessively high burdens it required antitrust plaintiffs to meet in *In Re Lipitor*.
1330. *See* for instance CARRIER, Payment After Actavis, 2014, pp. 44-47.
1331. CARRIER, Pharma Complexity, 2014, pp. 11-12.
1332. CARRIER, LEVIDOW, KESSELHEIM, Daraprim Price Increase, 2017, p. 1384.

be obtained only through one source.[1333] Hospitals were prevented from obtaining the drug through a general wholesaler and patients could no longer find Daraprim in a local drug store, while there were no FDA-approved generic substitutes for the drug.[1334] Turing's conduct is allegedly exclusionary and is expected to be the object of a future antitrust monopolization claim.[1335]

A Risk Evaluation and Mitigation Strategies

More subtle cases of abuse related to drug distribution concern Risk Evaluation and Mitigation Strategies (REMS). The Food and Drug Administration Amendments Act of 2007 (FDAAA) gave FDA the authority to require from brand-name drug manufacturers REMS.[1336] REMS are approved safety strategies and policies to manage a known or potential risk associated with a medicine and to safeguard the distribution of certain drugs or biological products.[1337] A REMS may require that pharmacies selling the respective drug are enrolled in the REMS and pharmacists may be expected to verify if the drug's prescriber and patient are also enrolled, before dispensing the drug.[1338] On certain instances, REMS may be used by brand-name manufacturers to prevent generic entry, a danger that was readily identified by the US Congress: under the FDAAA it is explicitly prohibited for a brand-name manufacturer to make use of the REMS to "block or delay approval" of a generic competitor's ANDA.[1339] In order to launch a generic drug version, a generic manufacturer needs to conduct bioequivalence testing in order to demonstrate that its generic formulation is therapeutically equivalent to the brand-name drug.[1340] The following sections discuss cases in which REMS were employed by brand-name drug manufacturers to prevent generic competitors from having access to the samples of the brand-name drugs they needed in order to conduct this bioequivalence testing.

1333. CARRIER, KESSELHEIM, Price Hike, 2015; CARRIER, LEVIDOW, KESSELHEIM, Daraprim Price Increase, 2017, pp. 1378-1381. Daraprim is a drug used to treat toxoplasmosis, a fatal parasitic brain infection usually occurring to patients with weakened immune systems such as patients with last-stage HIV infection.
1334. CARRIER, LEVIDOW, KESSELHEIM, Daraprim Price Increase, 2017, pp. 1387, 1392-1393.
1335. CARRIER, LEVIDOW, KESSELHEIM, Daraprim Price Increase, 2017, pp. 1397-1407.
1336. Food and Drug Administration Amendments Act of 2007 (FDAAA), 121 Stat. 823, Public Law 110-85, (September 27, 2007); See also FDA, A Brief Overview of Risk Evaluation and Mitigation Strategies (REMS). Available at: http://www.fda.gov/AboutFDA/Transparency/Basics/ucm325201.htm. (last accessed on March 31, 2018).
1337. See FDA, Approved Risk Evaluation and Mitigation Strategies (REMS), for the approved REMS approved in 2016. Available at: http://www.accessdata.fda.gov/scripts/cder/rems/index.cfm (last accessed on March 31, 2018), for the currently approved REMS.
1338. FTC Brief as Amicus Curiae, Actelion Pharms Ltd. v. Apotex Inc., Case No. 1:12-cv-05743-NLH-AMD, (March 11, 2013), p. 7. Available at: https://www.ftc.gov/policy/advocacy/amicus-briefs/2013/03/actelion-pharmaceuticals-ltd-et-al-v-apotex-inc. [cited as: FTC, Amicus Brief, Actelion Pharms v. Apotex].
1339. 21 U.S.C. § 355-1(f)(8).
1340. See supra Chapter 2, Part 2; OECD, U.S. Note, 2014, p. 16, point 51.

B Preventing Generics from Buying Samples of the Branded Drug

1 Actelion Pharms Ltd. v. Apotex Inc.

In *Actelion Pharmaceuticals*, three generic manufacturers alleged that the brand-name drug manufacturer Actelion imposed distribution restrictions that prevented them from buying samples of the drug through customary distribution channels, while Actelion also refused to sell the drugs directly to them;[1341] thereby the generic manufacturers were precluded from meeting the FDA's requirements and from developing their generic versions of the brand-name drug.[1342] Actelion argued that it was under "no duty or no obligation" to sell its drug products to its potential generic competitors; its distribution restrictions were required by the FDA and its right to refuse to sell to the generic companies was nearly absolute.[1343] The FTC filed an amicus curiae brief strongly disagreeing with Actelion's position, stressing that it could pose a significant threat to competition in the pharmaceutical industry by jeopardising the functioning of the Hatch-Waxman Act.[1344] The district court allowed the case to proceed noting that according to the US Supreme Court's jurisprudence refusals to deal are "fact specific" and "industry specific;" the FDA does not have the regulatory power to compel samples and the generic company did not have any other potential remedy available for the alleged anticompetitive conduct suffered.[1345] Nevertheless, the case did not move further since the litigating parties entered a settlement whose terms were not disclosed.

2 Mylan Pharms v. Celgene Corp.

A nearly identical case is *Mylan Pharms v. Celgene Corp.*, a case that concerns two blockbuster cancer drugs.[1346] Mylan is alleging that Celgene abused its REMS to prevent generic competitors from acquiring the brand-name drug samples which were necessary for the bioequivalence testing. Further, Celgene allegedly delayed the generic's efforts to obtain the drug samples *via* burdensome and unnecessary requests of information, in an attempt to foreclose potential generic competition. The FTC argued that refusing to sell drug samples to potential generic competitors may constitute exclusionary conduct and should be subject to antitrust analysis since it is

---

1341. Transcript of Motions Hearing, *Actelion Pharm. Ltd. v. Apotex, Inc.*, 1:12-cv-05743, (D.N.J. October17 2013).
1342. FTC Press Release, *FTC Amicus Brief: Improper Use of Restricted Drug Distribution Programs May Impede Generic Competition* (March 12, 2013). Available at: https://www.ftc.gov/news-events/press-releases/2013/03/ftc-amicus-brief-improper-use-restricted-drug-distribution (last accessed on March 31, 2018).
1343. Idem.
1344. FTC, *Amicus* Brief, *Actelion Pharms v. Apotex*, pp. 15-17.
1345. Transcript of Motions Hearing, *Actelion Pharm. Ltd. v. Apotex, Inc.*, 1:12-cv-05743, at *115-116, (D.N.J. October 17, 2013).
1346. *Mylan Pharms. v. Celgene Corp.*, Case No. 2:14-cv-02094 (D.N.J., December 22, 2014). The concerned drugs are Thalomid and Revlimid.

liable to undermine the objectives of the Hatch-Waxman Act.[1347] The district court denied the defendants' motion to dismiss the REMS allegations, finding that the plaintiffs alleged facts sufficient to support an antitrust claim for denying a generic competitor access to patented drug samples distributed in accordance with an REMS programme.[1348] Two class actions were filed against Celgene on behalf of direct and indirect purchasers of the drug, sustaining that Celgene had unlawfully perpetuated its monopoly not only by using distribution restrictions but also by fraudulently obtaining "use" patents and engaging in sham litigation.[1349]

IV Product Reformulations and Product-Hopping

The term "product reformulation" refers to a strategic behaviour of brand-name drug manufacturers, consisting of physically changing their drug products. One of the main aims behind this strategy may be to prevent the substitutability of the new version of their brand-name drugs by generic drug versions, so that the tactic is also known as product-hopping.[1350] Before the statutory MMA amendments of 2003, brand-name manufacturers were adding new patents and stacking up consecutive 30-month stays in order to extend their exclusivity on the brand-name drug and to prevent generic competitors from entering the market.[1351] When multiple 30-month stays were no longer possible, another strategy emerged: "stacking-up" drug products through product-hopping.[1352] Already in 2010, CARRIER stressed the need for courts and commentators to focus on the combination of anticompetitive reverse settlements with product-hopping strategies, noting that the latter may eliminate any meaningful competition *post* generic entry.[1353]

A *Defining Product-Hopping*

Product-hopping in the context of pharmaceutical products occurs when a brand-name drug manufacturer seeks to swift the demand from a drug product A – whose patent protection is about to expire – to drug product B which is usually a modified version of the drug product A enjoying a longer term of remaining patent protection.[1354] As one

---

1347. FTC Brief as *Amicus Curiae*, *Mylan Pharms. v. Celgene Corp.*, Case No. 2:14-cv-2094-ES-MAH, (June 17, 2014), pp. 8-9, 15-17. Available at: https://www.ftc.gov/policy/advocacy/amicus-briefs/2014/06/mylan-pharmaceuticals-inc-v-celgene-corporation.
1348. *Mylan Pharms. v. Celgene Corp.*, Case No. 2:14-cv-02094 (D.N.J., December 22, 2014).
1349. See *In re Thalomid and Revlimid Antitrust Litigation*, Civil No.: 14-6997 (KSH) (CLW), (D.N.J. 2015), on the consolidated class actions of *International Union of Bricklayers, et al. v. Celgene Corporation*, Case No. 14-6997 (D.N.J. November 7, 2014); *City of Providence v. Celgene Corporation*, Case No. 2:15-cv-01605 (D.N.J. 2015), dismissing Celgene's motion to dismiss all counts in plaintiffs' complaints.
1350. See SHADOWEN, LEFFLER, LUKENS, Market Discipline, 2011, pp. 698-704.
1351. See *supra*, Chapter 2, Part 2, Section II.D.2 and Section IV.A, discussing consecutive 30-month stays and the 2003 MMA amendments respectively.
1352. NOAH, Product Hopping, 2015, pp. 165-169.
1353. CARRIER, Real-World, 2010, pp. 1033-1036.
1354. GINSBURG, WONG-ERVIN, WRIGHT, Micromanaging Innovation, 2015, p. 2.

commentator put it "[w]hen the brand-manufacturer kills demand for its old formulation, demand for rival generics dies with it."[1355] There are two different tactics available: "hard" switches, where the brand company introduces drug product B to the market and withdraws drug product A from the market, and "soft" switches, where the brand-name manufacturer does not withdraw the drug product A but continues to market it, shifting however all of its promotion and marketing efforts to drug product B.[1356] The distinction between hard and soft switches is not always easy to make. For instance, a brand manufacturer may not withdraw product A from the market but may instead increase its price to prohibitive levels, practically removing it from the market by making it unaffordable.[1357] Reducing the price of the new drug product is another option which may lead to a successful switch.[1358] Another subtler tactic is to seek the withdrawal of the FDA's licence for older versions of the drug, in order to block the approval of its generic copies that would undercut the sales of the new version of the drug, as arguably happened in the *OxyContin* case.[1359]

B Generic Substitution

The mechanism of generic substitution and the strategy of product-hopping are closely related. In essence, the main goal of product-hopping is to block the way to generic substitution and to prevent a demand shift from the brand-name drug – whose patent protection expired – to its generic equivalents. The following sections outline how generic substitution works in order to better understand how product-hopping may be employed as a mean to delay generic entry.

1 The Mechanism of Generic Substitution

Generic substitution is the substitution of brand-name drugs by therapeutically equivalent and much less expensive generic drug versions. A generic drug is bioequivalent or "AB rated" if it contains the same active ingredient as the brand-name drug, has the same dosage and the same form. Moreover, "the rate and extent of absorption" of the generic drug's active ingredient must be the same as those of the brand-name drug.[1360] If a study demonstrating bioequivalence was submitted for a generic drug product, it will be given an AB-rating by the FDA in the *Orange Book*.[1361] As explained in Chapter 2 of this book, the Orange Book contains therapeutic equivalence evaluations for "approved multisource prescription drug products," which serve as public information

---

1355. CHENG, Product Hopping, 2008, p. 1488.
1356. SHEPHERD, Subsidize Competitors, 2016, pp. 668-672.
1357. *Idem*, noting that this tactic would be generally considered as a soft switch, but in reality would have the same effect as a hard switch.
1358. Ho, Patentable, 2015, pp. 317-321.
1359. NOAH, Product Hopping, 2015, pp. 172-179, describing how upon Purdue's application, FDA withdrew its approval for the original version of OxyContin on safety grounds. NOAH argues that this withdrawal deferred generic competition for more than twelve years.
1360. 21 U.S.C. § 355(j)(8)(B)(i).
1361. FDA Website, "Orange Book Preface," 38th edition.

and advice to State health agencies, prescribers and pharmacists in order to promote public education on drug product selection and the containment of healthcare costs.[1362]

Generic substitution generates increasingly larger cost savings: there is evidence that in 2016, savings from the substitution of brand-name drugs by generics amounted to $253 billion, while in 2010 generic savings amounted to $138 billion.[1363] The use of generic drugs saved the US healthcare system and consumers approximately $1.67 trillion between 2007 and 2016.[1364] The importance of generic substitution schemes is huge, if one considers that generic substitution rates may reach up to almost 90% of the market when there are generic drug versions available.[1365] In 2016, generic drugs accounted for 89% of prescriptions dispensed in the US, amounting to only 26% of total drug costs.[1366]

The FDA is not responsible for generic substitution which is regulated through State laws and regulations.[1367] A considerable number of US States, including the State of New York and the District of Columbia have adopted FDA's AB-rating system and only permit generic substitution if the generic drug received an AB-rating in the Orange Book. Additionally, some States require pharmacists to substitute generic drugs, unless otherwise prescribed by the physician.[1368] The mechanism of generic substitution is designed to correct a type of an agency problem: a market failure arising from the prescription drug system, namely the disconnect between the physician who chooses to prescribe a specific drug and patients and insurers who incur the cost of this drug.[1369]

2 Biosimilar or Interchangeable Drugs and Generic Substitution

Healthcare savings are expected to increase further through the introduction of the new generation low-cost biosimilar or interchangeable drugs. Biosimilars are biological products approved by the FDA not under the Hatch-Waxman Act but through an abbreviated pathway on the basis of Obama's Patient Protection and Affordable Care

---

1362. *See supra* Chapter 2, Part 1, Section I on FDA's Orange Book; FDA Website, "Orange Book Preface," 38th edition.
1363. AAM, *Generic Drug Access & Savings in the U.S.*, Report, (2017), pp. 39. Available at: https://accessiblemeds.org/resources/blog/2017-generic-drug-access-and-savings-us-report (last accessed on March 31, 2018). [cited as: AAM, Generic Drug Access & Savings Report, 2017], p. 39.
1364. *Idem. See also*, GPhA, *Generic Annual Drug Cost Savings in the U.S.*, 7th Annual Edition, 2015, pp. 1. Available at: http://www.gphaonline.org/gpha-media/gpha-resources/2015-gpha-annual-report (last accessed on March 31, 2018). [cited as: GPhA, Generic Savings, 2015], finding savings of $1.68 trillion between 2005 and 2014; IMS, Savings Estimation, 2013, p. 2, also arguing that the use of generic drugs resulted in savings of $1.7 trillion between 2002 and 2010.
1365. FTC, *Pay-for-Delay*, 2010, p. 8; AsPE, Expanding Generics, 2010, pp. 3-4; SHEPPARD, Essential Contributors, 2010, pp. 3-4.
1366. AAM, Generic Drug Access & Savings Report, 2017, p. 16.
1367. AsPE, Expanding Generics, 2010, p. 3; FDA Website, "Orange Book Preface," 38th edition.
1368. *Mylan Pharmaceuticals Inc. v. Warner Chilcott PLC et al*, Civ. No. 12-3824, (E.D. Pa. 2015), pp. 7-8.
1369. FTC Brief as *Amicus Curiae* Supporting Plaintiff-Appellant, *Mylan Pharmaceuticals Inc. v. Warner Chilcott PLC et al.*, (September 30, 2015), pp. 25-26. [cited as: FTC, *Amicus* Brief, *Mylan Pharms. v. Warner* Chilcott, 2015].

Act (commonly known as Affordable Care Act or Obamacare (ACA)),[1370] after showing that they are highly similar to a FDA-approved biological product and that they meet FDA's standard of safety and efficacy.[1371] An interchangeable biological product is biosimilar to an FDA-approved reference product and can be substituted for the reference product by a pharmacist, without the intervention of the healthcare provider who prescribed the reference brand-name product.[1372] To meet the interchangeability criteria, an applicant must demonstrate biosimilarity by showing that the biological product is expected to produce the same clinical result as the reference product and that the risk of safety or diminished efficacy in case of switching between the reference product and the biological product is not greater than using the reference product without any alteration or switch.[1373] On March 6, 2015, the first biosimilar product obtained full FDA approval,[1374] marking the beginning of a new era which is however likely to lead to new antitrust concerns.[1375]

C Anticompetitive Product-Hopping Strategies

1 The Timing of Drug Product Reformulation

The US regulatory framework may create opportunities for brand-name drug manufacturers to make medically trivial but economically crucial changes to their drug products, especially since neither patent law nor FDA regulations require that the reformulated drug is superior compared to the original product.[1376] The timing of product reformulations often raises controversy. It is alleged that the majority of

---

1370. H.R. 3590, *Patient Protection and Affordable Care Act*, Public Law No: 111-148, 24 Stat. 119 through 124 Stat. 1025, 111th Congress, (2009-2010). This abbreviated pathway is provided in the *Biologics Price Competition and Innovation Act (BPCI Act)*, which was passed as part of the ACA, amending 42 U.S.C. Public Health Service Act (PHS Act), Public Law No. 78-410, 58 Stat. 682, Chapter 373 (1944). *See also* FDA, CDER, CBER, *Guidance for Industry, Biosimilars: Questions and Answers Regarding Implementation of the Biologics Price Competition and Innovation Act of 2009*, April 2015, pp. 3-4. Available at: http://www.fda.gov/downloads/Drugs/GuidanceComplianceRegulatoryInformation/Guidances/UCM444661.pdf. (last accessed on March 31, 2018). [cited as: FDA, Q&A Biosimilars, 2015].
1371. FDA Website, *Biosimilars*, (2015). Available at: http://www.fda.gov/Drugs/DevelopmentApprovalProcess/HowDrugsareDevelopedandApproved/ApprovalApplications/TherapeuticBiologicApplications/Biosimilars/ (last accessed on March 31, 2018).
1372. FDA, *Biosimilars*, (2015).
1373. 42 U.S.C. 262(k)(4), 351(k)(4) of the PHS Act, added by the BPCI Act; *See also* FDA, Q&A Biosimilars, 2015, p. 4. For a great overview of US State laws and legislation on biologic medications and the substitution of biosimilars *see* CAUCHI, 2017.
1374. FDA Press Release, *FDA Approves First Biosimilar Product Zarxio*, (March 6, 2015). Available at: http://www.fda.gov/NewsEvents/Newsroom/PressAnnouncements/ucm436648.htm (last accessed on March 31, 2018).
1375. *See* for instance TUCKER, WELLS, Biologics, 2014, pp. 102-105, analysing the anticompetitive issues that may arise in the context of biologic drugs and arguing that the *Actavis* scrutiny could be extended to settlements between reference drug manufacturers and follow-on biologics manufacturers. *See* however FISHER LIETZAN, 2017, submitting that the framework for competition and innovation in drug products may be mostly irrelevant when it comes to biologics.
1376. SHADOWEN, LEFFLER, LUKENS, Product Changes, 2009, pp. 5-7.

pharmaceuticals' reformulations are temporarily unrelated to imminent generic entry.[1377] On the flipside, it is also argued that substantial numbers of product reformulations occur near the end of the respective drug's patent life and concern incremental changes, such as switches from one drug form to another or changes to the drug's dosology (e.g., from thrice per day to once per day), at a huge cost to generic competition.[1378] What is undisputed is that the timing of drug reformulation is a crucial matter and that brand-name drug manufacturers have a great interest in switching the market to their new drug product before generic entry occurs.[1379]

2 Product-Hopping Effects to Generic Substitution

Brand-name drug manufacturers can delay generic competition in two ways through a "hard" switch: by making trivial changes to their drug product and by withdrawing in parallel the older version of the drug from the market. Similarly to previous forms of evergreening, product-hopping may cause a new set of Orange Book filings, paragraph IV certifications, Hatch-Waxman patent infringement litigation and 30-month stays. Even in the absence of new patent claims related to the newer version of the brand-name drug, the generic challenger must file a second ANDA application for the new branded drug and undergo the same time-consuming FDA review process as it did for its first ANDA.[1380] This strategy has a great impact in limiting the market share of generic drugs. Whereas generic AB-rated and bioequivalent versions of a drug may capture up to 90% of prescriptions for a molecule,[1381] this is not the case for drugs that brand-name manufacturers "secured" through product-hopping.[1382] In *TriCor*, the brand-name manufacturer reformulated twice the relevant drug and withdrew the older versions of the drug from the market in a hard switch; as a result, generics only managed to capture 2.2% of unit sales, five years subsequent to generic entry.[1383] Even in the soft-switch case of *Prilosec*, five years after generic entry, the generics only managed to capture a rough 25% of annual unit sales.[1384]

Even though a generic manufacturer is still allowed to market the first generic version for which it gained FDA approval, this is of no use if the brand-name drug

---

1377. Shadowen, Leffler, Lukens, Product Changes, 2009, pp. 21-27, 78, finding that out of 425 product changes, only 81 occurred either 3 years before the approval of the relevant generic version or 1 year after the approval of the generic drug by the FDA, a 4-year period referred in the study as "Generic Window."
1378. Ho, Patentable, 2015, pp. 317-321; Hughes, Ferner, Disinvestment and NICE, 2010, p. 691; Shadowen, Leffler, Lukens, Market Discipline, 2011, pp. 701-704, "[a]lthough many product reformulations appear to be legitimate efforts by the brand manufacturer to fill out a product line, improve the product, or satisfy 'niche' demands for the products, many other reformulations appear to be designed principally to impair generic competition."
1379. Carrier, Real-World, 2010, pp. 1020-1022.
1380. See further, Hovenkamp, Janis, Lemley, Leslie, *IP And Antitrust*, 2015, pp. 15-78.3-15-81.
1381. FTC, Pay-for-Delay, 2010, p. 8.
1382. Shadowen, Leffler, Lukens, Product Changes, 2009, pp. 71-72.
1383. *Teva Pharmaceuticals USA, Inc. et al. v. Abbott Laboratories et al.*, No. 02-1512 (D. Del. November 12, 2008); Downing, Ross, Jackevicius, Krumholz, Abbott's Franchise, 2012, pp. 71-72.
1384. Walgreen Co. et al., First Amended Complaint and Demand for Jury Trial, *Walgreen Co. v. AstraZeneca Pharm. L.P.*, No. 1:06-cv-02084-RWR (2006), para. 106.

manufacturer successfully managed to coerce the majority of patients into switching to its new version of the brand-name drug.[1385] All State laws governing generic substitution in the US prohibit the substitution of brand-name drugs by generic drugs which are not "therapeutically equivalent."[1386] Nevertheless, there is not one uniform definition of "therapeutic equivalence."[1387] Under State substitution laws, the ability of pharmacists to substitute the first generic version with the "new" branded drug is limited, until the second paragraph IV ANDA of the generic challenger obtains FDA approval.[1388] While it is true that monopolists have no general duty to facilitate their competitors' entry into the market,[1389] or to continue selling a particular product,[1390] they must refrain from acts whose sole purpose or effect is to exclude competition from the market.[1391] Merely introducing a new product in the market – irrespectively of whether this product is superior or not – does not itself amount to exclusionary conduct. Moreover, there is merit to the arguments of brand-name manufacturers that they cannot be held liable for stopping the marketing of a drug product.[1392] However, such actions may be problematic from an antitrust perspective if combined with a wrongful conduct such as disparaging the old drug product, raising false safety concerns, coercing consumers or reducing the market's ambit.[1393]

3 Hard and Soft Product Switches as Monopolisation Strategies

Section 2 of Sherman Act prohibits monopolisation, attempts to monopolise or conspiracies to monopolise interstate or international commerce.[1394] Product-hopping strategies through which the brand-name drug manufacturer allegedly attempts to monopolise the market are to be evaluated primarily under Section 2 of the Sherman Act, but they may also raise claims under Section 1 of the Sherman Act.[1395] In order to

---

1385. See for instance CARRIER, Pharma Complexity, 2014, pp. 4-6, 8-9 "[i]f brands can switch the market before generic entry, patients would not experience the benefits of lower prices and would be unlikely to make a second switch to the generic."
1386. ASPE, Expanding Generics, 2010, Appendix A, *List of State Laws Governing Generic Substitution by Pharmacists*. Available at: http://aspe.hhs.gov/basic-report/expanding-use-generic-drugs (last accessed on March 31, 2018).
1387. *New York v. Actavis PLC, Forest Labs LLC*, 787 F.3d 638, 644-646, (2nd Cir. 2015). See also JESSE, Generic Substitution, 2008.
1388. See further, HOVENKAMP, JANIS, LEMLEY, LESLIE, *IP And Antitrust*, 2015, p. 15-78.4.
1389. See for instance CHENG, Product Hopping, 2008, pp. 1500-1503, arguing that brand-name manufacturers are not under the duty to "serve as the sales force of generic manufacturers" and that antitrust law should not condemn product hopping merely on this ground.
1390. HOVENKAMP, JANIS, LEMLEY, LESLIE, *IP And Antitrust*, 2015, p. 15-78.
1391. *United States v. Grinnell Corp. et al.*, 86 S. Ct. 1698, 1704, (January 13, 1966), condemning a behaviour under Section 2 of the Sherman Act which was "plainly and explicitly" for the single purpose of wilfully acquiring and maintaining monopoly power; *United States v. Microsoft Corp.* 253 F.3d 34, 65 (D.C. Cir. 2001), finding that "[j]udicial deference to product innovation, however, does not mean that a monopolist's product design decisions are *per se* lawful."
1392. HOVENKAMP, JANIS, LEMLEY, LESLIE, *IP And Antitrust*, 2015, 2015, p. 15-78.
1393. *In re Suboxone Antitrust Litigation*, 64 F. Supp. 3d 665, 682 (E.D. Pa. 2014).
1394. 15 U.S.C. § 2.
1395. See for instance *Mylan Pharmaceuticals Inc. v. Warner Chilcott PLC et al.*, 838 F.3d 421, 431-433 (3rd Cir. 2016), where the antitrust plaintiffs argued that the product hopping strategy

support a claim for actual monopolisation, the plaintiff shall prove: (1) the possession of market power in the relevant market, and; (2) the wilful acquisition or maintenance of that power.[1396]

Harsher antitrust scrutiny is typically applied to hard product switches in the pharmaceutical sector, compared to soft switches. Even the *threat* of a hard switch combined with fabricated safety concerns targeting competing drug products may constitute an exclusionary conduct that could coerce patients and doctors into switching.[1397] Long before the decision of the Supreme Court in *Actavis*, there were product-hopping cases in the pharmaceutical market. For instance, in 2006, the Delaware District Court employed a rule of reason analysis in *Abbott Labs. v. Teva Pharmaceuticals* and found that the plaintiffs had sufficiently supported an antitrust claim by alleging that Abbott engaged in a hard switch that blocked generic competition.[1398]

On the other hand, soft switches are not always seen as antitrust violations. In the 2008 decision of *Walgreen Comp. et al. v. AstraZeneca Pharmaceuticals*, the district court found that a soft product switch did not amount to consumers' coercion but merely offered them a new product choice.[1399] The court's *rationale* was criticised as "insupportable" for largely ignoring that prescription pharmaceutical markets are different from ordinary markets.[1400] Nevertheless, other commentators supported this distinction between hard and soft product switches; since the *Walgreen* case concerned the introduction of a new product without withdrawal of the product's previous version from the market and absent a gaming of the regulatory system by the brand-name manufacturer, this soft switch represented substantially lower antitrust risks.[1401]

The following sections analyse three prominent product-hopping cases in the US pharmaceutical market that were decided after the Supreme Court's decision in *FTC v. Actavis*. All three cases concerned allegedly incremental brand-name drug changes through which automatic generic substitution was estopped.

3.1 Hard Product Switch and Coercion of Patients

The *New York v. Actavis PLC, Forest Labs LLC* (the *Namenda* case) – which was decided two years after *Actavis* – provides a good illustration of a product-hopping

---

at issue violated both Section 1 and Section 2 of the Sherman Act. For an excellent analysis of the US jurisprudence on product-hopping and a detailed proposal on the antitrust analysis of such conduct *see* CARRIER, SHADOWEN, Product Hopping, 2016.
1396. *Mylan Pharmaceuticals Inc. v. Warner Chilcott PLC et al.*, 838 F.3d 421, 433-434 (3rd Cir. 2016).
1397. *In re Suboxone Antitrust Litigation*, 64 F. Supp. 3d. 665, 679-685 (E.D. Pa. 2014).
1398. *Abbott Labs. v. Teva Pharms. USA Inc.*, 432 F. Supp. 2d. 408, 422-424 (D. Del. 2006).
1399. *Walgreen Comp. et al. v. AstraZeneca Pharms. et al.*, 534 F. Supp. 2d.146, 148-152 (D.D.C. 2008).
1400. *See* for instance SHADOWEN, LEFFLER, LUKENS, Product Changes, 2009, pp. 65-77.
1401. HOVENKAMP, JANIS, LEMLEY, LESLIE, *IP And Antitrust*, 2015, pp. 15-78.3-15.80, arguing that if the generic has lost any market share it was most probably "because of the desirability of the patent owner's new product."

strategy. Similarly to previous drug product-hopping cases,[1402] the brand-name drug manufacturers allegedly attempted to switch Alzheimer patients from Namenda IR – a drug which was reaching the end of its patent exclusivity in July 2015 – to Namenda XR, before the generic versions of Namenda IR entered the market.[1403] Namenda IR and Namenda XR have the same therapeutic effect and the same active ingredient; the medical difference between the drugs is that Namenda IR is administered twice a day since it is released immediately in the bloodstream and Namenda XR is administered only once, since it is released gradually.[1404] As part of their "product extension" strategy in order to avoid the patent cliff, Namenda's manufacturers stopped actively marketing Namenda IR while they spent high amounts to promote Namenda XR, which they sold at a discounted rate. Further, they issued rebates to health plans ensuring that patients would not have to make higher co-payments for Namenda XR than for Namenda IR.[1405]

The drug switch attempted was a "hard switch" which combined the planned withdrawal of Namenda IR from the market and the parallel introduction of Namenda XR.[1406] Namenda's manufacturers estimated that this hard switch would convert 80% to 100% of Namenda IR patients to Namenda XR, before generic entry occurred, leaving "few to no prescriptions" where generics would be eligible to compete.[1407] The removal of Namenda IR from the market prior to the release of generic versions of the drug and the "forced switch" of patients was criticised for going far beyond a mere attempt to minimise the impact of new competition and having severe effects on consumer welfare in the form of fewer drug choices and diminished price competition.[1408] Before Namenda IR was removed entirely from the market, the New York State filed a complaint alleging that the drug's withdrawal from the market would violate antitrust laws. The district court for the Southern District of New York issued a preliminary injunction barring the brand-name manufacturers from restricting patients' access to Namenda IR prior to the entry of generic IR versions.[1409]

The 2nd Circuit affirmed the district court's preliminary injunction and found that this conduct resulted into *coercing* consumers rather than persuading them on the merits to switch drugs. The court found that the planned hard product switch would likely impede generic competition by precluding the generic substitution through State drug substitution laws.[1410] Coercing patients to switch to Namenda XR would largely prevent generic substitution, because generic versions of Namenda IR are not AB-rated

---

1402. *Abbott Labs. v. Teva Pharms. USA Inc.*, 432 F. Supp. 2d. 408, 422-424 (D. Del. 2006); *In re Suboxone Antitrust Litigation*, 64 F. Supp. 3d. 665, 679-685 (E.D. Pa. 2014); *Walgreen Comp. et al. v. AstraZeneca Pharms. et al.*, 534 F. Supp. 2d.146, 148-152 (D.D.C. 2008).
1403. *New York v. Actavis PLC, Forest Labs LLC*, 787 F.3d 638, 642-643, 647-648 (2nd Cir. 2015).
1404. *New York v. Actavis PLC, Forest Labs LLC*, 787 F.3d 638, 647 (2nd Cir. 2015).
1405. *New York v. Actavis PLC, Forest Labs LLC*, 787 F.3d 638, 647-648 (2nd Cir. 2015).
1406. *New York v. Actavis PLC, Forest Labs LLC*, 787 F.3d 638, 654 (2nd Cir. 2015).
1407. *New York v. Actavis PLC, Forest Labs LLC*, 787 F.3d 638, 654-655 (2nd Cir. 2015).
1408. Aspe, Generic Drug Market, 2015, pp. 5-7.
1409. *See also The People of New York v. Actavis PLC, Forest Labs LLC*, No. 14 Civ. 7473, (S.D.N.Y. 2014), at 104-109, discussing the anticompetitive conduct of the defendants; at 117-123, granting the preliminary injunction.
1410. *New York v. Actavis PLC, Forest Labs LLC*, 787 F.3d 638, 654 (2nd Cir. 2015); *Berkey Photo, Inc. v. Eastman Kodak Co.*, 603 F.2d 263, 274-275, 287 (2nd Cir. 1979), finding Kodak's conduct

for Namenda XR and could not substitute the latter.[1411] Despite the fact that generic manufacturers could still promote generic versions of Namenda IR, incurring such additional expenses would be ineffective and impractical. The generic manufacturers were deprived of the most cost-efficient means of generic distribution: generic substitution.[1412] This was not the first time a court found that preventing generic substitution through allegedly manipulative and unjustifiable formulation changes is a restriction of competition.[1413]

The decision of the 2nd Circuit was criticised by certain commentators, arguing that product-hopping should be per se lawful and be scrutinised under antitrust law in hard switches only when there is objective evidence of sham innovation leading to zero or negative consumer welfare effects.[1414] This approach of per se lawfulness seems rather radical given the difficulty to make a distinction between hard and soft switches, while it would render ironclad from antitrust scrutiny conduct possibly aiming to foreclose generic substitution. A rule of reason analysis of alleged product-hopping cases, that would allow courts to examine the facts and the particularities of each case and to rule on whether the product hop reflected a genuine innovation or a mere anticompetitive tactic of the brand-name manufacturer would be an option much closer to the spirit of the *Actavis* decision.

3.2 Multiple Product Reformulations and Aggressive Marketing

Another case that deals with hard product switches *post Actavis* is *Mylan Pharmaceuticals v. Warner Chilcott PLC* (the *Doryx* case). In 1994, Mayne Pharmaceuticals and Warner Chilcott entered into an exclusive licensing agreement with regard to Doryx, a prescription antibiotic used for the treatment of acne.[1415] The parties were accused of product-hopping since they allegedly made marginal changes to the drug which did not

---

not anticompetitive since consumers were not coerced but persuaded to buy Kodak's new film product and Kodak had not removed any older films from the market when it introduced this new one.
1411. *New York v. Actavis PLC, Forest Labs LLC*, 787 F.3d 638, 655 (2nd Cir. 2015).
1412. *New York v. Actavis PLC, Forest Labs LLC*, 787 F.3d 638, 655-656 (2nd Cir. 2015); *United States v. Microsoft Corp.* 253 F.3d 34, 63 (D.C. Cir. 2001), finding that barring competitors from the cost efficient means of distribution constitutes an antitrust violation; *United States v. Dentsply International, Inc.*, 399 F.3d 181, 191 (3rd Cir. 2005), ruling that the test for a Section 2 violation of the Sherman Act is not total foreclosure but whether a substantial amount of rivals is barred or the market's ambit is severely restricted. See however *In re Suboxone (Buprenorphine Hydrochloride & Naloxone) Antitrust Litig.*, 13-MD-2445, (ED. Pa. 2016), at *20, arguing that the *Namenda* decision did not hold as a matter of law that automatic generic substitution is the only cost-efficient means of generic competition in every pharmaceutical antitrust case.
1413. *Abbott Labs. v. Teva Pharms. USA Inc.*, 432 F. Supp. 2d. 408, 423 (D. Del. 2006).
1414. GINSBURG, WONG-ERVIN, WRIGHT, Micromanaging Innovation, 2015, pp. 3-4, arguing also that incremental drug product innovation can generate significant consumer benefits. *See also* SHEPHERD, Subsidize Competitors, 2016, pp. 693-707, criticising the decision and arguing that product hopping is "the predictable legal response to the incentives created by patent law and state substitution laws," while product shifting frustrates generic manufacturers because they can no longer rely on the marketing efforts of the brand-name drug manufacturers.
1415. *Mylan Pharmaceuticals Inc. v. Warner Chilcott PLC et al.*, Civ. No. 12-3824, (E.D. Pa. April 16, 2015), pp. 5-9. Doryx is the branded version of delayed-release doxycycline hyclate. Doryx capsules were not patent protected and were first marketed by Mayne in 1985.

provide significant improvements but made impossible the automatic substitution of Doryx prescriptions with generic equivalents.[1416] Initially Doryx was available in the form of capsules. In 2005, when Doryx tablets of 75 mg and 100 mg were approved by the FDA, Mayne and Warner Chilcott took aggressive steps to switch the market from capsules to tablets. In 2008, the FDA approved a 150 mg, single-scored Doryx tablet; soon after this approval, Mayne and Warner Chilcott stopped promoting the 75 mg and 100 mg tablets, starting an aggressive marketing programme of the new tablet. Later on, Mayne and Warner Chilcott, introduced a dual-scored 150 mg tablet and an unscored 200 mg Doryx tablet. Mylan alleged that all these product changes were anticompetitive product hops and tactical modifications intended to delay generic entry, while the internal documents of the defendants also referred to the Doryx product changes as defence strategies to generic competition.[1417]

The district court of the Eastern District of Pennsylvania found that Mylan failed to prove that the defendants held monopoly power in the relevant market and that they engaged in anticompetitive conduct; thus it rejected the plaintiff's allegations.[1418] The court found that the development and the marketing on new Doryx versions combined with the parallel withdrawal of previous Doryx forms were not anticompetitive. Misunderstanding the mechanism of generic substitution the court estimated that despite the product hops pharmacists remained free to substitute Doryx with generics; on the contrary, the defendants did not have any obligation to keep older Doryx versions in the market and facilitate generics' business plans.[1419]

Mylan appealed against the district court's decision and the FTC filed a brief as amicus curiae supporting the appeal. The FTC argued that the district court's product definition was overly broad, since functional interchangeability between products does not automatically mean that the prospect of drug substitution is strong enough to keep drug prices at competitive levels.[1420] The agency argued that product-hopping strategies can be evidence of monopoly power, since minor changes to a drug product formulation may indicate that the brand-name manufacturer wishes to maintain substantial profits that would be undermined by generic drug versions.[1421] Additionally, automatic substitution is the main distribution mechanism of generic competitors and thus merits antitrust protection: as the *Namenda* court found, product-hopping is foreclosing generic competitors from their most efficient distribution channel and

---

1416. *Mylan Pharmaceuticals Inc. v. Warner Chilcott PLC et al.*, Civ. No. 12-3824, (E.D. Pa. 2015), pp. 5-6.
1417. *Mylan Pharmaceuticals Inc. v. Warner Chilcott PLC et al.*, Civ. No. 12-3824, (E.D. Pa. 2015), pp. 9-17.
1418. *Mylan Pharmaceuticals Inc. v. Warner Chilcott PLC et al.*, Civ. No. 12-3824, (E.D. Pa. 2015), pp. 20-35.
1419. *Mylan Pharmaceuticals Inc. v. Warner Chilcott PLC et al.*, Civ. No. 12-3824, (E.D. Pa. 2015), pp. 35-41; *Verizon Commc'ns Inc. v. Law Offices of Curtis V. Trinko*, LLP, 124 S. Ct. 872, 883 (2004), finding that judges do not have *carte blanche* to insist that a monopolist alters its way of business so as to increase competition. *See* however, CARRIER, SHADOWEN, Product Hopping, 2016, pp. 179-178, analysing the price disconnect and the regulatory regime of generic substitution.
1420. FTC, *Amicus Brief, Mylan Pharms. v. Warner Chilcott*, 2015, pp. 17-21.
1421. FTC, *Amicus Brief, Mylan Pharms. v. Warner Chilcott*, 2015, pp. 19-21.

amounts to a violation of Section 2 of the Sherman Act.[1422] Even though innovation concerns are important, they should not bar *ipso facto* antitrust liability, especially in the pharma industry where the potential for anticompetitive product redesign is high.[1423] Thus, the FTC argued that the district court erred in its analysis by adopting a "broad-brush opposition to product-hopping liability in all circumstances."[1424]

The 3rd Circuit disagreed with the appellants and confirmed the decision of the district court, finding that Mylan failed to demonstrate that the defendants possessed monopoly power in the relevant market and to provide sufficient evidence of the defendants' anticompetitive conduct.[1425] The 3rd Circuit Court ruled that Mylan was not foreclosed from entering the market, while the defendants had provided strong evidence of their non-pretextual purposes behind the several product hops they engaged into.[1426] There were several elements differentiating the case at issue from the *Namenda* case: unlike the latter, the product reformulations were not merely a defence against a patent cliff neither did they have the result of foreclosing generics from the market.[1427] Nevertheless, the 3rd Circuit Court acknowledged that product reformulations combined with coercive conduct may lead to the imposition of antitrust liability, especially given the need of balancing innovation incentives and the protection of consumers and of competition.[1428] The decision of the 3rd Circuit in the *Doryx* case was widely criticised for not sufficiently appreciating the anticompetitive concerns that product-hopping raises, for misapplying the law on monopoly power and exclusionary conduct and for creating considerable conflict with the standard set by the *Namenda* decision.[1429] Mylan petitioned for rehearing, while the FTC and the American Antitrust Institute (AAI) both submitted amicus curiae briefs in support of Mylan's Petition, but the 3rd Circuit declined to rehear the case.[1430]

1422. FTC, *Amicus* Brief, *Mylan Pharms. v. Warner Chilcott*, 2015, pp. 22-27. See *New York v. Actavis PLC, Forest Labs LLC*, 787 F.3d 638, 656 (2nd Cir. 2015).
1423. FTC, *Amicus* Brief, *Mylan Pharms. v. Warner Chilcott*, 2015, pp. 27-28.
1424. FTC, *Amicus* Brief, *Mylan Pharms. v. Warner Chilcott*, 2015, p. 30.
1425. *Mylan Pharmaceuticals Inc. v. Warner Chilcott PLC et al.*, 838 F.3d 421, 434-438, 441 (3rd Cir. 2016).
1426. *Mylan Pharmaceuticals Inc. v. Warner Chilcott PLC et al.*, 838 F.3d 421, 438-439 (3rd Cir. 2016).
1427. *Mylan Pharmaceuticals Inc. v. Warner Chilcott PLC et al.*, 838 F.3d 421, 439-440 (3rd Cir. 2016).
1428. *Mylan Pharmaceuticals Inc. v. Warner Chilcott PLC et al.*, 838 F.3d 421, 440-441 (3rd Cir. 2016).
1429. CARRIER, Doryx, 2016, pp. 3-6. See also CARRIER, MINNITI, Citizen Petitions, 2016, pp. 347-349, arguing that a citizen petition (urging the FDA to refrain from granting any ANDA referencing Doryx unless it concerned the drug's reformulated version) was combined with product hopping in order to supplement Warner Chilcott's life cycle management strategy.
1430. See FTC Brief as *Amicus Curiae* in Support of Plaintiff-Appellant Mylan Pharmaceuticals Inc.'s Petition for Rehearing and Rehearing *Ex Banc*, *Mylan Pharmaceuticals Inc. v. Warner Chilcott PLC et al.*, (October 19, 2016); Brief for the American Antitrust Institute as *Amicus Curiae* in Support of Plaintiff-Appellant Mylan Pharmaceuticals Inc.'s Petition for Rehearing and Rehearing *Ex Banc*, *Mylan Pharmaceuticals Inc. v. Warner Chilcott PLC et al.*, (October 19, 2016).

3.3 Product-Hopping Combined with No-AG Commitment

A third very interesting case is *FTC v. Endo*, in which no-AG commitments and side-deals on development and co-promotion were combined with alleged product-hopping. On March 2016, the FTC sued Endo Pharmaceuticals Inc. and generic pharmaceutical companies for allegedly violating antitrust laws by concluding a set of reverse payment settlements concerning two of Endo's most important drugs Opana ER and Lidoderm.[1431] Endo settled with Watson Laboratories Inc. (part of Teva Pharmaceuticals at the moment of this writing), the first generic challenger which attempted to enter the Lidoderm patch market, allegedly paying it to forgo entry of its generic version following a similar twofold mode of payment; Endo agreed to refrain from launching an authorised generic drug for the first 7.5 months of Watson's generic sales, while it also agreed to provide Watson with branded Lidoderm patches valued at $96 to $240 million, "at no cost."[1432] However, Endo's settlement with the generic challenger Impax concerning the drug Opana ER is much more interesting and provides a vivid illustration of the increasing sophistication of Hatch-Waxman litigation settlement strategies.

Opana ER was a highly successful and rapidly growing opioid drug; its patent protection was set to expire in 2008 and its new dosage form exclusivity was set to expire in 2009.[1433] Facing the threat of generic entry, Endo had been working on a reformulated version of Opana ER, aiming to prevent automatic generic substitution. The timing was crucial for the strategy to be successful: the launch of the drug's reformulated version and the conversion of patents to the reformulated Opana ER should be completed before generic entry occurred.[1434] The generic manufacturer Impax was the first generic challenger to file a paragraph IV ANDA for Opana ER on December 2007. As a result of Impax's ANDA filing, Endo would not have sufficient time to obtain FDA approval for the reformulated Opana ER and to convert the market before Impax would have entered the generic market.

The FTC alleged that Endo paid the generic manufacturer Impax in order for the latter to abandon its patent challenge and to postpone its entry to the market of Opana ER for 2.5 years.[1435] According to the FTC, Endo purchased the time it needed by concluding an agreement with Impax, just a week before the latter was expected to obtain FDA approval for its generic version of Opana ER.[1436] Endo's payment to Impax was twofold. First, the brand-name manufacturer committed not to launch an authorised generic version, according Impax an absolute generic monopoly during the

---

1431. FTC, Complaint, *FTC v. Endo Pharmaceuticals et al.*, Case 2:16-cv-01440-PD, (March 30, 2016). [cited as: FTC, Complaint, *FTC v. Endo Pharmaceuticals et al.*, 2016]. *See also* FTC Press Release, *FTC Sues Endo Pharmaceuticals Inc. and Others for Illegally Blocking Lower-Cost Generic Versions of the Branded Drugs Opana ER and Lidoderm*, (March 30, 2016). Available at: https://www.ftc.gov/news-events/press-releases/2016/03/ftc-sues-endo-pharmaceuticals-inc-others-illegally-blocking-lower (last accessed on March 31, 2018).
1432. FTC, Complaint, *FTC v. Endo Pharmaceuticals et al.*, 2016, pp. 3, 18-19.
1433. FTC, Complaint, *FTC v. Endo Pharmaceuticals et al.*, 2016, pp. 11-12.
1434. FTC, Complaint, *FTC v. Endo Pharmaceuticals et al.*, 2016, pp. 15-16.
1435. FTC, Complaint, *FTC v. Endo Pharmaceuticals et al.*, 2016, pp. 2-3.
1436. FTC, Complaint, *FTC v. Endo Pharmaceuticals et al.*, 2016, p. 16.

180-day exclusivity period. In order to ensure the generic manufacturer that it would receive the supracompetitive profits promised by the settlement, Endo undertook the obligation to pay Impax in case its reformulation strategy succeeded and resulted in the devaluation of the no-AG commitment. The FTC alleges that this was indeed the case, leading Endo to make an additional payment of more than $102 million to Impax.[1437] Second, Endo agreed to pay Impax $40 million purportedly for an independent co-promotion and development deal concerning another drug.[1438] The district court judge for the district of Pennsylvania found that the FTC's claims concerned two separate drugs, separate undertakings and separate markets, thus they did not arise from the same circumstances or occurrences. The judge granted the defendants' motions and severed under Rule 21.[1439] A month later, the FTC voluntarily dismissed its complaint and in January 2017 the agency refiled charges related to the settlement agreements on Lidoderm and Opana ER which are pending before courts at the moment of this writing,[1440] while Endo chose to settle with FTC.[1441]

CONCLUSIONS

It is difficult to assess whether the ruling of the US Supreme Court in *FTC v. Actavis* has solved the problem of reverse payment settlements, and if so to what extent. The most fundamental achievement of the *FTC v. Actavis* decision is that it put an end to the use of the scope of the patent test as the applicable test for the evaluation of reverse payment settlements. After the Supreme Court's ruling, granting antitrust immunity to an otherwise anticompetitive settlement, merely on the basis of a patent, is no longer possible. However, the problem of delaying generic entry persists and continues to preoccupy antitrust specialists and enforcement authorities. The Supreme Court chose the rule of reason as the applicable legal standard for the adjudication of reverse

---

1437. FTC, Complaint, *FTC v. Endo Pharmaceuticals et al.*, 2016, pp. 17-20.
1438. FTC, Complaint, *FTC v. Endo Pharmaceuticals et al.*, 2016, p. 3.
1439. *FTC v. Endo Pharmaceuticals et al.*, Civ. No. 16-1440, (E.D. Pa. 2016).
1440. FTC, Complaint, *FTC v. Allergan et al.*, Case No. 17-cv-00312, (January 23, 2017); FTC, Complaint, *FTC v. Impax Laboratories Inc.*, Docket No. 9373, (January 19, 2017). *See also In re Lidoderm Antitrust Litigation*, Case No. 14-md-02521-WHO, (N.D. Cal. 2017), in which purchasers of Lidoderm won class certification in the antitrust multidistrict litigation against Endo Pharmaceuticals; *In re Opana ER Antitrust Litigation*, 162 F. Supp. 3d 704, 716-719, (N.D. Ill. February 10, 2016), finding that the plaintiffs have sufficiently pleaded the existence of a large reverse payment under *Actavis* when they alleged a payment in the form of a no-AG commitment and a development and co-promotion agreement. *See* however *In re Opana ER Antitrust Litigation*, MDL Docket No. 2580, Case No. 14 C 10150, (N.D. Ill. February 25, 2016), at *28-29, finding that the plaintiffs sufficiently alleged the existence of a reverse payment in the settlement, but were required to provide some reliable foundation to show an estimated value of the reverse payment and how it was calculated; without such an estimation, the court deemed it impossible to determine whether the payment was large and unjustified.
1441. *See* FTC Press Release, *Endo Pharmaceuticals Inc. Agrees to Abandon Anticompetitive Pay-for-Delay Agreements to Settle FTC Charges; FTC Refiles Suits Against Generic Defendants*, (January 23, 2017). Available at: https://www.ftc.gov/news-events/press-releases/2017/01/endo-pharmaceuticals-inc-agrees-abandon-anticompetitive-pay-delay (last accessed on March 31, 2018).

payment settlements, pushing lower courts gently towards the sliding scale of reasonableness. No rule is perfect nor flawless and neither is the one pronounced by the *Actavis* decision. The questions of valid justifications for payments, of whether and to what extent the relevant market needs to be defined and the market power of the brand-name manufacturer needs to be shown are still to be addressed.

The most important question *post Actavis* concerns the adjudication of patent settlements containing non-cash payments and value transfers. It is imperative that lower courts abandon a formalistic reading of the *Actavis* decision and uniformly apply the rule of reason analysis also to reverse payment settlements which are not limited to cash payments but include other forms of value transfer, concealed in no-AG commitments, side-deals, forgiveness of damages, poison-pill clauses, etc. Unilateral anticompetitive strategies which aim to prevent generic entry, such as abuses of restricted drug distribution and product-hopping shall be promptly addressed under the rule of reason and in the light of the Supreme Court's reasoning in *Actavis*.

Reverse payment settlements and anticompetitive strategies in the pharmaceutical sector are not a US monopoly; very similar strategies occupy European competition enforcement authorities and courts. The US experience on these types of anticompetitive behaviour largely affected the treatment of similar conduct in European jurisdictions, while the criteria used by the Supreme Court in *Actavis* were also used by European courts. Despite the large differences between the two legal orders, the American experience was indispensable in preventing and confronting anticompetitive conduct in the European pharmaceutical market.

Part III Pharma Settlements in the EU

Chapter 5 and Chapter 6 of this book focus on the analysis of reverse payment settlements in the European Union. Chapter 5 presents the European regulatory framework on patent protection and drug entry to the market, while it also analyses the fundamentals of European competition law. The main focus of analysis remains the intersection between competition law and intellectual property law and the specificities of the pharmaceutical sector. Chapter 6 presents the antitrust analysis of reverse payment settlements under European competition laws, focusing on the two major cases of *Lundbeck* and *Servier* and also analysing decisions of national competition law authorities concerning other types of anticompetitive and abusive strategies aiming to delay generic drug entry to the market.

Chapter 5

The European Regulatory Framework

Chapter 5 serves as an introduction to the European regulatory framework, first with regard to the entry of pharmaceuticals to the market and second with regard to the core competition law provisions which are indispensable for the analysis of reverse payment settlements under European Competition law.

Part 1 of this chapter discusses the patent system and patent grants in the European Union, while it also focuses on the drug entry in the EU market, both for brand-name pharmaceutical products and generic ones. The pharmaceutical sector is heavily regulated both on a European Union level and on European Member State national levels. The three regulatory areas that are of particular relevance for the analysis of the pharmaceuticals' markets are: (1) patent laws and particularly the European Patent Convention, national Member States' patent laws and the European Regulation on Supplementary Protection Certificates (SPCs); (2) marketing authorisations which are governed by both European and national laws; and (3) pricing and reimbursement that are governed solely by national rules. For the purposes of this book, only the first two areas are analysed in this chapter, leaving aside the national legislation of European Member States.

Part 2 of this chapter presents the fundamentals of European competition law, since no sector-specific competition rules are in place for pharmaceutical products. The procedural aspects of competition law enforcement are discussed, focusing on the relationship between the European Commission and the National Competition Enforcement Authorities of European Member States. The two foundations of European competition law, Article 101 TFEU and Article 102 TFEU are then presented, along with examples of anticompetitive agreements and practices. The focus remains on the sensitive balance between competition law and intellectual property law, by analysing the Block Exemption Regulations that may be applicable in reverse payment settlement cases in the pharmaceutical sector. The dichotomy between restrictions by object and restrictions by effect is extensively discussed. Finally, abuses of dominance which were linked to the exercise of intellectual property rights are presented, in order to provide the essential foundations before proceeding with the analysis of reverse payment settlements in the pharmaceutical sector as alleged violations of Article 101 TFEU and Article 102 TFEU.

PART 1 THE EUROPEAN PHARMA REGULATORY FRAMEWORK

The primary objective of the European Union legislation on pharmaceutical products is to safeguard public health. Similarly to the US, patentable inventions in the European pharmaceutical industry relate to new active ingredients, new formulations of existing active ingredients – commonly known as "primary," "basic" or "compound" patents – or to new ways of producing and administering active ingredients, sometimes referred to as "secondary" patents; there is however no requirement that a new drug product should be more effective in therapeutic action than an existing medicine. In general, the means employed for the protection of public health shall not hinder the development of the pharmaceutical industry and especially the free movement of medicinal products within the internal European market. The free movement of goods is one of the fundamental freedoms of European law: it is codified in Article 26 and Articles 28-37 of the TFEU and has a concrete and direct impact on the structure of the European market, even with regard to pharmaceutical products. For example, pursuant to Article 28 TFEU, parallel imports of medicinal products are a lawful form of trade within the internal EU market, provided that they do not pose a threat to public health or to the industrial and commercial property.[1442]

I Patent System and Patent Grants in Europe

Apart from the national patents which are granted by the European Member States' national patent offices pursuant to national laws, the European Patent office (EPO) may grant European patents on the basis of the European Patent Convention (EPC).[1443] Both national patent laws and the EPC must respect the standards set by the WTO TRIPS Agreement: not only the European Union but also the currently twenty-eight European Member States are WTO members,[1444] while nearly all contracting states of the European Patent Convention are members of the WTO, so that the Convention implements the relevant provisions of the TRIPS Agreement.[1445] National patent laws

---

1442. EU Commission, *Communication from the Commission on parallel imports of proprietary medicinal products for which marketing authorisations have already been granted*, COM(2003) 839 final, Brussels, 30.12.2003, p. 6, clarifying that parallel importation of medicinal products is a lawful form of trade within the internal EU market on the basis of Article 28 TFEU and is subject to the derogations of Article 36 TFEU. Available at: http://eur-lex.europa.eu/legal-content/EN/TXT/?uri = celex:52003DC0839 (last accessed on March 31, 2018).
1443. See further, the official website of the European Patent office (EPO): https://www.epo.org/index.html (last accessed on March 31, 2018).
1444. WTO Website, *The European Union and the WTO*. Available at: https://www.wto.org/english/thewto_e/countries_e/european_communities_e.htm#trips (last accessed on March 31, 2018).
1445. EPO Website, *A.III. Relationship to Other International Conventions*. Available at: http://www.epo.org/applying/european/Guide-for-applicants/html/e/ga_a_iii.html (last accessed on March 31, 2018).

Chapter 5: The European Regulatory Framework

are not discussed in detail, since national European Member States' laws fall outside the scope of this book. The following sections focus on the mechanism of the European Patent, of Supplementary Protection Certificates (SPCs) and on other sorts of exclusivities granted pursuant to European Union law.

A The European Patent Convention and EPO

The Convention on the Grant of European Patents – commonly known as the European Patent Convention (EPC) – is an international treaty binding all Member States of the European Union and a number of other states such as Switzerland, Albania, Iceland, Norway Liechtenstein and Turkey.[1446] The EPC establishes a common system for the law of patent grants and a centralised procedure for the grant of European patents by EPO.[1447] A European Patent confers the same rights, has the same effects and is subject to the same conditions as a national patent granted in an EPC contracting state.[1448] After its grant, a European Patent is split into a bundle of national patents which have to be validated in each EPC contracting state for which the patent was requested by the submission of a translation in case the patent is not issued in one of the official languages of that state.[1449] Any infringement of a European Patent is to be treated under national laws,[1450] while Member States to the EPC can provide for less protection than that conferred by the Convention.[1451]

1 The European Patent with Unitary Effect

To the day of this writing, it is impossible to obtain a unitary patent that is valid and enforceable in all European Member States. The unitary patent or "European Patent with unitary effect" is destined to be a European patent, granted by the EPO in accordance with the rules and procedures of the European Patent Convention, which will have unitary effect in the territory of the twenty-six participating Member States.[1452] The unitary patent will confer to its holder the right to prevent any third party from committing acts for which the patent provides protection; the scope of that right and any limitations shall be uniform in all Member States for which the patent has

---

1446. Convention on the Grant of European Patents (European Patent Convention) of 5 October 1973, as revised by the Act revising Article 63 EPC of 17 December 1991 and the Act revising the EPC of 29 November 2000. *See also* EPO Website, *Member States*. Available at: https://www.epo.org/about-us/organisation/member-states.html (last accessed on March 31, 2018).
1447. Articles 1-3 of Convention on the Grant of European Patents (European Patent Convention), 16th Edition, June 2016 (EPC).
1448. Article 64 EPC.
1449. Article 65 EPC.
1450. Article 64(3) EPC.
1451. Article 67(2) EPC.
1452. EPO Website, *FAQ – Unitary Patent*. Available at: http://www.epo.org/service-support/faq/procedure-law/faq.html (last accessed on March 31, 2018). For a detailed account on the history of the European patent with unitary effect *see* PLOMER, Unified Patent, 2015, pp. 510-529.

unitary effect.¹⁴⁵³ The EPO will be responsible for administering the patentees' requests for unitary effect, for issues related to renewal fees for unitary patents and also for keeping a register of unitary patents and their legal status (licences, transfers, revocation, limitation, etc.).¹⁴⁵⁴ The unitary patent is regulated by Regulation No. 1260/2012 and Regulation No. 1257/2012,¹⁴⁵⁵ which were accepted through the "enhanced cooperation" legislative procedure of the EU.¹⁴⁵⁶ Both regulations entered into force in January 2013, but will only apply from the date that the Agreement on the UPC enters into force.¹⁴⁵⁷ Even though the Agreement was signed by twenty-six EU Member States it is not in yet force, since it has not been ratified by the minimum number of thirteen states.¹⁴⁵⁸

2 The Increasing Number of Patent Applications and Patentability Criteria

The increasing rates of patent applications and granted patents is not a phenomenon that is limited to the US territory. The high number of patent applications and the surcharge of the patent offices worldwide arguably have a negative impact on the quality of the issued patents.¹⁴⁵⁹ In 2017 EPO granted 105,635 published patents, while in 2016 it had granted 95,940 patents, an increase of 40% when compared to 2015.¹⁴⁶⁰

1453. Article 5, Regulation (EU) No. 1257/2012 of the European Parliament and of the Council of 17 December 2012 implementing enhanced cooperation in the area of the creation of unitary patent protection.
1454. Article 9, Regulation (EU) No. 1257/2012 of the European Parliament and of the Council of 17 December 2012 implementing enhanced cooperation in the area of the creation of unitary patent protection. *See also* EPO Website, *Unitary Patent*. Available at: https://www.epo.org/law-practice/unitary/unitary-patent.html (last accessed on March 31, 2018).
1455. Council Regulation (EU) No. 1260/2012 of 17 December 2012 implementing enhanced cooperation in the area of the creation of unitary patent protection with regard to the applicable translation arrangements, OJ L 361, 31.12.2012, p. 89-92; Regulation (EU) No. 1257/2012 of the European Parliament and of the Council of 17 December 2012 implementing enhanced cooperation in the area of the creation of unitary patent protection OJ L 361, 31.12.2012, p. 1-8. *See also* EU Commission Press Release, *Unitary Patent Protection*, 2013.
1456. Article 118, para. 2, TFEU; 2011/167/EU: Council Decision of 10 March 2011 authorising enhanced cooperation in the area of the creation of unitary patent protection, OJ L 76, 22.3.2011, p. 53-55. Spain submitted an action for annulment arguing that Article 118 TFEU was not an adequate legal basis for said regulation, an objection which was rejected by the CJEU in Judgment of the Court of 5 May 2015, Case C-146/13, *Kingdom of Spain v. European Parliament and Council of the European Union*, ECLI:EU:C:2015:298.
1457. Article 7, Council Regulation (EU) No. 1260/2012; Article 18, Regulation (EU) No. 1257/2012; Agreement on a Unified Patent Court, OJ C 175, 20.6.2013, p. 1-40.
1458. EPO Website, *Unified Patent Court*. Available at: http://www.epo.org/service-support/faq/procedure-law/faq.html (last accessed on March 31, 2018). For the ratification status of the Agreement on a Unified Patent Court *see* Council of the European Union Website, *Agreement on a Unified Patent Court (UPC)*. Available at: http://www.consilium.europa.eu/en/documents-publications/agreements-conventions/agreement/?aid=2013001 (last accessed on March 31, 2018).
1459. *See* further *supra* Chapter 3, Part 2, Section III.B.1, discussing the high rates of patent invalidation in the US. For a useful and detailed comparison between the USPTO and the EPO *see* CHIEN, KESAN, USPTO and EPO, 2016.
1460. EPO Website, *Annual Report 2017*. Available at: https://www.epo.org/about-us/annual-reports-statistics/annual-report/2017/statistics/granted-patents.html#tab1 (last accessed on March 31, 2018).

A total of 310,784 patent applications were filed with EPO in 2017 alone.[1461] The highest number of European patent applications originated from the EPO contracting States, the US, Japan and China while the top technical fields concerned were medical technology, digital communications and computer technology.[1462]

Under the EPC, the three cumulative criteria to determine patentability are: (1) that the invention is new; (2) that the invention involves an inventive step; and (3) that the invention is susceptible of industrial application.[1463] An invention is new if it does not form part of the "state of the art," a concept encompassing everything that was made publicly available, in any form or shape, prior to the patent application's filing.[1464] As far as the inventive step criterion is concerned, it is fulfilled if the invention involves an improvement which is not obvious to a person skilled in the art.[1465] Finally, an invention is considered to be susceptible of industrial application if it can be made or used in any kind of industry.[1466] There are of course exceptions to patentability. For example, scientific theories and mathematical methods cannot be patented; neither can schemes, rules or methods for performing mental acts or doing business.[1467] Inventions whose commercial application would be against the public order, plant or animal varieties or biological processes for the production of plants or animals and treatment and diagnostic methods are not patentable either.[1468]

3 Patent Opposition Before the EPO and National Patent Authorities

In order to safeguard the quality of the issued patents, European patents are open to opposition and appeal from third parties without any presumption from the EPO regarding their status: anyone may oppose a patent grant within nine months from the publication of the mention of its grant.[1469] A decision by the EPO during opposition proceedings is retro-actively effective in all the states in which the European Patent is valid.[1470] 3.7% of the granted patents were the object of opposition procedures in 2017, leading to 4,070 opposition decisions by EPO.[1471] More than one-fourth of the relevant patents were revoked (27%), while 73% were upheld as granted or in an amended form.[1472]

1461. EPO Website, *Annual Report 2017: Statistics and Indicators*. Available at: https://www.epo.org/about-us/annual-reports-statistics/annual-report/2017/statistics.html (last accessed on March 31, 2018).
1462. EPO Website, *Annual Report 2017*. Available at: https://www.epo.org/about-us/annual-reports-statistics/annual-report/2017.html (last accessed on March 31, 2018).
1463. Article 52(1) EPC.
1464. Articles 54, 55 EPC.
1465. Article 56 EPC.
1466. Article 57 EPC.
1467. Article 52(2) EPC.
1468. Article 53 EPC.
1469. Article 99 EPC.
1470. Article 105(b) EPC.
1471. EPO Website, *Annual Report 2017: Searches, Examinations, Oppositions*. Available at: http://www.epo.org/about-us/annual-reports-statistics/annual-report/2017/download-centre.html (last accessed on March 31, 2018).
1472. Idem.

Another mean to challenge the validity of issued patents are civil and/or administrative opposition procedures before national patent offices or before national courts. As the European patent is a "bundle" of national patents, a finding of invalidity or even the annulment of a patent in one national jurisdiction does not automatically invalidate the patents in all other national jurisdictions of the contracting EPC states, even if those patents are based on the same European Patent granted by the EPO. This is the reason why no conclusive inferences can be drawn regarding the quality of the issued patents solely on the basis of the EPO statistics,[1473] since there are no official statistics on the rates of patent invalidation before national state courts and national patent offices.

II The Entry of Pharmaceuticals to the European Market

The European Union adopted in 2004 a new pharmaceutical regulatory package which aimed to strengthen competitiveness in the European pharmaceutical industry. The two main pillars of the 2004 package were the new rules on pharmaceutical data exclusivity and the European "Bolar" provision which are discussed in the following sections. Data exclusivity signifies the period during which a drug manufacturer cannot cross-refer to the data which supported another marketing authorisation in order to obtain marketing authorisation for its own pharmaceutical product. The term "marketing exclusivity" signifies the time-period in which a generic, hybrid or biosimilar drug cannot be placed on the market. In 2010, the European pharmacovigilance legislation – focusing on the monitoring of medicinal products after they have been placed on the market – was amended through Regulation 1235/2010 and Directive 2010/84/EU which strengthened and rationalised the system of monitoring safety of pharmaceutical products in the European market.[1474] In 2012, the European pharmacovigilance framework was further amended as new requirements and procedures were laid down by means of Regulation 1027/2012 and Directive 2012/26/EU.[1475]

1473. *See* for instance SCELLATO ET AL., 2011, pp. 62-88, analysing opposition cases involving EPO patents and finding that there is no robust evidence supporting the quality deterioration of granted patents.
1474. Regulation (EU) No. 1235/2010 of the European Parliament and of the Council of 15 December 2010, OJ L-348, p. 1-16; Directive 2010/84/EU. *See also* European Commission, DG Health and Food Safety, *The EU Pharmacovigilance System*. Available at: http://ec.europa.eu/health/human-use/pharmacovigilance/index_en.htm#geninf; (last accessed on March 31, 2018). Available at: http://ec.europa.eu/health/human-use/pharmacovigilance/index_en.htm#geninf (last accessed on March 31, 2018); European Medicines Agency Website, *Guidelines on Good Pharmacovigilance Practices*. Available at: http://www.ema.europa.eu/ema/index.jsp?curl = pages/regulation/document_listing/document_listing_00 0345.jsp&mid = WC0b01ac058058f32c (last accessed on March 31, 2018) [cited as: EMA Website, *Guidelines on Good Pharmacovigilance Practices*].
1475. Regulation 1027/2012 of the European Parliament and of the Council of 25 October 2012, amending Regulation (EC) No. 726/2004 as regards pharmacovigilance, OJ L 316, p. 38-40; Directive 2012/26/EU amending Directive 2001/83/EC as regards pharmacovigilance.

A Marketing Authorisation of Medicinal Products

In order to ensure the quality, safety and efficacy of brand-name and generic medicinal products, a marketing authorisation shall be obtained before they can be put on the European Economic Area (EEA) market.[1476] The marketing authorisation procedures for medicinal products are completely harmonised in the European Union, through Regulation No. 726/2004 with respect to centrally authorised medicinal products and Directive 2001/83/EC with respect to nationally authorised medicinal products.[1477] The underlying objective of the marketing authorisation mechanism and the risk-benefit balancing it entails is the need to protect public health.[1478] It is important to note that when deciding whether to grant a marketing authorisation to a generic drug, EEA marketing authorisation authorities are not allowed to take into consideration the patent status of the brand-name drug. Simply put, the non-infringement of a patent is not a requirement in order to obtain a marketing authorisation in the EEA.[1479] Only when the originator successfully carries the burden of showing (at least prima facie) before a national court of a Member State that its patent is infringed by a generic drug, the generic undertaking may be injucted by the court not to sell its generic product.[1480]

1 Three Types of Marketing Authorisations in the European Union

There are three different possibilities in order to obtain a marketing authorisation in the European Union: (1) a national market authorisation; (2) a Union authorisation; and (3) a mutual recognition procedure. The national authorities of the Member States are generally competent to grant national marketing authorisations for medicinal products on the basis of Directive 2001/83/EC. According to Directive 2001/83/EC, in order to obtain a marketing authorisation for a drug product, innovators are required to show the safety and efficacy of the concerned drug on the basis of detailed data collected in

---

1476. The European Economic Area (EEA) is the area formed by the twenty-eight (soon to be twenty-seven after United Kingdom's 2016 Brexit referendum) European Member States, plus Norway, Iceland and Lichtenstein. The latter three states have adopted through the EEA agreement the totality of the existing EU Law on medicinal products. See EU Commission, *Pharma Legislation Notice: Chapter 1*, 2015, p. 5.
1477. Directive 2001/83/EC on the Community code relating to medicinal products for human use; Regulation (EC) No. 726/2004 of the European Parliament and of the Council of 31 March 2004 laying down Community procedures for the authorisation and supervision of medicinal products for human and veterinary use and establishing a European Medicines Agency (OJ L 136/1, 30.04.2004, p. 1-33).
1478. EU Commission, *Pharma Sector Inquiry*, 2009, point 299.
1479. Case AT.39226 – Lundbeck, Commission Decision of 19 June 2013, relating to a proceeding under Article 101 of the Treaty on the Functioning of the European Union and Article 53 of the EEA Agreement, C(2013) 3803 final, Brussels, 19.6.2013, para. 624 [cited as: EU Commission Decision, *Lundbeck*, 2013]; CASE AT.39612 – Perindopril (Servier), Commission Decision of 9 July 2014, relating to a proceeding under Article 101 and Article 102 of the Treaty on the Functioning of the European Union, C(2014) 4955 final, Brussels, 9.7.2014, para. 75 [cited as: EU Commission Decision, *Servier*, 2014].
1480. EU Commission Decision, *Lundbeck*, 2013, para. 624.

different phases of clinical trials.[1481] Directive 2001/83/EC introduced the concept of "global marketing authorisation:" once a drug product obtains an initial marketing authorisation, any subsequent additional strengths, forms, administration routes, presentation, variations and extensions shall also be granted a marketing authorisation or be included in the initial marketing authorisation. All these marketing authorisations are considered to belong to the same global marketing authorisation.[1482]

Products which fall under Regulation No. 726/2004 are granted a Union marketing authorisation by the European Commission through a centralised procedure, relying on the opinion of the European Medicines Agency (EMA).[1483] This single authorisation allows direct access to the whole European market.[1484] Regulation No. 726/2004 requires that one single name is used to identify a medicinal product authorised under the centralised procedure,[1485] while it limits the ability of applicants to obtain more than one marketing authorisation per medicinal product.[1486] Products falling under the mandatory scope of Regulation No. 726/2004 are for instance biotechnology medicinal products, orphan medicinal products and medicinal products with a new active substance whose therapeutic indication is the treatment for specific diseases.[1487] Some medicinal products fall under the optional scope of Regulation No. 726/2004, if for instance it can be shown that they constitute a significant therapeutic, scientific or technical innovation; these products may be authorised either under the centralised or the national (decentralised/mutual recognition) procedure on the choice

---

1481. Article 6(1), Directive 2001/83/EC. This global marketing authorisation encompasses all marketing authorisations granted by different MS and under different names. *See* further EU Commission, *Pharma Legislation Notice: Chapter 1*, 2015, pp. 9-10.
1482. Articles 6, 8, Directive 2001/83/EC.
1483. *See* further, EU Commission, *Pharma Legislation Notice: Chapter 1*, 2015, pp. 7-9, describing the Union marketing authorisation system. Available at: http://ec.europa.eu/health/files/eudralex/vol-2/a/vol2a_chap1_201507.pdf (last accessed on March 31, 2018).
1484. Regulation (EC) No. 726/2004 of the European Parliament and of the Council of 31 March 2004 laying down Community procedures for the authorisation and supervision of medicinal products for human and veterinary use and establishing a European Medicines Agency (OJ L 136/1, 30.04.2004, p. 1-33). The scientific evaluation of the application is done by the Committee for Medicinal Products for Human Use (CHMP) of the EMA. *See also* EMA Website, *Q&A Presubmission Guidance*. Available at: http://www.ema.europa.eu/ema/index.jsp?curl=pages/regulation/q_and_a/q_and_a_detail_000021.jsp&mid=WC0b01ac0580022711 (last accessed on March 31, 2018). Available at: http://www.ema.europa.eu/ema/index.jsp?curl=pages/regulation/q_and_a/q_and_a_detail_000021.jsp&mid=WC0b01ac0580022711. (last accessed on March 31, 2018).
1485. Article 6(1), Regulation 726/2004.
1486. Article 82(1), Regulation 726/2004. *See* further, European Commission, DG Health and Consumers, *Handling of Duplicate Marketing Authorisation Applications*, Ref. Ares 2011)1044649, 03.10.2011, p. 1-11. Available at: https://ec.europa.eu/health/sites/health/files/files/latest_news/2011_09_duplicates_note_upd_01.pdf (last accessed on March 31, 2018), analysing the duplicate marketing authorisation applications under Article 82(1), Regulation 726/2004.
1487. Article 3(1) and Annex, Regulation 726/2004. *See also* EU Commission, *Pharma Sector Inquiry*, 2009, para. 305, fn. 236. Those diseases are AIDS, cancer, diabetes and neurodegenerative diseases.

of the applicant.[1488] Additionally, biological pharmaceutical products (products whose active substance is made or derived by a living organism) which were manufactured by means of a biotechnological process have to be authorised *via* the centralised route.[1489]

The mutual recognition procedure concerns medicinal products which are subject to national authorisation processes and for which marketing authorisation was granted in one Member State, commonly known as the "reference member state."[1490] In this case, the holder of the marketing authorisation may submit an application in other European Member States using the mutual recognition procedure.[1491] These Member States shall recognise the marketing authorisation by approving the assessment report, the summary of the product characteristics, the labelling and the package leaflet and shall grant a marketing authorisation accompanied with the latter three elements.[1492]

2 Duration of Marketing Authorisation and Exclusivities

Decisions taken *via* the centralised procedure are valid in all European Member States so that the relevant drug product may be put on all of the respective markets.[1493] Marketing authorisations obtained through the centralised procedure are initially valid for five years and may be renewed;[1494] once renewed, they are normally valid for an unlimited period.[1495] Within three years after the grant of the marketing authorisation, the approved drug product must be put on the market; if this is not the case, the

---

1488. Article 3(2), Regulation 726/2004. *See also idem* Article 14(11); it should be noted that the Regulation does not define in detail what constitutes a "significant" improvement, merely using the rather vague phrasing of "significant clinical benefit in comparison with existing therapies."
1489. EU Commission, *Pharma Sector Inquiry*, 2009, para. 308.
1490. Article 28(1), Directive 2001/83/EC.
1491. *Idem. See also* European Commission, *EudraLex – Pharmaceutical Legislation Notice to applicants and regulatory guidelines medicinal products for human use*, Volume 2 A, Chapter 2, Mutual Recognition, (February 2007), pp. 9-11. Available at: http://ec.europa.eu/health/documents/eudralex/vol-2/index_en.htm. (last accessed on March 31, 2018) [cited as: EU Commission, *Pharma Legislation Notice: Chapter 2*, 2007], briefly describing the mutual recognition procedure.
1492. Articles 11, 28, 54, 55, 59 and 63, Directive 2001/83/EC; EU Commission, *Pharma Sector Inquiry*, 2009, para. 332. *See further*, EU Commission, *Pharma Legislation Notice: Chapter 2*, 2007.
1493. Article 76, Directive 2001/83/EC. *See also*, European Commission, DG Health and Food Safety, *The Centralised Procedure*. Available at: http://ec.europa.eu/health/authorisation-procedures-centralised_en.htm (last accessed on March 31, 2018). Available at: http://ec.europa.eu/health/authorisation-procedures-centralised_en.htm (last accessed on March 31, 2018).
1494. Article 14(1), Regulation No. 726/2004; Article 24, Directive 2001/83/EC.
1495. Article 14(3), Regulation No. 726/2004. *See also* European Medicines Agency, *Guideline on the processing of renewals in the centralised procedure*, EMA/CHMP/2990/00 Rev. 4, 22 June 2012, pp. 1-17. Available at: http://ec.europa.eu/health/files/eudralex/vol-2/2012-06_gpr.pdf (last accessed on March 31, 2018), pp. 2-3, and; EU Commission, *Pharma Legislation Notice: Chapter 1*, 2015, p. 11.

marketing authorisation will be withdrawn.[1496] A marketing authorisation will also be withdrawn in case the drug was initially put on the market but was subsequently absent for three consecutive years.[1497]

Once a marketing authorisation is granted, the reference drug product is accorded an 8-year data exclusivity period, during which other generic manufacturers cannot rely on the data submitted in the marketing authorisation application of the reference product.[1498] A 10-year market exclusivity period is also granted to the drug product, which runs parallel to the data exclusivity period.[1499] During this market exclusivity period, generic manufacturers may apply for an abridged marketing authorisation, cross-referring to the data in support of the marketing authorisation of the reference product. However, during the 10-year market exclusivity, generic, hybrid or biosimilar products may not be placed on the market, even if they were already granted a marketing authorisation.[1500] An additional year of market exclusivity is granted if the holder of the marketing authorisation obtains an authorisation for one or more therapeutic indications that bring significant clinical benefits to existing therapies, during the 8-year data exclusivity period.[1501] Further, an additional year of data exclusivity may be granted if significant clinical or preclinical studies were carried out by the applicant in relation to this new therapeutic indication.[1502] Finally, in case the classification of the medicinal product changed on the basis of significant preclinical tests or clinical trials, one more year of data exclusivity is granted.[1503]

3 The EU Bolar Exemption and the Abridged Marketing Authorisation

In order to facilitate generic drug companies to conduct the bioequivalence trials necessary to develop their generic versions of patent-protected pharmaceuticals, certain acts related to the R&D of drug products are legally exempted and do not constitute patent infringement. As above-analysed, these exemptions are commonly known as the "Bolar" exemptions and are stipulated in the Hatch-Waxman Act in the US.[1504] In the European Union, before 2004 prepatent expiry R&D was regulated only on a national level, causing legal uncertainty.[1505] The Bolar exemption is currently found in Article 10(6) of Directive 2001/83/EC as amended by Directive 2004/27/EC,[1506] according to which conducting the necessary studies and trials in order to apply for a marketing authorisation shall not be regarded as infringing patent rights or SPCs

---

1496. EU Commission, *Pharma Sector Inquiry*, 2009, para. 314.
1497. *Idem*.
1498. Article 14(11), Regulation No. 726/2004; Article 10(1), Directive 2001/83/EC.
1499. Article 14(11), Regulation No. 726/2004.
1500. Article 10(1), Directive 2001/83/EC. *See also* EU Commission, *Pharma Sector Inquiry*, 2009, para. 326, referring to this system as the 8+2(+1) Formula.
1501. Article 14(11), Regulation No. 726/2004; Article 10(1), Directive 2001/83/EC.
1502. Article 10(5), Directive 2001/83/EC.
1503. Article 74(a), Directive 2001/83/EC.
1504. *See supra*, Chapter 2, Part 2, Section I, on the etymology of the "Bolar" exemptions and the Hatch-Waxman Act enactment.
1505. EU Commission, *Pharma Sector Inquiry*, 2009, para. 371.
1506. Directive No. 2004/27/EC, amending Directive No. 2001/83/EC on the Community code relating to medicinal products for human use.

for medicinal products.[1507] This Bolar exemption is not perfectly harmonised across all European Member States, since its scope and interpretations vary across the EU.[1508]

An abridged application may be filed in order to obtain marketing authorisation for a generic drug version of a brand-name drug which has already received marketing authorisation on the basis of Directive 2001/83/EC.[1509] In this abridged procedure, the applicant is not required to prove the safety and efficacy of its generic drug version, since the EMA relies on the tests and trials conducted for the reference drug product.[1510] It should be noted that the generic manufacturer can rely on the marketing authorisation of the reference product even if this marketing authorisation was withdrawn or if it was granted in another European Member State.[1511] Under the rules on data exclusivity, an abridged application cannot be granted before the eight years from the grant of the marketing authorisation for the reference drug product have elapsed.[1512]

Biological medicinal products which are similar to a reference drug product that has already received marketing authorisation, can also obtain marketing authorisation through the abridged procedure. However, for these drugs additional information on the toxicological and clinical profile of the biosimilar must be submitted in order to establish the drug's safety and efficacy.[1513] In case the holder of the marketing authorisation for the reference drug wishes to market a generic version of the same drug, it must file an application for the marketing authorisation of the drug's generic version pursuant to Article 82(1) of Regulation No. 726/2004.

B Pricing and Reimbursement of Pharmaceuticals in the EU

The national authorities of European Member States are free to determine the prices of pharmaceutical products and to designate the treatments which are reimbursed under their national social security systems.[1514] The pricing and reimbursement systems are rather complex and vary from one Member State to another: different schemes and policies are used, adapted to each Member State's health and economic needs.[1515] In

---

1507. Article 10(6), Directive 2001/83/EC. *See also* Article 27(d), Agreement on a Unified Patent Court, OJ C 175, 20.6.2013, p. 1-40, (UPC Agreement, upholding the exemption of Article 10(6), Directive 2001/83/EC.
1508. TRIDICO, JACOBSTEIN, WALL, 2014, discussing which MS adopt a broader and which a narrower reading of the exemption.
1509. Article 10, Directive 2001/83/EC; EU Commission, *Pharma Sector Inquiry*, 2009, para. 307.
1510. Idem.
1511. Before 2004 it was questionable whether generics could rely on a marketing authorisation which was withdrawn. *See* further *infra*, Chapter 5, Part 2, Section III.E.3 analysing this problem in the *AstraZeneca* case.
1512. EU Commission, *Pharma Sector Inquiry*, 2009, para. 319.
1513. Recital 15, Directive 2004/27/EC; EU Commission, *Pharma Sector Inquiry*, 2009, para. 308.
1514. EU Commission Website, *Pricing and Reimbursement of Medicinal Products*. Available at: https://ec.europa.eu/growth/sectors/healthcare/competitiveness/products-pricing-reimbursement_en (last accessed on March 31, 2018).
1515. For an overview of the National Pharmaceutical Pricing and Reimbursement Systems *see* the relevant Document List of the EU Commission, available at: http://ec.europa.eu/DocsRoom/documents?locale=en&tags=Pharmaceutical%20pricing%20and%20reimbursement%20systems (last accessed on March 31, 2018).

many Member States a pharmaceutical product can only be marketed after a decision on its price and on its reimbursement status has been taken, which determine the commercial terms of access to the market.[1516] These pricing policies aim to ensure that patients have access to necessary medicines and that health budgets are kept at reasonable levels, contributing to the sustainability of the health system, while originator companies have adequate incentives to continue innovating.[1517] In order to preserve originators' incentives to innovate, Member States typically set the price of innovative pharmaceutical products at high levels.

Pharmaceuticals' pricing and reimbursement are closely connected to the attainment of the European policy objectives of the internal market, of pharmaceutical competitiveness, of sustainable R&D and of the protection of human health.[1518] In order to ensure that the pricing and reimbursement policies of Member States are transparent and do not interfere with the operation of the internal market, Directive 89/105/EEC was adopted, commonly known as the Transparency Directive.[1519] The three main requirements set by the Transparency Directive are that pricing and reimbursement individual decisions: (1) are made within a specific time-frame (90 to 180 days); (2) are communicated to the applicant and contain a statement of reasons on the basis of objective and verifiable criteria; and (3) can be appealed judicially at a national level.[1520]

Even though EU Member States are free to determine the prices and reimbursement of pharmaceutical products as long as they respect the relevant European law provisions, this does not mean that price levels in one Member State are unaffected by price levels in other Member States. The most common pharmaceuticals pricing policy in EU Member States is external price referencing (EPR), on the basis of which the price levels of pharmaceutical products are set based on price comparisons with other EU Member States, that are for instance geographical neighbours or in a comparable economic situation.[1521] Therefore, generic entry in one EU Member State and the impact it has in decreasing the price levels of the brand-name pharmaceutical product

---

1516. EU Commission, *Pharma Sector Inquiry*, 2009, para. 145; EU Commission Decision, *Servier*, 2014, para. 81.
1517. EU Commission, *Pharma Sector Inquiry*, 2009, para. 145; EU Commission Decision, *Servier*, 2014, para. 81.
1518. EU Commission Website, *Pricing and Reimbursement of Medicinal Products*.
1519. Council Directive 89/105/EEC of 21 December 1988 relating to the transparency of measures regulating the prices of medicinal products for human use and their inclusion in the scope of national health insurance systems, OJ L 40, 11.2.1989, p. 8-11.
1520. *See* Articles 5 and 6, Council Directive 89/105/EEC; EU Commission Website, *Transparency Directive*. Available at: https://ec.europa.eu/growth/sectors/healthcare/competitiveness/products-pricing-reimbursement/transparency-directive_en (last accessed on March 31, 2018).
1521. *See* European Commission, DG Health and Food Safety Health systems, medical products and innovation, *Study on enhanced cross-country coordination in the area of pharmaceutical product pricing*, February 24, 2016. Available at: https://ec.europa.eu/health/sites/health/files/systems_performance_assessment/docs/pharmaproductpricing_frep_en.pdf Last accessed on March 31, 2018), pp. 5-6, 19-40, describing in detail the different EPR systems of EU Member States, their benefits and limitations.

may also affect the price levels in other EU Member States where generic entry has not yet occurred but where this first Member State is used as a reference state in order to determine prices. The free movement of goods within the EU and the legitimate possibility of parallel imports of medicinal products may also have a great impact on price levels of pharmaceutical products across the European Union.

C Extending the Market Exclusivity of Medicinal Products

1 Supplementary Protection Certificates

According to Article 63 of the EPC, the total term of patent protection granted by a European patent is twenty years from the filing of the patent application. Due to the time-consuming procedures related to drug marketing authorisation and to bringing drug products to the market, the effective patent term is considerably shorter. In order to compensate for the time-period between the filing of an application for a new drug product and the authorisation to place that product on the market, the mechanism of Supplementary Protection Certificates (SPCs) was created in the European Union, on the basis of Regulation No. 1768/92, which was subsequently replaced by Regulation No. 469/2009.[1522] The following conditions shall be fulfilled in order to obtain an SPC: (1) the relevant medicinal product shall be protected by a basic patent in force; (2) there must be a valid authorisation to place the medicinal product on the market, which is also the first authorisation to place the product on the market as a medicinal product; and (3) the relevant medicinal product was not already granted an SPC.[1523]

Similarly to the patent term extension to compensate FDA review in the US,[1524] an SPC confers the same rights as the ones conferred by the basic patent for up to five years,[1525] so as to ensure that the holder of both a patent and an SPC enjoys an overall maximum of fifteen years of exclusivity from the moment the drug product in question obtains authorisation to be placed on the EU market.[1526] An SPC takes effect at the end of the lawful patent term of the basic patent and may only be granted once for each medicinal product.[1527] This extension of the patent term aims to restore the reduced period of market exclusivity and to recoup the patent holder's investment into the

---

1522. Council Regulation (EEC) No. 1768/92 of 18 June 1992, concerning the creation of a supplementary protection certificate for medicinal products, OJ L 182/1, 2.7.1992, p. 1-5, replaced by Regulation (EC) No. 469/2009 of the European Parliament and of the Council of 6 May 2009, concerning the supplementary protection certificate for medicinal products, OJ L 152/1, 16.6.2009, p. 1-10.
1523. Article 3, Regulation (EC) No. 469/2009.
1524. *See supra* Chapter 2, Part 2, Section III.A, on patent term extension to compensate FDA review in the US.
1525. Article 4 and Article 13, Regulation (EC) No. 469/2009. Article 1(c), Regulation (EC) No. 469/2009 defines the basic patent is defined as "a patent which protects a product as such, a process to obtain a product or an application of a product, and which is designated by its holder for the purpose of the procedure for grant of a certificate."
1526. Recital 9, Regulation (EC) No. 469/2009.
1527. Article 13, Regulation (EC) No. 469/2009. *See also* Judgment of the Court of 8 December 2011, Case C-125/10, *Merck Sharp & Dohme Corp. v. Deutsches Patent- und Markenamt*, EU:C:2011:812, paras 25-39, finding that an SPC can be granted when less than five years have

research and discovery of the new drug product.[1528] The ultimate goal is to preserve the incentives for future innovation in the field of pharmaceuticals.

2 Orphan Drug Market Exclusivity in the European Union

Similarly to the US,[1529] also in the European Union orphan medicinal products concern the diagnosis, prevention or treatment of serious or life-threatening but also rare health conditions which affect up to 5 in 10,000 people in the EU.[1530] Even though the prevalence of such conditions is typically low, in 2014 such diseases affected 68% of the EU population.[1531] Regulation 141/2000 provides incentives for originator companies to engage in the research, development and marketing of designated orphan drug products.[1532] If a marketing authorisation is granted for an orphan drug product, the European Union and the European Member States shall not accept any other application for a marketing authorisation of a similar medicinal product for the same therapeutic indication for a period of ten years.[1533] The orphan drug market exclusivity runs in parallel with the normal market and data exclusivities. Other incentives are also provided, such as protocol assistance, fee waivers associated with the marketing authorisation procedure and access to the centralised authorisation procedure which is mandatory for all orphan drug products.[1534] Between 2000 and September 2015, the EU Commission approved 1,544 applications for the designation of orphan drugs, while 117 orphan drugs were authorised – the vast majority of which have new active substances.[1535]

---

elapsed between the date of application for the basic patent and the date of the first marketing authorisation. *See also infra* Chapter 6, Part 2, Section II, discussing SPCs in the context of divisional patent applications.
1528. Recitals 4-9, Regulation (EC) No. 469/2009.
1529. *See supra*, Chapter 2, Part 2, Section III.B.3. Orphan drug exclusivity in the US is up to 7 years and concerns conditions either affecting less than 200,000 people in the US or drugs for which the costs of R&D development are not reasonably expected to be recouped by their sales.
1530. Recital 5, Regulation (EC) No. 141/2000 of the European Parliament and of the Council of 16 December 1999 on orphan medicinal products, OJ L 18, 22.1.2000, p. 1-5. *See also* European Commission, DG Health and Food Safety, *Orphan Medicinal Products*. Available at: http://ec.europa.eu/health/human-use/orphan-medicines/index_en.htm (last accessed on March 31, 2018).
1531. European Union Committee of Experts for Rare Diseases, 2014 *Report on the State of the Art of Rare Diseases Activities in Europe – Part I: Overview of Rare Disease Activities in Europe*, July 2014, pp. 1-68. Available at: http://www.eucerd.eu/?page_id=163 (last accessed on March 31, 2018), p. 6; European Commission, *Inventory of Union and Member State incentives to support research into, and the development and availability of, orphan medicinal products*, SWD(2015) 13 FINAL, State of Play 2015, p. 1. Available at: http://ec.europa.eu/health/human-use/orphan-medicines/developments/index_en.htm. (last accessed on March 31, 2018) [cited as: EU Commission, *Orphan Drugs Incentives Inventory*, 2015].
1532. Article 1, Regulation (EC) No. 141/2000.
1533. Article 8(1), Regulation (EC) No. 141/2000. See however, Article 8(2), Regulation (EC) No. 141/2000, stating that this exclusivity period can be decreased to 6 years under certain conditions.
1534. EU Commission, *Orphan Drugs Incentives Inventory*, 2015, pp. 3-4.
1535. *Idem*; 82% of the authorised orphan drugs contain new active substances.

3 Paediatric Exclusivity in the European Union

As in the US,[1536] conducting clinical trials in order to determine the safety and efficacy of a given drug for paediatric populations is rewarded by an extension of the brand-name drug manufacturer's exclusivity period in the European Union. In 2007, Regulation 1901/2006 and Regulation 1902/2006 were enacted, jointly known as the "Paediatric Regulation,"[1537] aiming to encourage high-quality research into the development of medicines for children, guarantee that the majority of the drugs are specifically authorised for such use and to ensure that accurate and helpful information on paediatric drugs is available. In exchange for conducting paediatric trials, the holder of the relevant patent or SPC is entitled to a 6-month extension to its patent term or SPC.[1538] In 2015, twenty-eight active substances benefited from this 6-month extension.[1539]

D Differences Between the EU and US Regulatory Frameworks

Before a medicinal product is put on the EU market, it must be subjected to an administrative authorisation procedure laid down in Regulation No. 726/2004 and in Directive 2001/83/EC.[1540] The marketing authorisation decision, for both brand-name and generic drugs, is taken on the basis of strictly scientific criteria of quality, safety and efficacy of the concerned medicinal product; economic or other considerations are strictly excluded.[1541] Unlike US, in the European Union the existence of a patent right covering the brand-name drug does not constitute an obstacle for the marketing authorisation of the respective generic drug version.

The biggest and most noticeable difference between the US and the European regulatory framework is the absence of a piece of legislation even remotely similar to the Hatch-Waxman Act in the European Union. There is neither an ANDA application process in order for generics to enter to the market nor an approval bottleneck due to the approval of the first generic drug version, nor an exclusivity period for the first

---

1536. See supra, Chapter 2, Part 2, Section II.B.4.
1537. Regulation (EC) No. 1901/2006 of the European Parliament and of the Council of 12 December 2006 on medicinal products for paediatric use and amending Regulation (EEC) No. 1768/92, Directive 2001/20/EC, Directive 2001/83/EC and Regulation (EC) No. 726/2004, OJ L 378, 27.12.2006, p. 1-19; Regulation (EC) No. 1902/2006 of the European Parliament and of the Council of 20 December 2006 amending Regulation 1901/2006 on medicinal products for paediatric use, OJ L 378, 27.12.2006, p. 20-21.
1538. Article 36(1), Regulation (EC) No. 1901/2006.
1539. European Medicines Agency, *2015 Report to the European Commission on the Application of the Paediatric Regulation*, pp. 1-75. Available at: http://ec.europa.eu/health/human-use/paediatric-medicines/index_en.htm. (last accessed on March 31, 2018), pp. 16-20.
1540. Directive 2001/83/EC of the European Parliament and of the Council of 6 November 2001 on the Community code relating to medicinal products for human use (OJ L 311/67, 28.11.2001, pp. 67-128). See also Directive 2001/82/EC on the Community code relating to veterinary medicinal products. See further EU Commission, *Compendium of EU Pharmaceutical Law*, 2015.
1541. Recital 13, Article 37 and Article 81, Regulation (EC) No. 726/2004. See also Articles 116, 117 and 126, Directive 2001/83/EC.

generic challenger.¹⁵⁴² Due to the absence of regulatory rules similar to the Hatch-Waxman Act in the EU, a patent settlement agreement between the brand-name drug manufacturer and just one generic competitor cannot have a market foreclosure effect for the totality of the EU market. Typically, such an agreement will only have a rather limited anticompetitive effect, when compared to the effect it would have had in the US market.

Due to the absence of the 180-day exclusivity period and of the approval bottleneck, even if the brand-name company and the first generic entrant in the EU enter into a reverse payment settlement agreement, such an agreement will not impede or discourage the entry of subsequent generic challengers in the market, which will be allowed if the relevant safety and efficacy requirements are met for their respective generic drug versions. The two main points that should be kept in mind are first, that a patent right does not bar the regulatory market authorisation of generic drugs in the EU and second that the regulatory market authorisation of the first generic drug version in the EU market does not in the least impede or withhold the authorisation of subsequent generic versions of the drug. Of course, this does not mean that generic entrants in the EU will not face patent infringement lawsuits by the brand-name manufacturer when entering the market. As extensively analysed in Chapter 6, these are the reasons why reverse payment settlements in the European Union typically concern more than one generic competitor and are generally combined with other types of anticompetitive strategies, such as product-hopping or "name and shame" campaigns, in order to reassure a broader foreclosure effect.¹⁵⁴³

PART 2 FUNDAMENTALS OF EUROPEAN COMPETITION LAW

The core provisions of European competition law which are the necessary foundation for the antitrust analysis of reverse payment settlements under European competition law are Article 101 and Article 102 TFEU – which articulate the broad prohibition of anticompetitive agreements and of abuse of dominant position – and Regulation 1/2003, which outlines the majority of the procedural rules to be followed in antitrust enforcement. Articles 101 TFEU and 102 TFEU bear no great resemblances to Sections 1 and 2 of the Sherman Act. On a first level, the historical and political background of the respective provisions is fundamentally different. In the European Union, Articles 101 and 102 TFEU form part of the foundations of the common integrated European market, whereas Sections 1 and 2 of the Sherman Act do not reflect any kind of coordinated effort to integrate the US economy.¹⁵⁴⁴ On a second level, the antitrust analysis employed differs considerably.¹⁵⁴⁵ In the US, the main question the rule of reason analysis seeks to address is whether a particular restraint on trade triggers Sherman Act liability. By contrast, in the European Union agreements that distort

---

1542. *See* further *supra* Chapter 2, Part 2, Section IV, on the problems caused by the Hatch-Waxman framework.
1543. *See* further *infra*, Chapter 6, Part 1.
1544. HOVENKAMP, JANIS, LEMLEY, LESLIE, *IP And Antitrust*, 2015, p. 45-12.1.
1545. *See* further JONES, KOVACIC, *Anticompetitive Agreements*, 2017, comparatively analysing the applicable framework on anticompetitive agreements in the EU and the US.

competition – whether reasonable or not – can escape antitrust liability if they fall under the exceptions of Article 101(3) TFEU.[1546]

Based largely on Articles 101 TFEU and 102 TFEU, EU Member States have developed their national systems of competition law.[1547] Some of the Member States require that their domestic laws are interpreted consistently with European competition rules. Even if there is no such explicit rule, many cases are likely to have the same outcome whether they are adjudicated under European or under national competition law.[1548] However, despite the high degree of convergence between EU and Member States' competition laws, a different outcome is not excluded and depends on which system of law will be applied. In case of a clash between domestic and EU competition law provisions, the general principle is that European Union law takes precedence over national laws, and this principle naturally applies also with regard to competition law.[1549]

I Competition Enforcement and Procedural Aspects

A number of reverse payment cases and other practices which allegedly delayed the entry of generic pharmaceuticals in the European Union were dealt by National Competition Enforcement Authorities.[1550] Before these cases are analysed in Chapter 6 of this book, it is important to explain the competences of the National Competition Enforcement Authorities and the procedural aspects of competition law enforcement in the European Union.

A National Competition Enforcement Authorities

The European Union law grants EU Member States the flexibility to create their National Competition Enforcement Authorities (NCAs). According to Article 35 of Regulation 1/2003, EU Member States are required to designate the authorities responsible for the application of Articles 101 and 102 TFEU, which will ensure that the provisions of Regulation 1/2003 are effectively complied with.[1551] According to the EU

1546. HOVENKAMP, JANIS, LEMLEY, LESLIE, *IP And Antitrust*, 2015, p. 45-12.1.
1547. Article 107 TFEU on state aid is the third pillar of European competition law, but will not be discussed as it falls outside the scope of this book.
1548. WHISH, BAILEY, *Competition Law*, 2015, pp. 77-78, providing the example of the UK law. See Section 60 of the Competition Act of 1998, "[...] questions arising under this Part in relation to competition within the United Kingdom are dealt with in a manner which is consistent with the treatment of corresponding questions arising in Community law in relation to competition within the Community."
1549. Judgment of the Court of 13 February 1969, Case 14-68, *Walt Wilhelm v. Bundeskartellamt*, EU:C:1969:4, para. 6, "[c]onsequently, conflicts between the rules of community and national rules in the matter of the law on cartels must be resolved by applying the principle that community law takes precedence."
1550. *See infra* Chapter 6, Part 3, focusing on the decisions of National Competition Enforcement Authorities concerning agreements and conduct that aimed in delaying generic drug entry to the market.
1551. Article 35, Regulation No. 1/2003. *See also* European Commission Website, *European Competition Network*. Available at: http://ec.europa.eu/competition/ecn/competition_

Commission, two basic institutional models of NCAs exist: (1) the administrative model, whereby a single administrative authority investigates cases and takes enforcement decisions which are subject to judicial control, and; (2) the judicial model, on the basis of which an administrative authority carries out the investigation and then brings the cases to national courts for them to issue a decision on the substance or to impose sanctions.[1552] NCAs' decisions should be free from external influence; indeed the EU Commission reports that NCAs are in their vast majority independent, to a degree that varies from one Member State to another,[1553] while they also enjoy organisational, financial and operational independence.[1554] The procedures followed and the sanctions that can be imposed by NCAs are not harmonised on an EU level;[1555] however they are subject to the principles of equivalence and effectiveness and shall respect the fundamental rights stipulated in the Charter of the Fundamental Rights of the European Union[1556] and the European Convention on Human Rights.[1557] The European Competition Network (ECN)[1558] – the network through which the EU Commission collaborates with NCAs – has launched leniency programmes and issued several reports and recommendations related to the investigative and decision-making powers of NCAs, in an effort to promote convergence among them.[1559] Virtually all Member State jurisdictions have voluntarily converged to the provisions of Regulation 1/2003, regarding the procedures followed by NCAs.[1560]

---

authorities.html (last accessed on March 31, 2018) [cited as: EU Commission Website, *European Competition Network*], providing lists of all NCAs. Available at: http://ec.europa.eu/competition/ecn/competition_authorities.html. (last accessed on March 31, 2018).

1552. European Commission, Staff Working Document, *Enhancing competition enforcement by the Member States' competition authorities: institutional and procedural issues*, accompanying the Communication from the Commission, SWD (2014 231 final), Brussels, 9.7.2014, paras 10-11. Available at: http://ec.europa.eu/competition/consultations/2015_effective_enforcers/index_en.html. (last accessed on March 31, 2018) [cited as: EU Commission, *Enhancing NCA enforcement*, 2014].

1553. EU Commission, *Enhancing NCA enforcement*, 2014, para. 12.

1554. EU Commission, *Enhancing NCA enforcement*, 2014, para. 15. *See also* Judgment of the Court of 16 October 2012, Case C-614/10, *European Commission v. Republic of Austria*, EU:C:2012:631, paras. 36-66, finding that operational independence does not guarantee complete independence of an NCA.

1555. EU Commission, *Enhancing NCA enforcement*, 2014, para. 43.

1556. Charter of Fundamental Rights of the European Union, OJ C 326, 26.10.2012, p. 391-407.

1557. European Convention for the Protection of Human Rights and Fundamental Freedoms, as amended by Protocols Nos 11 and 14, Rome, 4.XI.1950.

1558. *See* further EU Commission Website, *European Competition Network*. Available at: http://ec.europa.eu/competition/ecn/index_en.html. (last accessed on March 31, 2018).

1559. *See* for instance, European Competition Network, *Recommendation on Investigative Powers, Enforcement Measures and Sanctions in the Context of Inspections and Requests for Information*, December 2013, pp. 1-14. Available at: http://ec.europa.eu/competition/ecn/documents.html. (last accessed on March 31, 2018).

1560. EU Commission, *Enhancing NCA enforcement*, 2014, paras 60-61. However, the EU Commission also notes that most NCAs do not have a complete set of powers at their disposal so as to effectively apply Articles 101 and 102 TFEU.

B Procedural Issues and Regulation 1/2003

A competition law challenge to a particular practice can by initiated before the EU Commission either by a private party or on the Commission's own initiative. The Commission has the power to investigate the alleged antitrust violation and to render an opinion on whether the relevant TFEU provisions have been violated; it can also impose fines or seek other types of remedies.[1561] The Commission's decisions are reviewed on a first instance by the General Court of the EU, and on a second instance by the Court of Justice of the European Union (CJEU). It is settled case law of the CJEU that European Union law and national competition laws apply in parallel;[1562] this principle has not changed with the enactment of Regulation No. 1/2003.[1563] Regulation 1/2003 provides answers to a wide range of questions that occur regarding the application and the relationship between EU competition law and national competition laws.[1564] The European Commission is not the sole actor that has the competence to apply Articles 101 and 102 TFEU; on the basis of Article 3 of Regulation 1/2003, NCAs and national courts shall also apply Articles 101 and 102 TFEU alongside their national competition laws, to agreements, concerted practices or decisions which may affect trade between Member States.[1565]

1 The Convergence Rule

The need to create a "level playing field" for agreements in the internal market is stressed in Regulation No. 1/2003 through the so-called "convergence rule"; if an agreement is not prohibited under EU competition law, NCAs and national courts are generally not allowed to apply stricter scrutiny to it on the basis of harsher national laws.[1566] If a practice affects trade between Member States, but does not restrict competition under the meaning of Article 101(1) TFEU, or if the conditions of

---

1561. See Recital 12 and Article 7, Regulation 1/2003, referring to the possibility for the Commission to impose behavioural or structural remedies which are necessary to bring the infringement to an end. See further, RITTER, 2016.
1562. Judgment of the Court of 14 February 2012, Case C-17/10, *Toshiba Corporation and Others v. Úřad pro ochranu hospodářské soutěže*, EU:C:2012:72, para. 81; Judgment of the Court of 13 February 1969 Case 14/68, *Walt Wilhelm and others v. Bundeskartellamt*, ECLI:EU:C:1969:4, para. 3; Judgment of the Court of 9 September 2003, Case C-137/00, *The Queen v. The Competition Commission, Secretary of State for Trade and Industry and The Director General of Fair Trading, ex parte Milk Marque Ltd and National Farmers' Union*, EU:C:2003:429, para. 61; Judgment of the Court of 13 July 2006, Joined Cases C-295/04 to C-298/04, *Vincenzo Manfredi v. Lloyd Adriatico Assicurazioni SpA (C-295/04), Antonio Cannito v. Fondiaria Sai SpA (C-296/04) and Nicolò Tricarico (C-297/04) and Pasqualina Murgolo (C-298/04) v. Assitalia SpA*, EU:C:2006:461, para. 38.
1563. Judgment of the Court of 14 February 2012, Case C-17/10, *Toshiba Corporation and Others v. Úřad pro ochranu hospodářské soutěže*, ECLI:EU:C:2012:72, paras 79-92.
1564. Council Regulation (EC) No. 1/2003 of 16 December 2002 on the implementation of the rules on competition laid down in Articles 81 and 82 of the Treaty, OJ L 1/1, 4.1.2003, p. 1-25.
1565. Article 3(1), Regulation No. 1/2003.
1566. Recital 8 and Article 3(2), Regulation No. 1/2003. See also European Commission, Notice, *Guidelines on the application of Article 81(3) of the Treaty*, OJ C 101, 27.4.2004, para. 14. [cited as: EU Commission, *Article 81(3) Guidelines*, 2004].

exemption under Article 101(3) TFEU are fulfilled, such a practice may not be condemned under national competition laws.[1567] However, the convergence rule does not apply to unilateral conduct: Member States may adopt in their territory stricter national competition laws prohibiting or imposing sanctions on unilateral conduct by undertakings.[1568] Stricter rules have been adopted by several Member States: France, Italy, Germany, Portugal, Spain, Ireland and Slovakia enacted stricter national laws concerning the abuse of economic dependence.[1569] Some national laws also regulate the "abuse of superior bargaining power" or the "abuse of significant influence," in an effort to regulate disparities of bargaining power in distribution relationships even in cases where neither the distributor nor the supplier are dominant on the relevant market.[1570]

2 Avoiding Conflicting Decisions

In cases where trade between Member States may be affected, NCAs and national courts are *obliged* to apply EU competition law.[1571] According to the Commission, the enactment of Regulation 1/2003 – and in particular its Article 3(1) – has led to a significant increase in the application of Articles 101 and 102 TFEU.[1572] If the EU Commission initiates proceedings against an alleged restrictive practice, NCAs are relieved from their competence to apply Articles 101 and 102 TFEU and their respective national competition laws.[1573] The power of NCAs is restored once the EU Commission's proceedings are concluded, on which point NCAs may apply national competition law, provided that they comply with EU law.[1574] NCAs are further prohibited from contradicting a previous decision of the EU Commission when they are scrutinising decisions, agreements or practices that have already been the subject matter of a

---

1567. Article 3(2), Regulation No. 1/2003; *see also idem* Recitals 8 and 9, on the relationship between national and EU competition laws. See however *idem* Article 3(3), clarifying that Articles 3(1) and 3(2) do not apply when national courts or NCAs apply national merger control laws or provisions of national laws which pursue an objective different that the objectives pursued by Articles 101 and 102 TFEU.
1568. Recital 8 and Article 3(2), Regulation No. 1/2003; EU Commission, *Article 81(3) Guidelines*, 2004, para. 14.
1569. European Commission Staff Working Paper, *Accompanying the Report on the functioning of Regulation No. 1/2003*, COM(2009) 206 final, Brussels, 29.4.2009, paras 162-169 [cited as: EU Commission, *Staff Working Paper Regulation No. 1/2003*, 2009].
1570. EU Commission, *Staff Working Paper Regulation No. 1/2003*, 2009, para. 162.
1571. Recitals 8 and 9, Regulation No. 1/2003.
1572. European Commission, Communication, *Ten Years of Antitrust Enforcement under Regulation 1/2003: Achievements and Future Perspectives*, COM(2014) 453 Final, Brussels, 9.7.2014, pp. 3-8, noting that from 2004 until 2013 the application of EU competition laws has grown at a remarkable rate.
1573. Judgment of the Court of 14 February 2012, Case C-17/10, *Toshiba Corporation and Others v. Úřad pro ochranu hospodářské soutěže*, EU:C:2012:72, paras 74-78, examining the combined effect of Articles 3(1) and Article 11(6) of Regulation 1/2003.
1574. Judgment of the Court of 14 February 2012, Case C-17/10, *Toshiba Corporation and Others v. Úřad pro ochranu hospodářské soutěže*, EU:C:2012:72, paras 79-92.

Commission decision, in an effort to boost legal certainty and the uniform application of competition law rules throughout the EU and to avoid conflicting decisions.[1575]

3 Burden and Standard of Proof

The proceedings initiated by the EU Commission on the basis of Articles 101 and 102 TFEU are of administrative nature. However, the fines imposed for the alleged infringement of EU competition law are punitive fines, which are treated as de facto criminal charges falling within the scope of Article 6(1) of the ECHR.[1576] Thus, the presumption of innocence resulting from Article 6(2) of the ECHR, but also from Article 6(2) of the Treaty on European Union[1577] and Article 47 of the Charter of Fundamental Rights of the European Union,[1578] applies to procedures relevant to the infringement of competition laws which can potentially result to fines or periodic penalty payments.[1579]

According to Article 2 of Regulation No. 1/2003, the burden to prove an infringement lies with the Commission or any other person alleging an infringement of Article 101(1) or Article 102 TFEU; once satisfied, the burden shifts to the defendants claiming the benefit of Article 101(3) TFEU, who shall meet the paragraph's conditions.[1580] In order to satisfy the initial burden of proof, the Commission or any other antitrust plaintiff shall establish "sufficiently precise and coherent proof" of an infringement through a consistent body of evidence.[1581] The quality of proof required is not that of beyond reasonable doubt: even if the court has doubts on the existence of infringement, it can still find that the plaintiff has successfully carried its burden, while any remaining doubt will benefit the antitrust defendant.[1582]

1575. Article 16(2), Regulation No. 1/2003; *See also idem* Recital 22; Judgment of the Court of 14 February 2012, Case C-17/10, *Toshiba Corporation and Others v. Úřad pro ochranu hospodářské soutěže*, EU:C:2012:72, paras 84-87.
1576. See for instance ECHR Judgment, *A. Menarini Diagnostics S.R.L. v. Italy*, No. 43509/08, §§ 38-47, 27 September 2011.
1577. Article 6, Treaty on European Union. *See also* Consolidated version of the Treaty on European Union, 2016/C 202/1, p. 13-46.
1578. Charter of Fundamental Rights of the European Union, OJ C 326, 26.10.2012, p. 391-407.
1579. Judgment of the General Court of 25 October 2011, Case T-348/08, *Aragonesas Industrias y Energía, SAU v. European Commission*, EU:T:2011:621, para. 94; Judgment of the Court of 8 July 1999, Case C-235/92 P, *Montecatini SpA v. Commission of the European Communities*, EU:C:1999:362, paras 175-176; Judgment of the Court of 8 July 1999, Case C-199/92 P, *Hüls AG v. Commission of the European Communities*, EU:C:1999:358, paras 149-150.
1580. Article 2, Regulation No. 1/2003.
1581. Judgment of the Court of 28 March 1984, Joined Cases 29/83 and 30/83, *Compagnie Royale Asturienne des Mines SA and Rheinzink GmbH v. Commission of the European Communities*, EU:C:1984:130, para. 20 (Judgment of the Court of 28 March 1984, Joined Cases 29/83 and 30/83, *Compagnie Royale Asturienne v. Commission*).
1582. Judgment of the Court of First Instance of 8 July 2008, Case T-53/03, *BPB plc v. Commission of the European Communities*, EU:T:2008:254, para. 64, rejecting the defendant's argument that the Commission should adduce "proof beyond reasonable doubt" of the existence of infringement; Judgment of the General Court of 12 April 2013, Case T-442/08, *International Confederation of Societies of Authors and Composers (CISAC) v. European Commission*, EU:T:2013:188, para. 91; Judgment of the General Court of 25 October 2011, Case T-348/08, *Aragonesas Industrias y Energía, SAU v. European Commission*, EU:T:2011:621, paras 92-93.

On the basis of the CJEU's jurisprudence, individuals can claim damages for a violation of Article 101 or 102 TFEU, if they can establish a causal relationship between the alleged harm and the prohibited practice.[1583] Directive 2014/104/EU, coordinating the enforcement of competition rules by competition authorities and their enforcement in damages actions before national courts, was signed into law on November 26, 2014 and was to be implemented in the legal systems of the EU Member States until December 27, 2016.[1584] This directive aims to remove the obstacles to compensation for the victims of infringement of EU competition law by granting parties easier access to evidence, setting clear limitation period rules and regulating the interplay between the public enforcement of competition laws and private damages actions.[1585]

II Article 101 TFEU

Article 101 TFEU is comprised of three paragraphs and articulates a broad prohibition of agreements which have as their object or effect the prevention, restriction or distortion of competition within the common EU market.[1586] Indicative examples of such agreements are provided in a short list in its first paragraph: (1) fixing purchase or selling prices or other trading conditions directly or indirectly; (2) limiting or controlling production, markets, technical development or investment; (3) sharing markets or sources of supply; (4) applying dissimilar conditions to equivalent transactions with other trading parties thereby placing them at a competitive disadvantage; and (5) making the conclusion of contracts subject to the acceptance of supplementary obligations which have no connection with the subject of such contracts.[1587] The prohibitions of Article 101(1) TFEU apply not only to horizontal agreements between actual and potential competitors but also to vertical agreements, between undertakings operating at different market levels.[1588]

1583. Judgment of the Court of 13 July 2006, Joined Cases C-295/04 to C-298/04, *Vincenzo Manfredi v. Lloyd Adriatico Assicurazioni SpA (C-295/04), Antonio Cannito v. Fondiaria Sai SpA (C-296/04) and Nicolò Tricarico (C-297/04) and Pasqualina Murgolo (C-298/04) v. Assitalia SpA*, EU:C:2006:461, paras 60-64; Judgment of the Court of 20 September 2001, Case C-453/99, *Courage Ltd v. Bernard Crehan and Bernard Crehan v. Courage Ltd and Others*, EU:C:2001:465, paras 26-29.
1584. Article 21, Directive 2014/104/EU. *See* further European Commission, *Directive on Antitrust Damages Actions*. Available at: http://ec.europa.eu/competition/antitrust/actionsdamages/directive_en.html (last accessed on March 31, 2018) [cited as: EU Commission Website, *Antitrust Damages Directive*]. Available at: http://ec.europa.eu/competition/antitrust/actionsdamages/directive_en.html (last accessed on March 31, 2018); European Commission, DG Competition, *Competition Policy Brief: The Damages Directive: Towards a More Effective Enforcement of the EU Competition Rules*, Issue 2015-1, (January 2015). Available at: http://ec.europa.eu/competition/publications/cpb/2015/001_en.pdf (last accessed on March 31, 2018).
1585. Recitals 6, 11-17, 36, Directive 2014/104/EU. *See also* EU Commission Website, *Antitrust Damages Directive*.
1586. Article 101(1) TFEU.
1587. *Idem*.
1588. Judgment of the Court of 13 July 1966, Joined Cases 56 and 58/64, *Établissements Consten S.à.R.L. and Grundig-Verkaufs-GmbH v. Commission of the European Economic Community*, EU:C:1966:41, p. 342.

The second paragraph of Article 101 TFEU provides the sanction of automatic voidness of the anticompetitive provisions of agreements or decisions: "[a]ny agreements or decisions prohibited pursuant to this article shall be automatically void."[1589] According to the CJEU, this nullity concerns only the clauses of the agreement at issue which are prohibited by Article 101 TFEU; an agreement will only be void in its totality if the infringing clauses are not severable from the remaining terms of the agreement.[1590] The question of whether the infringing clauses are severable or not from the rest of the agreement is to be addressed under national laws and not under EU law.[1591]

Finally, the third paragraph of Article 101 TFEU provides for the exceptions to the applicability of paragraph (1) and the subsequent voidness of paragraph (2), if an agreement, a decision, or a concerted practice contributes to improving the production or distribution of goods or to promoting technical or economic progress, while attributing to consumers a fair share of the resulting benefit.[1592] In addition, such an agreement, decision or concerted practice shall not impose on the concerned undertakings restrictions which are not indispensable to the attainment of these objectives, while it shall not accord to the undertakings the possibility of eliminating competition in respect of a substantial part of the concerned products.[1593]

A Defining the Concept of Undertakings

The term "undertaking" has the same meaning in both Articles 101 and 102 TFEU and it is not defined in the TFEU; European courts have provided the term's definition in their jurisprudence.[1594] The concept of an undertaking generally encompasses every entity which engages in an economic activity, no matter what the legal status of that entity is and regardless of the way in which it is financed.[1595] Not only companies and partnerships qualify as undertakings: trade associations,[1596] agricultural

---

1589. Article 101(2) TFEU.
1590. Judgment of the Court of 30 June 1966, C-56/65, *Société Technique Minière (L.T.M.) v. Maschinenbau Ulm GmbH (M.B.U.)*, EU:C:1966:38, p. 250; Judgment of the Court of 14 December 1983, Case 319/82, *Société de Vente de Ciments et Bétons de l'Est SA v. Kerpen & Kerpen GmbH und Co. KG*, EU:C:1983:374, para. 11.
1591. Judgment of the Court of 30 June 1966, C-56/65, *Société Technique Minière (L.T.M.) v. Maschinenbau Ulm GmbH (M.B.U.)*, EU:C:1966:38, p. 250; Judgment of the Court of 14 December 1983, Case 319/82, *Société de Vente de Ciments et Bétons de l'Est SA v. Kerpen & Kerpen GmbH und Co. KG*, EU:C:1983:374, para. 11. See further CAUFFMAN, 2012, pp. 29-54, on the impact of voidness for the infringement of Article 101(1) TFEU.
1592. Article 101(3) TFEU.
1593. Idem.
1594. Judgment of the Court of First Instance of 8 July 2008, T-99/04AC, *Treuhand AG v. Commission of the European Communities*, EU:T:2008:256, para. 144; WHISH, BAILEY, *Competition Law*, 2015, p. 85.
1595. Judgment of the Court of 23 April 1991, Case C-41/90, *Klaus Höfner and Fritz Elser v. Macrotron GmbH*, EU:C:1991:161, para. 21.
1596. See for instance Judgment of the Court of 8 November 1983, *NV IAZ International Belgium and others v. Commission of the European Communities*, Joined Cases 96-102, 104, 105, 108 and 110/82, EU:C:1983:310, paras 19-20.

cooperatives,[1597] and natural persons[1598] – not acting as employees or final consumers purchasing goods or services – have been held to be undertakings.[1599] Moreover, members of several professions have been held to be undertakings for the purpose of competition laws: custom agents,[1600] lawyers,[1601] accountants,[1602] geologists[1603] and also attestation agents[1604] and self-employed medical specialists.[1605]

1 Economic Activity and Definition of Undertaking

Generally, a functional and not a formalistic approach shall be adopted in order to define whether an entity engages *in concreto* in a particular activity as an undertaking for the purpose of competition law scrutiny.[1606] The very same legal entity may be

---

1597. Judgment of the Court of 25 March 1981, Case 61/80, *Coöperatieve Stremsel – en Kleurselfabriek v. Commission of the European Communities*, EU:C:1981:75, paras 9-16.
1598. Judgment of the Court of 30 January 1985, Case 35/83, *BAT Cigaretten-Fabriken GmbH v. Commission of the European Communities*, EU:C:1985:32, paras. 7-11, 23, 37 (Judgment of the Court of 30 January 1985, Case 35/83, *BAT Cigaretten-Fabriken GmbH v. Commission*) finding that the owner of a German trademark and the owner of an international registered trademark were undertakings. See also Judgment of the Court of First Instance of 13 December 2006, Joined Cases T-217/03 and T-245/03, *Fédération nationale de la coopération bétail et viande (FNCBV) (T-217/03) and Fédération nationale des syndicats d'exploitants agricoles (FNSEA) and Others (T-245/03) v. Commission of the European Communities*, EU:T:2006:391, paras 46-60, finding that in the case at hand farmers could be regarded as undertakings for the purpose of applying Article 101 TFEU (then Article 81 TEC); upheld by Judgment of the Court of 18 December 2008, *Coop de France bétail et viande (C-101/07 P) and Fédération nationale des syndicats d'exploitants agricoles (FNSEA) and Others (C-110/07 P) v. Commission of the European Communities*, EU:C:2008:741.
1599. See *a contrario* Judgment of the Court of 12 September 2000, Joined Cases C-180/98 to C-184/98, *Pavel Pavlov and Others v. Stichting Pensioenfonds Medische Specialisten*, EU:C:2000:428, paras 78-81, finding that medical specialists making contributions to their supplementary pension scheme could not be regarded as final consumers and were acting as undertakings. See also Judgment of the Court of 16 September 1999, *Criminal proceedings against Jean Claude Becu, Annie Verweire, Smeg NV and Adia Interim NV*, EU:C:1999:419, paras 26-27, finding that dockers cannot be regarded as undertakings for the duration of an employment relationship during which they perform work under the direction of others.
1600. Judgment of the Court of 18 June 1998, Case C-35/96, *Commission of the European Communities v. Italian Republic*, EU:C:1998:303, paras 33-44 (Judgment of the Court of 18 June 1998, Case C-35/96, *Commission of the European Communities v. Italian Republic*).
1601. Judgment of the Court of 19 February 2002, Case C-309/99, *J. C. J. Wouters, J. W. Savelbergh and Price Waterhouse Belastingadviseurs BV v. Algemene Raad van de Nederlandse Orde van Advocaten, intervener: Raad van de Balies van de Europese Gemeenschap*, EU:C:2002:98, paras 45-49.
1602. Judgment of the Court of 28 February 2013, Case C-1/12, *Ordem dos Técnicos Oficiais de Contas v. Autoridade da Concorrência*, EU:C:2013:127, paras 34-38.
1603. Judgment of the Court of 18 July 2013, *Consiglio nazionale dei geologi v. Autorità garante della concorrenza e del mercato and Autorità Garante della Concorrenza e del Mercato v. Consiglio nazionale dei geologi*, EU:C:2013:489, paras 41-45.
1604. Judgment of the Court of 12 December 2013, Case C-327/12, *Ministero dello Sviluppo economico and Autorità per la vigilanza sui contratti pubblici di lavori, servizi e forniture v. SOA Nazionale Costruttori – Organismo di Attestazione SpA*, EU:C:2013:827, paras 26-35.
1605. Judgment of the Court of 12 September 2000, Joined Cases C-180/98 to C-184/98, *Pavel Pavlov and Others v. Stichting Pensioenfonds Medische Specialisten*, EU:C:2000:428, paras 73-77.
1606. Opinion of Advocate General Jacobs in Case C-67/96, *Albany International BV v. Stichting Bedrijfspensioenfonds Textielindustrie*, EU:C:1999:28, para. 207; WHISH, BAILEY, *Competition Law*, 2015, p. 87.

acting as an undertaking when carrying one activity but not when engaging in another, so that the classification of an activity as economic or as falling within the exercise of public powers must be carried out separately for each activity exercised by the entity.[1607] According to well-established jurisprudence of the CJEU, any activity which consists of offering goods or services within a given market is an economic activity.[1608] On the contrary, three activities are non-economic: (1) social protection activities provided on a solidarity basis, such as pensions, health insurance, social security, etc.;[1609] (2) the exercise of public powers by state-owned entities, public authorities or private entities entrusted with the provision of a public service or task;[1610] and (3) procurement related to a non-economic activity.[1611]

An entity acting as a "facilitator" to a cartel – even if not producing the cartelised goods or services – may be considered as an undertaking.[1612] Moreover, even if the mere holding of shares does not automatically signify that the owner of the shares is an undertaking who engages in economic activity, the analysis changes if that shareholder is actually exercising control and is involved in the management of the undertakings;

1607. Judgment of the Court of 1 July 2008, Case C-49/07, *Motosykletistiki Omospondia Ellados NPID (MOTOE) v. Elliniko Dimosio*, EU:C:2008:376, para. 25.
1608. Judgment of the Court of 12 September 2000, Joined Cases C-180/98 to C-184/98, *Pavel Pavlov and Others v. Stichting Pensioenfonds Medische Specialisten*, EU:C:2000:428, para. 75; Judgment of the Court of 16 June 1987, Case 118/85, *Commission of the European Communities v. Italian Republic*, EU:C:1987:283, para. 7; Judgment of the Court of 18 June 1998, Case C-35/96, *Commission of the European Communities v. Italian Republic*, para. 36; Judgment of the Court of 16 November 1995, Case C-244/94, *Fédération Française des Sociétés d'Assurance, Société Paternelle-Vie, Union des Assurances de Paris-Vie and Caisse d'Assurance et de Prévoyance Mutuelle des Agriculteurs v. Ministère de l'Agriculture et de la Pêche*, EU:C:1995:392, para. 14; Judgment of the Court of 11 December 1997, Case C-55/96, *Job Centre coop. arl.*, EU:C:1997:603, para. 21.
1609. See for instance Judgment of the Court of 22 January 2002, Case C-218/00, *Cisal di Battistello Venanzio & C. Sas v. Istituto nazionale per l'assicurazione contro gli infortuni sul lavoro (INAIL)*, EU:C:2002:36, paras 31-46, finding that a body entrusted by law with the management of a scheme providing insurance against accidents at work and occupational diseases is not an undertaking within the meaning of Articles 85 and 86 of the EC Treaty.
1610. Judgment of the Court of 19 January 1994, Case C-364/92, *SAT Fluggesellschaft mbH v. Eurocontrol*, EU:C:1994:7, paras 30-31, finding that the supervision and control of air space constitute typical activities of a public authority; Judgment of the Court of 18 March 1997, Case C-343/95, *Diego Calì & Figli Srl v. Servizi ecologici porto di Genova SpA (SEPG)*, EU:C:1997:160, paras 14-25, ruling that a private company engaging in the public task of anti-pollution surveillance of Genoa's harbour was not acting as an undertaking with regard to that particular activity; Judgment of the Court of 12 July 2012, Case C-138/11, *Compass-Datenbank GmbH v. Republik Österreich*, EU:C:2012:449, para. 36. See also JONES, SUFRIN, 2014, pp. 129-133, for an analysis of the CJEU's jurisprudence on public bodies and bodies performing public functions which are not economic.
1611. Judgment of the Court of First Instance of 4 March 2003, Case T-319/99, *Federación Nacional de Empresas de Instrumentación Científica, Médica, Técnica y Dental (FENIN) v. Commission of the European Communities*, EU:T:2003:50, paras 35-37, finding that an association purchasing medical goods and equipment in order to use them in an activity of purely social nature does not act as an undertaking.
1612. Judgment of the Court of First Instance of 8 July 2008, Case T-99/04, *AC-Treuhand AG v. Commission of the European Communities*, EU:T:2008:256, paras 122, 150; Judgment of the General Court of 6 February 2014, Case T-27/10, *AC-Treuhand AG v. European Commission*, EU:T:2014:59, para. 44.

in the latter case the shareholder will be regarded as engaging in economic activity.[1613] Non-profit organisations or organisations without an economic purpose may also engage in economic activity; a Federal Employment Office was found to fall under the definition of undertaking despite providing services free of charge.[1614] Practicing football by a football club was also found to constitute an economic activity.[1615]

2 Associations of Undertakings

The prohibitions of Article 101(1) TFEU also apply to "decisions by associations of undertakings."[1616] Even if such an association does not engage in economic activity, its decisions may still fall within the scope of competition law; on the contrary Article 101(1) TFEU will not apply to its agreements if the association does not qualify as an undertaking. But what is an "association of undertakings"? Trade associations and professional bodies such as associations of accountants have been considered as associations of undertakings by the CJEU.[1617] With regard to trade associations, they can be considered as associations of undertakings even if they have been subsequently approved by a public authority or their members are appointed by the state and not elected.[1618] There is a wide margin of flexibility in a characterisation of a body as an association of undertakings: a body may be considered as an association of undertakings when performing some of its tasks but not when performing others.[1619]

1613. Judgment of the Court of 10 January 2006, Case C-222/04, *Ministero dell'Economia e delle Finanze v. Cassa di Risparmio di Firenze SpA, Fondazione Cassa di Risparmio di San Miniato and Cassa di Risparmio di San Miniato SpA*, EU:C:2006:8, paras 111-113.
1614. Judgment of the Court of 23 April 1991, Case C-41/90, *Klaus Höfner and Fritz Elser v. Macrotron GmbH*, EU:C:1991:161, paras 20-24.
1615. Judgment of the Court of First Instance of 26 January 2005, Case T-193/02, *Laurent Piau v. Commission of the European Communities*, EU:T:2005:22, paras 69-72, finding that FIFA also constitutes an association of undertakings.
1616. Article 101(1) TFEU.
1617. Judgment of the Court of 19 February 2002, Case C-309/99, *J. C. J. Wouters, J. W. Savelbergh and Price Waterhouse Belastingadviseurs BV v. Algemene Raad van de Nederlandse Orde van Advocaten, intervener: Raad van de Balies van de Europese Gemeenschap*, EU:C:2002:98, paras 50-71; Judgment of the Court of 28 February 2013, Case C-1/12, *Ordem dos Técnicos Oficiais de Contas v. Autoridade da Concorrência*, EU:C:2013:127, paras 39-59. See also Judgment of the Court of 18 July 2013, Case C-136/12, *Consiglio nazionale dei geologi v. Autorità Garante della Concorrenza e del Mercato and Autorità Garante della Concorrenza e del Mercato v. Consiglio nazionale dei geologi*, EU:C:2013:489, paras 41-45, finding that the National Association of Geologists in Italy should be regarded as an association of undertakings when adopting rules of professional conduct.
1618. 82/896/EEC: Commission Decision of 15 December 1982 relating to a proceeding under Article 85 of the EEC Treaty (IV/29.883 – AROW/BNIC), OJ L 379, 31.12.1982, paras 48-54; 95/188/EC: Commission Decision of 30 January 1995 relating to a proceeding under Article 85 of the EC Treaty (IV/33.686 – Coapi), OJ L 122, 2.6.1995, paras 32-33.
1619. See for instance Judgment of the Court of 19 February 2002, Case C-309/99, *J. C. J. Wouters, J. W. Savelbergh and Price Waterhouse Belastingadviseurs BV v. Algemene Raad van de Nederlandse Orde van Advocaten, intervener: Raad van de Balies van de Europese Gemeenschap*, EU:C:2002:98, paras 50-71; Opinion of Advocate General Jacobs delivered on January 28, 1999, in Case C-67/96, *Albany International BV v. Stichting Bedrijfspensioenfonds Textielindustrie*, EU:C:1999:28, para. 214. See also WHISH, BAILEY, *Competition Law*, 2015, p. 95, advocating in favour of a "functional approach" towards the concept of association of

Chapter 5: The European Regulatory Framework

MasterCard was considered to be an association of undertakings when owned by several banks on behalf of which it operated the MasterCard payment system – even when MasterCard was no longer owned by those institutions, the latter retained some residual decision-making powers and shared a "commonality of interests" with MasterCard, which remained an "institutionalised form of coordination on the conduct of the banks."[1620]

B Agreements and Concerted Practices under Article 101(1) TFEU

1 The Definition of Agreement under Article 101(1) TFEU

In order to have an agreement within the meaning of Article 101(1) TFEU, it is sufficient that the undertakings concerned have expressed their joint intention to conduct themselves on the market in a specific way.[1621] The term "agreement" is not limited to formal contracts but also encompasses informal agreements, decisions of trade associations and concerted practices. The term "concerted practice" concerns a form of coordination between the undertakings where an agreement has not yet been concluded; however, the practical cooperation among the undertakings knowingly substitutes the risks of competition.[1622] The concept of concerted practice requires concertation between the undertakings concerned, subsequent concerted conduct in the market and a cause-effect relationship between the two.[1623]

An agreement is regarded as concluded under Article 101(1) TFEU even if the specific characteristics of the envisaged restriction are still under negotiation: the main requirement is a concurrence of wills on imposing a restriction on competition.[1624] The term "agreement" under Article 101(1) TFEU is vastly broad; indicatively, patent

---

undertakings; JONES, SUFRIN, 2014, pp. 147-149, discussing the complexity of determining whether an entity is acting as an association of undertakings or as a single undertaking, especially in cases it was found to be both.

1620. Judgment of the Court of 11 September 2014, Case C-382/12 P, *MasterCard Inc. and Others v. European Commission*, EU:C:2014:2201, paras 62-77.

1621. Judgment of the Court of First Instance of 17 December 1991, Case T-7/89, *SA Hercules Chemicals NV v. Commission of the European Communities*, EU:T:1991:75, para. 256; Judgment of the Court of First Instance of 20 March 2002, Case T-9/99, *HFB Holding für Fernwärmetechnik Beteiligungsgesellschaft mbH & Co. KG and Others v. Commission of the European Communities*, ECR, EU:T:2002:70, para.199.

1622. Judgment of the Court of 4 June 2009, C-8/08, *T-Mobile Netherlands BV, KPN Mobile NV, Orange Nederland NV and Vodafone Libertel NV v. Raad van bestuur van de Nederlandse Mededingingsautoriteit*, EU:C:2009:343, para. 26; Judgment of the Court of 8 July 1999, Case C-49/92 P, *Commission of the European Communities v. Anic Partecipazioni SpA*, EU:C:1999:356, para. 115 (Judgment of the Court of 8 July 1999, Case C-49/92 P, *Commission of the European Communities v. Anic*); Judgment of the Court of 8 July 1999, Case C-199/92 P, *Hüls AG v. Commission of the European Communities*, EU:C:1999:358, para. 158. See also European Commission, Communication, *Guidelines on the applicability of Article 101 of the Treaty on the Functioning of the European Union to horizontal co-operation agreements*, OJ C 11/1, 14.1.2011, paras 60-63. [cited as: EU Commission, *101 TFEU Guidelines*, 2011].

1623. Judgment of the Court of 8 July 1999, Case C-199/92 P, *Hüls AG v. Commission of the European Communities*, EU:C:1999:358, para. 161; JONES, SUFRIN, 2014, pp. 164-172.

1624. Judgment of 20 March 2002, T-9/99, *HFB and Others v. Commission*, EU:T:2002:70, paras 151-157, 206.

settlement agreements,[1625] "gentlemen's agreements,"[1626] oral agreements[1627] and contractual terms and conditions in a standard form contract,[1628] can all qualify as agreements under Article 101(1) TFEU. However, Article 101(1) TFEU does not apply to collective bargaining agreements, insofar as those agreements relate to the improvement of work and employment conditions.[1629]

2 Potential Competition

The examination of conditions of competition at a certain market must be based not only on existing competition between undertakings already present in that market, but also on *potential* competition. The goal is to ascertain whether there are concrete possibilities for the undertakings concerned to compete among themselves or for a new undertaking to enter the market and compete with the established ones, in the light of the market's structure and the legal and economic context within which it functions.[1630] An undertaking can only be described as a potential competitor if its entry to the market is economically viable; such demonstration shall not constitute a mere hypothesis but must be supported by evidence and an analysis of the relevant market's structure.[1631] Thus, the undertaking's *ability* to enter the market is the essential factor

---

1625. European Commission, Communication, *Guidelines on the application of Article 101 of the Treaty on the Functioning of the European Union to technology transfer agreements*, OJ C 89/3, 28.3.2014, paras 234-243 [cited as: EU Commission, *Technology Transfer Agreements Guidelines*, 2014]. See infra Chapter 6, analysing pharma patent settlement agreements under EU competition laws.
1626. Judgment of the Court of 15 July 1970, Case 41/69, *ACF Chemiefarma NV v. Commission of the European Communities*, EU:C:1970:71, paras 106-114; Judgment of the Court of First Instance of 8 July 2008, Case T-53/03, *BPB plc v. Commission of the European Communities*, EU:T:2008:254, paras 76-87.
1627. Judgment of the Court of 20 January 2016, Case C-373/14 P, *Toshiba Corporation v. European Commission*, EU:C:2016:26, paras 23-35, finding an oral agreement to constitute a restriction by object, confirming the Judgment of the General Court of 21 May 2014, Case T-519/09, *Toshiba Corp. v. European Commission*, EU:T:2014:263, para. 228. See also Judgment of the Court of 20 June 1978, Case 28/77, *Tepea BV v. Commission of the European Communities*, EU:C:1978:133, para. 41, finding that oral agreements were mutually binding and constituted an agreement within the meaning of Article 85(1) of the EEC Treaty, now Article 101(1) TFEU.
1628. 79/68/EEC: Commission Decision of 12 December 1978 relating to a proceeding under Article 85 of the EEC Treaty (IV/29.430 – Kawasaki), OJ L 16/9, 23.1.1979, p. 9-16, paras 41-42; 87/409/EEC: Commission Decision of 13 July 1987 relating to a proceeding under Article 85 of the EEC Treaty (IV/31.741 – Sandoz), OJ L 222/28, 10.8.1987, 1987, p. 28-34, paras 25-29.
1629. Judgment of the Court of 21 September 1999, Case C-67/96, *Albany International BV v. Stichting Bedrijfspensioenfonds Textielindustrie*, EU:C:1999:430, paras 46-64; Judgment of the Court of 21 September 1999, Joined Cases C-115/97 to C-117/97, *Brentjens' Handelsonderneming BV v. Stichting Bedrijfspensioenfonds voor de Handel in Bouwmaterialen*, EU:C:1999:434, para. 57.
1630. Judgment of the Court of First Instance of 15 September 1998, Joined Cases T-374/94, T-375/94, T-384/94 and T-388/94, *European Night Services Ltd (ENS), Eurostar (UK) Ltd, formerly European Passenger Services Ltd (EPS), Union internationale des chemins de fer (UIC), NV Nederlandse Spoorwegen (NS) and Société nationale des chemins de fer français (SNCF) v. Commission of the European Communities*, EU:T:1998:198, para. 137; Judgment of the Court of 28 February 1991, Case C-234/89, *Stergios Delimitis v. Henninger Bräu AG*, EU:C:1991:91, para. 21.
1631. Judgment of the General Court of 14 April 2011, Case T-461/07, *Visa Europe Ltd and Visa International Service v. European Commission*, EU:T:2011:181, paras 167-171. See also

Chapter 5: The European Regulatory Framework

for it to be considered as a potential competitor; its *intention* to enter the market is of secondary importance.[1632] The time-frame of the potential entry also plays a role: such entry shall take place with sufficient speed so as to form a constraint on market participants.[1633]

One of the core criteria in detecting the existence of potential competition is the perception of market incumbents on whether potential credible competition exists.[1634] The possible lack of commercial interest in entering the market is irrelevant and does not renter the alleged restraint of competition devoid of its purpose to eliminate the residual risk of a future entry on the long-term.[1635] Additionally, the existence of objective barriers to entry does not exclude potential competition, as long as potential competitors are technically able to enter the market.[1636] The notion of potential competition is of particular importance in the analysis of reverse payment settlements under European competition law. As discussed in Chapter 6, generic manufacturers are considered to be potential competitors of brand-name drug manufacturers, since they have a number of concrete possibilities to enter the market, e.g., by launching at risk or by requesting the revocation of the patent.[1637]

3 Eliminating or Reducing Market Uncertainty

Article 101(1) TFEU precludes any direct or indirect contact between economic operators that could potentially influence the market conduct of an actual or potential competitor. It also precludes revealing to actual or potential competitors the conduct which an economic operator has decided or contemplates to adopt, where the object or effect of either of these contacts is to restrict competition.[1638] The overriding principle established in the jurisprudence of the CJEU on Article 101(1) TFEU is that each economic operator shall determine independently the policy it intends to adopt in the

---

Judgment of the Court of First Instance of 4 July 2006, Case T-177/04, *easyJet Airline Co. Ltd v. Commission of the European Communities*, EU:T:2006:187, paras 123-125.
1632. Judgment of the General Court of 14 April 2011, Case T-461/07, *Visa Europe Ltd and Visa International Service v. European Commission*, EU:T:2011:181, para. 168.
1633. Judgment of the General Court of 14 April 2011, Case T-461/07, *Visa Europe Ltd and Visa International Service v. European Commission*, EU:T:2011:181, para. 189.
1634. Judgment of the General Court of 12 July 2011, Case T-112/07, *Hitachi Ltd, Hitachi Europe Ltd and Japan AE Power Systems Corp. v. European Commission*, EU:T:2011:342, paras 90, 226, 319.
1635. Judgment of the General Court of 12 July 2011, Case T-112/07, *Hitachi Ltd, Hitachi Europe Ltd and Japan AE Power Systems Corp. v. European Commission*, EU:T:2011:342, paras 158, 160.
1636. Judgment of the General Court of 12 July 2011, Case T-112/07, *Hitachi Ltd, Hitachi Europe Ltd and Japan AE Power Systems Corp. v. European Commission*, EU:T:2011:342, paras 111, 157, 160. See also Judgment of the General Court of 21 May 2014, Case T-519/09, *Toshiba Corp. v. European Commission*, EU:T:2014:263, para. 230.
1637. See infra, Chapter 6, Part 1, Section II.B.2.
1638. Judgment of the Court of 8 July 1999, Case C-49/92 P, *Commission of the European Communities v. Anic*, paras 116-117.

market.[1639] Conduct which results in the elimination or the reduction of uncertainty in the market with regard to the future conduct of actual or potential competitors and in coordination, under the form of obligations or arrangements that regulate the conduct of at least one party by causing a change in its incentives, is not tolerated under Article 101(1) TFEU.[1640]

4 Article 101(1) TFEU and the "Single Economic Entity" Doctrine

Legal persons who form a single economic entity in essence form one single undertaking and there is no agreement between them that could fall within the scope of Article 101(1) TFEU. In order for distinct legal persons to form one single economic entity – so that an agreement between them is regarded as an internal allocation of functions within a single undertaking and not as a restrictive agreement among independent undertakings – certain criteria need to be met. First, the legal persons concerned shall consist of a "unitary organisation of personal, tangible and intangible elements."[1641] Second, this unitary organisation shall pursue a long-term specific economic aim, and third, it shall contribute to the commission of an infringement under Article 101(1) TFEU.[1642] If subsidiaries or different companies within a corporate group do not determine their conduct on the market independently, they form a single economic entity and thus an undertaking under Article 101(1) TFEU; in such cases, the European Commission is able to address the decision imposing a fine to the parent company of the group.[1643] Thus, Article 101(1) TFEU does not in principle apply to agreements between a parent company and one or more of its subsidiaries,[1644] agreements between

---

1639. Judgment of the Court of 20 November 2008, Case C-209/07, *Competition Authority v. Beef Industry Development Society Ltd and Barry Brothers (Carrigmore) Meats Ltd*, EU:C:2008:643, paras 33-35; EU Commission, *Article 81(3) Guidelines*, 2004, para. 14.
1640. EU Commission, *Article 81(3) Guidelines*, 2004, para. 15.
1641. Judgment of the Court of First Instance of 12 December 2007, *Akzo Nobel NV and Others v. Commission of the European Communities*, EU:T:2007:381, para. 57; Judgment of the Court of First Instance of 20 March 2002, Case T-9/99, *HFB Holding für Fernwärmetechnik Beteiligungsgesellschaft mbH & Co. KG and Others v. Commission of the European Communities*, EU:T:2002:70, para. 54.
1642. Judgment of the Court of First Instance of 12 December 2007, *Akzo Nobel NV and Others v. Commission of the European Communities*, EU:T:2007:381, paras 57-58; *See also* JONES, SUFRIN, 2014, pp. 137-147, discussing the single economic entity doctrine and its consequences on the application of Articles 101 and 102 TFEU.
1643. Judgment of the Court of First Instance of 12 December 2007, *Akzo Nobel NV and Others v. Commission of the European Communities*, EU:T:2007:381, paras 57-58; Judgment of the Court of First Instance of 30 September 2003, Case T-203/01, *Manufacture française des pneumatiques Michelin v. Commission of the European Communities*, EU:T:2003:250, para. 290.
1644. Judgment of the Court of First Instance of 12 January 1995, Case T-102/92, *VIHO Europe BV v. Commission of the European Communities*, EU:T:1995:3, paras 47-51; upheld by Judgment of the Court of 24 October 1996, Case C-73/95 P, *Viho Europe BV v. Commission of the European Communities*, EU:C:1996:405, paras 14-18. *See also* ODUDU, BAILEY, 2014, pp. 1727-1733.

Chapter 5: The European Regulatory Framework

principals and their agents[1645] and also agreements between contractors and their subcontractors.[1646]

C Anticompetitive Object or Effect of the Agreement

In order for an agreement to fall under the scope of prohibition of Article 101(1) TFEU, it shall have as its *object* or *effect* the prevention, restriction or distortion of competition in the internal market. According to settled case law starting from 1965, the conditions of object or effect are not cumulative but alternative conditions,[1647] so that it is necessary to first consider the object of an agreement.[1648] As analysed in the following section, no strict parallels can be drawn between the tests and antitrust analysis employed in the European Union and in the US. It should be stressed that a characterisation of a restriction as a restriction by object is not the equivalent of per se illegality under US antitrust law, whereas the examination of alleged restrictive effects a restriction may have on competition is not the mirror equivalent of a rule of reason analysis under US antitrust laws. The distinction between restrictions by object and by effect is particularly relevant for the analysis of reverse payment settlements under European competition law. One of the most important debates is whether reverse payments should fall under the by object or the by effect category, given the tremendous consequences such a categorisation has on the legal analysis of the conduct at issue.

1 Restrictions by Object

Restrictions by object are the restrictions to competition which "by their nature" are regarded as harmful to the proper functioning of normal competition, independently of any concrete effect that they may have.[1649] Once the anticompetitive object of an

---

1645. Judgment of the Court of 16 December 1975, Joined Cases 40 to 48, 50, 54 to 56, 111, 113 and 114-73, *Coöperatieve Vereniging "Suiker Unie" UA and others v. Commission of the European Communities*, EU:C:1975:174, paras 478-483; European Commission, Notice, *Guidelines on Vertical Restraints*, SEC/2010/0411 final, Brussels, 10.5.2010, paras 12-21 [cited as: EU Commission, Guidelines on Vertical Restraints, 2010]. See especially para. 18, "[s]ince the principal bears the commercial and financial risks related to the selling and purchasing of the contract goods and services all obligations imposed on the agent in relation to the contracts concluded and/or negotiated on behalf of the principal fall outside Article 101(1)."
1646. See European Commission, Notice of 18 December 1978 concerning its assessment of certain subcontracting agreements in relation to Article 85 (1) of the EEC Treaty, OJ C 1, 3.1.1979.
1647. Judgment of the Court of 30 June 1966, Case 56/65, *Société Technique Minière (L.T.M.) v. Maschinenbau Ulm GmbH (M.B.U.)*, EU:C:1966:38, p. 249.
1648. Judgment of the Court of 16 July 2015, Case C-172/14, *ING Pensii – Societate de Administrare a unui Fond de Pensii Administrat Privat SA v. Consiliul Concurenţei*, EU:C:2015:484, para. 30.
1649. Judgment of the Court of 1 February 1978, Case 19/77, *Miller International Schallplatten GmbH v. Commission of the European Communities*, EU:C:1978:19, para. 7; Judgment of the Court of 20 November 2008, Case C-209/07, *Competition Authority v. Beef Industry Development Society Ltd and Barry Brothers (Carrigmore) Meats Ltd*, EU:C:2008:643, para. 17; Judgment of the Court of 13 December 2012, Case C-226/11, *Expedia Inc. v. Autorité de la concurrence and Others*, EU:C:2012:795, para. 37.

agreement is established, it is unnecessary to examine its effects on competition.[1650] The *potential* of an agreement to have a negative impact on competition is sufficient for it to fall under Article 101(1) TFEU, if the agreement is capable of resulting in the prevention, restriction or distortion of competition in the internal market.[1651]

In order to assess if an agreement involves a restriction by object, one shall examine the context of its provisions, the objectives that the agreement seeks to attain and the agreement's legal and economic context.[1652] Taking into consideration the nature of the goods or services affected by the agreement, as well as the real conditions of functioning and structure of the market(s) at question, is vital in order to determine that context.[1653] The parties' intention in concluding the agreement is not a necessary factor in determining whether an agreement constitutes a restriction by object, but it may be taken into consideration by either the Commission or the European courts.[1654] The anticompetitive object of an agreement may be deducted by the content of its clauses, the conduct of the concerned undertakings or their intention as arising from the "genesis" of the agreement or the circumstances under which the agreement was implemented.[1655]

1650. Judgment of the Court of 14 March 2013, Case C-32/11, *Allianz Hungária Biztosító Zrt. and Others v. Gazdasági Versenyhivatal*, EU:C:2013:160, paras 28-30, 34-35 (Judgment of the Court of 14 March 2013, Case C-32/11, *Allianz Hungária v. Gazdasági Versenyhivatal*); Judgment of the Court of 13 December 2012, Case C-226/11, *Expedia Inc. v. Autorité de la concurrence and Others*, EU:C:2012:795, paras 35-36; Case C-209/07, *Beef Industry Development Society and Barry Brothers*, November 20, 2008, [2008] ECR I-8637, para. 17; Judgment of the Court of 30 January 1985, Case 123/83, *Bureau national interprofessionnel du cognac v. Guy Clair*, EU:C:1985:33, para. 22; Judgment of the Court of 4 June 2009, C-8/08, *T-Mobile Netherlands BV, KPN Mobile NV, Orange Nederland NV and Vodafone Libertel NV v. Raad van bestuur van de Nederlandse Mededingingsautoriteit*, EU:C:2009:343, para. 31; Joined Judgments in *GlaxoSmithKline Services and Others v. Commission and Others*, C-501/06 P, C-513/06 P, C-515/06 P, and C-519/06 P, EU:C:2009:610, para. 55.
1651. Judgment in *T-Mobile Netherlands and Others*, C-8/08, EU:C:2009:343, para. 31; Judgment in *Allianz Hungária Biztosító and Others*, C-32/11, EU:C:2013:160, paras 35-38.
1652. Judgment of the Court of 20 January 2016, Case C-373/14 P, *Toshiba Corporation v. European Commission*, EU:C:2016:26, para. 27; Judgment of the Court of 16 July 2015, Case C-172/14, *ING Pensii – Societate de Administrare a unui Fond de Pensii Administrat Privat SA v. Consiliul Concurenței*, EU:C:2015:484, para. 33; Joined Judgments in *GlaxoSmithKline Services and Others v. Commission and Others*, C-501/06 P, C-513/06 P, C-515/06 P, and C-519/06 P, EU:C:2009:610, para. 25; Judgment in *Beef Industry Development and Barry Brothers*, C-209/07, EU:C:2008:643, paras 16-21.
1653. Judgment of the Court of 14 March 2013, Case C-32/11, *Allianz Hungária v. Gazdasági Versenyhivatal*, para. 36; Joined Judgments in *GlaxoSmithKline Services and Others v. Commission and Others*, C-501/06 P, C-513/06 P, C-515/06 P, and C-519/06 P, EU:C:2009:610, para. 58; Judgment of the Court of 13 October 2011, Case C-439/09, *Pierre Fabre Dermo-Cosmétique SAS v. Président de l'Autorité de la concurrence and Ministre de l'Économie, de l'Industrie et de l'Emploi*, EU:C:2011:649, para. 35.
1654. Judgment of the Court of 8 November 1983, *NV IAZ International Belgium and others v. Commission of the European Communities*, Joined Cases 96-102, 104, 105, 108 and 110/82, EU:C:1983:310, paras 23-25; Judgment of the Court of 6 October 2009, C-501/06 P, C-513/06 P, C-515/06 P, and C-519/06 P, *GlaxoSmithKline Services and Others v. Commission and Others*, EU:C:2009:610, para. 58.
1655. Judgment of the Court of 8 November 1983, *NV IAZ International Belgium and others v. Commission of the European Communities*, Joined Cases 96-102, 104, 105, 108 and 110/82, EU:C:1983:310, paras 23-25; Judgment of the Court of 28 March 1984, Joined Cases 29/83 and 30/83, *Compagnie Royale Asturienne des Mines SA and Rheinzink GmbH v. Commission of the*

Chapter 5: The European Regulatory Framework

The fact that an agreement may also pursue other legitimate objectives and not have as its sole aim the restriction of competition does not necessarily bar the finding of a restriction by object.[1656] Restrictions by object are not necessarily restrictions which *obviously* restrict competition, while they are neither exhausted nor limited by the indicative list of examples provided in Article 101(1) TFEU.[1657] A restriction by object may fall outside the scope of Article 101 when it can be objectively justified, for instance on the grounds of protecting safety or health.[1658] From May 1, 2004 until April 13, 2015 the Commission adopted ninety decisions concerning Article 101 TFEU; seventy-seven out of them concerned alleged restrictions by object.[1659]

1.1 Expanding the Group of Restrictions by Object

One of the main characteristics of the doctrine of anticompetitive object is that it is founded upon a "box" approach: instead of a case-by-case assessment of the relevant restraint, it adopts a categorical approach that condemns restraints which fall within certain categories *quasi*-automatically.[1660] Even though restrictions of competition by object cannot be reduced to an exhaustive list, some restraints of competition are particularly liable to be found to be restrictions by object: price fixing (either horizontal or vertical) and exchanges of information on future prices,[1661] market sharing, quotas, collective exclusive dealing,[1662] controlling outlets or export bans,[1663] are some infamous examples.

European Communities, EU:C:1984:130, para. 26; Opinion of Advocate General Tizzano delivered on 25 October 2005 in the case of *General Motors v. European Commission*, C-551/03 P, EU:C:2006:229, paras 77-78.

1656. Judgment in *Beef Industry Development and Barry* Brothers, C-209/07, EU:C:2008:643, para. 21; Judgment of the Court of 8 November 1983, Joined Cases 96-102, 104, 105, 108 and 110/82, *NV IAZ International Belgium and others v. Commission of the European Communities*, EU:C:1983:310, para. 25; Judgment of the Court of 30 January 1985, Case 35/83, *BAT Cigaretten-Fabriken GmbH v. Commission*, para. 33.
1657. Opinion of Advocate General Trstenjak delivered on September 4, 2008 on Case C-209/07, *Competition Authority v. Beef Industry Development Society Ltd and Barry Brothers (Carrigmore) Meats Ltd.*, EU:C:2008:643, paras 47-48. See also the Judgment of the Court of 13 October 2011, Case C-439/09, *Pierre Fabre Dermo-Cosmétique SAS v. Président de l'Autorité de la concurrence and Ministre de l'Économie, de l'Industrie et de l'Emploi*, EU:C:2011:649, para. 47, for an example of a non-obvious restriction by object, finding that in the context of a selective distribution system, a contractual clause which required sales of cosmetics and personal care products to be made in a physical space and in the presence of a qualified pharmacist, thus resulting in the ban of sales though internet, amounted to a restriction by object.
1658. EU Commission, *Guidelines on Vertical Restraints*, 2010, para. 60; *see also* EU Commission, *Article 81(3) Guidelines*, 2004, para. 18; WHISH, BAILEY, *Competition Law*, 2015, pp. 124-125.
1659. BRUZZONE, CAPOZZI, 2015, p. 4.
1660. *See* for instance, NAGY CSONGOR, 2015, pp. 154-155; WHISH, BAILEY, *Competition Law*, 2015, pp. 129-133.
1661. Judgment of the Court of 4 June 2009, C-8/08, *T-Mobile Netherlands BV, KPN Mobile NV, Orange Nederland NV and Vodafone Libertel NV v. Raad van bestuur van de Nederlandse Mededingingsautoriteit*, EU:C:2009:343, para. 43.
1662. Judgment of the Court of 20 November 2008, C-209/07, *Beef Industry Development and Barry Brothers*, EU:C:2008:643, paras 33-34.

Certain decisions by the CJEU seemed to broaden the group of restrictions by object and to lower the burden for finding such a restriction. In *T-mobile* and in *Allianz Hungária*, the CJEU found that the potential of a restraint having a negative impact on competition is sufficient to establish the anticompetitive object of a practice, stressing that Article 101 TFEU was enacted to protect competition "as such;" thus, it is not necessary to demonstrate a direct effect of a restriction by object neither on prices nor on end users.[1664] The EU Commission's findings of new types of restrictions by object, notably with regard to pay-for-delay agreements in the pharmaceutical sector in the *Lundbeck* and *Servier* cases,[1665] in conjunction with the view that all hardcore restrictions in EU Block Exemption Regulations shall be regarded as restrictions by object,[1666] reinforced the impression that the group of restrictions by object is constantly enlarging. The characterisation of certain restrictions such as the joint setting of multilateral interchange fees in the payment card market as a restriction by object – despite the lack of jurisprudential or other legal precedent on the matter – seems to confirm the expansion of the restrictions by object group.[1667]

1.2   The Judgment of CJEU in *Cartes Bancaires*

The 2014 judgment of the CJEU in *Cartes Bancaires* arguably put an end to this expanding tendency and restored the court's "traditional" approach with regard to

---

1663. Judgment of the Court of 6 April 2006, Case C-551/03 P, *General Motors BV v. Commission of the European Communities*, EU:C:2006:229, paras 64-80. See however Judgment of the Court of 6 October 2009, C-501/06 P, C-513/06 P, C-515/06 P, and C-519/06 P, *GlaxoSmithKline Services and Others v. Commission and Others*, EU:C:2009:610, paras 59-60, finding that in the specific and unusual pharmaceuticals' context, an indirect ban in export was not a restriction by object but it did restrict competition by effect.
1664. Judgment of the Court of 4 June 2009, C-8/08, *T-Mobile Netherlands BV, KPN Mobile NV, Orange Nederland NV and Vodafone Libertel NV v. Raad van bestuur van de Nederlandse Mededingingsautoriteit*, EU:C:2009:343, paras 31, 36-39. See also Judgment of the Court of 14 March 2013, Case C-32/11, *Allianz Hungária v. Gazdasági Versenyhivatal*, para. 38, repeating the wording of *T-Mobile*; Judgment of the General Court of 14 April 2011, Case T-461/07, *Visa Europe Ltd and Visa International Service v. European Commission*, EU:T:2011:181, para. 126.
1665. See *infra*, Chapter 6, on the analysis of reverse payment settlements cases in the pharma sector in the EU.
1666. European Commission, *Notice on agreements of minor importance which do not appreciably restrict competition under Article 101(1) of the Treaty on the Functioning of the European Union (De Minimis Notice)*, OJ C 291/1, 30.8.2014, para. 13. [cited as: EU Commission, *De Minimis Notice*, 2014], "[...] the Commission will not apply the safe harbour created by those market share thresholds to agreements containing any of the restrictions that are listed as hardcore restrictions in any current or future Commission block exemption regulation, which are considered by the Commission to generally constitute restrictions by object."
1667. European Commission, Staff Working Document, *Guidance on restrictions of competition "by object" for the purpose of defining which agreements may benefit from the De Minimis Notice*, Brussels, 25.6.2014, SWD(2014) 198 final, pp. 6-7. [cited as: EU Commission, *Guidance on restrictions by object*, 2014], including in the list of price fixing restrictions by object the Case AT.39398 – Visa MIF, Commission Decision of 26 February 2014, relating to a proceeding under Article 101 of the Treaty on the Functioning of the European Union and Article 53 of the EEA Agreement, C(2014) 1199 final, Brussels 26.02.2014, pp. 7-9, where the joint setting of Multilateral Interchange Fees was considered to be price fixing. See the DG Competition Website for all the material realted to the case. Available at: http://ec.europa.eu/competition/elojade/isef/case_details.cfm?proc_code=1_39398 (last accessed on March 31, 2018).

Chapter 5: The European Regulatory Framework

restrictions by object.[1668] Previously, the General Court had agreed with the Commission's finding that *Cartes Bancaires*, a fee structure established by nine members of a payment card system, was a restriction by object and effect, preventing new banks from entering into that specific sector.[1669] The CJEU annulled the decision of the General Court, finding that it misinterpreted and misapplied Article 101(1) TFEU by characterising the restrictions at issue as restrictions by object.[1670] The court stressed that "the essential legal criterion for ascertaining whether coordination between undertakings involves such a restriction of competition 'by object' is the finding that such coordination reveals in itself a sufficient degree of harm to competition," rendering needless an examination of the restriction's effects.[1671]

One of the main points of the decision is that the CJEU made clear the need for a *restrictive* interpretation of the concept of restriction by object under Article 101(1) TFEU.[1672] This is the reason that the *Cartes Bancaires* decision was greeted as the return of the CJEU to a more conservative approach, putting an end to the wave of expansion of the concept of restriction by object.[1673] A second important point of the *Cartes Bancaires* is that the CJEU required a rather detailed consideration of the alleged restriction by object, entailing an examination of the content of the agreement at issue, its objectives and its economic and legal context.[1674] In determining an agreement's context, the court further required an elaborate factual consideration of the nature of the affected goods or services and the real conditions of the functioning and of the structure of the relevant market, as it has done previously in its decision in *Allianz Hungária*.[1675] Of course some analysis of the agreement in question is necessary in order to determine whether it constitutes a restriction by object.[1676] However, the elaborate analysis illustrated in *Cartes Bancaires* seems to blur the lines of the object-effect distinction, nearly eliminating its primary purpose: avoiding the detailed examination of any anticompetitive effects restrictions by object may have.[1677]

1668. Judgment of the Court of 11 September 2014, Case C-67/13 P, *Groupement des cartes bancaires (CB) v. European Commission*, EU:C:2014:2204, paras 48-58.
1669. Judgment of the General Court of 29 November 2012, Case T-491/07, *Groupement des cartes bancaires "CB" v. European Commission*, EU:T:2012:633, paras 148, 232. *See also* Case No COMP/D1/38606 – Groupement Des Cartes Bancaires "CB," Commission Decision of 17 October 2007 relating to a proceeding pursuant to Article 81 of the EC Treaty, Brussels, 17.10.2007, pp. 70-90.
1670. Judgment of the Court of 11 September 2014, *Groupement des cartes bancaires (CB) v. European Commission*, EU:C:2014:2204, paras 56-87.
1671. Judgment of the Court of 11 September 2014, *Groupement des cartes bancaires (CB) v. European Commission*, EU:C:2014:2204, paras 57-58.
1672. *Idem*.
1673. Whish, Bailey, *Competition Law*, 2015, p. 126.
1674. Judgment of the Court of 11 September 2014, *Groupement des cartes bancaires (CB) v. European Commission*, EU:C:2014:2204, para. 53.
1675. *Idem*; Judgment of the Court of 14 March 2013, Case C-32/11, *Allianz Hungária v. Gazdasági Versenyhivatal*, para. 36.
1676. *See* for instance Pereira Cardoso, 2014, pp. 273-274, greeting the *Cartes Bancaires* decision for rejecting excessive formalism and demanding an effects-based approach with the support of economic analysis.
1677. Whish, Bailey, *Competition Law*, 2015, pp. 126-127. *See also* Opinion of Advocate General Kokott, delivered on 19 February 2009 on Case C-8/08, *T-Mobile Netherlands BV, KPN Mobile NV, Orange Nederland NV and Vodafone Libertel NV v. Raad van bestuur van de Nederlandse*

2 Restrictions by Effect

If it is not clear that the object of an agreement is to restrict competition, an extensive analysis of its *effects* on the market shall be conducted, in order to determine whether it restricts actual or potential competition within the meaning of Article 101(1) TFEU. The notion of market power is central to this analysis: anticompetitive effects could occur when the parties to an agreement have or acquire market power, either individually or collectively, and the agreement at issue contributes to creating, maintaining or strengthening such market power, or simply allows the parties to exploit it.[1678] Empirical facts and a robust analysis of the structure of the relevant market shall be presented before courts in order to show the anticompetitive effects of the alleged restriction.[1679] A "counterfactual" examination of the actual legal and economic context that would occur in the absence of the agreement is necessary in order to compare the two situations and to determine whether and to what extent an agreement has restrictive effects on actual or potential competition.[1680] The assessment of the agreement's restrictive effects shall be based on the content of the agreement and the facts at the time of the settlement, taking into consideration how the agreement was actually implemented.[1681]

The Commission's Horizontal Guidelines contain a definition of agreements that restrict competition by effect. Such agreements shall have, or be likely to have an appreciable adverse impact on at least one of the competition parameters: price, output, product quality, product variety or innovation.[1682] Such effects can be produced by agreements appreciably reducing competition between the parties – or one of them and third parties – by reducing their decision-making independence, e.g., through obligations contained in the agreement which regulate the parties' market conduct or by changing the parties' incentives and thus influencing their conduct.[1683]

Mededingingsautoriteit, EU:C:2009:110, paras 42-49, stressing that "a finding of an anti-competitive object does not depend on an assessment of the actual impact of a concerted practice but simply the *capacity in an individual case* for that concerted practice to produce an anti-competitive impact."

1678. EU Commission, *Article 81(3) Guidelines*, 2004, para. 25.
1679. Judgment of the General Court of 14 April 2011, Case T-461/07, *Visa Europe Ltd and Visa International Service v. European Commission*, EU:T:2011:181, para. 167; Judgment of the Court of First Instance of 15 September 1998, Joined Cases T-374/94, T-375/94, T-384/94 and T-388/94, *European Night Services Ltd (ENS), Eurostar (UK) Ltd, formerly European Passenger Services Ltd (EPS), Union internationale des chemins de fer (UIC), NV Nederlandse Spoorwegen (NS) and Société nationale des chemins de fer français (SNCF) v. Commission of the European Communities*, EU:T:1998:198, paras 142-145.
1680. Judgment of the Court of 30 June 1966, Case 56/65, *Société Technique Minière (L.T.M.) v. Maschinenbau Ulm GmbH (M.B.U.)*, EU:C:1966:38, p. 250; Judgment of the Court of First Instance of 2 May 2006, Case T-328/03, *O2 (Germany) GmbH & Co. OHG v. Commission of the European Communities*, EU:T:2006:116, para. 77, noting that the Commission must carry out an objective analysis of the impact of the agreement on the competitive situation. *See also* EU Commission, *101 TFEU Guidelines*, 2011, para. 29.
1681. *See* EU Commission Decision, *Servier*, 2014, para. 1220.
1682. EU Commission, *101 TFEU Guidelines*, 2011, para. 27.
1683. Judgment of the Court of First Instance of 12 June 1997, T-504/93, *Tiercé Ladbroke SA v. Commission of the European Communities*, EU:T:1997:84, paras 154-162; EU Commission, *101 TFEU Guidelines*, 2011, para. 27.

Chapter 5: The European Regulatory Framework

3 A European Rule of Reason Analysis?

The rule of reason analysis under US antitrust laws, its main elements and characteristics and the "sliding scale of reasonableness" have been discussed in Chapter 4. Suffice to recall – risking oversimplification – that under the US rule of reason, a case-by-case analysis is conducted, aiming to weigh a practice's anticompetitive consequences against its prospective procompetitive benefits. The main goal is to determine the effect of the challenged practice on market output: increasing or decreasing it.[1684] The rule of reason analysis is reserved for practices which have a certain potential for both competitive harm and possible social gains.

European competition law and US antitrust law are materially different on multiple levels and these differences should not be blurred by the importation of US terminology to the European Union.[1685] European competition law specialists have argued against the adoption of a European reasonableness test modelled upon the US rule of reason.[1686] The EU Commission has also stressed that such an approach would entail the risk of diverting Article 101(3) TFEU from its purpose, especially since this provision already contains all the elements of a "rule of reason" analysis.[1687] In its decision in *Métropole*, the General Court rejected the view that a rule of reason analysis lies under Article 101(1) TFEU, making it necessary to weigh the procompetitive and anticompetitive effects of an alleged restriction in order to determine if Article 101 applies.[1688] Instead, the court noted that such balancing was part of determining whether a restraint benefits from the exemption of Article 101(3).[1689]

The judgment of the CJEU in *Wouters* muddied the waters on the subject, since the court declined to apply Article 101(1) TFEU and found that the objectives of a regulatory rule adopted by the Dutch Bar and governing the formation of multidisciplinary partnerships should be balanced against an alleged restriction on competition. The court stressed that account should be taken of the overall context in which the restraint was imposed and of its objectives; additionally, it should also be considered whether the restrictive effects to competition are inherent in these objectives.[1690] The CJEU found that the rule at issue was liable to limit production and technical

---

1684. See *supra* Chapter 4, Part 1, Section II.C on the analysis of rule of reason analysis under US antitrust law. See also HOVENKAMP, JANIS, LEMLEY, Anticompetitive Settlements, 2003, p. 1728.
1685. WHISH, BAILEY, *Competition Law*, 2015, pp. 142-145.
1686. *Idem*.
1687. European Commission, *White Paper on Modernisation of the Rules Implementing Articles 85 and 86 of the EC Treaty*, Commission Programme No 99/027, OJ C 132/1, Brussels, 28.04.1999, para. 57.
1688. Judgment of the Court of First Instance of 18 September 2001, Case T-112/99, *Métropole télévision (M6), Suez-Lyonnaise des eaux, France Télécom and Télévision française 1 SA (TF1) v. Commission of the European Communities*, EU:T:2001:215, paras 72-76.
1689. Judgment of the Court of First Instance of 18 September 2001, Case T-112/99, *Métropole télévision (M6), Suez-Lyonnaise des eaux, France Télécom and Télévision française 1 SA (TF1) v. Commission of the European Communities*, EU:T:2001:215, para. 74.
1690. Judgment of the Court of 19 February 2002, Case C-309/99, *J. C. J. Wouters, J. W. Savelbergh and Price Waterhouse Belastingadviseurs BV v. Algemene Raad van de Nederlandse Orde van Advocaten, intervener: Raad van de Balies van de Europese Gemeenschap*, EU:C:2002:98, para. 97.

development within the meaning of what is now Article 101(1) TFEU, while it also had an effect on trade between Member States. Nevertheless, the court considered that despite its inherent restrictive effects to competition, the relevant regulation was necessary for the proper practice of the legal profession in the Netherlands.[1691] It should be stressed that the *Wouters* decision does not amount to a strict application of a rule of reason analysis by the CJEU in line with the US standards. However, it seems to be clashing with the views expressed by the EU Commission and by the General Court in *Métropole*, which were both rather hostile to a balancing of procompetitive and anticompetitive effects as a step of determining whether an alleged restriction falls within the ambit of Article 101(1) TFEU.

D Affecting Trade Between Member States

In order for Articles 101 and 102 TFEU to apply, an agreement or abuse of dominance respectively shall affect trade in between EU Member States. This is not a high burden to meet; in essence, an impact on the cross-border economic activity involving at least two Member States must be shown.[1692] The application of the effect on trade criterion is independent of the definition of relevant geographic markets; trade in between Member States may be affected even in cases where the relevant market is national or sub-national.[1693] Even an IP licensing agreement between parties in the same EU Member State, limited to activities performed in that same Member State, may have an effect on trade between EU Member States, by affecting for instance licensing opportunities in other Member States.[1694]

Articles 101 and 102 TFEU may apply irrespectively of where the undertakings concerned are located: the main criterion is that the implemented agreement or practice produces effects within the EU market.[1695] Finally, a concerned agreement or practice "may affect" trade if it is possible to foresee with a sufficient degree of probability,

---

1691. Judgment of the Court of 19 February 2002, Case C-309/99, *J. C. J. Wouters, J. W. Savelbergh and Price Waterhouse Belastingadviseurs BV v. Algemene Raad van de Nederlandse Orde van Advocaten, intervener: Raad van de Balies van de Europese Gemeenschap*, EU:C:2002:98, paras 97-110. *See also* WHISH, BAILEY, *Competition Law*, 2015, pp. 138-142, analysing the *Wouters* decision.
1692. European Commission, Notice, *Guidelines on the effect on trade concept contained in Articles 81 and 82 of the Treaty*, OJ C 101/81, 27.4.2004, para. 21. [cited as: EU Commission, *Guidelines: effect on trade in Articles 81 & 82*, 2004].
1693. EU Commission, *Guidelines: effect on trade in Articles 81 & 82*, 2004, para. 22.
1694. EU Commission, *Guidelines: effect on trade in Articles 81 & 82*, 2004, paras 21-22.
1695. Judgment of the Court of 27 September 1988, Joined Cases 89, 104, 114, 116, 117 and 125 to 129/85, *Ahlström Osakeyhtiö and others v. Commission of the European Communities*, EU:C:1988:447, paras 11-23, finding that a cartel between undertakings in several non-EU countries, that was implemented within the EU fell within the territorial scope of Article 101(1) TFEU; Judgment of the General Court of 12 June 2014, Case T-286/09, *Intel Corp. v. European Commission*, EU:T:2014:547, paras 231-258, relying both on *Wood Pulp* and on the qualified effects doctrine to establish jurisdiction. *See also* Judgment of the Court of 28 April 1998, Case C-306/96, *Javico International and Javico AG v. Yves Saint Laurent Parfums SA (YSLP)*, EU:C:1998:173, para. 28, finding that an export ban imposed upon distributors in Ukraine and Russia could have an appreciable effect on trade and undermine the objectives of the common market.

based on objective factors of law or fact, the possible direct or indirect, actual or potential influence it could have on interstate trade.[1696] As analysed in the following sections, in order for an agreement to "affect trade between Member States" under Article 101(1) TFEU, three basic elements must be met: (1) trade between Member States shall be affected; (2) a probability that the agreement affects trade must be established; and (3) the effect on trade of the agreement must be appreciable.

1   An Appreciable Effect on Interstate Trade as a Jurisdictional Criterion

If an agreement as a whole is capable of having an appreciable effect on trade between Member States, there is EU law jurisdiction over its entirety, covering also any of its parts that do not affect interstate commerce.[1697] The concept of effect on trade is a jurisdictional matter and has been interpreted broadly in CJEU's jurisprudence.[1698] It is generally accepted that the EU has no jurisdiction over cases where the effects of the relevant agreement or conduct are confined to one single Member State;[1699] however, an agreement which operates within only one Member State may be capable of affecting interstate trade.[1700] The notion of trade also extends beyond traditional exchanges of goods and services and covers all cross-border activity, such as the cross-border establishment of undertakings or the creation of branches or subsidiaries in other Member States.[1701]

The effect on trade criterion incorporates the quantitative element of appreciability, which can be appraised on the basis of the position and importance of the relevant undertakings into the market for the concerned products.[1702] The assessment of appreciability is done on a case-by-case basis and depends on the nature of the agreement or practice, the nature of the covered products and the market position of the concerned undertakings; the definition of the relevant market and the calculation of the respective market shares are not necessary.[1703] If an agreement does not have an effect on interstate trade or has insignificant effects, it falls outside the scope of European competition law and Article 101(1) TFEU will not apply; instead, the agreement will be analysed under national competition laws of the concerned Member State.

1696. EU Commission, *Guidelines: effect on trade in Articles 81 & 82*, 2004, para. 23.
1697. Judgment of the Court of 9 July 1969, Case 5/69, *Franz Völk v. S.P.R.L. Ets J. Vervaecke*, EU:C:1969:35, p. 302 paras 5/7; Judgment of the Court of 30 June 1966, Case 56/65, *Société Technique Minière (L.T.M.) v. Maschinenbau Ulm GmbH (M.B.U.)*, EU:C:1966:38, p. 249. See also EU Commission, *Guidelines: effect on trade in Articles 81 & 82*, 2004, para. 14.
1698. JONES, SUFRIN, 2014, pp. 181-186.
1699. Judgment of the Court of 31 May 1979, Case 22/78, *Hugin Kassaregister AB and Hugin Cash Registers Ltd v. Commission of the European Communities*, EU:C:1979:138, para. 17.
1700. See for instance, Judgment of the Court of 28 February 1991, Case C-234/89, *Stergios Delimitis v. Henninger Bräu AG*, EU:C:1991:91, paras 28-33.
1701. EU Commission, *Guidelines: effect on trade in Articles 81 & 82*, 2004, paras 19, 30.
1702. EU Commission, *Guidelines: effect on trade in Articles 81 & 82*, 2004, para. 44; Judgment of the Court of First Instance of 1 April 1993, T-65/89, *BPB Industries Plc and British Gypsum Ltd v. Commission of the European Communities*, EU:T:1993:31, para.138.
1703. EU Commission, *Guidelines: effect on trade in Articles 81 & 82*, 2004, paras 45, 48.

2 Agreements of Minor Importance and the Notion of Appreciability

2.1 *De Minimis*: The Lack of Appreciable Impact on Interstate Trade

In *Völk v. Vervaecke* the CJEU formulated for the first time the *de minimis* doctrine by holding that agreements which affect competition within the meaning of Article 101 TFEU will not fall within its scope if they do not have an appreciable impact on competition or on trade between Member States.[1704] This rule of double appreciability is recurring in the jurisprudence of the CJEU[1705] but has been abandoned with regard to restrictions by object in the *Expedia* judgment.[1706] Restraints which have as their object the restriction of competition and produce an effect on trade between Member States are automatically found to violate Article 101(1) TFEU, without any further need of demonstrating their concrete effects on competition.[1707] The *Expedia* decision and the 2010 revision of the Vertical and Horizontal Block Exemption Regulations were the main reasons for the Commission to amend its *de minimis* notice, so that restrictions by object cannot longer benefit from the safe harbour of the *de minimis* even if they fall below the given thresholds.[1708]

A distinction must be made between the notions of "appreciability" of a restriction and the requirement that a restrictive agreement has to be capable of appreciably affecting trade between Member States. If a restriction is not appreciable, normally it will not have an appreciable effect on trade between Member States either. However,

---

1704. Judgment of the Court of 9 July 1969, Case 5/69, *Franz Völk v. S.P.R.L. Ets J. Vervaecke*, EU:C:1969:35, p. 302, paras 5-7. The notion of "appreciability" was introduced for the first time in Judgment of the Court of 30 June 1966, C-56/65, *Société Technique Minière (L.T.M.) v. Maschinenbau Ulm GmbH (M.B.U.)*, EU:C:1966:38, p. 249.

1705. Judgment of the Court of 28 May 1998, Case C-7/95 P, *John Deere Ltd v. Commission of the European Communities*, EU:C:1998:256, para. 77; Judgment of the Court of 21 January 1999, Joined Cases C-215/96 and C-216/96, *Carlo Bagnasco and Others v. Banca Popolare di Novara soc. coop. arl. (BNP) (C-215/96) and Cassa di Risparmio di Genova e Imperia SpA (Carige) (C-216/96)*, EU:C:1999:12, para. 34; Judgment of the Court of 23 November 2006, Case C-238/05, *Asnef-Equifax, Servicios de Información sobre Solvencia y Crédito, SL v. Asociación de Usuarios de Servicios Bancarios (Ausbanc)*, EU:C:2006:734, para. 50 (Judgment of the Court of 23 November 2006, Case C-238/05, *Asnef-Equifax v. Ausbanc*).

1706. Judgment of the Court of 13 December 2012, Case C-226/11, *Expedia Inc. v. Autorité de la concurrence and Others*, EU:C:2012:795, paras 36-38. See also European Commission, *Notice on agreements of minor importance which do not appreciably restrict competition under Article 81(1) of the Treaty establishing the European Community (de minimis)*, OJ C 368/13, 22.12.2001, para. 2. [cited as: EU Commission, *De Minimis Notice*, 2001], referring to the *Expedia* judgment.

1707. Judgment of the Court of 13 December 2012, Case C-226/11, *Expedia Inc. v. Autorité de la concurrence and Others*, EU:C:2012:795, paras 36-38; WHISH, BAILEY, *Competition Law*, 2015, p. 148; *See also* ORTEGA GONZALEZ, 2013, pp. 463-465, arguing that the appreciability condition is presumed with regard to by object restrictions after the *Expedia* ruling. VAN DER VIJVER, VOLLERING, 2013, pp. 1139-1143, noting that according to the *Expedia* decision there is no need for an appreciability test after an agreement was found to be a restriction by object. (full pp.1133-1144).

1708. European Commission, *FAQs, Antitrust: Commission adopts revised safe harbours for minor agreements ("De Minimis Notice") and provides guidance on "by object" restrictions of competition*, MEMO/14/440, Brussels 25.06.2014, pp. 1-2. Available at: http://europa.eu/rapid/press-release_MEMO-14-440_en.htm. (last accessed on March 31, 2018). *See also* WAGNER-VON PAPP, 2015.

there are cases in the context of trans-border trade, in which a restriction – despite not being appreciable – is found to have an appreciable effect on trade. Determining the appreciability or the lack thereof of a restraint is not a simple task. As analysed in the following section, the Commission uses market thresholds in an attempt to establish a safe harbour within which restraints do not presumptively have an appreciable effect on competition. Another approach is the qualitative one, whereby even if the parties to an agreement have market power, the agreement itself may have insignificant effects on competition.[1709]

2.2 The EU Commission's *De Minimis* Notices

Before analysing the provisions of the Commission's *de minimis* notices it should be stressed that these notices have no binding legal effect for NCAs or courts;[1710] they have however a "self-binding" effect for the EU Commission.[1711] The 2001 *de minimis* notice followed a relatively simple structure. On the basis of the notice, horizontal restraints below a market share of 15% and non-horizontal restrains below a market share of 10% benefited from the safe harbour of the *de minimis* notice, except hardcore, anticompetitive by object restraints which were prohibited irrespective of the relevant market share.[1712] The 2001 notice contained an exhaustive negative checklist of hardcore restrictions which could *not* benefit from the *de minimis* notice, making the assessment of the possibility of exemption simple and rather predictable.[1713]

In 2014, the EU Commission published a new *de minimis* notice which replaced the 2001 version. The scope of the 2014 notice is narrower and excludes *all* restrictions by object, while it only covers agreements which may have as their effect the prevention, restriction or distortion of competition in the internal market.[1714] Nevertheless, restrictions by object may still fall outside the prohibition of Article 101(1)

1709. *See* for instance Judgment of the Court of 12 September 2000, Joined Cases C-180/98 to C-184/98, *Pavel Pavlov and Others v. Stichting Pensioenfonds Medische Specialisten*, EU:C:2000:428, paras 90-97, finding that because of the cost imposed by a decision had only a marginal and indirect influence on the final cost of the services offered, the restriction did not have an appreciable effect, not linking this finding to the market power of the concerned medical specialists.
1710. Judgment of the Court of 28 June 2005, Joined Cases C-189/02 P, C-202/02 P, C-205/02 P to C-208/02 P and C-213/02 P, *Dansk Rørindustri A/S (C-189/02 P), Isoplus Fernwärmetechnik Vertriebsgesellschaft mbH and Others (C-202/02 P), KE KELIT Kunststoffwerk GmbH (C-205/02 P), LR af 1998 A/S (C-206/02 P), Brugg Rohrsysteme GmbH (C-207/02 P), LR af 1998 (Deutschland) GmbH (C-208/02 P) and ABB Asea Brown Boveri Ltd (C-213/02 P) v. Commission of the European Communities*, EU:C:2005:408, para. 209; Judgment of the Court of 29 September 2011, Case C-520/09 P, *Arkema SA v. European Commission*, EU:C:2011:619, para. 88; Judgment of the Court of 14 June 2011, Case C-360/09, *Pfleiderer AG v. Bundeskartellamt*, EU:C:2011:389, para. 21; Opinion of Advocate General Kokott, delivered on 6 September 2012, Case C-226/11, *Expedia Inc.*, EU:C:2012:544, paras 26-34.
1711. WAGNER-VON PAPP, 2015.
1712. EU Commission, *De Minimis Notice*, 2001, paras 2, 7, 8. *See also* Judgment of the Court of 13 December 2012, Case C-226/11, *Expedia Inc. v. Autorité de la concurrence and Others*, EU:C:2012:795, para. 38.
1713. EU Commission, *De Minimis Notice*, 2001, paras 2-3.
1714. EU Commission, *De Minimis Notice*, 2014, p. 1-4, para. 14. *See also* PAZZI, 2014, pp. 246-249.

TFEU, in the unlikely case they fulfil the conditions of the Article 101(3) TFEU exemption or because they are – in exceptional cases – objectively necessary for an agreement to exist or for a legitimate goal to be attained.[1715] The exhaustive list of hardcore restrictions that did not benefit from *de minimis* was replaced in the 2014 Notice by an illustrative list of hardcore restrictions,[1716] "which is without prejudice to any developments in the case law and in the Commission's decisional practice."[1717]

Agreements covered by block exemptions benefit from the *de minimis* safe harbour, to the extent that they contain restraints which are not listed as hardcore, but nevertheless are not covered by block exemptions.[1718] The safe harbour market share thresholds, which are used as a proxy to determine the lack of market power of the undertakings involved, remained the same in the 2014 notice.[1719] Restrictions falling below the market shares of 15% (for horizontal restrictions) and of 10% (for non-horizontal restrictions) are still considered not to have an appreciable effect on competition. These thresholds do create safe harbours for agreements falling below them, but do not establish a presumption of appreciability for the agreements exceeding them: the latter may also have a negligible effect on competition and not be caught by Article 101(1) TFEU.[1720] The 2014 notice does not define what constitutes an appreciable effect on trade between Member States and merely refers to the Commission's Notice on effect on trade.[1721] Nevertheless it does acknowledge that agreements of minor importance between small and medium size undertakings (SMEs) are rarely capable of appreciably affecting trade.[1722]

The Commission's 2014 guidance on restrictions by object which may benefit from the *de minimis* notice does not define which agreements may fall under the *de minimis* exception; on the contrary it focuses on the definition of agreements which do *not* fall under it. This approach was criticised as problematic; if a restraint is not included in the illustrative list of the *de minimis* notice, it shall be assessed on a case-by-case basis in order to determine whether it falls under the notice or not, diminishing the effectiveness and utility of the safe-harbour exception which is designed to avoid exactly this kind of analysis.[1723]

E *Exceptions under Article 101(3) TFEU*

In case a restriction on competition is found to fall under Article 101(1) TFEU, but the conditions set in Article 101(3) TFEU are satisfied, the agreement at issue shall not be

---

1715. EU Commission, *Guidance on restrictions by object*, 2014, pp. 3-4.
1716. EU Commission, *De Minimis Notice*, 2014, para. 13.
1717. EU Commission, *Guidance on restrictions by object*, 2014, p. 5.
1718. EU Commission, *De Minimis Notice*, 2014, para. 14.
1719. EU Commission, *De Minimis Notice*, 2014, para.8; EU Commission, *De Minimis Notice*, 2001, para. 7.
1720. EU Commission, *De Minimis Notice*, 2014, para. 3.
1721. EU Commission, *De Minimis Notice*, 2014, para. 4, referring to EU Commission, *Guidelines: effect on trade in Articles 81 & 82*, 2004, paras 44-57.
1722. EU Commission, *De Minimis Notice*, 2014, para. 4, fn. 5.
1723. Nagy Csongor, 2015, p. 158.

prohibited and no prior decision to that effect is required.[1724] The antitrust defendant claiming the benefit of the exception of Article 101(3) TFEU bears the burden of proving that the conditions of this exception are met.[1725]

1 Four Cumulative Conditions for an Exemption under Article 101(3) TFEU

Four cumulative conditions must be met in order for an agreement to be exempted from Article 101(1) TFEU: (1) the agreement shall contribute to improving the production or distribution of goods or to promoting technical or economic progress; (2) it shall attribute to consumers a fair share of the resulting benefit; (3) it shall not impose on the concerned undertakings restrictions which are not indispensable in order to attain these objectives; and (4) it shall not accord the undertakings the possibility to eliminate competition in a substantial part of the products in question.[1726] If all four conditions are fulfilled, then the agreement arguably enhances competition in the relevant market since it leads to the production and offer of better or lower-priced products to consumers, thereby compensating them for any adverse effects produced by the restriction imposed on competition.[1727] The goal of compensating consumers and offsetting such compensation with the relevant anticompetitive harm of the agreement shows that the consumer welfare approach is not limited within the US borders but prevails in the competition laws of the European Union too.

A claim for an exception under Article 101(3) TFEU needs to be substantiated to allow the verification of the following elements: (1) the nature of the claimed efficiencies; (2) the causal link between agreement and claimed efficiencies; (3) the likelihood and magnitude of each efficiency; and (4) how and when the efficiency could be achieved.[1728] In case an antitrust defendant is claiming cost efficiencies, it must calculate or estimate – as reasonably possible and through verifiable data – the value of the claimed efficiency gain while describing in detail how the amount was computed. The method through which the efficiency gain was achieved shall also be described.[1729]

2 From Individual Exemptions to Self-Assessment

Before the enactment of Regulation No. 1/2003, the EU Commission had the sole power of granting individual exemptions to agreements notified to it on the basis of Regulation

---

1724. Article 1(2), Regulation No. 1/2003.
1725. Article 2, Regulation No. 1/2003. *See also* EU Commission, *Article 81(3) Guidelines*, 2004, para. 11.
1726. Article 101(3) TFEU; Judgment of the Court of 23 November 2006, Case C-238/05, *Asnef-Equifax v. Ausbanc*, para. 65; Judgment of the Court of 7 February 2013, Case C-68/12, *Protimonopolný úrad Slovenskej republiky v. Slovenská sporiteľňa a.s.*, EU:C:2013:71, para. 36. *See also* EU Commission, *Article 81(3) Guidelines*, 2004, para. 34.
1727. EU Commission, *Article 81(3) Guidelines*, 2004, para. 34.
1728. EU Commission, *Article 81(3) Guidelines*, 2004, para. 51. *See also* EU Commission Decision, *Servier*, 2014, para. 2066, referring to the Guidelines.
1729. EU Commission, *Article 81(3) Guidelines*, 2004, para. 56.

17 of 1962.[1730] The system of notifications aiming at the grant of individual exemptions was problematic and overburdened the Commission, preventing it from concentrating on the pursuit of cartels and abusive behaviour, while it imposed high costs on undertakings.[1731] Regulation No. 1/2003 replaced the system of notifications to a "self-assessment" by the undertakings, which are responsible for conducting their own analysis of the agreement under the conditions of Article 101(3) TFEU. Despite the initial scepticism on the administrability of the self-assessment system, business and law firms were able to successfully adapt to it[1732] with the assistance of reports and best practices publications by the Commission.[1733] Under Regulation No. 1/2003, there are three possible ways for the Commission to find that an agreement satisfies the requirements of Article 101(3) TFEU: (1) accepting undertakings' legally binding commitments under Article 9 of Regulation No. 1/2003; (2) a finding of inapplicability of Article 101(1) TFEU on the basis of Article 10 of Regulation No. 1/2003, and (3) a provision of informal guidance in cases presenting novel or unresolved questions.[1734]

3   Restrictions by Object Can Also Fall under Article 101(3) TFEU

In its decision in *Matra*, the General Court of the EU (then Court of First Instance) has held that in principle *any* anticompetitive practice can be exempted under Article 101(3) TFEU, no matter its effects on the market.[1735] This position has been affirmed multiple times by the CJEU, which confirmed that undertakings are entitled to assert an exception under Article 101(3) TFEU "in all circumstances."[1736] There are severe restrictions of competition which are unlikely to fulfil the conditions of Article 101(3)

1730. EEC Council, Regulation No. 17: First Regulation implementing Articles 85 and 86 of the Treaty, Official Journal 013, 21/02/1962, p. 0204-0211.
1731. Recital 3, Regulation No. 1/2003; WHISH, BAILEY, *Competition Law*, 2015, p. 176.
1732. EU Commission, *Staff Working Paper Regulation No. 1/2003*, 2009, paras 11-12.
1733. See for instance European Commission, *Practical methods to assess efficiency gains in the context of Article 81(3) of the EC Treaty*, Final report, May 6, 2005. See also European Commission DG Competition, *Best practices for the submission of economic evidence and data collection in cases concerning the application of Articles 101 and 102 TFEU and in Merger cases*, 2010, pp. 1-20. Available at: http://ec.europa.eu/competition/consultations/2010_best_practices/best_practice_submissions.pdf. (last accessed on March 31, 2018).
1734. Recital 38, Articles 9-10, Regulation No. 1/2003. See also WHISH, BAILEY, *Competition Law*, 2015, pp. 268-276, analysing the above-mentioned articles of Regulation No. 1/2003.
1735. Judgment of the Court of First Instance of 15 July 1994, Case T-17/93, *Matra Hachette SA v. Commission of the European Communities*, EU:T:1994:89, para. 85.
1736. See for instance Judgment of the Court of 13 October 2011, Case C-439/09, *Pierre Fabre Dermo-Cosmétique SAS v. Président de l'Autorité de la concurrence and Ministre de l'Économie, de l'Industrie et de l'Emploi*, EU:C:2011:649, para. 57, "an undertaking has the option, in all circumstances, to assert, on an individual basis, the applicability of the exception provided for in Article 101(3) TFEU." See also Judgment of the Court of 20 November 2008, Case C-209/07, *Competition Authority v. Beef Industry Development Society Ltd and Barry Brothers (Carrigmore) Meats Ltd*, EU:C:2008:643, paras 21, 39, finding that any justifications for a restriction by object would have to be made under Article 101(3) TFEU; Judgment of the Court of 6 October 2009, Joined Cases C-501/06 P, C-513/06 P, C-515/06 P and C-519/06 P, *GlaxoSmithKline Services Unlimited v. Commission of the European Communities (C-501/06 P) and Commission of the European Communities v. GlaxoSmithKline Services Unlimited (C-513/06 P) and European Association of Euro Pharmaceutical Companies (EAEPC) v. Commission of the European Communities (C-515/06 P) and Asociación de exportadores*

TFEU, such as price fixing and limiting, controlling or sharing markets. These restrictions may lead to transfers of value from consumers to producers without providing any countervailing value to consumers.[1737]

A finding by the Commission of a restriction by object is not the equivalent of a per se offence under Section 1 of the Sherman Act. An agreement that constitutes a restriction by object could still fall under the exception of Article 101(3) TFEU if the conditions of said provision are met.[1738] This is not the case with per se illegal restraints under US antitrust law. If a restraint belongs to the per se illegal restraints, a conclusive presumption of illegality applies; the parties do not have the possibility to claim any procompetitive justifications, while courts do not need to examine the intent behind the constraint nor the restraint's actual effect on competition.[1739] The possibility for a restriction by object to fall under the exemption of Article 101(3) is not merely theoretical: in *Société Air France*, the Commission allowed an extensive alliance between two airlines which amounted to a restriction by object.[1740]

F Block Exemption Regulations and Guidelines

Another way to fulfil the conditions of exemption under Article 101(3) TFEU is to draft an agreement satisfying one of the block exemptions issued by the European Council or the Commission: if an agreement falls under a block exemption, it is valid without the need to first consider whether it violates Article 101(1) TFEU.[1741] Once an agreement is

---

españoles de productos farmacéuticos (Aseprofar) v. Commission of the European Communities (C-519/06 P), EU:C:2009:610, paras 159-164.
1737. EU Commission, *Article 81(3) Guidelines*, 2004, para. 46.
1738. Speech of Alexander Italianer, Director-General for Competition, European Commission, "Competitor agreements under EU competition law," September 26, 2013, New York, U.S.A., Fordham Competition Law Institute. Available at: http://ec.europa.eu/competition/speeches/text/sp2013_07_en.pdf, pp. 7-8.
1739. *Arizona v. Maricopa County. Medical Soc.*, 102 S. Ct. 2466, 2473 (1982); *National College Athletic Ass'n ("NCAA") v. Board of Regents*, 104 S. Ct. 2948, 2959 (1984); *Eastman Kodak Co. v. Image Technical Services, Inc.*, 112 S. Ct. 2072, 2091-2092 (1992) (Judge Scalia, dissenting), "Per se rules of antitrust illegality are reserved for those situations where logic and experience show that the risk of injury to competition [...] is so pronounced that it is needless and wasteful to conduct the usual judicial inquiry into the balance between the behavior's procompetitive benefits and its anticompetitive costs." See further *supra*, Chapter 3, Part 1, on per se illegal restraints under US antitrust laws.
1740. 2004/841/EC: Commission Decision of 7 April 2004 relating to a proceeding pursuant to Article 81 of the EC Treaty concerning case COMP/A.38284/D2 – Société Air France/Alitalia Linee Aeree Italiane SpA (notified under document number C(2004) 1307), OJ L 362, 9.12.2004, p. 17-20; Case AT.39595 – Continental/United/Lufthansa/Air Canada, Commission Decision of 23 May 2013, relating to proceedings pursuant to Article 101(3) of the Treaty on the Functioning of European Union, C(2013) 2836 final, Brussels, 23.5.2013, paras 55-79; WHISH, BAILEY, *Competition Law*, 2015, pp. 161-163.
1741. Judgment of the Court of 2 April 2009, Case C-260/07, *Pedro IV Servicios SL v. Total España SA*, EU:C:2009:215, para. 36; EU Commission, *Guidelines on Vertical Restraints*, 2010, para. 101.

covered by a block exemption, it is automatically exempt from the prohibition of Article 101(1) TFEU; there is a rebuttable presumption that the cumulative conditions of Article 101(3) are met and parties are relieved from the relevant burden of proof.[1742] Agreements that are valid under a block exemption cannot be declared invalid by a national court;[1743] on the contrary, the Commission and the NCAs have in certain circumstances the power to withdraw the benefit of a block exemption.[1744] If an agreement does not fall under the scope of a block exemption, a national court may not extend the block exemption's scope so as for it to cover the agreement. The general rule regarding block exemptions is that if the conditions of exemption are not met, then the regulations cease to apply in their entirety.[1745]

The Commission is authorised to grant block exemptions to vertical agreements and to bilateral licences of intellectual property rights.[1746] It is also authorised to grant block exemptions with regard to standardisation agreements, R&D agreements and specialisation agreements;[1747] the insurance sector;[1748] agreements between SMEs in

---

1742. EU Commission, *Article 81(3) Guidelines*, 2004, para. 35.
1743. EU Commission, *Article 81(3) Guidelines*, 2004, para. 2.
1744. Article 29, Regulation No. 1/2003.
1745. JONES, SUFRIN, 2014, p. 264. However, under the block exemptions on vertical and technology transfer agreements, some of the relevant agreements' provisions may benefit from the block exemption, while the exemption may be inapplicable for other provisions of the same agreement.
1746. On the basis of Regulation No. 19/65/EEC of 2 March of the Council on application of Article 85(3) of the Treaty to certain categories of agreements and concerted practices, OJ 36, 6.3.1965, p. 533-535, as amended by Council Regulation (EC) No. 1215/1999 of 10 June 1999 amending Regulation No. 19/65/EEC on the application of Article 81(3) of the Treaty to certain categories of agreements and concerted practices OJ L 148, 15.6.1999, p. 1-4, the following Block Exemption Regulations are in force: Commission Regulation (EU) No. 330/2010 of 20 April 2010 on the application of Article 101(3) of the Treaty on the Functioning of the European Union to categories of vertical agreements and concerted practices, OJ L 102, 23.4.2010, p. 1-7; Commission Regulation (EU) No. 461/2010 of 27 May 2010 on the application of Article 101(3) of the Treaty on the Functioning of the European Union to categories of vertical agreements and concerted practices in the motor vehicle sector, OJ L 129, 28.5.2010, p. 52-57, and; Commission Regulation (EU) No. 316/2014 of 21 March 2014 on the application of Article 101(3) of the Treaty on the Functioning of the European Union to categories of technology transfer agreements, OJ L 93, 28.3.2014, p. 17-23.
1747. On the basis of Regulation (EEC) No. 2821/71 of the Council of 20 December 1971 on application of Article 85(3) of the Treaty to categories of agreements, decisions and concerted practices, OJ L 285, 29.12.1971, p. 46-48, two Block Exemption Regulations are in force: Commission Regulation (EU) No. 1217/2010 of 14 December 2010 on the application of Article 101(3) of the Treaty on the Functioning of the European Union to certain categories of research and development agreements, OJ L 335, 18.12.2010, p. 36-42, and; Commission Regulation (EU) No. 1218/2010 of 14 December 2010 on the application of Article 101(3) of the Treaty on the Functioning of the European Union to certain categories of specialisation agreements, OJ L 335, 18.12.2010, p. 43-47.
1748. Council Regulation (EEC) No. 1534/91 of 31 May 1991 on the application of Article 85(3) of the Treaty to certain categories of agreements, decisions and concerted practices in the insurance sector, OJ L 143, 7.6.1991, p. 1-3, based on which the Commission adopted Commission Regulation (EU) No. 267/2010 of 24 March 2010 on the application of Article 101(3) of the Treaty on the Functioning of the European Union to certain categories of agreements, decisions and concerted practices in the insurance sector, OJ L 83, 30.3.2010, p. 1-7.

Chapter 5: The European Regulatory Framework

the road and inland waterway sectors;[1749] consortia between liner shipping companies[1750] and agreements in the air-transport sector.[1751] Block exemptions are adopted for a certain period of time and kept under constant review during that period.[1752] Before 1999, Block Exemption Regulations ordinarily specified a narrow category of restrictions that could be permissible in an agreement and a list of prohibited, black-listed restrictions.[1753] After the adoption of Regulation No. 2790/1990, Block Exemption Regulations follow an economic approach: agreements which meet specific market thresholds, satisfy the set conditions and do not contain hardcore restraints are generally unlikely to raise anticompetitive concerns.[1754] Hardcore restraints are listed in various Block Exemption Regulations and their presence in an agreement precludes the application of the exemption; in the Commission's view, hardcore restraints presumptively violate Article 101(1) TFEU and are generally unlikely to satisfy the conditions of Article 101(3) TFEU.

Understanding the block exemptions which could potentially apply to horizontal agreements is essential before analysing patent settlements between actual or potential competitors in the pharmaceutical sector. Parties to reverse payment settlements in the European Union in both the *Lundbeck* and the *Servier* case invoked the provisions of Block Exemption Regulations in order to avoid the application of Article 101(1) TFEU.[1755] The following sections present the European Union rules on horizontal cooperation agreements: the 2011 Guidelines on horizontal cooperation agreements;[1756] the Research & Development Block Exemption Regulation 1217/2010;[1757] and Regulation 1218/2010, the Block Exemption Regulation for specialisation agreements.[1758] The Technology Transfer Block Exemption Regulation 316/2014 is also

---

1749. Council Regulation (EC) No. 169/2009 of 26 February 2009 applying rules of competition to transport by rail, road and inland waterway, OJ L 61, 5.3.2009, p. 1-5.
1750. Council Regulation (EC) No. 246/2009 of 26 February 2009 on the application of Article 81(3) of the Treaty to certain categories of agreements, decisions and concerted practices between liner shipping companies (consortia), OJ L 79, 25.3.2009, p. 1-4.
1751. Council Regulation (EC) No. 487/2009 of 25 May 2009 on the application of Article 81(3) of the Treaty to certain categories of agreements and concerted practices in the air-transport sector, OJ L 148, 11.6.2009, p. 1-4.
1752. *See also* JONES, SUFRIN, 2014, pp. 263-266, discussing block exemptions.
1753. JONES, SUFRIN, 2014, p. 265.
1754. *Idem.*
1755. *See infra* Chapter 6, Part 1, Sections II and III on the analysis of the *Lundbeck* and the *Servier* cases respectively.
1756. EU Commission, *101 TFEU Guidelines*, 2011, replacing European Commission, Notice, *Guidelines on the applicability of Article 81 of the EC Treaty to horizontal cooperation agreements*, OJ C 3, 6.1.2001.
1757. Commission Regulation (EU) No. 1217/2010 of 14 December 2010, on the application of Article 101(3) of the Treaty on the Functioning of the European Union to certain categories of research and development agreements, OJ L 335, 18.12.2010, p. 36-42, replacing Commission Regulation (EC) No. 2659/2000 of 29 November 2000 on the application of Article 81(3) of the Treaty to categories of research and development agreements, OJ L 304, 5.12.2000, p. 7-12.
1758. Commission Regulation (EU) No. 1218/2010 of 14 December 2010, on the application of Article 101(3) of the Treaty on the Functioning of the European Union to certain categories of specialisation agreements, OJ L 335, 18.12.2010, p. 43-47.

discussed.[1759] However, the Block Exemption Regulation 330/2010 on the application of Article 101(3) on vertical agreements and concerted practices is not discussed, since it does not apply to vertical agreements concluded between competing undertakings.[1760] The vertical Block Exemption Regulation does not apply exceptionally if both parties to a vertical agreement – such as a distribution agreement – are manufacturers of the goods in question, a situation that may be typical in distribution agreements of pharmaceuticals.[1761]

1 Guidelines on Horizontal Cooperation Agreements

In 2011, the EU Commission published new guidelines on horizontal cooperation agreements, replacing the 2001 edition.[1762] The 2011 Guidelines concern cooperation agreements between actual and potential competitors and touch upon a plurality of subjects such as information exchange, R&D, production, purchasing, commercialisation and standardisation. Cooperation agreements may lead to substantial economic benefits and be used to share risk, save costs, while increasing investment and innovation and enhancing product quality and variety.[1763] However, such agreements may also lead to competition problems, if for instance they enable parties to maintain or increase market power.[1764] The purpose of the guidelines on horizontal cooperation Agreements is to provide an analytical framework for the most common types of such agreements with the aim to ensure that effective competition is maintained.[1765] Adapting to the evolving reality of horizontal cooperation agreements, the 2011 Guidelines considerably extended the scope of the R&D Block Exemption Regulation, which now covers not only joint R&D activities but also "paid-for research agreements."[1766] The new Guidelines also revised substantially the provisions on

---

1759. Commission Regulation (EU) No. 316/2014 of 21 March 2014 on the application of Article 101(3) of the Treaty on the Functioning of the European Union to categories of technology transfer agreements, OJ L 93, 28.3.2014, p. 17-23.
1760. Article 2(4), Commission Regulation (EU) No. 330/2010 of 20 April 2010 on the application of Article 101(3) of the Treaty on the Functioning of the European Union to categories of vertical agreements and concerted practices, OJ L 102, 23.4.2010, p. 1-7.
1761. See Article 2(4), Regulation (EU) No. 330/2010. See also EU Commission Decision, *Lundbeck*, 2013, para. 720, finding that said regulation did not apply to the distribution parts of the agreement between Lundbeck, Merck and Ranbaxy. See further *infra*, Chapter 6, Part 1, Section II on the analysis of the Lundbeck decision.
1762. EU Commission, *101 TFEU Guidelines*, 2011. See also European Commission, Public Consultation, *Revised Rules for the Assessment of Horizontal Cooperation Agreements under EU Competition Law*, from 04.05.2010 to 25.06.2010. Available at: http://ec.europa.eu/competition/consultations/2010_horizontals/. (last accessed on March 31, 2018); DREXL ET AL., 2010.
1763. EU Commission, *101 TFEU Guidelines*, 2011, para. 2.
1764. EU Commission, *101 TFEU Guidelines*, 2011, para. 3.
1765. EU Commission, *101 TFEU Guidelines*, 2011, paras 4-5.
1766. EU Commission, *101 TFEU Guidelines*, 2011, paras 111-149. See also, European Commission, *FAQs, Commission Adopts Revised Competition Rules on Horizontal Co-operation Agreements*, MEMO/10/676, Brussels, 14 December 2010. Available at: http://europa.eu/rapid/press-release_MEMO-10-676_en.htm?locale=en. (last accessed on March 31, 2018) [cited as: EU Commission, *FAQs: Horizontal Co-operation Agreements*, 2010].

standardisation and introduced new provisions on information exchange,[1767] while stressing the need for self-assessment by undertakings.[1768]

2 The Research and Development Block Exemption Regulation

Regulation 1217/2010 is the current version of the R&D Block Exemption Regulation which replaced Regulation 2659/2000 and will be in force until the end of 2022.[1769] In line with the objectives set by Article 179(2) TFEU,[1770] the R&D Block Exemption Regulation aims to encourage undertakings of all sizes to engage into R&D and to support their efforts of cooperation, while effectively protecting competition.[1771] A R&D agreement is defined as an agreement entered to by two or more parties relating to the conditions under which the parties pursue: (1) joint R&D of contract products or technologies, including or excluding the joint exploitation of its results; (2) joint exploitation of the results of R&D on contract products or technologies, carried out in accordance with a prior agreement; (3) paid-for R&D of contract products or technologies, including or excluding the joint exploitation of its results; (4) joint exploitation of the results of paid-for R&D of contract products or technologies pursuant to a prior agreement between the same parties.[1772]

R&D agreements may be exempted from the application of Article 101(1) TFEU, pursuant to Article 101(3) TFEU and the provisions of the R&D Block Exemption Regulation.[1773] The block exemption also extends to the provisions of R&D agreements on the assignment or licensing of IP rights, under the condition that these provisions do not constitute the primary object of the R&D agreement but are directly related and necessary for the agreement's implementation.[1774] For a block exemption to be granted to an R&D agreement, the conditions of Article 3 of Regulation 1217/2010 must be met: one of the most fundamental ones is that all parties shall have full access to the final results of the joint R&D or paid-for R&D, for the purposes of further research, development or exploitation. Nevertheless, access to exploitation may be limited by the parties or may require compensation.[1775] If the agreement provides only for joint R&D

1767. EU Commission, *101 TFEU Guidelines*, 2011, Chapter 7 on standardisation agreements; Chapter 2 on the competitive assessment of information exchange.
1768. *See also* EU Commission, *FAQs: Horizontal Co-operation Agreements*, 2010.
1769. Commission Regulation (EU) No. 1217/2010 of 14 December 2010, on the application of Article 101(3) of the Treaty on the Functioning of the European Union to certain categories of research and development agreements, OJ L 335, 18.12.2010, p. 36-42, replacing Commission Regulation (EC) No. 2659/2000 of 29 November 2000 on the application of Article 81(3) of the Treaty to categories of research and development agreements, OJ L 304, 5.12.2000, p. 7-12.
1770. Recital 2, Regulation 1217/2010, referring to Article 179(2) TFEU, which calls upon the EU to encourage undertakings, including SMEs, to engage in R&D and to cooperate with one another.
1771. Recital 2, Regulation 1217/2010.
1772. Article 1(1)(a), Regulation 1217/2010.
1773. Article 2, Regulation 1217/2010.
1774. Article 2(2), Regulation 1217/2010.
1775. Article 3(2), Regulation 1217/2010. With regard to access to exploitation, *see further* WHISH, BAILEY, *Competition Law*, 2015, p. 633, giving the example of a pharmaceutical company which enters into an R&D agreement with a university, and can require under Article 3(2),

or paid-for R&D, it shall also provide that each party shall be granted access to any preexisting know-how of the other parties, if indispensable for exploiting the obtained results.[1776] Under an R&D agreement, any joint exploitation may only concern results protected under IP rights or know-how which are indispensable for the manufacture of the contract products or the application of the contract technologies.[1777] Finally, in the context of exploitation, parties charged with the manufacture of contract products must be required to fulfil orders for supplies from the other parties, except if joint distribution is provided for in the agreement.[1778]

The duration of the exemption granted by the R&D block exemption depends on whether the parties are competitors or not; if the parties are not competitors, it may extend to the whole duration of the R&D agreement and may continue to apply seven years after the relevant products or technologies are first put in the EU market, where the results are jointly exploited.[1779] If the parties are not competitors, their market shares are irrelevant; however, if they are competitors, their joint market share at the time of the agreement shall not exceed 25%.[1780] The R&D Block Exemption Regulation contains a list of hardcore restrictions that cannot benefit from the block exemption, such as the restriction of the parties' possibility to carry R&D independently in a field unrelated to the R&D agreement, the limitation of output or sales (with certain exceptions), the fixing of prices when selling the contract product or technologies to third parties, etc.[1781] Additionally, two restrictions are listed as excluded from the R&D block exemption: (1) the obligation not to challenge the validity of the IP rights held by the parties in the internal market and relevant to the R&D agreement, and; (2) the obligation not to grant licences to third parties allowing them to manufacture the contract products or to apply the contract technologies, unless if the agreement provides for the exploitation of said products or technologies in the internal market by at least one of the parties, vis-à-vis third parties.[1782] As is the case with all block exemptions, the benefit of the R&D block exemption may be withdrawn by the Commission or the NCAs, pursuant to Article 29 of Regulation 1/2003, if the agreement is found to have effects which are incompatible with Article 101(3) TFEU.[1783]

Regulation 1217/2010, its partner not to exploit the results commercially but to limit itself only to further research. The goal is to prevent the commercialisation of the results by the partner, which would be a major disincentive for the company to engage in beneficial R&D agreements.

1776. Article 3(3), Regulation 1217/2010; the agreement may also provide for compensation for giving such access to know-how, under the condition that such compensation is not so high as to impede effective access to the know-how.
1777. Article 3(4), Regulation 1217/2010.
1778. Article 3(5), Regulation 1217/2010.
1779. Article 4(1), Regulation 1217/2010.
1780. Article 4(2), Regulation 1217/2010. *See also idem* Article 7, on the application of the market share threshold.
1781. *See* further Article 5, Regulation 1217/2010.
1782. Article 6, Regulation 1217/2010.
1783. Article 29, Regulation 1/2003. *See also* Recitals 18-21, Regulation 1217/2010, discussing the withdrawal of the benefit of the R&D Block Exemption.

3 The Block Exemption Regulation on Specialisation Agreements

Regulation 1218/2010 is the Block Exemption Regulation for specialisation agreements, covering unilateral and reciprocal specialisation agreements and joint production agreements which may improve the production or distribution of goods by enabling parties to operate more efficiently and supply cheaper products.[1784] A specialisation agreement is defined as an agreement by virtue of which one or more parties agree to fully or partly cease production of certain products or to refrain from producing them and to purchase them from another party, which agrees to produce and supply these products.[1785] A joint production agreement, as plainly revealed by its name, is an agreement under which two or more parties agree to produce products jointly.[1786]

Pursuant to Article 2 of the Block Exemption Regulation on specialisation agreements and Article 101(3) TFEU, a block exemption from the application of Article 101(1) is granted.[1787] This exemption shall apply to specialisation agreements containing clauses relating to the assignment and licensing of IP, provided that they do not constitute the primary objective of the agreement,[1788] while it shall also apply to specialisation agreements providing for an exclusive purchase or supply obligation, under which the parties jointly distribute the products.[1789] The combined market share of all parties shall not exceed 20% on any relevant market for the block exemption to apply.[1790] However, in case this threshold is exceeded, there is no presumption that Article 101(1) TFEU is infringed or that the conditions of Article 101(3) TFEU are not satisfied; an individual assessment of the agreement is required.[1791] The Block Exemption Regulation on specialisation agreements also contains a list of hardcore restrictions such as price fixing when selling the relevant products to third parties, the limitation of output or sales and the allocation of markets or consumers: the inclusion of these restrictions will normally mean that the agreement falls outside the scope of the block exemption as a whole.[1792] Similarly to the other block exemptions, the benefit of the block exemption on specialisation agreements may be withdrawn by either the

---

1784. Article 1, Commission Regulation (EU) No. 1218/2010 of 14 December 2010, on the application of Article 101(3) of the Treaty on the Functioning of the European Union to certain categories of specialisation agreements, OJ L 335, 18.12.2010, p. 43-47. *See idem* Recitals 6, 7, presenting the efficiency arguments in favour of the specialisation agreements.
1785. Article 1(1), Regulation 1218/2010. In unilateral specialisation agreements one party only ceases or refrains from production, while in reciprocal agreements both parties cease or refrain from production and purchase the relevant products from another party.
1786. Article 1(1), Regulation 1218/2010.
1787. Article 2(1), Regulation 1218/2010.
1788. Article 2(2), Regulation 1218/2010.
1789. Article 2(3), Regulation 1218/2010.
1790. Article 3, Regulation 1218/2010. *See also idem*, Article 5, setting rules for the application of this market threshold.
1791. Recital 10, Regulation 1218/2010.
1792. Article 4, Regulation 1218/2010. It should be noted that the article itself provides for some exceptions: for instance the setting of sales targets in the context of joint distribution is not considered to be a hardcore restriction, albeit limiting sales. Similarly, fixing prices charged to immediate consumers, in the context of joint distribution is not considered to be a hardcore restriction.

Commission or an NCA if the agreement's effects on the market are incompatible with Article 101(3) TFEU, e.g., in case the market is already highly concentrated so that competition is already weak.[1793]

4 The Technology Transfer Block Exemption Regulation

4.1 The 2014 Technology Transfer Block Exemption Regulation

The Technology Transfer Block Exemption Regulation (TTBER) is a Block Exemption Regulation which is of major importance for the analysis of patent settlements in the pharmaceutical sector under EU competition law. In 2014, Regulation 316/2014 replaced the previous TTBER Regulation 772/2004, in an attempt to facilitate the sharing of IP and to provide clear guidance on licensing agreements which stimulate competition.[1794] The TTBER will only apply if the Block Exemption Regulation on R&D agreements[1795] and the Block Exemption Regulation on specialisation agreements[1796] are not applicable.[1797]

The TTBER provides for a block exemption of technology transfer agreements, to which Article 101(1) TFEU shall not apply.[1798] Technology transfer agreements are licensing agreements in which the licensor authorises the licensee(s) to use the former's technology in order to produce goods or services.[1799] Under the TTBER, technology is defined as know-how and patents, utility models, designs, topographies or semiconductor products, SPCs for medicinal products, plant breeders' rights and software copyright.[1800] It should be stressed that the exemptions granted by the TTBER are only valid as long as the underlying licensed IP right has not expired, lapsed or been declared invalid.[1801] The block exemption will apply until the date on which the last underlying IP right expires, becomes invalid or enters the public domain.[1802]

Under the 2014 TTBER, the block exemption also applies to the provisions of the technology transfer agreement which do not constitute technology rights and relate to

---

1793. Recitals 13-15, Regulation 1218/2010.
1794. European Commission, *FAQs, Antitrust: Commission adopts revised competition regime for technology transfer agreements – frequently asked questions*, Brussels, 21 March 2014. Available at: http://europa.eu/rapid/press-release_MEMO-14-208_en.htm (last accessed on March 31, 2018) [cited as: EU Commission, *FAQs: Revised TTBER*, 2014].
1795. Commission Regulation (EU) No. 1217/2010 of 14 December 2010 on the application of Article 101(3) of the Treaty on the Functioning of the European Union to certain categories of research and development agreements, OJ L 335, 18.12.2010, p. 36-42.
1796. Commission Regulation (EU) No. 1218/2010 of 14 December 2010 on the application of Article 101(3) of the Treaty on the Functioning of the European Union to certain categories of specialisation agreements, OJ L 335, 18.12.2010, p. 43-47.
1797. Recital 7, Article 9, Regulation 316/2014.
1798. Article 2(1), Regulation 316/2014.
1799. Article 1(1)(c), Regulation 316/2014.
1800. Article 1(1)(b), Regulation 316/2014.
1801. Article 2(2), Regulation 316/2014. In case of know-how, the Article clarifies that the block exemption applies as long as the know-how remains secret; if however the know-how becomes public as a result of an action by the licensee, the exemption shall apply for the licensing agreement's duration.
1802. Article 2(2), Regulation 316/2014.

the purchase of products by the licensee or to the licensing and assignment of other IP rights or know-how, if those provisions are directly related to the production or sale of the contract products.[1803] It thus makes it easier for ancillary provisions to benefit from the block exemption, in comparison to its predecessor, TTBER 2004, which applied to ancillary provisions only if they did not constitute the primary object of the agreement and so long as they were directly related to the application of the licensed technology.[1804] Another amendment brought by the 2014 TTBER is that unlike the 2004 TTBER,[1805] it does not provide for an exemption for a restriction on passive sales by licensees to exclusive territories or customer groups. Under the 2014 TTBER, such restrictions on passive sales by licensees – while normally hardcore restrictions – may fall outside Article 101(1) TFEU, for a limited time-period of generally two years, if they are objectively necessary for the licensee to penetrate a new market.[1806]

The TTBER covers only bilateral licensing agreements, concluded between two undertakings for the purpose of production of contract products by the licensee or its subcontractors.[1807] However, the Commission's 2014 Guidelines on technology transfer agreements also cover multiparty patent pool agreements.[1808] In particular, the TTBER exempts from the prohibition of Article 101 TFEU licensing agreements concluded between companies which have limited market power: agreements between competitors whose combined market shares do not exceed 20% and agreements between non-competitors whose individual market shares do not exceed 30% are exempted, provided that they do not contain certain severely anticompetitive restrictions.[1809] These low market shares create the presumption that the agreements at issue do not contain certain severe anticompetitive restrictions, they lead to the improvement of production or distribution and allow consumers a certain share of the resulting

---

1803. Article 2(3), Regulation 316/2014. For an overview of the 2014 TTBER amendments *see* LUGARD, 2014, pp. 51-59.
1804. Recital 9, Article 1(1)(b), Commission Regulation (EC) No. 772/2004 of 27 April 2004 on the application of Article 81(3) of the Treaty to categories of technology transfer agreements, OJ L 123, 27.4.2004, p. 11-17. *See also* WHISH, BAILEY, *Competition Law*, 2015, p. 826.
1805. *See* Article 4(2)(b)(ii), Commission Regulation (EC) No. 772/2004 of 27 April 2004 on the application of Article 81(3) of the Treaty to categories of technology transfer agreements, OJ L 123, 27.4.2004, p. 11-17.
1806. EU Commission, *Technology Transfer Agreements Guidelines*, 2014, para. 126. According to the 2014 Guidelines, such restrictions will be "objectively necessary," if for example a licensee aims to enter a new market and needs to substantially invest in order to do so. In that case, the licensee may be protected from other licensees' passive sales in the first two years of operating in the market, without infringing Article 101(1) TFEU.
1807. Article 1(1)(c), Regulation 316/2014; EU Commission, *Technology Transfer Agreements Guidelines*, 2014, paras 56, 60, noting that the TTBER does not apply to technology licence agreements allowing for sub-licensing. *See also* Recital 7, Regulation 316/2014 noting that the TTBER applies only to licensing agreements in wpahich a licensor permits the licensee to exploit the licensed technology for the production of goods or services.
1808. EU Commission, *Technology Transfer Agreements Guidelines*, 2014, paras 57, 244-273, replacing the European Commission, Notice, Guidelines on the application of Article 81 of the EC Treaty to technology transfer agreements, OJ C 101, 27.4.2004. *See also* WHISH, BAILEY, *Competition Law*, 2015, pp. 834-838, discussing the application of Article 101 TFEU to technology pools.
1809. Recitals 10, 11 and Article 3(2), 3(3) Regulation 316/2014. *See also* EU Commission, *Technology Transfer Agreements Guidelines*, 2014, paras 82-85.

benefits.[1810] Nevertheless, there is no presumption that agreements between undertakings which exceed these market thresholds are infringing Article 101(1) TFEU.[1811]

Article 4 TTBER lists a number of restrictions – contained in both horizontal and vertical agreements – which are considered to be "hardcore," do not fall under the TTBER and are unlikely to benefit from the exemptions of Article 101(3) TFEU.[1812] If an agreement contains any of these hardcore restrictions, it is excluded in its entirety from the benefit of the block exemption. Such restrictions in horizontal agreements are for instance restrictions on a party's ability to determine its prices towards third parties, some agreements having as their object the limitation of output, the allocation of markets and customers or agreements imposing restrictions on the licensee's ability to exploit its own technology.[1813] With regard to vertical agreements, hardcore restrictions that fall outside the scope of the TTBER are restrictions concerning prices, territories and customer groups or sales within selective distribution systems.[1814] The Commission considers that licensing agreements containing one of Article's 4 hardcore restrictions shall be viewed as restrictions by object.[1815] On some occasions, restrictions are treated as hardcore only if the relevant agreement is reciprocal.[1816]

The underlying concern of the Commission in establishing this list of hardcore restrictions is that competitors may use technology transfer agreements in order to conceal agreements which are or have the effect of cartels.[1817] However, there is no presumption that agreements which fall out of the scope of the TTBER are caught under the prohibition of Article 101(1) TFEU and cannot benefit from the exemption of Article 101(3) TFEU.[1818] This lack of "negative" presumptions would be rather unlikely in the 1970s-1980s and marks the Commission's shift towards a more economics-oriented approach to the application of competition laws.[1819] Generally, the TTBER follows the logic that if something is not explicitly prohibited in its provisions, it is allowed. The Commission could thus only take action and allege that a technology transfer agreement falls under Article 101(1) TFEU, by arguing that it imposes one of the hardcore restrictions of Article 4 TTBER, or that it constitutes an "excluded restriction" within

---

1810. Recitals 10, 11, Regulation 316/2014; EU Commission, *Technology Transfer Agreements Guidelines*, 2014, para. 5. It should be noted that the market shares have not changed in the 2014 TTBER Regulation. For a synopsis of the main substantive changes brought by the 2014 TTBER *see* EU Commission, *FAQs: Revised TTBER*, 2014.
1811. EU Commission, *Technology Transfer Agreements Guidelines*, 2014, para. 43.
1812. Article 4, Regulation 316/2014; EU Commission, *Technology Transfer Agreements Guidelines*, 2014, para. 18.
1813. Article 4(1), Regulation 316/2014.
1814. Article 4(2), Regulation 316/2014.
1815. EU Commission, *Technology Transfer Agreements Guidelines*, 2014, para. 14.
1816. *See* Article 1(1)(d), 1(1)(e), Regulation 316/2014, for the definitions of reciprocal and non-reciprocal agreements under the TTBER. *See also* Article 4(1)(b), 4(1)(c) Regulation 316/2014, and the distinctions it draws between reciprocal and non-reciprocal agreements, and EU Commission, *Technology Transfer Agreements Guidelines*, 2014, para. 98, discussing this distinction.
1817. EU Commission, *Technology Transfer Agreements Guidelines*, 2014, paras 97-116.
1818. EU Commission, *Technology Transfer Agreements Guidelines*, 2014, para. 43.
1819. WHISH, BAILEY, *Competition Law*, 2015, p. 825. *See idem* pp. 823-834, analysing the provisions of Regulation 316/2014.

the meaning of Article 5 TTBER, or alternatively by withdrawing the benefit of the regulation on the basis of Article 6 TTBER.[1820]

Article 5 TTBER mentions three excluded restrictions: (1) the imposition of a direct obligation to the licensee to grant an exclusive licence to the licensor on its own improvements to the licensed technology; (2) a direct or indirect non-challenge clause, under which a party undertakes the obligation not to challenge the validity of the IP rights the other party holds in the EU; and (3) any direct or indirect obligation of the licensee not to exploit its own technology or any limitation of either party's ability to conduct R&D, when the parties are not competitors.[1821] The matter of non-challenge clauses was among the 2014 amendments. Under the 2004 TTBER, the licensor had the possibility to terminate the agreement and deny to the licensee the right to use the relevant technology in case the licensee challenged the validity of the relevant patent rights.[1822] However, non-challenge clauses may be anticompetitive under certain circumstances: under the 2014 TTBER, non-challenge clauses combined with termination provisions are exempted from the benefit of the block exemption only in the context of exclusive licence agreements.[1823] These restrictions of Article 5 TTBER are excluded from the block exemption in an effort to protect incentives to innovate; nevertheless, in contrast to the hardcore restrictions of Article 4 TTBER, the block exemption could still apply to the remaining clauses of the technology transfer agreement which includes excluded restrictions, provided that the remaining clauses are severable from the excluded clauses.[1824]

Agreements below the TTBER's defined market thresholds which do not include any of the hardcore restrictions of Article 4 TTBER or the excluded restrictions of Article 5 TTBER do not normally eliminate competition in a substantial part of the concerned products.[1825] However, Article 6 TTBER grants the Commission or NCAs the possibility to proceed to such a withdrawal if the technology transfer agreement has effects which are incompatible with Article 101(3) TFEU.[1826] The burden of proof lies with the withdrawing authority, which shall show that the agreement falls under Article 101(1) TFEU and that the conditions of Article 101(3) TFEU are not satisfied.

1820. Articles 4, 5, 6, Regulation 316/2014; WHISH, BAILEY, *Competition Law*, 2015, p. 825.
1821. Article 5, Regulation 316/2014. With regard to non-challenge clauses, the TTBER allows however the existence of a clause terminating an exclusive technology transfer agreement in case the licensee challenges the validity of any of the challenged technology rights. Moreover, limitations to exploit own technology or on the parties' ability to conduct R&D can be exceptionally permitted if indispensable to prevent the disclosure of the licensed know-how to third parties.
1822. Article 5(1)(c), Regulation 772/2004.
1823. Article 5(1)(b), Regulation 316/2014.
1824. Recital 15, Regulation 316/2014.
1825. Recital 16, Regulation 316/2014.
1826. Recitals 17, 18, Article 6, Regulation 316/2014. Such withdrawal of the TTBER Block Exemption benefit is done on the basis of Article 29(1), Regulation 1/2003, when for instance access of third parties' technologies or access of potential licences to the market is restricted.

4.2 The 2014 TTBER Guidelines

The Commission published new guidelines on the application of the 2014 TTBER which included one significant amendment that is of particular relevance for this book since it concerns settlement agreements.[1827] The 2014 Guidelines recognise that settlement agreements in the context of technology disputes on whether a patent is valid or infringed are generally a legitimate and efficient way to reach a compromise to a dispute; nevertheless, the public interest in the elimination of weak or invalid patents shall also be borne in mind since such patents constitute a barrier to innovation and economic activity.[1828] Even though licensing is not generally caught under Article 101(1) TFEU, since it is not as restrictive of competition and allows parties to exploit the licensed technologies, individual terms and conditions of settlement agreements may still fall under the prohibition.[1829] For instance, settlements which may limit or delay the licensee's ability to launch the relevant product in any of the concerned markets may be prohibited.[1830]

Importantly, the 2014 Guidelines refer to pay-for-delay agreements and note that such settlements do not ordinarily involve any technology transfer and are thus caught by Article 101(1) TFEU.[1831] Taking into consideration the evolving types of settlements, the Commission notes that pay-for-delay settlements which are combined with a licensing agreement of the technology rights concerned in the underlying dispute, may fall under Article 101(1) TFEU if they result in a delayed or limited ability for the licensee to launch the relevant product on any of the markets concerned; such settlements shall be analysed under Article 4(1)(c) and 4(1)(d) of the TTBER as they will be considered hardcore restrictions and will not fall within the scope of the TTBER exemptions.[1832] The risk of market allocation/market sharing in such settlement agreements will increase if the parties are actual or potential competitors and if there was a large value transfer from the licensor to the licensee.[1833] The block exemption will not apply to the technology transfer agreement as a whole if it includes such hardcore provisions.[1834]

With regard to cross-licensing agreements which impose restrictions on the use of the licensed technologies and on the licensing to third parties, the Guidelines note that

---

1827. EU Commission, *Technology Transfer Agreements Guidelines*, 2014, replacing EU Commission, *Article 81(3) Guidelines*, 2004.
1828. EU Commission, *Technology Transfer Agreements Guidelines*, 2014, para. 235.
1829. EU Commission, *Technology Transfer Agreements Guidelines*, 2014, paras 236-237.
1830. EU Commission, *Technology Transfer Agreements Guidelines*, 2014, paras 236-243.
1831. EU Commission, *Technology Transfer Agreements Guidelines*, 2014, para. 238. *See also*, EU Commission Decision, *Lundbeck*, 2013, para. 677, finding that the TTBER Guidelines did not apply since there was no transfer of technology in any of the relevant agreements, without employing any further analysis. *See* however, EU Commission Decision, *Servier*, 2014, paras 2097-2012, analysing in detail why the Servier settlements could not benefit from the TTBER Block Exemption. *See* further Chapter 6, Part 1, Sections II and III analysing the Lundbeck and the Servier Commission decisions.
1832. EU Commission, *Technology Transfer Agreements Guidelines*, 2014, para. 239; Article 4(1)(c), 4(1)(d), Regulation 316/2014.
1833. EU Commission, *Technology Transfer Agreements Guidelines*, 2014, para. 239.
1834. EU Commission, *Technology Transfer Agreements Guidelines*, 2014, para. 95.

they are likely to be caught by the prohibition of Article 101(1) TFEU if the parties have a strong market position and the agreement's restrictions go beyond what is necessary in order to unblock.[1835] If such an agreement extends to future developments, the agreement's impact on the parties' incentives to innovate shall also be assessed: if the parties have significant market power and the agreement prevents the parties from gaining a competitive lead over each other, the agreement is likely to fall under Article 101(1) TFEU and unlikely to satisfy the exemption conditions of 101(3) TFEU.[1836]

Finally, non-challenge clauses, whereby the parties agree not to challenge *ex post* the underlying IP rights of the dispute, are inherent in settlement agreements and generally fall outside the prohibition of Article 101(1) TFEU.[1837] The Commission raises a crucial point and notes that "the restriction of the freedom to challenge an intellectual property right *is not* part of the specific subject matter of an intellectual property right and may restrict competition."[1838] It should be stressed that if the underlying IP right was granted on the basis of misleading or fraudulent information – and is thus likely invalid – a non-challenge clause may be anticompetitive and fall under Article 101(1) TFEU.[1839] If the licensee is financially or otherwise induced by the licensor not to challenge the validity of the licensed technology rights or if these rights are a necessary input for the licensee's production, the scrutiny of any non-challenge clauses is necessary.[1840]

III Article 102 TFEU

Before providing an overview of the main points concerning Article 102 TFEU, it should be noted that this book focuses on horizontal patent settlement agreements between competitors and potential competitors in the pharmaceutical sector under Article 101 TFEU. However, due to the increasing sophistication of the settlement agreements and of other techniques developed in order to delay generic drug entry in both the EU and the US, this analysis would not be complete without a reference – even if limited – to competition law provisions targeting the abuse of dominance position and related strategies. As analysed in Chapter 6, cases involving reverse payment settlements were also combined with other strategies, e.g., SPCs or naming and shaming strategies

---

1835. EU Commission, *Technology Transfer Agreements Guidelines*, 2014, para. 240, noting also that Article 101(1) is particularly likely to apply if the parties share markets or fix reciprocal running royalties which have a significant impact on prices.
1836. EU Commission, *Technology Transfer Agreements Guidelines*, 2014, para. 241. See also ROBERT, FALCONI, 2006, pp. 526-527, discussing the antitrust analysis of cross-licensing, which differs depending on whether the licensed technologies are competing or complementary. If the parties are not competitors, cross-licensing is unlikely to cause antitrust concerns; however, if the cross-licensing covers substitutable technologies or the alleged blocking position is a mere sham, then it is most likely problematic from an antitrust perspective.
1837. EU Commission, *Technology Transfer Agreements Guidelines*, 2014, para. 242.
1838. EU Commission, *Technology Transfer Agreements Guidelines*, 2014, para. 243.
1839. *Idem.*
1840. *Idem.*

which are scrutinised under Article 102 TFEU, rather than Article 101 TFEU. Articles 101 and 102 TFEU are not mutually exclusive and may apply simultaneously to the same contractual agreements.[1841]

A Introduction to Article 102 TFEU

Article 102 TFEU deals with monopoly and market power, focusing on the unilateral behaviour of undertakings which hold a dominant position. It prohibits dominant undertakings from eliminating a competitor and from strengthening their position through the use of methods which are outside the scope of competition on the merits.[1842] Moreover, it imposes on dominant undertakings a special responsibility not to impair genuine undistorted competition in the internal market through their conduct, irrespectively of the reasons due to which they obtained a dominant position.[1843] The prohibition of abuse of dominance does not only aim at practices or behaviour which may cause damage to consumers directly, but also at practices which are detrimental for consumers through their impact on the structure of effective competition.[1844]

Article 102 TFEU prohibits any abuse by one or more undertakings having a dominant position within the internal market or a substantial part of the internal market, to the extent that such abuse may affect trade between Member States.[1845] The requirement of appreciability of the abuse under Article 102 TFEU is identical to the same requirement under Article 101 TFEU: the concept of "effects on trade" is

---

1841. Judgment of the Court of 13 February 1979, Case 85/76, *Hoffmann-La Roche & Co. AG v. Commission of the European Communities*, EU:C:1979:36, para. 116; Judgment of the Court of 16 March 2000, Joined Cases C-395/96 P and C-396/96 P, *Compagnie maritime belge transports SA (C-395/96 P), Compagnie maritime belge SA (C-395/96 P) and Dafra-Lines A/S (C-396/96 P) v. Commission of the European Communities*, EU:C:2000:132, para. 112 (Judgment of the Court of 16 March 2000, Joined cases C-395/96 P and C-396/96 P, *Compagnie maritime belge Transports and others v. Commission*; Judgment of the Court of 21 February 1973, Case 6/72, *Europemballage Corporation and Continental Can Company Inc. v. Commission of the European Communities*, EU:C:1973:22, para. 33. See also IBÁÑEZ COLOMO, 2016, pp. 728-730, discussing how exclusive dealing may be a restriction of competition by effect under Article 101 TFEU but is a prima facie prohibited when it falls under Article 102 TFEU.
1842. Judgment of the Court of 6 December 2012, C-457/10 P, *AstraZeneca AB and AstraZeneca plc v. European Commission*, EU:C:2012:770, para. 75 (Judgment of the General Court of 1 July 2010, Case T-321/05, *AstraZeneca v. Commission*); Judgment of the Court of First Instance of 7 October 1999, T-228/97, *Irish Sugar plc v. Commission of the European Communities*, EU:T:1999:246, para. 111; Judgment of the Court of 3 July 1991, Case C-62/86, *AKZO Chemie BV v. Commission of the European Communities*, EU:C:1991:286, para. 70 (Judgment of the Court of 3 July 1991, Case C-62/86, *AKZO Chemie BV v. Commission*).
1843. Judgment of the Court of 9 November 1983, Case 322/81, *NV Nederlandsche Banden Industrie Michelin v. Commission of the European Communities*, EU:C:1983:313, para. 57; Judgment of the Court of 27 March 2012, Case C-209/10, *Post Danmark A/S v. Konkurrencerådet*, EU:C:2012:172, para. 23.
1844. Judgment of the Court of 17 February 2011, C-52/09, *Konkurrensverket v. TeliaSonera Sverige AB*, EU:C:2011:83, para. 24.
1845. Article 102 TFEU.

Chapter 5: The European Regulatory Framework

interpreted in the same fashion for both articles.[1846] Both exclusionary and exploitative abuses by a dominant undertaking, which extend in more than one Member State, are normally considered to be capable of affecting trade between Member States by their very nature.[1847]

The concept of undertaking under Article 102 is identical to the concept of undertaking under Article 101 TFEU.[1848] Typically, dominant undertakings are operating under *quasi*-monopolistic conditions and are able to restrict output and increase prices without losing substantial sales to competitors: this is the kind of abuse that Article 102 TFEU aims to prevent. The prohibition of Article 102 TFEU applies only to the conduct of undertakings which are already dominant at the market at the time of abuse; however, it does not apply to anticompetitive conduct through which an undertaking achieves dominance or to abuses by non-dominant undertakings which cause consumer harm despite the lack of dominance.[1849] In order for Article 102 TFEU to apply, four elements shall be established: (1) the presence of one or more undertakings; (2) a dominant position, held within the internal market or a substantial part of it; (3) an abuse; and (4) an effect on trade between Member States.

The main problems on the application of Article 102 TFEU are linked to the notions of dominance and of abuse. The high difficulties of showing that an undertaking is dominant or that it has committed an abuse, along with the severe consequences such a finding has, make the application of Article 102 TFEU rather problematic for the European Commission and for European courts. Not all exclusionary practices are subject to the same principles;[1850] conduct such as exclusive dealing or royalty rebates are typically considered as prima facie illegal irrespective of their impact on competition,[1851] whereas other practices like margin squeeze or refusals to deal are only prohibited if their exclusionary effects have been shown.[1852] It is argued that some types of rebates and discounts are treated as per se illegal since their foreclosure effects can be *inferred* and thus need not to be proven;[1853] however, since there is the

---

1846. *See supra*, Chapter 5, Part 2, Section II.D.1, on the analysis of the appreciability requirement under Article 101 TFEU.
1847. EU Commission, *Guidelines: effect on trade in Articles 81 & 82*, 2004, paras 73-76.
1848. *See supra* Chapter 5, Part 2, Section II.A analysing the concept of undertaking under Article 101 TFEU.
1849. JONES, SUFRIN, 2014, p. 270.
1850. *See further* IBÁÑEZ COLOMO, 2016, pp. 712-720, discussing the legal status of some of the main categories of exclusionary behaviour.
1851. Judgment of the Court of First Instance of 30 September 2003, Case T-203/01, *Manufacture française des pneumatiques Michelin v. Commission of the European Communities*, EU:T:2003:250, paras 235-246; Judgment of the Court of 15 March 2007, Case C-95/04 P, *British Airways plc v. Commission of the European Communities*, EU:C:2007:166, paras 96-100 (Judgment of the Court of 15 March 2007, Case C-95/04 P, *British Airways plc v. Commission*).
1852. Judgment of the Court of 14 October 2010, Case C-280/08 P, *Deutsche Telekom AG v. European Commission*, EU:C:2010:603, paras 250-251, confirming that anticompetitive effects need to be demonstrated in case of a pricing practice by a dominant undertaking which leads to the margin squeeze of its equally efficient competitors; confirmed in Judgment of the Court of 17 February 2011, C-52/09, *Konkurrensverket v. TeliaSonera Sverige AB*, EU:C:2011:83, para. 61.
1853. *See* for instance Judgment of the Court of First Instance of 30 September 2003, Case T-203/01, *Manufacture française des pneumatiques Michelin v. Commission of the European Communities*, EU:T:2003:250, paras 56, 65-66; WAELBROECK, 2005, pp. 152-160, criticising the *Michelin*

possibility to objectively justify such rebates, it is obvious that they are treated as presumptively illegal and not as illegal per se.[1854]

B Defining and Detecting Dominance in the Internal Market

Article 102 TFEU does not contain a definition of dominance nor does it determine a procedure in order to declare an undertaking as dominant. In its settled case law, the CJEU defines dominance as a position of economic strength an undertaking enjoys, enabling it to prevent the maintenance of effective competition on the relevant market and granting it the ability to behave independently of its competitors, customers and consumers.[1855] A dominant position does not preclude the existence of *some* competition in the market but allows the dominant undertaking to determine or exercise an appreciable influence onthe conditions of competition.[1856] The possibilities of competition shall be examined within a market comprising the totality of products which are particularly suitable to satisfy constant needs with respect to their characteristics and are interchangeable with other products only to a limited extent; these possibilities of competition shall be assessed with regard to competitive conditions and the structure of both demand and supply.[1857] Dominance can be found both on the buying and on the selling side. The Commission must define the market and analyse the conditions of competition in each and every decision applying Article 102 TFEU, while it cannot rely

---

II decision for rejecting the effect criterion and for concluding that any pricing behaviour by a dominant undertaking is per se illegal. *See also* Judgment of the General Court of 9 September 2010, Case T-155/06, *Tomra Systems ASA and Others v. European Commission*, EU:T:2010:370, paras 208-210, stating that on the basis of a consistent line of decisions, a fidelity rebate by a dominant undertaking is contrary to Article 82 EC (now Article 102 TFEU).

1854. *See* for example Judgment of the General Court of 12 June 2014, Case T-286/09, *Intel Corp. v. European Commission*, EU:T:2014:547, paras 81, 94, referring to the possibility of objectively justify such a restriction by means of an efficiency defence.

1855. Judgment of the Court of 14 February 1978, Case 27/76, *United Brands Company and United Brands Continentaal BV v. Commission of the European Communities, Chiquita Bananas*, EU:C:1978:22, para. 65; Judgment of the Court of 13 February 1979, Case 85/76, *Hoffmann-La Roche & Co. AG v. Commission of the European Communities*, EU:C:1979:36, para. 38. *See also* Judgment of the Court of 17 February 2011, C-52/09, *Konkurrensverket v. TeliaSonera Sverige AB*, EU:C:2011:83, para. 23; Judgment of the Court of 14 October 2010, Case C-280/08 P, *Deutsche Telekom AG v. European Commission*, EU:C:2010:603, para. 170; Judgment of the Court of 2 April 2009, Case C-202/07 P, *France Télécom SA v. Commission of the European Communities*, EU:C:2009:214, para. 103. For a critical discussion of the criterion to act "independently of consumers and customers" *see*, WALKER, AZEVEDO, 2002, pp. 364-365.

1856. Judgment of the Court of 13 February 1979, Case 85/76, *Hoffmann-La Roche & Co. AG v. Commission of the European Communities*, EU:C:1979:36, para. 39.

1857. Judgment of the General Court of 1 July 2010, Case T-321/05, *AstraZeneca v. Commission*, para. 31; Judgment of the Court of 9 November 1983, Case 322/81, *NV Nederlandsche Banden Industrie Michelin v. Commission of the European Communities*, EU:C:1983:313, para. 37; Judgment of the Court of First Instance of 21 October 1997, Case T-229/94, *Deutsche Bahn AG v. Commission of the European Communities*, EU:T:1997:155, para. 54; Judgment of the Court of First Instance of 17 December 2003, *British Airways plc v. Commission*, para. 91.

Chapter 5: The European Regulatory Framework

on previous findings of dominance.[1858] The concerned undertakings typically favour a wide market definition, since the broader the market, the more unlikely is a finding of dominance.[1859]

1   Product Market Definition

In order to examine whether an undertaking is dominant within a given market, the first essential step of analysis is to define the relevant market.[1860] The relevant market is generally comprised by all the products or services which are regarded as substitutable by consumers, due to their characteristics, prices and intended use.[1861] The purpose of defining the relevant market is to identify the undertakings which are capable of constraining the behaviour of the allegedly dominant undertaking and to prevent it from behaving independently of "effective competitive pressure."[1862] Such competitive constraints are demand and supply substitutability and potential competition.[1863]

1.1   Qualitative Versus Quantitative Criteria and the SSNIP Test

There are two different groups of criteria on the basis of which the relevant product market can be defined: qualitative and quantitative. In a number of decisions the CJEU has opted for an analysis of qualitative elements in order to determine the relevant product market. For instance, in *United Brands* the CJEU found that the relevant product market was limited to bananas: relying on specific physical, functional and economic characteristics of bananas, such as their easy handling, softness and taste, the court found that there was a small degree of interchangeability between bananas and other kinds of fresh fruit.[1864]

The Commission generally favours quantitative over qualitative criteria in order to measure the relevant substitutability of products and has adopted the SSNIP test for

---

1858. Judgment of the Court of First Instance of 22 March 2000, Joined Cases T-125/97 and T-127/97, *The Coca-Cola Company and Coca-Cola Enterprises Inc. v. Commission of the European Communities*, EU:T:2000:84, para. 82.
1859. *See* however Judgment of the Court of 3 July 1991, Case C-62/86, *AKZO Chemie BV v. Commission*, paras 34, 37-45, where AKZO argued for a narrow market definition but the Court confirmed the Commission's definition of the relevant market.
1860. Judgment of the Court of 21 February 1973, Case 6/72, *Europemballage Corporation and Continental Can Company Inc. v. Commission of the European Communities*, EU:C:1973:22, para. 32. In *Continental Can* the Court annulled the EU Commission's decision for failing to properly define the market on the supply side.
1861. Judgment of the General Court of 1 July 2010, Case T-321/05, *AstraZeneca v. Commission*, para. 31. European Commission, *Commission Notice on the definition of relevant market for the purposes of Community competition law*, OJ C 372, 9.12.1997, para. 7. [cited as: EU Commission, *Notice on the definition of relevant market*, 1997].
1862. *See* further EU Commission, *Notice on the definition of relevant market*, 1997, para. 2.
1863. EU Commission, *Notice on the definition of relevant market*, 1997, para. 13.
1864. Judgment of the Court of 14 February 1978, Case 27/76, *United Brands Company and United Brands Continentaal BV v. Commission of the European Communities, Chiquita Bananas*, EU:C:1978:22, paras 12-35. *See also* JONES, SUFRIN, 2014, pp. 306-309, criticising the decision.

measuring the elasticity of demand.[1865] The main inquiry under the SSNIP test is to determine whether a small but significant non-transitory increase on the price of product A will shift purchasers to buy sufficient of the substitute product B so as to render product A's price increase unsustainable.[1866] If after such a price increase consumers switch from product A to product B, then the two products form part of the same market. The SSNIP test has been approved by the General Court in *AstraZeneca*;[1867] however, the test raises practical problems in its application, such as the difficulties in accurately predicting consumers' reactions. Another major problem is the infamous "cellophane fallacy:" high cross-elasticity of demand between products may occur because of monopoly power and not because of the consumers' belief that the concerned products are good substitutes for one another.[1868] The Commission further recognises that the prevailing price charged by the allegedly dominant undertaking is most probably raised above competitive levels since it was determined in the absence of effective competition.[1869] The SSNIP test is not able to identify whether the current price of the product is already a monopoly price which results from the exercise of market power: this could lead to an overbroad definition of the relevant market.

1.2 Product Market Definition in the Pharmaceutical Sector

Certain specific features of the pharmaceutical sector differentiate it from other industries and shall be taken into consideration when defining the relevant market. Such features are for instance the existence of a classification system on the basis of which drug products are grouped according to their functional interchangeability. The market of pharmaceuticals is publicly regulated to a high degree, especially with regard to market authorisation, pricing and reimbursement rules, while the demand side is

---

1865. See further OECD Roundtable, *Note by the European Union*, 2012, pp. 3-6, describing the process of defining the relevant market in the EU practice. Available at: http://ec.europa.eu/competition/international/multilateral/2012_jun_market_definition_en.pdf (last accessed on March 31, 2018). *See* however *idem* p. 5, noting that the Commission increasingly uses quantitative economic tools such as price correlation analysis, critical loss analysis and demand estimation in order to refine its market definition analysis.
1866. European Commission, Communication, *Guidance on the Commission's enforcement priorities in applying Article 82 of the EC Treaty to abusive exclusionary conduct by dominant undertakings*, OJ C 45/7, 24.2.2009, paras 17-18 [cited as: EU Commission, *Guidance in applying Article 82*, 2009].
1867. Judgment of the General Court of 1 July 2010, Case T-321/05, *AstraZeneca v. Commission*, paras 86-87.
1868. The "cellophane fallacy" originates from the US Supreme Court decision of *United States v. E. I. du Pont de Nemours & Co.*, 76 S. Ct. 994 (1956), commonly known as the Cellophane case, in which the Supreme Court erroneously concluded that Du Pont did not have significant market power since cellophane did not constitute a separate relevant market but directly and closely competed with packaging materials such as polythen, aluminium foil or wax paper. *See* further BAKER J., Market Definition, 2007, extensively discussing the problem of cellophane fallacy.
1869. EU Commission, *Notice on the definition of relevant market*, 1997, para. 19. *See also* European Commission, *DG Competition discussion paper on the application of Article 82 of the Treaty to exclusionary abuses*, Brussels, December 2005, p. 7, para. 13. Available at: http://ec.europa.eu/competition/antitrust/art82/discpaper2005.pdf. (last accessed on March 31, 2018) [cited as: EU Commission, *Discussion Paper Article 82*, 2005].

Chapter 5: The European Regulatory Framework

characterised by a low degree of patients' involvement in the choice of their treatment since prescribing doctors are the main determinant of demand.[1870] The potential substitutability of medicines or therapies in day-to-day medical practice and the actual trends in the consumption of prescribed medicines are key-factors for assessing competitive constraints between different categories of medicines.[1871]

The "price disconnect" that was already analysed in the US part of this book, also applies in the EU: prescribing doctors are primarily guided by the drug's therapeutic advantages, effectiveness and appropriateness and not by its price. This price disconnect extends to patients, who despite being the drugs' ultimate consumers, do not normally bear the entire cost of the prescription medicine; in an effort to remedy this disconnect, public authorities have instituted a high degree of price control. The influence on the pricing of pharmaceuticals exercised by public health systems confers *more* market power to pharmaceutical companies, compared to a system where the final consumer would bear the full cost of medication, due to the inelastic demand in the pharmaceuticals' markets in the EEA.[1872] This inelasticity derives from both the above-described "price disconnect" of the prescribing doctor who does not bear the cost for the prescribed medication and from the fact that the final consumer is most usually fully or partially insured against the cost of the medication.[1873]

The general principles of market definition also apply to the pharma sector cases: in order to define the relevant market, one shall not examine whether products compete against each other on the broad sense but whether the products concerned are sufficiently substitutable to significantly constrain each other's market power, especially as far as pricing is concerned.[1874] Not all functionally interchangeable products need to be included in the relevant market: products shall be considered as differentiated even if they can be broadly used for the same purposes but differ in terms of price, quality, consumer preferences or other important attributes.[1875] Thus, in order to define the functional interchangeability of medicines in the context of product market definition, it does not suffice to determine the different medicines that are prescribed for the same general health condition; the varying degrees of medicines' efficiency and appropriateness are also crucial factors and may result to the definition of different and possibly narrower product markets.[1876] Even though such differentiated products could potentially compete on some dimensions, the relevant market definition in competition

---

1870. 2006/857/EC: Commission Decision of 15 June 2005 relating to a proceeding under Article 82 of the EC Treaty and Article 54 of the EEA Agreement (Case COMP/A.37.507/F3 – AstraZeneca) (notified under document number C(2005) 1757), OJ L 332, 30.11.2006, para. 362 [cited as: EU Commission Decision, *AstraZeneca*, 2005].
1871. *Idem*.
1872. EU Commission Decision, *AstraZeneca*, 2005, para. 554.
1873. *Idem*.
1874. EU Commission Decision, *AstraZeneca*, 2005, para. 370.
1875. *Idem. See also* Judgment of the Court of 6 December 2012, Case C-457/10 P, *AstraZeneca v. Commission*, para. 59.
1876. EU Commission Decision, *AstraZeneca*, 2005, para. 381.

law cases should include only products which can considerably constrain an undertaking's behaviour and prevent it from behaving independently of effective competitive pressure.[1877]

In order to define markets in the pharmaceutical sector, the Commission uses as a starting point the third level of the WHO/European Pharmaceutical Marketing Research Association (EphMRA) Anatomical Therapeutical Chemical Classification System (ATC3),[1878] on the basis of which pharmaceutical products are grouped into categories according to their therapeutic indications, e.g., intended use.[1879] If it is clear that the undertakings concerned face sufficiently strong competitive restraints at another level and the ATC3 class does not lead to a correct market definition, the Commission alternatively refers to the fourth level of the WHO/EphMRA Anatomical Therapeutical Chemical Classification System (ATC4), which constitutes a further subdivision based on therapeutic and pharmacological criteria such as molecule class, formulation or mode of action,[1880] or the fifth level (ATC5) which refers to individual active substances.[1881] The Commission occasionally left the exact definition of the relevant product market open because of serious doubts, taking however into consideration the closeness of substitution due to overlaps at a molecule level or an ATC4 level.[1882]

On some instances, the drug's *molecule* is found to be the relevant market: on genericised drug markets against serious health conditions, competition occurs among drugs with the same molecule.[1883] Nevertheless, if it is established that drugs with other molecules are indeed substitutable, then the molecule is excluded from being the relevant market.[1884] The specific characteristics of hospital use and demand are also taken into consideration in the definition of product market. With regard to drugs

---

1877. EU Commission Decision, *AstraZeneca*, 2005, para. 370.
1878. See further EphMRA Website, *Classifications*. Available at: http://www.ephmra.org/ Classification. (last accessed on March 31, 2018).
1879. *See* for instance Case No COMP/M.5476 – PFIZER / WYETH, Commission Decision of 17 July 2009, Regulation (EC) No 139/2004 Merger Procedure – Article 6(1)(b) in conjunction with Article 6(2), EUR-lex document number: 32009M5476, Date: 17/07/2009, paras 15-19, on a merger in the pharmaceutical sector, where the Commission relied on ATC3 level classification for the definition of the relevant market.
1880. *See* Case No COMP/M.5253 – SANOFI-AVENTIS / ZENTIVA, Commission Decision of 4 February 2009, Regulation (EC) No 139/2004 Merger Procedure-Article 6(2) in conjunction with Art 6(2), EUR-lex document number: 32009M5253 Date: 04/02/2009, paras 12-16 [cited as: EU Commission Decision, *SANOFI-AVENTIS / ZENTIVA*, 2009], where the Commission relied on ATC4 level classification. *See also* Greenaway, Jakab, Johansson, Kundan, 2009, p. 64.
1881. EU Commission Decision, *AstraZeneca*, 2005, paras 371-372.
1882. Greenaway, Jakab, Johansson, Kundan, 2009, pp. 64-65, referring to EU Commission Decision, *SANOFI-AVENTIS / ZENTIVA*, 2009, paras 223, 246, on the ATC4 level indicating the closeness of substitution and paras 454, 461, 469, referring to the molecule level.
1883. *See* for instance, Case No COMP/M.5295 – TEVA/BARR, Commission Decision of 19 December 2008, Regulation (EC) No 139/2004 Merger Procedure-Article 6(1)(b) in conjunction with Art 6(2), EUR-lex document number: 32008M5295, Date: 19/12/2008, paras 28-45 [cited as: EU Commission Decision, *TEVA/BARR*, 2008]; Greenaway, Jakab, Johansson, Kundan, 2009, p. 64.
1884. EU Commission Decision, *TEVA/BARR*, 2008, paras 116, 158, 164; EU Commission Decision, *SANOFI-AVENTIS / ZENTIVA*, 2009, paras 109, 140-145, 174-175.

Chapter 5: The European Regulatory Framework

purchased by hospitals, competition occurs between drugs having the same molecule: as far as serious illnesses are concerned, hospitals do not consider switching to drugs based on another molecule even if the drug's price increases considerably.[1885] *Price* can also be an indicator to consider for product market definition, but is by no means conclusive.[1886] The factor of price is of much greater importance in genericised markets than in drug markets where generic entry has not occurred.[1887] Actual demand in terms of sales in relation to pharmaceutical's prices shall be examined as evidence of competitive restraints in the relevant market, taking into consideration the specificities of the pharmaceutical sector.[1888]

A distinction that is highly important for the definition of the product market is the distinction between "over-the-counter" drugs (OTC drugs), which are available without a doctor's prescription, and prescription drug products. The medical indications, the side effects but also the legal framework and the distribution and marketing rules for OTC and prescription drugs can differ considerably, even if their active ingredients are identical. For instance, OTC drugs may be advertised whereas prescription drugs' advertising is generally restricted; OTC drugs are not prescribed and they are not reimbursed in most cases, while prescription drugs must be prescribed by a doctor and part of their purchase price may be reimbursed by the Member State's public healthcare system: these are some of the reasons for which the marketing of prescription drugs is targeting prescribers and not patients.[1889] The EU Commission often relies on this distinction but has clarified that it does not always lead to separate relevant markets.[1890]

Relying on the pharmaceuticals' *modes of action* is an alternative way to define the relevant product market. This approach has been used by the Commission in a number of decisions concluding that drugs with different modes of action did not belong to the same product market.[1891] For instance, in *AstraZeneca*, the Commission

---

1885. EU Commission Decision, *SANOFI-AVENTIS / ZENTIVA*, 2009, paras 80, 292-294, 297-299; EU Commission Decision, *TEVA/BARR*, 2008, para. 17.
1886. EU Commission Decision, *AstraZeneca*, 2005, para. 368, "the degree of price correlation is strongest as between products containing the same active substance (notably an original substance and its generic counterparts);" *See* however, EU Commission Decision, *SANOFI-AVENTIS / ZENTIVA*, 2009, paras 81, 95, stating that price is not a conclusive indicator for defining the product market.
1887. EU Commission Decision, *SANOFI-AVENTIS / ZENTIVA*, 2009, paras 80, 292-294, 297-299; EU Commission Decision, *TEVA/BARR*, 2008, para. 16.
1888. EU Commission Decision, *AstraZeneca*, 2005, para. 400.
1889. EU Commission Decision, *TEVA/BARR*, 2008, para. 12.
1890. EU Commission Decision, *TEVA/BARR*, 2008, paras 12-13, finding that OTC and prescription pharmaceuticals constituted separate product markets; EU Commission Decision, *AstraZeneca*, 2005, para. 384, noting that H2 blockers were OTC, while the vast majority of PPI were prescription drugs (with only one exception for one strength of a PPI that was available as an OTC in Sweden). *See* however EU Commission Decision, *SANOFI-AVENTIS / ZENTIVA*, 2009, paras 51-54, 58-59, not distinguishing between OTC and prescription drug products for the definition of the relevant product market.
1891. Cas No COMP/M.1397 SANOFI / SYNTHELABO, Décision de la Commission de 17 mai 1999, Règlement (CEE) n° 4064/89 sur les concentrations, Article 6, paragraphe 1, point b), CELEX Database: Document No 399M1403 Date: 17/05/1999, para. 30, finding that drugs using different modes of operation (antiplatelet agents, acting on the platelet structure and oral anticoagulants, acting on the coagulation cascade) did not belong in the same product market;

relied on the proton pump inhibitors' (PPI) fundamentally distinct mode of action which differentiated them from histamine receptor antagonists (H2 blockers) and other medicines used in the field of acid-related gastrointestinal conditions: PPIs were therapeutically superior and thus constituted the relevant product market.[1892] The General Court upheld the Commission's definition of product market.[1893] However, this does not mean that two drugs with different modes of action can never belong to the same product market: in *Pfizer/Pharmacia* the Commission found that even though two drugs had different modes of action, they did have an identical indication and a similar diagnosis profile, thus were substitutable.[1894]

2 Geographic Market Definition

2.1 General Criteria of Geographic Market Definition

According to the Commission, the relevant geographic market is defined as the area in which the undertakings concerned are involved in the supply and demand of products or services and in which the conditions of competition are sufficiently homogeneous so that it can be distinguished from neighbouring areas where the conditions of competition are appreciably different.[1895] Already in 1978, in *United Brands*, the CJEU stressed the importance of geographic market definition and provided a nearly identical definition.[1896] The condition of "homogeneity" of conditions of competition does not imply perfect homogeneity; similar or sufficiently homogeneous conditions suffice.[1897] In order to define the geographic market, the Commission takes a preliminary view on the basis of broad indications on the distribution of market shares between the relevant

---

Case No COMP/M.1403 – ASTRA / ZENECA, Commission Decision of 26 February 1999, Regulation (EEC) No 4064/89, Merger Procedure, Article 6(1)(b), CELEX Database: Document No 399M1403, Date: 26/02/1999, paras 37-38, finding that local and general anaesthetics can constitute separate product markets.

1892. EU Commission Decision, *AstraZeneca*, 2005, para. 370. See also Judgment of the Court of 6 December 2012, Case C-457/10 P, *AstraZeneca v. Commission*, paras 373-379. PPIs had a direct blocking effect on the proton pump in the stomach's cells, directly blocking the source of acid secretion in the stomach, in contrast to H2s which acted indirectly and had no direct impact on the pump itself.

1893. Judgment of the General Court of 1 July 2010, Case T-321/05, *AstraZeneca v. Commission*, para. 106. See also Judgment of the Court of 6 December 2012, C-457/10 P, *AstraZeneca v. Commission*, paras 27-60, rejecting both grounds of appeal on the definition of the product market and upholding the General Court's ruling.

1894. Case No COMP/M.2922 – PFIZER / PHARMACIA, Commission Decision of 27 February 2003, Regulation (EEC) No 4064/89, Merger Procedure, Article 6(2), CELEX Database: Document No 303M2922, Date: 27/02/2003, para. 28, finding that Cardura (an alpha-blocker with peripheral action) and Adesipress (an alpha-blocker with central action) competed against each other and were substitutable.

1895. EU Commission, *Notice on the definition of relevant market*, 1997, para. 8.

1896. Judgment of the Court of 14 February 1978, Case 27/76, *United Brands Company and United Brands Continentaal BV v. Commission of the European Communities*, EU:C:1978:22, para. 11.

1897. Judgment of the Court of First Instance of 21 October 1997, Case T-229/94, *Deutsche Bahn AG v. Commission of the European Communities*, EU:T:1997:155, para. 92; Judgment of the Court of First Instance of 6 October 1994, Case T-83/91, *Tetra Pak International SA v. Commission of the European Communities*, EU:T:1994:246, paras 91-92.

parties and their competitors. Pricing and price differences at a national and EU or EEA level are also examined.[1898] National regulation of Member States may create national markets,[1899] while EU regulation may also lead to the creation of narrow markets.[1900] Other factors of influence are high transport costs, consumer preference,[1901] language differences and marketing infrastructures. On these grounds, geographic markets may be defined as the entire territory or part of a Member State, or as a number of Member States.[1902] Finally, it is possible to distinguish between demand-side substitution (which can be based on the SSNIP test) and supply-side substitution also in the geographic dimension of markets.[1903]

2.2 Geographic Market Definition in the Pharmaceutical Sector

All three Commission decisions concerning pharmaceutical products in *AstraZeneca*, in *Lundbeck* and in *Servier* have defined the relevant geographic markets as national.[1904] This national nature of pharmaceuticals' markets derives from the great differences among the national EU Member States' regulatory frameworks on marketing authorisation, pricing and reimbursement rules and on the different incentives and public policies for cheaper generic products and parallel imports.[1905] The harmonisation of rules on a European level is limited to rules on the marketing authorisation of medicinal products, concerning the safety, quality and efficacy requirements for pharmaceuticals, which were analysed in Part 1 of this chapter.[1906] The systems of drug distribution differ widely from one Member State to another, while brand-name drug

---

1898. EU Commission, *Notice on the definition of relevant market*, 1997, para. 28. *See also idem* paras 44-52, on the kind of evidence the Commission uses in order to reach a conclusion as to the geographic market.
1899. *See* for instance, Judgment of the Court of 3 July 1991, Case C-62/86, *AKZO Chemie BV v. Commission*, paras 35, 39, where the market was confined to UK and Ireland which were the only Member States to allow the use of bleaching factors in flour.
1900. 88/518/EEC: Commission Decision of 18 July 1988 relating to a proceeding under Article 86 of the EEC Treaty (Case No IV/30.178 Napier Brown – British Sugar), OJ L 284, 19.10.1988, paras 43-49, defining Great Britain as the relevant geographic market, also due to the effect of Community regulations concerning the quantity of beet-origin sugar.
1901. 92/553/EEC: Commission Decision of 22 July 1992 relating to a proceeding under Council Regulation (EEC) No. 4064/89 (Case No IV/M.190 – Nestlé/Perrier), para. 34, relying on French consumers' preference for national brands among other factors and concluding the relevant geographic market was France.
1902. *See also* Judgment of the Court of 14 February 1978, Case 27/76, *United Brands Company and United Brands Continentaal BV v. Commission of the European Communities*, EU:C:1978:22, paras 36-57, the Court affirming the Commission's definition of the geographic market comprised by the Federal Republic of Germany, Denmark, Ireland, the Netherlands and the Belgium–Luxembourg Economic Union (BLEU).
1903. *See further* PEEPERKORN, VEROUDEN, 2014, pp. 51-52, analysing demand-side substitution and supply-side substitution in the context of geographic market definition.
1904. *See* EU Commission Decision, *AstraZeneca*, 2005, para. 503; EU Commission Decision, *Lundbeck*, 2013, para. 592; EU Commission Decision, *Servier*, 2014, para. 2547.
1905. EU Commission Decision, *AstraZeneca*, 2005, para. 503; EU Commission Decision, *Lundbeck*, 2013, para. 592.
1906. *See infra*, Chapter 6, Part 1. *See also* EU Commission Decision, *AstraZeneca*, 2005, para. 503.

manufacturers use different branding and packaging.[1907] Even the prescribing practices of doctors in different Member States may differ in certain cases.[1908]

3 Defining the Temporal Market

The relevant temporal market is not at all mentioned in the Commission Notice on the definition of the relevant market. The temporal dimension of markets is often ignored, while many markets do not have a temporal dimension.[1909] Nevertheless, the temporal dimension of the market may be essential or even inherent to the definition of product markets in some cases, such as transport markets.[1910] Temporal developments and time factors may still influence the relevant market and the market positions and the Commission takes them into consideration indirectly in the definition of relevant market.[1911] With regard to pharmaceutical product markets, in *Servier* the Commission examined the time-dimension for the purposes of relevant market definition and noted that price rigidity, demand for the relevant drug and switching barriers remained unchanged from 2000 to 2009, for the entire time-period under investigation.[1912]

C Assessing Market Power and Dominance

Once the relevant market is defined, the position of the undertaking in that market and any competitive restraints it faces shall be examined, by analysing the market share of the undertaking concerned and any other factors which may indicate dominance such as barriers to entry and to expansion. The Commission's Guidance Paper on enforcement priorities in applying Article 102 TFEU includes a section on market power: nearly

---

1907. EU Commission Decision, *AstraZeneca*, 2005, para. 503; EU Commission Decision, *Servier*, 2014, para. 2547.
1908. EU Commission Decision, *Servier*, 2014, para. 2547.
1909. JONES, SUFRIN, 2014, pp. 330-331; *See also* Judgment of the Court of 9 November 1983, Case 322/81, *NV Nederlandsche Banden Industrie Michelin v. Commission of the European Communities*, EU:C:1983:313, para. 59, "[...] it must be observed that temporary unprofitability or even losses are not inconsistent with the existence of a dominant position."
1910. *See* for instance Judgment of the Court of First Instance of 15 September 1998, Joined Cases T-374/94, T-375/94, T-384/94 and T-388/94, *European Night Services Ltd (ENS), Eurostar (UK) Ltd, formerly European Passenger Services Ltd (EPS), Union internationale des chemins de fer (UIC), NV Nederlandse Spoorwegen (NS) and Société nationale des chemins de fer français (SNCF) v. Commission of the European Communities*, EU:T:1998:198, paras 84-87, where the Commission argued that ENS's share in the business travel segment should be measured in relation to late evening and early morning flights rather than by reference to all the flights around the clock on a given day; *See also idem* paras 93-105, where the Court noted that the Commission first asserted this narrower market definition in the state of proceedings before the Court and found that the contested Commission decision did not contain a sufficient statement of reasons on the market shares of ENS in the relevant market and on whether ENS's agreements had an appreciable effect on trade between MS; thus it annulled the contested decision.
1911. *See* for instance EU Commission, *Notice on the definition of relevant market*, 1997, para. 12, "[t]he different time horizon considered in each case might lead to the result that different geographic markets are defined for the same products [...]."
1912. EU Commission Decision, *Servier*, 2014, para. 2548.

equating dominance with power over prices, the Commission argues that an undertaking which is able to sustain price increases above the competitive level for a significant time-period can generally be regarded as dominant.[1913]

For Article 102 TFEU to apply, the undertaking shall be dominant within the internal market or a substantial part of it. In order to determine whether a specific territory constitutes "a substantial part of the common market," one has to examine the pattern and volume of both the product's production and consumption. The habits and economic opportunities of sellers and purchasers shall also be considered.[1914] The territory of an individual Member State or even parts thereof have been found to be a substantial part of the internal market in the CJEU's jurisprudence.[1915] The notion of "substantial part" of the internal market is not static and may depend on other factors such as the nature of the market at issue; for instance, in transport cases, very small geographic areas such as harbours were considered to be substantial parts of the internal market.[1916]

Finding that an undertaking is dominant in the relevant market may have severe consequences. For instance, unilateral anticompetitive acts such as the imposition of export bans or resale prices are not prohibited under Article 101 TFEU, which applies only to agreements, decisions and concerted practices.[1917] If an undertaking engaging in such conduct is not dominant, then the conduct falls outside the scope of Article 102 TFEU as well and is thus legal. Therefore, a wrong finding of dominance may lead to the condemnation of an undertaking's procompetitive behaviour as abusive conduct prohibited by Article 102 TFEU, a Type 1 "false positive" error.[1918]

1   Market Shares

If an undertaking has a statutory monopoly in a relevant market, it is beyond doubt in a dominant position. However, if this is not the case, the first step in assessing

---

1913. EU Commission, *Guidance in applying Article 82*, 2009, paras 9-11.
1914. Judgment of the Court of 16 December 1975, Joined Cases 40 to 48, 50, 54 to 56, 111, 113 and 114-73, *Coöperatieve Vereniging "Suiker Unie" UA and others v. Commission of the European Communities*, EU:C:1975:174, para. 371.
1915. *See* for example Judgment of the Court of 27 March 1974, Case 127-73, *Belgische Radio en Televisie and société belge des auteurs, compositeurs et éditeurs v. SV SABAM and NV Fonior*, EU:C:1974:25, para. 5, ruling that exercising a quasi-monopoly within Belgium amounted to an occupation of a dominant position within the internal market; Judgment of the Court of 11 November 1986, Case 226/84, *British Leyland Public Limited Company v. Commission of the European Communities*, EU:C:1986:421, paras 11-34, finding that the UK qualified as a substantial part of the internal market within which there was an abuse of dominant position.
1916. 94/19/EC: Commission Decision of 21 December 1993 relating to a proceeding pursuant to Article 86 of the EC Treaty (IV/34.689 – *Sea Containers v. Stena Sealink* – Interim measures), OJ L 15, 18.1.1994, para. 77.
1917. *See* for instance Judgment of the Court of 6 January 2004, Joined Cases C-2/01 P and C-3/01 P, *Bundesverband der Arzneimittel-Importeure eV and Commission of the European Communities v. Bayer AG*, EU:C:2004:2, paras 70, 88, on unilateral conduct concerning export bans; Judgment of the Court of 13 July 2006, Case C-74/04 P, *Commission of the European Communities v. Volkswagen AG*, EU:C:2006:460, paras 13, 54, on unilateral conduct concerning resale prices.
1918. JONES, SUFRIN, 2014, p. 272.

dominance is determining the undertaking's market share.[1919] The calculation of market shares is analysed in the Commission's notice on market definition and is based on the undertaking's sales of the relevant product in the relevant area.[1920] The general principle is that the higher the market share, the more likely it is that the undertaking is dominant: a market share of 70%-80% or 90% is itself evidence of a dominant position.[1921] Market shares may vary from one market to another and other factors – such as the absence of barriers to entry – are also relevant in determining dominance.[1922] In the EU, a market share above 50% raises a presumption of dominance, a threshold that is often criticised for being too low.[1923] In the US, this threshold is indeed higher: firms which have market shares between 60% and 99% are roughly described as dominant; if a defendant in a well-defined market, protected by sufficient entry barriers, has a market share that exceeds 70%-75% for a period of five years, it could be reasonably presumed to be dominant.[1924] Back in the EU, undertakings with market shares lower than 50% can be found to be dominant if for instance they hold a market share twice as large as their closest competitor. Generally, the market share of an allegedly dominant undertaking shall be examined vis-à-vis the market shares of its competitors.[1925]

2 Other Factors Indicating Dominance and Barriers to Entry

An undertaking's own statements or internal documentation may be indicative of its dominance: the EU courts and the Commission have relied on statements of

---

1919. See Judgment of the Court of 13 February 1979, Case 85/76, *Hoffmann-La Roche & Co. AG v. Commission of the European Communities*, EU:C:1979:36, paras 39-41. See also EU Commission, *Guidance in applying Article 82*, 2009, para. 13, stating that market shares provide "the first useful indication" of the market structure and of the relative importance of undertakings present in the market.
1920. EU Commission, *Notice on the definition of relevant market*, 1997, para. 53.
1921. Judgment of the Court of First Instance of 12 December 1991, Case T-30/89, *Hilti AG v. Commission of the European Communities*, EU:T:1991:70, paras 91-94, holding that the existence of a market share between 70% and 80% is "a clear indication of the existence of a dominant position;" Judgment of the Court of First Instance of 6 October 1994, Case T-83/91, *Tetra Pak International SA v. Commission of the European Communities*, EU:T:1994:246, paras 109-110, finding that having a 90% market share was evidence of a dominant position.
1922. Judgment of the Court of 13 February 1979, Case 85/76, *Hoffmann-La Roche & Co. AG v. Commission of the European Communities*, EU:C:1979:36, para. 41; Judgment of the Court of 6 December 2012, C-457/10 P, *AstraZeneca v. Commission*, para. 176.
1923. Judgment of the Court of 3 July 1991, Case C-62/86, *AKZO Chemie BV v. Commission*, para. 60, noting that a market share of 50% is in itself evidence of dominant position. See for instance JONES, SUFRIN, 2014, pp. 338-339.
1924. HOVENKAMP, AREEDA, *Fundamentals of Antitrust*, 2014, pp. 8-5 – 8-9.
1925. Judgment of the Court of 14 February 1978, Case 27/76, *United Brands Company and United Brands Continentaal BV v. Commission of the European Communities, Chiquita Bananas*, EU:C:1978:22, paras 97-129, finding that UBC, whose market share was estimated by the Commission at 45%, held a dominant position in the relevant market; Judgment of the Court of First Instance of 17 December 2003, Case T-219/99, *British Airways plcv. Commission of the European Communities*, EU:T:2003:343, paras 189-225, finding that British Airways held a dominant position, despite having a market share of 39.7%.

Chapter 5: The European Regulatory Framework

undertakings considering themselves "the world leader" in the market;[1926] even a plain admission of a high market share and of a dominant position in internal documents is not as rare as expected.[1927] Profits or an undertaking's economic performance may also be used as a proxy to identify the market power of an undertaking.[1928] Nevertheless, a lack of profit or even the existence of losses are not incompatible with a finding of a dominant position. On the contrary, they may also be indicative of the undertaking's economic strength.[1929] The undertaking's overall size, strength and range of products may be relevant indicators of dominance.[1930] Finally, constraints imposed by the threatened future expansion of actual competitors or by the entry to the market of potential competitors shall be taken into consideration in the assessment of dominance.[1931] An undertaking may not increase prices if expansion or entry of competitors is likely, timely and sufficient.[1932] The importance of barriers to entry and expansion, such as tariffs, quotas, economies of scale and scope,[1933] privileged access to essential inputs,[1934] etc., lies in the difficulties they impose on competitors that wish to enter or to expand on the market and to threaten the incumbent's market share.[1935]

3   Countervailing Buyer Power

Countervailing buyer power refers to the constraints imposed to an undertaking by the bargaining strength of its customers and is one of the factors taken into consideration when assessing dominance.[1936] Dominance is defined as the power of an undertaking

---

1926. Judgment of the Court of 3 July 1991, Case C-62/86, *AKZO Chemie BV v. Commission*, para. 61, "AKZO regards itself as the world leader in the peroxides market."
1927. See for instance Case No COMP/E-1/38.113 – Prokent-Tomra, Commission decision of 29 March 2006, relating to proceedings under Article 82 of the Treaty and Article 54 of the EEA Agreement, C(2006)734, Brussels, 29.03.2006, paras 60-64.
1928. See for example Judgment of the Court of 13 February 1979, Case 85/76, *Hoffmann-La Roche & Co. AG v. Commission of the European Communities*, EU:C:1979:36, para. 48.
1929. Judgment of the Court of 14 February 1978, Case 27/76, *United Brands Company and United Brands Continentaal BV v. Commission of the European Communities, Chiquita Bananas*, EU:C:1978:22, paras 126-128; Judgment of the Court of 9 November 1983, Case 322/81, *NV Nederlandsche Banden Industrie Michelin v. Commission of the European Communities*, EU:C:1983:313, para. 59.
1930. Judgment of the Court of 9 November 1983, Case 322/81, *NV Nederlandsche Banden Industrie Michelin v. Commission of the European Communities*, EU:C:1983:313, para. 55; Judgment of the General Court of 1 July 2010, Case T-321/05, *AstraZeneca v. Commission*, paras 284-286.
1931. EU Commission, *Guidance in applying Article 82*, 2009, paras 12, 16.
1932. EU Commission, *Guidance in applying Article 82*, 2009, para. 16.
1933. Judgment of the Court of 14 February 1978, Case 27/76, *United Brands Company and United Brands Continentaal BV v. Commission of the European Communities, Chiquita Bananas*, EU:C:1978:22, para. 122, discussing the exceptionally high capital investments required for running a banana plantation and the financial risks and costs which are irrecoverable if the attempt fails.
1934. 89/22/EEC: Commission Decision of 5 December 1988 relating to a proceeding under Article 86 of the EEC Treaty (IV/31.900, *BPB Industries plc*), OJ L 10, 13.1.1989, para. 120, where new entrants to the market needed to have access to the raw material of gypsum, but this was only possible if they would incur the great financial risk of opening a new mine of gypsum or of importing it.
1935. EU Commission, *Guidance in applying Article 82*, 2009, paras 16-17.
1936. EU Commission, *Guidance in applying Article 82*, 2009, para. 12.

to behave to an appreciable extent independently not only from its competitors but also from its customers.[1937] An undertaking is less likely to be dominant if it can be constrained by powerful buyers who have the power to protect not only themselves, but also the market itself against price increases, facilitating the entry of new competitors and the expansion of existing ones.[1938] Even an undertaking with a large market share may not be able to act independently of customers with high bargaining strength.[1939] Such countervailing market power may for instance be the result of the customers' size, their commercial significance, or the customers' ability to switch quickly to competing suppliers.[1940] Nevertheless, in the context of pharmaceuticals, national health services may not always be able to constrain the behaviour of a dominant undertaking despite being the drug's only buyer within a national market. For instance, the originator of an innovative new drug, which is the only or at least the most-effective cure for a disease, will not be severely restrained by national health services. In such a case, national health services are normally in a weak bargaining position and incapable of influencing the drug's price level or the undertaking's market share.[1941]

D The Concept of Abuse of Dominance

The concept of abuse refers to the conduct of a dominant undertaking which is liable to influence the structure of a market in which competition is already weakened due to its presence.[1942] The abuse of dominant position is an objective concept and implies no intention to cause harm.[1943] Through methods which differ from those governing

---

1937. Judgment of the Court of 13 February 1979, Case 85/76, *Hoffmann-La Roche & Co. AG v. Commission of the European Communities*, EU:C:1979:36, para. 38.
1938. See EU Commission, *Guidance in applying Article 82*, 2009, para. 18. "[b]uyer power may not, however, be considered a sufficiently effective constraint if it only ensures that a particular or limited segment of customers is shielded from the market power of the dominant undertaking;" JONES, SUFRIN, 2014, pp. 359-360.
1939. EU Commission, *Guidance in applying Article 82*, 2009, para. 18; Judgment of the Court of First Instance of 7 October 1999, Case T-228/97, *Irish Sugar plc v. Commission of the European Communities*, EU:T:1999:246, paras 97-104, considering whether the alleged lack of independence of an undertaking from its customers could be considered an an exceptional circumstance preventing the finding of a dominant position; the court found that it could not.
1940. EU Commission, *Guidance in applying Article 82*, 2009, para. 18.
1941. See EU Commission Decision, *AstraZeneca*, 2005, paras 553-561, rejecting AstraZeneca's argument that monopsony buyers and price regulation in the pharmaceutical markets deprive pharmaceutical companies of the ability to determine the drugs' prices or exercise market power with regard to prices.
1942. Judgment of the Court of 6 December 2012, C-457/10 P, *AstraZeneca v. Commission*, para. 74; Judgment of the Court of 13 February 1979, Case 85/76, *Hoffmann-La Roche & Co. AG v. Commission of the European Communities*, EU:C:1979:36, para. 91; Judgment of the Court of 3 July 1991, Case C-62/86, *AKZO Chemie BV v. Commission*, para. 69; Judgment of the Court of 11 December 2008, Case C-52/07, *Kanal 5 Ltd and TV 4 AB v. Föreningen Svenska Tonsättares Internationella Musikbyrå (STIM) upa*, EU:C:2008:703, para. 25; Judgment of the Court of 17 February 2011, Case C-52/09, *TeliaSonera Sverige*, EU:C:2011:83, para. 27.
1943. Judgment of the General Court of 1 July 2010, Case T-321/05, *AstraZeneca v. Commission*, para. 359; Judgment of the Court of First Instance of 12 December 2000, Case T-128/98, *Aéroports de Paris v. Commission of the European Communities*, EU:T:2000:290, para. 173.

Chapter 5: The European Regulatory Framework

normal competition, the dominant undertaking hinders the maintenance or the further growth of competition still existing in the market.[1944] There are two main categories of abuse that Article 102 TFEU covers: exploitative and exclusionary.[1945] Exploitative abuses aim to the exploitation of consumers, whereas exclusionary abuses signify the anticompetitive conduct by the dominant undertaking aiming to exclude actual or potential competitors from the market.[1946] Exploitative and exclusionary abuses are not mutually exclusive, meaning that the same abusive conduct may qualify as both.[1947] Dominant undertakings are not prevented from protecting their own economic interests through reasonable steps; however, behaviour whose purpose is to strengthen the undertaking's dominant position and to abuse it is prohibited under Article 102 TFEU.[1948] The means and procedure by which such abuse is achieved are irrelevant.[1949] Behaviour which could have been deemed to be unproblematic if the undertaking concerned was not dominant in the relevant market, may be prohibited because of a finding of dominance.

Some examples of abuses, which shall not be read as an exhaustive list,[1950] are provided in the text of Article 102 TFEU: (1) the direct or indirect imposition of unfair purchase or selling prices or other trading conditions; (2) the limitation of production, markets, technological development to the prejudice of consumers; (3) the application of dissimilar conditions to equivalent transactions with other trading parties, placing them at a competitive disadvantage; and (4) subjecting the conclusion of contracts to the condition of acceptance by the counterparties of supplementary obligations which

---

1944. Judgment of the Court of 6 December 2012, C-457/10 P, *AstraZeneca v. Commission*, para. 74; Judgment of the Court of 13 February 1979, Case 85/76, *Hoffmann-La Roche & Co. AG v. Commission of the European Communities*, EU:C:1979:36, para. 91; Judgment of the Court of 3 July 1991, Case C-62/86, *AKZO Chemie BV v. Commission*, para. 69; Judgment of the Court of 11 December 2008, Case C-52/07, *Kanal 5 Ltd and TV 4 AB v. Föreningen Svenska Tonsättares Internationella Musikbyrå (STIM) upa*, EU:C:2008:703, para. 25; Judgment of the Court of 17 February 2011, Case C-52/09, *TeliaSonera Sverige*, EU:C:2011:83, para. 27.
1945. EU Commission, *Guidelines: effect on trade in Articles 81 & 82*, 2004, para. 73.
1946. Judgment of the Court of 21 February 1973, Case 6-72, *Europemballage Corporation and Continental Can Company Inc. v. Commission of the European Communities*, EU:C:1973:22, para. 25. See also EU Commission, *Guidance in applying Article 82*, 2009, paras 1-8, dealing only with exclusionary abuses and setting the enforcement priorities of the EU Commission with regard to Article 102 TFEU.
1947. See for instance Judgment of the Court of 15 March 2007, Case C-95/04 P, *British Airways plc v. Commission*, paras 143-150, holding that discriminatory prices offered to consumers may also exclude competitors from the market.
1948. Judgment of the Court of First Instance of 1 April 1993, T-65/89, *BPB Industries Plc and British Gypsum Ltd v. Commission of the European Communities*, EU:T:1993:31, para. 69.
1949. Judgment of the Court of 17 February 2011, C-52/09, *Konkurrensverket v. TeliaSonera Sverige AB*, EU:C:2011:83, paras 26-27; Judgment of the Court of 2 April 2009, Case C-202/07 P, *France Télécom SA v. Commission of the European Communities*, EU:C:2009:214, paras 105-106.
1950. Judgment of the Court of 15 March 2007, Case C-95/04 P, *British Airways plc v. Commission*, para. 57; Judgment of the Court of 14 November 1996, Case C-333/94 P, *Tetra Pak International SA v. Commission of the European Communities*, EU:C:1996:436, para. 37; Judgment of the Court of 16 March 2000, Joined Cases C-395/96 P and C-396/96 P, *Compagnie maritime belge Transports and others v. Commission*, para. 112; Judgment of the Court of 21 February 1973, Case 6/72, *Europemballage Corporation and Continental Can Company Inc. v. Commission of the European Communities*, EU:C:1973:22, para. 26.

have no connection to the subject of such contracts, by their nature or commercial usage. On the basis of CJEU's jurisprudence, the following practices may fall under the prohibition of Article 102 TFEU: predatory pricing, margin squeeze, exclusive purchasing contracts, discount and rebate schemes, tying and bundling, refusal to supply, etc. The totality of these practices and related jurisprudence are not analysed under this chapter, since a number of them fall outside the scope of this book. On the contrary, abuses of dominance which are related to the exercise of IP-related rights are discussed in the following section.

E Abuse of Dominance and the Exercise of IP-Related Rights

Before providing examples in the European Courts' jurisprudence in which the abuse of dominance at issue was related to the exercise of IP rights, it should be stressed that the mere possession of IP rights does not automatically confer a dominant position.[1951] If the relevant market is wider than the patented product and also comprises of substitutable products, the legal monopoly granted by the IP right does not amount to an economic monopoly, since the IP right does not enable its holder to prevent effective competition. However, if access to the market is protected by IP rights, they may be considered to be barriers to entry and may contribute to a finding of dominance.

1 TetraPak and the Acquisition of Exclusive Licences

The relevant legal question in the *TetraPak I* case was whether the acquisition of an exclusive licence (related to a new technological method for the sterilisation of cartons suitable for long-life milk) constituted an abuse of dominance within the meaning of Article 102 TFEU by TetraPak, the largest producer for milk cartons and machines for packaging milk in the EEA.[1952] The Commission argued in its decision that this acquisition strengthened TetraPak's considerable dominance by reinforcing its technical advantages against the minimum competition it faced. Additionally, this exclusive licence prevented or at least delayed any new competitor from entering the market.[1953] The Court of First Instance agreed that abuse may occur in cases where competitive entry is merely delayed and not altogether prevented.[1954] The court noted that even though the acquisition of an exclusive licence by a dominant undertaking does not constitute an abuse of dominant position per se, the acquisition at issue was an abuse

---

1951. Judgment of the Court of 29 February 1968, Case 24-67, *Parke, Davis and Co. v. Probel, Reese, Beintema-Interpharm and Centrafarm*, EU:C:1968:11, p. 72; Judgment of the Court of 6 April 1995, Joined Cases C-241/91 P and C-242/91 P, *Radio Telefis Eireann (RTE) and Independent Television Publications Ltd (ITP) v. Commission of the European Communities*, EU:C:1995:98, para. 46.
1952. European Commission, Press Release, *TetraPak I*, IP-88-497, Brussels 1988. Available at: http://europa.eu/rapid/press-release_IP-88-497_en.htm. (last accessed on March 31, 2018).
1953. 88/501/EEC: Commission Decision of 26 July 1988 relating to a proceeding under Articles 85 and 86 of the EEC Treaty (IV/31.043 – Tetra Pak I (BTG licence), paras 26-52, analysing why TetraPak's acquisition constituted an abuse of dominance and its effects on the market.
1954. Judgment of the Court of First Instance of 10 July 1990, Case T-51/89, *Tetra Pak Rausing SA v. Commission of the European Communities*, EU:T:1990:41, para. 23.

Chapter 5: The European Regulatory Framework

based on the facts of the case, despite the fact that the licence agreement did not breach Article 101 TFEU as it fell under the Block Exemption Regulation on patent licensing agreements.[1955]

2   *Standard-Essential Patents and Refusals to License*

Dominant undertakings are not generally obliged to deal with rivals and their refusal to grant an IP licence does not in itself constitute an abuse of dominant position.[1956] However, such refusal may exceptionally fall under the prohibition of Article 102 TFEU, if it can be shown that the relevant IP right is indispensable in order to compete in a neighbouring market and that a refusal to license results in the elimination of effective competition.[1957] Undertakings define technical or quality requirements though agreements setting specific industry standards. The patents which are essential to the technology incorporated in these standardisation agreements are known under the term "standard-essential patents" (SEPs). Since it is not possible for these undertakings to manufacture products meeting the set standard without obtaining a licence for the relevant SEPs, the holders of SEPs shall generally license these patents to third parties under fair, reasonable and non-discriminatory (FRAND) terms.[1958] Holders of SEPs may have significant market power so that the commitment to license their patents under FRAND terms is a mechanism to ensure effective access to the set

---

1955. Judgment of the Court of First Instance of 10 July 1990, Case T-51/89, *Tetra Pak Rausing SA v. Commission of the European Communities*, EU:T:1990:41, paras 23-30. At the time the relevant Block Exemption Regulation was Commission Regulation (EEC) No. 2349/84 of 23 July 1984 on the application of Article 85(3) of the Treaty to certain categories of patent licensing agreements, OJ L 113, 26.4.1985, p. 34-34, (replaced by Commission Regulation (EC) No. 240/96 of 31 January 1996 on the application of Article 85(3) of the Treaty to certain categories of technology transfer agreements, OJ L 31, 9.2.1996, p. 2-13, subsequently replaced by Commission Regulation (EC) No. 772/2004 of 27 April 2004 on the application of Article 81(3) of the Treaty to categories of technology transfer agreements, OJ L 123, 27.4.2004, p. 11-17. In 2014, the Commission Regulation (EU) No. 316/2014 of 21 March 2014 on the application of Article 101(3) of the Treaty on the Functioning of the European Union to categories of technology transfer agreements, OJ L 93, 28.3.2014, p. 17-23, was adopted.
1956. Judgment of the Court of 6 April 1995, Joined Cases C-241/91 P and C-242/91 P, *Radio Telefis Eireann (RTE) and Independent Television Publications Ltd (ITP) v. Commission of the European Communities*, EU:C:1995:98, para. 49; Judgment of the Court of 5 October 1988, Case 238/87, *AB Volvo v. Erik Veng (UK) Ltd*, EU:C:1988:477, paras 7-8.
1957. Judgment of the Court of 6 April 1995, Joined Cases C-241/91 P and C-242/91 P, *Radio Telefis Eireann (RTE) and Independent Television Publications Ltd (ITP) v. Commission of the European Communities*, EU:C:1995:98, paras 50-57; Judgment of the Court of First Instance of 17 September 2007, Case T-201/04, *Microsoft Corp. v. Commission of the European Communities*, EU:T:2007:289, paras 560-564; Judgment of the Court of 16 July 2015, Case C-170/13, *Huawei Technologies Co. Ltd v. ZTE Corp. and ZTE Deutschland GmbH*, EU:C:2015:477, paras 51-53 (Judgment of the Court of 16 July 2015, Case C-170/13, *Huawei Technologies v. ZTE Corp. and ZTE Deutschland GmbH*), finding that the refusal of the proprietor of a standard-essential patent to grant a licence on FRAND terms may constitute an abuse of dominant position under Article 102 TFEU.
1958. *See* further European Commission, DG Competition, *Competition Policy Brief: Standard Essential Patents*, Issue 8, June 2014, pp. 1-5. Available at: http://ec.europa.eu/competition/publications/cpb/2014/008_en.pdf (last accessed on March 31, 2018).

standard for all market players and to prevent a "hold-up."[1959] The ultimate goal is to allow consumers a wider choice of interoperable products while ensuring a fair compensation for the SEPs holders.[1960]

2.1 The Commission's Investigations in the *Samsung* and *Motorola* Cases

The *Samsung* case is illustrative of how SEPs can be linked to an alleged abuse of dominance. Even though seeking injunctions is a legitimate remedy against patent infringements, seeking such injunctions against a company willing to enter into a licence agreement on the Standard Essential Patent (SEP) on FRAND terms may constitute an abuse of dominant position if the SEP holder has voluntarily committed to enter such a licensing agreement. Samsung owned SEPs on mobile telecommunication standards and has agreed to license them on FRAND terms; however, it started seeking injunctions against Apple on the basis of these SEPs. The Commission considered that Apple was a willing licensee and informed Samsung that its conduct could constitute an abuse of dominant position breaching Article 102 TFEU.[1961] As a result of the Commission's investigation, Samsung committed not to seek injunctions on its SEPs on mobile services in the European Union for a period of five years, against any potential licensee willing to accept a specific licensing framework.[1962] Potential issues of patent infringement, invalidity or essentiality are to be taken into consideration by the arbitration tribunal determining the FRAND terms of such licensing.[1963] The Commission accepted Samsung's commitments and made them legally binding on the basis of Article 9, Regulation 1/2003, closing the investigation.[1964]

The same day, the Commission found that Motorola had abused its dominant position and infringed Article 102 TFEU by seeking and enforcing injunctions against

---

1959. See for instance, European Commission, Press Release, *Antitrust: Commission accepts legally binding commitments by Samsung Electronics on standard essential patent injunctions*, IP/14/490, Brussels, 29 April 2014. Available at: http://europa.eu/rapid/press-release_IP-14-490_en.htm. (last accessed on March 31, 2018) [cited as: EU Commission Press Release, *Samsung Commitments*, 2014].
1960. EU Commission Press Release, *Samsung Commitments*, 2014. See also Pentheroudakis Chryssoula, Baron Justus A., "Licensing Terms of Standard Essential Patents: A Comprehensive Analysis of Cases," EU Commission, JRC Science for Policy Report, (2017), EUR 28302 EN; doi:10.2791/32230, pp. 21-32, explaining the economic function of FRAND licensing terms and the incentives they contribute to standard development.
1961. European Commission, *Samsung – Enforcement of ETSI Standards Essential Patents (SEPs)*, Brussels, MEMO/12/1021, 21 December 2012. Available at: http://europa.eu/rapid/press-release_MEMO-12-1021_en.htm. (last accessed on March 31, 2018); European Commission, Press Release, *Antitrust: Commission sends Statement of Objections to Samsung on potential misuse of mobile phone standard-essential patents*, IP/12/1448, Brussels, 21 December 2012. Available at: http://europa.eu/rapid/press-release_IP-12-1448_en.htm. (last accessed on March 31, 2018).
1962. CASE AT.39939 – SAMSUNG – Enforcement of UMTS standard essential patents, Commission Decision of 29 April 2014, relating to proceedings under Article 102 of the Treaty on the Functioning of the European Union and Article 54 of the EEA Agreement, C(2014) 2891 final Brussels, 29.4.2014, paras 80, 97-104 [cited as: EU Commission Decision, *SAMSUNG*, 2014], on Samsung's final commitments.
1963. EU Commission Decision, *SAMSUNG*, 2014, para. 99.
1964. EU Commission Decision, *SAMSUNG*, 2014, paras 126-128.

Apple before a German court on the basis of SEPs on smartphones.[1965] Motorola Mobility had declared some of its patents essential for the GPRS standard and committed to license them on FRAND terms; however it seeked and enforced injunctions against Apple, despite the fact that Apple proposed six times to enter into a licence agreement and to be bound by the determination of the FRAND royalties as determined by the competent German court.[1966] The Commission requested Motorola to bring this infringement to an end and not repeat it in the future; nevertheless, it did not impose a fine, taking note of the lack of EU jurisprudence on similar conduct by an SEP holder at the time and the conflicting positions of national courts on the matter.[1967]

The Commission's decisions in *Samsung* and *Motorola* provide a safe harbour for willing licensees wishing to avoid the risk of injunctions on the basis of SEPs. Importantly, a potential licensee who challenges the validity, the essentiality or the infringement of SEPs is not considered to be "unwilling:" on the contrary potential licensees remain free to challenge the SEPs on the above-mentioned grounds and to serve the public interest in eliminating invalid patents.[1968]

2.2 The CJEU Rules on SEP-Related Abuses of Dominance in *Huawei*

The *Huawei* decision in 2015 was the first decision of the CJEU on an abuse of dominance related to an SEP. Huawei Technologies, a multinational telecommunications company, owned an SEP essential to the Long-Term Evolution standard and undertook to license it to third parties on FRAND terms.[1969] Huawei brought an action against ZTE Corp. for infringement of its SPE, seeking an injunction prohibiting the infringement, the rendering of accounts, the recall of products and an award for damages. The two parties had extensively negotiated the possibility to conclude a licensing agreement on FRAND terms, but had not succeeded to do so.[1970]

The decision of the CJEU in *Huawei* closely follows the reasoning of the Commission decisions on *Samsung* and *Motorola*, focusing also on the concept of the "willing licensee."[1971] The Court found that the refusal to grant a licence by a proprietor of an SEP, who has committed to license it on FRAND terms and thus created legitimate

---

1965. European Commission, Press Release, *Antitrust: Commission finds that Motorola Mobility Infringed EU competition rules by misusing standard essential patents*, IP/14/489, Brussels, 29 April 2014. Available at: http://europa.eu/rapid/press-release_IP-14-489_en.htm. (last accessed on March 31, 2018).
1966. European Commission, CASE AT.39985 – MOTOROLA – ENFORCEMENT OF GPRS STANDARD ESSENTIAL PATENTS, ANTITRUST PROCEDURE, Article 7, Regulation 1/2003, Brussels, 29.4.2014, C(2014) 2892 final, paras 279-321, describing Motorola's conduct [cited as: EU Commission Decision, *MOTOROLA*, 2014].
1967. EU Commission Decision, *MOTOROLA*, 2014, paras 557-561.
1968. European Commission, *FAQs, Antitrust decisions on standard essential patents (SEPs) – Motorola Mobility and Samsung Electronics*, MEMO/14/322, Brussels, 29 April 2014. Available at: http://europa.eu/rapid/press-release_MEMO-14-322_en.htm (last accessed on March 31, 2018).
1969. Judgment of the Court of 16 July 2015, Case C-170/13, *Huawei Technologies*, paras 21-23.
1970. Judgment of the Court of 16 July 2015, Case C-170/13, *Huawei Technologies*, paras 24-27.
1971. Judgment of the Court of 16 July 2015, Case C-170/13, *Huawei Technologies*, para. 70.

expectations to third parties in this regard, constitutes an abuse of dominant position under Article 102 TFEU.[1972] According to *Huawei*, Article 102 must be interpreted as meaning that the proprietor of an SEP who seeks an injunction prohibiting the infringement of its patent or the recall of products for the production of which the SEP has been used, is obliged to comply with the following legal requirements when bringing actions against alleged infringers: (1) the proprietor shall alert the alleged infringer by designating the SEP and specifying the way in which it was infringed; (2) the proprietor shall present to the alleged infringer a specific, written licensing offer on FRAND terms. On the other hand, the alleged infringer must also diligently respond to the offer by accepting it or submitting a counter-offer, also on FRAND terms.[1973] The CJEU attempted to strike a fair balance between the parties' interests by putting the burden on both parties to satisfy the necessary conditions during the FRAND negotiation process.[1974] The *Huawei* judgment was greeted for balancing the abusive recourse to injunctions with the legitimate interests of SEP holders to receive a fair remuneration for licensing their invention.[1975]

3 The Manipulation of IP Rights in the AstraZeneca Case

In 2005, the European Commission fined AstraZeneca €60 million for abusing the patent system and the system for the authorisation of medicines with the aim to delay competition from generic drugs and parallel imports to its blockbuster drug Losec.[1976] The abuse of AstraZeneca was twofold: first, misleading information and dates were provided to a number of national patent offices and national courts aiming to gain additional patent protection for Losec in the form of supplementary protection certificates (SPCs).[1977] Second, the marketing authorisation procedures were misused and AstraZeneca engaged in product-hopping by switching Losec from a capsule to a tablet form, so as to inhibit generic entry, generic substitution and parallel imports.[1978]

1972. Judgment of the Court of 16 July 2015, Case C-170/13, *Huawei Technologies*, paras 51-54.
1973. Judgment of the Court of 16 July 2015, Case C-170/13, *Huawei Technologies*, paras 59-71, 77. See also, Opinion of Advocate General Wathelet delivered on 20 November 2014, Case C-170/13, *Huawei Technologies Co. Ltd v. ZTE Corp. and ZTE Deutschland GmbH*, EU:C:2014:2391, which the CJEU largely followed in its ruling.
1974. HENNINGSSON, FRAND, 2016, p. 449.
1975. BANASEVIC, 2015, pp. 463-464; HENNINGSSON, FRAND, 2016, pp. 446-449.
1976. EU Commission Decision, *AstraZeneca*, 2005, paras 773, 860. See also EU Commission, Press Release, *Competition: Commission fines AstraZeneca €60 million for misusing patent system to delay market entry of competing generic drugs*, IP/05/737, Brussels, 15 June 2000. Available at: http://europa.eu/rapid/press-release_IP-05-737_en.htm?locale=en. (last accessed on March 31, 2018).
1977. Instead of providing the dates in which the drug was granted authorisation by the national authorities, AstraZeneca provided the later dates in which national pricing authorities approved the price of omeprazole and omeprazole sodium. See Judgment of the Court of 6 December 2012, C-457/10 P, *AstraZeneca v. Commission*, paras 77-99.
1978. See EU Commission Decision, *AstraZeneca*, 2005, paras 143-146; 255-257.

3.1 AstraZeneca's Product-Hopping Strategy

Some of the product-hopping strategies employed in the US were briefly discussed in Chapter 4 of this book.[1979] In both the US and the EU, product-hopping strategies are largely similar and entail for example switching the form of the drug – as in the *AstraZeneca* case – incremental changes in the drug's chemical composition while keeping the same active ingredient, or creating "combination products" by combining in one product two or more pharmaceutical compositions that used to be marketed separately.[1980] The timing of a drug product switch is crucial and shall occur before generics enter the market in order to prevent the substitution of the brand-name drug by its generic version.[1981] In order to maximise the effect of this product switch, AstraZeneca withdrew the capsule version of the drug and deregistered its marketing authorisation, preventing generic drug manufacturers from using simplified marketing authorisation procedures which at that time were only available if the marketing authorisation of the original product was still in force.[1982] After the revision of Directive 2001/83/EC by Directive 2004/27/EC, the withdrawal of the marketing authorisation of the brand-name reference drug does not in principle prevent the generic companies from relying on the abridged authorisation procedure.[1983]

3.2 Providing Misleading Information and Eliminating Competition

In its decision in *AstraZeneca*, the General Court agreed that the misrepresentation of certain dates by AstraZeneca amounted to providing misleading information and noted that the abuse of dominance within the meaning of Article 102 TFEU is not necessarily limited to abuses of economic power.[1984] A dominant undertaking has the special responsibility not to impair genuine undistorted competition within the internal market by conduct which falls outside the scope of competition on the merits. Submitting misleading information to public authorities, information which is liable to lead them in the erroneous grant of an exclusive right to which the dominant undertaking is not entitled – or to which it is entitled but for a shorter time-period – constitutes such

---

1979. *See supra*, Chapter 4, Part 3, Section IV.C.
1980. *See* further SHADOWEN, LEFFLER, LUKENS, Product Changes, 2009, pp. 21-36, analysing different kinds of product hopping and their timing *vis-à-vis* generic entry. *See also* EU Commission, *Pharma Sector Inquiry*, 2009, paras 1012-1019, discussing the second-generation products and their effect on generic entry.
1981. EU Commission, *Pharma Sector Inquiry*, 2009, paras 1007-1010, 1024-1031.
1982. EU Commission Decision, *AstraZeneca*, 2005, paras 263-264, 314-315, 527-529, 856.
1983. Revised Article 10(1) of Directive 2001/83/EC, as amended by Directive 2004/27/EC of the European Parliament and of the Council of 31 March 2004, OJ L 136, p. 34-57. *See also* EU Commission, *Pharma Sector Inquiry*, 2009, para. 1041.
1984. Judgment of the General Court of 1 July 2010, Case T-321/05, *AstraZeneca v. Commission*, paras 352-361. *See also* Judgment of the Court of 21 February 1973, Case 6/72, *Europemballage Corporation and Continental Can Company Inc. v. Commission of the European Communities*, EU:C:1973:22, para. 27; Judgment of the Court of 13 February 1979, Case 85/76, *Hoffmann-La Roche & Co. AG v. Commission of the European Communities*, EU:C:1979:36, para. 91.

abusive conduct.[1985] In order to determine whether AstraZeneca's conduct was liable to raise regulatory obstacles to competition, the court took into consideration the limited discretion and the absence of an obligation for the public authorities to verify the accuracy and the truthfulness of the information submitted. The special responsibility of undertakings to inform the public authorities of any error made was also stressed.[1986] Despite the objective nature of the concept of abuse, the intention of the undertaking shall be taken into consideration to support a finding of abuse of dominant position.[1987] Whether the public authorities were actually misled or not and whether the erroneously granted rights were subsequently revoked was irrelevant for the assessment of AstraZeneca's abusive conduct.[1988] The court also found that the finding of an abuse of dominant position did not require the enforcement of the exclusive right which was granted as a result of the misleading representations, since the mere possession of that exclusive right kept competitors away.[1989]

Finally, the General Court stressed that the elimination of *all* competition was not a necessary condition for a finding of abuse of dominance, making a distinction between the *AstraZeneca* and the *TetraPak* case, but also noting that the *TetraPak* decision did not necessarily require such elimination of *all* competition for Article 102 TFEU to be applied.[1990] Even though prescription drugs are researched, developed, marketed and sold differently than other products and interact strongly with intellectual property laws, an argument of difference in the application of competition law requires a more fact-specific basis in order to succeed under the *AstraZeneca* standards.[1991] The existence of specific patent law related remedies does not mean that proof of anticompetitive effects is required.[1992] However, the General Court decreased the fines imposed by the Commission from €60 million to €52.5 million, finding that the Commission failed to prove that AstraZeneca's conduct prevented or restricted parallel imports in Norway and in Denmark.[1993]

1985. Judgment of the General Court of 1 July 2010, Case T-321/05, *AstraZeneca v. Commission*, para. 354.
1986. Judgment of the General Court of 1 July 2010, Case T-321/05, *AstraZeneca v. Commission*, paras 357-359.
1987. Judgment of the General Court of 1 July 2010, Case T-321/05, *AstraZeneca v. Commission*, para. 359.
1988. Judgment of the General Court of 1 July 2010, Case T-321/05, *AstraZeneca v. Commission*, para. 360.
1989. Judgment of the General Court of 1 July 2010, Case T-321/05, *AstraZeneca v. Commission*, para. 362.
1990. Judgment of the General Court of 1 July 2010, Case T-321/05, *AstraZeneca v. Commission*, para. 365.
1991. KENT, 2010, p. 3.
1992. Judgment of the General Court of 1 July 2010, Case T-321/05, *AstraZeneca v. Commission v*, para. 367.
1993. Judgment of the General Court of 1 July 2010, Case T-321/05, *AstraZeneca v. Commission*, paras 852-855, 913.

3.3 The CJEU Affirms the Abuse of Dominant Position

On appeal, the CJEU largely affirmed the General Court's decision.[1994] One of the most important points in the decision of the CJEU in *AstraZeneca* is that it upheld that the exercise of legal rights by an undertaking can also constitute an abuse of a dominant position.[1995] Another important point of the decision is that the anticompetitive nature of the alleged violations shall be evaluated within the time-frame in which the relevant acts were committed.[1996] The decision of *AstraZeneca* was criticised for imposing strict limits on strategies related to managing the life cycle of pharmaceutical products and to extracting the maximum return from innovation-related investments.[1997] It was argued that under the General Court's standard even a "genuine and honest error" made by a dominant undertaking during the patent application process could amount to abuse, irrespectively of whether it was ultimately corrected.[1998] However, as the CJEU noted in its decision on appeal on *AstraZeneca*, the General Court did not hold neither that undertakings have to be infallible in their dealings with regulatory authorities nor that every objectively wrong representation constitutes an abuse of dominant position;[1999] on the contrary, such assessment shall be made *in concreto*: a consistent and linear conduct of highly misleading representations – which was manifestly not transparent – clearly fell outside the scope of competition on the merits.[2000]

F   Objective Justifications under Article 102 TFEU

Unlike Article 101(3), Article 102 TFEU does not contain a codified exception provision, while no *de minimis* rule applies in abuses of dominance. A dominant undertaking may justify its conduct by demonstrating that it is objectively necessary or that it produces substantive efficiencies, outweighing any anticompetitive effects it may have

---

1994. Judgment of the Court of 6 December 2012, C-457/10 P, *AstraZeneca v. Commission*.
1995. See also the subsequent case of *Reckitt Benckiser*, which was fined £10.2 million by the UK Office of Fair Trading for abusing its dominant position by withdrawing and delisting Gaviscon Original which had lost patent protection and replacing it with Gaviscon Advanced which still enjoyed patent protection. See further Gov.UK, Competition and Markets Authority case, *Reckitt Benckiser: alleged abuse of a dominant position, 2008-2011*. Related Documents available at: https://www.gov.uk/cma-cases/reckitt-benckiser-alleged-abuse-of-a-dominant-position. (last accessed on March 31, 2018).
1996. Judgment of the Court of 6 December 2012, C-457/10 P, *AstraZeneca v. Commission*, para. 110.
1997. JONES, SUFRIN, 2014, pp. 558-564.
1998. BUSHELL, Case C-457/10 P, 2012.
1999. Judgment of the Court of 6 December 2012, C-457/10 P, *AstraZeneca v. Commission*, para. 99. See however, PODSZUN, 2014, pp. 287-289, arguing that the Court's standard may lead to far-reaching obligations for dominant undertakings.
2000. Judgment of the General Court of 1 July 2010, Case T-321/05, *AstraZeneca v. Commission*, para. 357; Judgment of the Court of 6 December 2012, C-457/10 P, *AstraZeneca v. Commission*, paras 93-99. See also, DE LA MANO, NAZZINI, ZENGER, 2014, pp. 493-494, arguing that this approach of the court is sound from an economic viewpoint; *see* however GERADIN, Pfizer/Pharmacia, 2014, pp. 347-352, criticising the vagueness of the concept of "competition on the merits" in the *AstraZeneca* decisions.

on consumers.[2001] There is not a concrete theoretical framework on the concept of "objective justification" established in the CJEU's jurisprudence: it is unclear whether and under which circumstances anticompetitive effects will be considered as objectively necessary or as efficiency producing.[2002] Conduct which is necessary to protect public interest objectives such as the health and safety of consumers could be justified as objectively necessary, even though the protection of health and safety is normally the task of public authorities.[2003] This necessity shall be based on objective factors applying to all undertakings in the market in general, which are external to the dominant undertaking.[2004] An undertaking may also attempt to justify its conduct on the ground of efficiencies arguably guaranteeing that no net consumer harm is likely to arise.[2005] The dominant undertaking shall carry the burden of proving that the relevant conduct is indispensable for the realisation of the claimed efficiencies,[2006] by proving for instance that absent the restraint, the relevant products cannot or will not be produced or distributed in the market.[2007]

Conclusions

The patent system of the European Union differs substantially from the US patent system. The European Patent Convention established the system of the European Patent, but national laws of Member States remain largely important. There is a rather high degree of harmonisation with regard to drug marketing authorisations: the Union marketing authorisation is granted by the European Commission and allows direct access to the totality of the EU market, while the mutual recognition procedure facilitates the recognition of national marketing authorisations to other Member States, through simplified procedures. In an effort to preserve innovation incentives, patent term extensions also apply in the EU, by means of Supplementary Protection Certificates, orphan drug market exclusivity and paediatric market exclusivity. In parallel, the EU strives to facilitate generic entry to the market through the Bolar exemption and the abridged marketing authorisation mechanism. The EU Commission's initiatives

---

2001. Judgment of the Court of 14 February 1978, Case 27/76, *United Brands Company and United Brands Continentaal BV v. Commission of the European Communities, Chiquita Bananas*, EU:C:1978:22, para. 184; Judgment of the Court of First Instance of 12 December 1991, Case T-30/89, *Hilti AG v. Commission of the European Communities*, EU:T:1991:70, paras 102-119; Judgment of the Court of First Instance of 6 October 1994, Case T-83/91, *Tetra Pak International SA v. Commission of the European Communities*, EU:T:1994:246, paras 136, 207; Judgment of the Court of 15 March 2007, Case C-95/04 P, *British Airways plc v. Commission*, paras 69, 86; Judgment of the Court of 27 March 2012, Case C-209/10, *Post Danmark A/S v. Konkurrencerådet*, EU:C:2012:172, para. 48; Judgment of the Court of 17 February 2011, C-52/09, *Konkurrensverket v. TeliaSonera Sverige AB*, EU:C:2011:83, para. 76. See also EU Commission, *Guidance in applying Article 82*, 2009, paras 28-31.
2002. JONES, SUFRIN, 2014, p. 385.
2003. EU Commission, *Discussion Paper Article 82*, 2005, pp. 24-25, paras 77-79; EU Commission, *Guidance in applying Article 82*, 2009, para. 29.
2004. EU Commission, *Guidance in applying Article 82*, 2009, para. 29.
2005. EU Commission, *Guidance in applying Article 82*, 2009, para. 30.
2006. EU Commission, *Guidance in applying Article 82*, 2009, paras 30-31.
2007. EU Commission, *Discussion Paper Article 82*, 2005, p. 25, para. 80.

against anticompetitive conduct which delays generic entry to the market also play a central role to this effort. It should be borne in mind that in the absence of a regulatory framework remotely similar to the Hatch-Waxman Act in the European Union, the existence of a patent right covering the brand-name drug does not constitute and obstacle for the marketing authorisation of the respective generic drug version in the EU market.

The distinction between restrictions by object and restrictions by effect under Article 101 TFEU is of fundamental importance for the adjudication of reverse payment settlements. The exemptions of Article 101(3) TFEU and the Block Exemption Regulations also play a key role in this analysis of patent settlements in the pharmaceutical sector under European competition law. As reverse payment settlements evolved through time in the European Union, Article 102 TFEU and abuses of dominant position became increasingly relevant for a "global" analysis of strategies employed to delay generic entry. Product market definition in the pharmaceutical markets shall be tailored to the specificities of the pharmaceuticals at issue, whereas the exercise of IP rights may constitute an abuse of dominant position. As is analysed in Chapter 6, the mere existence of an intellectual property right does not grant its holder a shelter from the application of European competition laws.

CHAPTER 6

Delaying Generic Entry in the EU

INTRODUCTION

This chapter analyses the main cases and decisions concerning pharmaceutical patent settlements involving reverse payments in the European Union. As an introduction, the European Commission's Pharma Sector Inquiry Reports and their main conclusions are briefly presented. Second, the first decisions of the European Commission against anticompetitive patent settlements in the European Union on the *Lundbeck* and the *Servier* cases are discussed. The first decision of the European General Court on reverse payments in *Lundbeck v. Commission* is critically analysed, emphasising on the influence the US Supreme Court's decision in *FTC v. Actavis* had had upon the General Court's reasoning. The main focus in the legal analysis of anticompetitive reverse payments as part of patent settlements remains on Article 101 TFEU, since the European General Court and the European Commission primarily consider them as horizontal agreements between (potential) competitors, cartelising the relevant drug markets. Notwithstanding this focus, the Commission's decision in *Servier* analyses for the first time anticompetitive patent settlements under both Articles 101 and 102 TFEU, since the settlements at issue were considered to be part of the brand-name manufacturer's strategy aiming to protect its dominance in the relevant market. Finally, other kinds of anticompetitive conduct aiming to delay generic entry are presented, through a number of relevant decisions of Member States' National Competition Authorities.

I The EU Commission Pharma Sector Inquiry

In 2008, the European Commission launched the first pharmaceutical sector inquiry, based on indications that competition in the European pharmaceutical market was not working properly.[2008] Fewer new pharmaceuticals appeared to the market, while generic entry seemed to be delayed in certain cases. The Commission identified a plethora of strategies employed by originators in order to prolong the life of their patents and to avoid generic competition for the longest period possible: various patenting strategies, patent-related exchanges and litigation, launch of follow-on drug products and different types of settlements with generic drug manufacturers.[2009] It was thus necessary to examine whether patent settlements between originators and generic challengers infringed Article 101 TFEU and whether originators created artificial barriers to entry through misusing patent rights, sham litigation or through other conduct violating Article 102 TFEU.[2010] The Commission's final inquiry report was adopted on July 8, 2009. Since then, the Commission has been publishing annual reports on the monitoring of patent settlements.[2011]

In its final 2009 report on the Pharma Sector Inquiry, the Commission identified types of pharma patent settlements which may be problematic from a competition law perspective. Such settlements are for instance: (1) settlements that lead to delays in generic entry in return for a value transfer; (2) settlements containing restrictions beyond the exclusionary scope of the patent (the patent's geographic scope, its period of protection or its exclusionary scope); and (3) settlement agreements covering patents which do not meet the patentability criteria (e.g., patents granted on the basis of misleading or incomplete information).[2012] As analysed in the following sections, a generic company's ability to enter the market can be limited through several means in a settlement agreement: non-challenge and non-compete clauses, licences granted by the originator company not allowing the generic manufacturer to enter the market with its own generic product under its own commercialisation conditions, distribution agreements stipulating that the generic manufacturer will distribute the relevant drug of the originator or will source its supplies of the Active Pharmaceutical Ingredient (API) from the originator, etc.[2013] The form of value transfers in pharmaceutical patent

---

2008. European Commission Press Release, *Antitrust: Commission Launches Sector Inquiry into Pharmaceuticals with Unannounced Inspections*, IP/08/49, January 16, 2008. Available at: http://europa.eu/rapid/press-release_IP-08-49_en.htm?locale=en. (last accessed on March 31, 2018).
2009. For the detailed analysis of the issues regarding competition between originators and generic manufacturers *see* EU Commission, *Pharma Sector Inquiry*, 2009, pp. 181-368.
2010. European Commission Press Release, "Antitrust: Commission Launches Sector Inquiry into Pharmaceuticals with Unannounced Inspections," IP/08/49, January 16, 2008.
2011. For all the information and reports relating to the Pharma Sector Inquiry visit the website of the European Commission, *Pharma Sector Inquiry and Follow-up*. Available at: http://ec.europa.eu/competition/sectors/pharmaceuticals/inquiry/ (last accessed on March 31, 2018).
2012. EU Commission, *Pharma Sector Inquiry*, 2009, pp. 520-533, summarising the EU Commission's conclusions from the Pharma Sector Inquiry; EU Commission, *8th Patent Settlements Report*, 2018, p. 2.
2013. EU Commission, *8th Patent Settlements Report*, 2018, p. 3. On the contrary, royalty-free licences allowing the generic company to immediately launch its generic version without imposing any further constraints are considered to be unproblematic. *See* further *supra*, Chapter 6, Part 2, on the analysis of the *Servier* settlements.

settlements varies, ranging from direct monetary transfers to distribution agreements, side-deals or licences to the generic manufacturer.[2014]

The Commission proposed a categorisation of patent settlement agreements between originators and generic manufacturers as follows: (1) A-type agreements, which do not restrict the generic company's ability to market its own generic product; (2) B-type settlements which limit generic entry (B.I type concerns settlements not including a value transfer from the originator to the generic; B.II type settlements foresee such a value transfer).[2015] Type A settlements are normally unproblematic from a competition law perspective; the same applies to type B.I. settlements, unless they fall outside the exclusionary scope of the patent, or they concern a patent which does not meet the patentability criteria to the knowledge of the originator.[2016] The most problematic category, which is likely to attract a high degree of competition law scrutiny, is type B.II settlements which limit access to the market and contain a value transfer to the generic manufacturer. Table 6.1 below is based on the EU Commission's 8th report on the Monitoring of Patent Settlements (published on March 9, 2018) and provides a clear overview of the settlement agreements concluded in the EU from 2000 until 2016.[2017]

2014. EU Commission, *8th Patent Settlements Report*, 2018, pp. 3-4.
2015. EU Commission, *8th Patent Settlements Report*, 2018, p. 4.
2016. EU Commission, *8th Patent Settlements Report*, 2018, p. 4.
2017. EU Commission, *8th Patent Settlements Report*, 2018, p. 9, Table 2. The indication "PT-related" concerns settlement agreements which are related to Portuguese legislation enacted in 2012, mandating arbitration proceedings between originators and marketing authorisation applicants; then the originator's IPRs are not contested by the generic applicant, the proceedings are immediately settled. *See* further *idem* p. 8, where the EU Commission explains the relevant Portuguese legislative context.

Table 6.1 EU Commission, Categories of Patent Settlements (in %), 2000-2016

Type	2000 - 2Q 2008 (%)	2Q 2008-2009 (%)	2010 (%)	2011 (%)	2012 (%)	
					All	Excluding PT-related
A	52	57	61	70	43	61
B.I	26	33	36	19	51	30
B.II	22	10	3	11	7	10

Type	2013 (%)		2014 (%)		2015 (%)		2016 (%)	
	All	Excluding PT-related	All	Excluding PT-related	All	Excluding PT-related	All	Excluding PT-related
A	45	67	49	74	26	38	27	45
B.I	47	22	39	7	64	48	62	40
B.II	8	11	12	20	10	14	11	15

In 2016, type A settlements amounted to 27% of all patent settlements in the EU, type B.I. settlements amounted to 62% and type B.II. for only 11% of the settlements.[2018] The Commission found that its constant monitoring and the antitrust scrutiny which was imposed on patent settlement agreements between originators and generic challengers did not hinder companies from concluding settlements in general, but led to a decrease in the number of B.II. anticompetitive settlements.[2019]

II Health Expenditures in European Member States

Due to the large differences among European Member States' national health systems, total health spending varies greatly across the European Union. Even though the organisation and financing of health systems differs from one Member State to another,[2020] more than 70% of health expenditures are funded by the public sector in two-thirds of the Member States.[2021] In 2014, €200 billion were spent on pharmaceuticals in the European Union.[2022] In 2015, health spendings averaged at 15% of total European Member States' government expenditures and at 7.8% of the GDP in the EU as a whole. However, not all Member States are close to this average: in Hungary, health expenditures rose up to 20% of total government expenditures, while in Cyprus they only amounted to 7.2%.[2023] The Member States with the highest share of publicly funded health expenditures in 2016 were Germany, Sweden and Denmark which covered more than 84% of total health expenditures.[2024]

Despite these discrepancies, health spending is one of the largest and fastest growing expenditures for Member States' governments: the rising incomes, ageing population and the expectations for higher quality health services are expected to further increase the share of public health expenditures of Member States' GDP until

---

2018. EU Commission, *8th Patent Settlements Report*, 2018, pp. 9-13.
2019. EU Commission, *8th Patent Settlements Report*, 2018, pp. 14-15.
2020. European Commission, Economic Policy Committee (AWG), *Joint Report on Health Systems*, Occasional Papers 74, December 2010, p. 1-191. Available at: http://ec.europa.eu/economy_finance/publications/occasional_paper/2010/pdf/ocp74_en.pdf. (last accessed on March 31, 2018), pp. 81-142, analysing in detail the different MS health system characteristics (insurance coverage, expenditure control mechanisms, etc.).
2021. European Commission, European Semester Thematic Fiche: Health and Health Systems, 2017, pp. 3-4. Available at: https://ec.europa.eu/info/sites/info/files/european-semester_thematic-factsheet_health-systems_en_0.pdf (last accessed on March 31, 2018). [cited as: EU Commission, *Health Systems*, 2017]. *See also* Eurostat Website, *Healthcare Expenditure Statistics*, presenting key statistics on expenditure and financial aspects of healthcare in the European Union. Available at: http://ec.europa.eu/eurostat/statistics-explained/index.php/Healthcare_expenditure_statistics (last accessed on March 31, 2018).
2022. OECD, European Commission, *Health at a Glance: Europe 2016 – State of Health in the EU Cycle*, December 2016, pp. 1-199. Available at: http://www.oecd.org/health/health-at-a-glance-europe-23056088.htm (last accessed on March 31, 2018), p. 120.
2023. EU Commission, *Health Systems*, 2017, p. 4, Figure 3, presenting data from 2013 or most recent.
2024. EU Commission, *Health Systems*, 2017, pp. 3-4, Figure 2, presenting data from 2016 or most recent.

2060.[2025] Ensuring the sustainability of public finances on a European Union level is directly linked to the projected impact of age-related public spending on healthcare[2026] and explains why restraining the costs related to public healthcare is among the top priorities of the European Commission.

The Commission's efforts to that effect are not solely focused on the scrutiny of patent settlements between brand-name manufacturers and generic companies and on anticompetitive strategies potentially delaying generic entry. Indicatively, the EU Commission opened in May 2017 the first formal investigation concerning allegedly excessive drug pricing practices against Aspen Pharma, with the aim to examine whether the latter abused its dominant position within the meaning of Article 102 TFEU.[2027] The opening of the Commission's investigation on Aspen Pharma came after the brand-name manufacturer received a fine of more than €5 million by the Italian Competition Authority (ICA) in October 2016, finding that Aspen Pharma had fixed unfair prices by increasing up to 1500% the price for life-saving cancer drugs, in breach of Article 102 TFEU.[2028] It is worth noting that Aspen Pharma lost its appeal against this decision, on all grounds.[2029] This was not the only fine imposed by a National Competition Authority: in December 2016, UK's CMA fined the drug manufacturer Pfizer and the drug distributor Flynn Pharma £90 million for allegedly charging excessive and unfair prices in the UK for an anti-epilepsy drug.[2030]

A   The Importance of Generic Entry in the European Union

Generic entry in the pharmaceuticals market has a profound effect in the market's structure as it changes it from a monopoly market of the brand-name drug to a

---

2025. European Commission, *The 2015 Ageing Report: Economic and budgetary projections for the 28 EU Member States (2013-2060)*, European Economy 3/2015, pp. 1-424. Available at: http://ec.europa.eu/economy_finance/publications/european_economy/2015/pdf/ee3_en.pdf (last accessed on March 31, 2018), pp. 138-141.
2026. EU Commission, *Health Systems*, 2017, p. 6.
2027. EU Commission Press Release, *Antitrust: Commission opens formal investigation into Aspen Pharma's pricing practices for cancer medicines*, IP/17/1323, Brussels, May 15, 2017. Available at: http://europa.eu/rapid/press-release_IP-17-1323_en.htm. (last accessed on March 31, 2018).
2028. Autorità Garante della Concorrenza et del Mercato (Italian Competition Authority), Press Release, *A480 – Price increases for cancer drugs up to 1500%: the ICA imposes a 5 million Euro fine on the multinational Aspen*, October 14, 2016. Available at: http://www.agcm.it/en/newsroom/press-releases/2339-a480-price-increases-for-cancer-drugs-up-to-1500-the-ica-imposes-a-5-million-euro-fine-on-the-multinational-aspen.html. Last accessed on March 31, 2018).
2029. Tribunale Amministrativo Regionale per il Lazio, *Aspen Pharma Trading Limited et al. c. Autorità Garante della Concorrenza e del Mercato*, N. 08945/2017 REG.RIC., 26/7/2017. Available at: https://www.giustizia-amministrativa.it/cdsintra/wcm/idc/groups/public/documents/document/mday/ntm4/~edisp/5e2rmfwdi3oqyig55npxxhkhmu.html (last accessed on March 31, 2018).
2030. Competition and Markets Authority (CMA), Press Release, *CMA fines Pfizer and Flynn £90 million for drug price hike to NHS*, December 7, 2016. Available at: https://www.gov.uk/government/news/cma-fines-pfizer-and-flynn-90-million-for-drug-price-hike-to-nhs. (last accessed on March 31, 2018).

competitive market where more sources of supply are available.[2031] Also in the European Union, the most radical effects of generic entry are observed on the average price levels of the concerned drug product and on the sales' volumes of originators.[2032] In 2009, the price of generic medicines when they first entered the European Union market was on average 25% lower than the price of the relevant brand-name drug; two years later, when more generic drug versions were available in the market, prices were on average 40% lower than the monopoly price of the brand-name drug.[2033] The market share of generics was on average 30% within a year from the first generic entry to the relevant market, rising up to 45% after two years.[2034]

The timing of generic entry differs greatly among European Member States; for instance in the UK, Denmark and Ireland the average time of generic entry is rather short following the end of patent protection and market exclusivities, while it may exceed six months in other Member States such as Germany, France, Italy or Hungary.[2035] In order to further reduce medicines' prices and to shift demand to available generic versions, Member States use budget control mechanisms such as reference pricing, differentiation of reimbursement levels, by encouraging generic substitution, etc..[2036] In 2014, off-patent medicines that no longer enjoyed patent protection accounted for 92% of the treatment volume in the European Union, saving tax-payers an estimated €100 billion and contributing to higher access to medicines for patients of many EU countries.[2037]

Generic substitution is not harmonised in the European Union but is instead regulated in the national legislation of EU Member States.[2038] For instance, the markets of Member States in Central and Eastern Europe are typically branded generic markets, where there is no automatic generic substitution and prescriptions refer to the brand-name drug.[2039] The level and speed of generic penetration differs from one Member State to another and is generally higher in markets with automatic generic substitution, where the drug prescriptions are made by the International Nonproprietary Name (INN)[2040] rather than the brand of the relevant

---

2031. EU Commission, *Pharma Sector Inquiry*, 2009, pp. 77-78.
2032. EU Commission, *Pharma Sector Inquiry*, 2009, pp. 77-90.
2033. EU Commission, *Pharma Sector Inquiry*, 2009, pp. 94, 521.
2034. EU Commission, *Pharma Sector Inquiry*, 2009, p. 521.
2035. EU Commission, *Pharma Sector Inquiry*, 2009, p. 71.
2036. EU Commission Decision, *Lundbeck*, 2013, paras 88-96.
2037. IMS Institute, *The Role of Generic Medicines in Sustaining Healthcare Systems: a European Perspective*," June 2015, pp. 6-8. Available at: https://www.imshealth.com/files/web/IMSH%20Institute/Healthcare%20Briefs/IIHI_Generics_Healthcare_Brief.pdf. (last accessed on March 31, 2018).
2038. *See* indicatively EU Commission Decision, *Servier*, 2014, para. 2284, discussing generic substitution in the UK; para. 2321, discussing generic substitution in France; para. 2342, discussing generic substitution in Poland.
2039. EU Commission Decision, *Servier*, 2014, para. 1726.
2040. An International Nonproprietary Name (INN), also known as generic name is a unique name that is public property, is globally recognised and facilitates the identification of pharmaceutical substances or active pharmaceutical ingredients. *See* further WHO Website, *International Nonproprietary Names*. Available at: http://www.who.int/medicines/services/inn/en/ (last accessed on March 31, 2018).

drug.[2041] Generic substitution is mandatory in a handful of Member States, such as Italy, Denmark, Finland, Spain and Sweden.[2042]

B The Elimination of Adversity Between Competitors in the EU

As analysed in the US part of this book, the Hatch-Waxman Act largely eliminated the adversity between originators and generic manufacturers, by aligning their interests and making it more profitable for both parties to conclude a settlement and to collude instead of litigating.[2043] Despite the absence of a legal act remotely similar to the Hatch-Waxman Act in the European Union, originators and generic challengers may be better off by concluding a reverse payment settlement agreement, than by continuing their independent course and rivalry.[2044] The stakes for the settling parties in the European Union are nearly identical to the stakes in the US: the originator faces the risk of a court ruling of non-infringement, which would allow the concerned generic to enter the market, or even worse, of a finding of patent invalidity, which could amount to a *carte blanche* for other generics to enter the market with their respective generic versions. The protection of rivalry between pharmaceutical companies relates to the general principle of Article 101 TFEU, which requires each economic operator to determine *independently* the policy it intends to adopt in the market.[2045] In the context of a patent settlement between a generic challenger and the brand-name drug manufacturer, the two parties are at least potential competitors and should in principle pursue opposite commercial interests.[2046]

In both the European Union and the US, the risks of generic entry for the generic manufacturer, along with the high economic losses the originator would incur in case of generic entry, make a payment to the generic challenger in exchange for a commitment not to enter the market a highly attractive option, setting aside the competition law related consequences of such a payment.[2047] It makes economic sense for an originator to prevent generic entry by making a payment to the generic: the originator's loses subsequent to generic entry exceed the generic company's gains from competing. The difference in these amounts would normally accrue to consumers, in the form of lower drug prices.[2048] By settling, the originator further avoids the risks of:

2041. EU Commission, *Pharma Sector Inquiry*, 2009, pp. 72, 76, 86. See also EU Commission Decision, *Servier*, 2014, para. 1726.
2042. BELLONI, MORGAN, PARIS, Pharma Expenditures, 2016, pp. 30-31. See also EU Commission Decision, *Lundbeck*, 2013, para. 95, providing a list of examples of different generic substitution and reimbursement regimes in a number of EU Member States, in the period concerned by the decision.
2043. See supra Chapter 2, Part 2, Section IV.B.
2044. EU Commission Decision, *Lundbeck*, 2013, para. 643; EU Commission Decision, *Servier*, 2014, para. 1139; EU Commission, *Article 81(3) Guidelines*, 2004, point 14.
2045. EU Commission Decision, *Lundbeck*, 2013, para. 657; EU Commission Decision, *Servier*, 2014, para. 1147.
2046. EU Commission Decision, *Lundbeck*, 2013, para. 643.
2047. EU Commission Decision, *Lundbeck*, 2013, paras 641-644; EU Commission Decision, *Servier*, 2014, paras 1146-1154. For the analysis of the effects of rivalry in the US. *see supra* Chapter 2, Part 2, Section IV.B.
2048. EU Commission Decision, *Servier*, 2014, para. 1149.

(1) not obtaining an interim injunction against the generic drug versions; (2) patent invalidation; (3) a court finding of non-infringement; and (4) significant losses if generic entry would eventually occur.[2049] The originator's incentives to make a payment to delay generic entry increase majorly if there is an appreciable risk that the relevant patent is invalid or not infringed. From the generic manufacturer's point of view, a patent settlement with a significant value transfer is highly attractive: the generic receives a payment higher than its projected profits from entering the market, without incurring the risks attached to litigation, market entry, regulatory drug approval and the risks of competition from the originator and from other generic entrants.[2050]

Absent the anticompetitive consequences, a substantial payment for delaying generic entry without incurring the risks and costs of a generic drug launch, of patent litigation and of price competition would be a one-way street for both parties.[2051] Nevertheless these anticompetitive consequences do exist and two undertakings are not allowed to enter into reverse payment settlement agreements which block patent challenges of potentially invalid or weak patents while delaying generic entry to the market, on the basis of rent sharing.[2052] Applying competition law scrutiny to such reverse payment settlements is a necessary remedy to a market failure: the economically optimal choice for two competing pharmaceutical companies is detrimental to the competition in the drug market and subsequently to consumers and to national healthcare systems. The application of competition law scrutiny to such anticompetitive agreements attempts to remedy this market failure and negates general competition law immunity to the patent holder, but also to the settling generic company. Imposing competition law liability to these two parties for colluding, will normally remove the incentives for the parties to enter such settlements and restore the rivalry between them in both the US and the European Union markets, if not completely at least to a considerable extent.

PART 1   THE EU COMMISSION ENFORCEMENT CASES

INTRODUCTION

Following the opening of the Pharma Sector Inquiry in 2009, the European Commission undertook a number of antitrust enforcement actions against practices allegedly preventing or delaying generic entry to the market. *Lundbeck* and *Servier* are the first decisions of the European Commission on anticompetitive patent settlements between originators and generic challengers, which set the European legal standards for the antitrust analysis of patent settlements involving reverse payments; both decisions were appealed by the parties before the General Court of the European Union. The evolution and sophistication in the structure of patent settlements is clear when one

---

2049. EU Commission Decision, *Lundbeck*, 2013, para. 708.
2050. EU Commission Decision, *Servier*, 2014, para. 1150.
2051. EU Commission Decision, *Lundbeck*, 2013, paras 642, 709.
2052. EU Commission Decision, *Servier*, 2014, para. 1153.

compares the settlements at issue in *Lundbeck* and the settlements in *Servier*. Whereas the *Lundbeck* case principally concerned payments from the originator to the generic challengers, *Servier* concerns a net of complicated transactions between the generic manufacturers and the originator, comprising of side-deals, distribution and licensing agreements, etc. The Commission's antitrust analysis also evolved to a great extend from *Lundbeck* to *Servier*: whereas in both decisions the Commission found that the settlement agreements restricted competition by object, the *Servier* decision contains a detailed analysis of the effects that the agreements allegedly had had on the market, while it also expands the antitrust analysis to both Articles 101 and 102 TFEU, finding that Servier had used the settlement agreements in the context of a broader strategy to preserve its market share, abusing its dominant position.

I The Fentanyl and the Modafinil Cases

Before proceeding to the analysis of the two major antitrust enforcement cases of the European Commission in *Lundbeck* and *Servier*, it is interesting to briefly present the *Fentanyl* case and the antitrust fines that the EU Commission imposed on the US company Johnson & Johnson and on the Swiss enterprise Novartis. The major difference of the *Fentanyl* case compared to *Lundbeck*, *Servier* and the *Modafinil* cases is that Johnson & Johnson's patent protection had expired at the time of the parties' agreement: there was no dispute over the validity or infringement of the brand-name drug manufacturer's patent rights, so that the *Fentanyl* case does not fall within the categories of pharma patent settlements that are analysed in this book.

The *Modafinil* case is a case of major interest since it is the third and most recent pay-for-delay investigation launched by the European Commission. In July 2017, the Commission sent a statement of objections to Teva with its preliminary view that the agreement Teva concluded with Cephalon was in breach of EU antitrust rules. At the moment of this writing there is limited information publicly available on this case; however, for the sake of completeness the main points of the Commission's statement of objections are presented.

A Delaying the Entry of Generic Fentanyl in the Dutch Market

On December 10, 2013 the Commission imposed fines of approximately €16 million on Johnson & Johnson and on Novartis, whose Dutch subsidiaries concluded anticompetitive agreements delaying the entry of generic versions of the pain-killer Fentanyl.[2053] Johnson & Johnson had developed and commercialised Fentanyl since the

---

2053. European Commission Press Release, *Antitrust: Commission fines Johnson & Johnson and Novartis €16 million for delaying market entry of generic pain-killer fentanyl*, IP/13/1233, Brussels, December 10, 2013. Available at: http://europa.eu/rapid/press-release_IP-13-1233_en.htm. (last accessed on March 31, 2018).

1960s.[2054] In 2005, the patent protection for the Fentanyl depot patch expired in the Netherlands and Novartis' subsidiary Sandoz was at the verge of launching its generic Fentanyl version. However, instead of entering the market, Sandoz concluded a "co-promotion agreement" with Janssen-Cilag, the Dutch subsidiary of Johnson & Johnson.[2055] This agreement provided Sandoz strong incentives not to enter the market, in the form of monthly payments exceeding Sandoz's projected profits if it would have entered the generic market. In December 2006, when another generic manufacturer was about to launch generic Fentanyl, the agreement ceased. The Commission found that this agreement infringed Article 101 TFEU by object, since it delayed the market entry of cheaper generics in the Netherlands for seventeen months, keeping prices artificially high to the expense of patients and tax-payers financing the Dutch health system.[2056] The agreement's aim was to preserve Fentanyl's high price and to split part of the resulting profits, as demonstrated by the following facts: (1) before concluding the agreement Janssen-Cilag had not considered any other potential co-promotion partner; (2) Sandoz engaged to very limited (or none) co-promotion activities; (3) the payment exceeded Sandoz's potential generic profits. Neither Johnson & Johnson nor Novartis appealed against the Commission's fines.

B The Settlement Between Teva and Cephalon on Modafinil

In 2011, the EU Commission opened an antitrust investigation to assess whether an agreement between the US-based pharmaceutical manufacturer Cephalon and the generic manufacturer Teva may had had the object or effect of hindering generic competition in the EEA area. The agreement concerned the drug Modafinil, a medicine used for treating certain types of sleeping disorders, marketed under the brand-name Provigil.[2057] Cephalon held patents on Provigil and on its manufacture; when certain compound patents expired in the EEA, Teva entered the UK market for a short time-period.[2058] After Cephalon sued for the alleged infringement of its process patents on Modafinil, the two parties settled the litigation in December 2005, by entering a worldwide agreement settling the suits in the US and in the UK.[2059] In the context of the

---

2054. Case AT.39685 – Fentanyl, Commission Decision of 10 December 2013, relating to a proceeding under Article 101 of the Treaty on the Functioning of the European Union C(2013) 8870 final, Brussels, 10.12.2013, paras 68-88. [cited as: EU Commission Decision, *Fentanyl*, 2013].
2055. For a detailed description of the co-promotion agreement and the supply agreement between Sandoz and Janssen-Cilag *see* EU Commission Decision, *Fentanyl*, 2013, paras 109-203.
2056. EU Commission Decision, *Fentanyl*, 2013, paras 211-399, analysing the Commission's rationale in finding a restriction of competition by object. *See idem* paras 400-439, rejecting the parties' arguments for an exemption under Article 101(3) TFEU.
2057. EU Commission Press Release, *Antitrust: Commission sends Statement of Objections to Teva on "pay-for-delay" pharma agreement*, IP/17/2063, Brussels, July 17, 2017. Available at: http://europa.eu/rapid/press-release_IP-17-2063_en.htm (last accessed on March 31, 2018) [cited as: EU Commission Press Release, *Modafinil*, 2017]. *See* further European Commission Press Release, *Antitrust: Commission opens investigation against pharmaceutical companies Cephalon and Teva*, IP/11/511, April 28, 2011. Available at: http://europa.eu/rapid/press-release_IP-11-511_en.htm?locale=en. (last accessed on March 31, 2018).
2058. EU Commission Press Release, *Modafinil*, 2017.
2059. *Idem*.

settlement, Teva committed not to launch its generic Modafinil products in the EEA markets before October 2012. In the US, Cephalon did not only settle with Teva but also with Barr, Mylan and Ranbaxy; all settlements concerned the drug Provigil and were subject to an antitrust complaint by the FTC, which was settled in 2015.[2060]

On July 2017, the EU Commission informed Teva of its preliminary view that its agreement with Cephalon concerning Modafinil was in breach of EU competition law.[2061] In its statement of objections, the Commission stressed that Provigil was a blockbuster drug and that Teva received a substantial transfer of value from Cephalon through a series of cash payments and other agreements.[2062] Unfortunately, the details of the settlement and of the value transfers from Cephalon to Teva are not yet public. However, the Commission's preliminary view is that the settlement constituted a pay-for-delay agreement, which may have caused substantial harm to European patients and healthcare budgets by delaying the entry of cheaper generic drug versions. If the Commission's view is confirmed, this settlement amounts to an infringement of Article 101 TFEU. Given that both Cephalon and Teva do not have their seats within the European Union, it is interesting to see whether the Commission's jurisdiction on the alleged conduct will be challenged by the parties. This may not be an easy endeavour especially given CJEU's ruling in *Intel* in 2017, which confirmed that the European Commission's jurisdiction to find and punish conduct that was adopted outside the European Union may be established on the basis of either the implementation test (if the conduct at issue was implemented in the EU) or the qualified effects test (if this conduct had anticompetitive effects liable to have an impact within the EU market – even if it was not adopted in the EU).[2063]

II *Lundbeck v. Commission*

Lundbeck, a Danish drug manufacturer, developed and marketed Cipramil, an antidepressant drug with the active ingredient citalopram. After the basic patent for the drug's molecule expired, Lundbeck held a number of process patents. In 2002, Lundbeck settled with the generic manufacturers Merck (GUK), Alpharma, Arrow and Ranbaxy, concluding six agreements with a duration ranging from ten to twenty-two months, covering the markets of the UK, the EEA, Norway, Denmark and

---

2060. FTC Press Release, *FTC Settlement of Cephalon Pay-for-delay Case Ensures $1.2 Billion in Ill-Gotten Gains Relinquished; Refunds Will Go To Purchasers Affected By Anticompetitive Tactics*, May 28, 2015. Available at: https://www.ftc.gov/news-events/press-releases/2015/05/ftc-settlement-cephalon-pay-delay-case-ensures-12-billion-ill. (last accessed on March 31, 2018). The FTC action led to the decision of *King Drug Co. of Florence, Inc. v. Cephalon, Inc.*, 702 F. Supp. 2d 514 (E.D. PA. 2010); *see also supra* Chapter 3, Part 2, Section IV.B.
2061. In 2011, Cephalon became a subsidiary of Teva, so that the EU Commission's statement of objections was addressed to Teva and its subsidiary Cephalon. *See* European Commission Press Release, *Mergers: Commission approves the acquisition of Cephalon by Teva, subject to conditions*, IP/11/1193, October 14, 2011. Available at: http://europa.eu/rapid/press-release_IP-11-1193_en.htm. (last accessed on March 31, 2018).
2062. EU Commission Press Release, *Modafinil*, 2017.
2063. Judgment of the Court of 6 September 2017, Case C-413/14 P, *Intel Corporation Inc. v. Commission*, EU:C:2017:632, paras. 40-47.

Switzerland.²⁰⁶⁴ In return for the generics' commitment not to enter the citalopram market, Lundbeck paid them significant amounts and provided other incentives: indicatively, pursuant to two settlements covering the UK and the EEA market, Lundbeck transferred to Merck GUK the equivalent of €31.4 million.

In 2013, the European Commission found that these settlements constituted restrictions of competition by object and imposed a fine of €93.7 million on Lundbeck and €52.2 million on the generic undertakings.²⁰⁶⁵ Lundbeck and all the generic manufacturers appealed the Commission's decision before the General Court of the European Union. On September 8, 2016 the General Court published the *Lundbeck* decision, its first decision on patent settlements involving reverse payments. The General Court dismissed all actions brought by the undertakings, confirmed the Commission's fines and ruled that the settlements at issue constituted restrictions of competition by object.²⁰⁶⁶ The following sections present in parallel the main points of the Commission's decision and of the General Court's ruling on *Lundbeck*. For the shake of brevity, the rest of the Court's decisions on the generic manufacturers' appeals are not be discussed,²⁰⁶⁷ since the reasoning, position and findings of the General Court remain nearly identical to its decision on Lundbeck's appeal.

A The Role of the Patent in the Antitrust Analysis

1 *The Presumption of Patent Validity in the Commission's Decision*

As in the US, also in the European Union a patent is assumed to be valid and the patent holder's ownership of the patent right is considered to be lawful.²⁰⁶⁸ However, this assumption does not bar legal court actions challenging the patent validity.²⁰⁶⁹ The specific subject matter of the patent cannot be interpreted as affording protection against competitors' actions brought in order to challenge patent validity, given the public interest in the elimination of erroneously granted patents that create obstacles to

---

2064. Judgment of the General Court of 8 September 2016, Case T-472/13, *H. Lundbeck A/S and Lundbeck Ltd v. European Commission*, EU:T:2016:449 (Judgment of the General Court of 8 September 2016, Case T-472/13, *Lundbeck v. Commission*),.
2065. European Commission, Press Release, *Antitrust: Commission fines Lundbeck and other pharma companies for delaying market entry of generic medicines*, IP/13/563, Brussels, June 19, 2013. Available at: http://europa.eu/rapid/press-release_IP-13-563_en.htm?locale=en. (last accessed on March 31, 2018).
2066. For an analysis of the main points of the General Court's decision in Case T-472/13, *Lundbeck v. Commission*, see ATHANASIADOU, Lundbeck v. Commission, 2016.
2067. Judgment of the General Court of 8 September 2016, Case T-460/13, *Sun Pharmaceutical Industries Ltd, formerly Ranbaxy Laboratories Ltd and Ranbaxy (UK) Ltd v. European Commission*, EU:T:2016:453; Judgment of the General Court of 8 September 2016, Case T-467/13, *Arrow Group ApS and Arrow Generics Ltd v. European Commission*, EU:T:2016:450; Judgment of the General Court of 8 September 2016, Case T-470/13, *Merck KGaA v. European Commission*, EU:T:2016:452; Judgment of the General Court of 8 September 2016, Case T-471/13, *Xellia Pharmaceuticals ApS and Alpharma, LLC, formerly Zoetis Products LLC v. European Commission*, EU:T:2016:460.
2068. Judgment of the General Court of 1 July 2010, T-321/05, *AstraZeneca v. Commission*, para. 362.
2069. EU Commission Decision, *Lundbeck*, 2013, para. 628.

economic activity.[2070] Such generic challenges to patent validity are an essential element of the competitive process between generic companies that seek to enter the market and originators invoking their patents against generic entry.[2071]

Similarly to the US, in the European Union the assumption of patent validity is used by courts in order to allocate the burden of proof: an originator claiming patent infringement by the generic entrant bears the burden of proving such infringement, while a generic challenger alleging patent invalidity shall carry the relevant burden of proof.[2072] However, the assumed validity of a patent can be highly irrelevant in cases where the potential generic entrant does not infringe the patent. This was the case in *Lundbeck* according to the Commission, which found that the assumed validity of Lundbeck's process patent was not sufficient to exclude generic competition with respect to the drug's compound.[2073] The Commission adopted an *ex ante* perspective, examining the legality of Lundbeck's settlements at the time these settlements were concluded.[2074] At the time of settlements, both Lundbeck and the generic companies believed there was a concrete possibility that Lundbeck's process patents would be found to be invalid, either partially or entirely.[2075] Moreover, the generic challengers never admitted the validity of Lundbeck's patent in their respective settlement agreements.[2076] At the time of settlements, Lundbeck could not claim as an objective fact that an infringement existed or that it had the right to exclude the generics from the market.[2077] Lundbeck could have used national court procedures to enforce its patents or it could have settled relying solely on the strength of its patents, if it were convinced that they were valid and infringed. However, in the one instance that Lundbeck tried to enforce its process patent before UK courts, it failed.[2078]

The European Commission linked the likelihood of patent invalidity to the size of the reverse payment: the higher the chance of a finding of patent invalidity or non-infringement and the higher the originator's damages from generic entry, the bigger the reverse payment would be.[2079] The Commission identified as "exclusion payments" payments by the originator to the generic which result in the latter accepting commercial limitations which it would not normally accept on the basis of its assessment of likelihood of patent invalidity or infringement. Such a promise would

---

2070. Judgment of the Court of 25 February 1986, Case 193/83, *Windsurfing International Inc. v. Commission of the European Communities*, EU:C:1986:75, para. 92; Judgment of the General Court of 1 July 2010, T-321/05, *AstraZeneca v. Commission*, para. 367.
2071. EU Commission Decision, *Lundbeck*, 2013, para. 1036.
2072. EU Commission Decision, *Lundbeck*, 2013, para. 78.
2073. EU Commission Decision, *Lundbeck*, 2013, para. 668.
2074. EU Commission Decision, *Lundbeck*, 2013, para. 669.
2075. EU Commission Decision, *Lundbeck*, 2013, para. 669, stating that the generics considered Lundbeck's crystallisation process patent "high school chemistry," while Lundbeck itself had estimated there was a 60% possibility that the patent would be invalidated by a UK court.
2076. EU Commission Decision, *Lundbeck*, 2013, para. 669.
2077. EU Commission Decision, *Lundbeck*, 2013, para. 674.
2078. *Idem*, noting that Lundbeck failed to enforce its crystallisation patent in the Lagap litigation before UK courts.
2079. EU Commission Decision, *Lundbeck*, 2013, para. 640. *See also supra* Chapter 4, Part 1, Section III.2, analysing the position of the Supreme Court in *FTC v. Actavis* that the size of an unjustified reverse payment is a strong indicator of the patent's weakness.

mean that the generic agrees to give up its independent efforts to enter the market – at least for the duration of the settlement.[2080] The idea behind the Commission's reasoning is identical to the one expressed by the US Supreme Court in *FTC v. Actavis*: the anticompetitive harm of such patent settlements is the prevention of even a small risk of generic competition in the market.[2081]

2 Potential Competition and the Presumption of Patent Validity

In its decision in *Lundbeck*, the General Court discussed the presumption of patent validity in connection with the issue of potential competition. Lundbeck argued that the launch of generic products that infringe third parties' IP rights is not the expression of potential competition under Article 101(1) TFEU.[2082] The General Court rejected this argument, which was based on the erroneous premises that: (1) the generic drug versions infringed Lundbeck's patents beyond doubt, and; (2) that Lundbeck's patents were ironclad to the invalidity claims raised in the generic undertakings' infringement actions.[2083]

The General Court stressed that the presumption of patent validity shall not be equated with a presumption of illegality of generic drugs validly placed on the market: while a patent is presumed valid until expressly revoked or invalidated, this presumption of patent validity shall not be equated with a presumption of patent infringement by *all* potential generic drug versions.[2084] Generic entry "at risk" is not unlawful *ipso facto*: the burden of proof lay with Lundbeck to prove before national courts that these generic drug versions infringed its process patents.[2085] In the context of the patent litigation, the generic entrants were free to seek a declaration of invalidity of the patents invoked by Lundbeck, while Lundbeck itself estimated the probability of invalidation of its crystallisation patent at 50%-60%.[2086] Thus, Lundbeck's process patents were not necessarily insurmountable barriers to generic entry.[2087]

At the time of settlements, the generic challengers had a number of concrete possibilities to enter the market: (1) launching at risk; (2) requesting a court declaration of non-infringement; (3) opposing the patent before the national authorities or

---

2080. EU Commission Decision, *Lundbeck*, 2013, para. 640.
2081. *FTC v. Actavis, Inc.*, 133 S. Ct. 2223, 2236 (2013). *See also supra* Chapter 4, Section III.2.
2082. Judgment of the General Court of 8 September 2016, Case T-472/13, *Lundbeck v. Commission*, para. 115.
2083. Judgment of the General Court of 8 September 2016, Case T-472/13, *Lundbeck v. Commission*, para. 120.
2084. Judgment of the General Court of 8 September 2016, Case T-472/13, *Lundbeck v. Commission*, para. 121.
2085. Judgment of the General Court of 8 September 2016, Case T-472/13, *Lundbeck v. Commission*, para. 122.
2086. Judgment of the General Court of 8 September 2016, Case T-472/13, *Lundbeck v. Commission* para. 122, relying on evidence in the EU Commission Decision, *Lundbeck*, 2013, paras 157, 745.
2087. Judgment of the General Court of 8 September 2016, Case T-472/13, *Lundbeck v. Commission*, paras 124-127.

EPO and requesting it to be revoked or narrowed, etc.[2088] These possibilities represented the expression of potential competition: the drug's API patent and some other process patents had expired at the time the agreements were concluded, while there were other non-infringing processes in order to produce generic citalopram.[2089] Moreover, the generic undertakings were ready to enter the market and to accept the risks attached to such an entry: they have taken steps and made investments to that effect and have also obtained or could readily obtain a marketing authorisation for their generic drug versions.[2090] The generic manufacturer Merck had even entered the market: its distributor NM Pharma had been selling generic citalopram in Sweden for five months before the conclusion of the settlement agreement and Merck also sold generic tablets of citalopram in the UK for a value of £3.3 million, before obtaining a second extension of its settlement agreement with Lundbeck on the UK market.[2091] The generics' readiness and preparations to enter the market and Merck's effective entry at risk amounted to potential competition, despite Lundbeck's allegations of the unlawfulness of generic entry and the possibility for it to prevent this entry by relying on its process patents.[2092] Therefore, the General Court rejected the applicants' argument that the presumption of patent validity and the related IP rights prevented the finding that the parties were potential competitors at the time of settlements.[2093]

3 The Rejection of the Scope of the Patent Test

3.1 The EU Commission's Rationale for Rejecting the Scope of the Patent Test

In its decision in *Lundbeck,* the European Commission stressed that an agreement involving a considerable payment from the originator to the generic challenger in return for the latter's promise not to enter the market for a certain period of time merits full competition law scrutiny.[2094] A patent grants its holder the right to oppose possible patent infringements but not the right to pay actual or potential competitors in order to stay out of the market or to refrain from challenging the patent's validity.[2095] Any limitations imposed by patent settlement agreements between generic challengers and originators shall fall within the scope of the patent at issue and not exceed it.[2096] The

---

2088. Judgment of the General Court of 8 September 2016, Case T-472/13, *Lundbeck v. Commission,* paras 97, 128.
2089. Judgment of the General Court of 8 September 2016, Case T-472/13, *Lundbeck v. Commission,* paras 127,129.
2090. Judgment of the General Court of 8 September 2016, Case T-472/13, *Lundbeck v. Commission,* paras 129, 131, referring to EU Commission Decision, *Lundbeck,* 2013, paras 738 to 743 and 827 to 832 as regards Merck (GUK), paras 877 to 883 and 965 to 969 as regards Arrow, paras 1016 to 1018 as regards Alpharma and paras 1090 to 1102 as regards Ranbaxy.
2091. Judgment of the General Court of 8 September 2016, Case T-472/13, *Lundbeck v. Commission,* para. 131.
2092. *Idem.*
2093. Judgment of the General Court of 8 September 2016, Case T-472/13, *Lundbeck v. Commission,* paras 131-132. *See also* EU Commission Decision, *Lundbeck,* 2013, paras 621-636, finding that the settling parties were potential competitors.
2094. EU Commission Decision, *Lundbeck,* 2013, para. 640.
2095. EU Commission Decision, *Lundbeck,* 2013, para. 641.
2096. EU Commission Decision, *Lundbeck,* 2013, para. 659.

scope of the patent test was explicitly rejected by the Commission, since it would allow originators to financially induce generics to abandon any effort to enter the market even after the expiry of the patent covering the drug's compound: such a test would decrease competition in the pharma sector and would preserve the high cost of drug products whose patent protection has expired.[2097] The EU Commission did not accept that a *payment* to delay generic entry could fall within the scope of the patent. The means that patent holders use in order to defend their rights matter and not all are compatible with European competition laws.[2098] An exclusion payment to a competitor – in return for the latter's commitment not to enter the market – is not a right granted by patent law and is not a legitimate mean for the protection of patent rights.[2099] The "specific subject matter" of a patent covers the right to oppose and not the right to buy off competition; therefore, the Commission found that Lundbeck's settlements fell outside the patent's subject matter.[2100]

A valid patent prevents generic competitors from using the patented invention. During the patent exclusivity period, amounting in practice to a maximum of fifteen years,[2101] the patent holder may be able to charge for the brand-name drug a price which considerably exceeds the drug's marginal cost of production, in order to recoup its significant investment costs on R&D. Once the drug's compound patent and any SPCs have expired, the drug's active ingredient can in principle be used by generic manufacturers in order to produce and market their generic drug versions.[2102] The compound's original patent application shall indicate how the invention can be reproduced,[2103] so that the patent protection for the original production method of the drug's active ingredient normally expires simultaneously with the patent protecting the drug's active ingredient.[2104]

If a drug's molecule patent and original process patent have expired (including any granted SPCs), the generic competitors can legitimately use processes which are not protected by patent rights in order to produce and market their generic drug versions.[2105] Lundbeck only owned process patents on citalopram, limited to a particular process for the production of the active ingredient.[2106] According to the Commission, such process patents did not justify a commitment from generic competitors not to sell citalopram for a certain time-period, irrespectively of whether the processes the generic manufacturers used infringed Lundbeck's remaining patents;

2097. EU Commission Decision, *Lundbeck*, 2013, para. 698.
2098. EU Commission Decision, *Lundbeck*, 2013, para. 641.
2099. EU Commission Decision, *Lundbeck*, 2013, para. 698.
2100. *Idem*.
2101. Recital 9, Regulation (EC) No. 469/2009. *See also supra*, Chapter 5, Part 1, Section III.B.1 on Supplementary Protection Certificates.
2102. EU Commission Decision, *Lundbeck*, 2013, para. 68.
2103. *See* further Article 83 EPC, "[t]he European patent application shall disclose the invention in a manner sufficiently clear and complete for it to be carried out by a person skilled in the art;" Article 29 TRIPS Agreement, "Members shall require that an applicant for a patent shall disclose the invention in a manner sufficiently clear and complete for the invention to be carried out by a person skilled in the art […]."
2104. EU Commission Decision, *Lundbeck*, 2013, para. 68.
2105. EU Commission Decision, *Lundbeck*, 2013, para. 642.
2106. EU Commission Decision, *Lundbeck*, 2013, paras 144-147.

thus, the agreement's object was to commit generic competitors to stay out of the citalopram market entirely.[2107] The scope of the settlement agreements was broader than the scope of Lundbeck's patents, while the commitments that the generic challengers accepted went beyond what a court enforcement of Lundbeck's process patents could have achieved.[2108]

The Commission's message in *Lundbeck* is clear: even if patent settlement agreements fall within the temporal, territorial and substantive scope of the relevant patents, the fundamental legal analysis of these settlements remains unchanged.[2109] The settling parties in *Lundbeck* have advocated in favour of the scope of the patent test: provided that a genuine dispute existed and that there was no "restriction of competition beyond that legitimately created by the patent itself," settlements should not attract antitrust scrutiny regardless of the existence of a payment.[2110] Lundbeck further argued that any restrictive effects of the agreements were inherent to the underlying intellectual property right.[2111] The Commission stressed that even if the limitations to the generic company's commercial autonomy do not go beyond the material scope of the patent, they can still infringe Article 101 TFEU if they result from the transfer of value and not from the parties' independent assessment of the patent right.[2112] Restrictions that fall outside the substantive scope of the patent are identified as restrictions which could not have been obtained by the patentee's rights to oppose alleged infringement before a court.[2113] According to the Commission, Lundbeck obtained extensive limitations to generic entry through its six settlement agreements with the generic manufacturers, limitations which it could not have obtained through enforcing its process patents before national courts.[2114] Four of the settlement agreements went beyond the scope of Lundbeck's process patent, excluding from the market future citalopram products which could be produced in a non-infringing manner.[2115]

3.2 The General Court Rejects the Scope of the Patent Test

The General Court largely upheld the EU Commission's rejection of the scope of the patent test as the relevant standard for the analysis of reverse payments under European competition laws. One of the core points the General Court made in *Lundbeck* is that the application of Article 101(1) TFEU to patent settlement agreements is by no means excluded: an agreement is not exempt from competition laws merely because it concerns a patent or is intended to solve a patent dispute.[2116] The exercise of industrial property rights under the legislation of Member States is generally not

---

2107. EU Commission Decision, *Lundbeck*, 2013, para. 642.
2108. EU Commission Decision, *Lundbeck*, 2013, para. 675.
2109. EU Commission Decision, *Lundbeck*, 2013, para. 698.
2110. *Idem*.
2111. *Idem*.
2112. EU Commission Decision, *Lundbeck*, 2013, para. 641.
2113. EU Commission Decision, *Lundbeck*, 2013, para. 642.
2114. EU Commission Decision, *Lundbeck*, 2013, paras 692-693.
2115. EU Commission Decision, *Lundbeck*, 2013, para. 693.
2116. Judgment of the General Court of 8 September 2016, Case T-472/13, *Lundbeck v. Commission* paras 117, 459.

affected by Article 101(1) TFEU. Nevertheless, the conditions of exercise of such a right may fall under Article 101(1)'s prohibitions in cases where this exercise is seemingly the object, means or consequence of an agreement, decision or concerted practice.[2117] The General Court relied on the *Windsurfing* judgment and noted that even though the EU Commission is not competent to determine the scope of the patent, it may take action when this scope is relevant for determining whether an infringement of Article 101 or Article 102 TFEU occurred.[2118] The General Court agreed that the specific subject matter of the patent did not afford protection against actions challenging the validity of the patent, given the public interest in eliminating obstacles to the economic activity arising from erroneous patent grants.[2119]

The applicants in *Lundbeck* asserted that agreements containing restrictions inherent to the exercise of patent rights should not be covered by Article 101(1) TFEU, arguing in favour of the scope of the patent test as the relevant standard for the analysis of reverse payment settlements.[2120] The General Court upheld the EU Commission's decision and rejected the application of the scope of the patent test: "[f]irst, [the scope of the patent test] leads to a presumption that a generic medicinal product infringes the originator undertaking's patent and thus allows the generic medicinal product to be excluded on that basis, when the question whether it infringes any patents is an unresolved issue. Secondly, it is based on the premiss that any patent invoked in the context of a settlement agreement will be held valid if its validity is challenged, although there is no basis in law or in practice for that outcome [...]. The 'scope of the patent' test is therefore based on a subjective assessment, by the applicants, of the scope of their patents and of their validity, whereas a national court or competent authority may have taken a different view."[2121]

Drawing inspiration from *FTC v. Actavis*,[2122] the General Court noted that the question of whether a particular restraint lies beyond the limits of the patent monopoly is a conclusion that follows from the examination of the scope and validity of the patent and not the starting point of analysis.[2123] An important point made in the *Lundbeck* decision is that even if the restrictions imposed by the settlement agreements potentially fell within the scope of the relevant patents, these agreements went *beyond* the subject matter of intellectual property rights, which includes the right to oppose

---

2117. Judgment of the General Court of 8 September 2016, Case T-472/13, *Lundbeck v. Commission*, para. 117, citing Judgment of the Court of 31 October 1974, Case 15-74 *Centrafarm BV and Adriaan de Peijper v. Sterling Drug Inc.*, EU:C:1974:114, para. 9.
2118. Judgment of the General Court of 8 September 2016, Case T-472/13, *Lundbeck v. Commission*, para. 119, citing Judgment of the Court of 25 February 1986, Case 193/83, *Windsurfing International Inc. v. Commission of the European Communities*, EU:C:1986:75, (Case 193/83, *Windsurfing v. Commission*), para. 26.
2119. Judgment of the General Court of 8 September 2016, Case T-472/13, *Lundbeck v. Commission*, para. 119, citing Case 193/83, *Windsurfing*, para. 92.
2120. Judgment of the General Court of 8 September 2016, Case T-472/13, *Lundbeck v. Commission*, paras 478-484, 499.
2121. Judgment of the General Court of 8 September 2016, Case T-472/13, *Lundbeck v. Commission*, para. 491.
2122. *See supra* Chapter 4, Part 1, analysing the *FTC v. Actavis* decision of the US Supreme Court.
2123. Judgment of the General Court of 8 September 2016, Case T-472/13, *Lundbeck v. Commission*, paras 492, 493, referring to *FTC v. Actavis*, 133 S. Ct. 2223, 2231-2232 (2013).

infringements but *not* the right to pay actual or potential competitors in order for them not to enter the market.[2124] The General Court noted that the Commission had not successfully carried the burden of establishing that the UK settlement between Lundbeck and Merck went beyond the scope of Lundbeck's patents;[2125] however, this did not alter the finding of a restriction by object.[2126]

B Lawful Patent Settlements

1 Settlements Falling Outside the Scope of Article 101(1) TFEU

In its decision in *Lundbeck* the EU Commission outlined the patent settlements which could fall outside the scope of Article 101(1) TFEU, staying close to the *dicta* of the US Supreme Court in *FTC v. Actavis*.[2127] First, a settlement based on the parties' assessment of the probability of the patent being held invalid or not infringed by a court will not normally infringe Article 101 TFEU if: (1) it is reached without an inducement, and; (2) the limitations agreed in the settlement do not go beyond the rights granted by patent law.[2128] Such an agreement may contain an obligation for the generic competitor not to use the invention covered by the patent during part or for the totality of the patent term, since this limitation will normally be based on the parties' competing interests and on their perceptions concerning the strength of the patent.[2129] Due to the parties' adversity and conflicting interests, the generic competitor concluding such a settlement is not likely to accept stricter limitations on its entry conditions than the ones it estimates that it is bound to accept due to the patent's strength.[2130]

Second, even a patent settlement containing a payment could fall outside the scope of Article 101(1) TFEU if such a payment is instrumental in concluding a settlement accepted by both parties.[2131] According to the Commission, a payment from the generic entrant to the originator (thus not a "reverse" payment) may be legitimate, if for example the generic has entered the market and in the course of litigation, a high likelihood emerges that the relevant patent is valid or infringed. In such a case, the generic company may agree to withdraw its product from the market and to pay damages to the patent holder.[2132] In its decision in *Lundbeck*, the Commission also provided an example of a legitimate reverse payment: if the generic competitor has stayed out of the market as a result of legal threats or court action by the originator but later on there is a high likelihood that the patent was not infringed or that it was invalid,

---

2124. Judgment of the General Court of 8 September 2016, Case T-472/13, *Lundbeck v. Commission*, paras 495, 539.
2125. Judgment of the General Court of 8 September 2016, Case T-472/13, *Lundbeck v. Commission*, para. 569.
2126. Judgment of the General Court of 8 September 2016, Case T-472/13, *Lundbeck v. Commission*, paras 570-574, 599.
2127. *See supra* Chapter 4, Part 1, Sections III, IV.
2128. EU Commission Decision, *Lundbeck*, 2013, paras. 638, 659.
2129. EU Commission Decision, *Lundbeck*, 2013, para. 638.
2130. *Idem.*
2131. EU Commission Decision, *Lundbeck*, 2013, para. 639.
2132. *Idem.*

the originator may allow the generic to immediately enter the market but may also include a payment to compensate the generic company for the damages suffered.[2133] The Commission's position on permissible patent settlements was upheld in its entirety by the General Court, which noted that the existence of a reverse payment is not always problematic, especially when such a payment: (1) is linked to the strength of the patent as perceived by the settling parties; (2) is a necessary element in order to find an acceptable and legitimate solution for both parties; and (3) is not accompanied by restrictions intending to delay generic entry.[2134]

2 The Legitimate Settlement Between Neolab and Lundbeck

An example of an unproblematic patent settlement is the settlement between Lundbeck and Neolab. When Neolab launched a generic version of citalopram in the UK, Lundbeck started infringement proceedings against it; Neolab in return counterclaimed that Lundbeck's patent was invalid.[2135] Neolab accepted voluntary injunctions and refrained from selling its generic drug, while Lundbeck committed to pay damages if its patent was found to be invalid. According to Lundbeck's internal documents, there was a 90% possibility of such an invalidity finding, so the company preferred to settle.[2136] On the basis of this settlement, Lundbeck agreed to pay Neolab damages for the year the generic was prevented from selling its drug due to the voluntary injunctions and released Neolab from any claims for past and future sales, reserving its patent rights for the period after March 2004. Neolab from its side released Lundbeck from any claims for damages.[2137] The Commission found that this settlement, including a payment from the originator to the generic, was unproblematic even though it was clear that the settlement prevented a highly likely invalidation of Lundbeck's patent.[2138] As a result of this settlement with Neolab and of Lundbeck's settlement with Lagap, the validity of the crystallisation patent was never decided by a UK court.[2139]

The General Court confirmed the Commission's finding that Neolab's settlement with Lundbeck was unproblematic, despite Lundbeck's payment to Neolab. This reverse payment was made in exchange for Neolab's commitment not to seek damages before courts, while Lundbeck had committed not to bring any claims under its patents against Neolab for a certain time-period.[2140] The court noted that there was a first settlement between Neolab and Lundbeck which provided for the delay in generic entry pending the outcome of the Lagap litigation; however that settlement did not involve a transfer of value and was conditional upon Lundbeck paying Neolab

---

2133. EU Commission Decision, *Lundbeck*, 2013, para. 639.
2134. Judgment of the General Court of 8 September 2016, Case T-472/13, *Lundbeck v. Commission*, paras 350, 360, referring to EU Commission Decision, *Lundbeck*, 2013, paras 638, 639.
2135. EU Commission Decision, *Lundbeck*, 2013, para. 164.
2136. *Idem.*
2137. *Idem.*
2138. EU Commission Decision, *Lundbeck*, 2013, para. 165.
2139. *Idem.*
2140. Judgment of the General Court of 8 September 2016, Case T-472/13, *Lundbeck v. Commission*, para. 350, referring to EU Commission Decision, *Lundbeck*, 2013, paras 164, 639.

damages in case of an unfavourable judgment.[2141] After Lundbeck settled with Lagap,[2142] Neolab still had an interest in invalidating Lundbeck's patent and obtaining damages. Lundbeck's commitment not to make any patent claims in the event Neolab entered the market was of crucial importance and differentiated the Neolab settlement from the rest of Lundbeck's reverse payment settlements.[2143] Unlike the latter, the payment in the Neolab settlement was accompanied by an acceptance of non-infringement and a commitment by Lundbeck not to impede generic entry, so that it was clear that the payment was *not* made in exchange for generic exclusion from the market.[2144] The reverse payment's actual object was to settle the dispute between the parties without delaying the market entry of generics.[2145]

C Restriction of Competition by Object

The concept of restriction of competition by object under European competition law has been analysed in Chapter 5 of this book. Suffice to recall that an agreement whose objective aim, inherent tendency or necessary consequence is to restrict competition falls under the category of restrictions by object.[2146] In its decision in *Lundbeck* the European Commission examined for the first time a set of reverse payment settlements and concluded that they constituted restrictions of competition by object,[2147] a finding that was subsequently upheld by the General Court, as discussed in the following sections.

1 The Commission's Criteria for Determining a Restriction by Object

The case-by-case assessment of the facts and the specific circumstances of each case is necessary in order to determine whether patent settlements are based on each party's individual assessment of the strength of the patent and whether the limitations imposed by the agreement fall within the scope of the patent.[2148] According to the Commission, the key elements for the assessment of a reverse payment settlement are: (1) whether certain limitations were imposed on the generic manufacturer's behaviour,

---

2141. Judgment of the General Court of 8 September 2016, Case T-472/13, *Lundbeck v. Commission*, para. 351.
2142. *See* further EU Commission Decision, *Lundbeck*, 2013, paras 152-163, analysing Lagap's generic entry to the market and its settlement with Lundbeck.
2143. Judgment of the General Court of 8 September 2016, Case T-472/13, *Lundbeck v. Commission*, para. 351.
2144. *Idem.*
2145. Judgment of the General Court of 8 September 2016, Case T-472/13, *Lundbeck v. Commission*, para. 350.
2146. *See supra* Chapter 5, Part 2, Section II.C.1, on restrictions of competition by object under EU competition laws.
2147. EU Commission Decision, *Lundbeck*, 2013, paras 736-1174, examining one by one all the settlement agreements between the parties and finding that they constitute restrictions of competition by object of Article 101(1) TFEU.
2148. EU Commission Decision, *Lundbeck*, 2013, para. 659.

and; (2) whether those limitations were achieved by means of a payment from the originator to the generic manufacturer – irrespectively of whether they fell within or outside the scope of the patent.[2149]

The Commission outlines in *Lundbeck* three decisive criteria for determining whether a reverse payment settlement constitutes a restriction of competition by object: (1) whether the generic manufacturer and the originator were at least potential competitors at the time of settlement; (2) whether the generic manufacturer committed to limit its independent efforts to enter with its generic drug version one or more EEA markets for the duration of the agreement; (3) whether the agreement was linked to a transfer of value from the originator to the generic manufacturer, which considerably reduced the incentives of the generic undertaking to independently pursue its efforts to enter one or more EEA markets.[2150] The Commission also outlined additional important factors particular in the *Lundbeck* case, such as the fact that the originator's value transfers to the generic manufacturers took into consideration their expected profits if they would have succeeded in entering the market. The Commission also stressed the absence of a commitment by Lundbeck to refrain from initiating infringement proceedings if the generics entered the market following the settlement's expiry and noted that Lundbeck could not have achieved the agreement's limitations through the enforcement of its process patents, since these limitations went beyond the rights granted to holders of process patents.[2151]

2 The General Court Confirms the Restriction of Competition by Object

Even though the General Court upheld the Commission's finding of restriction by object in this particular case, this finding does not amount to the categorical condemnation of *all* patent settlements containing reverse payments as restrictions by object.[2152] According to the General Court's decision in *Lundbeck*, when a reverse payment is combined with the exclusion of generic competitors from the market or with a limitation of their incentives to pursue generic entry, this limitation may not arise exclusively from the parties' individual perceptions on the strength of the patent; on the contrary, it is likely obtained through the payment and constitutes a "buying-off" of competition.[2153] The EU General Court benefited from the US experience on reverse payment settlements and was influenced to a great extent by the reasoning of *FTC v. Actavis*.[2154]

2149. EU Commission Decision, *Lundbeck*, 2013, para. 660.
2150. EU Commission Decision, *Lundbeck*, 2013, para. 661.
2151. EU Commission Decision, *Lundbeck*, 2013, para. 662.
2152. Judgment of the General Court of 8 September 2016, Case T-472/13, *Lundbeck v. Commission*, para. 354.
2153. Judgment of the General Court of 8 September 2016, Case T-472/13, *Lundbeck v. Commission*, para. 352.
2154. *FTC v. Actavis*, 133 S. Ct. 2223 (2013). For an analysis of the Supreme Court's decision *see* further ATHANASIADOU, FTC v. Actavis, 2015. Available at: http://papers.ssrn.com/sol3/papers.cfm?abstract_id=2737870 (last accessed on March 31, 2018).

2.1 The Size and the Disproportionate Nature of the Reverse Payments

As analysed in Chapter 4 of this book, in 2013 the US Supreme Court held in *FTC v. Actavis* that a large and unjustified reverse payment in a patent settlement may provide a workable surrogate for the patent's weakness, without the necessity for the court to conduct a detailed analysis of patent validity.[2155] Following the same line of reasoning three years later, the General Court of the EU highlighted that the *size* of a reverse payment may indicate the settling parties' perceptions regarding the strength or weakness of the patent at the time of the settlement; it may also indicate the originator's doubts on its chances of succeeding in patent infringement litigation.[2156] As the applicants seemingly acknowledged in their written pleadings in *Lundbeck*, the higher the chances of a patent being held invalid or not infringed and the higher the projected damages to the originator in case of successful generic entry, the higher the reverse payment will be in order to avoid these risks.[2157] The General Court stressed that if the applicants would have been so confident on their patent's validity and on its infringement by the generic drug versions, they could have prevented generic entry by obtaining orders before national courts, while they could have also obtained damages in case the generic manufacturers had unlawfully entered the market.[2158]

The disproportionate nature of the reverse payments in the *Lundbeck* settlements was combined with other important elements: (1) the fact that the payments seemed to correspond to the generic manufacturers' anticipated profits had they entered the market; (2) the absence of a commitment by Lundbeck not to initiate patent infringement actions if the generic manufacturers launched their products to the market after the expiry of the settlement agreement; and (3) the presence of restrictions which went beyond the scope of Lundbeck's patents.[2159] It was on the basis of these elements, which were particular in the settlements at hand, that the Commission reached the conclusion that the agreements had as their object the restriction of competition within the meaning of Article 101(1) TFEU.[2160] The General Court affirmed the Commission's position, stressing that the existence of reverse payments and their disproportionate nature were relevant factors in establishing whether the agreements at issue constituted restrictions of competition "by object" for the purpose of Article 101 TFEU: these payments by the originator were employed as an incentive for the generic undertakings

---

2155. Judgment of the General Court of 8 September 2016, Case T-472/13, *Lundbeck v. Commission*, para. 353, referring to *FTC v. Actavis*, 133 S. Ct. 2223, 2236-2237 (2013).
2156. Judgment of the General Court of 8 September 2016, Case T-472/13, *Lundbeck v. Commission*, para. 353. See also *FTC v. Actavis*, 133 S. Ct. 2223, 2235-2237 (2013).
2157. Judgment of the General Court of 8 September 2016, Case T-472/13, *Lundbeck v. Commission*, para. 353, noting that the applicants cited para. 640 of the EU Commission Decision, *Lundbeck*, 2013, in their written pleadings.
2158. Judgment of the General Court of 8 September 2016, Case T-472/13, *Lundbeck v. Commission*, para. 384.
2159. Judgment of the General Court of 8 September 2016, Case T-472/13, *Lundbeck v. Commission*, para. 354.
2160. Judgment of the General Court of 8 September 2016, Case T-472/13, *Lundbeck v. Commission*, para. 354, referring to paras 661, 662 of the EU Commission Decision, *Lundbeck*, 2013.

not to continue their independent efforts of market entry.[2161] Settlements which contain significant reverse payments and reduce or even eliminate the generic manufacturers' incentives to enter the market for a set time-period, without resolving the underlying patent dispute, fall under the prohibition of Article 101(1) TFEU.[2162]

2.2 Exchanging Uncertainty for Certainty Through a Value Transfer

The notion of replacing uncertainty for certainty through reverse payments is not novel in the antitrust analysis of pharma patent settlements. As the Supreme Court held in *FTC v. Actavis*, a patent "may or may not be valid, may or may not be infringed," so that referring to what the holder of a valid patent could do does not itself answer the antitrust question.[2163] A large unjustified payment likely seeks to prevent the *risk* of competition and that consequence constitutes the relevant anticompetitive harm.[2164] In *Lundbeck*, the settling parties were in a dispute over the strength of Lundbeck's patents, while all of the settlements at issue were concluded at a time where there was considerable uncertainty on whether these patents constituted sufficient barriers to generic entry.[2165] The Commission found that the parties' settlement agreements restricted the generic manufacturers' ability to enter the market and their autonomy of decision-making, reducing or even eliminating Lundbeck's commercial uncertainty on the issue of generic entry.[2166]

The General Court noted that Lundbeck's patents could not have been the underlying reason for the generic manufacturers' commitment not to enter the market: the decisive element behind the non-entry commitments were the payments which served as a "deal clincher."[2167] The Commission had stressed in its decision that the *form* of the payment is irrelevant and it should cover any kind of *value transfer* which is unexplainable or which considerably exceeds the value of any counter-performance by the generic manufacturer.[2168] The General Court did not limit its *Lundbeck* ruling to cash payments when holding that reverse payments in patent settlements distort the generics' incentives to enter the market: the transfer of *value* replaces the parties' autonomous assessment of the patent strength and of the generic manufacturers' chances of succeeding in potential litigation.[2169] In contrast to the US Supreme Court's ruling in *FTC v. Actavis*, the General Court did not even once refer to a *cash*

2161. Judgment of the General Court of 8 September 2016, Case T-472/13, *Lundbeck v. Commission*, para. 354.
2162. Judgment of the General Court of 8 September 2016, Case T-472/13, *Lundbeck v. Commission*, paras 353, 360.
2163. *FTC v. Actavis*, 133 S. Ct. 2223, 2230-2231 (2013).
2164. *FTC v. Actavis*, 133 S. Ct. 2223, 2236 (2013).
2165. EU Commission Decision, *Lundbeck*, 2013, para. 633.
2166. EU Commission Decision, *Lundbeck*, 2013, para. 609.
2167. Judgment of the General Court of 8 September 2016, Case T-472/13, *Lundbeck v. Commission*, para. 361.
2168. EU Commission Decision, *Lundbeck*, 2013, para. 660.
2169. Judgment of the General Court of 8 September 2016, Case T-472/13, *Lundbeck v. Commission*, paras 353, 360.

payment:[2170] instead the court uniformly used the term "transfer of value," leaving no room for controversy on whether its reasoning in the *Lundbeck* decision only applies to reverse payments in cash.[2171]

Additionally, Lundbeck had not disputed that the payments were tailored on the expected profits or on the turnover the generics would have made, had they entered the market for the term of the agreements.[2172] Finally, according to evidence on the time-period before the settlements, the generic undertakings had made considerable preparations for their market entry and were not dissuaded by Lundbeck's patents.[2173] Even though there was uncertainty on whether the generic drug versions infringed the relevant patents, the generic undertakings had a real chance of prevailing in the event of patent litigation.[2174] Establishing the existence of a restriction by object did not require that the Commission showed irrefutably that Lundbeck doubted the validity of its patent, since the evidence of the case showed that the generic manufacturers were confident on their chances of entering the market.[2175] The decisive element was the considerable *uncertainty* at the time of the settlements on the possibility for the generics to successfully enter the market without being subject to infringement actions or injunctions and on the possibility to successfully challenge the patent's validity.[2176] As a result of these significant reverse payments, the originator exchanged that *uncertainty* for the *certainty* that the generics would abstain from entering the market by means of significant reverse payments: thus, *all* competition on the market, even potential, was eliminated for the duration of the settlement agreements.[2177]

2.3   Reverse Payments and the *Cartes Bancaires* Decision

The applicants in *Lundbeck* attempted to use the CJEU's decision in *Cartes Bancaires* in order to rebut the Commission's finding of a restriction by object.[2178] In 2014, pending the appeal against the Commission decision in *Lundbeck*, the Court of Justice of the

---

2170. The only time the word "cash" appears in the Judgment of the General Court of 8 September 2016, Case T-472/13, *Lundbeck v. Commission*, is para. 406, where the applicants unsuccessfully argued that the standard applied by the Commission to assess agreements that provide for early market entry leads to "different results depending on whether the value transfer takes the form of a cash payment or a rapid entry to the market".
2171. *See supra* Chapter 4, Part 2, discussing *FTC v. Actavis* and whether it applies to non-cash payments.
2172. Judgment of the General Court of 8 September 2016, Case T-472/13, *Lundbeck v. Commission*, para. 362.
2173. Judgment of the General Court of 8 September 2016, Case T-472/13, *Lundbeck v. Commission*, para. 363.
2174. Judgment of the General Court of 8 September 2016, Case T-472/13, *Lundbeck v. Commission*, para. 363, referring to *idem* para. 122; EU Commission Decision, *Lundbeck*, 2013, paras 75, 76.
2175. Judgment of the General Court of 8 September 2016, Case T-472/13, *Lundbeck v. Commission*, para. 369.
2176. *Idem*.
2177. Judgment of the General Court of 8 September 2016, Case T-472/13, *Lundbeck v. Commission*, paras 363, 369, 382.
2178. Judgment of the General Court of 8 September 2016, Case T-472/13, *Lundbeck v. Commission*, para. 432.

European Union (CJEU) issued its decision in *Cartes Bancaires*. In this decision, the CJEU stressed the need for a *restrictive* interpretation of the concept of restriction by object under Article 101(1) TFEU[2179] and required a rather detailed consideration of the alleged restriction by object, including an examination of the content of the agreement at issue, its objectives and its economic and legal context.[2180] In determining the agreement's context, it is necessary to consider the nature of the affected goods or services, as well as the real conditions of the functioning and structure of the relevant market.[2181] The applicants in *Lundbeck* argued that the Commission's decision ignored the CJEU's call for restrictively interpreting the concept of restriction by object, seeking to avoid the factual analysis and burden of proving a restriction of competition based on the settlements' effects.[2182]

The General Court noted that the *Cartes Bancaires* decision did not question the basic principles applying to restrictions of competition by object.[2183] On the basis of the Commission's decision in *Lundbeck*, the relevant agreements were comparable to market exclusion agreements: excluding competitors from the market is an extreme form of market sharing and falls among the most serious restrictions of competition.[2184] The Commission had taken into consideration Lundbeck's process patents but concluded that even if they were valid, they did not allow the exclusion of *all* generic competition from the market.[2185] Furthermore, there was considerable uncertainty on the validity of the patents at the time of settlements, in the absence of a court ruling on the matter.[2186]

The undertakings' argument that "it took the Commission more than a decade to formulate a legal standard with respect to reverse payment settlements" while in the meantime such settlements were considered to fall within a grey area, was rejected by the General Court which stressed that a finding of restriction by object did not necessitate a previous condemnation of reverse payment settlements by the Commission.[2187] Even though reverse payment settlements were not previously found to be restrictive of competition by object, the Commission had followed an individual and detailed examination of the settlements in question, with regard to their content, purpose and context.[2188] The role of experience on a restrictive behaviour, mentioned

---

2179. Case C-67/13 P, *Cartes Bancaires*, paras 57-58.
2180. Case C-67/13 P, *Cartes Bancaires*, para. 53.
2181. Case C-67/13 P, *Cartes Bancaires*, para. 53, citing the Judgment of the Court of 14 March 2013, Case C-32/11, *Allianz Hungária v. Gazdasági Versenyhivatal*, para. 36.
2182. Judgment of the General Court of 8 September 2016, Case T-472/13, *Lundbeck v. Commission*, para. 432.
2183. Judgment of the General Court of 8 September 2016, Case T-472/13, *Lundbeck v. Commission*, para. 434.
2184. Judgment of the General Court of 8 September 2016, Case T-472/13, *Lundbeck v. Commission*, para. 435.
2185. *Idem*.
2186. *Idem*.
2187. Judgment of the General Court of 8 September 2016, Case T-472/13, *Lundbeck v. Commission*, para. 438. This argument was previously rejected by the Commission, *see* EU Commission Decision, *Lundbeck*, 2013, para. 652.
2188. Judgment of the General Court of 8 September 2016, Case T-472/13, *Lundbeck v. Commission*para. 438.

in *Cartes Bancaires* as a criterion for finding a restriction by object,[2189] does not concern a specific category of agreements within a particular sector; it refers to certain forms of collusion which are so likely to have negative effects on competition, that it is not necessary to demonstrate these effects in the relevant case, as was the case with the restrictions imposed by the settlements in *Lundbeck*.[2190]

2.4 Patent Settlements and the *Beef Industry* Agreements

The settling parties in *Lundbeck* argued that their settlement agreements were not comparable to the agreements in the *Beef Industry* case and to other classic market-sharing cases not related to patent enforcement, using the following arguments.[2191] First, the *Beef Industry* agreements were not intended to preserve a patent conferring on its holder the right of preventing the market entry of infringing products and the irreparable damage following generic entry.[2192] Second, absent the agreements in *Beef Industry*, the concerned undertakings would have certainly competed, but this certainty did not exist in the *Lundbeck* settlements.[2193] Third, even absent any payment, the *Beef Industry* agreements would have been deemed to be restrictive of competition by object.[2194]

The General Court rejected these arguments: the Commission's analogy between the agreements in *Beef Industry* and the *Lundbeck* settlements was not vitiated by any error of law.[2195] The concerned undertakings in *Beef Industry* were active in the beef processing market in Ireland and created a mechanism through which some of them agreed to stay out of that market for two years in exchange for payments from the undertakings that stayed active in the market.[2196] In *Lundbeck*, the patent owner – the only undertaking in the countries covered by the settlement agreements – paid its potential competitors to stay out of the market for a certain period.[2197] Therefore, in both cases the relevant agreements limited the ability of competing economic operators to independently determine their market policies by impeding the normal operation of the competitive process.[2198]

2189. Case C-67/13 P, *Cartes Bancaires*, para. 51.
2190. Judgment of the General Court of 8 September 2016, Case T-472/13, *Lundbeck v. Commission*, para. 438-439.
2191. Judgment of the General Court of 8 September 2016, Case T-472/13, *Lundbeck v. Commission*, paras 417-418, referring to the Case C-209/07, *Beef Industry*.
2192. Judgment of the General Court of 8 September 2016, Case T-472/13, *Lundbeck v. Commission*, para. 419.
2193. Judgment of the General Court of 8 September 2016, Case T-472/13, *Lundbeck v. Commission*, para. 420.
2194. Judgment of the General Court of 8 September 2016, Case T-472/13, *Lundbeck v. Commission*para. 421.
2195. Judgment of the General Court of 8 September 2016, Case T-472/13, *Lundbeck v. Commission*, para. 423.
2196. Case C-209/07, *Beef Industry*, paras 32-33.
2197. Judgment of the General Court of 8 September 2016, Case T-472/13, *Lundbeck v. Commission*, para. 424.
2198. Judgment of the General Court of 8 September 2016, Case T-472/13, *Lundbeck v. Commission*, para. 425, also referring to Case C-209/07, *Beef Industry*, paras 33-35.

Lundbeck's new process patents did not prevent the General Court from finding that the settling generic manufacturers were Lundbeck's potential competitors.[2199] The fact that the settlements concerned a patent or were intended to settle a patent dispute did not exempt them from competition laws, while other legitimate objectives which may have been pursued by the settlements did not preclude a finding of a restriction by object.[2200] The General Court noted that even though the undertakings in *Beef Industry* were actual competitors, the CJEU did not require the Commission to demonstrate that absent the settlements the excluded undertakings would have stayed in the market.[2201] The *Beef Industry* agreements were in conflict with Article 101(1) TFEU whose aim is to prohibit coordination between undertakings deliberately substituting the risks of competition with practical cooperation between them.[2202]

The agreements in *Lundbeck* replaced the inherent risks of the normal competitive process and the uncertainty concerning the validity of Lundbecks' patents and their alleged infringement by the generics, with the certainty that the generic manufacturers would refrain from entering the market. Thus, it was irrelevant whether the generics would have undoubtedly entered the market, since the possibility of generic entry was eliminated by the agreements.[2203] The *Lundbeck* settlements served as a means for the parties to share a part of Lundbeck's monopoly profits to the detriment of consumers paying higher drug prices than the ones they would have paid if generic drugs would have entered the market.[2204] Both in *Beef Industry* and in *Lundbeck* the payments played a decisive role in inducing undertakings to withdraw from the market; absent the payments, the generic undertakings in *Lundbeck* would not have unilaterally agreed to stay out of the market.[2205]

D Justifications in the General Court's Decision

1 Justifications for the Value Transfers as Part of the Settlements

In order to rebut the Commission's finding of an infringement of Article 101(1) TFEU, the applicants in *Lundbeck* unsuccessfully attempted to justify the value transfers in their settlements. The General Court rejected all their arguments, which are briefly discussed in the following sections.

2199. Judgment of the General Court of 8 September 2016, Case T-472/13, *Lundbeck v. Commission*, para. 426.
2200. Judgment of the General Court of 8 September 2016, Case T-472/13, *Lundbeck v. Commission*, para. 427.
2201. Judgment of the General Court of 8 September 2016, Case T-472/13, *Lundbeck v. Commission*, para. 428.
2202. Idem.
2203. Judgment of the General Court of 8 September 2016, Case T-472/13, *Lundbeck v. Commission*, para. 429.
2204. Idem.
2205. Judgment of the General Court of 8 September 2016, Case T-472/13, *Lundbeck v. Commission*, paras 430-431.

1.1 The Risk Asymmetry Between Originators and Generic Manufacturers

The first argument used by the applicants in order to justify the value transfers in the settlements was that of the "asymmetry of risks" between originators and generic undertakings: while Lundbeck risked sustaining considerable and irreversible damage by the infringement of generic undertakings, the latter faced little to no risk.[2206] The Commission had recognised in its decision that due to the downward price spiral caused by generic entry, the damages which the generic manufacturers would be required to pay would often be much lower than the damage suffered by the originator if a generic would enter the market, so that it would make *commercial sense* for the originator to pay the generics the amount of its expected loses.[2207]

The General Court rejected this line of argumentation. The court acknowledged that this asymmetry of risks existed, especially given that the patented Cipramil product was the "flagship" product of Lundbeck and represented most of its turnover.[2208] Nevertheless, the application of Article 101 TFEU is in no way excluded by the fact that the anticompetitive behaviour is the most-effective or the least risky course of action for an undertaking, especially if it entails paying actual or potential competitors not to enter the market and splitting the profits resulting from the absence of generic competition in the market to the detriment of consumers, as had happened in the *Lundbeck* settlements.[2209] The General Court stressed the even if a reverse payment constitutes the *only* means to "bridge the gap" between the parties and to reach a settlement, this neither elevates a payment to a legitimate mean of settlement, nor exempts the agreement from the application of competition law.[2210] Further aggravating elements exist where: (1) the payment amount appears linked to the projected profits of the generic undertakings had they entered the market; (2) the agreement does not resolve the underlying patent dispute; and (3) the restrictions imposed by the settlements go beyond the scope of the relevant patents.[2211]

1.2 The Irreparable Harm Caused by Generic Entry

The General Court acknowledged that it was possible that Lundbeck could have suffered irreparable harm in the event of unlawful generic entry, as a result of the

---

2206. Judgment of the General Court of 8 September 2016, Case T-472/13, *Lundbeck v. Commission*, paras 370-374.
2207. EU Commission Decision, *Lundbeck*, 2013, paras 96, 644 and fn. 180.
2208. Judgment of the General Court of 8 September 2016, Case T-472/13, *Lundbeck v. Commission*, para. 379, referring to EU Commission Decision, *Lundbeck*, 2013, paras 26 and 120.
2209. Judgment of the General Court of 8 September 2016, Case T-472/13, *Lundbeck v. Commission*, para. 380, citing Judgment of the Court of First Instance of 8 July 2004, Case T-48/00, *Corus UK Ltd, formerly British Steel plc v. Commission of the European Communities*, EU:T:2004:219, para.73; Judgment of the Court of First Instance of 8 July 2004, Case T-50/00, *Dalmine SpA v. Commission of the European Communities*, EU:T:2004:220, para. 211.
2210. Judgment of the General Court of 8 September 2016, Case T-472/13, *Lundbeck v. Commission*, para. 383.
2211. Judgment of the General Court of 8 September 2016, Case T-472/13, *Lundbeck v. Commission*, paras. 354-383, referring to EU Commission Decision, *Lundbeck*, 2013, paras 661 and 662.

irreversible price falls such generic entry would cause.[2212] Nevertheless, regulatory price cuts – following the expiry of the patent covering the active pharmaceutical ingredient (API) of a drug – are a well-known characteristic of pharma markets and constitute *a normal commercial risk* that could not justify the conclusion of anticompetitive agreements.[2213] Moreover, such price cuts result from regulatory intervention and illustrate the balance struck by EU Member States between the patent protection afforded to the originator on the one hand and the savings which are achieved by generic entry for both Member States' budgets and for consumers on the other.[2214]

Accepting the irreparable harm argument would amount to allowing originators to shield themselves against such irreversible price falls through reverse payment settlements.[2215] The result would be the maintenance of higher prices for brand-name drug products, to the detriment of consumers and healthcare budgets, a result that could not have been attained even if the originators had successfully brought patent infringement actions before national courts.[2216] The General Court ruled that such an outcome would be manifestly contrary to the TFEU provisions on competition, intended also to protect consumers from unjustified price increases resulting from competitors colluding.[2217] Given that Lundbeck's defence before national courts could not, even in the most favourable scenario, lead to the same negative consequences for both competition and consumers, there was no reason to suppose that the collusion in the case at issue was lawful.[2218] The General Court recalled that it is unacceptable for undertakings to mitigate the effects of legal rules they consider unfavourable by entering into restrictive agreements with the intention to offset those disadvantages.[2219]

2   Justifications under Article 101(3) TFEU

The General Court found that the applicants failed to demonstrate any beneficial effects these settlements might have had on competition or on consumers and rejected their arguments invoking the exception of Article 101(3) TFEU.

2212. Judgment of the General Court of 8 September 2016, Case T-472/13, *Lundbeck v. Commission*, para. 385.
2213. *Idem.*
2214. *Idem.*
2215. Judgment of the General Court of 8 September 2016, Case T-472/13, *Lundbeck v. Commission*, para. 386.
2216. *Idem.*
2217. Judgment of the General Court of 8 September 2016, Case T-472/13, *Lundbeck v. Commission*, para. 386, referring also to Judgment of the Court of 19 March 2015, Case C-286/13 P, *Dole Food Company, Inc. and Dole Fresh Fruit Europe v. European Commission*, EU:C:2015:184, para. 115 and the case law cited; Judgment of the Court of 9 July 2015, Case C-231/14 P, *InnoLux Corp. v. European Commission*, EU:C:2015:451, para. 61.
2218. Judgment of the General Court of 8 September 2016, Case T-472/13, *Lundbeck v. Commission*, para. 386.
2219. Judgment of the General Court of 8 September 2016, Case T-472/13, *Lundbeck v. Commission*, para. 387, referring to Judgment of the Court of First Instance of 27 July 2005, Cases T-49/02 to T-51/02, *Brasserie nationale and Others v. Commission*, EU:T:2005:298, para. 81 and the case law cited.

2.1 The Avoidance of Litigation Costs

One of the most popular arguments in favour of reverse payments in patent settlements is that such payments allow the avoidance of significant litigation costs. Lundbeck also argued that its settlements would have allowed the avoidance of high litigation costs in various Member States and would also mitigate the risk of conflicting national courts' decisions.[2220] The General Court noted that most of the settlements at issue made no specific reference nor estimated the avoided litigation costs, while Lundbeck had not provided evidence regarding the method of calculation of the reverse payments; it merely stated that they resulted from negotiations with the generics.[2221]

The court stressed that the underlying patent dispute was not genuinely resolved by the settlement, since Lundbeck was not prevented from bringing infringement actions against the generics before different EEA Member States' courts, after the expiry of the settlements.[2222] While it was true that Lundbeck did not initiate any patent infringement actions after the expiry of its settlement agreements with the generics, this was because generic citalopram entry had already occurred at that time point, so that such actions were no longer meaningful for Lundbeck.[2223] In any case, it was unlikely that the costs of litigation in various EEA countries would have been higher than Lundbeck's reverse payments which amounted to several million euros.[2224] Pharmaceutical undertakings do not normally initiate patent infringement litigation in *all* EU Member States simultaneously and do not bring multiple actions before different courts when the same issues are at stake; instead, they focus on a few test cases.[2225] Thus, the General Court found that the applicants' estimations of several million of euros of avoided legal costs were irrelevant, since it was not certain that these costs would have been incurred in the absence of the settlements.[2226]

The settling parties indeed had the right to enter into settlements in order to avoid potential litigation costs but they could not substitute their own assessment of the validity of their patents and of the generic drugs' infringing nature with that of an

---

2220. Judgment of the General Court of 8 September 2016, Case T-472/13, *Lundbeck v. Commission*, para. 388. *See also* EU Commission Decision, *Lundbeck*, 2013, paras 1221-1231, summarising the parties' arguments on the claimed efficiency gains of the settlement agreements, which were rejected by the Commission.
2221. Judgment of the General Court of 8 September 2016, Case T-472/13, *Lundbeck v. Commission*, para. 388.
2222. Judgment of the General Court of 8 September 2016, Case T-472/13, *Lundbeck v. Commission*, paras 718-719.
2223. Judgment of the General Court of 8 September 2016, Case T-472/13, *Lundbeck v. Commission*, para. 718. For instance, the generic undertaking Lagap had already entered the UK market with its generic citalopram version.
2224. Judgment of the General Court of 8 September 2016, Case T-472/13, *Lundbeck v. Commission*, para. 389.
2225. Judgment of the General Court of 8 September 2016, Case T-472/13, *Lundbeck v. Commission* *Commission*, para. 389, referring also to the *Lagap* case in the UK, where the applicants decided to focus on a few test cases, and ultimately settled in order to avoid a court defeat that would be used against them in other jurisdictions. *See* further EU Commission Decision, *Lundbeck*, 2013, para. 160.
2226. Judgment of the General Court of 8 September 2016, Case T-472/13, *Lundbeck v. Commission*, para. 718.

independent judge, neither were they entitled to pay the generic undertakings to comply with that assessment and refrain from entering the market for a certain time-period.[2227] Even if the settlements at issue allowed the avoidance of certain litigation costs, the settling parties had not established that the restrictions imposed by these settlements were indispensable for achieving that objective, while they could have opted instead for a procompetitive type of settlement, as was the *Neolab* settlement.[2228]

2.2 Preserving the Incentives to Innovate and Benefits to Consumers

In its appeal before the General Court, Lundbeck argued that the settlement agreements were essential to preserve its incentives to innovate, without however demonstrating neither how these settlements contributed to this incentive nor how the four conditions of Article 101(3) TFEU were satisfied.[2229] The General Court stressed that the agreements at issue sought to delay generic market entry and were not essential to preserve the originator's incentives to innovate. The agreements did not provide any commitment from Lundbeck to authorise generic entry on the market after their expiration, while they prevented generics from immediately entering the market.[2230] It was difficult to discern any benefits these agreements may have had for consumers, since no explanation was provided on how the latter would have obtained a fair share of the settlements' alleged benefits.[2231] These agreements merely allowed Lundbeck to "gain time" and to delay generic entry against payments of significant amounts to its potential competitors.[2232]

E *The Importance of Lundbeck and Its Comparison with* **Actavis**

The much awaited decision of the General Court in *Lundbeck* set the legal standard for the analysis of reverse payments under European competition law. Two points are of particular interest for the purposes of this book and are analysed in the following sections: whether the standard adopted by the European General Court is likely to have a dissuasive effect on the conclusion of patent settlements and whether it is more

---

2227. Judgment of the General Court of 8 September 2016, Case T-472/13, *Lundbeck v. Commission*, para. 390.
2228. Judgment of the General Court of 8 September 2016, Case T-472/13, *Lundbeck v. Commission*, para. 719.
2229. Judgment of the General Court of 8 September 2016, Case T-472/13, *Lundbeck v. Commission*, para. 713. *See also* EU Commission Decision, *Lundbeck*, 2013, paras 710-713, Lundbeck arguing that patent settlements containing reverse payments preserve the incentives to innovate and may be good for consumers even on the short term.
2230. Judgment of the General Court of 8 September 2016, Case T-472/13, *Lundbeck v. Commission*, paras 716-717.
2231. Judgment of the General Court of 8 September 2016, Case T-472/13, *Lundbeck v. Commission*, paras 713-715, 718-720.
2232. Judgment of the General Court of 8 September 2016, Case T-472/13, *Lundbeck v. Commission*, paras 716-717.

stringent than the standard adopted by the US Supreme Court in *FTC v. Actavis*. Finally, Lundbeck's pleas in its appeal against the General Court's decision are critically analysed.

1 How Does the Lundbeck *Ruling Affect the Decision to Settle?*

The applicants in *Lundbeck* argued that a finding of a restriction by object within the meaning of Article 101(1) TFEU would have a dissuasive effect on concluding settlements allowing early generic entry.[2233] The General Court rejected this argument as manifestly unfounded: the agreements at issue violated competition laws because their object was to delay generic entry and not to facilitate it, while Lundbeck had not committed to refrain from patent infringement proceedings in the event of generic entry after the agreements' expiry.[2234] On the contrary, patent settlements which allow for immediate generic entry are not problematic even if they include reverse payments as was the case in the Neolab settlement.[2235] Therefore, the argument that this finding of restriction by object would remove any incentive to conclude patent settlements, leading to an "avalanche of litigation" was rejected.[2236]

Even though the General Court ruled that the settlements in *Lundbeck* constituted restrictions by object, the court made clear that this decision did not amount to the categorisation of *all* patent settlements involving reverse payments as restrictions by object. The General Court stressed at several points of its decision that the Commission's finding of restriction by object in the *Lundbeck* decision was based on an individual and detailed examination of the content, purpose and context of the settlements in question.[2237] The *Lundbeck* settlements were particularly problematic since they involved reverse payments which broadly corresponded to the projected profits of the generic undertakings had they entered the market or to the damages they would have obtained had they succeeded in the litigation against Lundbeck.[2238] These payments were sufficiently high for the generics to accept limitations on their autonomy and for considerably reducing – if not eliminating – their incentives to enter the market.[2239]

As above-analysed, the General Court provided examples of legitimate reverse payments, which resolve the underlying patent dispute and allow early generic entry.

2233. Judgment of the General Court of 8 September 2016, Case T-472/13, *Lundbeck v. Commission*, paras 405-408.
2234. Judgment of the General Court of 8 September 2016, Case T-472/13, *Lundbeck v. Commission*, para. 410.
2235. Judgment of the General Court of 8 September 2016, Case T-472/13, *Lundbeck v. Commission*, para. 411; *see also supra* Chapter 6, Part 1, Section II.C.2, on the settlement between Lundbeck and Neolab.
2236. Judgment of the General Court of 8 September 2016, Case T-472/13, *Lundbeck v. Commission*, para. 412.
2237. *See* for instance Judgment of the General Court of 8 September 2016, Case T-472/13, *Lundbeck v. Commission*, paras 61-67, 332-336.
2238. Judgment of the General Court of 8 September 2016, Case T-472/13, *Lundbeck v. Commission* paras 388, 414.
2239. Judgment of the General Court of 8 September 2016, Case T-472/13, *Lundbeck v. Commission* para. 414, referring to EU Commission Decision, *Lundbeck*, 2013, para. 644.

On the flipside, agreements intended to delay generic market entry in exchange for significant reverse payments, transforming the uncertainty in relation to whether the generic drugs infringed the originator's patent into certainty and limiting the generic manufacturers' autonomy, likely lead to the elimination of actual and potential competition from the market. If the General Court's decision could potentially have a dissuasive effect, this effect would be limited to the latter kind of agreements which are similar to market exclusion agreements and would not extend to efficient settlements which increase consumer welfare. Had the settling parties in *Lundbeck* been able to foresee the General Court's ruling when they had settled back in 2002, they would have probably avoided settlements involving large pay-for-delay value transfers, which did not resolve the underlying patent dispute; instead they would have attempted to conclude a settlement closer to the examples of legitimate settlements outlined by both the General Court and the EU Commission.

2 Comparing the Tests in Lundbeck and FTC v. Actavis

It is interesting to contrast the General Court's approach in *Lundbeck* with the US Supreme Court's ruling in *FTC v. Actavis*. As analysed in Chapter 4 of this book, the US Supreme Court opted for the rule of reason as the applicable legal standard for the adjudication of reverse payments settlements and held that the likelihood of a reverse settlement creating anticompetitive effects depends on: (1) the payment's size; (2) the payment's scale vis-à-vis the anticipated litigation costs; (3) the payment's independence from other services provided to the patent holder; and (4) the lack of any other convincing justification.[2240] Nevertheless, the US Supreme Court clarified that its choice of the rule of reason did not require lower courts or the FTC to litigate the patent's validity, to present every possible supporting fact or to refute every possible defence. Instead, the Supreme Court invited lower courts to structure their own rule of reason analysis, noting that there is a "sliding scale" in accepting reasonableness, while the quality of required proof should vary with the circumstances.[2241] The influence of *FTC v. Actavis* is evident in the General Court's decision: the main criteria and principles for the adjudication of reverse payments are closely similar, so that it would be redundant to argue that the General Court embraced a rule harsher than the one adopted by the Supreme Court in *FTC v. Actavis*, in all but name.

Similarly to the *Actavis* standard, under the standard set by *Lundbeck*, a patent settlement with a disproportionately high payment from the originator – in exchange for the exclusion of generic competitors from the market – raises a red flag and may constitute a restriction of competition by object. On the contrary, a settlement agreement including the originator's acceptance of non-infringement and its commitment not to hinder generic entry will most probably fall outside the scope of Article 101 TFEU, even if it involves a justified reverse payment. The rejection of the scope of the patent test as the relevant standard for the adjudication of patent settlements is an

---

2240. *FTC v. Actavis, Inc.*, 133 S. Ct. 2223, 2237 (2013).
2241. *FTC v. Actavis, Inc.*, 133 S. Ct. 2223, 2237-2238 (2013).

important point of *Lundbeck*: the test that was rejected by the US Supreme Court in *FTC v. Actavis* was not revived in the European Union.

The General Court may have affirmed the restriction by object of competition in the *Lundbeck* case, but did not categorically condemn all patent settlements containing reverse payments. Under the court's standard in *Lundbeck*, settlements which provide for early generic entry and resolve the underlying patent dispute will not most probably fall under the prohibition of Article 101(1) TFEU. Both the *Lundbeck* and the *Actavis* decisions rely on the size of payment as an indicator of the strength of the patent and do not require the competition authorities to assess the validity of the patent. Moreover, both decisions do not accept that an exclusion payment to a competitor could fall within the subject matter of a patent and stress that the existence of a patent does not immunise a settlement agreement from antitrust scrutiny.

Both the *Actavis* and the *Lundbeck* decisions insist that the presumption of patent validity shall not be elevated into a presumption of patent infringement: a patent does not necessarily preclude *all* generic competition from the market, since it is possible that it is either not infringed by the generic drug versions or that it is simply invalid. Finally, both standards offer to the concerned parties the possibility to provide justifications for the restrictions imposed on competition by the settlements and do not categorically condemn patent settlement agreements including payments. Pharmaceutical companies have the right to enter into patent settlement agreements in order to avoid litigation costs but patent holders may not pay their potential generic competitors in order to concede that the originator's patent is valid or infringed by the generic versions. On the basis of the General Court's ruling, the avoidance of litigation costs may serve as a valid justification for reverse payments in patent settlements under the following conditions: (1) the avoided litigation costs shall be estimated in the settlement agreements, and; (2) the method of calculation of the reverse payments shall be supported by evidence.[2242] A patent settlement must resolve the underlying patent dispute: the crucial element is a commitment from the patent holder *not* to bring patent infringement actions against the settling generic manufacturers entering the market after the expiry of the settlement agreements. In any case, even if the settlements allow the avoidance of litigation costs, the parties shall demonstrate that any restrictions on competition imposed by the settlements are indispensible.[2243]

3 Lundbeck's Appeal Before the CJEU

On November 2016, Lundbeck appealed against the General Court's decision.[2244] Lundbeck alleges that the General Court erred in law in upholding that the agreements

---

[2242]. Judgment of the General Court of 8 September 2016, Case T-472/13, *Lundbeck v. Commission*, paras 388-391.

[2243]. Judgment of the General Court of 8 September 2016, Case T-472/13, *Lundbeck v. Commission*, para. 719.

[2244]. Case C-591/16 P: Appeal brought on 18 November 2016 by H. Lundbeck A/S, Lundbeck Ltd against the judgment of the General Court (Ninth Chamber) delivered on 8 September 2016 in

had the object of restricting competition. Arguing in essence in favour of a revival of the scope of the patent test, Lundbeck submits that the General Court erred in law in finding that the settlements at issue restricted competition by object even in case they fell within the scope of Lundbeck's patents. Lundbeck also argues that the settlements cannot be considered by their nature harmful to competition, since they contain restrictions *comparable* to those that a patent holder could have obtained through court rulings enforcing its patents, while a "mere payment" cannot render an otherwise legitimate and unproblematic settlement which falls within the scope of the patent into a restriction of competition by object.[2245] Lundbeck further alleges that the General Court did not examine whether there was a "meeting of minds" of the settling parties on the aim to impose restrictions exceeding the scope of Lundbeck's patents, and argues instead that the settlements fell within the subject matter of the underlying patents.[2246] Alternatively, even if the agreements fell outside the scope of the patent, Lundbeck submits that they did not constitute restrictions of competition by object, since they were not by their nature harmful to competition or comparable to market-sharing agreements.[2247]

These arguments fail to take into consideration that the settlements between Lundbeck and the generic manufacturers removed *any* risk of a finding of patent invalidation or non-infringement, rendering in essence Lundbeck's patents ironclad, in return for value transfers. At the time the settlements were concluded, there was considerable uncertainty on the issues of patent validity and of patent infringement.[2248] The settlements offered Lundbeck a 100% certainty that the generics would stay off the market until the end of the term of the settlements, a certainty that Lundbeck could not have obtained through the enforcement of its patents. On the basis of the evidence presented in the EU Commission's decision, the exclusion of the generic manufacturers was based on Lundbeck's payments to the generics and such reverse payments do not fall within the exclusionary scope of a patent: the patent scope does not encompass the right to pay generic competitors in order for them not to challenge patent validity and not to enter the market.

Lundbeck also appealed against the General Court's finding that the settling parties were actual or potential competitors at the time of the agreements, regardless of whether the generic drug versions infringed Lundbeck's patents.[2249] Lundbeck argues that it did not doubt the validity of its patents, while it invokes: (1) scientific evidence allegedly showing that the generics or their API producers infringed the relevant

---

Case T-472/13: *H. Lundbeck A/S, Lundbeck Ltd v. European Commission.* OJ C 30, 30.1.2017, p. 25-26 (Case C-591/16 P: Appeal by H. Lundbeck A/S, Lundbeck Ltd against the judgment of the General Court in Case T-472/13).

2245. Case C-591/16 P: Appeal by H. Lundbeck A/S, Lundbeck Ltd against the judgment of the General Court in Case T-472/13, p. 25, first plea.
2246. Case C-591/16 P: Appeal by H. Lundbeck A/S, Lundbeck Ltd against the judgment of the General Court in Case T-472/13, p. 25, second plea.
2247. Case C-591/16 P: Appeal by H. Lundbeck A/S, Lundbeck Ltd against the judgment of the General Courtin Case T-472/13, p. 25, third plea.
2248. Case T-472/13, *Lundbeck v. Commission*, para. 369.
2249. Case C-591/16 P: Appeal by H. Lundbeck A/S, Lundbeck Ltd against the judgment of the General Court in Case T-472/13, p. 26, fourth plea.

patents; (2) national court orders granting preliminary injunctions and other forms of relief to Lundbeck; and (3) EPO's confirmation of the validity of Lundbeck's crystallisation patent. Therefore, Lundbeck argues that the General Court should have assessed if the generic versions infringed the patents at issue, in order to determine whether the generic manufacturers had real and concrete possibilities of entering the market.[2250]

Nevertheless, a large and otherwise unjustified reverse payment from an originator to a generic challenger in order for the latter to refrain from entering the market provides a proxy of the patent holder's doubts on the matter of patent validity or patent infringement. As acknowledged by both the General Court of the European Union and the US Supreme Court, a patent holder confident on the validity of its patent or on the fact that it is infringed by a generic manufacturer has no reason to pay a generic manufacturer in order for the latter to respect its patent. Additionally, the burden of proof in order for a court to grant a preliminary injunction or other forms of relief has to be carried by patent holders and largely differs from one European Member State to another.[2251] In any case, such a grant of preliminary relief does not demonstrate *ipso facto* that the relevant patent was indeed valid or infringed. Even if the validity of the relevant crystallisation patent was upheld by EPO subsequent to the settlement agreements, the fact that a patent is valid does not automatically mean that it is also infringed by the relevant generic drug versions and that it undoubtedly has the potential to prevent *all* generic competition. Examining whether the relevant generic versions infringed the relevant patents is not a necessary step in order to determine whether the generic manufacturers were Lundbeck's potential competitors. As analysed, in the European Union generic manufacturers may enter the market even if they infringe the patent(s) covering the reference brand-name drug, since obtaining a marketing authorisation for a generic drug is not contingent on showing that the relevant patent(s) are not infringed.[2252] According to the evidence on which the Commission and the General Court based their decisions in *Lundbeck*, the generic undertakings had made considerable preparations for their market entry and were not

---

2250. Case C-591/16 P: Appeal by H. Lundbeck A/S, Lundbeck Ltd against the judgment of the General Court in Case T-472/13, p. 26, fourth plea.
2251. *See* for instance European Observatory of Counterfeiting and Piracy, *Injunctions in Intellectual Property Rights*, 2011, pp. 1-118. Available at: http://ec.europa.eu/internal_market/iprenforcement/docs/injunctions_en.pdf. (last accessed on March 31, 2018), p. 7, noting that the level of evidence required to satisfy the burden that the applicant is the rights-holder and his rights are being infringed, or that such infringement is imminent, is generally at the courts' discretion; idem pp. 8-9, reporting differences between European Member States concerning the burden of proof and the possibility of success in provisional/precautionary measures. *See also* European Observatory of Counterfeiting and Piracy, *Evidence and Right of Information in Intellectual Property Rights*, 2011, pp. 5-6. Available at: http://ec.europa.eu/internal_market/iprenforcement/docs/evidence_en.pdf. (last accessed on March 31, 2018), analysing the different burdens of proof that need to be carried by the patent holder in order for temporary injunctions/ seizure and search orders to be granted.
2252. EU Commission Decision, *Lundbeck*, 2013, para. 624; EU Commission Decision, *Servier*, 2014, para. 75. *See supra* Chapter 5, Part 1, Section II.A.

Chapter 6: Delaying Generic Entry in the EU

dissuaded by Lundbeck's patents,[2253] while despite the uncertainty on the issue of patent infringement, the generics had a real chance of winning in patent litigation.[2254]

It is of particular interest to see how the CJEU will treat Lundbeck's appeal after its decision in *Genetech* in 2016. In *Genetech*, the court found that the patent licensing agreement at issue which required the licensee to pay a royalty for the entire period the agreement was in effect – even in case the relevant patent was *revoked* or *not infringed* by the licensee – did not constitute a violation of Article 101(1) TFEU, *if the licensee could freely terminate it by giving reasonable notice*.[2255] The CJEU's *rationale* in *Genetech* seems to be at odds with the reasoning of the General Court in *Lundbeck* regarding the definition of the exclusionary potential of a patent. One of the core notions in the *Lundbeck* decision is that a patent holder cannot legitimately exclude from the market non-infringing competition. Nevertheless, pursuant to *Genetech*, a patentee has a legitimate right to require the licensee to pay royalties even if the relevant patent was subsequently revoked or if the licensee is not infringing it; the sole conditions are that the licence agreement is still valid and that the licensee can freely terminate it.[2256] In essence *Genetech* seems to legitimise a patentee's behaviour that extends *beyond* the exclusionary scope of a patent. Since a patentee cannot legitimately exclude or impede the market entry of non-infringing competition, granting it the right to request royalties for a revoked patent seems rather absurd. While the reasoning of the CJEU in the *Genetech* decision may make sense from a commercial and contract law perspective, it seems to be distorting the sensitive balance between patent law and EU competition law.

Even if the CJEU upholds the General Court's decision in *Lundbeck*, the challenges raised by patent settlements do not end here. From the conclusion of the *Lundbeck* settlements in 2002 pharma patent settlements have become increasingly sophisticated and no longer include big cash payments. Value transfers from originators to generic competitors may nowadays take the form of side-deals or non-compete commitments at an authorised generics' level, further complicating the task of courts and antitrust enforcers who need to promptly adapt to the ever-changing reality of patent settlements. The settlements in the *Servier* case which is analysed in the next sections provide a vivid illustration of the evolution in the form of patent settlements.

2253. Judgment of the General Court of 8 September 2016, Case T-472/13, *Lundbeck v. Commission*, paras 363, 369.
2254. Judgment of the General Court of 8 September 2016, Case T-472/13, *Lundbeck v. Commission*, para. 363, referring to *idem* para. 122; EU Commission Decision, *Lundbeck*, 2013, paras 75-76.
2255. Judgment of the Court of 7 July 2016, Case C-567/14, *Genentech Inc. v. Hoechst GmbH and Sanofi-Aventis Deutschland GmbH*, EU:C:2016:526 (Judgment of the Court of 7 July 2016, Case C-567/14, *Genentech Inc. v. Hoechst GmbH*), paras 40-43. The CJEU largely relied on the Judgment of the Court of 12 May 1989, Case 320/87, *Kai Ottung v. Klee & Weilbach A/S and Thomas Schmidt A/S*, EU:C:1989:195.
2256. Judgment of the Court of 7 July 2016, Case C-567/14, *Genentech Inc.*, para. 40. *See also* Opinion of Advocate General Wathelet delivered on 17 March 2016, Case C-567/14, *Genentech Inc. v. Hoechst GmbH and Sanofi-Aventis Deutschland GmbH*, EU:C:2016:177, paras 85-97.

III Commission v. Servier

The *Commission v. Servier* decision is the second pay-for-delay case of the European Commission after *Lundbeck*. The following sections analyse in detail the EU Commission decision of 2014, finding that a number of patent settlement agreements between the brand-name manufacturer Servier and five generic manufacturers infringed both Article 101 and Article 102 TFEU.

A The Facts

1 Servier's Settlements and Technology Acquisitions

Perindopril is a blockbuster blood pressure control drug marketed by the French pharmaceutical company Servier. In 2006 and 2007, Perindopril was Servier's best-selling product, accounting for 30% of the company's total turnover.[2257] Servier held significant market power on the perindopril molecule: no other antihypertension medicines apart from perindopril's generic versions were able to meaningfully constrain its sales and prices.[2258] In 2003, perindopril's molecule patent expired for the most part, but Servier still held a number of "secondary" process patents which blocked generic entry.[2259] Servier had already started employing its "anti-generics" strategy in the late 1990s: it obtained a number of process and crystalline form patents[2260] and also acquired two competing technologies in order to remove competition from the market.[2261] Through these acquisitions, Servier not only eliminated direct competition from the holders of the patents covering these competing technologies but also removed them as a source of essential inputs for potential generic competitors, which could have obtained active pharmaceutical ingredients (APIs) and licences on these competing technologies.[2262]

When generic manufacturers started preparing their entry to the perindopril market and applied for marketing authorisations, Servier tried to dissuade them by sending warning letters and by making use of litigation and injunction proceedings.[2263] Between 2005 and 2007, Servier concluded five patent settlement agreements with the

---

2257. EU Commission Decision, *Servier*, 2014, paras 1-2.
2258. EU Commission Press Release, *Antitrust: Commission fines Servier and five generic companies for curbing entry of cheaper versions of cardiovascular medicine*, IP/14/799, Brussels, July 9, 2014. Available at: http://europa.eu/rapid/press-release_IP-14-799_en.htm. (last accessed on March 31, 2018) [cited as: EU Commission Press Release, *Servier*, 2014].
2259. *Idem.*
2260. EU Commission Decision, *Servier*, 2014, para. 5, referring to Servier's "alpha crystalline form patent" or '947 patent, which was perceived by the generic companies as the most important obstacle to generic entry. This patent was ultimately annulled, first by certain MS jurisdictions and finally revoked by the EPO in 2009. *See* further *idem*, paras 124-129. *See also idem*, para. 118, arguing that Servier's patenting strategy consisted of filing as many "blocking" patents as possible.
2261. EU Commission Decision, *Servier*, 2014, para. 6. *See* further *idem*, paras 246-420, analysing the development of competing APIs by other drug manufacturers and their acquisition by Servier.
2262. EU Commission Decision, *Servier*, 2014, para. 6.
2263. EU Commission Decision, *Servier*, 2014, para. 7.

most advanced generic challengers: Niche/Unichem, Matrix, Teva, Krka, Lupin.[2264] In return for inducements and significant payments exceeding in total €120 million – payments which were linked to the generic manufacturers' projected sales and gross profits if they have would entered the market –[2265] the generic companies undertook the obligation not to challenge Servier's patents and not to enter, directly or indirectly, the generic market for a number of years.[2266]

It is interesting to take a closer look to the inducements Servier used in those settlements. In the Niche/Unichem settlement, Servier offered to pay an amount equivalent to several years of Niche's expected generic profits; in return Niche/Unichem agreed not to challenge Servier's patents and to restrict their ability to compete.[2267] With regard to Teva, Servier offered a one-off payment (ranging from £0-£10 million) and eleven monthly payments (ranging from £0-£2 million),[2268] which according to the Commission can be compared to Teva's earning expectations in the first year of its generic market presence.[2269] Servier's settlements with Krka and Lupin included the transfer of certain patents from the generic manufacturers to Servier.[2270] Krka transferred to Servier two process patent applications, receiving a grant-back licence from Servier.[2271] Krka was also granted a licence on Servier's '947 patent, which effectively shielded the generic manufacturer from competition of other generic undertakings in seven CEE Member States where Krka's presence was already strong.[2272] Finally, Servier acquired from Lupin three process patent applications for €40 million, granting the generic manufacturer a royalty-free licence to the technology it had sold to Servier.[2273]

The geographical scope of nearly all the settlements extended to the entire EU territory.[2274] In 2014, the EU Commission imposed fines rising up to €427.7 million to Servier and the settling generic companies.[2275] The Commission found that the reverse payment settlements at issue amounted to anticompetitive agreements within the

---

2264. *See* further EU Commission Decision, *Servier*, 2014, paras 19-40, describing the generic manufacturers.
2265. EU Commission Decision, *Servier*, 2014, para. 7, referring to Niche commenting on the value transfer "[s]ettlement was equivalent to over 10 year planned sales and 20 years planned gross profit."
2266. EU Commission Decision, *Servier*, 2014, para. 7.
2267. EU Commission Decision, *Servier*, 2014, paras 1338-1347.
2268. The exact amounts of these payments are not indicated in the public version of the EU Commission Decision in *Servier*.
2269. EU Commission Decision, *Servier*, 2014, paras 1600-1607.
2270. EU Commission Decision, *Servier*, 2014, para. 7; *see idem* para. 1040 on the acquisition of Lupin's three process patent applications by Servier for €40 million; paras 1765-1773 on the acquisition of Krka's two patents by Servier.
2271. *See infra* Chapter 6, Part 1, Section III.C, on side-deals as value transfers in the Servier settlements.
2272. EU Commission Decision, *Servier*, 2014, paras 1721-1749; in exchange Krka withdrawn from twenty EU markets among which were UK and France, Servier's biggest markets world-wide.
2273. EU Commission Decision, *Servier*, 2014, paras 1037-1048, 1937-1978.
2274. EU Commission Decision, *Servier*, 2014, para. 7. The only exception was the settlement agreement between Servier and Teva which covered only the UK territory.
2275. *See also* EU Commission Decision, *Servier*, 2014, para. 44. Already in 2008 the Commission had started an *ex officio* investigation with unannounced inspections of the premises of the concerned undertakings.

meaning of Article 101 TFEU, while Servier's patent acquisitions combined with the reverse payment settlements amounted to an abuse of dominant position within the meaning of Article 102 TFEU.[2276]

2   Servier's Hard Product Switch to Second Generation Perindopril

In an effort to extend the life cycle of perindopril, Servier developed and introduced a second-generation product which allegedly had no superior medical effect, but served as its "principal weapon" against generic entry.[2277] The replacement of salts in the second-generation product generated new patent protection for Servier until 2023, while Servier also changed the drugs' dosages.[2278] The Commission found that Servier's launch of this second-generation product was linked to the regulatory framework on generic substitution: pharmacists could not substitute a drug with one salt for a drug with another salt in a certain number of Member States, nor could they substitute medicines with different dosages.[2279] According to the Commission, the main objective of Servier's product switch was to block generic substitution due to the different salt and the different dosages of its new drug product.[2280]

Servier carefully planned the timing of the product switch from the first to the second generation of perindopril, with the parallel withdrawal of the first generation drug from the market.[2281] Many generic competitors considered the launch of Servier's second-generation product as evergreening and the most important non-patent barrier to generic entry in the perindopril market.[2282] It was almost impossible for generics to enter the markets where Servier had already successfully switched to the second-generation drug before generic entry occurred, as was the case in Belgium, Ireland or Denmark.[2283]

B   Settlements Violating Article 101(1) TFEU

In order to determine if the patent settlement agreements in *Servier* constituted restrictions by object, the European Commission applied a test largely similar to the

---

2276. EU Commission Decision, *Servier*, 2014, para. 9; EU Commission Press Release, *Servier*, 2014.
2277. EU Commission Decision, *Servier*, 2014, paras 217-228. See especially *idem* paras 225-226, citing internal document of Servier and Teva, mentioning the replacement of the erbumine with the arginine salt lacked added therapeutic benefits but was likely to impede or block generic entry.
2278. EU Commission Decision, *Servier*, 2014, para. 8. Due to the different molecular weight of the new salt, this second-generation drug was sold in different dosages. See also *idem*, paras 223-228, arguing that the second version of perindopril did not have superior medical effects when compared to the first version of the drug.
2279. EU Commission Decision, *Servier*, 2014, paras 233-234, citing Servier's internal documents. See also supra Chapter 4, Section IV, analysing generic substitution and product-hopping strategies in the US.
2280. EU Commission Decision, *Servier*, 2014, para. 242.
2281. EU Commission Decision, *Servier*, 2014, paras 234-237.
2282. EU Commission Decision, *Servier*, 2014, para. 239.
2283. EU Commission Decision, *Servier*, 2014, para. 240-241, mentioning the UK as an exception where generics entered the market after Servier's product switch.

Chapter 6: Delaying Generic Entry in the EU

one it had previously applied in its decision in *Lundbeck*, in essence affirming the latter. The Commission repeated that it needed to assess whether: (1) the generic manufacturers and the brand-name manufacturer were at least potential competitors; (2) the generic manufacturers voluntarily limited their independent efforts to enter the EU market; and (3) the settlement agreement involved a value transfer, substantially reducing the generic manufacturers' incentives to enter the market.[2284] The answer to all three of these questions was positive according to the Commission; its reasoning in the *Servier* decision is closely similar to its reasoning in *Lundbeck*, so that it is of little interest to repeat it. Briefly put, similarly to the settlements in *Lundbeck*, the *Servier* settlements imposed restrictions lasting throughout the patent term, while they did not include any commitment by Servier not to initiate patent infringement proceedings if the generics would enter the market after the expiry of the settlements. Additionally, the value transfers were linked to the generics' projected turnover and profits, had they entered the market, while the restrictions imposed by the settlements exceeded the scope of the underlying patent dispute and what Servier could have obtained through the successful enforcement of its patents.[2285] Naturally, Servier challenged the Commission's finding of a restriction by object in its action before the EU General Court, arguing that the three factors on which the Commission relied for its finding of a restriction by object are overly broad and thus ineffective.[2286]

It is highly interesting to analyse the points of the Commission's decision in *Servier* which distinct it from the *Lundbeck* case. For instance, side-deals were a core element of Servier's settlements with the generic manufacturers. The settlements in *Servier* were polyvalent and highly complex, forming a net of licensing, distribution and acquisition agreements whose exhaustive analysis in the Commission's decision is neither easy to understand nor to structure in a useful way.[2287] For the sake of clarity and brevity, the following sections analyse the most important of these side-deals, focusing on the acquisition of Krka's and Lupin's patent applications by Servier and the side-deals on the distribution of authorised generics.[2288]

C Side-Deals as Value Transfers in the Servier Settlements

In its decision in *Servier*, the Commission noted that the inducement to a generic competitor in order for it to refrain from entering the market may result from different forms of commercial arrangements.[2289] A side-deal, dependent on the generic's acceptance of the settlement terms, may also be employed as an inducement to delay generic

---

2284. EU Commission Decision, *Servier*, 2014, para. 1154.
2285. EU Commission Decision, *Servier*, 2014, para. 1155.
2286. Case T-691/14: Action brought on 21 September 2014, *Servier SAS and Others v. Commission*, OJ C 462, 22.12.2014, p. 26, pleas 4-12 (Case T-691/14: Action brought on 21 September 2014, *Servier SAS and Others*).
2287. Suffice to state that the EU Commission Decision, *Servier*, 2014 is 805 pages long; the EU Commission decision, *Lundbeck*, 2013 is 464 pages long.
2288. *See* for instance EU Commission Decision, *Servier*, 2014, paras 910-922, describing Servier's exclusive licence agreement on the '947 patent to Krka; *idem* paras 1349-1354, describing Servier's generic subsidy Biogaran's licence and supply agreement with Niche/Unichem.
2289. EU Commission Decision, *Servier*, 2014, para. 1190.

entry.²²⁹⁰ In order to determine whether such a side-deal is used by the originator as an inducement, two elements shall be analysed: (1) the *link* between the side-deal and the patent settlement, and; (2) the commercial importance of the side-deal.²²⁹¹ According to the Commission, the significance of an inducement shall be examined compared to the alternative competitive scenarios absent the settlement, so as to determine the opportunity costs of the settlement for the generic company.²²⁹² As the General Court held in *Lundbeck*, a value transfer corresponding to the projected profits of the generic company, had it entered the market, could be an indication of significant inducement.²²⁹³ Going further, the Commission argued in *Servier* that even inferior value transfers could be considered as inducements not to enter the market,²²⁹⁴ rejecting in essence a presumption of legality forming a safe harbour for value transfers which are inferior to the generics' projected profits in case of entry to the market. Two of Servier's settlements, with Lupin and with Krka, involved side-deals transferring patent rights from the generic manufacturers to Servier.²²⁹⁵ Before analysing these acquisitions, it should be stressed that the acquired intellectual property rights were not further developed by Servier.²²⁹⁶

1   Servier's Acquisition of Lupin's Generic Patent Applications

Lupin sold three process patent applications to Servier for €40 million: the generic manufacturer gave no explicit assurance on the non-infringing status or the validity of those patent applications, while Servier licensed all of them back to Lupin on a non-exclusive, royalty-free licence.²²⁹⁷ The Commission found that Lupin's patent applications were of no commercial value to Servier: the latter had limited knowledge of the patent applications it acquired, did not insist on the validity or functionability of Lupin's patent applications as a precondition for the purchase and did not follow its normal policy of conducting a feasibility study before acquiring the respective intellectual property rights.²²⁹⁸ Finally, neither Servier nor Lupin provided a plausible description of the factors that lead to the determination of €40 million as the value of the patent applications.²²⁹⁹ Thus, the Commission concluded that the payment did not reflect the perceived value, the validity or usefulness of the patent applications to

---

2290. EU Commission Decision, *Servier*, 2014, para. 1190.
2291. *Idem*.
2292. EU Commission Decision, *Servier*, 2014, para. 1191.
2293. Judgment of the General Court of 8 September 2016, Case T-472/13, *Lundbeck v. Commission*, para. 354; EU Commission Decision, *Servier*, 2014, para. 1191.
2294. EU Commission Decision, *Servier*, 2014, para. 1191.
2295. EU Commission Decision, *Servier*, 2014, para. 1040 on the acquisition of Lupin's three process patent applications by Servier for €40 million; paras 1765-1773 on the acquisition of Krka's two patents by Servier.
2296. EU Commission Decision, *Servier*, 2014, para. 380; the only exception is one of Krka's patent applications which arguably contributed to some improvement of Servier's production processes.
2297. EU Commission Decision, *Servier*, 2014, para. 1040. *See also idem* paras 1960-1966, analysing the value of Lupin's patent applications.
2298. EU Commission Decision, *Servier*, 2014, paras 1940-1954.
2299. EU Commission Decision, *Servier*, 2014, para. 1955.

Servier which was negligible; on the contrary Servier's payment constituted a reverse payment, was primarily an inducement for Lupin to settle with Servier and reflected the value of shielding Servier's profits that would have been foregone if Lupin's technology would have led to generic entry.[2300]

2 Servier's Acquisition and Licence Agreement with Krka

On the basis of an Acquisition and Licence Agreement (mentioned in the Commission's decision as ALA) Krka transferred to Servier two process patent applications and received €30 million and a licence-back from Servier.[2301] The ALA – combined with the patent settlement agreement between Servier and Krka – stipulated that no technology could be available from the generic manufacturer earlier than two to three years from the conclusion of the settlements, providing to Servier absolute protection from any remaining potential competition.[2302] The Commission found that Krka was prohibited from supplying to any third party perindopril covered by the '947 patent (produced based on the assigned technology) and that the generic manufacturer was only limited to commercialise its own perindopril in the seven Member States covered by the ALA.[2303] Similarly to the acquisition of Lupin's patent applications, Servier did not conduct any studies on the feasibility of Krka's patent applications or their potential benefits to Servier's technology.[2304] Krka did not provide any guarantee on the validity or non-infringement of its patent applications, did not conduct full due diligence and did not transfer to Servier any know-how on the exploitation of the acquired technology.[2305] As was the case with the patent applications acquired from Lupin, the patent applications of Krka had negligible commercial value and their acquisition by Servier formed part of a "joint activity to control the market."[2306] The acquisition of Krka's patent applications by Servier entailed an immediate one-off distortion of competition within the meaning of Article 101 TFEU: Servier had foreclosed the potential competition based on the use of Krka's technology by removing the generic manufacturer's ability to license or assign its technology to third parties.[2307] Servier arguably admitted that the €30 million payment was linked to the patent settlement[2308] while the Commission stressed that this payment was disconnected from the patent applications and served as a form of "rent sharing" between the parties.[2309]

2300. EU Commission Decision, *Servier*, 2014, paras 1955-1978.
2301. EU Commission Decision, *Servier*, 2014, paras 1768-1770, 1774. *See idem* paras 923-928 on the details of the ALA between Servier and Krka.
2302. EU Commission Decision, *Servier*, 2014, paras 1765-1773.
2303. EU Commission Decision, *Servier*, 2014, para. 1773.
2304. EU Commission Decision, *Servier*, 2014, paras 1777-1779.
2305. EU Commission Decision, *Servier*, 2014, paras 1779-1781.
2306. EU Commission Decision, *Servier*, 2014, paras 1790-1810.
2307. EU Commission Decision, *Servier*, 2014, paras 1772-1773.
2308. EU Commission Decision, *Servier*, 2014, paras 1790-1799; since Krka did not forego the use of its technology, the Commission argued that the additional payment of €30 million "represented a windfall for Krka."
2309. EU Commission Decision, *Servier*, 2014, paras 1804-1810.

What is of particular interest in the Commission's analysis is the finding that the patent settlement and the ALA between Krka and Servier formed part of *a single and continuous activity* to restrict competition through market sharing.[2310] The two agreements were concluded within a short time-period, both contained restrictions that pursued the objective of market sharing between the parties and followed a similar method of restricting competition through inducements to Krka.[2311] The Commission found that Servier and Krka shared markets and entered into a de facto duopoly in seven Member States, while Krka agreed to withdraw from the market of eighteen Member States.[2312]

3 Side-Deals on the Distribution of Authorised Generics

Servier used side-deals not only as mechanisms of value transfer but also as a defence mechanism in case its patents would be invalidated. Servier's strategy to engage generic manufacturers as distributors of authorised generics was a key element in order to defend its market shares in the perindopril market and would only be activated in case patent '947 was invalidated.[2313] Authorised generic distribution arrangements can be used as a mechanism of "controlled generic entry," since the generic companies commit not to launch and compete with their own generic versions, whereas the originator retains some degree of control over commercial parameters such as the launch date of the authorised generic, prices, quantities, etc.[2314] The authorised generic launch was considered to be a "nuclear weapon" and Servier planned to use it strategically, since it instructed its "friendly" generic manufacturers to be prepared for an authorised generic launch, but to only proceed "in case of *absolute* necessity."[2315] These agreements were used as an efficient *ultimum remedium* to maintain a good income on perindopril and keep volumes in case of generic entry.[2316]

Servier concluded a total of ten distribution agreements with generic companies, one of which was concluded with Teva, concerning the UK market.[2317] On the basis of an exclusive purchasing agreement, Servier agreed to supply Teva with generic perindopril. In case of failure to supply by Servier, Teva had no other right or remedy apart from receiving a payment of liquidated damages; it could not terminate the agreement, neither could it source perindopril from third parties.[2318] This exclusive purchasing agreement, combined with the non-challenge and the non-compete clauses – which are analysed in the following sections – secured Servier's position in the perindopril market.

2310. EU Commission Decision, *Servier*, 2014, para. 1807-1811.
2311. EU Commission Decision, *Servier*, 2014, paras 1811-1812.
2312. EU Commission Decision, *Servier*, 2014, paras 1803-1810.
2313. EU Commission Decision, *Servier*, 2014, para. 758, citing an internal communication of Sevier.
2314. EU Commission Decision, *Servier*, 2014, para. 203.
2315. EU Commission Decision, *Servier*, 2014, para. 203.
2316. EU Commission Decision, *Servier*, 2014, para. 205.
2317. *Idem.*
2318. EU Commission Decision, *Servier*, 2014, paras 744, 748.

Chapter 6: Delaying Generic Entry in the EU

When its '947 patent was initially upheld by the EPO opposition division on July 2006, Servier decided to seek injunctive relief against Apotex (the generic manufacturer which had already entered the UK market) and chose not to supply Teva with generic perindopril but to pay liquidated damages instead.[2319] Servier knew that if it would have launched the authorised generic, the whole perindopril market would become generic, making it nearly impossible for Servier to regain its pre-generic entry market position: the downward price spiral following generic entry and the lost market shares would cause Servier great damages.[2320] However, when the '947 patent was invalidated by the UK High Court, there were no obstacles to the generic entry of Apotex.[2321] Changing its strategy, Servier made use of its last resort and gave Teva its consent to start marketing perindopril authorised generics.[2322]

D *The Analysis of the Anticompetitive Effects of the Settlements*

Even though the Commission found that the settlement agreements in *Servier* constituted restrictions of competition by object, it decided to analyse their likely restrictive effects on competition "for the sake of completeness."[2323] Such an analysis of anticompetitive effects was completely absent in the Commission's decision in *Lundbeck*. The complexity of the *Servier* settlements, which formed a net of patent settlements and side-deals, is likely one of the main reasons of the Commission's effects analysis.[2324] It should also be noted that the Commission's decision in *Servier* was taken before *Lundbeck* was decided by the General Court, at a time of legal uncertainty concerning the legal standard the court would opt for. The Commission's finding of a restriction by object in *Lundbeck* was being heavily criticised by legal practitioners[2325] and the CJEU's decision in *Cartes Bancaires* – noting that the notion of restriction by object should be interpreted restrictively – was used as one of the main arguments against the Commission's decision.[2326] Thus, it is not surprising that the Commission decided to include an analysis of the effects of the settlements at issue in its *Servier* decision, since it faced the risk of the General Court overturning its finding of a restriction by object in

---

2319. EU Commission Decision, *Servier*, 2014, paras 750-769.
2320. *See* EU Commission Decision, *Servier*, 2014, para. 762, citing a witness statement.
2321. EU Commission Decision, *Servier*, 2014, para. 776. *See* further SIMON & SIMON, Pharma, IP & Competition in the EU, 2011, pp. 268-269, describing Servier's patent infringement suit against Apotex and the UK High Court's decision invalidating Servier's patent. Subsequently the Canadian Federal Court upheld the validity of a related patent covering perindopril.
2322. EU Commission Decision, *Servier*, 2014, paras 776-779.
2323. EU Commission Decision, *Servier*, 2014, para. 1213.
2324. *See supra* Chapter 6, Part 1, Section III.C on the analysis of Servier's side deals with the generic manufacturers.
2325. *See* indicatively, KILLICK, JOURDAN, DICKINSON, Lundbeck, 2015.
2326. *See* for instance STRAUS, Servier, 2016, pp. 540-544, arguing that treating patent settlements involving value transfers as restrictions by object has far-reaching "criminal consequences" and is against the *Cartes Bancaires* judgment. *See* further *supra* Chapter 5, Part 2, Section II.C.1.2, discussing the decision of *Cartes Bancaires*. *See also supra* Chapter 6, Part 1, Section II.C.2.3, on the General Court's decision in *Lundbeck* ruling that the Commission's finding of a restriction by object was not in conflict with the *Cartes Bancaires* decision.

Lundbeck. What remained unchanged in the Commission's decision in *Servier* was the rejection of the scope of the patent test as the applicable test for the analysis of reverse payment settlements.[2327]

The restrictive effects of an agreement shall be assessed in comparison with the actual legal and economic context, where competition would occur absent the settlements.[2328] Such assessment shall look into the degree of actual and potential competition between the settling parties and from third parties, if the settlements would not have been concluded.[2329] In *Servier*, the Commission's assessment of anticompetitive effects focused on the following elements: (1) market power, since negative effects on competition are most likely to occur when the parties individually or jointly have some degree of market power, created, maintained or strengthened through the agreement; (2) the content of the agreement and its inducements; (3) the competitive behaviour the generics would have likely engaged in, absent the settlements; and (4) whether competition would be restricted if other relevant sources of competition existed in the relevant market.[2330]

1 The Relevant Market and Servier's Position Within It

In *Servier*, the Commission opted for a narrow market definition and defined the original perindopril drug as the relevant product market. Even though there were many other similar medicines available in the market, their functional similarities were not adequate so as to establish that they represented sufficiently close substitutes which constrained Servier's market behaviour.[2331] The degree of substitutability of a given molecule with other molecules depends, among other things: (1) on the doctors' inertia (the doctors' natural tendency to prescribe new patients with the medicines that were effective for their previous patients), and; (2) on the relative proportion of continued-use patients compared to all patients treated with a certain medicine.[2332] Servier's brand-name drug benefited from both effects: already prior to the Commission's investigation it had accumulated a large base of continued-use patients, while a group of "loyal prescribers" continuously provided for a flow of new patients.[2333] The Commission concluded that the substitutability between other available therapies and perindopril was effectively restricted by the *ex ante* uncertain effects of treatments and the doctors' personal experience.[2334] Moreover, price decreases on other drug products intended for the same use did not negatively affect perindopril's sales, due to the

---

2327. EU Commission Decision, *Servier*, 2014, paras 1188-1194.
2328. EU Commission, *101 TFEU Guidelines*, 2011, para. 29; EU Commission Decision, *Servier*, 2014, para. 1221.
2329. *Idem*.
2330. EU Commission Decision, *Servier*, 2014, paras 1224-1227.
2331. EU Commission Decision, *Servier*, 2014, para. 1230.
2332. EU Commission Decision, *Servier*, 2014, paras 1232-1233.
2333. EU Commission Decision, *Servier*, 2014, para. 1234.
2334. EU Commission Decision, *Servier*, 2014, para. 1235.

doctors' general disregard towards prices and price rigidities, the so-called "price disconnect" which has been discussed in previous chapters.[2335]

On the contrary, the constraints imposed by generic entry in the perindopril market (mentioned in the Commission's decision as the "generic constraint") were critical for the assessment of the relevant product market and outweighted by far the above-mentioned potential constraints posed by alternative medicines.[2336] Generic perindopril could challenge *all* the existing sales of Servier's brand-name product.[2337] As a result of generic entry in the perindopril market, the average prices of perindopril decreased within a range of 17% to 90%, while the sale volumes were shifted from Servier's patented product to the perindopril generic substitutes.[2338] Since the generic constraint massively outweighted other potential constraints the Commission defined the market narrowly, limited only to perindopril,[2339] a definition that is being challenged by Servier in its action before the EU General Court.[2340]

The EU Commission found that Servier held high market shares in the perindopril market, given its market exclusivity on the patented product for the relevant time-period.[2341] Additionally, Servier's secondary process patents on perindopril constituted important barriers, further strengthening its market position. To the extent that the company's ability to charge supracompetitive prices was linked to the settlement agreements at issue, it was possible to show the settlements' direct anticompetitive effects.[2342] The Commission found that the delay in the entry of generic perindopril resulted in much higher consumer spendings, while each national market covered by the settlements was a multimillion market in terms of Servier's annual turnover.[2343]

2   The Non-challenge and the Non-compete Clauses of the Settlements

All of the *Servier* settlements with the generic manufacturers contained non-challenge and non-compete clauses which are extensively analysed in the Commission's decision.[2344] Pursuant to these non-challenge clauses, the generic manufacturers were

---

2335. EU Commission Decision, *Servier*, 2014, para. 1236. For a brief discussion on the "price disconnect" as a parameter in product market definition *see supra*, Chapter 5, Part 2, Section III, B.1.2.
2336. EU Commission Decision, *Servier*, 2014, paras 1240-1241.
2337. EU Commission Decision, *Servier*, 2014, para. 1238, noting that contrary to other drugs, generic perindropil was not affected by the doctors' inertia or limited by the existence of continued-use patient base, while EU regulatory frameworks promoted price competition between brand-name and generic perindropil.
2338. EU Commission Decision, *Servier*, 2014, para. 1239.
2339. EU Commission Decision, *Servier*, 2014, para. 1240.
2340. Case T-691/14: Action brought on 21 September 2014, *Servier SAS and Others*, pp. 26-27, pleas 14-16, arguing that the Commission wrongly defined the relevant market as the single molecule for perindopril and incorrectly found that Servier had a dominant position in the relevant technology market.
2341. EU Commission Decision, *Servier*, 2014, para. 1241. The investigated period was from 2000 until 2009; *see idem*, para. 6.
2342. EU Commission Decision, *Servier*, 2014, para. 1243.
2343. *Idem*.
2344. *See* the Commission's analysis on the non-challenge and non-compete clauses, EU Commission Decision, *Servier*, 2014, paras 1305-1317 on the settlement with Niche/Unichem; paras

blocked from challenging and possibly invalidating Servier's patents, while on the basis of the non-compete clauses the generics were prevented from competing on the perindopril market. In sum, Servier obtained a 100% certainty that the generics did not represent a competitive threat and avoided the objective legal review of the validity and of the (non-)infringement of its patents. The Commission stressed that non-challenge clauses do not fall within the subject matter of the patent and that a patent holder cannot buy certainty against the risks inherent in litigation and still obtain immunity from competition law.[2345]

2.1 The Non-challenge Clauses and Their Effects

All five settlement agreements between Servier and the generic manufacturers included non-challenge clauses, obliging the generics to abstain from invalidity and non-infringement actions against Servier's patent rights. Further, pursuant to the settlements Niche/Unichem, Krka[2346] and Lupin were obliged to withdraw their oppositions before the EPO concerning Servier's '947 patent.[2347] The non-challenge obligations were generally broad, even though the material scope of these clauses was not identical in all settlements; for instance Niche/Unichem committed to abstain from invalidity and non-infringement actions against *any* of Servier's patent rights,[2348] while Matrix was prohibited from seeking any declaration of non-infringement and only allowed to defend itself if Servier initiated infringement actions against it.[2349] The territorial scope of the non-challenge obligations varied in each generic settlement: in the Matrix settlement it extended to all the countries in which Servier's corresponding patent rights existed with the exception of the US;[2350] in the Krka settlement the non-challenge obligation had worldwide scope,[2351] while in the Teva settlement it only covered the UK market.[2352]

1438-1448 on the settlement with Matrix, paras 1544-1574 on the settlement with Teva; paras 1711-1720 on the settlement with Krka; paras 1905-1926 on the settlement with Lupin.
2345. EU Commission Decision, *Servier*, 2014, para. 1153.
2346. EU Commission Decision, *Servier*, 2014, para. 1712. The Commission found that object of the Krka settlement was to remove the immediate competitive threat Krka represented to Servier, given that it was one of the few generic companies which was involved in patent challenges before national courts and considered that its arguments regarding the opposition procedure before the EPO were stronger.
2347. EU Commission Decision, *Servier*, 2014, para. 1305 on the settlement with Niche/Unichem; para. 1711 on the settlement with Krka; paras 1905-1906 on the settlement with Lupin. *See* however *idem* para. 1546 on the settlement with Teva; Teva was not obliged to withdraw its EPO opposition concerning Servier's '947 patent; however, the agreement prevented the generic from directly challenging the said patent in the period between EPO's final determination and the expiry of the settlement.
2348. EU Commission Decision, *Servier*, 2014, para. 1305.
2349. EU Commission Decision, *Servier*, 2014, para. 1438.
2350. *Idem*.
2351. EU Commission Decision, *Servier*, 2014, para. 1711. *See also idem* 1715; at the time of settlements, Krka and Apotex were the only two generic companies that managed to complete the independent development of generic perindopril and to receive marketing authorisations in a number of EU Member States.
2352. EU Commission Decision, *Servier*, 2014, para. 1544.

The material scope of the non-challenge obligations also varied in each settlement agreement. For instance, the non-challenge clause in the Lupin settlement was not limited to Servier's '947 patent but also vaguely extended to "any [other] patent owned by Servier or its affiliates covering the relevant [drug] products."[2353] The Commission interpreted this clause as encompassing not only any drug product containing perindopril API but also any alternative salt of perindopril; thus, the settlement went far beyond the commitment not to challenge the '947 patent – which was the subject matter of the patent litigation – extending also to the patent covering Servier's secondgeneration product.[2354] The purpose of the settlement agreement went beyond putting an end to the pending patent litigation: instead, its aim was to impose on Lupin commitments that could not have been imposed through the exclusionary power of Servier's patents.[2355]

The Commission found that these non-challenge clauses prevented the generic manufacturers from establishing that the technologies they have developed were *de iure* non-infringing technologies and could be legitimately used for the production of non-infringing generic perindopril.[2356] These non-challenge clauses in essence prevented the objective legal review of the validity of Servier's patents, disabling any possible benefit for generic producers in case of patent invalidation.[2357] Servier was thus guaranteed a 100% certainty that its patent position would not be threatened by generic manufacturers.[2358]

2.2 The Non-compete Clauses

Niche/Unichem had developed in collaboration with Matrix a process for the production of perindopril. However, on the basis of the non-compete obligations included in their respective settlement agreements with Servier, the generics were not allowed to carry out any kind of "restricted act" relating to perindopril, in any country of the world where Servier's respective patents existed.[2359] Niche, Unichem, Matrix and their distribution partners were contractually prevented from commercialising in the EU perindopril produced through the process they have developed until September 2008.[2360] This prohibition was broad: in the Niche/Unichem settlement it extended to *all* EU Member States;[2361] in the Matrix settlement it extended to all countries where Servier held its three process patents (with the exception of the US),[2362] irrespective of whether the settling parties have been litigating or of whether the generics had pending

---

2353. EU Commission Decision, *Servier*, 2014, para. 1909.
2354. *See* EU Commission Decision, *Servier*, 2014, paras 1910-1911, where the Commission rejected Servier's narrow interpretation of this clause, and found that the non-challenge obligation extended to Servier's process patents.
2355. EU Commission Decision, *Servier*, 2014, para. 1915.
2356. EU Commission Decision, *Servier*, 2014, paras 1306, 1438, 1546-1548, 1712.
2357. EU Commission Decision, *Servier*, 2014, paras 1308, 1438, 1712.
2358. EU Commission Decision, *Servier*, 2014, paras 1308, 1915.
2359. EU Commission Decision, *Servier*, 2014, para. 1309.
2360. EU Commission Decision, *Servier*, 2014, paras 1310-1317.
2361. EU Commission Decision, *Servier*, 2014, para. 1317.
2362. EU Commission Decision, *Servier*, 2014, para. 1442.

marketing authorisation applications.[2363] Additionally, after the expiry of Servier's process patents, Niche and Unichem were not allowed to enter the market with a product containing the alpha crystalline form claimed in Servier's '947 patent,[2364] while Matrix and Niche were obliged to suspend their cooperation agreement until the expiry of Servier's process patents.[2365]

The non-compete clause in the Teva settlement did not prevent Teva from producing and marketing generic perindopril using new processes not infringing Servier's patents.[2366] However, the Teva settlement included an exclusive purchasing obligation, under which Teva had to buy all the required perindopril erbumine for distribution in the UK from Servier.[2367] As above-analysed, Teva was unable to terminate this exclusive purchasing agreement and to sell possibly non-infringing perindopril, even in case Servier failed to supply.[2368] The combination of various clauses of the settlement led the Commission to the conclusion that Teva could not sell its own generic product, while it did not have any incentive to develop a new generic version of perindopril.[2369] The parties' arguments on the procompetitive nature of this exclusive purchasing obligation were rejected by the Commission, which found that no early-entry option was foreseen by the agreement.[2370] On the contrary, the non-compete obligation was employed by Servier as a means to control Teva's market behaviour and to ensure that Teva would not supply perindopril in the UK if that would be detrimental for Servier's interests. Further, pursuant to the settlement, Teva could be converted into a distributor of Servier's authorised generics and be used as a defence mechanism against generic entry, in case Servier's patents would be invalidated.[2371] Under the non-compete obligation, Teva could not sell perindopril in the UK for the duration of its settlement agreement with Servier; instead it received a lump sum payment from Servier and liquidated damages.[2372]

Krka on the other hand, one of the two generic manufacturers which managed to complete the independent development of generic perindopril,[2373] was prevented from launching its existing generic drug, either directly or indirectly, except if expressly authorised by Servier.[2374] The non-compete clause excluded the alleged generic infringer from the market without the need for Servier to establish before a court that its patent was indeed infringed.[2375] In return for Krka's commitment, Servier granted

---

2363. EU Commission Decision, *Servier*, 2014, para. 1317.
2364. *Idem*. This restriction applied both to situations where Niche would supply generic perindopril directly and where it would supply the market though a local partner.
2365. EU Commission Decision, *Servier*, 2014, para. 1448.
2366. EU Commission Decision, *Servier*, 2014, para. 1549.
2367. See *supra* Chapter 6, Part 1, Section III.C.3.
2368. EU Commission Decision, *Servier*, 2014, para. 1574.
2369. EU Commission Decision, *Servier*, 2014, para. 1552.
2370. EU Commission Decision, *Servier*, 2014, paras 1557-1560.
2371. EU Commission Decision, *Servier*, 2014, para. 1570.
2372. See EU Commission Decision, *Servier*, 2014, para. 1574. Teva received liquidated damages during the period starting from the settlement's conclusion until the beginning of the actual supply.
2373. EU Commission Decision, *Servier*, 2014, para. 1715.
2374. EU Commission Decision, *Servier*, 2014, para. 1716.
2375. EU Commission Decision, *Servier*, 2014, para. 1720.

the generic a licensing agreement on the '947 patent, expressly authorising Krka to commercialise generic perindopril in seven CEE Member States;[2376] thus, the non-compete obligation only applied to eighteen to twenty EU Member States.[2377] Therefore, Krka was induced to abandon its prerogatives under patent law, since it was prevented from marketing generic perindopril in the restricted Member States where Servier did not grant it a licence, even though Krka had obtained or would imminently obtain marketing authorisations.[2378]

Finally, on the basis of the non-compete clause in the Lupin settlement, Lupin and its affiliates were obliged to refrain from selling any perindropil products in any country covered by the settlement.[2379] Lupin was prevented from selling the perindopril it had developed by itself, but also any other perindopril (newly developed or acquired by third parties), irrespectively of whether it was infringing Servier's patents.[2380] Thus, Lupin did not have any incentive to develop a new non-infringing perindopril version, while it made its generic launch fully dependent on third parties' generic entry and on Servier's inability to prevent such entry.[2381]

3 Assessment of the Value Transfers in the Settlements

The identification of the value transfers in the *Servier* settlements was necessary for their assessment as restrictions by object. In order to assess the value transfers, the Commission attempted to determine the exact purpose of each value transfer from Servier to the settling generic manufacturers and also the values transferred to Servier in return.[2382] The settling undertakings referred to the following elements as value transfers in the agreements: (1) the non-challenge and the non-compete obligations; (2) the generics' commitments not to request new marketing authorisations; and (3) the termination/suspension of existing consumer relationships or of their programmes to develop and manufacture perindopril.[2383] However, the Commission found that Servier had not gained any commercial value by compensating the generic undertakings for their "substantial costs and potential liabilities:" the generics' costs for ceasing their perindopril programme did not represent a separate benefit to Servier, while their

---

2376. EU Commission Decision, *Servier*, 2014, para. 910.
2377. EU Commission Decision, *Servier*, 2014, para. 1716. The licensing agreement concerned the following states: the Czech Republic, Hungary, Lithuania, Latvia, Poland, Slovakia and Slovenia. For the period between 27 October 2006 and 31 December 2006, the Commission's assessment only covers eighteen Member States.
2378. EU Commission Decision, *Servier*, 2014, para. 1718.
2379. EU Commission Decision, *Servier*, 2014, paras 1916-1917. This non-compete obligation would only be lifted if: (1) an authorised generic was put on the market; (2) all the perindopril relevant patents expired in the relevant jurisdiction, and; (3) another party sold generic perindopril on the market and Servier did not initiate interim injunctions against such sales.
2380. EU Commission Decision, *Servier*, 2014, para. 1918.
2381. EU Commission Decision, *Servier*, 2014, para. 1919.
2382. *See* for instance EU Commission Decision, *Servier*, 2014, paras 1320-1354 on the assessment of the value transferred by Servier to Niche/Unichem.
2383. EU Commission Decision, *Servier*, 2014, paras 1320-1354 on Servier's settlement with Niche/Unichem; paras 1449-1467 on Servier's settlement with Matrix; paras 1575-1608 on Servier's settlement with Teva.

commitments on abstaining from requesting marketing authorisations merely reinforced their non-compete obligations.[2384] Three out of the five settlements in *Servier* did not mention any specific goods, rights or services provided by the generic manufacturers to Servier.[2385] The sole exceptions were Servier's settlements with Lupin and Krka, which contained a transfer of value from both directions.[2386] Therefore, the Commission found that Servier would have paid the generic manufacturers irrespectively of the validity or usefulness of the acquired patents whose inherent commercial value was negligible; the payments served as an inducement for the generic manufacturers to settle with Servier.[2387]

The Commission found that there was a clear link between the value transfers in the settlements and the limitations imposed to generic entry; the payments from Servier to the generics were a net value transfer, since the costs and liabilities of the generics were of no commercial value to Servier and could not serve as legitimate justifications for the value transfers.[2388] Even if these costs could have been considered as acceptable legitimate justifications, they exceeded the generic manufacturers' incurred costs, while the parties have not given *any* explanation on the method of calculation of the value transfers.[2389] The net value transfer from Servier was used as an inducement to conclude the settlement which represented a rent-sharing arrangement, in return for the generics' commitment not to compete; in return for these value transfers, Servier secured its monopoly on perindopril and its market position for multiple years, possibly until the expiration of the '947 patent in 2021.[2390]

E Justifications under Article 101(3) TFEU

The settling parties in *Servier* tried to justify the restrictions imposed by their settlements on the basis of Article 101(3) TFEU, alleging efficiency gains from: (1) the avoidance of litigation costs; (2) the improvement of Servier's perindopril production processes through the acquisition of generic companies' technology; (3) the improvement of Servier's product distribution; (4) Teva's alleged expedited generic entry and Krka's licence; (5) the reverse payment settlements securing the generics' incentives to

---

2384. EU Commission Decision, *Servier*, 2014, paras 1322-1331 on Servier's settlement with Niche/Unichem; paras 1456-1464 on Servier's settlement with Matrix; paras 1586-1591 on Servier's settlement with Teva.
2385. EU Commission Decision, *Servier*, 2014, para. 1321 on Servier's settlement with Niche/Unichem; paras 1459-1460 on Servier's settlement with Matrix; para. 1587 on Servier's settlement with Teva.
2386. *See supra* Chapter 6, Part 1, Section III.C.
2387. *See supra* Chapter 6, Part 1, Section III.C on Servier's acquisition of Lupin's and Krka's patent applications.
2388. EU Commission Decision, *Servier*, 2014, paras 1331-1332 on Servier's settlement with Niche/Unichem; paras 1967-1978 on Servier's settlement with Lupin.
2389. EU Commission Decision, *Servier*, 2014, para. 1337 on Servier's settlement with Niche/Unichem; paras 1459-1464 on Servier's settlement with Matrix; paras 1592-1599 on Servier's settlement with Teva.
2390. EU Commission Decision, *Servier*, 2014, paras 1338-1348 on Servier's settlement with Niche/Unichem; para. 1467 on Servier's settlement with Matrix; para. 1608 on Servier's settlement with Teva; paras 1967-1978 on Servier's settlement with Lupin.

challenge patents and to enter the market.[2391] The Commission found that the parties failed to submit the necessary evidence in order to show that the four conditions for the application of Article 101(3) TFEU were fulfilled.[2392] Further, the restrictions by object imposed by the agreements were not necessary in order to achieve the claimed efficiencies;[2393] the objective nature of these efficiency gains was not substantiated;[2394] while the parties had not demonstrated that the consumers in the restricted markets would have received a fair share of any claimed efficiency.[2395]

1 Avoided Litigation Costs and the Acquired Technologies

The parties in *Servier* did not substantiate their alleged savings from the avoided litigation costs while the payments to the generics exceeded their projected litigation costs.[2396] The Commission stressed that litigation forms an essential part of competition between patent holders and generic companies: the avoided litigation costs are merely savings achieved through a reduction of output into patent litigation which is a key element in successfully invalidating the relevant patent and for enabling viable generic entry.[2397] The parties could have settled without any value transfers, on the basis of their assessment of Servier's patents vis-à-vis the generic drug version concerned, e.g., through an early-entry agreement or a distinct distribution agreement or technology transfer agreement,[2398] and the market sharing created by the settlements could have been avoided.[2399] Servier argued that the settlements allowed it to acquire the generics' patent applications and to possibly advance its technology while reducing its costs.[2400] Nevertheless, Servier had not reported any use for four out of the five acquired technologies, while it failed to demonstrate any expected savings from the use of the acquired patent applications.[2401] The Commission also rejected the parties' allegations on efficiency gains arising from the improvement of the distribution of Servier's products and the facilitation of Teva's generic entry to the market.[2402]

2391. EU Commission Decision, *Servier*, 2014, para. 2069, summarising the alleged efficiency gains identified by the Commission.
2392. EU Commission Decision, *Servier*, 2014, para. 2071.
2393. *See* further EU Commission Decision, *Servier*, 2014, paras 2062-2122, analysing and rejecting the alleged efficiencies of the settlement agreements.
2394. *See* for instance Judgment of the Court of 13 July 1966, Joined Cases 56 and 58/64, *Établissements Consten S.à.R.L. and Grundig-Verkaufs-GmbH v. Commission of the European Economic Community*, EU:C:1966:41, p. 348, requiring the demonstration of "an objectively ascertainable improvement in the production and distribution of goods" in order for the Commission to assess whether the imposed restrictions were indispensable to attain the alleged efficiency gains.
2395. EU Commission Decision, *Servier*, 2014, para. 2072.
2396. EU Commission Decision, *Servier*, 2014, para. 2076.
2397. EU Commission Decision, *Servier*, 2014, para. 2075.
2398. EU Commission Decision, *Servier*, 2014, para. 2072.
2399. *Idem*.
2400. EU Commission Decision, *Servier*, 2014, para. 2078.
2401. EU Commission Decision, *Servier*, 2014, paras 2078-2081. *See also idem* para. 2082, where the Commission noted that the non-challenge and non-compete clauses of the settlement agreements were not necessary in order to conclude a technology transfer agreement.
2402. EU Commission Decision, *Servier*, 2014, paras 2083-2095.

2 Outside the Scope of the Technology Transfer Block Exemption

Finally, the Commission refused to exempt the settlement between Krka and Servier on the basis of the Technology Transfer Block Exemption Regulation and the Technology Transfer Guidelines.[2403] Despite Servier's licence to Krka covering seven CEE Member States, the Krka settlement contained restrictions removing Krka's competition from markets in which the generic manufacturer was previously present as a potential competitor.[2404] The conditions for the application of the TTBER were not met: Servier held a monopoly in perindopril in the vast majority of Member States and enjoyed significant market power largely exceeding TTBER's thresholds.[2405] The settlement's restrictions went far beyond the TTBER's field-of-use restrictions and restrictions of active sales and had the object of market allocation: in the eighteen to twenty non-licensed Member States' territories, Krka was barred from selling perindopril products based on its own technology and from attempting to remove Servier's patent barriers from the market.[2406] The Commission found that the Krka agreement could be seen as a hardcore "restriction of the licensee's ability to exploit its own technology" due to its non-challenge and non-compete clauses.[2407] Pursuant to the settlement Krka had withdrawn from the market of eighteen to twenty Member States: in those markets there was no licensing enhancing competition between the parties.[2408] Before the conclusion of the settlement, Krka was Servier's actual or potential competitor in all twenty-five to twenty-seven Member States markets; after the settlement Krka remained Servier's competitor only in the seven licenced Member States' markets, thereby denying consumers any possible benefits from the licence in the seven licensed markets and any benefit from Krka's generic entry in the non-licensed markets.[2409]

F Servier's Abuse of Dominance under Article 102 TFEU

The Commission's analysis of reverse payment settlements as an abuse of dominance by Servier is of particular importance, given that *Servier* is the first Commission decision which argues that a reverse payment settlement may constitute a violation of both Article 101 and Article 102 TFEU. Article 102 TFEU is likely to play an increasingly important role in the analysis of patent settlements and other strategies potentially delaying generic entry, especially given the constant evolution of such strategies and their combination with other types of unilateral conduct that may be potentially anticompetitive. Originator companies are ordinarily dominant in the relevant drug

---

2403. EU Commission Decision, *Servier*, 2014, paras 2096-2102.
2404. EU Commission Decision, *Servier*, 2014, paras 2096-2097.
2405. EU Commission Decision, *Servier*, 2014, para. 2098. The TTBER exempts from the prohibition of Article 101 TFEU licensing agreements concluded between competing companies whose market shares do not exceed 20% and agreements between non-competitors whose market shares do not exceed 30% are exempted. *See* further *supra* Chapter 5, Part 2, Section II.F.4. on the TTBER.
2406. EU Commission Decision, *Servier*, 2014, paras 2098, 2100.
2407. Article 4(d) TTBER.
2408. EU Commission Decision, *Servier*, 2014, para. 2099.
2409. EU Commission Decision, *Servier*, 2014, para. 2101.

market before generic entry occurs, due to the patent monopoly they enjoy. Given that the General Court in *Lundbeck* did not discuss the reverse payments at issue under Article 102 TFEU, the Commission's reasoning in *Servier* provides – at the moment of this writing – the only existing standard for the analysis of reverse payments as potential abuses of dominance under Article 102 TFEU.[2410]

1   Defining the Relevant Market and Servier's Market Position

As above-analysed, the Commission defined the relevant product market in *Servier* as being limited to perindopril, patent protected and generic.[2411] Servier's branded perindopril did not face any significant price constraints from potentially competing products, a fact that came in sharp contrast with Servier's vulnerability as far as perindopril's generic versions were concerned.[2412] The Commission chose to examine separately the markets supplied through the retail (pharmacies) and hospital distribution channels, focusing its analysis of Servier's alleged abuse of dominant position on the retail channel.[2413] As far as the geographic market was concerned, the Commission did not divert from its earlier practice on pharmaceutical cases and found that the relevant geographic markets were national: France, the Netherlands, Poland and the UK.[2414] The temporal dimension of the market was from 2000 to 2009, the entire period of the Commission's investigation.[2415]

Two time-periods were of particular importance for the assessment of Servier's dominance in the relevant market: from 2000 to 2004, when Servier acquired the Azad technology and from 2005 to 2007 when Servier concluded the settlement agreements with the generic manufacturers.[2416] During part of the first period, Servier's compound patent on perindopril was still in force, while after its expiration Servier held three process patents which it did not license; the only two alternative enabling technologies were not considered as sufficiently substitutable to Servier's technology.[2417] Servier remained the main holder of the perindopril production technology during the second period and was the only marketer of perindopril with the limited exceptions of Krka and Apotex: Krka had launched generic perindopril in a number of CEE Member States for which it had received a licence by Servier in the context of their settlement, while

---

2410. *See also* GALLASCH, 2016, pp. 143-144, arguing that reverse payment patent settlements should not only trigger an investigation under Article 101 TFEU but also under Article 102 TFEU if they are used by a dominant firm in order to facilitate a broader unilateral conduct.
2411. *See supra*, Chapter 6, Part 2, Section III.B.1. *See also* EU Commission Decision, *Servier*, 2014, para. 2403 repeating this market definition in the analysis of Servier's abuse of dominant position under Article 102 TFEU; and *idem* paras 2535-2546, presenting in detail the Commission's analysis with regard to the relevant product market.
2412. EU Commission Decision, *Servier*, 2014, paras 2494-2495. *See also supra* Chapter 6, Part 2, Section III.B.1.
2413. EU Commission Decision, *Servier*, 2014, paras 2408-2412.
2414. EU Commission Decision, *Servier*, 2014, paras 2547, 2549 referring to EU Commission Decision, *AstraZeneca*, 2005, para. 503. *See supra* Chapter 5, Part 2, Section III.B.2.2.
2415. EU Commission Decision, *Servier*, 2014, para. 2548.
2416. EU Commission Decision, *Servier*, 2014, para. 2741.
2417. EU Commission Decision, *Servier*, 2014, paras 2742-2749.

Apotex had launched its own generic version at risk in the UK market on 2006.[2418] The Commission found Servier should be considered to hold a dominant position also during this second time-period, since no other company had any market share in the perindopril market or a technology sufficiently substitutable with Servier's technology.[2419]

2 Servier's Continuous Exclusionary Strategy

The acquisition of the Azad technology and the conclusion of the reverse payment settlements were complimentary and formed Servier's broader strategy to delay or block generic entry upon the expiration of perindopril's compound patent.[2420] Servier consistently targeted and settled with most of the generic manufacturers posing a competitive threat, while there was a high degree of concentration characterising the company's behaviour.[2421] The Commission found that this conduct constituted a single and continuous exclusionary strategy which infringed Article 102 TFEU.[2422]

2.1 Servier's Acquisition of Azad's Non-infringing Production Process

Technology transfers are usually procompetitive since they can help in diffusing the use of the acquired technology, leading to improved drug formulations or lower production costs.[2423] However, a technology acquisition may deviate from competition on the merits and be liable to contribute to an overall infringement of Article 102 TFEU.[2424] In 2004, Servier acquired the competing technology of the Swiss company Azad which had developed perindopril at its own risk and expenses.[2425] The preamble of the acquisition agreement included Servier's finding that Azad's patent applications did not infringe Servier's patents and stated that the rationale behind this acquisition was to strengthen Servier's defence mechanism on its own perindopril.[2426] Azad terminated its project on the development of perindopril shortly after Servier acquired its technology, disrupting its planned collaboration projects with other generic manufacturers.[2427]

2418. EU Commission Decision, *Servier*, 2014, paras 2751-2752.
2419. EU Commission Decision, *Servier*, 2014, paras 2754-2758.
2420. EU Commission Decision, *Servier*, 2014, para. 2961-2963.
2421. EU Commission Decision, *Servier*, 2014, para. 2962, mentioning that the Azad acquisition and all the reverse payment patent settlements were signed by the same representative of Servier.
2422. EU Commission Decision, *Servier*, 2014, para. 2961. *See idem* paras 2964-2987, analysing the combined effects of Servier's single and continuous exclusionary strategy.
2423. EU Commission Decision, *Servier*, 2014, para. 2799. *See supra* Chapter 5, Part 2, Section II.F.4 on the TTBER.
2424. EU Commission Decision, *Servier*, 2014, para. 2800.
2425. EU Commission Decision, *Servier*, 2014, paras 306-372. *See also idem* paras 246-305, analysing Servier's acquisition of another company's technology regarding the development of perindopril API.
2426. EU Commission Decision, *Servier*, 2014, para. 369.
2427. EU Commission Decision, *Servier*, 2014, para. 381.

In *Servier*, the Commission examined three elements in order to assess Servier's acquisition of Azad's technology: (1) whether the acquired technology was potentially enabling (e.g., sufficiently advanced) and therefore a source of potential competition to Servier;[2428] (2) whether this technology was effectively removed from the market as a potentially viable source of competition;[2429] and (3) whether this acquisition made generic entry difficult or impossible, leading to significant delays.[2430] The specific characteristics of the pharmaceutical markets were also taken into consideration: (1) the fact that an API is an indispensable input in a drug's formulation; (2) the years of development work required for generic entry; (3) the consumer harm caused to both patients and social security schemes by any delay in generic entry; (4) the price-inelasticity of demand prior to generic entry; and (5) the considerable difference in the price of the concerned drug in a monopolised market vis-à-vis its price in a competitive market.[2431]

The Commission relied on the *TetraPak I* decision and argued that the competitive effects of an outright technology transfer may be similar to those of an exclusive licence.[2432] The exclusive licence at issue in *TetraPak I* had strengthened Tetra's dominance and prevented or at least delayed the entry of competitors to the relevant market, fettering competition substantially.[2433] Even though the acquisition of an exclusive licence by a dominant undertaking was not found to be abusive per se, the decisive factor was whether this acquisition deprived potential competitors from the means to effectively compete with the dominant undertaking.[2434] Such an abuse of dominance may occur not only when competitive entry is altogether prevented but also when it is considerably delayed.[2435]

After conducting due diligence, Servier itself explicitly recognised in the preamble of the Azad agreement that Azad's technology did *not* infringe the originator's patents;[2436] the technology's acquisition was described as "protective measures against generics" in Servier's internal documents.[2437] The Commission concluded that this acquisition had the object of effectively removing a non-infringing source of perindopril API from the market and of ensuring that Azad had neither the capacity nor the incentives to develop generic perindopril.[2438] At the time of the acquisition, no other generic company had managed to launch generic perindopril: Servier controlled the

---

2428. EU Commission Decision, *Servier*, 2014, para. 2800.
2429. The Commission examined for instance whether the transferor remained free to use or license the technology or parts of it or whether the transferee was willing or able to license it out.
2430. EU Commission Decision, *Servier*, 2014, paras 2800, 2818.
2431. EU Commission Decision, *Servier*, 2014, para. 2801.
2432. EU Commission Decision, *Servier*, 2014, para. 2803, referring to Judgment of 6 October 1994, *Tetra Pak v. Commission*, T-83/91, EU:T:1994:246.
2433. EU Commission Decision, *Servier*, 2014, para. 2804.
2434. EU Commission Decision, *Servier*, 2014, paras 2808-2809, referring to Judgment of 6 October 1994, *Tetra Pak v. Commission*, T-83/91, EU:T:1994:246.
2435. EU Commission Decision, *Servier*, 2014, paras 2808-2809, referring to Judgment of 6 October 1994, *Tetra Pak v. Commission*, T-83/91, EU:T:1994:246.
2436. EU Commission Decision, *Servier*, 2014, para. 2820.
2437. EU Commission Decision, *Servier*, 2014, para. 2852.
2438. EU Commission Decision, *Servier*, 2014, para. 2851.

entire production of perindopril API and did not offer it to third parties.[2439] Azad was the most immediate threat to Servier: its perindopril API was non-infringing, was available to various generic partners and could have potentially allowed generic entry in 2007. This acquisition impeded and delayed generic entry: since Azad's technology was rendered inaccessible as an input to generic companies, a number of advanced generic perindopril projects were excluded and needed to be started from scratch.[2440] Further, the emerging competitive structure of perindopril API's market and of the potential supply of non-infringing perindopril API was distorted; the acquisition of Azad's technology was capable of contributing to the foreclosure of the market, while it also deviated from competition on the merits.[2441] Azad's technology was excluded from the market not due to the superiority of Servier's technology but due to fact that Servier sought to strengthen its position against generic entry by acquiring this independent source of competition and removing it from the market.[2442]

The Commission rejected Servier's arguments on the alleged efficiencies of the Azad acquisition, noting that Servier had never used Azad's technology;[2443] in any case, the acquisition was not objectively necessary to achieve the claimed efficiencies and could not be objectively justified.[2444] The acquisition constituted abusive behaviour and contributed to Servier's overall single and continuous exclusionary strategy which was infringing Article 102 TFEU.[2445] The Commission stressed that this finding was limited to the circumstances of the case and should *not* be read as a general prohibition of technology acquisitions by dominant undertakings.[2446] However, it is difficult to imagine a situation in which the acquisition of the only non-infringing technology available in the market by the patent holder and dominant undertaking would not fall under the prohibition of 102 TFEU, on the basis of the criteria set in the Commission decision in *Servier*.

2.2 Servier's Settlements as Abuses of Dominance under Article 102 TFEU

Both Articles 101 and 102 TFEU may apply concurrently to an agreement concluded between two undertakings, provided that there is a "supplementary element."[2447] On

---

2439. EU Commission Decision, *Servier*, 2014, para. 2855. *See idem*, paras 2862-2871, discussing the technologies that were being developed at the time by Cipla and Sandoz, but arguably were at least one year behind Azad's timeline for perindopril development.
2440. EU Commission Decision, *Servier*, 2014, paras 2874, 2917. The Commission mentions that the generic companies had even ordered significant quantities of Azad's perindopril API.
2441. EU Commission Decision, *Servier*, 2014, para. 2917.
2442. EU Commission Decision, *Servier*, 2014, para. 2881.
2443. EU Commission Decision, *Servier*, 2014, paras 2891-2899.
2444. EU Commission Decision, *Servier*, 2014, paras 2900-2916.
2445. EU Commission Decision, *Servier*, 2014, para. 2917.
2446. EU Commission Decision, *Servier*, 2014, para. 2917.
2447. Judgment of the Court of 13 February 1979, Case 85/76, *Hoffmann-La Roche & Co. AG v. Commission of the European Communities*, EU:C:1979:36, para. 116; Judgment of the Court of 11 April 1989, Case C-66/86, *Ahmed Saeed Flugreisen v. Zentrale zur Bekampfung unlauteren Wettbewerb*, EU:C:1989:140, para. 37 (Judgment of the Court of 11 April 1989, Case C-66/86, *Ahmed Saeed Flugreisen v. Zentrale*); Judgment of the Court of First Instance of 10 July 1990, Case T-51/89, *Tetra Pak Rausing SA v. Commission of the European Communities*,

the basis of the European Courts' jurisprudence, such supplementary elements are for instance: (1) the pressure imposed by the dominant undertaking to the other settling party;[2448] (2) the practical effect of precluding all competition from the market through the acquisition of an exclusive licence,[2449] or; (3) the inducement of retailers in order for them to obtain supplies exclusively from the dominant undertaking.[2450]

Servier's settlement agreements with the generic manufacturers were not only found to violate Article 101 TFEU; the Commission examined the unilateral aspects of these settlements under the light of Article 102 TFEU and found that Servier's unilateral conduct was abusive.[2451] Servier was a dominant undertaking and offered its generic competitors, which threatened its market position, inducements in order for them to stay out of the market and not to challenge the '947 patent.[2452] The importance of the '947 patent to Servier is also demonstrated by the fact that *all* the relevant patent settlement agreements included a non-challenge commitment concerning this patent, even when there was no actual or threatened patent litigation between the settling parties.[2453]

The patent settlement agreements were seen as a unilateral strategy by Servier, using all possible means to protect itself from generic entry: one of those means was to use its market power and part of its substantial monopoly perindopril profits to "fend off" generic challengers.[2454] Servier's settlement strategy was consistent and followed a clear pattern as of its first generic patent litigation with Niche.[2455] This unilateral conduct was possible due to the key-patents held by Servier and due to its market power: more than €90 million were paid out to the generic companies in order for them not to enter the market and not to challenge the validity of Servier's patent.[2456] The amounts paid were self-financing since they allowed Servier to preserve its monopoly rents for a longer period.[2457] The chain of the concluded settlements had a cumulative self-reinforcing effect, stronger than that of each individual agreement, maximising the potential restrictive effect on competition.[2458] The Commission concluded that these five settlement agreements, which were part of Servier's single and continuous

---

EU:T:1990:41, paras 21, 25, 30; Judgment of the Court of 16 March 2000, Joined Cases C-395/96 P and C-396/96 P, *Compagnie maritime belge Transports and others v. Commission*, para. 33. See also EU Commission, *101 TFEU Guidelines*, 2011, point 16.

2448. Judgment of the Court of 11 April 1989, Case 66/86, *Ahmed Saeed Flugreisen*, para. 46.
2449. Judgment of the Court of First Instance of 10 July 1990, Case T-51/89, *Tetra Pak Rausing SA v. Commission of the European Communities*, EU:T:1990:41, para. 24, "The additional element lies in the very context of the case – in the fact that Tetra Pak's acquisition of the exclusive licence had the practical effect of precluding all competition in the relevant market."
2450. 98/531/EC: Commission Decision of 11 March 1998 relating to a proceeding under Articles 85 and 86 of the EC Treaty (Case Nos IV/34.073, IV/34.395 and IV/35.436 Van den Bergh Foods Limited), OJ L 246, 4.9.1998, paras 263-266.
2451. EU Commission Decision, *Servier*, 2014, paras 2926-2933.
2452. EU Commission Decision, *Servier*, 2014, paras 2927-2928.
2453. EU Commission Decision, *Servier*, 2014, para. 2928. *See also supra*, Chapter 6, Part 2, Section III.D.2.1, on the non-challenge clauses in the Servier settlement agreements.
2454. EU Commission Decision, *Servier*, 2014, para. 2933.
2455. EU Commission Decision, *Servier*, 2014, para. 2936.
2456. EU Commission Decision, *Servier*, 2014, para. 2937.
2457. EU Commission Decision, *Servier*, 2014, paras 2938.
2458. EU Commission Decision, *Servier*, 2014, paras 2938-2942.

strategy, were capable of foreclosing competition on the upstream EU market of perindopril API technology and in the national markets of France, Poland, the Netherlands and the UK for perindopril formulations, hindering numerous projects on the development of generic perindopril.[2459] Servier's conduct considerably affected the competitive structure of the market and was capable of harming consumers by delaying generic entry, while it could not be objectively justified.[2460]

3 The Effects of Servier's Abuse of Dominance

An abuse of dominant position is prohibited under Article 102 TFEU "in so far as it may affect trade between Member States."[2461] Abuses which have an effect on the competitive structure in the markets of more than one EU Member States are by their nature capable of affecting trade between Member States,[2462] while a probability that interstate trade is affected suffices: the pattern of trade must be capable of being affected by the abuse at issue while trade does not necessarily need to be reduced.[2463] Finally, the abuse's effect on trade must be appreciable and is mainly assessed with reference to the position of the concerned undertakings in the relevant product market.[2464]

Servier's single and continuous infringement covered the entire EU: the settlement agreements were capable of precluding competition on the perindopril API technology market in the entire EU and on the perindopril formulation markets in four national Member States' markets (France, Poland, the UK and the Netherlands).[2465] The Commission found that the infringement was by its very nature capable of affecting trade between the Member States; the actual and potential effects of Servier's abuse in the EU market were appreciable due to the magnitude of perindopril sales in the Member States concerned and due to generic competition's characteristic of quickly replacing originators' sales.[2466] Servier's anticompetitive strategy resulted in market foreclosure effects, likely delayed generic entry in the perindopril market and caused consumer harm by sustaining higher perindopril prices for both patients and healthcare systems.[2467]

G Servier's Action for Annulment Before the EU General Court

In September 2014, Servier brought an action for the annulment of the EU Commission's decision before the EU General Court.[2468] Servier's action consists of seventeen pleas in law, while the respective oral proceedings before the General Court lasted for

---

2459. EU Commission Decision, *Servier*, 2014, para. 2957.
2460. EU Commission Decision, *Servier*, 2014, paras 2957-2980.
2461. Article 102 TFEU. *See* further *supra* Chapter 5, Part 2, Section III, analysing Article 102 TFEU.
2462. EU Commission Decision, *Servier*, 2014, para. 2989.
2463. EU Commission Decision, *Servier*, 2014, para. 2990.
2464. EU Commission Decision, *Servier*, 2014, para. 2991.
2465. EU Commission Decision, *Servier*, 2014, para. 2992.
2466. EU Commission Decision, *Servier*, 2014, paras 2993-2996.
2467. EU Commission Decision, *Servier*, 2014, para. 2997.
2468. Case T-691/14: Action brought on 21 September 2014, *Servier SAS and Others*, pp. 25-27.

four consecutive days in June 2017. Even though the decision of the court is pending at the moment of this writing, it is worth to briefly mention the main grounds of Servier's action. First, Servier argues that the Commission's decision was the product of "hypothesis-confirmation" bias, since its main point was to make the statement that the pharmaceutical sector was "rotten."[2469] Servier is further alleging the violation of procedural requirements but also of its right to an effective remedy, stressing that the Commission's decision was extremely lengthy and did not take into consideration the constraints of time and form that had to be respected when lodging an appeal.[2470] The action for annulment further targets the Commission's finding of a restriction by object and the Commission's analysis of the alleged effects of the settlements, arguing that the settlements at issue did not have an actual effect on the market.[2471] Another important point raised by Servier is that the Commission's definition of the relevant market as the market of the perindopril molecule was erroneous and led to the incorrect finding of Servier's dominance.[2472] Interestingly, Servier makes an argument against the prevailing case law of the CJEU[2473] by arguing that the simultaneous application of Article 101 and Article 102 TFEU to the same facts is not possible, while it is also sustained that the conclusion of the settlement agreements and the acquisition of technology do not amount to abuses of dominant position.[2474] Given the complexity of the underlying facts and legal questions and the lack of previous jurisprudence on reverse payment settlement strategies as abuses of dominance under Article 102 TFEU, the decision of the General Court in *Servier* is expected with great eagerness and will likely to lead to even more fiery debates that the court's decision in *Lundbeck*.

PART 2 NATIONAL COMPETITION AUTHORITIES' DECISIONS

The decisions of the EU Member States National Competition Authorities (NCAs) provide a good overview of the plethora of anticompetitive strategies employed by brand-name drug manufacturers in the EU in order for them to preserve their monopoly rents and delay generic entry. The following sections briefly present a number of selected cases and decisions of NCAs condemning the anticompetitive behaviour of undertakings as breaches of Article 101 and Article 102 TFEU.

2469. Case T-691/14: Action brought on 21 September 2014, *Servier SAS and Others*, pp. 25-27, plea 1.
2470. *Idem*, pleas 2-3.
2471. *Idem*, pleas 4-12.
2472. *Idem*, pleas 14-16. Servier also alleges that the Commission's definition of the "technology market" was insufficiently clear and lead to the finding that Servier was dominant in that hypothetical market.
2473. Judgment of the Court of 13 February 1979, Case 85/76, *Hoffmann-La Roche & Co. AG v. Commission of the European Communities*, EU:C:1979:36, para. 116; Judgment of the Court of 16 March 2000, Joined Cases C-395/96 P and C-396/96 P, *Compagnie maritime belge Transports and others v. Commission*, para. 112; Judgment of the Court of 21 February 1973, Case 6/72, *Europemballage Corporation and Continental Can Company Inc. v. Commission of the European Communities*, EU:C:1973:22, para. 33. See also supra Chapter 5, Part 2, Section III.
2474. Case T-691/14: Action brought on 21 September 2014, *Servier SAS and Others*, plea 17.

I Preventing Substitution and Disparaging Generic Drugs

The mechanism of generic substitution and the different ways in which it may be hindered by drug product switches in the US were extensively discussed in Chapter 4.[2475] Product-hopping is not of course limited to the US territory. Two years before the EU Commission found that Servier had allegedly engaged in a hard product switch aiming to prevent generic substitution,[2476] the CJEU had ruled on product-hopping in the pharmaceutical market in its landmark decision of *Astra Zeneca*.[2477] The following sections discuss three decisions by the UK and the French National Competition Authorities, which examine strategies employed by originators allegedly having the aim of hindering generic substitution.

A Hard Product Switch as an Infringement of Article 102 TFEU

One of the earliest product-hopping cases after the *Astra Zeneca* decision of the CJEU was the case of Reckitt Benckiser in the UK. In 2010, Reckitt Benckiser admitted that it had abused its dominant position in the market for UK's National Health System supply of alginate and antacid heartburn medicines and got fined £10.2 million.[2478] In June 2005, the drug manufacturer withdrew and delisted Gaviscon Original, its drug product whose patent protection had expired, replacing it with Gaviscon Advanced, a newer version of the drug which was patent protected.[2479] As a result, doctors' ability to write "open" prescriptions which allow pharmacists to substitute brand-name drugs with their generic versions was hindered: when doctors used their prescribing software and typed "Gaviscon," only the drug's newer version was listed, for which there were no generic versions.[2480]

The UK Office of Fair Trading concluded that Reckitt Benckiser's conduct constituted an abuse of dominant position within the meaning of Article 102 TFEU, finding that the originator foresaw that the effect of the drug's withdrawal would be to hinder the development of full generic competition to the relevant market by denying

---

2475. *See supra* Chapter 4, Part 3, Section IV, analysing product reformulations and product hopping strategies in the US.
2476. EU Commission Decision, *Servier*, 2014, paras 218-245, analysing Servier's selective product switch. *See supra*, Chapter 6, Part 1, Section III.A.2.
2477. Judgment of the Court of 6 December 2012, C-457/10 P, *AstraZeneca v. Commission*. *See supra* Chapter 5, Part 2, Section III.E.3, analysing the *Astra Zeneca* decision of the CJEU.
2478. Office of Fair Trading, Press Release, *OFT Issue Decision in Reckitt Benckiser Case*, April 13, 2011. Available at: http://webarchive.nationalarchives.gov.uk/20140402142426/http://www.oft.gov.uk/news-and-updates/press/2011/53-11. (last accessed on March 31, 2018).
2479. Office of Fair Trading, Decision No. CA98/02/2011 *Reckitt Benckiser*, 2011, pp. 9-13, 23-27. Non-confidential version of the decision available at: https://www.gov.uk/cma-cases/reckitt-benckiser-alleged-abuse-of-a-dominant-position (last accessed on March 31, 2018).
2480. *See* Office of Fair Trading, Decision No. CA98/02/2011 *Reckitt Benckiser*, 2011, pp. 53-60, describing the doctors' drug prescribing system in the UK. *See idem*, pp. 83-120, on Reckitt Benckiser's drug withdrawal.

pharmacists the choice of product on receipt of the relevant prescriptions.[2481] Reckitt Benckiser predicted that generic entry was imminent in 2005 and anticipated that it would lead to a significant loss of market share.[2482] Had it not withdrawn Gaviscon Original from the market, Reckitt Benckiser would allegedly be forced to offer significant discounts to pharmacies.[2483] Thus, the drug withdrawal was not "normal competition" or "competition on the merits:" its objective was to hinder the development of generic competition and to preserve Reckitt Benckiser's high market share and price levels.[2484]

B Disparaging Generic Drugs on the Prescription Level

In 2013, the French Competition Authority fined Sanofi-Aventis with €40.6 million for abusing its dominant position in the French market of clopidogrel by disparaging the generic versions of its blockbuster drug Plavix, used for the prevention of relapses in serious cardiovascular diseases.[2485] In 2008, Plavix was the world's 4th best seller drug and represented the highest cost of medicine reimbursement for the French public health system: €625 million.[2486] The main patent for Plavix expired in July 2008 but Sanofi-Aventis extended its patent protection until 2017 by obtaining complementary patents on new variations in the salts and therapeutic indications which according to the French Competition Authority had no impact on the bioequivalence or substitutability between Plavix and its generic versions.[2487]

Sanofi-Aventis arguably engaged in an elaborate global strategy aiming to prevent generic substitution: (1) at the prescription stage, by encouraging doctors to insert the indication "non-substitutable" to their prescriptions and; (2) at the substitution stage, by encouraging pharmacists to substitute Plavix with the authorised generic drug version of Sanofi-Aventis (Clopidogrel Winthrop).[2488] The medical visitors and

---

2481. Office of Fair Trading, Decision No. CA98/02/2011 *Reckitt Benckiser*, 2011, pp. 12-13, 253-317, analysing the withdrawal of Gaviscon Original from the market as an abuse of dominant position.
2482. Office of Fair Trading, Decision No. CA98/02/2011 *Reckitt Benckiser*, 2011, pp. 83-120, describing the withdrawal strategy and its effects on the market.
2483. Office of Fair Trading, Decision No. CA98/02/2011 *Reckitt Benckiser*, 2011, p. 13.
2484. Office of Fair Trading, Decision No. CA98/02/2011 *Reckitt Benckiser*, 2011, pp. 316-318.
2485. Autorité de la Concurrence, Communiqué de Presse, *L'Autorité de la concurrence sanctionne Sanofi-Aventis à hauteur de 40,6 million d'euros pour avoir mis en place une stratégie de dénigrement à l'encontre des génériques de Plavix®, l'un des médicaments les plus vendus dans le monde*, Mai 14, 2013. Available (also in English) at: http://www.autoritedelaconcurrence.fr/user/standard.php?id_rub = 482&id_article = 2090. Last accessed on March 31, 2018) [cited: Autorité de la Concurrence, Press Release, *Sanofi-Aventis*, 2013].
2486. Autorité de la Concurrence, Press Release, *Sanofi-Aventis*, 2013. *See also* the full decision of the French Competition Authority on Plavix: Autorité de la Concurrence, Press Release, *Sanofi-Aventis*, 2013. Available at: http://www.autoritedelaconcurrence.fr/user/avisdec.php?numero = 13D11 (last accessed on March 31, 2018).
2487. Sanofi-Aventis obtained a patent on the type of salt use in Plavix until 2013 and secured patent protection of the instruction on the treatment for acute coronary syndrome (ACS) in double therapy, by combining clopidogrel and acetylsalicylic acid, until 2017. *See* further Autorité de la Concurrence, Press Release, *Sanofi-Aventis*, 2013.
2488. Autorité de la Concurrence, Press Release, *Sanofi-Aventis*, 2013.

representatives of Sanofi-Aventis allegedly spread doubts on the efficiency and safety of generic drug versions of Plavix, implying that doctors and pharmacists could be held liable for any medical problems they could arise from these generic drugs, despite the fact that there was no scientific evidence confirming such hazards.[2489] This disparaging strategy was highly successful and led to abnormally low substitution rates for Plavix, while Sanofi-Aventis' own generic drug achieved an exceptional penetration rate, reaching a 34% market share in the relevant market.[2490] In 2016, the French Cour de Cassation upheld the decision and the fines of the French Competition Authority, rejecting the parties' appeal.[2491]

C   Unwarranted Discounts and Naming and Shaming

The French Competition Authority also fined Schering-Plough €15.3 million in 2013 for disparaging Arrow's generic drug and for granting unwarranted discounts to pharmacists. Schering-Plough and its parent company Merck & Co were also fined more than €400,000 for concluding an anticompetitive agreement with Reckitt Benckiser in an effort to close competitors off the market.[2492] The relevant drug was Subutex, prescribed for the treatment of opiate addiction; Reckitt Benckiser was the holder of the rights of the drug and had entrusted its marketing in France to Schering-Plough. Similarly to the strategy of Sanofi-Aventis,[2493] Schering-Plough allegedly organised seminars and meetings with the aim to alarm doctors and pharmacists on the alleged risks of prescribing Arrow's generic drug instead of branded Subutex. The disparaging strategy was successful on both key-stages of generic substitution: 67% of doctors' prescriptions contained the reference "non-substitutable," while at the dispensing stage pharmacists were provided with incentives not to substitute the remaining of the prescriptions.[2494] This resulted in very low substitution rates and costed an average of €77 million per year in reimbursement costs to the French public health system.

The decision of the French Competition Authority was not appealed by Schering-Plough, whose competition compliance commitments led to a reduction of the imposed fines. Reckitt Benckiser unsuccessfully appealed the decision before the Paris Court of

---

2489. Autorité de la Concurrence, Press Release, *Sanofi-Aventis*, 2013.
2490. *Idem.* According to the French Competition Authority, this is a market share four times greater than Sanofi-Aventis typical market shares in the French market.
2491. Arrêt n° 890 du 18 octobre 2016 (15-10.384) – Cour de cassation – Chambre commerciale, financière et économique – ECLI:FR:CCASS:2016:CO00890. Available at: https://www.courdecassation.fr/publications_26/arrets_publies_2986/chambre_commerciale_financiere_economique_3172/2016_7408/octobre_7799/890_18_35358.html (last accessed on March 31, 2018). For a summary of the decision in English *see*: KASTEN, Sanofi-Aventis, 2016.
2492. Reckitt Benckiser was also fined €318,000 for participating in this anticompetitive agreement. *See* Autorité de la Concurrence, Press Release, *Schering-Plough*, 2013. Available (also in English) at: http://www.autoritedelaconcurrence.fr/user/standard.php?id_rub=482&id_article=2283 (last accessed on March 31, 2018).
2493. *See supra* Chapter 6, Part 2, Section I.B, analysing the *Sanofi-Aventis* case.
2494. Autorité de la Concurrence, Press Release, *Schering-Plough*, 2013. *See also* the full text of the decision: Autorité de la Concurrence, *Décision Schering-Plough*, 2013. Available at: http://www.autoritedelaconcurrence.fr/pdf/avis/13d21.pdf (last accessed on March 31, 2018).

Appeal;[2495] it then contested the decision before the French Supreme Court. The French Supreme Court found that starting from October 2005, the two companies had agreed on a strategy in order to impede the entry of generic Subutex in the market and on actions aiming to implement this strategy, comprising of disparaging generic drugs and granting loyalty rebates to pharmacies.[2496] The fact that the parties had concluded a licensing agreement and that the parties' strategy was implemented unilaterally by Schering-Plough did not alter the finding of an anticompetitive agreement. The lack of a dominant position of Reckitt Benckiser in the market also did not alter the characterisation of the agreement as anticompetitive. The French Supreme Court stressed that it was not sanctioning quantity rebates as by object restrictions of competition. However, the parties' commercial strategy to delay generic entry through the disparagement of generic drugs and loyalty rebates constituted a restriction of competition by object, on the basis of the agreement's content, the objectives of the parties and the legal and economic context of the case.[2497]

II Divisional Patents as an Abuse of Dominance

Patent applicants have the possibility to file divisional patent applications before the EPO, relating to any pending earlier European patent application.[2498] By means of a divisional patent application, the patent applicant divides out from a pending patent application (parent patent application) one or more narrower patent applications (divisionals). After its filing, each divisional patent application is treated as an independent patent application,[2499] but has the same priority and application date as the parent patent.[2500] Such a divisional patent application may only be filed for a subject matter which does not extend beyond the content of the filed patent application.[2501] The usual reason for such a filing is that the parent patent application does not satisfy the requirements as to the unity of invention[2502] and that the patent applicant is

---

2495. See Arrêt n° 50 du 26 mars 2015, 2014/03330 – Cour d'appel de Paris – Pôle 5 – Chambre 5-7. Available at: http://www.autoritedelaconcurrence.fr/doc/ca_subutex_13d21.pdf (last accessed on March 31, 2018).
2496. Arrêt n° 33 du 11 janvier 2017 (15-17.134) – Cour de cassation – Chambre commerciale, financière et économique, ECLI:FR:CCASS:2017:CO00033. Available at: https://www.courdecassation.fr/publications_26/arrets_publies_2986/chambre_commerciale_financiere_economique_3172/2017_7954/janvier_7955/33_11_35890.html (last accessed on March 31, 2018).
2497. Arrêt n° 33 du 11 janvier 2017 (15-17.134) – Cour de cassation – Chambre commerciale, financière et économique, ECLI:FR:CCASS:2017:CO00033.
2498. See EPC, Implementing Regulations to the Convention on the Grant of European Patents, Rule 36.
2499. See further EPO Website, *Guide for Applicants: How to Get a European Patent*, D. VIII, "Divisional Applications," point 212.
2500. EU Commission, *Pharma Sector Inquiry*, 2009, p. 193.
2501. See further EPO Website, *Guide for Applicants: How to Get a European Patent*, D. VIII, "Divisional Applications," point 209.
2502. EPO Website, Guide for Applicants: How to Get a European Patent, C. II., "Unity of Invention," point 69, stating that European patent applications shall relate to only one single invention or to a group of inventions which are linked in a way which forms a single general

not content in limiting it.[2503] With regard to the possibility of obtaining an SPC for a divisional patent application, it should be stressed that on the basis of CJEU's jurisprudence each separate patent may confer entitlement to a new SPC only in so far as it covers a totally separate innovation.[2504] This could possibly mean that national patent offices should examine the claims of both the parent patent and the divisional patent in order to determine whether the relevant products covered by these patents are totally separate inventions within the meaning of the SPC Regulation (EC) No. 469/2009.[2505]

In 2012, Pfizer was fined €10.6 million by the ICA for abusing its dominant position in the market of glaucoma medicines.[2506] Pfizer marketed Xalatan, a global leader in the market for glaucoma medicines, and owned a 60% market share in the relevant market. The drug manufacturer undertook a complex strategy with the aim to protect its market share from the entry of equivalent drugs subsequent to the expiration of its patents in 2009. Pfizer applied before EPO for a divisional patent descending from Xalatan[2507] and obtained an SPC and a paediatric extension, prolonging its patent

---

inventive concept. Available at: http://www.epo.org/applying/european/Guide-for-applicants/html/e/ga_c_ii_2.html (last accessed on March 31, 2018).

2503. See further EPO Website, Guide for Applicants: How to Get a European Patent, D. VIII, "Divisional Applications," point 208. Available at: http://www.epo.org/applying/european/Guide-for-applicants/html/e/ga_d_viii.html (last accessed on March 31, 2018).

2504. See Judgment of the Court of 12 March 2015, Case C-577/13, *Actavis Group PTC EHF and Actavis UK Ltd v. Boehringer Ingelheim Pharma GmbH & Co. KG*, EU:C:2015:165, para. 39 (Judgment of the Court of 12 December 2013, Case C-443/12, *Actavis v. Boehringer Ingelheim*), interpreting Article 3(a) and 3(c), Regulation (EC) No. 469/2009 and concluding that "where a basic patent includes a claim to a product comprising an active ingredient which constitutes the sole subject matter of the invention, for which the holder of that patent has already obtained an SPC, as well as a subsequent claim to a product comprising a combination of that active ingredient and another substance, that provision precludes the holder from obtaining a second SPC for that combination." *See also* Judgment of the Court of 12 December 2013, Case C-443/12, *Actavis v. Boehringer Ingelheim*, paras 42-43, interpreting Article 3(c), Regulation (EC) No. 469/2009 as precluding a "patent holder from obtaining – on the basis of that same patent but a subsequent MA for a different medicinal product containing that active ingredient in conjunction with another active ingredient which is not protected as such by the patent – a second SPC relating to that combination of active ingredients."

2505. *See further* CARLING, PEARS, 2016, discussing the relevant case law of the CJEU and the decision of the UK Intellectual Property Office, *Merck Sharp & Dohme Corporation*, 2016, granting an SPC for an innovative combination product.

2506. Autorità Garante della Concorrenza et del Mercato (Italian Competition Authority), Press Release A431 – Pharmaceuticals: Pfizer sanctioned with 10.6 million euro fine for abuse of dominant position, January 17, 2012 (Autorità Garante della Concorrenza, Press Release, *Pfizer*, 2012). Available at: http://www.agcm.it/en/newsroom/press-releases/1986-pfizer-sanctioned-with-106-million-euro-fine-for-abuse-of-dominant-position.html (last accessed on March 31, 2018) The full text of ICA's decision Autorità Garante della Concorrenza, decision *Pfizer/Pharmacia*, 2012, (only in Italian). Available at: http://www.agcm.it/component/joomdoc/allegati-news/A431_chiusura.pdf/download.html (last accessed on March 31, 2018).

2507. This divisional patent was revoked by EPO in October 2010, subsequent to generic suppliers' opposition proceedings. See Autorità Garante della Concorrenza, decision *Pfizer/Pharmacia*, 2012, para. 96.

protection until 2012.[2508] Moreover, Pfizer warned generic producers against entering the market, engaged in allegedly abusive litigation against generic suppliers and put pressure on the Italian Medicines Agency in order for it not to authorise generic competitors to produce their drugs.[2509] According to the ICA, the effects of Pfizer's conduct were the following: (1) the increase of the effective market entry costs for the generic manufacturers; (2) the delay in the market entry of generic Xalatan versions by at least seven months; (3) the maintenance of a de facto exclusive monopolisation in the relevant market even after the expiration of its patent protection; (4) the loss of estimated €14 million in savings for the Italian National Healthcare System.[2510]

Despite the fact that Pfizer had used legitimate means to obtain the extension of its patent protection,[2511] the ICA found that the drug manufacturer strategically created uncertainty on whether generic entry could occur and abused its dominant position.[2512] Pfizer's divisional patent was never used by Pfizer in order to place new drugs in the market and was subsequently revoked by EPO. Drawing inspiration from the *AstraZeneca* decision, the ICA found that this divisional patent did not demonstrate Pfizer's intention to launch a new drug to the market but on the contrary, Pfizer's intention to exclude generic competition.[2513] Nevertheless, ICA's reasoning in *Pfizer* went much further than the CJEU's reasoning in the *AstraZeneca*. While in *AstraZeneca* the brand-name drug manufacturer had provided misleading information to the competent authorities, Pfizer had followed lawful proceedings for the extension of its patent protection.[2514] This was the main reason that the ICA's decision was widely criticised[2515] and subsequently overturned by the Regional Administrative Court of Lazio.[2516] However, the Italian Council of State (Italy's highest instance Administrative Court) upheld the original decision by the ICA: the Council of State found that Pfizer's conduct revealed its clear anticompetitive intent to defer the commercialisation of generic drugs to the damage of the Italian National Healthcare System. The court ruled that the lawfulness of Pfizer's divisional patent application was not of relevance since

---

2508. Muscolo Gabriella, ICA Statement: Pharma Competition, 2015. Available at: http://unctad.org/meetings/en/Presentation/CCPB_7RC2015_RTPharma_Italy_en.pdf (last accessed on March 31, 2018) Pfizer applied for a divisional patent only in the countries in which it forgot to apply for SPCs.
2509. Muscolo Gabriella, ICA Statement: Pharma Competition, 2015.
2510. Autorità Garante della Concorrenza, Press Release, *Pfizer*, 2012. For a detailed analysis & criticism on ICA's decision in *Pfizer/Pharmacia* see GERADIN, Pfizer/Pharmacia, 2014, pp. 348-352.
2511. The Italian Council of State also accepted that Pfizer's application for a divisional patent was a legitimate right pursuant to patent law. See D'AMORE, Pfizer, 2014, p. 79.
2512. Autorità Garante della Concorrenza, Press Release, *Pfizer*, 2012.
2513. Autorità Garante della Concorrenza, decision *Pfizer/Pharmacia*, 2012, paras 127, 179, 190, 196-197, 200.
2514. MUSCOLO, ICA Statement: Pharma Competition, 2015; DE STEFANO, Abuse, 2012, pp. 87-89. See also supra Chapter 5, Part 2, Section E.3 on the analysis of AstraZeneca's abusive conduct.
2515. For criticism against ICA's decision in Pfizer see for instance GERADIN, Pfizer/Pharmacia, 2014, pp. 349-352.
2516. Tribunale Amministrativo Regionale per il Lazio, *Pfizer et al. c. Autorita' garante della concorrenza e del mercato*, N. 09968/2011 REG.RIC., 3/9/2012. Available at: https://dottoratoblog.files.wordpress.com/2016/01/tar-lazio-pfizer_ratiopharm-copia.pdf (last accessed on March 31, 2018). See also D'AMORE, Pfizer, 2014, p. 78, briefly explaining the Regional Administrative Court's *rationale* in annulling ICA's decision.

ICA's decision concerned Pfizer's behaviour under antitrust law and not its compatibility with patent law, while unlawful behaviour is not a prerequisite for a finding of abuse of dominance.[2517]

III Preventing Off-Label Drug Use: The *Roche/Novartis* Case

The term "off-label use" refers to any intentional use of an authorised drug product which is not covered by its marketing authorisation, e.g., the use of a drug product for a different indication, the use of a different dosage or dosing frequency or the use of the drug by a different patient group.[2518] There are various drivers which influence the off-label drug use such as the withdrawal of a drug product from the market, factors related to pricing and reimbursement or patient-related factors.[2519] Off-label prescriptions are not regulated by European Union law; however, in some EU Member States, such as France and Hungary, there is national legislation on off-label drug use.[2520]

A *The Artificial Differentiation of Avastin and Lucentis*

On February 2014, the ICA found that the Swiss drug manufacturers Roche and Novartis infringed Article 101 TFEU by participating in an anticompetitive agreement in the ophthalmic drug market, concerning the drugs Avastin and Lucentis.[2521] Both Avastin and Lucentis were developed by the US company Genetech, whose parent company is Roche; Genetech granted the commercial exploitation of Avastin outside US to Roche, while it also concluded a licensing agreement with the Novartis Group entrusting it with the commercial exploitation of Lucentis outside the US.[2522] Therefore, Avastin is marketed by Roche and is used on-label for some cancer treatments and off-label for treating age-related muscular degeneration, which is the main cause of

---

2517. Il Consiglio di Stato, *Autorita' garante della concorrenza e del mercato c. Pfizer et al.*, N. 00116/2014REG.PROV.COLL., 15/1/2014. Available at: http://www.quotidianosanita.it/allegati/allegato4345250.pdf (last accessed on March 31, 2018). For a detailed analysis of the decision see D'AMORE, Pfizer, 2014, pp. 77-81. Available at: DOI: 10.12870/iar-9935.
2518. WEDA ET AL., *Study on Off-label Use in the EU*, 2017, p. 7.
2519. WEDA ET AL., *Study on Off-label Use in the EU*, 2017, pp. 49-55.
2520. WEDA ET AL., *Study on Off-label Use in the EU*, 2017, pp. 88-89.
2521. Autorità Garante della Concorrenza et del Mercato (Italian Competition Authority), Press Release, *I760 – Pharmaceuticals and Antitrust: the Italian Competition Authority fines Roche and Novartis over eur 180 million for cartelizing the sales of two major ophthalmic drugs, Avastin and Lucentis*, March 5, 2014. Available at: http://www.agcm.it/en/newsroom/press-releases/2106-i760-pharmaceuticals-and-antitrust-the-italian-competition-authority-fines-roche-and-novartis-over-eur-180-million-for-cartelizing-the-sales-of-two-major-ophthalmic-drugs-avastin-and-lucentis.html (last accessed on March 31, 2018) [Autorità Garante della Concorrenza, Press Release, *Roche/Novartis*, 2014].
2522. Judgment of the Court of 23 January 2018, Case C-179/16, *F. Hoffmann-La Roche Ltd., La Roche SpA, Novartis AG and Novartis Farma SpA v. Autorità Garante della Concorrenza e del Mercato*, EU:C:2018:25, para. 23 (Judgment of the Court of 23 January 2018, Case C-179/16, *Roche / Novartis*).

blindness in developed countries.²⁵²³ Lucentis is marketed by Novartis, is specifically addressed to treat age-related muscular degeneration and is sold at a price much higher than that of Avastin.²⁵²⁴

Before Lucentis entered the Italian market, Avastin was the sole available treatment for age-related muscular degeneration and was prescribed by doctors as an off-label treatment.²⁵²⁵ Under Italian national law at that time, such off-label use was only reimbursed if there were no authorised valid therapeutic alternatives ("on-label drugs") available in the market: once Lucentis entered the market it began replacing Avastin – the use of which was no longer reimbursed for off-label conditions – arguably increasing the costs for the Italian National Health Care Service by €45 million only in 2012.²⁵²⁶ According to the ICA, Novartis and Roche set up a complex strategy which entailed the artificial differentiation of the two drug products while raising uncertainty by undermining the results of independent research on Avastin's safety in order to persuade doctors not to prescribe it for the condition of age-related muscular degeneration.²⁵²⁷ Part of this strategy was Roche's request for the amendment of the summary of Avastin's product characteristics that were pending before the EMA, so as to mention certain alleged side effects of the drug associated with its use for the treatment of eye diseases not covered by its marketing authorisation, followed by a relevant formal communication to healthcare professionals.²⁵²⁸

The ICA found that Novartis and Roche (and their subsidiaries Novartis Italia and Roche Italia) colluded and imposed on them fines exceeding €180 million: the undertakings' agreement had an anticompetitive object and the effect of increasing the healthcare costs for the Italian National Health Care Service.²⁵²⁹ The decision was appealed by the parties before the Regional Administrative Tribunal of Lazio, which

---

2523. Muscolo, Roche-Novartis, 2015, pp. 219-222. Available at: https://www.epo.org/law-practice/legal-texts/official-journal/2015/etc/se5/p211.html; Autorità Garante della Concorrenza, Press Release, *Roche/Novartis*, 2014.
2524. Muscolo, Roche-Novartis, 2015, p. 219, fn. 2, noting that at the time of the decision one injection of Avastin costed €81.64 under safety standards and €15.29 without these standards, while an injection of Lucentis costed €902 ex works and €1,489 as the retail price.
2525. On the off-label use of drugs in the European Union *see further* Weda et al., *Study on Off-label Use in the EU*, 2017. For more information on the off-label drug use in the EU *see* for instance, European Commission, STAMP Commission Expert Group, *Repurposing of Established Medicines/ Active Substances*, June 28, 2016. Available at: http://ec.europa.eu/health/files/committee/stamp/2016-06_stamp5/3_repurposing_of_established_medicines_reflection_paper.pdf; (last accessed on March 31, 2018); European Commission, DG Health & Consumers, Pharmaceutical Committee, *Study on off-label use*, March 26, 2014, pp. 1-4. Available at: ec.europa.eu/health/files/committee/72meeting/pharm655.pdf. (last accessed on March 31, 2018).
2526. Muscolo, Roche-Novartis, 2015, p. 220, noting that under Italian law, a doctor who prescribes an off-label drug while an on-label drug treatment is available bears liability in case of diseases deriving from the off-label use.
2527. Muscolo, Roche-Novartis, 2015, p. 221. The companies also attempted to modify the wording of the European Public Assessment report for Avastin, so as to include the drug's ophthalmic risks and hinder the possible authorisation of the drug's off-label use.
2528. Judgment of the Court of 23 January 2018, Case C-179/16, *Roche / Novartis*, paras. 26-33.
2529. Autorità Garante della Concorrenza, Press Release, *Roche/Novartis*, 2014. *See also* Muscolo, Roche-Novartis, 2015, p. 222, noting that the Italian government issued a follow-up action before the court against the two companies, claiming more than €1 billion.

largely upheld the ICA's decision as to the anticompetitive effect of the companies' conduct.[2530] The court found that all arguments relating to the medical and scientific aspects of the drugs, to pharmacovigilance requirements or to the parties' licensing agreement went beyond the scope of the Competition Authority's powers; it concluded that Avastin and Lucentis were substitutable and comprised the relevant product market.[2531] It is noteworthy that subsequent to the *Avastin-Lucentis* case, Italy revised its national law so as to permit and reimburse the off-label use of an authorised drug, provided that its cost is cheaper than the cost of the on-label drug and that such off-label use is supported by medical and scientific research evidence.[2532]

B The CJEU Upholds the Finding of a Restriction by Object

The decision of the Regional Administrative Tribunal of Lazio was also appealed by the parties before the Italian Consilgio di Stato, which suspended the application of the first instance decision and made a request for a preliminary ruling to the CJEU.[2533] In January 2018, the CJEU upheld the findings of the ICA in its decision in *Roche/Novartis*.[2534]

According to the CJEU's judgment in *Roche/Novartis*, the relevant market for the purposes of the application of Article 101 TFEU may include not only pharmaceutical products which are authorised for the concerned diseases but also other pharmaceutical products whose marketing authorisation does not cover these diseases but which are nonetheless used to this effect and are in reality substitutable with the former.[2535] In essence the CJEU accepted that pharmaceutical products which are used off-label may be found to be part of the relevant market along with "on-label" drugs: as long as the drugs which are used off-label are compliant with the applicable provisions on production and marketing, the National Competition Authority shall examine their

---

2530. Tribunale Amministrativo Regionale per il Lazio, *Novartis e Roche contro Autorità Garante della Concorrenza e del Mercato*, N. 12168/2014 REG.PROV.COLL, 2/12/2014. Available at: https://www.giustizia-amministrativa.it/cdsintra/cdsintra/AmministrazionePortale/DocumentViewer/index.html?ddocname = UOXPTSFKKCFFCNJWOYADFYV42Y&q = Novartis (last accessed on March 31, 2018).
2531. For a brief analysis of the Italian Tribunal's decision in English *see* Accardo, Novartis-Roche, 2015. Available at: https://ttlfnews.wordpress.com/2015/01/21/italian-court-confirms-hefty-fines-on-novartis-and-roche/ (last accessed on March 31, 2018).
2532. L. n. 79/2014, Conversione in legge, con modificazioni, del decreto-legge 20 marzo 2014, n. 36. The amended law also requires that such off-label use satisfies the criteria of affordability and suitability, while it shall also be specifically authorised by the Italian Medicines Agency. Available at: http://www.federalismi.it/nv14/articolo-documento.cfm?Artid = 25047&content = Conversione + in + legge, + con + modificazioni, + del + decreto-legge + 20 + marzo + 2014, + n. + 36&content_author = (last accessed on March 31, 2018). *See also* McKenna, Off-Label Reimbursement, 2015.
2533. Il Consiglio di Stato, *F. Hoffmann-La Roche Ltd e Novartis Ag contro Autorità Garante della Concorrenza e del Mercato*, N. 00966/2016 REG.PROV.COLL., 11/03/2016; Case C-179/16: Request for a preliminary ruling from the Consiglio di Stato (Italy) lodged on 25 March 2016 – F. Hoffmann-La Roche AG, La Roche SpA, Novartis AG and Novartis Farma SpA v. Autorità Garante della Concorrenza e del Mercato, OJ C 222, 20.6.2016, p. 4-5.
2534. Judgment of the Court of 23 January 2018, Case C-179/16, *Roche / Novartis*.
2535. Judgment of the Court of 23 January 2018, Case C-179/16, *Roche / Novartis*, paras. 59-67.

effects on the structure of demand and supply.²⁵³⁶ Second, the CJEU confirmed that Article 101 TFEU may apply to an arrangement between two parties to a licensing agreement regarding the exploitation of a pharmaceutical product, if such arrangement aims to restrict the promotion of other pharmaceutical products by third parties (*in casu* healthcare professionals) and to reduce competitive pressure on the use of the licensed product; the court clearly stated that such an arrangement cannot be considered as ancillary.²⁵³⁷

One of the most crucial points of the decision is that the CJEU upheld that the dissemination of misleading information in the context of scientific uncertainty may amount to a restriction of competition by object within the meaning of Article 101 TFEU.²⁵³⁸ The court did not challenge the obligations of the marketing authorisation holder under the European pharmacovigilance regulations, especially with regard to any new information that may have an influence on the risk/benefit evaluation of the respective drug product.²⁵³⁹ However, these pharmacovigilance requirements apply only to the marketing authorisation holder and not to any of its competitors. According to the facts of the case, Roche and Novartis had colluded and adopted a common strategy aiming to the artificial differentiation of Avastin and Lucentis, on the basis of which an "alarmist" interpretation of the available scientific data was produced and disseminated, which could give rise to public concern on the safety of Avastin for ophthalmological uses and arguably influence the therapeutic choices of doctors.²⁵⁴⁰ The CJEU concluded that the disseminated misleading information was likely to influence doctors towards refraining from prescribing Avastin for such uses and result in reduced demand; thus, the arrangement between Roche and Novartis was sufficiently harmful to competition and an examination of its effects would have been superfluous.²⁵⁴¹

CONCLUSIONS

Even though pay-for-delay settlements have been the object of conflicting court decisions, heated debates and much attention in the US ever since 2001,²⁵⁴² the problematic aspects of reverse payment settlements in the European Union came into the spotlight rather recently. The European Commission's enforcement actions against

---

2536. Judgment of the Court of 23 January 2018, Case C-179/16, *Roche / Novartis*, paras. 48-67.
2537. Judgment of the Court of 23 January 2018, Case C-179/16, *Roche / Novartis*, paras. 68-75.
2538. Judgment of the Court of 23 January 2018, Case C-179/16, *Roche / Novartis*, paras. 76-95.
2539. The court referred to Article 16(2), Article 17, Regulation (EC) No. 726/2004 (as amended), which codify the obligation for the marketing authorisation holder to supply EMA, the Commission and the Member States any new information which may cause the variation of the required information for the issuance of the marketing authorisation, the risk/benefits evaluation etc. and to Article 106a, Directive 2001/83/EC, as amended by Directive 2004/27/EC, stipulating the conditions for the dissemination of information on medicinal products to healthcare professionals and the general public. *See* further Judgment of the Court of 23 January 2018, Case C-179/16, *Roche / Novartis*, paras. 82-88.
2540. Judgment of the Court of 23 January 2018, Case C-179/16, *Roche / Novartis*, paras. 89-95.
2541. Judgment of the Court of 23 January 2018, Case C-179/16, *Roche / Novartis*, paras. 92-95.
2542. The first Circuit court decision on reverse payment settlements in the US was the decision of *Andrx Pharmaceuticals., Inc. v. Biovail Corp. Int'l*, 256 F.3d 799, 806 (D.C. Cir. 2001).

anticompetitive settlements in the pharma sector started officially only in 2013, while the first European Court decision on patent settlements between originators and generic challengers, *Lundbeck v. Commission*, was published in September 2016. Unsurprisingly, the legal problems raised by patent settlements between generics and originators are largely similar on both sides of the Atlantic, while the evolution of the legal analysis but also of the various patent settlement strategies are largely parallel.

After the decision of the General Court of the EU in *Lundbeck*, patent settlements including otherwise unjustified value transfers from the originator to the generic challenger in return for the latter's commitment not to enter the market are highly likely to be found anticompetitive violations of Article 101(1) TFEU. Benefiting from the US experience and jurisprudence, the General Court rejected the application of the scope of the patent test and refused to grant antitrust immunity to patent settlements; moreover, it made no reference to "cash payments" but only to "value transfers," swiftly avoiding a phrasing that could lead to the same rocky debates *FTC v. Actavis* gave rise to. If the Commission's decision in *Servier* is upheld by the General Court, such settlements may also be viewed as part of a broader abusive strategy by the originator and constitute an abuse of dominant position infringing Article 102 TFEU.

As time passes and antitrust scrutiny becomes more elaborate and insightful, patent settlements in the pharmaceutical sector become increasingly complicated and sophisticated in both the US and the EU. Complex strategies involving side-deals, licensing agreements, concealed value transfers, combined with unilateral conduct such as product-hopping, naming & shaming, etc. have increasingly replaced the straightforward payments for delay of the past. Antitrust enforcers, governments, legislators and the judiciary need to keep up with the market players, which seem to always be several steps ahead.

Conclusion

Patent settlements in the pharmaceutical industry are described as one of the most difficult topics in the field of US antitrust and EU competition law. This exciting topic touches upon the sensitive balance between intellectual property law and antitrust/competition law, the difficulty of preserving innovation incentives while boosting up competition in the market and the socially sensitive issues of pharmaceuticals' prices and health expenditures. The highly technical and complicated legislative frameworks regulating the market entry of brand-name and generic pharmaceutical products, the different kinds of available exclusivities and a great number of other industry-specific issues render the analysis of patent settlements and other strategies in the pharmaceutical industry even more challenging.

Despite the striking disparities in the legal realities of the US and the European Union and the extreme differences in their regulatory frameworks, patent settlements and other strategies in the pharmaceutical industry raise largely similar issues and are subject to broadly similar standards on both sides of the pond. The following sections outline the applicable tests for adjudicating patent settlements in the pharmaceutical industry under US antitrust and EU competition law, attempting to increase legal security regarding the current standards applied in the US and the EU. The main findings follow: an overview of the types of patent settlements and other strategies which are legitimate, illegitimate or fall within grey areas. Finally, some practical guidance is provided with the aim to assist the pharmaceutical industry in its efforts of complying with antitrust and competition law and in avoiding sanctions and reputational damage.

PART 1 APPLICABLE TESTS IN THE US AND THE EU

One of the most important conclusions of this book is that the scope of the patent test cannot be used as the applicable legal test for the adjudication of reverse payment settlements, neither in the US nor in the European Union. Instead, a case-by-case analysis of patent settlements shall be applied, ideally adopting a sliding scale of reasonableness according to the specificities of each case.

I The Scope of the Patent Test Is Rejected

A *Reverse Payments Do Not Fall Within the Scope of Patents*

The scope of the patent test was applied by a number of US Circuit Courts adjudicating reverse payments, before it was rejected by the US Supreme Court in *FTC v. Actavis* in 2013. Under the scope of the patent test, reverse payment settlements including unjustified large value transfers were considered to fall within the "exclusionary potential of the patent" and were thus rendered antitrust immune. Upgrading the presumption of patent validity from a procedural device for the allocation of the burden of proof into a substantive right of the patentee to exclude all generic competition from the market, the US courts applying the scope of the patent test in essence ignored the issues of patent validity and patent infringement and the fact that a patent, even if valid, has the potential to exclude only infringing pharmaceutical products from the market. Courts applying the scope of the patent test overlooked the fact that a patent does not legitimise a payment aiming to exclude a potential competitor from the market and shielded from antitrust scrutiny settlements potentially prolonging unjustified monopolies which resembled market partitioning agreements. The Hatch-Waxman Act and its objectives of accelerating generic entry and encouraging the elimination of potentially invalid patents from the drug market was turned on its face, while the number of potentially problematic settlements increased.[2543] In its decision in *FTC v. Actavis*, the Supreme Court put an end to the problematic application of the scope of the patent test to reverse payment settlements, acknowledging their potential for genuine effects on competition and noting that both patent and antitrust policies are relevant in determining the "scope of patent monopoly."[2544]

The split among US Circuit Courts, the long and tense debate between antitrust specialists on the optimal applicable test and the decision of the Supreme Court in *FTC v. Actavis* highly influenced the analysis of patent settlements in the pharmaceutical sector under European competition law. Benefiting from the US experience, the European Commission and National Competition Authorities of EU Member States did not accept the application of the scope of the patent test for the analysis of reverse payment settlements, despite the settling parties' recurring argument that reverse payment settlements fell within the scope of the patent and outside the scope of Articles 101 and 102 TFEU. In 2016, the EU General Court confirmed the rejection of the scope of the patent test in its decision in *Lundbeck v. Commission*, affirming that Article 101 TFEU may apply to patent settlements since the existence of a patent does not exempt an agreement from the application of competition laws. Similarly to the US Supreme Court, the European General Court stressed that the scope of the patent test presumed that the originator's patent was not only valid but also infringed, allowing for the automatic exclusion of the generic drug version from the market. The General Court stressed that the subject matter of IP rights includes the right to oppose their

---

[2543]. *See* further *supra* Chapter 3, Part 2, extensively analysing the application of the scope of the patent test to reverse payment settlements and the criticisms against it.

[2544]. *See supra*, Chapter 4, Part 1, on the analysis of *FTC v. Actavis, Inc.*, 133 S. Ct. 2223 (2013).

infringement but does not encompass the right to pay actual or potential competitors in order to refrain from entering the market, highlighting that the elimination of obstacles arising from erroneous patent grants serves the public interest.[2545]

On the basis of the US Supreme Court's decision in *FTC v. Actavis* and of the EU General Court's decision in *Lundbeck v. Commission*, there is no umbrella antitrust immunity granted by patents. Both decisions explicitly rejected the application of the scope of the patent test to reverse payments, a test which misinterpreted the exclusionary potential of patents and which allowed potential competitors to collude and defer generic entry, eliminating any uncertainty concerning the possible invalidity or non-infringement of the patent at issue. Both in the US and in the EU an underlying patent does not shield a settlement agreement between (potential) competitors from antitrust scrutiny. Large unjustified value transfers from patent holders to alleged generic infringers in return for the generic manufacturers' commitment to defer generic entry are not ironclad from antitrust liability but need to be scrutinised closely, on a case-by-case basis.

B Restoring Uncertainty and the Balance Between IP and Antitrust

In both the US and the EU, a patent holder cannot legitimately use a large value transfer in order to exchange the *uncertainty* on the issues of patent validity, patent infringement and the possibility of legitimate generic entry with the *certainty* of prolonging its monopoly and foreclosing generic competition from the market. The relevant anticompetitive harm of reverse payment settlements is such a buying-off of uncertainty, an uncertainty which is necessary in order to preserve competition in the pharmaceutical markets.

The element of uncertainty is at the core of the relationship between intellectual property law and antitrust law and influences the analysis of reverse payments. Under the scope of the patent test, patents were seen as omnipotent, offering an undebatable monopoly and the power to exclude all generic competition from the market, without any further analysis on whether such competition was infringing or not. Reverse payment settlements were granted antitrust immunity, allowing the settling parties to enjoy guaranteed certainty on the lack of competition in the market. However, uncertainty is a fundamental element in preserving competition and has an impact not only on price levels, output quantity and quality but also on innovation incentives. Especially with regard to pharmaceutical patent settlements, the level of uncertainty directly affects the bargaining position of the parties and the timing and conditions of generic entry. The prohibition of large reverse value transfers and the insistence of courts that patent settlements should be negotiated on the basis of the parties' perceptions on patent validity and patent infringement were necessary steps in restoring the equilibrium between patent protection and competition.

2545. *See supra*, Chapter 6, Part 1, Section II, on the analysis of the *Lundbeck* case.

PART 2 GUIDANCE FOR THE PHARMA INDUSTRY

The core objective of this book is to provide guidance to the pharmaceutical industry with regard to which forms of patent settlements will most likely violate US antitrust and EU competition law, which ones are legitimate and which fall under a grey area and may be potentially problematic.

I Patent Settlements Which Are Likely Illegitimate

There are certain types of patent settlements which will almost always be found to infringe antitrust/competition law provisions in both the US and the EU. On the basis of the presumptions embraced by the US Supreme Court and the EU General Court, patent settlement agreements which involve large value transfers from the originator to the generic manufacturer that are: (1) disproportionate to the anticipated litigation costs; (2) closely corresponding or exceeding the generic manufacturer's projected profits had it entered the market; (3) independent from any other goods or services provided from the generic manufacturer to the originator; and (4) used as an inducement for the generic manufacturer to refrain from entering the market, will most likely be found to violate US antitrust and EU competition law in the absence of a legitimate justification. For such settlements, the sliding scale of reasonableness will heavily tilt towards the presumptive illegality approach in the US, while in the EU they will most likely be found to constitute restrictions of competition by object, buying-off uncertainty on the issues of patent validity and patent infringement and eliminating generic competition from the market. This holds also true even if a patent settlement with the above-mentioned characteristics allows for generic entry to the market before the expiration of the relevant patent, since the underlying reason for such a delay in generic entry and such limitation on the independent decision of the generic manufacturer to enter the market will most likely derive from the large unjustified value transfer and not from the exclusionary potential of the patent.

II Legitimate Patent Settlements

On the other side of the spectrum, there are categories of settlements which will not in principle cause US antitrust/EU competition law concerns. The main categories of unproblematic settlements are outlined in the following sections.

A *Patent Settlements Without a Reverse Value Transfer*

It is common ground that patent settlement agreements which do not involve a value transfer in any form from the patent holder to the generic challenger and do not contain limitations going beyond the exclusionary potential of the relevant patent will not normally be problematic under US antitrust or EU competition law.[2546] Due to the settling parties' adversity and conflicting interests, any limitation to generic entry imposed by such a settlement will normally derive from the parties' perceptions on the strength and exclusionary potential of the relevant patent(s), since – absent a value transfer – a generic challenger will not have any incentive to accept restrictions extending beyond this point.

B Settlements Allowing Generic Entry Prior to Patent Expiration

Patent settlements that allow for early generic entry prior to the expiry of the underlying patent are perceived as unlikely to raise antitrust concerns. However, this point should be seen with caution and always be examined in conjunction with the exclusionary potential of the relevant patent. For instance, if the brand-name manufacturer's drug version is only protected by a process patent and the generic challenger's drug version uses another non-infringing process, then the parties cannot legitimately enter a settlement agreement limiting the generic manufacturer's ability to enter the market, even if such a limitation ends before the expiry of the relevant patent. In such a case, the patent does not have the potential to exclude from the market non-infringing generic drug versions, so that *any* delay imposed on generic entry is likely to be perceived as a restriction on competition.

C Legitimate and Justified Value Transfers

Certain settlements involving a reverse payment from the brand-name manufacturer to the generic challenger may be legitimate under certain conditions. As acknowledged by the US Supreme Court, patent holders may legitimately reimburse generic challengers for their expected litigation costs, while they can also pay a fair value for any goods or services provided to them, e.g., pursuant to a co-promotion or a distribution agreement.[2547] Nevertheless, the existence of side-deals in the context of a patent settlement between a brand-name manufacturer and a generic challenger may enter in a "grey zone" of suspicious settlements under certain circumstances, as discussed in the following sections. With regard to the reimbursement of projected litigation costs, it should be noted that the Supreme Court did not create a safe harbour for settlements including reverse payments inferior to the litigation costs, which shall also be scrutinised under the rule of reason if there is evidence that the underlying reason of the payment was to delay generic entry.

In the EU, a reverse payment will not always be problematic when: (1) it is linked to the strength of the patent as perceived by the settling parties; (2) it is a necessary element in order to find an acceptable and legitimate solution for both parties; and (3)

2546. See *supra*, Chapter 4, Part 1, Section III.A, discussing permissible settlements on the basis of *FTC v. Actavis, Inc.*, 133 S. Ct. 2223 (2013); *supra*, Chapter 6, Part 1, Section II.B, providing examples of legitimate patent settlements in the EU General Court's decision in Case T-472/13, *Lundbeck v. Commission*.

2547. See *supra*, Chapter 4, Part 1, Section III.A.

it is not accompanied by restrictions intending to delay generic entry.[2548] The EU Commission provided a concrete example of an unproblematic reverse payment, affirmed by the EU General Court: if the generic manufacturer stayed out of the market as a result of the brand-name drug manufacturer's legal threats or court actions, but later on a high likelihood emerges that the relevant patent was not infringed or was invalid, the brand-name manufacturer may allow the generic to enter the market immediately and make a payment as a compensation to the generic challenger for the damages it suffered by not entering the market.[2549] Settlements including value transfers from the generic challengers to patent holders (therefore not reverse payments) may also be legitimate: in case the generic entered the market but in the course of patent litigation patent infringement appears to be likely, the generic challenger may legitimately pay damages to the patent holder and withdraw its generic drug from the market.[2550] As in the US, also in the EU originators may reimburse generic manufacturers for the avoided litigation costs, provided that these costs are estimated in the settlement agreements, that the method of calculation of the reverse payments is supported by evidence and that the settlement genuinely resolves the underlying patent dispute.

III Grey Areas and Questionable Strategies

The most interesting categories of patent settlements and pharmaceutical strategies are the ones that fall within a grey area and cannot be classified as legitimate or illegitimate in a unequivocal way. A great variety of such settlements and strategies and their treatment by US and EU courts and enforcement authorities was analysed in Chapter 4 and Chapter 6. The following sections provide the overview of antitrust/competition law concerns for some of the most complex "grey" settlements and strategies.

A *The Broad Definition of Payment in Settlements*

Due to the increasingly high antitrust scrutiny imposed on patent settlements between originators and generic manufacturers, naked reverse cash payments and value transfers have become increasingly rare and are often replaced by sophisticated settlement schemes. Reverse payments to delay generic entry may take different forms such as side-deals on co-promotion and distribution, licensing agreements or no-AG commitments. In both the US and the EU, a broad definition of payment prevailed, not limited to cash payments but encompassing a large variety of different forms of value transfers from originators to generic manufacturers which may be seen as inducements to delay generic entry.

2548. *See supra*, Chapter 6, Part 1, Section II.B.
2549. *See supra*, Chapter 6, Part 1, Section II.B.
2550. *See supra*, Chapter 6, Part 1, Section II.B; EU Commission Decision, *Lundbeck*, 2013, para. 639.

Conclusion

1 Side-Deals

Side-deals in the context of patent settlements may be problematic from an antitrust/competition law perspective, especially if they are contingent on the generic manufacturer's commitment to delay its market entry. A key element in order to assess whether a side-deal may be potentially problematic is to determine whether it is dependent on the generic manufacturer's acceptance of the settlement terms: this could indicate that it is likely employed as an inducement to delay generic entry. Such side-deals may serve as a vehicle of value transfers, by including for example overpayments from the originator to the generic manufacturer or underpayments from the generic to the originator for the provided goods or services. Another controversial example is a side-deal by means of which the originator forgives potentially high damages that the generic manufacturer is liable to pay for another unrelated litigation between the settling parties. The analysis of such deals by antitrust/competition law authorities is a highly daunting task, since evaluating their actual commercial value and determining their (in)dependence from the patent settlement can be challenging. In order to examine if a side-deal is used as an inducement to delay generic entry, competition law authorities will look into the link between the side-deal and the patent settlement, will aim to estimate the value transferred by means of the side-deal and will also attempt to assess its commercial importance.[2551]

2 Licensing Agreements

Licensing agreements which allow the generic challenger to enter the market prior to the expiration of the relevant patent may also have the potential to eliminate competition from the market and are not immune from antitrust scrutiny. Even though in *FTC v. Actavis* the originator's payments to the first generic challenger were combined with a licensing agreement allowing the generic to enter the market before the expiration of the patent, the settlement at issue had the potential for genuine adverse effects on competition. Settlements which allow for generic entry prior to the patent's expiration pursuant to a licence, without including any reverse payment, may also be found to be problematic from an antitrust/competition law perspective. While licensing is generally considered to be procompetitive as such, patent settlements involving licensing agreements are not given a *carte blanche* as robustly procompetitive and are not granted categorical antitrust immunity.

An example of a problematic licensing agreement is the one used in order to preserve in the market a patent that is likely to be found invalid, allowing the settling parties to collude under the guise of lawful patent licensing. Especially licensing agreements which include no-challenge clauses, prohibiting the licensee from challenging the validity of the patent, are likely to attract a high degree of antitrust/competition law scrutiny. In the EU, licensing agreements as part of patent settlements were found to form part of a single and continuous strategy to restrict competition and

---

2551. *See supra*, Chapter 6, Part 1, Section III.C.

to enter into de facto duopolies in the markets covered by such licences.[2552] Licensing agreements which contain restrictions to competition through inducements to the generic manufacturers, aiming at the objective of market sharing between the parties and excluding competition from the market will be closely scrutinised by antitrust and competition law authorities and are likely to be found problematic in both the US and the EU.

3 Authorised Generic Distribution Agreements and No-Launch Commitments

Agreements between originators and generic challengers which concern authorised generic drug versions will be closely scrutinised by antitrust/competition law authorities. The launch of an authorised generic drug version by the originator is a legitimate possibility in both the US and the EU and is usually employed in an effort to preserve the originator's market share by competing with the generic entrants in the generic market. The launch of an authorised generic drug version has a much stronger impact in the US than in the EU, where it transforms the 180-day exclusivity period of the first generic challenger from a monopoly into a duopoly, amounting to possible losses of 50% for the first generic challenger.[2553] Consequently, the value transferred to the generic challenger through a no-AG commitment is that of a 180-day monopoly in the generic drug market and is arguably used as an inducement to defer generic entry, eliminating also the risk of patent invalidation or a finding of non-infringement. Even though there was initially some disagreement among lower US Courts on whether no-AG commitments may be considered as unjustified value transfers which violate antitrust law, the prevailing opinion is that they do represent transfers of value and should be scrutinised under the rule of reason standard set by *FTC v. Actavis*.

In the EU, the European Commission found that the authorised generic licensing and distribution agreements at issue in the *Servier* case constituted a mechanism of "controlled generic entry," aiming to maintain high monopoly profits on the relevant drug and the sales volumes in case of generic entry.[2554] Pursuant to such agreements the settling generic companies committed not to enter the market with their own generic versions, in return for a licence on the authorised generic drug version of the originator; that way the latter retained some control over the date of the launch of the authorised generic drug, over prices and quantities, etc.[2555]

2552. *See* for instance EU Commission Decision, *Servier*, 2014, paras 1803-1810.
2553. LEIBOWITZ, Interim Report Statement, 2009; FTC, *Authorized Generics*, 2011, p. 33, finding that the expenditures of the first challenger's generic drug – a proxy for its revenues – were 40 to 52% lower when an AG was present.
2554. *See supra*, Chapter 6, Part 1, Section III; EU Commission Decision, *Servier*, 2014, para. 205.
2555. *See supra*, Chapter 6, Part 1, Section III; EU Commission Decision, *Servier*, 2014, para. 203.

B Other Types of Potentially Anticompetitive Strategies

1 Product Switches and the Prevention of Generic Substitution

It is a highly challenging task for the enforcement authorities and courts to determine with certainty whether certain product reformulations constitute genuinely innovative inventions or whether they represent incremental changes to older drug versions, forming part of broader evergreening strategies. Product-hopping occurs when brand-name manufacturers strategically use product reformulations in order to switch the demand from the older version of the brand-name pharmaceutical product to its reformulated version, aiming to prevent generic substitution.

Hard product switches occur when the brand-name drug manufacturer introduces a reformulated drug version, withdrawing in parallel the previous drug version from the market. On the contrary, in a soft product switch typically both versions of the brand-name drug remain on the market, but most promotion and marketing efforts of the brand-name manufacturer are focused on the reformulated drug version. Hard product switches are the object of much higher antitrust/competition law scrutiny, especially if they are combined with other types of anticompetitive conduct coercing prescribing doctors or patients into switching.[2556] Some product switching strategies cannot be easily classified as soft or hard and require a closer analysis, such as strategies under which both drug versions are kept in the market but whereby the price of the older drug version is increased to prohibitive levels, or the price of the reformulated drug version is decreased dramatically. This is not to say that brand-name manufacturers have a general duty to facilitate generic entry or that they cannot freely make decisions on launching new product versions or on withdrawing older ones from the market. That said, soft product switches may be found unproblematic under US antitrust or European competition law. On the contrary, product switching strategies through which originators allegedly attempt to monopolise the market may infringe Sections 1 and 2 of the Sherman Act in the US and Article 102 TFEU in the EU. Other types of strategies targeting the safety and efficacy of generic drug versions, in both the prescription stage or the dispensing stage with the aim to limit or even prevent generic substitution, are also likely to be found problematic.[2557]

2556. For the relevant U.S. jurisprudence *see supra* Chapter 4, Part 3, Section IV analysing *New York v. Actavis PLC, Forest Labs LLC*, 787 F.3d 638, 654-665 (2nd Cir. 2015), ruling that the hard product switch at issue resulted in the coercion of consumers to switch. *See* however *Mylan Pharmaceuticals Inc. v. Warner Chilcott PLC et al.*, 838 F.3d 421, 434-441 (3rd Cir. 2016), finding that the generic competition was not foreclosed from the market despite a hard product switch, but acknowledging that product reformulations combined with coercive conduct may lead to the imposition of antitrust liability. For the decision of the EU Commission on an alleged hard product switch by Servier *see supra* Chapter 6, Part 1, Section III.A.2, discussing the EU Commission Decision, *Servier*, 2014, paras 217-242.

2557. *See supra*, Chapter 6, Part 2, Section I, describing EU Member States national jurisprudence on strategies preventing generic substitution and disparaging generic drugs.

2 The Acquisition of Competing Pharmaceutical Technologies

In the EU, dominant undertakings are not generally prohibited from acquiring competing technologies or exclusive licences on competing technologies. The decisive factor in order to assess the legality of such acquisitions is whether they deprive potential competitors from the means of effectively competing with the dominant undertaking and whether they are used as a protective measure against generic entry. Based on the EU Commission's decision in *Servier*, side-deals on the acquisition of competing pharmaceutical technologies developed by potential competitors risk to be seen not only as a means of concealing a reverse payment aiming to delay generic entry but also as part of a broader strategy to remove non-infringing sources of generic competition from the market. By acquiring non-infringing competing technologies, an originator may not only eliminate direct competition by the holders of the relevant acquired patents but may also remove from the market essential inputs for other potential generic competitors.[2558] Such an acquisition may be found to constitute an abuse of dominant position within the meaning of Article 102 TFEU when it is used in order to foreclose potential competition from the market, especially in cases where the acquired intellectual property rights are not further developed or put in use by the originator.[2559] In order to assess whether such an acquisition is abusive or not, European enforcement authorities will assess whether the acquired technology was potentially viable and thus a source of potential competition; whether the technology was effectively removed from the market and whether it delayed generic entry or rendered it difficult or even impossible.[2560]

Acquisitions of competing technologies have not been part of Hatch-Waxman settlements to a great extent and were thus not discussed in the US part of this book. In the US, acquisitions of competing technologies are analysed under Section 7 of the Clayton Act[2561] and are prohibited if they have the effect of lessening competition or the tendency to create a monopoly. Two criteria are likely to be assessed: (1) whether the combination of already owned patents and of the acquired patents permits the patent holder to demand higher prices for the use of the patented technology, and; (2) whether this combination of patents provides the patent holder with a greater ability or the incentive to hinder downstream competition.[2562] If the acquisition of competing technologies by a brand-name manufacturer meets either of these criteria, it is likely to be found problematic and will be carefully assessed. In case such an acquisition is a side-deal to a patent settlement between an originator and a generic challenger, it may also be assessed whether it serves as a concealed value transfer aiming to delay generic entry.

2558. *See* for instance EU Commission Decision, *Servier*, 2014, para. 6.
2559. *See supra*, Chapter 6, Part 1, Section III; EU Commission Decision, *Servier*, 2014, paras 380, 1772-1773.
2560. *See supra*, Chapter 6, Part 1, Section III; EU Commission Decision, *Servier*, 2014, paras 2800, 2818.
2561. 15 U.S.C. § 18.
2562. *See* further MAIORANA, OLIVER, DELUARD, Patent Acquisitions, 2012; FTC, DoJ, *Horizontal Merger Guidelines*, 2010, pp. 3-4.

Conclusion

IV Practical Advice for the Pharma Industry

The following sections provide some practical advice with the aim to assist the pharmaceutical industry in minimising the risk of infringing US antitrust and EU competition law through patent settlements and other types of strategies. The three main issues that are discussed are the possibility of concluding a settlement with a legitimate side-deal, the need for close monitoring and compliance training and the need to foresee and predict potentially problematic strategies.

A Settling Without an Exclusionary Value Transfer

In both the EU and the US it is not possible to legitimately conclude a patent settlement with a large value transfer as an inducement to delay generic entry. There is of course some merit to the concern that prohibiting value transfers renders the settlement of patent disputes more difficult; parties need to meet halfway and win something out of the settlement in order to settle. However, the prohibition of exclusionary value transfers does not amount to a complete and absolute prohibition of any type of efficiency-creating transaction as part of a patent settlement agreement.

Paying the generic manufacturer its expected litigation costs and any damages for excluding it from the market without a legal justification is legitimate in both the US and the EU. Patent settlements may also be legitimately combined with other types of commercial side-deals between originators and generic manufacturers, as long as certain rather broad conditions are met. First, the value transferred in the context of such a side-deal from the originator to the generic challenger shall be *fair* value for any goods/services provided; side-deals shall not be used as a means to conceal a reverse payment to delay generic entry. Second, such side-deals must be actually performed and not stay dead letter: if the generic manufacturer never actually delivers the contracted goods or services, it becomes evident that the side-deal was not of actual commercial interest for both parties but was used as a vehicle for a value transfer. Even if both of these criteria are met, another crucial element is that the patent settlement should not stretch and extend the exclusionary potential of the patent. If the relevant patent is not infringed by the generic drug version, the parties cannot legitimately conclude an agreement that delays generic entry, even if such entry is scheduled to occur before the expiration of the patent term. Additionally, the side-deal shall not have the effect of rendering ironclad the relevant patent, by including for example a non-challenge obligation for the generic manufacturer or by foreclosing from the market other potential generic competitors.

B The Need for Close Monitoring and Compliance Training

Pharmaceutical companies may have hundreds or thousands of employees, so that it is normally extremely hard for the company's legal department to keep the overview of all the commercial strategies adopted. In order to avoid engaging in settlements and strategies which restrain competition and are likely to result in high fines and severe reputational damage, the legal departments of pharmaceutical companies must closely collaborate with the management and the various company departments in a transparent manner. Intensive compliance training is indispensable and shall focus on antitrust/competition law concerns certain types of conduct may give rise to, while special attention shall be given to conduct falling within grey areas, which cannot be strictly categorised as legitimate or problematic.

Beyond the type of concluded patent settlements and adopted strategies, another major concern may be the internal communications, documents, e-mails and statements of employees. Such documents were broadly used by enforcement authorities and courts as evidence in order to establish the parties' intent to delay generic entry through reverse payments. Memorable statements include direct confessions of the aim to delay generic entry, concrete numbers of payments and value transfers, or even plain acknowledgements of the relevant patent's weakness or invalidity. Compliance training efforts should also focus on the content of internal and external correspondence and documents, in order to avoid raising suspicions of anticompetitive conduct.

C Foreseeing Risks and Avoiding Problematic Strategies

The evolution and sophistication of patent settlements and other types of strategies in the pharmaceutical industry is extremely rapid and highly impressive. Enforcement authorities seem to be struggling to keep up with the ever-changing reality of patent settlements. Nevertheless, the lack of a concrete prohibition or relevant precedent prohibiting a specific type of settlement or strategy does not mean that such conduct will escape antitrust and competition law scrutiny. Pharmaceutical companies need to carefully assess each and every element before engaging in a novel type of settlement or other strategy, focusing on the potential impact it may have on generic entry. This is not to say that brand-name manufacturers are not entitled to use the legitimate means they have at their disposal in order to protect their rights or their patent monopoly, neither that they are obliged to facilitate generic entry. Nevertheless, buying-off generic competition, creating artificial barriers to generic entry or settling so as to create a bottleneck effect will not be tolerated from antitrust and competition law enforcement authorities, irrespectively of the form of the employed conduct. Another crucial element is that of coercion: any strategy which is liable to coerce pharmaceuticals' prescribers or patients to a specific version of a product or to create artificial concerns on the safety and efficacy of another pharmaceutical product (whether generic or brand-name) has an overwhelming probability of being problematic. Finally, pharmaceutical companies need to assess the exclusionary potential of their patent rights in an objective manner so as to recognise their potential limitations. If there is one lesson to be learned from this book, this is that patents do not constitute umbrella exceptions from the application of US antitrust and EU competition law.

CLOSING REMARKS

There is not one definitive answer to be given regarding the issue of patent settlements and other types of strategies in the pharmaceutical industry under US antitrust and EU competition law. Whether a settlement or strategy will be found to be legitimate or problematic depends on the specificities of each case, on the exclusionary potential of the relevant patent(s) and on the overall regulatory, economic and factual context. The applicable test for the analysis of settlements and strategies in the pharmaceutical industry also depends on the specificities of each case; these will determine how steep the sliding scale of reasonableness will be in the US and whether a specific conduct may constitute a restriction of competition by object or by effect in the EU. The aim of this book was not to give a black-or-white answer to these questions, but to provide concrete examples of legitimate and illegitimate settlements and strategies, highlighting which conduct may be potentially problematic and on the basis of which criteria. As patent settlements and strategies in the pharmaceutical industry evolve, so will the legal analysis and the standards applied by courts and enforcement authorities. However, the main points of analysis will most likely focus on whether the relevant settlement or strategy unjustifiably eliminates competition from the market and on whether it exceeds the exclusionary scope of the patent rights at issue. Having these two points in mind, the pharmaceutical industry shall be able to assess whether a new form of settlement or a novel strategy is likely to be problematic from an antitrust and competition law perspective and to take the necessary steps to eliminate such risk.

Bibliography

I Books

ANDERMAN Steven, EZRACHI Ariel (eds), *Intellectual Property and Competition Law: New Frontiers*, Oxford University Press, 2011.

BENACCHIO Gian Antonio, CARPAGNANO Michelle, (eds), *L'applicazione delle regole di concorrenza in Italia e nell'Unione europea. Atti del V Convegno biennale Antitrust di Trento*, Editoriale scientifica, 2015.

BESSEN James, MEURER Michael J., *Patent Failure: How Judges, Lawyers, and Bureaucrats Put Innovators at Risk*, Princeton University Press, 2008. [cited as: BESSEN, MEURER, *Patent Failure*, 2008].

BOLDRIN Michelle, LEVINE David K., *Against Intellectual Monopoly*, Cambridge University Press, 2008. Also Available at: http://levine.sscnet.ucla.edu/general/intellectual/againstfinal.htm (last accessed on March 31, 2018). [cited as: BOLDRIN, LEVINE, *Against Intellectual Monopoly*, 2008].

COOTER Robert B. Jr., ULEN Thomas, *Law and Economics*, Pearson Education Limited, 6th ed., 2014. [cited as: COOTER, ULEN, *Law and Economics*, 2014].

EUROPEAN COMMISSION, *Compendium of EU Pharmaceutical Law* – Eudrabook version 1.3 – European Union, May 2015. Available at: http://bookshop.europa.eu/en/eudrabook-pbND0615186/ (last accessed on March 31, 2018) [cited as: EU Commission, *Compendium of EU Pharmaceutical Law*, 2015].

DREXL Joseph, LEE Nari, (eds), *Pharmaceutical Innovation, Competition and Patent Law: A Trilateral Perspective*, Edward Elgar Publishing Inc., 2013.

FAULL Jonathan, NIKPAY Ali (eds), *The EU Law of Competition*, 3rd ed., Oxford University Press, 2014.

GARNER Bryan A., editor in Chief, *Black's Law Dictionary*, Thomson Reuters 2014, 10th ed. [cited as: *Black's Law Dictionary*, 2014].

HOVENKAMP Herbert J., AREEDA Philip E., *Fundamentals of Antitrust Law*, 4th ed., Supplement, Wolters Kluwer (2014). [cited as: HOVENKAMP, AREEDA, *Fundamentals of Antitrust*, 2014].

HOVENKAMP Herbert J., *Federal Antitrust Policy – The Law of Competition and its Practice*, 4th ed., West Publishing Co. (2011). [cited as: HOVENKAMP, *Federal Antitrust Policy*, 2011].

Bibliography

HOVENKAMP Herbert J., *Innovation and Competition Policy*, Chap. 4 (2nd ed.): Competition Policy and the Patent System (July 22, 2013). Available at SSRN: http://ssrn.com/abstract = 1938310 (last accessed on March 31, 2018); [cited as: HOVENKAMP, *Innovation and Competition*, 2013].

HOVENKAMP Herbert J., JANIS Mark D., LEMLEY Mark A., LESLIE Christopher R., *IP and Antitrust: An Analysis of Antitrust Principles Applied to Intellectual Property Law*, Wolters Kluwer 2006. [cited as: HOVENKAMP, JANIS, LEMLEY, LESLIE, *IP and Antitrust*, 2006].

HOVENKAMP Herbert J., JANIS Mark D., LEMLEY Mark A., LESLIE Christopher R., *IP and Antitrust: An Analysis of Antitrust Principles Applied to Intellectual Property Law*, Wolters Kluwer, 2nd ed. 2015. [cited as: HOVENKAMP, JANIS, LEMLEY, LESLIE, *IP and Antitrust*, 2015].

JONES Alison, SUFRIN Brenda, *EU Competition Law: Text, Cases, and Materials*, Oxford University Press, 5th ed. 2014. [cited as: JONES, SUFRIN, 2014].

POSNER Richard A., *Economic Analysis of Law*, Wolters Kluwer Law & Business, 9th ed. 2014. [cited as: POSNER, *Economic Analysis of Law*, 2014].

SAMOY I., LOOS M.B.M. (eds), *Linked Contracts*, (Ius Commune Europaeum), (2012).

SHAVELL Steven, *Foundations of Economic Analysis of Law*, The Belknap Press of Harvard University Press, 2004, [cited as: SHAVELL, *Foundations of Economic Analysis*, 2004].

SULLIVAN Thomas E., HOVENKAMP Herbert J., SHELANSKI Howard A., LESLIE Christopher R., *Antitrust Law, Policy, and Procedure: Cases, Materials, Problems*, 7th ed., LexisNexis (2014), [cited as: SULLIVAN, HOVENKAMP, SHELANSKI, LESLIE, *Antitrust Law*, 2014].

TOPAZ DRUCKMAN Karen, HECKENDORN URSCHELER Lukas (eds), *Les difficultés économiques en droit*, Schulthess Verlag, 2015.

WIPO, *WIPO Intellectual Property Handbook: Policy, Law and Use*, WIPO Publication No. 489 (E), 2nd ed., 2004. Available at: http://www.wipo.int/about-ip/en/iprm/ (last accessed on March 31, 2018). [cited as: WIPO, IP Handbook, 2004].

WHISH Richard, BAILEY David, *Competition Law*, 8th Ed., Oxford University Press, 2015. [cited as: WHISH, BAILEY, *Competition Law*, 2015].

II Articles and Book Chapters

ABBOTT Alden F., MICHEL Suzanne T., "The Right Balance of Competition Policy and Intellectual Property Law: A Perspective on Settlements of Pharmaceutical Patent Litigation," 46 *IDEA* 1 (2005), pp. 1-36. [cited as: ABBOTT, MICHEL, Right Balance, 2005].

ACCARDO Gabriele, "Italian Court Confirms Hefty Fines on Novartis and Roche," TTLF Newsletter on Transatlantic Antitrust and IPR Developments, January 21, 2015. Available at: https://ttlfnews.wordpress.com/2015/01/21/italian-court-confirms-hefty-fines-on-novartis-and-roche/ (last accessed on March 31, 2018). [cited as: ACCARDO, Novartis-Roche, 2015].

ADAMS Christopher P., BRANTNER Van V., "Estimating the Cost of New Drug Development: Is it Really $802 Million?," 25:2 *Health Affairs* 420, (March/April 2006), pp. 420-442. [cited as: ADAMS, BRANTNER, Cost of New Drug Development, 2006].

ADDANKI Sumanth, DASKIN, Alan J., "Patent Settlement Agreements," *in* ABA Section of Antitrust Law, 3: Chapter 85 *Issues in Competition* 2127, (2008), pp. 2127-2153. [cited as: ADDANKI, DASKIN, Patent Settlement Agreements, 2008].

ADDANKI Sumanth, BUTLER Henry N., "Activating Actavis: Economic Issues in Applying the Rule of Reason to Reverse Payment Settlements," 15:1 *Minn. J. L. Sci. & Tech.* 77, (2014) pp. 77-94. [cited as: ADDANKI, BUTLER, Activating Actavis, 2014].

ALLISON John R., LEMLEY Mark A., "Empirical Evidence on the Validity of Litigated Patents," 26 *AIPLA Q. J.* 185, (1998), pp. 185-275. [cited as: ALLISON, LEMLEY, Empirical Evidence, 1998].

ALLISON John R., LEMLEY Mark A., MOORE Kimberly A., TRUNKEY Derek R., "Valuable Patents," 92 *Geo. L.J.* 435, (March 2003), pp. 435-477. [cited as: ALLISON, LEMLEY, MOORE, Valuable Patents, 2003].

ALLISON John R., LEMLEY Mark A., WALKER Joshua, "Extreme Value or Trolls on Top? The Characteristics of the Most Litigated Patents," 158 *U. Pa. L. Rev.* 1, (December 2009), full pp. 1-33. [cited as: ALLISON, LEMLEY, WALKER, Trolls on Top, 2009].

ALLISON John R., LEMLEY Mark A., WALKER Joshua, "Patent Quality and Settlement Among Repeat Patent Litigants," 99 *Geo. L.J.* 677, (2011), pp. 677-712. [cited as: ALLISON, LEMLEY, WALKER, Patent Quality, 2011].

ANGELL Marcia, "The Truth About the Drug Companies," The New York Review of Books, (July 15, 2004). Available at: http://www.nybooks.com/articles/2004/07/15/the-truth-about-the-drug-companies/. [cited as: ANGELL, Drug Companies, 2004].

AREEDA Phillip, "The Rule of Reason in Antitrust Analysis: General Issues," Federal Judicial Center, Education and Training Series, (June 1981), pp. 1-47. Available at: http://www.fjc.gov/public/pdf.nsf/lookup/antitrust.pdf/$file/antitrust.pdf. [cited as: AREEDA, Rule of Reason, 1981].

ASPE Issue Brief, "Expanding the Use of Generic Drugs," (December 1, 2010). Available at: http://aspe.hhs.gov/basic-report/expanding-use-generic-drugs. [cited as: ASPE, Expanding Generics, 2010].

ASPE Issue Brief, Department of Health and Human Services, "Some Observations Related to the Generic Drug Market," (May 16, 2015). Available at: https://aspe.hhs.gov/sites/default/files/pdf/139331/ib_GenericMarket.pdf. [cited as: ASPE, Generic Drug Market, 2015].

ATHANASIADOU Amalia, "FTC v. Actavis: Are Reverse Payment Settlements Antitrust Immune?," *in* TOPAZ DRUCKMAN Karen, HECKENDORN URSCHELER Lukas (eds), *Les difficultés économiques en droit*, Schulthess Verlag (2015), pp. 249-273. Available at: https://papers.ssrn.com/sol3/papers.cfm?abstract_id=2737870 (last accessed on March 31, 2018). [cited as: ATHANASIADOU, FTC v. Actavis, 2015].

ATHANASIADOU Amalia, "Lundbeck v. Commission: the First Decision of the European General Court on Reverse Payments," *Jusletter*, October 10, 2016. Available at:

https://papers.ssrn.com/sol3/papers.cfm?abstract_id = 2851449 (last accessed on March 31, 2018). [cited as: ATHANASIADOU, Lundbeck v. Commission, 2016].

AYRES Ian, KLEMPERER Paul, "Limiting Patentees' Market Power Without Reducing Innovation Incentives: The Perverse Benefits of Uncertainty and Non-injunctive Remedies," 97 *Mich. L. Rev.* 985, (February 1999), pp. 985-1033. [cited as: AYRES, KLEMPERER, Perverse Benefits, 1999].

AYRES Ian, KAPCZYNSKI Amy, "Innovation Sticks: The Limited Case for Penalising Failures to Innovate," 82:4 *The U. Chi. L. Rev.* 1781, (Fall 2015), pp. 1781-1852. [cited as: AYRES, KAPCZYNSKI, Innovation Sticks, 2015].

BACKUS Scott A., "Reversing Course on Reverse Payment Settlements in the Pharmaceutical Industry: Has Schering-Plough Created the BluePrint For Defensible Antitrust Violations?," 60 *Okla. L. Rev.* 375, (Summer 2007), pp. 375-418. [cited as: BACKUS, Reversing Course, 2007].

BAGHERIAN Reza, "The Preserve Access to Affordable Generics Act: Will Congress's Response to Reverse Payment Patent Settlements Enhance Competition in the Pharmaceutical Market?," 7 *J. Marshall Rev. Intell. Prop. L.* 150 (Fall 2007), pp. 150-170. [cited as: BAGHERIAN, Congress's Response, 2007].

BAKER Brook K., "Ending Drug Registration Apartheid: Taming Data Exclusivity and Patent/Registration Linkage," 34 *Am. J.L. & Med.* 303, (2008), pp. 303-344. [cited as: BAKER, Drug Apartheid, 2008].

BAKER Jonathan B., "Market Definition: An Analytical Overview," 74:1 *Antitrust L. J.* 129, (2007), pp. 129-173. [cited as: BAKER J., Market Definition, 2007].

BALTO David A., "Pharmaceutical Patent Settlements: The Antitrust Risks," 55 *Food & Drug L.J.* 321, (2000), pp. 321-341. [cited as: BALTO, Antitrust Risks, 2000].

BANASEVIC Nicholas, "The Implications of the Court of Justice's Huawei/ZTE Judgment," 6:7 *J. Eur. Competition L. & Prac.* 463, (2015), pp. 463-464. [cited as: BANASEVIC, 2015].

BASHEER Shamnad, "Alternative Incentives for Pharmaceutical Innovation," 27 *Intell. Prop. J.* 13, (December 2014), pp. 13-63. [cited as: BASHEER, Alternative Incentives, 2014].

BELLONI Annalisa, MORGAN David, PARIS Valérie, "Pharmaceutical Expenditures and Policies: Past Trends and Future Challenges," OECD Health Working Papers No. 87, (April 2016), pp. 1-75. Available at: http://www.oecd.org/officialdocuments/publicdisplaydocumentpdf/?cote = DELSA/HEA/WD/HWP(2016)10&doclanguage = En (last accessed on March 31, 2018). [cited as: BELLONI, MORGAN, PARIS, Pharma Expenditures, 2016].

BERNARD Kent, "When Does Interpretation Become Rewriting? The FTC Runs with the Actavis Decision," *CPI Antitrust Chron.* (2), (September 2013), pp. 1-7. [cited as: BERNARD, Rewriting, 2013].

BERNDT Ernst R., AITKEN Murray L. "Brand Loyalty, Generic Entry and Price Competition in Pharmaceuticals in the Quarter Century after the 1984 Waxman-Hatch Legislation," 18:2 *Int'l J. Econ. Bus.* 177, (2011), pp. 177-201. [cited as: BERNDT, AITKEN, Brand Loyalty, 2011].

BESSEN James, MEURER Michael J., "Of Patents and Property," 31:4 *Reg.* 18, (Winter 2008-2009), pp. 18-26. [cited as: BESSEN, MEURER, Patents and Property, 2008].

BESSEN James, MASKIN Eric, "Sequential Innovation, Patents, and Imitation," 40:4 *RAND J. Econ.* 611, (Winter 2009), pp. 611-635. [cited as: BESSEN, MASKIN, Sequential Innovation, 2009].

BESSEN James, LOVE Bryan J., "Make the 'Patent Polluters' Pay: Using Pigovian Fees to Curb Patent Abuse," 4 *Cal. L. Rev. Cir.* 84, (August 2013), pp. 84-91. [cited as: BESSEN, LOVE, Patent Polluters, 2013].

BIERI Diane E., "Implications of FTC v. Actavis: a Reasonable Approach to Evaluating Reverse Payment Settlements," 15:1 *Minn. J. L. Sci. & Tech.* 135 (2014), pp. 135-144. [cited as: BIERI, Reasonable Approach, 2014].

BLAIR Roger D., COTTER Thomas F., "Are Settlements of Patent Disputes Illegal Per Se?," 47 *Antitrust L. Bull.* 491, (Summer-Fall 2002), pp. 491-539. [cited as: BLAIR, COTTER, Illegal Per Se, 2002].

BOLDRIN Michelle, LEVINE David K., "The Case Against Patents," 27:1 *J. Econ. Persps.* 3, (Winter 2013), pp. 3-22. [cited as: BOLDRIN, LEVINE, Against Patents, 2013].

BRONWYN Hall H., "Patents and Patent Policy," 23:4 *Oxford Rev. Econ. Policy* 568, (2007), pp. 568-587. [cited as: BRONWYN, 2007].

BRUZZONE Ginevra, CAPOZZI Sara, "Restrictions by Object in the Case Law of the Court of Justice: In Search of a Systematic Approach," *in* BENACCHIO G., CARPAGNANO M., (eds), *L'applicazione delle regole di concorrenza in Italia e nell'Unione europea. Atti del V Convegno biennale Antitrust di Trento*, Editoriale scientifica, 2015. [cited as: BRUZZONE, CAPOZZI, 2015].

BULOW Jeremy, "The Gaming of Pharmaceutical Patents," 4 *Innovation Policy and the Economy* 145, (February 2004), pp. 145-187. [cited as: BULOW, Gaming of Patents, 2004].

BURK Dan L., LEMLEY Mark A., "Is Patent Law Technology-Specific," 17 *Berkeley Tech. L.J.* 1155 (2002), pp. 1155-1206. [cited as: BURK, LEMLEY, Technology-Specific, 2002].

BUSHELL Gavin, "Case C-457/10 P, AstraZeneca v Commission," *Kluwer Competition L. Blog*, December 7, 2012. Available at: http://kluwercompetitionlawblog.com/2012/12/07/case-c-45710-p-astrazeneca-v-commission-judgment-of-6-december-2012/ (last accessed on March 31, 2018). [cited as: BUSHELL, Case C-457/10 P, 2012].

BUTLER Henry N., JAROSCH Jeffrey P., "Policy Reversal on Reverse Payments: Why Courts Should Not Follow the New DoJ Position on Reverse-Payment Settlements of Pharmaceutical Patent Litigation," 96 *Iowa L. Rev.* 57, (November 2010), pp. 57-125. [cited as: BUTLER, JAROSCH, Policy Reversal, 2010].

CARLING David, PEARS Michael, "Avoiding the Actavis SPC Trap," *Life Sci. Intell. Prop. Rev.*, (March 9, 2016). Available at: http://www.lifesciencesipreview.com/contributed-article/avoiding-the-actavis-spc-trap (last accessed on March 31, 2018). [cited as: CARLING, PEARS, 2016].

CARRIER Michael A., "Unsettling Drug Patent Settlements: A Framework for Presumptive Illegality," 108 *Mich. L. Rev.* 37, (October 2009), pp. 37-80. [cited as: CARRIER, Unsettling Settlements, 2009].

CARRIER Michael A., "A Real-World Analysis of Pharmaceutical Settlements: The Missing Dimension of Product-Hopping," 62 *Fla. L. Rev.* 1009, (2010), pp. 1009-1036. [cited as: CARRIER, Real-World, 2010].

CARRIER Michael A., "2025: Reverse-Payment Settlements Unleashed," 2 *CPI Antitrust J.* 1, (December 2010), pp. 1-5. [cited as: CARRIER, Unleashed, 2010].

CARRIER Michael A., "Why the Scope of the Patent Test Cannot Solve the Drug Patent Settlement Problem," 16 *Stan. Tech. L. Rev.* 1, (September 16, 2012), pp. 1-8. [cited as: CARRIER, Scope of the Patent Test, 2012].

CARRIER Michael A., "Actavis and Large and Unjustified Payments," Posted on SCOTUSblog, (July 25, 2013). Available at: http://www.scotusblog.com/2013/07/actavis-and-large-and-unjustified-payments/. (last accessed on March 31, 2018). [cited as: CARRIER, Unjustified Payments, 2013].

CARRIER Michael A., "Five Arguments Laid to Rest After Actavis," 13 *Antitrust Source, by the ABA* 1, (October 2013), pp. 1-11. [cited as: CARRIER, Five Arguments, 2013].

CARRIER Michael A., "Payment After Actavis," 100 *Iowa L. Rev.* 7, (2014), pp. 7-49. [cited as: CARRIER, Payment After Actavis, 2014].

CARRIER Michael A., "Pharmaceutical Antitrust Complexity," *CPI Antitrust Chron.* 1, November 2014 (2), pp. 1-12. [cited as: CARRIER, Pharma Complexity, 2014].

CARRIER Michael A., "A Response to Chief Justice Roberts: Why Antitrust Must Play a Role in the Analysis of Drug Patent Settlements," 15:1 *Minn. J. L. Sci. & Tech.* 31, (2014), pp. 31-40. [cited as: CARRIER, Response to Roberts, 2014].

CARRIER Michael A., "Eight Reasons Why "No-Authorized-Generic" Promises Constitute Payment," 67:3 *Rutgers U. L. Rev.* 697 (2015), pp. 697-720. [cited as: CARRIER, Eight Reasons, 2015].

CARRIER Michael A., "The U.S. Court of Appeals for the Third Circuit Concludes That the Actavis Ruling Applies to Non-cash Payments (Lamictal)," *e-Competitions Bull.*, No. 75208, (August 2015-II), pp. 1-6. [cited as: CARRIER, Non-cash Payments, 2015].

CARRIER Michael A., MINNITI Carl, "Citizen Petitions: Long, Late-Filed, and At-Last Denied," 66 *Am. U. L. Rev.* 305, (2016), pp. 305-352. [cited as: CARRIER, MINNITI, Citizen Petitions, 2016].

CARRIER Michael A., "Pleading Standards: the Hidden Threat to Actavis," 91 *New York U. L. Rev.* On Line 31, (2016), pp. 31-42. [cited as: CARRIER, Pleading Standards, 2016].

CARRIER Michael A., "The U.S. Court of Appeals for the Third Circuit Offers Misguided Analysis of Product-Hopping (Mayne/ Warner Chilcott/ Mylan)," *e-Competitions Bull.*, No. 81744, (October 2016-II). [cited as: CARRIER, Doryx, 2016].

CARRIER Michael A., "Why the Supreme Court Should Deny *Certiorari* in *King Drug*," *Competition Policy Int'l*, (September 2016), pp. 1-7. [cited as: CARRIER, King Drug, 2016].

CARRIER Michael A., KESSELHEIM Aaron S, "The Daraprim Price Hike and a Role for Antitrust," (October 21, 2015), Health Affairs Blog. Available at: http://healthaffairs.org/blog/2015/10/21/the-daraprim-price-hike-and-a-role-for-antitrust/ (last accessed on March 31, 2018). [cited as: CARRIER, KESSELHEIM, Price Hike, 2015].

CARRIER Michael A., LEVIDOW Nicole L., KESSELHEIM Aaron S., "Using Antitrust Law to Challenge Turing's Daraprim Price Increase," 31:3 *Berkley Tech. L. J.* 1379, (2017), pp. 1379-1407 [cited as: CARRIER, LEVIDOW, KESSELHEIM, Daraprim Price Increase, 2017].

CARRIER Michael A., SHADOWEN Steve D., "Product Hopping: A New Framework," 92:1 *Notre Dame L. Rev.* 167, (2016), pp. 167-230. [cited as: CARRIER, SHADOWEN, Product Hopping, 2016].

CATLIN C. Aaron, COWAN A. Cathy, "History of Health Spending in the United States, 1960-2013," (November 19, 2015), pp. 1-37. Available at: https://www.cms.gov/Research-Statistics-Data-and-Systems/Statistics-Trends-and-Reports/NationalHealthExpendData/Downloads/HistoricalNHEPaper.pdf (last accessed on March 31, 2018). [cited as: CATLIN, COWAN, U.S. Health Spending, 2015].

CAUCHI Richard, "State Laws and Legislation Related to Biologic Medications and Substitution of Biosimilars," National Conference of State Legislatures (NCSL) Website, (July 1, 2017). Available at: http://www.ncsl.org/research/health/state-laws-and-legislation-related-to-biologic-medications-and-substitution-of-biosimilars.aspx (last accessed on March 31, 2018). [cited as: CAUCHI, 2017].

CAUFFMAN Caroline, "The Impact of Voidness for Infringement of Article 101 TFEU on Linked Contracts," *in* SAMOY I., LOOS M.B.M. (eds), *Linked Contracts*, (Ius Commune Europaeum), (2012), pp. 29-54. [cited as: CAUFFMAN, 2012].

CHAVES MOSIER Richard D., RITCHESON Steven W., "In Re Cardizem and Valley Drug: A View From the Faultline Between Patent and Antitrust in Pharmaceutical Settlements," 20:2 *Santa Clara High Tech. L.J.* 497, (2003), pp. 497-515. [cited as: CHAVES MOSIER, RITCHESON, Faultline, 2003].

CHEN Liyan, *The Most Profitable Industries in 2016*, Forbes. Available at: http://www.forbes.com/sites/liyanchen/2015/12/21/the-most-profitable-industries-in-2016/#559e3ab47a8b. (last accessed on March 31, 2018). [cited as: CHEN, Most Profitable Industries, 2016].

CHENG Jessie, "An Antitrust Analysis of Product Hopping in the Pharmaceutical Industry," 108 *Col. L. Rev.* 1471, (October 2008), pp. 1471-1515. [cited as: CHENG, Product Hopping, 2008].

CHENG Thomas K., "A Developmental Approach to the Patent-Antitrust Interface," 33:1 *Nw. J. Intl. L. & Bus.* 46, (fall 2012), pp. 46-79. [cited as: CHENG, Developmental Approach, 2012].

CHENG Thomas, "Putting Innovation Incentives Back in the Patent-Antitrust Interface," 11:5 *Nw. J. Tech. & Intell. Prop.* 385, (2013), pp. 385-439. [cited as: CHENG T., Patent-Antitrust Interface, 2013].

CHENG Thomas K., "Antitrust Treatment of the No Challenge Clause," 5:2 *N.Y.U. J. Intell. Prop. & Ent. Law* 437, (Spring 2016), pp. 437-512. [cited as: CHENG T., No Challenge Clause, 2016].

CHIEN Colleen, KESAN Jay, "Comparing Patent Quality at the USPTO and EPO," Law 360, November 29, 2016. Available at: https://www.law360.com/ip/articles/863111/comparing-patent-quality-at-the-uspto-and-epo#fn2. (last accessed on March 31, 2018). [cited as: CHIEN, KESAN, USPTO and EPO, 2016].

Coggio Brian D., DeMasi Timothy E., "The Right to a Jury Trial in Actions for Patent Infringement and Suits for Declaratory Judgement," 13:1 *Fordham Intell. Prop., Media & Ent. L.J.* 205, (2002), pp. 205-230. [cited as: Coggio, DeMasi, Jury Trial, 2002].

Cotter Thomas F., "Refining the 'Presumptive Illegality' Approach to Settlements of Patent Disputes Involving Reverse Payments: A Commentary on Hovenkamp, Janis and Lemley," 87 *Minn. L. Rev.* 1789, (June 2003), pp. 1789-1816. [cited as: Cotter, Refining Presumptive Illegality, 2003].

Cotter Thomas F., "Antitrust Implications of Patent Settlements Involving Reverse Payments," 71 *Antitrust L. J.* (2004), pp. 1069-1097. [cited as: Cotter, Antitrust Implications, 2004].

Cotter Thomas F., "FTC v. Actavis, Inc.: When Is the Rule of Reason Not the Rule of Reason?," 15:1 *Minn. J. L. Sci. & Tech.* 41, (2014), pp. 41-49. [cited as: Cotter, Not the Rule of Reason, 2014].

Coughlin Daniel F., Dede Rochelle A., "Hatch-Waxman Game-Playing from a Generic Manufacturer Perspective," 25 *Biotech. L. Rep.* 525, (October 2006), pp. 525-533. [cited as: Coughlin, Dede, Game-Playing, 2006].

Coury Larry, "C'est what? Saisie! A Comparison of Patent Infringement Remedies Among the G7 Economic Nations," 13 *Fordham Intell. Prop. Media & Ent. L.J.* 1110, (Summer 2003), pp. 1110-1159. [cited as: Coury, Saisie, 2003].

Crane Daniel A., "Exit Payments in Settlement of Patent Infringement Lawsuits: Antitrust Rules and Economic Implications," 54 *Fla. L. Rev.* 747, (September 2002), pp. 747-797. [cited as: Crane, Exit Payments, 2002].

Crane Daniel A., "Actavis, the Reverse Payment Fallacy, and the Continuing Need for Regulatory Solutions," 15:1 *Minn. J. L. Sci. & Tech.* 51, (2014), pp. 51-59. [cited as: Crane, Reverse Payment Fallacy, 2014].

Cremers Katrin, Ernicke Max, Gaessler Fabian, Harhoff Dietman, Helmers Christian, Mc Donagh Luke, Schliessler Paula, Van Zeebroeck Nicolas, "Patent Litigation in Europe," 44:1 *Eur J. L. ECon* 1, (August 2017), pp. 1-44. [cited as: Cremers et al., EU Patent Litigation, 2017].

D'Amore Claudia, "The Administrative Supreme Court Confirms the ICA's Decision to Condemn Pfizer for Abuse of Dominant Position Aimed at Delaying the Market Entry of Generic Pharmaceutical Companies," 1 *Rivista Italiana d'Antitrust (Italian Antitrust Rev.)* 2014, pp. 77-81. [cited as: D'Amore, Pfizer, 2014].

Danzon Patricia M., Chao Li-Wei, "Does Regulation Drive Out Competition in Pharmaceutical Markets?" 43 *J.L. & Econ.* 311, (2000) pp. 311-357. [cited as: Danzon, Chao, Regulation, 2000].

Davis Joshua P., "Applying Litigation Economics to Patent Settlements: Why Reverse Payments Should Be Per Se Illegal," 41 *Rutgers L.J.* 255, (Fall & Winter 2009), pp. 255-307. [cited as: Davis, Per Se Illegal, 2009].

Davis Joshua P., McEwan Ryan J., "Deactivating Actavis: The Clash Between the Supreme Court and (Some) Lower District Courts," 67:3 *Rutgers U. L. Rev.* 557, (Spring 2015), pp. 557-584. [cited as: Davis, McEwan, Deactivating Actavis, 2015].

DAVIT Barbara M., NWAKAMA Patrick E., BUEHLER Gary J., CONNER Dale P., HAIDAR Sam H., PATEL Devvrat T., YANG Yongsheng, YU Lawrence X., WOODCOCK Janet, "Comparing Generic and Innovator Drugs: A Review of 12 Years of Bioequivalence Data from the United States Food and Drug Administration," 43 *The Annals of Pharmacotherapy* 1583, (October 2009), pp. 1583-1597. [cited as: DAVIT ET AL., Bioequivalence Data, 2009].

DE LA MANO Miguel, NAZZINI Renato, ZENGER Hans, "Article 102," Chapter 4 *in* FAULL Jonathan, NIKPAY Ali (eds), *The EU Law of Competition*, 3rd ed. (2014), pp. 329-538. [cited as: DE LA MANO, NAZZINI, ZENGER, 2014].

DE STEFANO Gianni, "Italy: Abuse of Dominant Position – pharmaceuticals," 33(6) *E.C.L.R.* 2012, pp. 87-89. [cited as: DE STEFANO, Abuse, 2012].

DICKEY Bret M., ORSZAG Jonathan, TYSON Laura, "An Economic Assessment of Patent Settlements in the Pharmaceutical Industry," 19 *Annals Health L.* 367, (Winter 2010), pp. 367-400. [cited as: DICKEY, ORSZAG, TYSON, Economic Assessment, 2010].

DICKEY Bret M., RUBINFELD Daniel L., "Would the Per Se Illegal Treatment of Reverse Payment Settlements Inhibit Generic Drug Investment?," 8:3 *J. Competition L. & Econ.* 615, (2012), pp. 615-625. [cited as: DICKEY, RUBINFELD, Generic Drug Investment, 2012].

DIMASI Joseph A., HANSEN Ronald W., GRABOWSKI Henry G., "The Price of Innovation: New Estimates of Drug Development Costs," 22 *J. Health Econ.* 151 (March 2003), pp. 151-185. [cited as: DIMASI ET AL., New Estimates, 2003].

DIMASI Joseph A., GRABOWSKI Henry G., "The Cost of Biopharmaceutical R&D: Is Biotech Different?," 28 *Manag. Decis. Econ.* 469, (2007), pp. 469-479. [cited as: DIMASI, GRABOWSKI, Biopharmaceutical R&D, 2007].

DIMASI Joseph A., FELDMAN Lanna, SECKLER Allison., WILSON Andrew, "Trends in Risks Associated with New Drug Development: Success Rates for Investigational Drugs," 87:3 *Clin. Pharmacology & Therapeutics* 272, (March 2010), pp. 272-277. [cited as: DIMASI ET AL., Success Rates, 2010].

DIMASI Joseph A., GRABOWSKI Henry G., HANSEN Ronald W., "Innovation in the Pharma Industry: New Estimates of R&D Costs," 47 *J. Health Econ.* 20, (2016), pp. 22-33. [cited as: DIMASI ET AL., R&D Costs, 2016].

DOLIN Gregory, "Reverse Settlements as Patent Invalidity Signals," 24:2 *Harv. J. L. & Tech.* 281, (Spring 2011), pp. 281-333. [cited as: DOLIN, Patent Invalidity Signals, 2011].

DOMEIJ Bengt, "Anticompetitive Marketing in the Context of Pharmaceutical Switching in Europe," *in* Drexl Joseph, Lee Nari, (eds), *Pharmaceutical Innovation, Competition and Patent Law: A Trilateral Perspective*, Edward Elgar Publishing Inc., 2013, pp. 273-289. [cited as: DOMEIJ, Pharmaceutical Switching, 2013].

DOWNING Nicholas S., ROSS Joseph S., JACKEVICIUS Cynthia A., KRUMHOLZ Harlan M., "How Abbott's Fenofibrate Franchise Avoided Generic Competition," 122 *Arch. Internal Med.* 724 (May 2012), pp. 724-730. [cited as: DOWNING, ROSS, JACKEVICIUS, KRUMHOLZ, Abbott's Franchise, 2012].

DREXL Josef, FRÜH Alfred, MACKENRODT Mark-Oliver, PICHT Peter, PULYER Boris, ULLRICH Hanns, "Comments of the Max Planck Institute for Intellectual Property,

Competition and Tax Law on the Draft Commission Block Exemption Regulation on Research and Development Agreements and the Draft Guidelines on Horizontal Cooperation Agreements," Max Planck Institute for Intellectual Property, Competition & Tax Law Research Paper Series No. 10-12, (2010), pp. 1-22. Available at: http://ec.europa.eu/competition/consultations/2010_horizontals/max_planck_institute_en.pdf (last accessed on March 31, 2018). [cited as: DREXL ET AL., 2010].

DRUSS Benjamin G., MARCUS Steven C., OLFSON Mark, PINCUS Harold Alan, "Listening to Generic Prozac: Winners, Losers, and Sideliners," 23:5 *Health Affairs* 210, (September/October 2004), pp. 210-216. [cited as: DRUSS ET AL., Prozac, 2004].

EDLIN Aaron S., HEMPHILL Scott C., HOVENKAMP Herbert J., SHAPIRO Carl, "Activating Actavis," 28:1 *Antitrust Magazine* (Fall 2013), pp. 16-23. [cited as: EDLIN, HEMPHILL, HOVENKAMP, SHAPIRO, Activating Actavis, 2013].

EDLIN Aaron S., HEMPHILL Scott C., HOVENKAMP Herbert J., SHAPIRO Carl, "The Actavis Inference: Theory and Practice," 67:3 *Rutgers U. L. Rev.* 585, Spring 2015, pp. 585-635. [cited as: EDLIN, HEMPHILL, HOVENKAMP, SHAPIRO, Actavis Inference, 2015].

EISENBERG Rebecca S., "The Problem of New Uses," 5 *Yale J. Health Pol'y, L. & Ethics* 717, (Summer 2005), pp. 717-739. [cited as: EISENBERG, 2005].

ELHAUGE Einer, KRUEGER Alex, "Solving the Patent Settlement Puzzle," 91 *Tex. L. Rev.* 283, (2012), pp. 283-330. [cited as: ELHAUGE, KRUEGER, Patent Settlement Puzzle, 2012].

FARRELL Joseph, SHAPIRO Carl, "How Strong Are Weak Patents?," 98:4 *Am. Econ. Rev.* 1347, (September 2008), pp. 1347-1369. [cited as: FARRELL, SHAPIRO, Weak Patents, 2008].

FELDMAN Robin, "Ending Patent Exceptionalism and Structuring the Rule of Reason: The Supreme Court Opens the Door for Both," 15:1 *Minn. J.L. Sci. & Tech.* 61, pp. 61-76 (2014). [cited as: FELDMAN, Patent Exceptionalism, 2014].

FISHER Ellison Sara, COCKBURN Iain, GRILICHES Zvi, HAUSMAN Jerry, "Characteristics of Demand for Pharmaceutical Products: An Examination of Four Cephalosporins," 28:3 *Rand J. Econ.* 426, (Autumn 1997), pp. 426-446. [cited as: FISHER, COCKBURN, GRILICHES, HAUSMAN, Demand, 1997].

FISHER LIETZAN Erika, "The Uncharted Waters of Competition and Innovation in Biological Medicines," 44 *Fla. St. U. L. Rev.*, 2017, Forthcoming. pp. 1-63. Draft available at SSRN: https://papers.ssrn.com/sol3/papers.cfm?abstract_id=2848606 (last accessed on March 31, 2018). [Cited as FISHER LIETZAN, 2017].

FISS Owen M., "Against Settlement," 93:6 *Yale L. J.* 1073, (May 1984), pp. 1073-1090. [cited as: FISS, Against Settlement, 1984].

FRANK Richard G., "Editorial: New Estimates of Drug Development Costs," 22 *J. Health Econ.* 325, (2003), pp. 325-330. [cited as: FRANK, New Estimates, 2003].

FRANK Richard G., "The Ongoing Regulation of Generic Drugs," 357 *New. Eng. J. Med.* 1993, (2007), pp. 1993-1996. [cited as: FRANK, 2007].

GAL Michal S., MILLER Alan, "Patent Challenge Clauses: A New Antitrust Offense?," 102:4 *Iowa L. Rev.* 1477, pp. 1477-1532, (May 2017). [cited as: GAL, MILLER, Challenge Clauses, 2017].

GALANTER Mark, "The Vanishing Trial: an Examination of Trials and Related Matters in Federal and State Courts," 1:3 *J. Empirical Leg. Stud.* 459, (November 2004), pp. 459-570. [cited as: GALANTER, Vanishing Trial, 2004].

GALANTER Mark, "A World Without Trials?," 2006:1 *J. Dis. Res.* 7, (2006), pp. 7-33. [cited as: GALANTER, World Without Trials, 2006].

GALLASCH Sven, "A New Dimension to EU Pharma Antitrust Product-Hopping and Unilateral Pay-for-Delay," 12:1 *Eur. Competition J.* 137, pp. 137-158. [cited as: GALLASCH, 2016].

GERADIN Damien, "The Uncertainties Created by Relying on the Vague 'Competition on the Merits' Standard in the Pharmaceutical Sector: The Italian Pfizer/Pharmacia Case," 5:6 *J. Eur. Competition L. & Prac.* 344, (2014), pp. 344-352. [cited as GERADIN, Pfizer/Pharmacia, 2014].

GHOSH Shubha, "Convergence?," 15:1 *Minn. J. L. Sci. & Tech.* 95, (2014), pp. 95-113). [cited as: GHOSH, Convergence, 2014].

GIACCOTTO Carmelo, SANTERRE Rexford, VERNON John, "Explaining Pharmaceutical R&D Growth Rates at the Industry Level: New Perspectives and Insights," Related Publication 03-31, (December 2003), pp. 1-21, [cited as: GIACCOTTO, SANTERRE, VERNON, R&D Growth Rates, 2003].

GINSBURG Douglas H., WONG-ERVIN Koren W., WRIGHT Joshua D., "Product-Hopping and the Limits of Antitrust: The Danger of Micromanaging Innovation," 12 *CPI Antitrust Chron.* 1, (December 2015), pp. 1-5. [cited as: GINSBURG, WONG-ERVIN, WRIGHT, Micromanaging Innovation, 2015].

GOODMAN Marc, NACHMAN Gary, CHEN Louise, "Quantifying the Impact from Authorized Generics," 9 *Morgan Stanley Research Report* 2004. [cited as: GOODMAN ET AL., 2004].

GRABOWSKI Kevin, LEWIS Tracy, GUHA Rahul, IVANOVA Zoya, SALGADO Maria, WOODHOUSE Sally, "Does Generic Entry Always Increase Consumer Welfare?," 67:3 *Food & Drug L. J.* 373, (2012), pp. 373-391. [cited as: GRABOWSKI ET AL., Consumer Welfare, 2012].

GRAGLIA Lino A., "Leegin Creative Leather Products Inc. v. PSKS, Inc.: The Strange Career of the Law of Resale Price Maintenance," 53 *Antitrust Bull.* 803 (2008), pp. 803-847. [cited as: GRAGLIA, Leegin Creative, 2007].

GRAHAM Joel, "The Legality of Hatch-Waxman Pharmaceutical Settlements: Is the Terazosin Test the Proper Prescription?," 84 *Wash. U. L. Rev.* 429 (2006), pp. 429-459. [cited as: GRAHAM, Terazosin Test, 2006].

GRAHAM Stuart J.H., VAN ZEEBROECK Nicolas, "Comparing Patent Litigation Across Europe: A First Look," 17 *Stan. Tech. L. Rev.* 655, (2014), pp. 655-708. [cited as: GRAHAM, VAN ZEEBROECK, Patent Litigation Across Europe, 2014].

GREENAWAY Sean, JAKAB Erika, JOHANSSON Dag; KUNDAN Jasmin, "Recent Commission Merger Control Decisions in the Pharmaceutical Sector: Sanofi-Aventis/Zentiva and Teva/Barr," 2 Competition Policy Newsletter 64, (2009), pp. 64-67. Available at: http://ec.europa.eu/competition/publications/cpn/ (last accessed on March 31, 2018). [cited as: GREENAWAY, JAKAB, JOHANSSON, KUNDAN, 2009].

GROSS Samuel R., SYVERUD Kent D., "Getting to No: A Study of Settlement Negotiations and the Selection of Cases for Trial," 90 *Mich. L. Rev.* 319, (1991), pp. 319-393. [cited as: GROSS, SYVERUD, Getting to No, 1991].

GUHA Rahul, LACY Andrew M., WOODHOUSE Sally, "Analyzing Competition in the Pharmaceutical Industry," 8:1 American Bar Association Section of Antitrust Law Economics Committee Newsletter 6, (Spring 2008) pp. 6-9. [cited as: GUHA, LACY, WOODHOUSE, Competition, 2008].

HAN Minsuk, "A Two-Branched Attack on the Jury Right in Patent Litigation," 99:3 *Cornell L. Rev.* 659, (March 2014), pp. 659-684. [cited as: HAN M., Jury Right in Patent Litigation, 2014].

HAN Shannon U., "Pay-to-Delay Settlements: The Circuit-Splitting Headache Plaguing Big Pharma," 15:4 *Vand. J. Ent. & Tech. L.* 913, (2013), pp. 913-947. [cited as: HAN, Circuit-Splitting Headache, 2013].

HANKS Kendyl, JACOBSON Sarah, MUSGROVE Kyle, SHEN Michael, "Pay-for-Delay Settlements: Antitrust Violation or Proper Exercise of Pharmaceutical Patent Rights?," *Business Law Today, American Bar Association*, (January 2011). Available at: http://www.americanbar.org/publications/blt/2011/01/02_hanks.html. (last accessed on March 31, 2018) [cited as: HANKS, JACOBSON, MUSGROVE, SHEN, Proper Exercise, 2011].

HARRIS Barry C., MURPHY Kevin M., WILLIG Robert D., WRIGHT Matthew B., "Activating Actavis: A More Complete Story," 28 *Antitrust* 83, (Spring 2014), pp. 83-89. [cited as: HARRIS, MURPHY, WILLIG, WRIGHT, Activating Actavis, 2014].

HASTINGS Ian, "Dynamic Innovative Efficiency in Pharmaceutical Patent Settlements," 13:1 *N. C. J. L. & Tech.* 31, (Fall 2011), pp. 31-68. [cited as: HASTINGS, Dynamic Innovative Efficiency, 2011].

HELED Yaniv, "Regulatory Competitive Shelters," 76 *Ohio St. L.J.* 299, (2015), pp. 299-356. [cited as: HELED, 2015].

HELLER Al, "A Pivotal Year for Generics Pricing," *Drug Store News*, (February 15, 1999) Available at: http://business.highbeam.com/413375/article-1G1-53989656/1999-pivotal-year-generics-pricing. (last accessed on March 31, 2018) [cited as: HELLER, Pivotal Year, 1999].

HEMPHILL Scott C., "Paying for Delay: Pharmaceutical Patent Settlement as a Regulatory Design Problem," 81 *NYULR* 1553, (November 2006), pp. 1553-1623. [cited as: HEMPHILL, Paying for Delay, 2006].

HEMPHILL Scott C., "Drug Patent Settlements Between Rivals: A Survey," Working Paper (March 13, 2007; last revised on December 28, 2013), pp. 1-49, Available at: http://papers.ssrn.com/sol3/papers.cfm?abstract_id=969492. (last accessed on March 31, 2018) [cited as: HEMPHILL, Drug Patent Settlements, 2007].

HEMPHILL Scott C., "An Aggregate Approach to Antitrust: Using New Data and Rulemaking to Preserve Drug Competition," 109:4 *Colum. L. Rev.* 629, (May 2009), pp. 629-688. [cited as: HEMPHILL, Aggregate Approach, 2009].

HEMPHILL Scott C., LEMLEY Mark A., "Earning Exclusivity: Generic Drug Incentives and the Hatch-Waxman Act," 77:3 *Antitrust L. J.* 947, (2011), pp. 947-989. [cited as: HEMPHILL, LEMLEY, Earning Exclusivity, 2011].

HEMPHILL Scott C., SAMPAT Bhaven N., "Evergreening, Patent Challenges and Effective Market Life in Pharmaceuticals," 31 *J. Health Econ.* 327, (March 2012), pp. 327-339. [cited as: HEMPHILL, SAMPAT, Evergreening, 2012].

HENRY Matthew D., "The Market Effects of Patent Litigation," 4:1 *Tech. & Inv.* 57, (2013), pp. 57-68. [cited as: HENRY, Market Effects, 2013].

HENNINGSSON Kristian, "Injunctions for Standard-Essential Patents under FRAND Commitment: A Balanced, Royalty-Oriented Approach," 47:4 *IIC* 438, (2016), pp. 438-469. [cited as: HENNINGSSON, FRAND, 2016].

HERMANN Michael R., "The Stay Dilemma: Examining Brand and Generic Incentives for Delaying the Resolution of Pharmaceutical Patent Litigation," 111 *Colum. L. Rev.* 1788, (2011), pp. 1788-1832. [cited as: HERMANN, 2011].

HERPER Matthew, "The Cost of Developing Drugs is Insane. That Paper that Says Otherwise Is Insanely Bad," Forbes, October 16, 2017. Available at: https://www.forbes.com/sites/matthewherper/2017/10/16/the-cost-of-developing-drugs-is-insane-a-paper-that-argued-otherwise-was-insanely-bad/#57057afa2d45 (last accessed on March 31, 2018). [cited as: HERPER, 2017].

HIRSCH Bradford R., BALU Suresh, Schulman Kevin A., "The Impact of Specialty Pharmaceuticals as Drivers of Health Care Costs," 33:10 *Health Affairs* 1714, (2014), pp. 1714-1720. [cited as: HIRSCH, BALU, Specialty Pharmaceuticals, 2014].

Ho Cynthia M., "Should All Drugs Be Patentable? A Comparative Perspective," 17 *Vand. J. Ent. & Tech. L.* 295, Winter 2015, pp. 295-384. [cited as: Ho, Patentable, 2015].

HOVENKAMP Erik, "Challenge Restraints and the Scope of the Patent," 1 *CPI Antitrust Chron.* 48, (Winter 2016), pp. 48-55. [cited as: HOVENKAMP E., Challenge Restraints, 2016].

HOVENKAMP Herbert J., JANIS M., LEMLEY Mark A., "Anticompetitive Settlements of Intellectual Property Disputes," 87 *Minn. L. Rev.* 1719, (June 2003), pp. 1719-1766. [cited as: HOVENKAMP, JANIS, LEMLEY, Anticompetitive Settlements, 2003].

HOVENKAMP Herbert J., "Competitor Collaboration after California Dental Association," 2000:1 *University of Chicago Legal Forum* 149, (2000), pp. 149-189. [cited as: HOVENKAMP, California Dental, 2000].

HOVENKAMP Herbert J., "Sensible Antitrust Rules for Pharmaceutical Competition," 39 *U.S.F.L. Rev.* 11, (Fall 2004), pp. 11-31. [cited as: HOVENKAMP, Sensible Antitrust Rules, 2004].

HOVENKAMP Herbert J., "Restraints on Innovation," 29:1 *Cardozo L. Rev.* 247, (2007), pp. 247-260. [cited as: HOVENKAMP, Restraints, 2007].

HOVENKAMP Herbert J., "Leegin, the Rule of Reason, and Vertical Agreement," University of Iowa Legal Studies Research Paper, Number 10-40, (December 2010) (revised), pp. 1-14. Available at SSRN: http://ssrn.com/abstract=1673519 or http://dx.doi.org/10.2139/ssrn.1673519 (last accessed on March 31, 2018). [cited as: HOVENKAMP, Leegin, 2010].

HOVENKAMP Herbert J., "Antitrust and Patent Law Analysis of Pharmaceutical Reverse Payment Settlements," (January 15, 2011). Available at SSRN: http://ssrn.com/abstract=1741162 or http://dx.doi.org/10.2139/ssrn.1741162 (last accessed on March 31, 2018). [cited as: HOVENKAMP, Reverse Payment, 2011].

Bibliography

HOVENKAMP Herbert J., "Implementing Antitrust's Welfare Goals," 81:5 *Fordham L. Rev.* 2471, (2013), pp. 2471-2496. [cited as: HOVENKAMP, Antitrust's Welfare Goals, 2013].

HOVENKAMP Herbert J., "Anticompetitive Patent Settlements and the Supreme Court's Actavis Decision," 15:1 *Minn. J. L. Sci. & Tech.* 3, (2014), pp. 3-30. [cited as: HOVENKAMP, Actavis, 2014].

HOVENKAMP Herbert J., "The Rule of Reason and the Scope of the Patent," University of Iowa, Legal Studies Research Paper, No. 14-29, 52 *San Diego L. Rev.* 515, pp. 515-554, (2015). [cited as: HOVENKAMP, Scope of the Patent, 2015].

HOVENKAMP Herbert J., "Antitrust and the Patent System: a Reexamination," 76:3 *Ohio State L. J.* 467, (2015), pp. 467-564. [cited as: HOVENKAMP, Reexamination, 2015].

HUBBARD Tim, LOVE James, "A New Trade Framework for Global Healthcare R&D," 2:2 *PLoS Biology* 0147, (February 2004), pp. 0147-0150. [cited as: HUBBARD, LOVE, Healthcare R&D, 2004].

HUGHES Dyfrig, FERNER Robin, "New Drugs for Old: Disinvestment and NICE," 340 *BMJ* (formerly the British Medical Journal) 690, (March 27, 2010), pp. 690-692. [cited as: HUGHES, FERNER, Disinvestment and NICE, 2010].

IBÁÑEZ COLOMO Pablo, "Beyond the 'More Economics-Based Approach': A Legal Perspective on Article 102 TFEU Case Law," Forthcoming in (2016) 53 *Com. Mkt. L. Rev.*, (2016), pp.709-740, [cited as: IBÁÑEZ COLOMO, 2016].

JACOBO-RUBIO Ruben, TURNER John L., WILLIAMS Jonathan W., "Generic Entry, Pay-for-Delay Settlements, and the Distribution of Surplus in the U.S. Pharmaceutical Industry," (March 28, 2016), pp. 1-42. Available at: http://www.economics.illinois.edu/seminars/documents/Turner.Pdf. (last accessed on March 31, 2018) [cited as: JACOBO-RUBIO, TURNER, WILLIAMS, 2016].

JACOBO-RUBIO Ruben, TURNER John L., WILLIAMS Jonathan W., "The Distribution of Surplus in the U.S. Pharmaceutical Industry: Evidence from Paragraph (iv) Patent Litigation Decisions," (March 15, 2017), pp. 1-47. Available at: https://papers.ssrn.com/sol3/papers.cfm?abstract_id=2481908. (last accessed on March 31, 2018). [cited as: JACOBO-RUBIO, TURNER, WILLIAMS, 2017].

JESSE Vivian C., "Generic Substitution Laws," *U.S. Pharmacist* (2008). Available at: http://www.uspharmacist.com/content/s/44/c/9787. (last accessed on March 31, 2018). [cited as: JESSE, Generic Substitution, 2008].

JONES Alison, KOVACIC William E., "Identifying Anticompetitive Agreements in the United States and the European Union: Developing a Coherent Antitrust Analytical Framework," 62 *Antitrust Bull.* 254, (2017), pp. 254-293. [cited as: JONES, KOVACIC, Anticompetitive Agreements, 2017].

KAPCZYNSKI Amy, SYED Talha, "The Continuum of Excludability and the Limits of Patents," 122 *The Yale L. J.* 1900, (2013), pp. 1900-1963. [cited as: KAPCZYNSKI, SYED, Continuum of Excludability, 2013].

KARST Kurt. R., "When Is 5-year NCE Exclusivity Less than 5 Years," HPM Website, FDA Law Blog, January 9, 2013. Available at: http://www.fdalawblog.net/fda_law_blog_hyman_phelps/2013/01/when-is-5-year-nce-exclusivity-less-than-5-years.html. (last accessed on March 31, 2018). [cited as: KARST, 2013].

KARST Kurt. R., "The Generic Drug Labeling Carve-Out Score Board," September 2, 2014, listing FDA Citizen Petition Responses & Letter Decisions Permitting a Labeling Carve-out. Available at: http://www.fdalawblog.net/fda_law_blog_hyman_phelps/2014/09/the-generic-drug-labeling-carve-out-scorecard.html. (last accessed on March 31, 2018). [cited as: KARST, 2014].

KASTEN Tim, "The French Supreme Court Confirms Fines Imposed on Undertaking for Abusive Limitation of Generic Entry (Sanofi-Aventis)," October 18, 2016, e-Competitions Bulletin November 2016, Art. N° 81972. [cited as: KASTEN, Sanofi-Aventis, 2016].

KENDALL Brent, "DoJ Shifts Policy on Generic Drug Patent Settlements," *Wall St. J.*, (July 6, 2009). Available at: http://www.wsj.com/articles/SB124691728092502381 (last accessed on March 31, 2018). [cited as: KENDALL, DoJ Shifts Policy, 2009].

KENT Bernard, "The AstraZeneca Decision of the General Court: Some Basic Observations and a Few Interesting Questions," 2 *CPI Antitrust J.* 1, September 2010, pp. 1-8. [cited as: KENT, 2010].

KESAN Jay P., BALL Gwendolyn G., "How Are Patent Cases Resolved? An Empirical Examination of the Adjudication and Settlement of Patent Disputes," 84:2 *Wash. U. L. Rev.* 237, (2006), pp. 237-312. [cited as: KESAN, BALL, Patent Disputes, 2006].

KESSELHEIM Aaron S., TAN Yongtian Tina, AVORN Jerry, "The Roles of Academia, Rare Diseases, and Repurposing in the Development of the Most Transformative Drugs," 34:2 *Health Affairs* 286, (February 2015), pp. 286-293. [cited as: KESSELHEIM, TAN, AVORN, Transformative Drugs, 2015].

KHATIBIFAR Tania, "The Need for a Patent-Centric Standard of Antitrust Review to Evaluate Reverse Payment Settlements," 23 *Fordham Intell. Prop. Media & Entert. L. J.* 1351, (May 17, 2013), pp. 1351-1394. [cited as: KHATIBIFAR, Patent-Centric Standard, 2013].

KHOURY Amir H., "Differential Patent Terms and the Commercial Capacity of Innovation," 18 *Tex. Intell. Prop. L. J.* 373, (Spring 2010), pp. 373-417. [cited as: KHOURY, Differential Patent Terms, 2010].

KILLICK James, JOURDAN Jérémie, DICKINSON Jerome, "The Commission's Lundbeck Decision: A Critical Review of the Commission's Test for Patent Settlement Agreements," *CPI*, February 24, 2015. Available at: https://www.competitionpolicyinternational.com/the-commissions-lundbeck-decision-a-critical-review-of-the-commissions-test-for-patent-settlement-agreements/ (last accessed on March 31, 2018). [cited as: KILLICK, JOURDAN, DICKINSON, Lundbeck, 2015].

KIM Marhi, SCHWARZ Bryan, "Economic Prizes: a New Model for Pharmaceutical Innovations," 6 *Asper Rev. Int'l Bus. & Trade L.* 1, (2005), pp. 1-63. [cited as: KIM, SCHWARZ, Economic Prizes, 2005].

KNUCKLES Ann L., "Reverse Payment Settlements: The Ongoing Dilemma After FTC v. Actavis," 8 *Brook. J. Corp. Fin. & Com. L.* 516, (Spring 2014), pp. 532-537. [cited as: KNUCKLES, Ongoing Dilemma, 2014].

KOBAYASHI Bruce H., WRIGHT Joshua D., GINSBURG Douglas H., TSAI Joanna, "Actavis and Multiple ANDA Entrants: Beyond the Temporary Duopoly," 29:2 *Antitrust*

Magazine 89, Spring 2015, pp. 89-97. [cited as: KOBAYASHI, WRIGHT, GINSBURG, TSAI, Multiple ANDA, 2015].

KORN David E., LIETZAN Erika, SHAW Scott W., "A New History and Discussion of 180-Day Exclusivity," 64 *Food & Drug L.J.* 335 (2009), pp. 335-390. [cited as: KORN ET AL., 2009].

KOVACIC William E., WINERMAN Marc, "The Federal Trade Commission as an Independent Agency: Autonomy, Legitimacy and Effectiveness," 100 *Iowa L. Rev.* 2085, (2015), pp. 2085-2113. [cited as: KOVACIC, WINERMAN, FTC, 2015].

KRUEGER Alexander, "Implementing Actavis: Three Tips for Future Courts Assessing Reverse Patent Settlements under the Rule of Reason," 15:1 *Minn. J. L. Sci. & Tech.* 115, (2014), pp. 115-121. [cited as: KRUEGER, Implementing Actavis, 2014].

KURLANDER David C., "Rebalancing Pay-For-Delay: Why No-Authorized Generic Commitments Should be Subject to Higher Antitrust Scrutiny," 32:1 *Cardozo Arts & Entert. L. J.* 683, pp. 683-715 (2015). [cited as: KURLANDER, Rebalancing Pay-For-Delay, 2015].

KUTCHER Marlee P., "Waiting Is the Hardest Part: Why the Supreme Court Should Adopt the Third Circuit's Analysis of Pay-for-Delay Settlement Agreements," 44 *Loy. U. Chi. L.J.* 1093, (Summer 2013), pp. 1093-1151. [cited as: KUTCHER, Waiting Is the Hardest Part, 2013].

LANGENFELD James, WENQING Li, "Intellectual Property and Agreements to Settle Patent Disputes: The Case of Settlement Agreements With Payments From Branded to Generic Drug Manufacturers," 70 *Antitrust L.J.* 777, (2003), pp. 777-818. [cited as: LANGENFELD, WENQING, Settlement Agreements With Payments, 2003].

LANGINIER Corinne, GIANCARLO Moschini, "The Economics of Patents: an Overview," Working Paper 02-WP 293, CARD Working Papers, Paper 335, Iowa State University, (2002), pp. 1-24. Available at: http://lib.dr.iastate.edu/card_workingpapers/335 (last accessed on March 31, 2018). [cited as: LANGINIER, GIANCARLO, Economics of Patents, 2002].

LANJOUW Jean O., SCHANKERMAN Mark, "Characteristics of Patent Litigation: A Window on Competition," 32:1 *The RAND J. Econ.* 129, (Spring 2001), pp. 129-151. [cited as: LANJOUW, SCHANKERMAN, Characteristics of Patent Litigation, 2001].

LARRIMORE Lisa Quellete, "How Many Patents does it Take to Make a Drug: Follow-on Pharmaceutical Patents and University Licensing," 17:1 *Mich. Telecomm. & Tech. L. Rev.* 299, (2010), pp. 299-336. [cited as: LARRIMORE, Follow-on Patents, 2010].

LEARY Thomas B., "Antitrust Issues in the Settlement of Pharmaceutical Patent Disputes," Part III, 30 *Seattle U. L. Rev.* 377, (Winter 2007), pp. 377-393. [cited as: LEARY, Antitrust Issues, 2007].

LEFFLER Keith, LEFFLER Christopher, "Want to Pay a Competitor to Exit the Market? Settle a Patent Infringement Case," 2:1 ABA Section of Antitrust Law Economics Committee Newsletter, (Spring 2002). [cited as: LEFFLER & LEFFLER, Pay a Competitor, 2002].

LEFFLER Keith, LEFFLER Christopher, "The Probabilistic Nature of Patent Rights: In Response to Kevin McDonald," 17 *Antitrust ABA* 77 (Summer 2003), pp. 77-82. [cited as: LEFFLER & LEFFLER, Response to Kevin McDonald, 2003].

LEMLEY Mark A., "Rational Ignorance at the Patent Office," 95:4 *Nw. U. L. Rev.* 1495, (Summer 2001), pp. 1459-1532. [cited as: LEMLEY, Rational Ignorance, 2001].

LEMLEY Mark A., SHAPIRO Carl, "Probabilistic Patents," 19:2 *J. Econ. Persps.* 75, (Spring 2005), pp. 75-98. [cited as: LEMLEY, SHAPIRO, Probabilistic Patents, 2005].

LEMLEY Mark A., "Industry-Specific Antitrust Policy for Innovation," Stanford Law and Economics Olin Working Paper No. 397, (September 2010), pp. 1-15. Available at SSRN: https://ssrn.com/abstract=1670197 (last accessed on March 31, 2018). [cited as: LEMLEY, Industry-Specific, 2010].

LEMLEY Mark A., LESLIE Christopher R., "Categorical Analysis in Antitrust Jurisprudence," 93 *Iowa L. Rev.* 1207, (May 2008), pp. 1207-1270. [cited as: LEMLEY, LESLIE, Categorical Analysis, 2008].

LEMLEY Mark A., KENDALL Jamie, MARTIN Clint, "Rush to Judgment? Trial Length and Outcomes in Patent Cases," 41:2 *AIPLA Q. J.* 169, (Spring 2013), pp. 169-204. [cited as: LEMLEY, KENDALL, MARTIN, Rush to Judgment, 2013].

LEMLEY Mark A., "Why Do Juries Decide if Patents are Valid?," 99:8 *Va. L. Rev.* 1673, (December 2013), pp. 1727-1733. [cited as: LEMLEY, Juries, 2013].

LIGHT Donald W., "Misleading Congress About Drug Development," 32:5 *J. Health Pol., Policy & L.* 895, October 2007, pp. 895-913. [cited as: LIGHT, Misleading Congress, 2007].

LOVE James, HUBBARD Tim, "The Big Idea: Prizes to Stimulate R&D for New Medicines," 82:3 *Chi.-Kent L. Rev.* 1519, (2007), pp. 1519-1554. [cited as: LOVE, HUBBARD, Prizes, 2007].

LUGARD Paul, "The New EU Technology Transfer Regime: Like a Rolling Stone?," 95 *Digiworld Econ. J.* 41, (3rd Q. 2014), pp. 41-59. [cited as: LUGARD, 2014].

LYNDON Mary L., "Secrecy and Innovation in Tort Law and Regulation," 23 *New Mexico L. Rev.* 1, (1993), pp. 1-55. [cited as: LYNDON, Secrecy and Innovation, 1993].

MAIORANA David R., OLIVER Geoffrey D., DELUARD Ausra O., "Antitrust Analyses of Patent Acquisitions – Quid Novi?," Jones Day Publications, 2012. Available at: http://awa2013.concurrences.com/business-articles-awards/article/antitrust-analyses-of-patent#nb5 (last accessed on March 31, 2018). [cited as: MAIORANA, OLIVER, DELUARD, Patent Acquisitions, 2012].

MANN Ronald J., UNDERWEISER Marian, "A New Look at Patent Quality: Relating Patent Prosecution to Validity," 9:1 *J. Empirical Leg. Stud.* 1, (March 2012), pp. 1-32. [cited as: MANN, UNDERWEISER, Patent Quality, 2012].

MANSFIELD Edwin, SCHWARTZ Mark, WAGNER Samuel, "Imitation Costs and Patents: An Empirical Study," 91:364 *Econ. J.* 907, (1981), pp. 907–918. [cited as: MANSFIELD, SCHWARTZ, WAGNER, Imitation Costs, 1981].

MARCO Alan C., VISHNUBHAKAT Saurabh, "Certain Patents," 16 *Yale J.L. & Tech.* 132, (2013), pp. 103-133. [cited as: MARCO, VISHNUBHAKAT, Certain Patents, 2013].

MC DONALD Kevin D., "Patent Settlements and Payments that Flow the 'Wrong' Way: The Early History of a Bad Idea," 15:4 *ABA Sec. Antitrust L. Healthcare Chron.* 1, (Winter 2002), pp. 1-14. [cited as: MCDONALD, Wrong Way, 2002].

MCDONALD Kevin D., "Hatch-Waxman Patent Settlements and Antitrust: On 'Probabilistic' Patent Rights and False Positives," 17:2 *Antitrust* 68, (Spring 2003), pp. 68-76. [cited as: MCDONALD, False Positives, 2003].

MCDONALD Kevin D., "Because I Said So: On the Competitive Rationale of FTC v. Actavis," 28:1 *Antitrust* 36 (Fall 2013), pp. 36-44. [cited as: MCDONALD, I Said So, 2013].

MCDONALD Stuart, "All my Own Work: Intellectual Property Rights and the Reinvention of Innovation," 35:1 *E.I.P.R.* 4, (2013), pp. 4-14. [cited as: MCDONALD S., Reinvention of Innovation, 2013].

MCKENNA Cameron, "Off-Label Reimbursement: A New Method for Reducing Drug Prices?," Lexology, February 20, 2015. Available at: http://www.lexology.com/library/detail.aspx?g=7473c2eb-16d6-431a-ad88-4c927f65f32b. (last accessed on March 31, 2018). [cited as: MCKENNA, Off-Label Reimbursement, 2015].

MEADOWS Michelle, "Greater Access to Generic Drugs: New FDA Initiatives to Improve Generic Drug Reviews and Reduce Legal Loopholes," *FDA Consumer Article*, September/October 2003. Available at: http://www.fda.gov/drugs/resourcesforyou/ucm134448.htm. (last accessed on March 31, 2018). [cited as: MEADOWS, 2003].

MOORE Kimberly A., "Judges, Juries, and Patent Cases – An Empirical Peek Inside the Black Box," 99 *Mich. L. Rev.* 365, (November 2000), pp. 365-409. [cited as: MOORE, Empirical Peek, 2000].

MOORE Kimberly A., "Worthless Patents," 20:4 *Berkeley Tech. L. J.* 1521 (September 2005), pp. 1521-1552. [cited as: MOORE, Worthless Patents, 2005].

MORRISON Alan, "Commentary: Subjecting Reverse Payments in Patent Cases to Antitrust Scrutiny: Sounds Like a Good Idea, but Can it Work?," posted on SCOTUSblog (July 25, 2013). Available at: http://www.scotusblog.com/2013/07/commentary-subjecting-reverse-payments-in-patent-cases-to-antitrust-scrutiny-sounds-like-a-good-idea-but-can-it-work/ (last accessed on March 31, 2018). [cited as: MORRISON, Antitrust Scrutiny, 2013].

MORSE Howard M., "Product Market Definition in the Pharmaceutical Industry," 71:2 *Antitrust L.J.* 633, (2003), pp. 633-676. [cited as: MORSE, Product Market Definition, 2003].

MUNGAN Murat C., "Reverse Payments, Perverse Incentives," 27 *Harv. J.L. & Tech.* 1 (Fall 2013), pp. 1-46. [cited as: MUNGAN, Perverse Incentives, 2013].

MUSCOLO Gabriella, "Recent Developments in European and National Patent Law and Case Law: Decision of 27 February 2014 in Roche-Novartis," *Official J. EPO*, Supplementary Publication, 5/2015, pp. 211-222. Available at: https://www.epo.org/law-practice/legal-texts/official-journal/2015/etc/se5/p211.html (last accessed on March 31, 2018). [cited as: MUSCOLO, Roche-Novartis, 2015].

NAGY CSONGOR István, "The New Concept of Anti-competitive Object: A Loose Cannon in EU Competition Law," 36:4 *E.C.L.R.* 154, pp. 154-159. [cited as: NAGY CSONGOR, 2015].

NOAH Lars, "Product-Hopping 2.0: Getting the FDA To Yank Your Original License Beats Stacking Patents," 19:2 *Marq. IP L. Rev.* 161 (2015), pp. 161-179. [cited as: NOAH, Product-Hopping, 2015].

ODUDU Okeoghene, BAILEY David, "The Single Economic Entity Doctrine in EU," 51 *Competition L. Com. Mkt. L. Rev.* 1721, (2014), pp. 1721-1758. [cited as: ODUDU, BAILEY, 2014].

OHLHAUSEN Maureen K., "Patent Rights in a Climate of Intellectual Property Rights Skepticism," 30:1 *Harv. J. L. & Tech.* 103, (Fall 2016), pp. 103-152. [cited as: OHLHAUSEN, IP Skepticism, 2016].

OKADA Seiko F., "In Re K-Dur Antitrust Litigation: Pharmaceutical Reverse Payment Settlements Go Beyond the Scope of the Patent," 14 *N.C. J. L. & Tech.* 303, (Fall 2012), pp. 303-340. [cited as: OKADA, Beyond the Scope, 2012].

OLSON Luke M., WENDLING Brett W., FTC, "Estimating the Effect of Entry on Generic Drug Prices Using Hatch-Waxman Exclusivity," Working Paper No. 317, (April 2013), pp. 1-32. Available at: https://www.ftc.gov/reports/estimating-effect-entry-generic-drug-prices-using-hatch-waxman-exclusivity (last accessed on March 31, 2018). [cited as: OLSON, WENDLING, Effect of Entry, 2013].

ORIOLA Taiwo A., "Strong Medicine: Patents, Market, and Policy Challenges for Managing Neglected Diseases and Affordable Prescription Drugs," 7 *Can. J. L. & Tech.* 57, (April 2009), pp. 57-123. [cited as: ORIOLA, Strong Medicine, 2009].

O'ROURKE Maureen A., BRODLEY Joseph F., "Preliminary Views: Patent Settlement Agreements," 16 *Antitrust* 53, (Summer 2002), pp. 53-57. [cited as: O'ROURKE, BRODLEY, Preliminary Views, 2002].

ORTEGA GONZALEZ, Angela, "Restrictions by Object and the Appreciability Test: The Expedia Case, a Surprising Judgment or a Simple Clarification?," 34:9 *E.C.L.R.* 457, (2013), pp. 457-465. [cited as: ORTEGA GONZALEZ, 2013].

OSTROFF Steven, *Building a Modern Generic Drug Review Process*, FDA Blog, (February 4, 2016). Available at: https://blogs.fda.gov/fdavoice/index.php/2016/02/building-a-modern-generic-drug-review-process/ (last accessed on March 31, 2018). [cited as: OSTROFF, Generic Drug Review, 2016].

OUTTERSON Kevin, "Patent Buy-Outs for Global Disease Innovations for Low – and Middle – Income Countries," 32 *Am. J. L. & Med.* 159, (2006), pp. 159-173. [cited as: OUTTERSON, Patent Buy-Outs, 2006].

OWENS Michael, "Cure for Collusive Settlements: The Case for a Per Se Prohibition on Pay-for-Delay Agreements in Pharmaceutical Patent Litigation A.," 78:4 *Mo. L. Rev.* 1353, (Fall 2013), pp. 1353-1399. [cited as: OWENS, Per Se Prohibition, 2013].

PANATONNI Laura E., "The Effect of Paragraph IV Decisions and Generic Entry Before Patent Expiration on Brand Pharmaceutical Firms," 30 *J. Health Econ.* 126, (2011), pp. 126-145. [cited as: PANATONNI, Generic Entry, 2011].

PATEL Ankur N., "Delayed Access to Generic Medicine: A Comment on the Hatch-Waxman Act and the Approval Bottleneck," 78 *Fordham L. Rev.* 1075, (2009), pp. 1075-1115. [cited as: PATEL, 2009].

PAUL Steven M., MYTELKA Daniel S., DUNWIDDIE Christopher T., PERSINGER Charles C., MUNOS Bernard H., LINDBORG Stacy R., SCHACHT Aaron L., "How to Improve R&D Productivity: The Pharmaceutical Industry's Grand Challenge," 9 *Nature Reviews Drug Discovery* 203, (March 2010), pp. 203-214. [cited as: PAUL ET AL., R&D Productivity, 2010].

PAZZI Maria Gaia, "The Review of the De Minimis Notice," 3 *Rivista Italiana di Antitrust* 245, (2014), pp. 246-249. [cited as: PAZZI, 2014].

PEEPERKORN Luc, VEROUDEN Vincent, "The Economics of Competition," Chapter 1 *in* FAULL Jonathan, NIKPAY Ali (eds), *The EU Law of Competition*, 3rd ed., Oxford University Press (2014), pp. 3-90. [cited as: PEEPERKORN, VEROUDEN, 2014].

PEREIRA CARDOSO Joao, "Groupement des Cartes Bancaires: Reshaping the Object Box," Comentário de Jurisprudência 265, C&R – Competition and Regulation, 2014, n.º 18, pp. 265-280. [cited as: PEREIRA CARDOSO, 2014].

PINCUS Laura B., "The Computation of Damages in Patent Infringement Actions," 5 *Harv. J.L. & Tech*, 95, (Fall 1991), pp. 95-143. [cited as: PINCUS, 1991].

PINCKNEY Richard, "Understanding the Transitional Provisions of the Agreement on the Unified Patent Court," 37:5 *E.I.P.R.* 268, (2015), pp. 268-277. [cited as: PINCKNEY, 2015].

PLOMER Aurora, "A Unified Patent for a (Dis)United Europe: the Long Shadow of History," 46:5 *Intl. Rev. Intell. Prop. & Competition L.* 508, (2015), pp. 508-533. [cited as: PLOMER, Unified Patent, 2015].

PODSZUN Rupprecht, "Can Competition Law Repair Patent Law and Administrative Procedures? AstraZeneca," 51 *Com. Mkt. L. Rev.* 281, (2014), pp. 281-294. [cited as: PODSZUN, 2014].

POSNER Richard A., "Intellectual Property: The Law and Economics Approach," 19:2 *J. Econ. Persps.* 57, (Spring 2005), pp. 57-73. [cited as: POSNER, Intellectual Property, 2005].

PRASAD Vinay, MAILANKODY Sham, "Research & Development Spending to Bring a Single Cancer Drug to Market and Revenues After Approval," 177:11 *JAMA Internal Med.* 1569, (2017), pp. 1569-1575. [cited as: PRASAD, MAILANKODY, R&D Spending, 2017].

QUINN Sean J., "Down on the Pharma, How Green-Lighting Generics can Be a Game Changer Against Off-Label Marketing By Brand-Name Offenders," 26 No. 5 *Health L.* 1, (June 2014), pp. 1-13. [cited as: QUINN, 2014].

RADER Randall R., "The Hatch-Waxman Act: Balancing Innovation and Affordable Drugs," 3 *SKKU J. Sci. & Tech. L.* 1 (2009), pp. 1-7. [cited as: RADER, Balancing Innovation, 2009].

RADLEY David C., FINKELSTEIN Stan N., STAFFORD Randall S., "Off Label Prescribing Among Office-Based Physicians" 166:9 *Archives of Internal Med.* 1021, (2006), pp. 1021-1026). [cited as: RADLEY, FINKELSTEIN, STAFFORD, 2006].

RAI Arti K., "Specialised Trial Courts: Concentrating Expertise on Fact," 17:2 *Berkley Tech. L. J.* 877, (March 2002), pp. 877-897. [cited as: RAI, Specialised Trial Courts, 2002].

RAI Arti, "Use Patents, Carve-Outs, and Incentives – a New Battle in the Drug Patent Wars," 367:6 *N. Engl. J. Med.* 491, (August 9, 2012), pp. 491-493. [cited as: RAI, 2012].

REID Jennifer, BALASEGARAM Manica, "Research & Development in the Dark: What Does it Take to Make One Medicine? And What *Could* it Take?," 22 *Clin. Microbiology & Infection* 655, (2016), pp. 655-657. [cited as: REID, BALASEGARAM, R&D in the Dark, 2016].

RESNIK Judith, "Migrating, Morphing, and Vanishing: The Empirical and Normative Puzzles of Declining Trial Rates in Courts," 1:3 *J. Empirical Leg. Stud.* 783, (November 2004), pp. 783-841. [cited as: RESNIK, Declining Trial Rates, 2004].

RESNIK Judith, "The Privatisation of Process: Requiem for and Celebration of the Federal Rules of Civil Procedure at 75," 162 *U. Pa. L. Rev.* 1793, (2014), pp. 1793-1838. [cited as: RESNIK, Privatisation of Process, 2014].

RITTER Cyril, "Remedies for Breaches of EU Antitrust Law," May 17, 2016, pp. 1-36. Available at: http://papers.ssrn.com/sol3/papers.cfm?abstract_id=2781441 (last accessed on March 31, 2018). [cited as: RITTER, 2016].

ROBERT Gavin, FALCONI Fabio, "Patent Litigation Settlement Agreements in the Pharmaceutical Industry: Marrying the Innovation Bride and Competition Groom," 27:9 ECLR 524, (2006), pp. 524-533. [cited as: ROBERT, FALCONI, 2006].

ROTH Vincent J., "Will FDA Data Exclusivity Make Biological Patents Passé," 29:2 *Santa Clara Computer & High Tech. L. J.* 249, (February 2013), pp. 249-304. [cited as: ROTH, 2013].

SANDOVAL Catherine J.K., "Pharmaceutical Reverse Payment Settlements: Presumptions, Procedural Burdens, and Covenants Not to Sue Generic Drug Manufacturers," 26 *Santa Clara Computer & High Tech. L. J.* 141, (2009-2010), pp. 141-183. [cited as: SANDOVAL, Covenants Not to Sue, 2009-2010].

SCANNELL Jack W., BLANCKLEY Alex, BOLDON Helen, WARRINGTON Brian, "Diagnosing the Decline in Pharmaceutical R&D Efficiency," 11 *Nature Reviews Drug Discovery* 191, (March 2012), pp. 191-200. [cited as: SCANNELL ET AL., Diagnosing the Decline, 2012].

SCELLATO Giuseppe, CALDERINI Mario, CAVIGGIOLI Federico, FRANZONI Chiara, UGHETTO Elisa, KICA Evisa, RODRIGUEZ Victor, "Study on the Quality of the Patent System in Europe," DG MARKT, PATQUAL, (March 2011), pp. 1-194. [cited as: SCELLATO ET AL., 2011].

SCHERER Frederic M., "The Link Between Gross Profitability and Pharmaceutical R&D Spending," 20:5 *Health Affairs* 216, (2001), pp. 216-220. [cited as: SCHERER, R&D Spending, 2001].

SCHERER Frederic M., "The Pharmaceutical Industry – Prices and Progress," 351:9 *The New Eng. J. Med.* 927, (August 26, 2004), pp. 927-932. [cited as: SCHERER, Prices and Progress, 2004].

SCHIPPER Susan, "Bad Medicine: FTC v. Actavis, Inc. and the Missed Opportunity to Resolve the Pay-for-Delay Problem," 73 *Md. L. Rev.* 1240, (2014), pp. 1240-1276. [cited as: SCHIPPER, Bad Medicine, 2014].

SCHILDKRAUT Marc G., "Patent-Splitting Settlements and the Reverse Payment Fallacy," 71 *Antitrust L.J.* 1033, (2004), pp. 1033-1068. [cited as: SCHILDKRAUT, Reverse Payment Fallacy, 2004].

SCHUHMACHER Alexander, GASSMANN Oliver, HINDER Markus, "Changing R&D Models in Research-Based Pharmaceutical Companies," 14 *J. Translational Med.* 105, (April 2016). Available at: https://translational-medicine.biomedcentral.com/articles/10.1186/s12967-016-0838-4 (last accessed on March 31, 2018). [cited as: SCHUHMACHER, GASSMANN, HINDER, Changing R&D, 2016].

Bibliography

SHADOWEN Steve D., LEFFLER, Keith B., LUKENS Joseph T., "Anticompetitive Product Changes in the Pharmaceutical Industry," 41: 1&2 *Rutgers L. J.* 1, Fall/Winter 2009, pp. 1-81. [cited as: SHADOWEN, LEFFLER, LUKENS, Product Changes, 2009].

SHADOWEN Steve D., LEFFLER Keith B., LUKENS Joseph T., "Bringing Market Discipline to Pharmaceutical Product Reformulations," 42:6 *IIC* 698, (2011), pp. 698-725. [cited as: SHADOWEN, LEFFLER, LUKENS, Market Discipline, 2011].

SHAPIRO Carl, "Antitrust Analysis of Patent Settlements Between Rivals," *Antitrust*, (Summer 2003), pp. 70-77. [cited as: SHAPIRO, Settlements Between Rivals, 2003].

SHAPIRO Carl, "Antitrust Limits to Patent Settlements," 34 *RAND J. Econ.* 391, (Summer 2003), pp. 391-411. [cited as: SHAPIRO, Antitrust Limits, 2003].

SHEPPARD Alan, "Generic Medicines: Essential Contributors to the Long-Term Health of Society," *IMS Health*, 2010, pp. 1-15. [cited as: SHEPPARD, Essential Contributors, 2010].

SHEPHERD Joanna, "Deterring Innovation: NY v. Actavis and the Duty to Subsidize Competitors' Market Entry," 17:2 *Minn. J. L., Sci. & Tech.* 663, (2016), pp. 663-707. [cited as: SHEPHERD, Subsidize Competitors, 2016].

SIMON Priddis, SIMON Constantine, "The Pharmaceutical Sector, Intellectual Property Rights, and Competition Law in Europe," *in* ANDERMAN Steven, EZRACHI Ariel (eds.), *Intellectual Property and Competition Law: New Frontiers*, Oxford University Press, 2011, pp. 241-275. [cited as: SIMON & SIMON, Pharma, IP & Competition in the EU, 2011].

SOEHNGE Holly, "The Drug Price Competition and Patent Term Restoration Act of 1984: Fine-Tuning the Balance Between the Interests of Pioneer and Generic Drug Manufacturers," 58 *Food & Drug L.J.* 51, (2003), pp. 51-80. [cited as: SOEHNGE, 2003].

SORENSEN David F., SHADOWEN Steve D., "Model Jury Instructions: Trial by Actavis," 67:3 *Rutgers U. L. Rev.* 637, (Spring 2015), pp. 637-695. [cited as: SORENSEN, SHADOWEN, Model Jury Instructions, 2015].

STAFFORD Randall S., "Off-label Use of Drugs and Medical Devices: A Review of Policy Implications," 91:5 *Clin. Pharmacology & Therapeutics* 920, (2012), pp. 920-925). [cited as: STAFFORD, 2012].

STRAUS Joseph, "Can Antitrust Adequately Assess Patent Settlement Agreements Disconnected from Patent Law Relevant Facts? The Servier Case – its Public Perception and its Underlying Facts," 38:9 *E.I.P.R.* 533, 2016, pp. 533-544. [cited as: STRAUS, Servier, 2016].

UHL KATHLEEN, "2017 Was Another Record-Setting Year for Generic Drugs," FDA Voice, February 7, 2018. Available at: https://blogs.fda.gov/fdavoice/index.php/2018/02/2017-was-another-record-setting-year-for-generic-drugs/ (last accessed on March 31, 2018). [cited as: UHL, FDA Voice, 2018].

ULLRICH Hanns, "Strategic Patenting by the Pharmaceutical Industry: Towards a Concept of Abusive Practices of Protection, *in* Drexl Joseph, Lee Nari, (eds.), *Pharmaceutical Innovation, Competition and Patent Law: A Trilateral Perspective*, Edward Elgar Publishing Inc., (2013), pp. 241-272. [cited as: ULLRICH, Strategic Patenting, 2013].

URBINATI Duccio, RÉMUZAT Cécile, KORNFELD Åsa, VATAIRE Anne-Lise, CETINSOY Laurent, ABALLÈA Samuel, MZOUGHI Olfa, TOUMI Mondher, "EU Pharmaceutical Expenditure Forecast," 2:1 *J. Mkt. Access & Health Policy* 23738, (October 30, 2014), [Open Access article distributed under the terms of the Creative Commons CC-BY 4.0 License (http://creativecommons.org/licenses/by/4.0/) (last accessed on March 31, 2018). [cited as: URBINATI ET AL., EU Pharma Expenditure, 2014].

UNDERSTAHL Beth, "Authorized Generics: Careful Balance Undone," 16 *Fordham Intell. Prop. Media & Ent. L.J.* 355, (Autumn 2005), pp. 355-393. [cited as: UNDERSTAHL, 2005].

THOMAS Jeff, "Schering-Plough and In Re Tamoxifen: Lawful Reverse Payments in the Hatch-Waxman Context," 22 *Berkley Tech. L.J.* 13, (2007), pp. 13-46. Available at: http://scholarship.law.berkeley.edu/btlj/vol22/iss1/3/.(last accessed on March 31, 2018) [cited as: THOMAS, Lawful Reverse Payments, 2007].

THOMAS John R., "Collusion and Collective Action in the Patent System: A Proposal for Patent Bounties," 2001:1 *U. Ill. L. Rev.* 305, (2001), pp. 305-353. [cited as: THOMAS J.R., Patent Bounties, 2001].

TOKIC Stijepko, "The Role of Defining the Relevant Product Market in the Post-Actavis Era," 27 *I.P.J.* 265, (April 2015), pp. 265-297. [cited as: TOKIC, Relevant Product Market, 2015].

TOWEY Jamie, ALBERT Brad, FTC, "Is FTC v. Actavis Causing Pharma Companies to Change their Behavior," FTC Blogs, Competition Matters, January 13, 2016. Available at: https://www.ftc.gov/news-events/blogs/competition-matters/2016/01/ftc-v-actavis-causing-pharma-companies-change-their?utm_source=go vdelivery (last accessed on March 31, 2018). [cited as: TOWEY, ALBERT, FTC, Change Behavior, 2016].

TRIDICO Anthony, JACOBSTEIN Jeffrey, WALL Leythem, "Facilitating Generic Drug Manufacturing: Bolar Exemptions Worldwide," *WIPO Magazine*, 3/2014, (June 2014), discussing which MS adopt a broader and which a narrower reading of the exemption. Available at: http://www.wipo.int/wipo_magazine/en/2014/03/article_0004.html (last accessed on March 31, 2018). [cited as: TRIDICO, JACOBSTEIN, WALL, 2014].

TU Shine (Sean), "Invalidated Patents and Associated Patent Examiners," 18 *Vand. J. Ent. & Tech. L.* 1:135, (Fall 2015), pp. 135-165. [cited as: TU, Invalidated Patents, 2015].

TUCKER Darren S., WELLS Gregory F., "Emerging Competition Issues Involving Follow-on Biologics," 29:1 *Antitrust* 100, (Fall 2014), pp. 100-106. [cited as: TUCKER, WELLS, Biologics, 2014].

VAN DER VIJVER, Tjarda, VOLLERING, Stefan, "Understanding Appreciability: The European Court of Justice Reviews the Journey in Expedia," 50 *CML Rev.* 1133, (2013), pp. 1133-1144. [cited as: VAN DER VIJVER, VOLLERING, 2013].

VAN DIJK Theon, "Patent Height and Competition in Product Improvements," 44:2 *The J. Indus. Econ.* 151, (June 1996), pp. 151-167. [cited as: VAN DIJK, Product Improvements, 1996].

WAELBROECK Denis, "Michelin II: A Per Se Rule Against Rebates by Dominant Companies?," 1:1 *J. Competition L. & Econ.* 149, (2005), pp. 149–171. [cited as: WAELBROECK, 2005].

WAGNER-VON PAPP Florian, "De Minimis: An Overview of EU and National Case Law," May 7, 2015, e-Competitions Bulletin, De minimis, Art. N° 72780, pp. 1-12. Available at: http://www.concurrences.com/Bulletin/Special-Issues/De-minimis/De-minimis-An-overview-of-EU-and-72780. (last accessed on March 31, 2018). [cited as: WAGNER-VON PAPP, 2015].

WALKER Mike, AZEVEDO Joao Pearce, "Dominance: Meaning and Measurement," 23:7 *E.C.L.R.* 363, (2002), pp. 363-367. [cited as: WALKER, AZEVEDO, 2002].

WANG Zhenghui, "Reanalyzing Reverse-Payment Settlements: A Solution to the Patentee's Dilemma," 99:5 *Cornell L. Rev.* 1227 (2014), pp. 1227-1258. [cited as: WANG, Patentee's Dilemma, 2014].

WANSHENG, Jerry Liu, "Balancing Accessibility and Sustainability: How to Achieve the Dual Objectives of the Hatch-Waxman Act While Resolving Antitrust Issues in Pharmaceutical Patent Settlement Cases," 18 *Alb. L.J. Sci. & Tech.* 441, (2008), pp. 441-492. [cited as: WANSHENG, 2008].

WHEATON James J., "Generic Competition and Pharmaceutical Innovation: The Drug Price Competition and Patent Term Restoration Act of 1984," 35 *Cath. U. L. Rev.* 433, (Winter 1986), pp. 433-487. [cited as: WHEATON, 1986].

WILLIG Robert D., BIGELOW John P., "Antitrust Policy Toward Agreements That Settle Patent Litigation," 49 *Antitrust Bull.* 655, (Fall 2004), pp. 655-698. [cited as: WILLIG, BIGELOW, Toward Agreements, 2004].

WOLFE Raymond M., National Center for Science and Engineering Statistics, *Businesses Spent $341 Billion on R&D Performed in the United States in 2014*, August 25, 2016, pp. 1-7. Available at: https://www.nsf.gov/statistics/2016/nsf16315/ (last accessed on March 31, 2018). [cited as: WOLFE, R&D, 2014].

WOUTERS Olivier J., KANAVOS Panos G., "A Comparison of Generic Drug Prices in Seven European Countries: a Methodological Analysis," *BMC Health Servs. Res.* 17:242, (March 31, 2017), pp. 1-7. Available at: https://bmchealthservres.biomedcentral.com/articles/10.1186/s12913-017-2184-5 (last accessed on March 31, 2018). [cited as: WOUTERS, KANAVOS, 2017].

YEAZELL Stephen C., "Getting What We Asked For, Get What We Paid For, and Not Liking What We Got: The Vanishing Civil Trial," 1 *J. Empirical Leg. Stud.* 943 (2004), pp. 943-971. [cited as: YEAZELL, What We Asked, 2004].

YELDERMAN Stephen, "Do Patent Challenges Increase Competition?," 83 *U. Chi. L. Rev.* 1943, (2016), pp. 1943-2026. [cited as: YELDERMAN, Patent Challenges, 2016].

III Reports & Statements

A Reports & Studies

1 FTC & DoJ

DOJ, *Summary of Antitrust Division Health Care Cases*, (2017). Available at: https://www.justice.gov/atr/file/783756/download. (last accessed on 31 March 2018). [cited as: DoJ, *Health Care Cases*, 2017].

FTC, *Authorized Generic Drugs: Short-Term Effects and Long-Term Impact*, (August 2011), pp. 1-153. Available at: https://www.ftc.gov/reports/authorized-generic-drugs-short-term-effects-long-term-impact-report-federal-trade-commission. (last accessed on March 31, 2018). [cited as: FTC, *Authorized Generics*, 2011].

FTC, *Generic Drug Entry Prior to Patent Expiration: An FTC study*, (2002), pp. 1-68. Available at: http://www.ftc.gov/sites/default/files/documents/reports/generic-drug-entry-prior-patent-expiration-ftc-study/genericdrugstudy_0.pdf. (last accessed on March 31, 2018). [cited as: FTC, *Generic Drug Entry*, 2002].

FTC, *One Page FTC Performance Snapshot*, February 2015. Available at: https://www.ftc.gov/about-ftc/performance. (last accessed on March 31, 2018). [cited as: FTC, *Snapshot*, 2015].

FTC, *Overview of FTC Actions in Pharmaceutical Products and Distribution*, April 2017. Available at: https://www.ftc.gov/system/files/attachments/competition-policy-guidance/overview_pharma_april_2017.pdf (last accessed on March 31, 2018). [cited as: FTC, *Overview of Pharma Actions*, 2017].

FTC Report, *Agreements Filed with the Federal Trade Commission under the Medicare, Prescription Drug, Improvement and Modernization Act of 2003: Overview of Agreements Filed in FY 2007*. Available at https://www.ftc.gov/tips-advice/competition-guidance/industry-guidance/health-care/pharmaceutical-agreement-filings (last accessed on March 31, 2018). [cited as: FTC, *Agreements Filed*, 2007].

FTC Report, *Agreements Filed with the Federal Trade Commission under the Medicare, Prescription Drug, Improvement and Modernization Act of 2003: Overview of Agreements Filed in FY 2008*. Available at https://www.ftc.gov/tips-advice/competition-guidance/industry-guidance/health-care/pharmaceutical-agreement-filings (last accessed on March 31, 2018). [cited as: FTC, *Agreements Filed*, 2008].

FTC Report, *Agreements Filed with the Federal Trade Commission under the Medicare, Prescription Drug, Improvement and Modernization Act of 2003: Overview of Agreements Filed in FY 2009*. Available at https://www.ftc.gov/tips-advice/competition-guidance/industry-guidance/health-care/pharmaceutical-agreement-filings (last accessed on March 31, 2018). [cited as: FTC, Agreements Filed, 2009].

Bibliography

FTC Report, *Agreements Filed with the Federal Trade Commission under the Medicare, Prescription Drug, Improvement and Modernization Act of 2003: Overview of Agreements Filed in FY 2010*. Available athttps://www.ftc.gov/tips-advice/competition-guidance/industry-guidance/health-care/pharmaceutical-agreement-filings (last accessed on March 31, 2018). [cited as: FTC, Agreements Filed, 2010].

FTC Report, *Agreements Filed with the Federal Trade Commission under the Medicare, Prescription Drug, Improvement and Modernization Act of 2003: Overview of Agreements Filed in FY 2011*. Available athttps://www.ftc.gov/tips-advice/competition-guidance/industry-guidance/health-care/pharmaceutical-agreement-filings (last accessed on March 31, 2018). [cited as: FTC, Agreements Filed, 2011].

FTC Report, *Agreements Filed with the Federal Trade Commission under the Medicare, Prescription Drug, Improvement and Modernization Act of 2003: Overview of Agreements Filed in FY 2012*. Available athttps://www.ftc.gov/tips-advice/competition-guidance/industry-guidance/health-care/pharmaceutical-agreement-filings (last accessed on March 31, 2018). [cited as: FTC, Agreements Filed, 2012].

FTC Report, *Agreements Filed with the Federal Trade Commission under the Medicare, Prescription Drug, Improvement and Modernization Act of 2003: Overview of Agreements Filed in FY 2013*. Available athttps://www.ftc.gov/tips-advice/competition-guidance/industry-guidance/health-care/pharmaceutical-agreement-filings (last accessed on March 31, 2018). [cited as: FTC, Agreements Filed, 2013].

FTC Report, *Agreements Filed with the Federal Trade Commission under the Medicare, Prescription Drug, Improvement and Modernization Act of 2003: Overview of Agreements Filed in FY 2014*. Available at: https://www.ftc.gov/tips-advice/competition-guidance/industry-guidance/health-care/pharmaceutical-agreement-filings (last accessed on March 31, 2018). [cited as: FTC, Agreements Filed, 2014].

FTC Report, *Agreements Filed with the Federal Trade Commission under the Medicare, Prescription Drug, Improvement and Modernization Act of 2003: Overview of Agreements Filed in FY 2015*. Available at: https://www.ftc.gov/system/files/documents/reports/agreements-filed-federal-trade-commission-under-medicare-prescription-drug-improvement-modernization/overview_of_fy_2015_mma_agreements_0.pdf (last accessed on March 31, 2018). [cited as: FTC, *Agreements Filed*, 2015].

FTC, U.S. Department of Justice, *Antitrust Guidelines for Collaborations between Competitors*, (April 2000), pp. 1-35. Available at: https://www.ftc.gov/sites/default/files/documents/public_events/joint-venture-hearings-antitrust-guidelines-collaboration-among-competitors/ftcdojguidelines-2.pdf. (last accessed on March 31, 2018). [cited as: FTC, DoJ, *Antitrust Guidelines*, 2000].

FTC, U.S. Department of Justice, *Horizontal Merger Guidelines*, (August 19, 2010), pp. 1-34. Available at: https://www.ftc.gov/sites/default/files/attachments/

mergers/100819hmg.pdf (last accessed on March 31, 2018). [cited as: FTC, DoJ, *Horizontal Merger Guidelines*, 2010].

FTC, U.S. Department of Justice, *Antitrust Guidelines for the Licensing of Intellectual Property*, (January 12, 2017), pp. 1-36. Available at: https://www.justice.gov/atr/IPguidelines/download (last accessed on March 31, 2018). [cited as: FTC, DoJ, *IP Licensing Antitrust Guidelines*, 2017].

FTC Staff Study, *Pay-for-Delay: How Drug Company Pay-Offs Cost Consumers Billions*, (January 2010), pp. 1-12. Available at: http://www.ftc.gov/reports/pay-delay-how-drug-company-pay-offs-cost-consumers-billions-federal-trade-commission-staff. (last accessed on March 31, 2018). [cited as: FTC, *Pay-for-Delay*, 2010].

2 USPTO

International Intellectual Property Institute (IIPI), USPTO, *Study on Specialized Intellectual Property Courts*, January 25, 2012, pp. 1-140. Available at: iipi.org/wp-content/uploads/2012/05/Study-on-Specialized-IPR-Courts.pdf (last accessed on March 31, 2018). [cited as: IIPI, USPTO, Specialised IP Courts, 2012].

USPTO, PPTMT, *U.S. Patent Statistic Chart, Calendar years 1963-2015*. Available at: https://www.uspto.gov/web/offices/ac/ido/oeip/taf/us_stat.htm. (last accessed on March 31, 2018). [cited as: PTMT, *Patent Statistic*, 1963-2015].

USPTO, *Performance and Accountability Report FY 2017*, pp. 1-208. Available at: https://www.uspto.gov/sites/default/files/documents/USPTOFY17PAR.pdf (last accessed on March 31, 2018). [cited as: USPTO, *2017 Performance and Accountability Report*].

3 FDA

FDA, CDER, *Novel Drug Approvals for 2017*. Available at: https://www.fda.gov/Drugs/DevelopmentApprovalProcess/DrugInnovation/ucm537040.htm (last accessed on March 31, 2018). [cited as: FDA, CDER, New Drugs, 2017].

FDA, CDER, *CDER New Drugs Program: 2017 Update*. Available at: https://www.fda.gov/downloads/AboutFDA/CentersOffices/OfficeofMedicalProductsandTobacco/CDER/UCM587690.pdf (last accessed on March 31, 2018). [cited as: FDA, CDER New Drugs Program, 2017 Update].

FDA, CDER, *2016 Novel New Drugs Summary*, pp. 1-17. Available at: https://www.fda.gov/drugs/developmentapprovalprocess/druginnovation/ucm534863.htm (last accessed on March 31, 2018). [cited as: FDA, CDER, New Drugs, 2016].

FDA, *A Brief Overview of Risk Evaluation and Mitigation Strategies (REMS)*. Available at: http://www.fda.gov/AboutFDA/Transparency/Basics/ucm325201.htm. (last accessed on March 31, 2018). [cited as: FDA, REMS Overview, 2016].

FDA, *Approved Risk Evaluation and Mitigation Strategies (REMS)*, for the approved REMS approved in 2016. Available at: http://www.accessdata.fda.gov/scripts/cder/rems/index.cfm (last accessed on March 31, 2018). [cited as: FDA, Approved REMS, 2016].

Bibliography

FDA, *Determining whether to Submit an ANDA or a 505(b)(2) Application – Draft Guidance for Industry*, (October 2017). Available at: https://www.fda.gov/downloads/Drugs/GuidanceComplianceRegulatoryInformation/Guidances/UCM579751.pdf. (last accessed on March 31, 2018). [cited as: FDA, *Draft Guidance for Industry*, 2017].

FDA, *Information on Biosimilars*, (2015). Available at: http://www.fda.gov/Drugs/DevelopmentApprovalProcess/HowDrugsareDevelopedandApproved/ApprovalApplications/TherapeuticBiologicApplications/Biosimilars/. (last accessed on March 31, 2018). [cited as: FDA, Biosimilars, 2015].

FDA, *Listing of Authorized Generics as of March 30, 2017*. Available at: https://www.fda.gov/AboutFDA/CentersOffices/OfficeofMedicalProductsandTobacco/CDER/ucm126391.htm. (last accessed on March 31, 2018). [cited as: FDA, Listing of Authorized Generics, 2017].

FDA, Office of Pharmaceutical Quality, *2017 Annual Report – One Quality Voice*, February 2018. Available at: https://www.fda.gov/downloads/AboutFDA/CentersOffices/OfficeofMedicalProductsandTobacco/CDER/UCM598727.pdf (last accessed on March 31, 2018). [cited as: FDA, Pharma Quality Annual Report, 2017].

4 Other

AAM, *Generic Drug Access & Savings in the U.S.*, Report, (2017), pp. 1-52. Available at: https://accessiblemeds.org/resources/blog/2017-generic-drug-access-and-savings-us-report (last accessed on March 31, 2018). [cited as: AAM, Generic Drug Access & Savings Report, 2017].

Andrx Corp., *Annual Report Pursuant to Section 13 or 15(d) of the Securities Exchange Act*, for the fiscal year ended on December 31, 2002. Available at: http://www.getfilings.com/o0000950144-03-004118.html (last accessed on March 31, 2018). [cited as: Andrx, Annual Report, 2002].

CBO, *How Increased Competition From Generic Drug Has Affected Prices and Returns in the Pharmaceutical Industry,* (July 1998), pp. 1-75. Available at: https://www.cbo.gov/sites/default/files/105th-congress-1997-1998/reports/pharm.pdf. (last accessed on March 31, 2018). [cited as: CBO, Prices and Returns, 1998].

CBO, *Research and Development in the Pharmaceutical Industry*, (October 2006), pp. 1-55. Available at: https://www.cbo.gov/sites/default/files/109th-congress-2005-2006/reports/10-02-drugr-d.pdf (last accessed on March 31, 2018). [cited as: CBO, Pharma R&D, 2006].

CBO, *Effects of Using Generic Drugs on Medicare's Prescription Drug Spending*, (September 2010), pp. 1-24. Available at: http://www.cbo.gov/sites/default/files/cbofiles/ftpdocs/118xx/doc11838/09-15-prescriptiondrugs.pdf. (last accessed on March 31, 2018). [cited as: CBO, Drug Spending, 2010].

CBO, *Competition and the Cost of Medicare's Prescription Drug Program*, (July 2014), pp. 1-48. Available at: https://www.cbo.gov/publication/45552. (last accessed on March 31, 2018). [cited as: CBO, Cost, 2014].

Bibliography

CMS, *National Health Care Expenditures Projections 2017-2026, Forecast Summary*, pp. 1-3. Available at: https://www.cms.gov/Research-Statistics-Data-and-Systems/Statistics-Trends-and-Reports/NationalHealthExpendData/NationalHealthAccountsProjected.html (last accessed on March 31, 2018). [cited as: CMS, Expenditures Projections, 2018].

GPhA, *Generic Annual Drug Cost Savings in the U.S.*, 7th Annual Edition, 2015, pp. 1-9. Available at: http://www.gphaonline.org/gpha-media/gpha-resources/2015-gpha-annual-report (last accessed on March 31, 2018). [cited as: GPhA, Generic Savings, 2015].

GPhA, *Generic Pharmaceutical Association Annual Report*, 2015, pp. 1-20. Available at: http://www.gphaonline.org/gpha-media/gpha-resources/2015-gpha-annual-report (last accessed on March 31, 2018). [cited as: GPhA, *Annual Report*, 2015].

IMS Institute, *Impact of Patent Settlements on Drug Costs: Estimation of Savings*, (June 2013), pp. 1-8. Available at: https://www.imshealth.com/files/web/IMSH%20Institute/Healthcare%20Briefs/Impact_of_Patent_Settlements_on%20Drug_Costs.pdf. (last accessed on March 31, 2018). [cited as: IMS, Savings Estimation, 2013].

IMS Institute, *The Role of Generic Medicines in Sustaining Healthcare Systems: a European Perspective,"* June 2015, pp. 1-28. Available at: https://www.imshealth.com/files/web/IMSH%20Institute/Healthcare%20Briefs/IIHI_Generics_Healthcare_Brief.pdf. (last accessed on March 31, 2018). [cited as: IMS, Role of Generics in EU, 2015].

IMS Institute, *Price Declines after Branded Medicines Lose Exclusivity in the U.S.*, January 2016, pp. 1-4. Available at: https://www.imshealth.com/files/web/IMSH%20Institute/Healthcare%20Briefs/PhRMA%20Generic%20Price%20Brief%20January%202016.pdf (last accessed on March 31, 2018). [cited as: IMS, After Exclusivity, 2016].

IMS Institute for Healthcare Informatics, *Medicines Use and Spending in the US: a Review of 2015 and Outlook to 2020*, April 2016, pp. 1-50. Available at: http://www.imshealth.com/en/thought-leadership/quintilesims-institute/reports/medicines-use-and-spending-in-the-us-a-review-of-2015-and-outlook-to-2020 Last accessed on March 31, 2018). [cited as: IMS, Medicines Use and Spending, 2016].

PhRMA, "2015 Biopharmaceutical Research Industry Profile," Washington DC, April 2015, pp. 1-67. Available at: http://www.phrma.org/sites/default/files/pdf/2015_phrma_profile.pdf. (last accessed on March 31, 2018). [cited as: PhRMA, BioPharma Profile, 2015].

PhRMA, *2016 Profile: Biopharmaceutical Research Industry*, pp. 1-76. Available at: phrma.org/sites/default/files/pdf/biopharmaceutical-industry-profile.pdf (last accessed on March 31, 2018). [cited as: PhRMA, *2016 Profile*].

QuintilesIMS Institute, *Outlook for Global Medicines through 2021: Balancing Cost and Value*, December 2016, pp. 1-54. Available at: http://www.imshealth.com/en/thought-leadership/quintilesims-institute/reports/outlook_for_global_medicines_through_2021 (last accessed on March 31, 2018). [cited as: QuintilesIMS, *Global Medicines through 2021*, 2016].

Bibliography

RBC Capital Markets, Pharmaceuticals: *Analyzing Litigation Success Rates*, (January 15, 2010), pp. 1-24. Available at http://www.amlawdaily.typepad.com/pharmareport.pdf. (last accessed on March 31, 2018). [cited as: RBC, Litigation Success Rates, 2010].

TEVA PHARMACEUTICAL INDUSTRIES LTD., *Annual Report 2008*, Form 20-F, (February 27, 2009), pp. 1-107. Available at: http://media.corporate-ir.net/media_files/IROL/73/73925/fr/2008/2008-ar-20f.pdf. (last accessed on March 31, 2018). [cited as: TEVA PHARMACEUTICAL INDUSTRIES LTD, *Annual Report 2008*, Form 20-F, (Feb. 27, 2009)].

UNIVERSITY OF HOUSTON LAW CENTER, PATSTATS: U.S. Patent Litigation Statistics, *Rulings in 2013*, Validity Decisions, 01-16. Available at: http://www.patstats.org/2013_Full_Year_Posting.html. (last accessed on March 31, 2018). [cited as: PATSTATS, Patent Litigation, 2013].

U.S. Department of Commerce, International Trade Administration, *2016 Top Markets Report: Pharmaceuticals – A Market Assessment Tool for U.S. Exporters*, May 2016, pp. 1-41. Available at: http://www.trade.gov/topmarkets/pdf/Pharmaceuticals_Top_Markets_Reports.pdf (last accessed on March 31, 2018). [cited as: U.S. Department of Commerce, *2016 Top Markets*].

U.S. Department of Health and Human Services Report to the Congress, *Prescription Drugs: Innovation, Spending, and Patient Access*, (December 7, 2016), pp. 1-147. Available at: http://apps.who.int/medicinedocs/en/d/Js23128en/ (last accessed on March 31, 2018). [cited as: U.S. Department of Health and Human Services, *2016 Innovation & Spending Report*].

B   Guidances & Education

FDA, CDER, *Draft Guidance for Industry, Applications Covered by Section 505(b)(2)*, (October 1999), pp. 1-12. Available at: http://www.fda.gov/downloads/Drugs/Guidances/ucm079345.pdf. (last accessed on March 31, 2018). [cited as: FDA, Section 505(b)(2) Applications, 1999].

FDA, CDER, *Guidance for Industry: 180-day Exclusivity When Multiple ANDAs Are Submitted on the Same Day*, (July, 2003), pp. 1-6. Available at: http://www.fda.gov/downloads/drugs/guidancecomplianceregulatoryinformation/guidances/ucm072851.pdf. (last accessed on March 31, 2018). [cited as: FDA, Multiple ANDAs Guidance, 2003].

FDA, CDER, *Draft Guidance for Industry, Listed Drugs, 30-month Stays and Approval of ANDAs under MMA of 2003, Q&As*, 69 Federal Register 213, 64314-64315, (November 4, 2004). Available at: http://www.fda.gov/OHRMS/DOCKETS/98fr/04-24675.pdf. (last accessed on March 31, 2018). [cited as: FDA, MMA Q&As, 2004].

FDA, CDER, *Guidance for Industry, ANDA Submissions – Refuse to Receive Standards*, (May 2015), pp. 1-22. Available at: http://www.fda.gov/downloads/Drugs/GuidanceComplianceRegulatoryInformation/Guidances/UCM370352.pdf. (last accessed on March 31, 2018). [cited as: FDA, Refuse ANDAs Guidance, 2015].

FDA, CDER, CBER, *Guidance for Industry, Biosimilars: Questions and Answers Regarding Implementation of the Biologics Price Competition and Innovation Act of 2009*, April 2015, pp. 1-16. Available at: http://www.fda.gov/downloads/Drugs/GuidanceComplianceRegulatoryInformation/Guidances/UCM444661.pdf. (last accessed on March 31, 2018). [cited as: FDA, Q&A Biosimilars, 2015].

FDA, CDER, CBER, *Guidance for Industry: 180-day Exclusivity: Questions and Answers* (January 2017), pp. 1-30. Available at: https://www.fda.gov/downloads/Drugs/GuidanceComplianceRegulatoryInformation/Guidances/UCM536725.pdf. (last accessed on March 31, 2018). [cited as: FDA, 180-day Exclusivity Guidance, 2017].

FDA, REdI, *Hatch-Waxman 101*, Generic Drugs Forum, Sheraton, (April 23-25, 2015), pp. 1-25. Available at: http://www.fda.gov/downloads/Drugs/DevelopmentApprovalProcess/SmallBusinessAssistance/UCM445610.pdf. (last accessed on March 31, 2018). [cited as: FDA, *Hatch-Waxman 101*, 2015].

TILL Mary C., Legal advisor of the USPTO, "Hatch-Waxman Bootcamp," Presentation, July 2010, pp. 1-23. Available at: http://www.uspto.gov/patents/law/exam/presentation/hatch_waxman_20jul1020.ppt. (last accessed on March 31, 2018). [cited as: TILL, Hatch-Waxman Bootcamp, 2010].

C Rules and Applications

FDA, Department of Health and Human Services, *Applications for FDA Approval to Market a New Drug: Proposed Rule*, 21 CFR Part 314, [Docket No. 02N–0417] (September 12, 2002), pp. 1-70. Available at: http://www.fda.gov/OHRMS/DOCKETS/98fr/PATENT.pdf. (last accessed on March 31, 2018). [cited as: FDA, NDA Proposed Rule, 2002].

FDA, Department of Health and Human Services, *Applications for FDA Approval to Market a New Drug*, Final Rule, 68 Federal Register 117, pp. 36676-36712, No. 117, (June 18, 2003). Available at: http://www.fda.gov/OHRMS/DOCKETS/98fr/061803a.pdf. (last accessed on March 31, 2018). [cited as: FDA, NDA Final Rule, 2003].

FDA, Orphan Drug Regulations, 21 C.F.R. Part 316, Final Rule, 78 Federal Register 113, pp. 35117-35135, June 12, 2013. Available at: http://www.gpo.gov/fdsys/pkg/FR-2013-06-12/pdf/2013-13930.pdf (last accessed on March 31, 2018). [cited as: FDA, Orphan Drug Final Rule, 2013].

FDA, Department of Health and Human Services, *Abbreviated New Drug Applications and 505(b)(2) Applications*, 21 CFR Parts 314 and 320, Final Rule, 81 Federal Register 194, pp. 69580-69658 (October 2016). Available at: https://www.gpo.gov/fdsys/pkg/FR-2016-10-06/pdf/2016-22690.pdf (last accessed on March 31, 2018). [cited as: FDA, ANDA & 505(b)(2) Applications Final Rule, 2016].

Bibliography

D Lists & Estimates

FDA, *Pediatric Exclusivity Determinations List*, April 2016, pp. 1-11. Available at: https://www.fda.gov/downloads/Drugs/DevelopmentApprovalProcess/DevelopmentResources/UCM223058.pdf (last accessed on March 31, 2018). [cited as: FDA, Pediatric Exclusivity List, 2016].

U.S. Department of Health and Human Services, National Institutes of Health (NIH), *Estimates of Funding for Various Research, Condition and Disease Categories (RCDC)*, February 10, 2016. Available at: https://report.nih.gov/categorical_spending.aspx (last accessed on March 31, 2018). [cited as: U.S. Department of Health and Human Services, *Estimates of Funding*, 2016].

E Statements, Testimonies, Comments & Remarks

Collins Francis S., Director, National Institutes of Health, *Testimony on the Fiscal Year 2017 Budget Request before the Senate Committee*, April 6, 2016, pp. 1-5. Available at: http://www.nih.gov/sites/default/files/about-nih/nih-director/testimonies/testimony-fiscal-year-2017-budget-request-before-senate-committee.pdf (last accessed on March 31, 2018). [cited as: Collins, *Testimony on Budget Request*, 2016].

FTC, *Comment of the Federal Trade Commission, In the Matter of Applications for FDA Approval to Market a New Drug; Patent Listing Requirements and Application of 30-Month Stays on Approval of Abbreviated New Drug Applications Certifying that a Patent Claiming a Drug is Invalid or Will Not Be Infringed*, Docket No. 02N-0417, December 23, 2002, pp. 1-21. Available at: https://www.ftc.gov/policy/policy-actions/advocacy-filings/2002/12/ftc-comment-food-and-drug-administration-concerning. (last accessed on March 31, 2018). [cited as: FTC, NDA Comment, 2002].

Leibowitz Jon, Oral Statement of FTC Commissioner, *Hearing of the Senate Special Committee on Aging*, July 20, 2006, pp. 1-3. Available at: https://www.ftc.gov/public-statements/2006/07/oral-statement-commissioner-jon-leibowitz-hearing-senate-special-committee (last accessed on March 31, 2018). [cited as: Leibowitz, Committee on Aging, 2006].

Leibowitz Jon, Statement of former FTC Chairman, *On the release of the Commission's Interim Report on Authorized Generics*, June 2009, pp. 1-2. Available at: https://www.ftc.gov/sites/default/files/documents/reports/authorized-generics-interim-report-federal-trade-commission/p062105authgenstatementleibowitz.pdf. (last accessed on March 31, 2018). [cited as: Leibowitz, Interim Report Statement, 2009].

National Institutes of Health, *History of Congressional Appropriations*, Fiscal Years 2000-2016, pp. 1-3. Available at: https://officeofbudget.od.nih.gov/pdfs/FY16/Approp%20History%20by%20IC%20FY%202000%20-%20FY%202016.pdf (last accessed on March 31, 2018). [cited as: National Institutes of Health, *Congressional Appropriations*, 2016].

POZEN Sharis A., Acting Assistant Attorney General, Antitrust Division, U.S. Department of Justice, *Promoting Competition and Innovation Through Vigorous Enforcement of the Antitrust Laws on Behalf of Consumers*, Washington D.C., April 23, 2012. Available at: http://www.justice.gov/atr/public/speeches/282515.pdf. (last accessed on March 31, 2018). [cited as: POZEN, Vigorous Enforcement, 2012].

RAMIREZ Edith, *Statement of FTC's Chairwoman before the U.S. Senate*, Washington DC, of July 23, 2013, pp. 1-4. Available at: http://www.ftc.gov/sites/default/files/documents/public_statements/statement-chairwoman-edith-ramirez-pay-delay-settlements/130923pfdopeningstatement_0.pdf. Last accessed on March 31, 2018). [cited as: RAMIREZ, FTC, Statement, 2013].

SENATOR HATCH Orrin, *On Greater Access to Pharmaceuticals Act*, 148 Cong. Rec. S7565 (July 30, 2002). Available at: http://www.gpo.gov/fdsys/pkg/CREC-2002-07-30/pdf/CREC-2002-07-30-pt1-PgS7565.pdf. (last accessed on March 31, 2018). [cited as: SENATOR HATCH, Access to Pharmaceuticals, 2002].

SENATOR METZENBAUM Howard M. (Ret.), Chairman of the Consumer Federation of America, *Testimony before the Senate Judiciary Committee, regarding Legislative and Regulatory Responses to the FTC Study on Barriers to Entry in the Pharmaceutical Marketplace*, (June 17, 2003), pp. 1-5. Available at: http://www.consumerfed.org/pdfs/61803Testimony.pdf. (last accessed on March 31, 2018). [cited as: SENATOR METZENBAUM, Entry Barriers, 2003].

TROY Daniel E., Chief Counsel, U.S. FDA, *Drug Price Competition and Patent Term Restoration Act of 1984 (Hatch-Waxman Amendments)*, before the Senate Committee and the Judiciary, August 1, 2003. Available at: http://www.fda.gov/newsevents/testimony/ucm115033.htm. (last accessed on March 31, 2018). [cited as: TROY, Amendments, 2003].

REPRESENTATIVE WAXMAN, 130 Cong. Rec. 24425, (September 6, 1984).

WOODCOCK Janet, Director of CDER, Department of Health and Human Services, FDA, *Implementation of the Pediatric Exclusivity Provisions*, May 8, 2001. Available at: http://www.fda.gov/newsevents/testimony/ucm115220.htm. (last accessed on March 31, 2018). [cited as: WOODCOCK, Pediatric Exclusivity, 2001].

WRIGHT Joshua D., Commissioner, FTC, Remarks, *FTC v. Actavis and the Future of Reverse Payment Cases*, (September 26, 2013), pp. 1-16. Available at: https://www.ftc.gov/sites/default/files/documents/public_statements/ftc-v.actavis-future-reverse-payment-cases/130926actavis.pdf. (last accessed on March 31, 2018). [cited as: WRIGHT, FTC, Future, 2013].

F Press Releases

Andrx Corp., Report (Form 8-K), Exhibit 99.1, *Andrx Corporation Reports Financial Results For the Third Quarter of 2002*, Press Release dated October 31, 2002. Available at: http://www.sec.gov/Archives/edgar/data/1123337/000095014402010970/g78973exv99w1.htm. (last accessed on March 31, 2018). [cited as: ANDRX, Exhibit 99.1, 2002].

Bibliography

FDA Press Release, *FDA Approves First Biosimilar Product Zarxio*, (March 6, 2015). Available at: http://www.fda.gov/NewsEvents/Newsroom/PressAnnouncements/ucm436648.htm (last accessed on March 31, 2018). [cited as: FDA, First Biosimilar Approval, 2015].

FTC, *Pay-for-delay: When Drug Companies Agree Not to Compete*, Compilation of Press Releases. Available at: https://www.ftc.gov/news-events/media-resources/mergers-competition/pay-delay. (last accessed on March 31, 2018). [cited as: FTC, Press Releases List].

FTC Press Release, *FTC Amicus Brief: Improper Use of Restricted Drug Distribution Programs May Impede Generic Competition*, (March 12, 2013). Available at: https://www.ftc.gov/news-events/press-releases/2013/03/ftc-amicus-brief-improper-use-restricted-drug-distribution (last accessed on March 31, 2018). [cited as: FTC Press Release, Restricted Distribution, 2013].

FTC Press Release, *FTC Settlement of Cephalon Pay-for-delay Case Ensures $1.2 Billion in Ill-Gotten Gains Relinquished; Refunds Will Go To Purchasers Affected By Anticompetitive Tactics*, May 28, 2015. Available at: https://www.ftc.gov/news-events/press-releases/2015/05/ftc-settlement-cephalon-pay-delay-case-ensures-12-billion-ill. (last accessed on March 31, 2018). [cited as: FTC Press Release, Cephalon, 2015].

FTC Press Release, *FTC Sues Endo Pharmaceuticals Inc. and Others for Illegally Blocking Lower-Cost Generic Versions of the Branded Drugs Opana ER and Lidoderm*, (March 30, 2016). Available at: https://www.ftc.gov/news-events/press-releases/2016/03/ftc-sues-endo-pharmaceuticals-inc-others-illegally-blocking-lower (last accessed on March 31, 2018). [cited as: FTC Press Release, *FTC Sues Endo Pharmaceuticals Inc. and Others*, 2016].

FTC Press Release, *Endo Pharmaceuticals Inc. Agrees to Abandon Anticompetitive Pay-for-Delay Agreements to Settle FTC Charges; FTC Refiles Suits Against Generic Defendants*, (January 23, 2017). Available at: https://www.ftc.gov/news-events/press-releases/2017/01/endo-pharmaceuticals-inc-agrees-abandon-anticompetitive-pay-delay (last accessed on March 31, 2018). [cited as: FTC, Press Release, *Endo*, 2017].

Press Release, Office of the Attorney General of the State of California, *Attorney General Lockyer Announces $80 Million Settlement of Antitrust Case Against Drug Makers For Limiting Access to Generic Heart Medication*, (January 27, 2003). Available at: http://oag.ca.gov/news/press-releases/attorney-general-lockyer-announces-80-million-settlement-antitrust-case-against (last accessed on March 31, 2018). [cited as: LOCKYER, Announces Settlement, 2003].

G Notes and Hearings

FED. R. CIV. P. 16(a), Notes of the Advisory Committee on Rules – 1983 Amendment

FED. R. CIV. P. 16(a), Notes of the Advisory Committee on Rules – 1993 Amendment.

OECD, Competition Committee, *Generic Pharmaceuticals – Note by the United States*, DAF/COMP/WD (2014)51, June 19, 2014, pp. 1-20. Available at: http://

www.oecd.org/officialdocuments/publicdisplaydocumentpdf/?cote=DAF/COMP/WD(2014)51&docLanguage=En (last accessed on March 31, 2018). [cited as: OECD, U.S. Note, 2014].

Hearing on H.R. 1706, *The Protecting Consumer Access to Generic Drugs Act of 2009*, before Subcommittee on Commerce, Trade, & Consumer Protection, Energy & Commerce Committee, 111th Cong., Serial No. 111-25, (March 31, 2009), pp. 1-320. Available at: https://archive.org/download/gov.gpo.fdsys.CHRG-111hhrg67822/CHRG-111hhrg67822.pdf (last accessed on March 31, 2018). [cited as: Hearing, Protecting Consumer Access to Generics, 2009].

Table of Cases

I United States

A List of Cases

Abbott Labs. v. Brennan, 952 F.2d 1346 (Fed. Cir. 1991), **158**
Abbott Lab. v. Geneva Pharms., Inc., 120 S. Ct. 796 (2000), **117**
Abbott Labs. v. Geneva Pharms., Inc., 182 F.3d 1315 (Fed. Cir. 1999), **117**
Abbott Labs. v. Geneva Pharms., Inc., et al., 1998 U.S. Dist. Nos. 96-C-3331, 96-C-5868,
    & 97-C-7587, (N.D. Ill. September 1, 1998), **116**
Abbott Labs. v. Teva Pharms. USA Inc., 432 F. Supp. 2d. 408 (D. Del. 2006), **208–210**
Actelion Pharm. Ltd. v. Apotex, Inc., 1:12-cv-05743, (D.N.J. 2013), **201**
Addyston Pipe & Steel Co. v. United States, 20 S. Ct. 96 (1899), **83, 84, 93**
Andrx Pharmaceuticals Inc. v. Elan Corporation, 421 F.3d 1227 (11th Cir. 2005), **101,
    102, 106, 144**
Andrx Pharmaceuticals Inc. v. Biovail Corp. Int'l, 256 F.3d 799 (D.C. Cir. 2001), **64, 81,
    87–92, 138, 375**
Andrx Pharms., Inc. v. Biovail Corp., 276 F.3d 1368 (Fed. Cir. 2002), **52**
Andrx Pharm., Inc. v. Friedman, 83 F. Supp. 2d 179 (D.D.C. 2000), **90**
Arizona v. Maricopa County. Medical Soc., 102 S. Ct. 2466 (1982), **82, 83, 93, 96, 263**
Albrecht v. Herald Co., 88 S. Ct. 869 (1968), **85**
Allen v. Dairy Farmers of America, Inc., 748 F. Supp. 2d 323 (D. Vt. 2010), **153**
American Academic Suppliers, Inc. v. Beckley-Cardy, Inc., 922 F.2d 1317 (7th Cir. 1991),
    157
American Needle, Inc. v. National Football League, 130 S. Ct. 2201 (2010), **187**
Apotex, Inc. v. Thomson, 347 F.3d 1335 (Fed. Cir. 2003), **74**
Arkansas Carpenters Health & Welfare Fund v. Bayer AG, 604 F.3d 98 (2nd Cir. 2010),
    65, 103, 105
Asahi Glass Co., Ltd. v. Pentech Pharmaceuticals, Inc., 289 F. Supp. 2d 986 (N.D. Ill.
    2003), **98, 125, 136**
AstraZeneca UK Ltd. v. Mylan Pharms., Inc., No. 00-2239 (W.D. Pa. 30 November
    2000), **104, 117**

Table of Cases

Avery Dennison Corp. v. Acco Brands, Inc., No. CV99-1877DT (MCX) (C.D. Cal. 2000), **156**
Barr Laboratories Inc. v. Abbott Laboratories, 978 F. 2d 98 (3rd Cir. 1992), **160**
Barry Wright Corp. v. ITT Grinnell Corp., 724 F.2d 227 (1st Cir. 1983), **153**
Bell Atlantic Co. et al. v. Thomas Twombly et al., 127 S. Ct. 1955 (2007), **185**
Berkey Photo, Inc. v. Eastman Kodak Co., 603 F.2d 263 (2nd Cir. 1979), **156, 209**
Broadcast Music, Inc., et al. v. CBS, Inc. et al., 99 S. Ct. 1551 (1979), **82, 83**
Brown Shoe Co. v. United States, 82 S. Ct. 1502 (1962), **156, 157**
Bogosian v. Gulf Oil Corp., 561 F.2d 434 (3rd Cir. 1977), **185**
Business Electronics Corp. v. Sharp Electronics Corp., 108 S. Ct. 1515 (1988), **82**
California Dental Ass'n v. Fed. Trade Comm'n, 119 S. Ct. 1604 (1999), **128, 152**
California Dental Ass'n v. Fed. Trade Comm'n, 224 F.3d 942 (9th Cir. 2000), **159**
Carbice Corp. of Am. v. Am. Patents Dev. Corp., 51 S. Ct. 334 (1931), **99**
Caraco Pharm. Labs., Ltd. v. Forest Labs., Inc., 527 F.3d 1278 (Fed. Cir. 2008), **52, 58, 59, 64, 74**
Caraco Pharmaceutical Laboratories, Ltd., et al. v. Novo Nordisk A/S et al., 132 S. Ct. 1670 (2012), **58**
Catalano, Inc. v. Target Sales, Inc., 100 S. Ct. 1925 (1980), **84**
CCPI, Inc. v. Am. Premier, Inc., 967 F. Supp. 813 (D. Del. 1997), **158**
CVD, Inc. v. Raytheon Co., 769 F.2d 842 (1st Cir. 1985), **156**
City of Providence v. Celgene Corporation, Case No. 2:15-cv-01605 (D.N.J. 2015), **202**
City of Pittsburgh v. West Penn Power Co., 147 F. 3d 256 (3rd Cir.1998), **90**
Crystal Semiconductor Corp. v. TriTech Microelectronics Int'l, Inc., 246 F.3d 1336 (Fed. Cir. 2001), **197**
C.R. Bard, Inc. v. M3 Systems, Inc., 157 F.3d 1340 (Fed. Cir. 1998), **158**
Continental T.V., Inc. et al. v. GTE Sylvania Inc., 97 S. Ct. 2549 (1977), **83, 86, 95, 159**
Copperweld Corp. v. Independence Tube Corp., 104 S. Ct. 2731 (1984), **159, 187**
Dawson Chem. Co. v. Rohm & Haas Co., 100 S. Ct. 2601 (1980), **106**
Delano Farms Co. v. California Table Grape Comm'n, 655 F.3d 1337 (Fed. Cir., 2011), **156**
Dr. Miles Medical Co. v. John D. Park & Sons Co., 31 S. Ct. 376 (1911), **85**
Dynair Electronics, Inc. v. Video Cable, Inc., 55 Cal. App. 3d 11 (Cal. Ct. App. 1976), **176**
Eastman Kodak Co. v. Image Technical Services, Inc., 112 S. Ct. 2072 (1992), **83, 162, 187, 263**
Edward Katzinger Co. v. Chicago Metallic Manufacturing Co., 67 S. Ct. 416 (1947), **126**
Egyptian Goddess, Inc. v. Swisa, Inc., 543 F. 3d 665 (Fed. Cir. 2008), **119**
Eli Lilly and Company v. Medtronic Inc., 110 S. Ct. 2683 (1990), **56, 58**
Envirotech Corp. v. Al George, Inc., 730 F.2d 753 (Fed. Cir. 1984), **119**
Fashion Originators' Guild of America, Inc., et al. v. FTC, 61 S. Ct. 703 (1941), **84**
Flex Foot, Inc. v. CRR, Inc., 238 F. 3d 1362 (Fed. Cir. 2001), **124**
Food & Commercial Workers Local 1776 v. Teikoku Pharma USA, Inc., 74 F. Supp. 3d 1052 (N.D. Cal. 2014), **186, 189, 192**
Foster v. Hallco Mfg. Co., 947 F. 2d 469 (Fed. Cir. 1991), **124**
FTC v. AbbVie Inc. et al., 107 F.Supp.3d 428 (E.D.Pa. May 6, 2015), **168**
FTC v. AbbVie Inc. et al., Civil Action No. 14-5151, (E.D. Pa. Sep. 15, 2017), **168**

FTC v. Actavis, 133 S. Ct. 2223 (2013), **49, 63, 154, 168, 190, 191, 321, 325–327**
FTC et al. v. Promedica Health System Inc., No. 3:11 CV 47. (N.D. Ohio 2011), **153**
FTC v. Indiana Federation of Dentists, 106 S.Ct. 2009 (1986), **128**
FTC v. Schering-Plough Corp. et al., 126 S. Ct. 2929 (2006), **49, 132**
FTC v. Superior Court Trial Lawyers Ass'n, 110 S. Ct. 768 (1990), **83**
FTC v. Watson Pharmaceuticals, 677 F.3d 1298 (11th Cir. 2012), **49, 63, 76, 100, 102, 105, 123, 125, 142–145, 149, 154, 159, 190, 191, 321, 325–327**
Glaxo Group Ltd. v. Apotex, Inc., 376 F.3d 1339 (Fed. Cir. 2004), **58**
Glaxo, Inc. v. Novopharm, Ltd., 110 F.3d 1562, 1569 (Fed. Cir. 1997), **58**
Geneva Pharms. Tech. Corp. v. Barr Labs., Inc., 201 F. Supp. 2d 236 (S.D.N.Y. 2002), **160**
George R. Whitten, Jr., Inc. v. Paddock Pool Builders, Inc., 508 F.2d 547 (1st Cir. 1974), **157**
Getz Bros. & Co. v. Federal Salt Company, 147 Cal. 115 (Cal. 1905), **167**
Handgards, Inc. v. Ethicon, Inc., 743 F.2d 1282 (9th Cir. 1984), **156**
Hartford-Empire Co. v. United States, 65 S. Ct. 373 (1945), **93**
Hill v. United States, 263 F.2d 885 (3rd Cir. 1959), **176**
Imperial Chem. Indus., PLC v. Barr Labs., Inc., 795 F. Supp. 619 (S.D.N.Y. 1992), **117**
Imperial Chem. Indus., PLC v. Heumann Pharma GmbH & Co., 991 F.2d 811, (Fed. Cir. 1993) (unpublished opinion), **117**
International Union of Bricklayers, et al. v. Celgene Corporation, Case No. 14-6997 (D.N.J. 2014), **202**
In re Actos End Payor Antitrust Litigation, No. 1:14-cv-02846 (S.D.N.Y.), **166, 186, 195**
In re Aggrenox Antitrust Litig., 94 F. Supp. 3d 224 (D. Conn. 2015), **162, 166, 167, 176, 186, 189, 190, 193**
In re AndroGel Antitrust Litigation (No. II), 687 F. Supp. 2d 1371 (ND Ga. 2010), **142–144**
In re Barr Lab., Inc., 930 F. 2d 72 (D.C. Cir. 1991), **90**
In re Cardizem CD Antitrust Litig., 332 F.3d 896 (6th Cir. 2003), **81, 86, 88, 92–94, 96, 99**
In re Cardizem CD Antitrust Litig., 105 F. Supp. 2d 618 (E.D. Mich. 2000), **92, 159**
In re Cipro Cases I & II, 348 P.3d 845 (Cal., May 7, 2015), **76, 92, 150, 155, 161, 164, 166, 167, 169, 173, 174, 191**
In re Ciprofloxacin Hydrochloride Antitrust Litig., 544 F. 3d 1323 (Fed. Cir. 2008), **65, 73, 77, 100, 102, 103, 106, 109, 122, 124, 126, 146**
In re Ciprofloxacin Hydrochloride Antitrust Litig., 363 F. Supp. 2d 514 (E.D.N.Y. 2005), **123, 127**
In re Ciprofloxacin Hydrochloride Antitrust Litigation, 261 F. Supp. 2d 188 (E.D.N.Y. 2003), **76**
In re Effexor XR Antitrust Litig., No. 11-CV-5479, (D.N.J. 2014), **183, 184, 193, 198, 199**
In re Indep. Serv. Orgs. Antitrust Litig., 203 F.3d 1322 (Fed. Cir. 2000), **158**
In re Ins. Brokerage Antitrust Litig., 618 F.3d 300 (3rd Cir. 2010), **185**
In re K-Dur Antitrust Litigation, 686 F.3d 197 (3rd Cir. 2012), **81, 82, 109, 111, 112, 113, 118, 119, 123, 124, 126, 135, 137, 138, 151, 159**
In re K-Dur Antitrust Litig., Nos. 10-2077, 10-2078, 10-4571 (3rd Cir., 2013), **134**

Table of Cases

In re K-Dur Antitrust Litig., Civil Action No. 01-cv-1652 (SRC)(CLW),MDL Docket No. 1419 (D.N.J., Feb. 25, 2016), **134**

In re Lamictal Direct Purchaser Antitrust Litigation, No. 12-cv-995 (WHW) (D. N.J. 2014), **148, 154, 182, 184, 186, 187, 188**

In re Loestrin 24 Fe Antitrust Litig., 45 F. Supp. 3d 180 (D.R.I. 2014), **148, 166, 172, 180, 182, 184, 185**

In re Loestrin 24 Fe Antitrust Litig., 814 F.3d 538 (1st Cir. 2016), **182, 185, 186**

In re Lidoderm Antitrust Litigation, Case No. 14-md-02521-WHO, (N.D. Cal. 2017), **214**

In re Lipitor Antitrust Litig., 46 F. Supp. 3d 523 (D.N.J. Sept. 12, 2014), **214**

In re Lipitor Antitrust Litig.; In re Effexor XR Antitrust Litig., Nos. 14-4202, 14-4203, 14-4204, 14-4205, 14-4206, 14-4602 & 14-4632, Nos. 15-1184, 15-1185, 15-1186, 15-1187, 15-1274, 15-1323 & 15-1342, 855 F.3d 126, (3rd Cir. 2017), **198**

In re Lipitor Antitrust Litig., In re Effexor XR Antitrust Litig., 868 F.3d 231 (3rd Cir. 2017), **183, 198, 199**

In re Modafinil Antitrust Litig., 837 F.3d 238 (3rd Cir. 2016), **169**

In Re Niaspan Antitrust Litig., 42 F. Supp. 3d. 735 (E.D. Pa. 2014), **166, 167, 176, 186, 189, 192, 197**

In re Nexium (Esomeprazole) Antitrust Litig., 968 F. Supp. 2d 367 (D. Mass. 2013), **162, 178, 186**

In re Opana ER Antitrust Litigation, 162 F. Supp. 3d 704 (N.D. Ill. Feb. 10, 2016), **185**

In re Opana ER Antitrust Litigation, MDL Docket No. 2580, Case No. 14 C 10150, (N.D. Ill. Feb. 25, 2016), **214**

In re Skelaxin (Metaxalone) Antitrust Litigation, Case No. 1:12-md-2343, (E.D. Tenn. 2013), **164**

In re Suboxone Antitrust Litigation, 64 F. Supp. 3d. 665 (E.D. Pa. 2014), **207–209**

In re Suboxone (Buprenorphine Hydrochloride & Naloxone) Antitrust Litig., 13-MD-2445, (ED. Pa. 2016), **210**

In re Terazosin Hydrochloride Antitrust Litig., 352 F. Supp. 2d 1279 (S.D. Fla. 2005), **86, 159**

In re Tamoxifen Citrate Antitrust Litigation, 466 F.3d 187 (2nd Cir. 2006), **64, 65, 73, 76, 77, 101–104, 106, 109, 110, 112, 117–128, 146**

In re Thalomid and Revlimid Antitrust Litigation, Civil No.: 14-6997 (KSH) (CLW), (D.N.J. 2015), **202**

In re Wellbutrin XL Antitrust Litig., No. 08-cv-2431, No. 08-cv-2433, (E.D. Pa. 2014), **184**

In re Wellbutrin XL Antitrust Litig., 868 F.3d 132, 160-163 (3rd Cir. 2017), **189, 190, 192**

In re Werner Kotzab, 217 F.3d 1365 (Fed. Cir. 2000), **47, 112**

International Salt Co. v. United States, 332 U.S. 392, 68 S. Ct. 12 (1947), **84**

Jefferson Parish Hosp. Dist. No. 2 v. Hyde, 104 S. Ct. 1551 (1984), **158**

Kiefer-Stewart Co. v. Joseph E. Seagram & Sons, Inc., 71 S. Ct. 259 (1951), **85**

King Drug Co. of Florence, Inc. v. Cephalon, Inc., 702 F. Supp. 2d 514 (E.D. PA. 2010), **123, 314**

King Drug Company of Florence, Inc. v. Cephalon Inc., et al., Order by Judge Mitchell S. Goldberg, (Civil Actions No. 2:06-cv-1797, No. 2:06-cv-1833, No. 2:06-cv-2768 (E.D. Pa. 2015), **169**

King Drug Company of Florence, Inc., et al. v. Smithkline Beecham Corp., et al., 791 F.3d 388 (3rd Cir. 2015), **154, 155, 178, 182, 185, 187–194**

Korkala v. Allpro Imaging, Inc., No. 08-2712 (D. N.J. 2009), **156**

Lear, Inc. v. Adkins, 89 S. Ct. 1902 (1969), **109**

Leegin Creative Leather Prods Inc. v. PSKS, Inc., 127 S. Ct. 2705 (2007), **85**

Mannington Mills, Inc. v. Congoleum Industries, Inc., 610 F.2d 1059 (3rd Cir. 1979), **193**

Matsushita Elec. Indus. Co. v. Zenith Radio Corp., 106 S. Ct. 1348 (1986), **157**

Merck & Co., Inc., Petitioner v. Louisiana Wholesale Drug Company Inc., et al., 133 S. Ct. 2849 (2013), **134**

Merck KGaA v. Integra Lifesciences I, Ltd., 125 S. Ct. 2372 (2005), **53**

Mercoid Corp. v. Mid-Continent Inv. Co., 64 S. Ct. 268 (1944), **99**

Monsanto Co. v. Spray-Rite Service Corp., 104 S. Ct. 1464 (1984), **86**

Moraine Prods. v. ICI America, Inc., 538 F.2d 134 (7th Cir. 1976), **193**

Morgenstern v. Wilson, 29 F.3d 1291 (8th Cir. 1994), **156**

Morton Salt Co. v. G.S. Suppiger Co., 62 S. Ct. 402 (1942), **158**

Motion Picture Parents Co. v. Universal Film Mfr. Co., 37 S. Ct. 416 (1917), **158**

Mova Pharm. Corp. v. Shalala, 955 F. Supp. 128 (D.D.C. 1997), **64**

Mylan Pharms. v. Celgene Corp., Case No. 2:14-cv-02094 (D.N.J. 2014), **201, 202**

Mylan Pharm., Inc. v. FDA, 454 F. 3d 270 (N.D. W. Va. 2005), **177, 178**

Mylan Pharmaceuticals Inc. v. Warner Chilcott PLC et al., Civ. No. 12-3824, (E.D. Pa. 2015), **210, 211**

Mylan Pharmaceuticals Inc. v. Warner Chilcott PLC et al., 838 F.3d 421 (3rd Cir. 2016), **207, 208, 212, 385**

N. Tex. Specialty Physicians v. FTC, 528 F.3d 346 (5th Cir. 2008), **131**

National Soc. of Professional Engineers v. United States, 98 S. Ct. 1355 (1978), **83**

National College Athletic Ass'n ("NCAA") v. Board of Regents, 104 S. Ct. 2948 (1984), **82–84, 95, 154, 263**

New York v. Actavis PLC, Forest Labs LLC, 787 F.3d 638 (2nd Cir. 2015), **207, 209, 210, 212, 385**

Northern Pacific Ry. Co. v. United States, 78 S. Ct. 514 (1958), **83, 84**

NYNEX Corp. v. Discon, Inc., 119 S. Ct. 493 (1998), **82**

Omega Environmental, Inc. v. Gilbarco Inc., 127 F.3d 1157 (9th Cir. 1997), **153**

Paddock Publications, Inc. v. Chicago Tribune Co. et al., 103 F.3d 42 (7th Cir.1996), cert. denied, 117 S. Ct. 2435 (1997), **153**

Palmer v. BRG of Georgia, 111 S. Ct. 401 (1990), **84, 86, 180, 193**

Precision Instrument Manufacturing Co. et al. v. Automotive Maintenance Machinery Co., 65 S. Ct. 993 (1945), **106**

Professional Real Estate Investors, Inc. v. Columbia Pictures Industries, Inc., 113 S. Ct. 1920 (1993), **171**

Polk Bros., Inc. v. Forest City Enters., Inc., 776 F.2d 185 (7th Cir. 1985), **84**

Poppenhusen v. Falke, 19 F. Cas. 1048 (C.C.S.D.N.Y. 1861) (No. 11,279), **53**

Table of Cases

Queen City Pizza v. Dominos Pizza, 124 F.3d 430 (3rd Cir. 1997), **156**
Rebel Oil Co., Inc. v. Atlantic Richfield Co., 51 F.3d 1421 (9th Cir. 1995), **153**
Rite-Hite Corp. v. Kelley Co., 56 F.3d 1538 (Fed. Cir. 1995), **197**
Roche Products, Inc. v. Bolar Pharmaceutical Co., 733 F.2d 858 (Fed. Cir. 1984), **53**
Roland Machinery Co. v. Dresser Industries Inc., 749 F.2d 380 (7th Cir. 1984), **153**
Rothery Storage & Van Co. v. Atlas Van Lines, Inc., 792 F. 2d 210 (D.C. Cir. 1986), **84, 91**
Sanofi-Aventis et al. v. Apotex Inc. et al., 659 F.3d 1171 (Fed. Cir. 2011), **178**
Schering-Plough Corp. v. FTC, 402 F.3d 1056 (11th Cir. 2005), **76, 100–102, 104, 106, 107, 120–122, 124, 125, 127, 128, 144, 149, 159**
Schering-Plough Corp., Upsher-Smith Labs. & Am. Home Prods. Corp., Initial Decision, FTC Docket, No. 9297 (June 27, 2002), **159, 160**
Simpson v. Union Oil Co., 84 S. Ct. 1051 (1964), **110**
SmithKline Beecham Corporation, et al. v. King Drug Company of Florence, Inc., et al., 137 S. Ct. 446, (S.Ct. 2016), **191**
SmithKline Diagnostics, Inc. v. Helena Labs. Corp., 859 F. 2d 878 (Fed. Cir. 1988), **118**
SmithKline Corp. v. Eli Lilly & Co., 427 F. Supp. 1089 (E.D. Pa. 1976), **161**
Sousa v. First Cal. Co., 101 Cal. App. 2d 533 (1950), **176**
Spectrum Sports, Inc. v. McQuillan, 113 S. Ct. 884 (1993), **158**
Staff Builders of Philadelphia, Inc. et al. v. Koschitzki et al., 989 F.2d 692 (3rd Cir. 1993), **176**
Standard Oil Co. of California and Standard Stations v. United States, 69 S. Ct. 1051 (1949), **84**
Standard Oil Co. v. United States, 51 S. Ct. 421 (1931), **103**
Standard Oil Co. v. United States, 31 S. Ct. 502 (1911), **152**
State Oil Co. v. Khan, 118 S. Ct. 275 (1997), **85**
Stratoflex, Inc. v. Aeroquip Corp., 713 F.2d 1530 (Fed. Cir. 1983), **108**
Tanaka v. Univ. of S. Cal., 252 F.3d 1059 (9th Cir. 2001), **159**
Texaco Inc. v. Dagher, 126 S. Ct. 1276 (2006), **84**
Teva Pharm. Indus. Ltd. v. Crawford, 410 F.3d 51 (D.C. Cir. 2005), **177, 178**
Teva Pharmaceuticals USA, Inc. et al. v. Abbott Laboratories et al., No. 02-1512 (D. Del. 2008), **206**
Teva Pharms. USA, Inc. v. Pfizer, Inc., 395 F.3d 1324 (Fed. Cir. 2005), **52, 59, 74**
Teva Pharm. USA, Inc. v. Novartis Pharm. Corp., 482 F.3d 1330 (Fed. Cir. 2007), **74**
The People of New York v. Actavis PLC, Forest Labs LLC, No. 14 Civ. 7473 (S.D.N.Y. 2014), **209**
Time Ins. Co. v. AstraZeneca AB, No. 14-4149, 52 F. Supp. 3d 705 (E.D. Pa. 2014), **186, 189**
Trans-Missouri Freight Ass'n v. United States, 17 S. Ct. 540 (1897), **83, 93**
Tunis Brothers Co., Inc. v. Ford Motor Co., 952 F.2d 715, 722 (3rd Cir. 1991), **156**
Under Sea Indus., Inc. v. Dacor Corp., 833 F.2d 1551 (Fed. Cir. 1987), **119**
United Food & Commercial Workers Local 1776 v. Teikoku Pharma USA, Inc., 74 F. Supp. 3d 1052 (N.D. Cal. 2014), **186, 189, 192**
United States v. Addyston Pipe & Steel Co. et al., 85 F. 271 (6th Cir. 1898), **83, 84, 93**
United States v. Arnold, Schwinn & Co., 87 S. Ct. 1856 (1967), **86**

United States v. Brown Univ., 5 F.3d 658 (3d Cir. 1993), **128**
United States v. Dentsply International, Inc., 399 F.3d 181 (3rd Cir. 2005), **210**
United States v. E. I. du Pont de Nemours & Co., 76 S. Ct. 994 (1956), **156, 158, 280**
United States v. E. I. du Pont de Nemours & Co., 77 S. Ct. 872 (1957), **156**
United States v. General Electric Co., 47 S. Ct. 192 (1926), **85, 110**
United States v. General Motors Corp., 86 S. Ct. 1321 (1966), **86**
United States v. Grinnell Corp. et al., 86 S. Ct. 1698 (1966), **207**
United States v. Line Material Co., 68 S. Ct. 550 (1948), **113, 146, 193**
United States v. Masonite Corp., 62 S. Ct. 1070 (1942), **113**
United States v. Microsoft Corp. 253 F.3d 34 (D.C. Cir. 2001), **207, 210**
United States v. New Wrinkle, Inc., 72 S. Ct. 350 (1952), **146, 193**
United States v. Studiengesellschaft Kohle, m.b.H., 670 F.2d 1122 (D.C.Cir. 1981), **126**
United States v. Socony-Vacuum Oil Co., 60 S. Ct. 811 (1940), **84**
United States v. Singer Mfg. Co., 83 S. Ct. 1773 (1963), **93, 104, 113, 146, 171**
Upsher-Smith Laboratories, Inc., Petitioner v. Louisiana Wholesale Drug Company Inc., et al., 133 S. Ct. 2849 (June 24, 2013), **134, 135**
U.S. Healthcare, Inc. v. Healthsource, Inc., 986 F.2d 589 (1st Cir. 1993), **153**
Valley Drug Co. v. Geneva Pharms, Inc., 344 F.3d 1294 (11th Cir. 2003), **76, 86, 100–102, 107, 113, 117, 119, 120, 125, 127, 128, 144, 159**
Verizon Commc'ns Inc. v. Law Offices of Curtis V. Trinko, LLP, 124 S. Ct. 872 (2004), **211**
Walgreen Comp. et al. v. AstraZeneca Pharms. et al., 534 F. Supp. 2d.146 (D.D.C. 2008), **208, 209**
Walker Process Equip., Inc. v. Food Mach & Chem. Corp., 86 S. Ct. 347 (1965), **106, 156, 158**
Warner-Lambert Co. v. Apotex, 316 F.3d 1348 (Fed. Cir. 2003), **57**
Water Tech. Corp. et al. v. Calco Ltd., 850 F.2d 660, 671 (Fed. Cir. 1988), **197**
White Motor Co. v. United States, 83 S. Ct. 696 (1963), **86**
Whittemore v. Cutter, 29 F. Cas. 1120 (C.C.D. Mass. 1813) (No. 17,600), **53**
W.L. Gore & Assocs., Inc. v. Garlock, Inc., 721 F.2d 1540 (Fed. Cir. 1983), **108**
W. Penn Allegheny Health Sys., Inc. v. UPMC, 627 F.3d 85 (3rd Cir. 2010), **185**
Yamanouchi Pharm. Co., Ltd. et al. v. Danburry Pharmacal, Inc., et al., 231 F.3d 1339, (Fed. Cir. 2000), **59**
Zeneca Ltd. v. Pharmachemie B.V., No. 96-12413 (D. Mass. 2000), **104, 117**
Zeneca Ltd. v. Novopharm Ltd., No. 96-1364, (Fed. Cir. 1997) (unpublished opinion), **104, 117**

B Briefs & Memoranda

1 United States Briefs

Brief for the United States in Response to the Court's Invitation, *Arkansas Carpenters Health & Welfare Fund v. Bayer AG*, (Nos. 05-2851-cv(L), 05-2852-cv (CON), 05-2863-cv (CON), on appeal from the United States District Court for the Eastern

District of New York, (July 7, 2009). [cited as: U.S., Response Brief, *Arkansas Carpenters v. Bayer*], **105**

Brief for the United States as *Amicus Curiae* on Petition for Writ of *Certiorari, FTC v. Schering-Plough Corp.*, (No. 05-273) (May 17, 2006). [cited as: U.S., Amicus Brief, *FTC v. Schering-Plough*], **132**

Brief for the United States as Amicus Curiae Supporting Plaintiffs-Appellants, *In re K-Dur Antitrust Litigation*, (Nos. 10-2077, 10-2078, 10-2079) (May 18, 2011). [cited as: U.S., Amicus Brief, *In re K-Dur*], **95**

Brief for the United States as *Amicus Curiae, Joblove v. Barr Labs., Inc.*, (No. 06-830) (May 23, 2007). [cited as: U.S., Amicus Brief, *Joblove v. Barr*], **105**

2 FTC Briefs

Brief for the FTC on Petition for a Writ of *Certiorari* to the United States Court of Appeals for the Eleventh Circuit, *FTC v. Schering-Plough Corp. et al.*, (No. 05-273) (Aug. 29, 2005). [cited as: FTC, Certiorari Brief, *FTC v. Schering-Plough*], **132**

Brief for the FTC as *Amicus Curiae* Supporting Appellants and Urging Reversal, *In re K-Dur Antitrust Litigation*, (Nos. 10-2078, 10-2077, 10-2079) (May 18, 2011). [cited as: FTC, Amicus Brief, *In re K-Dur*], **113, 131**

FTC Brief as Plaintiff-Appellant in *FTC v. Watson Pharmaceuticals, Inc., et al.*, (No. 10-12729-DD), (June 26, 2010). Available at: http://www.ftc.gov/sites/default/files/documents/cases/2010/07/100726androgelbrief.pdf (last accessed on March 31, 2018). [cited as: FTC, Appellant Brief, *FTC v. Watson Pharmaceuticals*, 2010], **144**

FTC Brief on Writ of *Certiorari* to the United States Court of Appeals for the Eleventh Circuit, *FTC v. Watson Pharmaceuticals Inc. et al.*, (No. 12-416) (Jan. 22, 2013). [cited as: FTC, Certiorari Brief, *FTC v. Watson Pharmaceuticals*], **95, 130, 134**

FTC Brief as *Amicus Curiae, Actelion Pharms Ltd. v. Apotex Inc.*, Case No. 1:12-cv-05743-NLH-AMD, (March 11, 2013). Available at: https://www.ftc.gov/policy/advocacy/amicus-briefs/2013/03/actelion-pharmaceuticals-ltd-et-al-v-apotex-inc. [cited as: FTC, Amicus Brief, *Actelion Pharms v. Apotex*], **200, 201**

FTC Brief as *Amicus Curiae, In re: Effexor XR Antitrust Litigation*, no. 11-5479 (PGS)(LHG), (August 14, 2013). [cited as: FTC, Amicus Brief, *In Re Effexor XR*], **183, 189**

FTC Brief as *Amicus Curiae, In re Wellbutrin XL Antitrust Litig.*, Case no.: 2:08-cv-2431, Case no.: 2:08-cv-2433, (Sept. 26, 2013). [cited as: FTC, Amicus Brief, *In Re Wellbutrin XL*], **189, 193**

FTC Brief as *Amicus Curiae* in Support of Plaintiffs-Appellants, *In Re Lamictal Direct Purchaser Antitrust Litigation, King Drug Company of Florence, Inc., et al. v. SmithKlineBeecham Corp. et al.*, (No. 14-1243), (April 28, 2014). Available at: https://www.ftc.gov/system/files/documents/amicus_briefs/re-lamictal-direct-purchaser-antitrust-litigation/140428lamictalbrief.pdf. [cited as: FTC, Amicus Brief, *In Re Lamictal*], **180, 187, 189 190, 192**

FTC Brief as *Amicus Curiae, Mylan Pharms. v. Celgene Corp.*, Case No. 2:14-CV-2094-ES-MAH, (June 17, 2014). Available at: https://www.ftc.gov/policy/advocacy/

amicus-briefs/2014/06/mylan-pharmaceuticals-inc-v-celgene-corporation. [cited as: FTC, *Amicus* Brief, *Mylan Pharms. v. Celgene*], **202**

FTC Brief as *Amicus Curiae* Supporting Plaintiff-Appellant, *Mylan Pharmaceuticals Inc. v. Warner Chilcott PLC et al.*, (Sept. 30, 2015). [cited as: FTC, *Amicus* Brief, *Mylan Pharms. v. Warner* Chilcott, 2015], **204, 211, 212**

FTC Brief as *Amicus Curiae* in Support of Plaintiff-Appellant Mylan Pharmaceuticals Inc.'s Petition for Rehearing and Rehearing *Ex Banc, Mylan Pharmaceuticals Inc. v. Warner Chilcott PLC et al.*, (Oct. 19, 2016). [cited as: FTC, *Amicus* Brief for Rehearing, *Mylan Pharms. v. Warner Chilcott*, 2016], **212**

The States of New York, Arizona, Arkansas et al. Brief as *Amici Curiae* in support of Petitioner for a Writ of *Certiorari, FTC v. Watson Pharmaceuticals, Inc., et al.*, no. 12-416, (November, 5, 2012), [cited as: States, *Amici* Brief, *FTC v. Watson Pharmaceuticals*], **151**

3 Other Briefs

Brief for Representative Henry A. Waxman as *Amicus Curiae* Supporting Petitioner, *FTC v. Schering-Plough Corp.*, (No. 05-273) (Sept. 30, 2005). [cited as: WAXMAN, *Amicus* Brief, *FTC v. Schering-Plough*], **132**

Brief of States as *Amici Curiae* Supporting FTC on petition for a Writ of *certiorari, FTC v. Schering-Plough*, (No. 05-273) (Sept. 30, 2005). [cited as: States, *Amici* Brief, *FTC v. Schering-Plough*], **132**

Consolidated Answering Brief for Defendant-Appellee Andrx Pharmaceuticals, Inc., *Biovail Corporation v. Andrx Pharmaceuticals*, (Nos. 00-5050, 00-5396) (Dec. 28, 2000). [cited as: Andrx, Answering Brief, *Biovail v. Andrx*], **90**

Corrected Brief for 28 Professors of Law, Business and Economics as *Amici Curiae* Supporting Appellants *In re Ciprofloxacin Hydrochloride Antitrust Litig.*, (No. 2008-1097) (Feb. 8, 2008). [cited as: 28 Professors, *Amici* Brief, *Ciprofloxacin*], **108**

Representative Henry A. Waxman Brief as *Amicus Curiae* in support of Petitioner for a Writ of *Certiorari* in *FTC v. Watson Pharmaceuticals, Inc., et al.*, (No. 12-416) (Jan. 29, 2013). [cited as: WAXMAN, *Amicus* Brief, *FTC v. Watson Pharmaceuticals*], **122**

118 Law, Economics, and Business Professors and the American Antitrust Institute Brief as *Amici Curiae* in *FTC v. Watson Pharmaceuticals, Inc. et al.*, no. 12-416, (January, 29, 2013). [cited as: 118 Professors, *Amici* Brief, *FTC v. Watson Pharmaceuticals*], **146**

48 Law, Economics and Business Professors and the American Antitrust Institute Brief as *Amici Curiae* in Support of Appellants, *In Re Lipitor Antitrust Litigation*, Nos. 14-4202, 14-4203, 14-4204, 14-4205, 14-4206, 14-6202, 14-4632, (Dec. 28, 2015). [cited as: 48 Professors, *Amici* Brief, *In Re Lipitor*], **185, 199**

Brief for the American Antitrust Institute as *Amicus Curiae* in Support of Plaintiff-Appellant Mylan Pharmaceuticals Inc.'s Petition for Rehearing and Rehearing *Ex Banc, Mylan Pharmaceuticals Inc. v. Warner Chilcott PLC et al.*, (Oct. 19, 2016).

[cited as: AAI, *Amicus* Brief for Rehearing, *Mylan Pharms. v. Warner Chilcott*, 2016], **212**

4 Memoranda

Supplemental Memorandum in Support of Teva Defendants' Motions to Dismiss, *In re: Effexor XR Antitrust Litigation*, no. 11-5479 (PGS)(LHG), (August 7, 2013). [cited as: Teva Defendants' Support Memorandum, *In re: Effexor XR*, 2013], **183**

Supplemental Memorandum in Further Support of Wyeth's Defendants' Motions to Dismiss All Complaints, *In re: Effexor XR Antitrust Litigation*, no. 11-05479, Doc. No. 231, (August 7, 2013). [cited as: Wyeth's Defendants' Support Memorandum, *In re: Effexor XR*, 2013], **183**

5 Speeches/Congressional Records

Senator HATCH Orrin, 148 Cong. Rec. 14437, (2002), **148**
Representative WAXMAN Henry A., 146 Cong. Rec. 18774, (2000), **148**

6 Websites

FDA WEBSITE, "Orange Book Preface," 38th edition. Available at: http://www.fda.gov/Drugs/DevelopmentApprovalProcess/ucm079068.htm. (last accessed on March 31, 2018), **46**

FDA Website, *Generic Drugs*. Available at: https://www.fda.gov/Drugs/ResourcesForYou/Consumers/BuyingUsingMedicineSafely/GenericDrugs/default.htm (last accessed on March 31, 2018), **26, 30, 45**

FDA, *New Drug Therapy Approvals Report for 2017*, (January 2018). Available at: https://www.fda.gov/downloads/AboutFDA/CentersOffices/OfficeofMedicalProductsandTobacco/CDER/ReportsBudgets/UCM591976.pdf (last accessed on March 31, 2018), **17, 44**

US Courts Website, *Federal Judicial Caseload Statistics*, Available at: http://www.uscourts.gov/statistics-reports/analysis-reports/federal-judicial-caseload-statistics (last accessed on March 31, 2018), **32**

US Department of Health and Human Services, National Institutes of Health (NIH), *Budget*. Available at: https://www.nih.gov/about-nih/what-we-do/budget (last accessed on March 31, 2018), **15**

7 Questions & Answers

FDA, *What are Biologicals: Questions & Answers*. Available at: http://www.fda.gov/AboutFDA/CentersOffices/OfficeofMedicalProductsandTobacco/CBER/ucm133077.htm (last accessed on March 31, 2018), **17**

8 Letters

CBO, ELMENDORF Douglas W., Letter to Congressman Paul Ryan, November 4, 2010. Available at: https://www.cbo.gov/sites/default/files/cbofiles/ftpdocs/116xx/doc11674/11-04-drug_pricing.pdf. (last accessed on March 31, 2018). [cited as: ELMENDORF, 2010], **14, 29**

C FTC's Opinions-Orders-Complaints

1 Decisions, Opinions, Orders

FTC, Decision, *Warner-Lambert Co.*, 87 F.T.C. 812, Docket 8850, (April 27, 1976). [cited as: FTC, Decision, *Warner-Lambert*, 1976], **161**

In re Schering-Plough Corp., Final FTC Order, 136 F.T.C. 956 (FTC 2003). [cited as: FTC, Final Order, *Schering-Plough*, 2003], **93**

FTC, Decision, *In re Bristol-Myers Squibb Co.*, 135 F.T.C. 444, Docket No. C-4076 (April 14, 2003). [cited as: FTC, Decision, *Bristol-Myers Squibb*, 2003], **165**

FTC, *Stipulated Order for Permanent Injunction with Teikoku Seiyaku Co., Ltd., and Teikoku Pharma USA, Inc.*, Case No. 2:16-cv-01440-PD, (Mar. 30, 2016). [cited as: FTC, *Order for Permanent Injunction with Teikoku*, 2016], **165**

FTC, *Stipulated Order for Permanent Injunction with Endo Pharmaceuticals Inc. and Endo International PLC*, Case No. 17-cv-00312, (Jan. 23, 2017). [cited as: FTC, *Order for Permanent Injunction with Endo*, 2017], **165**

2 Complaints

FTC, Second Amended Complaint for Injunctive and Other Equitable Relief, *FTC v. Watson Pharmaceuticals, Inc., et al.*, no. 1:09-CV-00955-TWT, (May 28, 2009). Available at: http://www.ftc.gov/sites/default/files/documents/cases/2009/05/090528androgelfinalcmpt.pdf (last accessed on March 31, 2018). [cited as: FTC, Amended Complaint, *Watson Pharms*, 2009], 143

FTC, Administrative Complaint, *In re Schering-Plough Corp., Upsher-Smith Laboratories, Inc., and American Home Products Corp.*, Docket No. 9297, (Mar. 30, 2001). [cited as: FTC, Administrative Complaint, *Schering-Plough*, 2001], **135**

FTC, Complaint, *Abbott Labs. & Geneva Pharm., Inc.*, FTC Docket Nos. C-3945, 3946 (May 22, 2000). [cited as: FTC, Complaint, *Abbott Labs. & Geneva Pharm.*, 2000], **160**

FTC, Complaint, *Hoechst Marion Roussel, Inc. & Andrx Corp.*, FTC Docket No. 9293 (Mar. 16, 2000). [cited as: FTC, Complaint, *Hoechst Marion Roussel, Inc. & Andrx Corp.*, 2000], **160**

FTC, Complaint for Injunctive and other Equitable Relief, *FTC v. AbbVie et al.*, Case 2:14-cv-05151-HB, (September 8, 2014). [cited as: FTC, Complaint, *FTC v. AbbVie et al.*, 2014], **143, 167**

FTC, Complaint, *FTC v. Endo Pharmaceuticals et al.*, Case 2:16-cv-01440-PD, (March 30, 2016). [cited as: FTC, Complaint, *FTC v. Endo Pharmaceuticals et al.*, 2016], **213**

FTC, Complaint, *FTC v. Impax Laboratories Inc.*, Docket No. 9373, (January 19, 2017). [cited as: FTC, Complaint, *FTC v. Impax Laboratories Inc.*, 2017], **214**

FTC, Complaint, *FTC v. Allergan et al.*, Case No. 17-cv-00312, (January 23, 2017). [cited as: FTC, Complaint, *FTC v. Allergan et al.*, 2017], **214**

Indirect Purchaser Class Plaintiffs' Consolidated Class Action Complaint and Jury Demand, *In re: Effexor XR Antitrust Litigation*, (September 1, 2012). [cited as: Indirect Purchaser Class Action, *In re: Effexor XR*, 2012], **183**

WALGREEN CO. et AL., First Amended Complaint and Demand for Jury Trial, *Walgreen Co. v. AstraZeneca Pharm. L.P.*, No. 1:06- cv-02084-RWR (2006). [cited as: WALGREEN, Amended Complaint, *Walgreen Co. v. AstraZeneca Pharm.*, 2006], **206**

II European Union

A List of Cases and AG Opinions

1 Decisions of the Court of Justice of the European Union

Judgment of the Court of 15 July 1970, Case 41/69, *ACF Chemiefarma NV v. Commission of the European Communities*, EU:C:1970:71, **246**

Judgment of the Court of 12 March 2015, Case C-577/13, *Actavis Group PTC EHF and Actavis UK Ltd v. Boehringer Ingelheim Pharma GmbH & Co. KG*, EU:C:2015:165, **370**

Judgment of the Court of 12 December 2013, Case C-443/12, *Actavis Group PTC EHF and Actavis UK Ltd v. Sanofi*, EU:C:2013:833, **370**

Judgment of the Court of 27 September 1988, Joined cases 89, 104, 114, 116, 117 and 125 to 129/85, *Ahlström Osakeyhtiö and others v. Commission of the European Communities*, EU:C:1988:447, **256**

Judgment of the Court of 5 October 1988, Case 238/87, *AB Volvo v. Erik Veng (UK) Ltd*, EU:C:1988:477, **293**

Judgment of the Court of 11 April 1989, Case C-66/86, *Ahmed Saeed Flugreisen v. Zentrale zur Bekampfung unlauteren Wettbewerb*, EU:C:1989:140, **362, 363**

Judgment of the Court of 3 July 1991, Case C-62/86, *AKZO Chemie BV v. Commission of the European Communities*, EU:C:1991:286, **276, 279, 285, 288–291**

Judgment of the Court of 21 September 1999, Case C-67/96, *Albany International BV v. Stichting Bedrijfspensioenfonds Textielindustrie*, EU:C:1999:430, **246**

Judgment of the Court of 23 November 2006, Case C-238/05, *Asnef-Equifax, Servicios de Información sobre Solvencia y Crédito, SL v. Asociación de Usuarios de Servicios Bancarios (Ausbanc)*, EU:C:2006:734, **258, 261**

Judgment of the Court of 29 September 2011, Case C-520/09 P, *Arkema SA v. European Commission*, EU:C:2011:619, **259**

Judgment of the Court of 6 December 2012, C-457/10 P, *AstraZeneca AB and AstraZeneca plc v. European Commission*, EU:C:2012:770, **276, 281, 284, 288, 290, 291, 296, 299, 366**

Judgment of the Court of 14 March 2013, Case C-32/11, *Allianz Hungária Biztosító Zrt. and Others v. Gazdasági Versenyhivatal*, EU:C:2013:160, **250, 252, 253, 329**

Judgment of the Court of 27 March 1974, Case 127-73, *Belgische Radio en Televisie and société belge des auteurs, compositeurs et éditeurs v. SV SABAM and NV Fonior*, EU:C:1974:25, **287**

Judgment of the Court of 30 January 1985, Case 35/83, *BAT Cigaretten-Fabriken GmbH v. Commission of the European Communities*, EU:C:1985:32, **242, 251**

Judgment of the Court of 30 January 1985, Case 123/83, *Bureau national interprofessionnel du cognac v. Guy Clair*, EU:C:1985:33, **250**

Judgment of the Court of 11 November 1986, Case 226/84, *British Leyland Public Limited Company v. Commission of the European Communities*, EU:C:1986:421, **287**

Judgment of the Court of 21 September 1999, Joined cases C-115/97 to C-117/97, *Brentjens' Handelsonderneming BV v. Stichting Bedrijfspensioenfonds voor de Handel in Bouwmaterialen*, EU:C:1999:434, **246**

Judgment of the Court of 6 January 2004, Joined cases C-2/01 P and C-3/01 P, *Bundesverband der Arzneimittel-Importeure eV and Commission of the European Communities v. Bayer AG*, EU:C:2004:2, **287**

Judgment of the Court of 15 March 2007, Case C-95/04 P, *British Airways plc v. Commission of the European Communities*, EU:C:2007:166, **277, 291, 300**

Judgment of the Court of 20 November 2008, Case C-209/07, *Competition Authority v. Beef Industry Development Society Ltd and Barry Brothers (Carrigmore) Meats Ltd*, EU:C:2008:643. [cited, Case C-209/07, *Beef Industry*], **248, 249, 262**

Judgment of the Court of 31 October 1974, Case 15-74 *Centrafarm BV and Adriaan de Peijper v. Sterling Drug Inc.*, EU:C:1974:114, **321**

Judgment of the Court of 25 March 1981, Case 61/80, *Coöperatieve Stremsel – en Kleurselfabriek v. Commission of the European Communities*, EU:C:1981:75, **242**

Judgment of the Court of 28 March 1984, Joined cases 29/83 and 30/83, *Compagnie Royale Asturienne des Mines SA and Rheinzink GmbH v. Commission of the European Communities*, EU:C:1984:130, **239, 250–251**

Judgment of the Court of 16 June 1987, Case 118/85, *Commission of the European Communities v. Italian Republic*, EU:C:1987:283, **243**

Judgment of the Court of 18 June 1998, Case C-35/96, *Commission of the European Communities v. Italian Republic*, EU:C:1998:303, **242, 243**

Judgment of the Court of 21 January 1999, Joined cases C-215/96 and C-216/96, *Carlo Bagnasco and Others v. Banca Popolare di Novara soc. coop. arl. (BNP) (C-215/96) and Cassa di Risparmio di Genova e Imperia SpA (Carige) (C-216/96)*, EU:C:1999:12, **258**

Judgment of the Court of 8 July 1999, Case C-49/92 P, *Commission of the European Communities v. Anic Partecipazioni SpA*, EU:C:1999:356, **245, 247**

Table of Cases

Judgment of the Court of 16 September 1999, *Criminal proceedings against Jean Claude Becu, Annie Verweire, Smeg NV and Adia Interim NV*, EU:C:1999:419, **242**

Judgment of the Court of 16 March 2000, Joined cases C-395/96 P and C-396/96 P, *Compagnie maritime belge transports SA (C-395/96 P), Compagnie maritime belge SA (C-395/96 P) and Dafra-Lines A/S (C-396/96 P) v. Commission of the European Communities*, EU:C:2000:132, **276**

Judgment of the Court of 20 September 2001, Case C-453/99, *Courage Ltd v. Bernard Crehan and Bernard Crehan v. Courage Ltd and Others*, EU:C:2001:465, **240**

Judgment of the Court of 22 January 2002, Case C-218/00, *Cisal di Battistello Venanzio & C. Sas v. Istituto nazionale per l'assicurazione contro gli infortuni sul lavoro (INAIL)*, EU:C:2002:36, **243**

Judgment of the Court of 13 July 2006, Case C-74/04 P, *Commission of the European Communities v. Volkswagen AG*, EU:C:2006:460, **287**

Judgment of the Court of 20 November 2008, Case C-209/07, *Competition Authority v. Beef Industry Development Society Ltd and Barry Brothers (Carrigmore) Meats Ltd*, EU:C:2008:643, **248, 249, 262**

Judgment of the Court of 18 December 2008, *Coop de France bétail et viande (C-101/07 P) and Fédération nationale des syndicats d'exploitants agricoles (FNSEA) and Others (C-110/07 P) v. Commission of the European Communities*, EU:C:2008:741, **242**

Judgment of the Court of 12 July 2012, Case C-138/11, *Compass-Datenbank GmbH v. Republik Österreich*, EU:C:2012:449, **243**

Judgment of the Court of 18 July 2013, *Consiglio nazionale dei geologi v. Autorità garante della concorrenza e del mercato and Autorità garante della concorrenza e del mercato v. Consiglio nazionale dei geologi*, EU:C:2013:489, **242**

Judgment of the Court of 18 March 1997, Case C-343/95, *Diego Calì & Figli Srl v. Servizi ecologici porto di Genova SpA (SEPG)*, EU:C:1997:160, **243**

Judgment of the Court of 28 June 2005, Joined cases C-189/02 P, C-202/02 P, C-205/02 P to C-208/02 P and C-213/02 P, *Dansk Rørindustri A/S (C-189/02 P), Isoplus Fernwärmetechnik Vertriebsgesellschaft mbH and Others (C-202/02 P), KE KELIT Kunststoffwerk GmbH (C-205/02 P), LR af 1998 A/S (C-206/02 P), Brugg Rohrsysteme GmbH (C-207/02 P), LR af 1998 (Deutschland) GmbH (C-208/02 P) and ABB Asea Brown Boveri Ltd (C-213/02 P) v. Commission of the European Communities*, EU:C:2005:408, **259**

Judgment of the Court of 14 October 2010, Case C-280/08 P, *Deutsche Telekom AG v. European Commission*, EU:C:2010:603, **277, 278**

Judgment of the Court of 19 March 2015, Case C-286/13 P, *Dole Food Company, Inc. and Dole Fresh Fruit Europe v. European Commission*, EU:C:2015:184, **333**

Judgment of the Court of 13 July 1966, Joined cases 56 and 58/64, *Établissements Consten S.à.R.L. and Grundig-Verkaufs-GmbH v. Commission of the European Economic Community*, EU:C:1966:41, **240, 357**

Judgment of the Court of 21 February 1973, Case 6-72, *Europemballage Corporation and Continental Can Company Inc. v. Commission of the European Communities*, EU:C:1973:22, **291, 297**

Judgment of the Court of First Instance of 15 September 1998, Joined cases T-374/94, T-375/94, T-384/94 and T-388/94, *European Night Services Ltd (ENS), Eurostar (UK) Ltd, formerly European Passenger Services Ltd (EPS), Union internationale des chemins de fer (UIC), NV Nederlandse Spoorwegen (NS) and Société nationale des chemins de fer français (SNCF) v. Commission of the European Communities*, EU:T:1998:198, **246, 254, 286**

Judgment of the Court of 16 October 2012, Case C-614/10, *European Commission v. Republic of Austria*, EU:C:2012:631, **236**

Judgment of the Court of 13 December 2012, Case C-226/11, *Expedia Inc. v. Autorité de la concurrence and Others*, EU:C:2012:795, **249, 250, 258, 259**

Judgment of the Court of 9 July 1969, Case 5/69, *Franz Völk v. S.P.R.L. Ets J. Vervaecke*, EU:C:1969:35, **257–258**

Judgment of the Court of 16 November 1995, Case C-244/94, *Fédération Française des Sociétés d'Assurance, Société Paternelle-Vie, Union des Assurances de Paris-Vie and Caisse d'Assurance et de Prévoyance Mutuelle des Agriculteurs v. Ministère de l'Agriculture et de la Pêche*, EU:C:1995:392, **243**

Judgment of the Court of 2 April 2009, Case C-202/07 P, *France Télécom SA v. Commission of the European Communities*, EU:C:2009:214, **278, 291**

Judgment of the Court of 6 April 2006, Case C-551/03 P, *General Motors BV v. Commission of the European Communities*, EU:C:2006:229, **251**

Judgment of the Court of 6 October 2009, Joined cases C-501/06 P, C-513/06 P, C-515/06 P and C-519/06 P, *GlaxoSmithKline Services Unlimited v. Commission of the European Communities (C-501/06 P) and Commission of the European Communities v. GlaxoSmithKline Services Unlimited (C-513/06 P) and European Association of Euro Pharmaceutical Companies (EAEPC) v. Commission of the European Communities (C-515/06 P) and Asociación de exportadores españoles de productos farmacéuticos (Aseprofar) v. Commission of the European Communities (C-519/06 P)*, EU:C:2009:610, **262–263**

Judgment of the Court of 11 September 2014, Case C-67/13 P, *Groupement des cartes bancaires (CB) v. European Commission*, EU:C:2014:2204 (cited: Case C-67/13 P, Cartes Bancaires), **253**

Judgment of the Court of 7 July 2016, Case C-567/14, *Genentech Inc. v. Hoechst GmbH and Sanofi-Aventis Deutschland GmbH*, EU:C:2016:526, **341**

Judgment of the Court of 13 February 1979, Case 85/76, *Hoffmann-La Roche & Co. AG v. Commission of the European Communities*, EU:C:1979:36, **276, 278, 288–291, 297, 362, 365**

Judgment of the Court of 31 May 1979, Case 22/78, *Hugin Kassaregister AB and Hugin Cash Registers Ltd v. Commission of the European Communities*, EU:C:1979:138, **257**

Judgment of the Court of 8 July 1999, Case C-199/92 P, *Hüls AG v. Commission of the European Communities*, EU:C:1999:358, **239, 245**

Judgment of the Court of 16 July 2015, Case C-170/13, *Huawei Technologies Co. Ltd v. ZTE Corp. and ZTE Deutschland GmbH*, EU:C:2015:477, **293, 295–296**

Judgment of the Court of 23 January 2018, Case C-179/16, *F. Hoffmann-La Roche Ltd., La Roche SpA, Novartis AG and Novartis Farma SpA v. Autorità Garante della Concorrenza e del Mercato*, EU:C:2018:25, **372**
Judgment of the Court of 16 July 2015, Case C-172/14, *ING Pensii – Societate de Administrare a unui Fond de Pensii Administrat Privat SA v. Consiliul Concurenței*, EU:C:2015:484, **249, 250**
Judgment of the Court of 9 July 2015, Case C-231/14 P, *InnoLux Corp. v. European Commission*, EU:C:2015:451, **333**
Judgment of the Court of 6 September 2017, Case C-413/14 P, *Intel Corporation Inc. v. Commission*, EU:C:2017:632, **314**
Judgment of the Court of 28 May 1998, Case C-7/95 P, *John Deere Ltd v. Commission of the European Communities*, EU:C:1998:256, **258**
Judgment of the Court of 28 April 1998, Case C-306/96, *Javico International and Javico AG v. Yves Saint Laurent Parfums SA (YSLP)*, EU:C:1998:173, **256**
Judgment of the Court of 11 December 1997, Case C-55/96, *Job Centre coop. arl.*, EU:C:1997:603, **243**
Judgment of the Court of 19 February 2002, Case C-309/99, *J. C. J. Wouters, J. W. Savelbergh and Price Waterhouse Belastingadviseurs BV v. Algemene Raad van de Nederlandse Orde van Advocaten, intervener: Raad van de Balies van de Europese Gemeenschap*, EU:C:2002:98, **242, 244, 255, 256**
Judgment of the Court of 12 May 1989, Case 320/87, *Kai Ottung v. Klee & Weilbach A/S and Thomas Schmidt A/S*, EU:C:1989:195, **341**
Judgment of the Court of 23 April 1991, Case C-41/90, *Klaus Höfner and Fritz Elser v. Macrotron GmbH*, EU:C:1991:161, **241, 244**
Judgment of the Court of 11 December 2008, Case C-52/07, *Kanal 5 Ltd and TV 4 AB v. Föreningen Svenska Tonsättares Internationella Musikbyrå (STIM) upa*, EU:C:2008:703, **290, 291**
Judgment of the Court of 17 February 2011, C-52/09, *Konkurrensverket v. TeliaSonera Sverige AB*, EU:C:2011:83, **276, 277, 278, 290, 291, 300**
Judgment of the Court of 5 May 2015, Case C-146/13, *Kingdom of Spain v. European Parliament and Council of the European Union*, ECLI:EU:C:2015:298, **222**
Judgment of the Court of 1 February 1978, Case 19/77, *Miller International Schallplatten GmbH v. Commission of the European Communities*, EU:C:1978:19, **249**
Judgment of the Court of 8 July 1999, Case C-235/92 P, *Montecatini SpA v. Commission of the European Communities*, EU:C:1999:362, **239**
Judgment of the Court of First Instance of 18 September 2001, Case T-112/99, *Métropole télévision (M6), Suez-Lyonnaise des eaux, France Télécom and Télévision française 1 SA (TF1) v. Commission of the European Communities*, EU:T:2001:215, **255**
Judgment of the Court of 10 January 2006, Case C-222/04, *Ministero dell'Economia e delle Finanze v. Cassa di Risparmio di Firenze SpA, Fondazione Cassa di Risparmio di San Miniato and Cassa di Risparmio di San Miniato SpA*, EU:C:2006:8, **244**
Judgment of the Court of 1 July 2008, Case C-49/07, *Motosykletistiki Omospondia Ellados NPID (MOTOE) v. Elliniko Dimosio*, EU:C:2008:376, **243**

Judgment of the Court of 8 December 2011, Case C-125/10, *Merck Sharp & Dohme Corp. v. Deutsches Patent- und Markenamt*, EU:C:2011:812, **231**

Judgment of the Court of 12 December 2013, Case C-327/12, *Ministero dello Sviluppo economico and Autorità per la vigilanza sui contratti pubblici di lavori, servizi e forniture v. SOA Nazionale Costruttori – Organismo di Attestazione SpA*, EU:C:2013:827, **242**

Judgment of the Court of 11 September 2014, Case C-382/12 P, *MasterCard Inc. and Others v. European Commission*, EU:C:2014:2201, **245**

Judgment of the Court of 8 November 1983, *NV IAZ International Belgium and others v. Commission of the European Communities*, Joined cases 96-102, 104, 105, 108 and 110/82, EU:C:1983:310, **241, 250**

Judgment of the Court of 9 November 1983, Case 322/81, *NV Nederlandsche Banden Industrie Michelin v. Commission of the European Communities*, EU:C:1983:313, **276, 278, 286, 289**

Judgment of the Court of 28 February 2013, Case C-1/12, *Ordem dos Técnicos Oficiais de Contas v. Autoridade da Concorrência*, EU:C:2013:127, **242, 244**

Judgment of the Court of 29 February 1968, Case 24-67, *Parke, Davis and Co. v. Probel, Reese, Beintema-Interpharm and Centrafarm*, EU:C:1968:11, **292**

Judgment of the Court of 12 September 2000, Joined cases C-180/98 to C-184/98, *Pavel Pavlov and Others v. Stichting Pensioenfonds Medische Specialisten*, EU:C:2000:428, **242, 243, 259**

Judgment of the Court of 2 April 2009, Case C-260/07, *Pedro IV Servicios SL v. Total España SA*, EU:C:2009:215, **263**

Judgment of the Court of 14 June 2011, Case C-360/09, *Pfleiderer AG v. Bundeskartellamt*, EU:C:2011:389, **259**

Judgment of the Court of 13 October 2011, Case C-439/09, *Pierre Fabre Dermo-Cosmétique SAS v. Président de l'Autorité de la concurrence and Ministre de l'Économie, de l'Industrie et de l'Emploi*, EU:C:2011:649, **250, 251, 262**

Judgment of the Court of 27 March 2012, Case C-209/10, *Post Danmark A/S v. Konkurrencerådet*, EU:C:2012:172, **276, 300**

Judgment of the Court of 6 April 1995, Joined cases C-241/91 P and C-242/91 P, *Radio Telefis Eireann (RTE) and Independent Television Publications Ltd (ITP) v. Commission of the European Communities*, EU:C:1995:98, **292, 293**

Judgment of the Court of 30 June 1966, C-56/65, *Société Technique Minière (L.T.M.) v. Maschinenbau Ulm GmbH (M.B.U.)*, EU:C:1966:38, **241, 258**

Judgment of the Court of 16 December 1975, Joined cases 40 to 48, 50, 54 to 56, 111, 113 and 114-73, *Coöperatieve Vereniging "Suiker Unie" UA and others v. Commission of the European Communities*, EU:C:1975:174, **249, 287**

Judgment of the Court of 14 December 1983, Case 319/82, *Société de Vente de Ciments et Bétons de l'Est SA v. Kerpen & Kerpen GmbH und Co. KG*, EU:C:1983:374, **241**

Judgment of the Court of 28 February 1991, Case C-234/89, *Stergios Delimitis v. Henninger Bräu AG*, EU:C:1991:91, **246, 257**

Judgment of the Court of 19 January 1994, Case C-364/92, *SAT Fluggesellschaft mbH v. Eurocontrol*, EU:C:1994:7, **243**

Table of Cases

Judgment of the Court of 20 June 1978, Case 28/77, *Tepea BV v. Commission of the European Communities*, EU:C:1978:133, **246**

Judgment of the Court of 14 November 1996, Case C-333/94 P, *Tetra Pak International SA v. Commission of the European Communities*, EU:C:1996:436, **291**

Judgment of the Court of 9 September 2003, Case C-137/00, *The Queen v. The Competition Commission, Secretary of State for Trade and Industry and The Director General of Fair Trading, ex parte Milk Marque Ltd and National Farmers' Union*, EU:C:2003:429, **237**

Judgment of the Court of 4 June 2009, C-8/08, *T-Mobile Netherlands BV, KPN Mobile NV, Orange Nederland NV and Vodafone Libertel NV v. Raad van bestuur van de Nederlandse Mededingingsautoriteit*, EU:C:2009:343, **245, 250–252**

Judgment of the Court of 14 February 2012, Case C-17/10, *Toshiba Corporation and Others v. Úřad pro ochranu hospodářské soutěže*, EU:C:2012:72, **237, 238**

Judgment of the Court of 20 January 2016, Case C-373/14 P, *Toshiba Corporation v. European Commission*, EU:C:2016:26, **246, 250**

Judgment of the Court of 14 February 1978, Case 27/76, *United Brands Company and United Brands Continentaal BV v. Commission of the European Communities, Chiquita Bananas*, EU:C:1978:22, **278**

Judgment of the Court of 24 October 1996, Case C-73/95 P, *Viho Europe BV v. Commission of the European Communities*, EU:C:1996:405, **248**

Judgment of the Court of 13 July 2006, Joined Cases C-295/04 to C-298/04, *Vincenzo Manfredi v. Lloyd Adriatico Assicurazioni SpA (C-295/04), Antonio Cannito v. Fondiaria Sai SpA (C-296/04) and Nicolò Tricarico (C-297/04) and Pasqualina Murgolo (C-298/04) v. Assitalia SpA*, EU:C:2006:461, **237, 240**

Judgment of the Court of 13 February 1969, Case 14-68, *Walt Wilhelm v. Bundeskartellamt*, EU:C:1969:4, **235**

Judgment of the Court of 25 February 1986, Case 193/83, *Windsurfing International Inc. v. Commission of the European Communities*, EU:C:1986:75. [cited: Case 193/83, *Windsurfing*], **316, 321**

2 General Court Decisions (Former Court of First Instance)

Judgment of the Court of First Instance of 12 December 2000, Case T-128/98, *Aéroports de Paris v. Commission of the European Communities*, EU:T:2000:290, **290**

Judgment of the Court of First Instance of 12 December 2007, *Akzo Nobel NV and Others v. Commission of the European Communities*, EU:T:2007:381, **248**

Judgment of the Court of First Instance of 8 July 2008, T-99/04, *AC, Treuhand AG v. Commission of the European Communities*, EU:T:2008:256, **241**

Judgment of the General Court of 1 July 2010, Case T-321/05, *AstraZeneca AB and AstraZeneca plc v. European Commission*, EU:T:2010:266, **276, 278–280, 284, 289, 290, 297–299**

Judgment of the General Court of 25 October 2011, Case T-348/08, *Aragonesas Industrias y Energía, SAU v. European Commission*, EU:T:2011:621, **239**

Judgment of the General Court of 6 February 2014, Case T-27/10, *AC-Treuhand AG v. European Commission*, EU:T:2014:59, **243**

Judgment of the General Court of 8 September 2016, Case T-467/13, *Arrow Group ApS and Arrow Generics Ltd v. European Commission*, EU:T:2016:450, **315**

Judgment of the Court of First Instance of 1 April 1993, T-65/89, *BPB Industries Plc and British Gypsum Ltd v. Commission of the European Communities*, EU:T:1993:31, **257, 291**

Judgment of the Court of First Instance of 17 December 2003, Case T-219/99, *British Airways plc v. Commission of the European Communities*, EU:T:2003:343, **288**

Judgment of the Court of First Instance of 27 July 2005, Cases T-49/02 to T-51/02, *Brasserie nationale and Others v. Commission*, EU:T:2005:298, **333**

Judgment of the Court of First Instance of 8 July 2008, Case T-53/03, *BPB plc v. Commission of the European Communities*, EU:T:2008:254, **239**

Judgment of the Court of First Instance of 8 July 2004, Case T-48/00, *Corus UK Ltd, formerly British Steel plc v. Commission of the European Communities*, EU:T:2004:219, **332**

Judgment of the Court of First Instance of 21 October 1997, Case T-229/94, *Deutsche Bahn AG v. Commission of the European Communities*, EU:T:1997:155, **278, 284**

Judgment of the Court of First Instance of 8 July 2004, Case T-50/00, *Dalmine SpA v. Commission of the European Communities*, EU:T:2004:220, **332**

Judgment of the Court of First Instance of 4 July 2006, Case T-177/04, *easyJet Airline Co. Ltd v. Commission of the European Communities*, EU:T:2006:187, **247**

Judgment of the Court of First Instance of 4 March 2003, Case T-319/99, *Federación Nacional de Empresas de Instrumentación Científica, Médica, Técnica y Dental (FENIN) v. Commission of the European Communities*, EU:T:2003:50, **243**

Judgment of the Court of First Instance of 13 December 2006, Joined cases T-217/03 and T-245/03, *Fédération nationale de la coopération bétail et viande (FNCBV) (T-217/03) and Fédération nationale des syndicats d'exploitants agricoles (FNSEA) and Others (T-245/03) v. Commission of the European Communities*, EU:T:2006:391, **242**

Judgment of the General Court of 29 November 2012, Case T-491/07, *Groupement des cartes bancaires "CB" v. European Commission*, EU:T:2012:633, **253**

Judgment of the Court of First Instance of 12 December 1991, Case T-30/89, *Hilti AG v. Commission of the European Communities*, EU:T:1991:70, **288, 300**

Judgment of the Court of First Instance of 20 March 2002, Case T-9/99, *HFB Holding für Fernwärmetechnik Beteiligungsgesellschaft mbH & Co. KG and Others v. Commission of the European Communities*, ECR, EU:T:2002:70, **245, 248**

Judgment of the General Court of 12 July 2011, Case T-112/07, *Hitachi Ltd, Hitachi Europe Ltd and Japan AE Power Systems Corp. v. European Commission*, EU:T:2011:342, **247**

Judgment of the Court of First Instance of 7 October 1999, T-228/97, *Irish Sugar plc v. Commission of the European Communities*, EU:T:1999:246, **276**

Judgment of the General Court of 12 April 2013, Case T-442/08, *International Confederation of Societies of Authors and Composers (CISAC) v. European Commission*, EU:T:2013:188, **239**

Table of Cases

Judgment of the General Court of 12 June 2014, Case T-286/09, *Intel Corp. v. European Commission*, EU:T:2014:547, **256, 278**

Judgment of the Court of First Instance of 26 January 2005, Case T-193/02, *Laurent Piau v. Commission of the European Communities*, EU:T:2005:22, **244**

Judgment of the General Court of 8 September 2016, Case T-472/13, *H. Lundbeck A/S and Lundbeck Ltd v. European Commission*, EU:T:2016:449, **315**

Judgment of the Court of First Instance of 15 July 1994, Case T-17/93, *Matra Hachette SA v. Commission of the European Communities*, EU:T:1994:89, **262**

Judgment of the Court of First Instance of 30 September 2003, Case T-203/01, *Manufacture française des pneumatiques Michelin v. Commission of the European Communities*, EU:T:2003:250, **248**

Judgment of the Court of First Instance of 17 September 2007, Case T-201/04, *Microsoft Corp. v. Commission of the European Communities*, EU:T:2007:289, **293**

Judgment of the General Court of 8 September 2016, Case T-470/13, *Merck KGaA v. European Commission*, EU:T:2016:452, **315**

Judgment of the Court of First Instance of 2 May 2006, Case T-328/03, *O2 (Germany) GmbH & Co. OHG v. Commission of the European Communities*, EU:T:2006:116, **254**

Judgment of the Court of First Instance of 17 December 1991, Case T-7/89, *SA Hercules Chemicals NV v. Commission of the European Communities*, EU:T:1991:75, **245**

Judgment of the General Court of 8 September 2016, Case T-460/13, *Sun Pharmaceutical Industries Ltd, formerly Ranbaxy Laboratories Ltd and Ranbaxy (UK) Ltd v. European Commission*, EU:T:2016:453, **315**

Judgment of the Court of First Instance of 10 July 1990, Case T-51/89, *Tetra Pak Rausing SA v. Commission of the European Communities*, EU:T:1990:41, **292, 293, 362–363**

Judgment of the Court of First Instance of 12 June 1997, T-504/93, *Tiercé Ladbroke SA v. Commission of the European Communities*, EU:T:1997:84, **254**

Judgment of the Court of First Instance of 6 October 1994, Case T-83/91, *Tetra Pak International SA v. Commission of the European Communities*, EU:T:1994:246, **284**

Judgment of the Court of First Instance of 22 March 2000, Joined cases T-125/97 and T-127/97, *The Coca-Cola Company and Coca-Cola Enterprises Inc. v. Commission of the European Communities*, EU:T:2000:84, **279**

Judgment of the General Court of 9 September 2010, Case T-155/06, *Tomra Systems ASA and Others v. European Commission*, EU:T:2010:370, **278**

Judgment of the General Court of 21 May 2014, Case T-519/09, *Toshiba Corp. v. European Commission*, EU:T:2014:263, **246, 247**

Judgment of the Court of First Instance of 12 January 1995, Case T-102/92, *VIHO Europe BV v. Commission of the European Communities*, EU:T:1995:3, **248**

Judgment of the General Court of 14 April 2011, Case T-461/07, *Visa Europe Ltd and Visa International Service v. European Commission*, EU:T:2011:181, **246, 247, 252, 254**

Judgment of the General Court of 8 September 2016, Case T-471/13, *Xellia Pharmaceuticals ApS and Alpharma, LLC, formerly Zoetis Products LLC v. European Commission*, EU:T:2016:460, **315**

3 Advocate General Opinions

Opinion of Advocate General Jacobs delivered on 28 January 1999, Case C-67/96, *Albany International BV v. Stichting Bedrijfspensioenfonds Textielindustrie*, EU:C:1999:28, **244**

Opinion of Advocate General Tizzano delivered on 25 October 2005, Case C-551/03 P, *General Motors v. European Commission*, EU:C:2006:229, **251**

Opinion of Advocate-General Trstenjak delivered on 4 September 2008, Case C-209/07, *Competition Authority v. Beef Industry Development Society Ltd and Barry Brothers (Carrigmore) Meats Ltd.*, EU:C:2008:643, **251**

Opinion of Advocate General Kokott, delivered on 6 September 2012, Case C-226/11, *Expedia Inc.*, EU:C:2012:544, **259**

Opinion of Advocate General Wathelet delivered on 20 November 2014, Case C-170/13, *Huawei Technologies Co. Ltd v. ZTE Corp. and ZTE Deutschland GmbH*, EU:C:2014:2391, **296**

Opinion of Advocate General Wathelet delivered on 17 March 2016, Case C-567/14, *Genentech Inc. v. Hoechst GmbH and Sanofi-Aventis Deutschland GmbH*, EU:C:2016:177, **341**

4 Requests for a Preliminary Hearing

Case C-179/16: Request for a preliminary ruling from the Consiglio di Stato (Italy) lodged on 25 March 2016 – *F. Hoffmann-La Roche Ltd., La Roche SpA, Novartis AG and Novartis Farma SpA v. Autorità Garante della Concorrenza e del Mercato*, OJ C 222, 20.6.2016, p. 4-5, **374**

5 Appeals & Actions Before EU Courts

Case C-591/16 P: Appeal brought on 18 November 2016 by H. Lundbeck A/S, Lundbeck Ltd against the judgment of the General Court (Ninth Chamber) delivered on 8 September 2016 in Case T-472/13: *H. Lundbeck A/S, Lundbeck Ltd v. European Commission*. OJ C 30, 30.1.2017, pp. 25-26, **338–339**

Case T-691/14: Action brought on 21 September 2014, *Servier SAS and Others v. Commission*, OJ C 462, 22.12.2014, pp. 25-27, **364**

6 European Court of Human Rights (ECHR)

ECHR Judgment, *A. Menarini Diagnostics S.R.L. v. Italy*, No. 43509/08, 27 September 2011, **239**

Table of Cases

B European Commission Decisions et al.

1 European Commission Decisions

79/68/EEC: Commission Decision of 12 December 1978 relating to a proceeding under Article 85 of the EEC Treaty (IV/29.430 – Kawasaki), OJ L 16/9, 23.1.1979, p. 9-16. [cited as: EU Commission Decision, *Kawasaki*, 1978], **246**

82/896/EEC: Commission Decision of 15 December 1982 relating to a proceeding under Article 85 of the EEC Treaty (IV/29.883 – AROW/BNIC), OJ L 379, 31.12.1982, p. 1-18. [cited as: EU Commission Decision, *AROW/BNIC*, 1982], **244**

87/409/EEC: Commission Decision of 13 July 1987 relating to a proceeding under Article 85 of the EEC Treaty (IV/31.741 – Sandoz), OJ L 222/28, 10.8.1987, p. 28-34. [cited as: EU Commission Decision, *Sandoz*, 1987], **246**

88/518/EEC: Commission Decision of 18 July 1988 relating to a proceeding under Article 86 of the EEC Treaty (Case No IV/30.178 Napier Brown – British Sugar), OJ L 284, 19.10.1988, p. 41-59. [cited as: EU Commission Decision, *Napier Brown – British Sugar*, 1988], **285**

88/501/EEC: Commission Decision of 26 July 1988 relating to a proceeding under Articles 85 and 86 of the EEC Treaty (IV/31.043 – Tetra Pak I (BTG licence), p. 27-46. [cited as: EU Commission Decision, *Tetra Pak I*, 1988], **292**

89/22/EEC: Commission Decision of 5 December 1988 relating to a proceeding under Article 86 of the EEC Treaty (IV/31.900, *BPB Industries plc*), OJ L 10, 13.1.1989, p. 50-72. [cited as: EU Commission Decision, *BPB Industries plc*, 1989], **289**

92/553/EEC: Commission Decision of 22 July 1992 relating to a proceeding under Council Regulation (EEC) No 4064/89 (Case No IV/M.190 – Nestlé/Perrier), p. 1-31. [cited as: EU Commission Decision, *Nestlé/Perrier*, 1992], **285**

94/19/EC: Commission Decision of 21 December 1993 relating to a proceeding pursuant to Article 86 of the EC Treaty (IV/34.689 – *Sea Containers v. Stena Sealink* – Interim measures), OJ L 15, 18.1.1994, p. 8-19. [cited as: EU Commission Decision, *Sea Containers v. Stena Sealink*, 1994], **287**

95/188/EC: Commission Decision of 30 January 1995 relating to a proceeding under Article 85 of the EC Treaty (IV/33.686 – Coapi), OJ L 122, 2.6.1995, p. 37-50. [cited as: EU Commission Decision, *Coapi*, 1995], **244**

98/531/EC: Commission Decision of 11 March 1998 relating to a proceeding under Articles 85 and 86 of the EC Treaty (Case Nos IV/34.073, IV/34.395 and IV/35.436 Van den Bergh Foods Limited), OJ L 246, 4.9.1998, p. 1-50. [cited as: EU Commission Decision, *Van den Bergh*, 1998], **363**

Case No COMP/M.1403 – ASTRA/ZENECA, Commission Decision of 26 February 1999, Regulation (EEC) No 4064/89, Merger Procedure, Article 6(1)(b), CELEX Database: Document No 399M1403, Date: 26/02/1999, p. 1-24. [cited as: EU Commission Decision, *ASTRA/ZENECA Merger*, 1999], **283-284**

Case No COMP/M.1397 SANOFI/SYNTHELABO, Décision de la Commission de 17 mai 1999, Règlement (CEE) n° 4064/89 sur les concentrations, Article 6, paragraphe

1, point b), CELEX Database: Document No 399M1403 Date: 17/05/1999, p. 1-21. [cited as: Décision de la Commission, *SANOFI/SYNTHELABO*, 1999], **283**

Case No COMP/M.2922 – PFIZER/PHARMACIA, Commission Decision of 27 February 2003, Regulation (EEC) No 4064/89, Merger Procedure, Article 6(2), CELEX Database: Document No 303M2922, Date: 27/02/2003, p. 1-44. [cited as: EU Commission Decision, *PFIZER/PHARMACIA*, 2003], **284**

2004/841/EC: Commission Decision of 7 April 2004 relating to a proceeding pursuant to Article 81 of the EC Treaty concerning case COMP/A.38284/D2 – Société Air France/Alitalia Linee Aeree Italiane SpA (notified under document number C(2004) 1307), OJ L 362, 9.12.2004, p. 17–20. [cited as: EU Commission Decision, *Société Air France/Alitalia*, 2004], **263**

2006/857/EC: Commission Decision of 15 June 2005 relating to a proceeding under Article 82 of the EC Treaty and Article 54 of the EEA Agreement (Case COMP/A.37.507/F3 – AstraZeneca) (notified under document number C(2005) 1757), OJ L 332, 30.11.2006, p. 24-25. [cited as: EU Commission Decision, *AstraZeneca*, 2005], **281–286, 290, 296, 297, 359**

Case No COMP/E-1/38.113 – Prokent-Tomra, Commission decision of 29 March 2006, relating to proceedings under Article 82 of the Treaty and Article 54 of the EEA Agreement, C(2006)734, Brussels, 29.03.2006, p. 1-163. [cited as: EU Commission Decision, *Prokent-Tomra*, 2006], **289**

Case No COMP/D1/38606 – Groupement Des Cartes Bancaires "CB," Commission Decision of 17 October 2007 relating to a proceeding pursuant to Article 81 of the EC Treaty, Brussels, 17.10.2007, p. 1-170. [cited as: EU Commission Decision, *Groupement Des Cartes Bancaires*, 2007], **253**

Case No COMP/M.5295 – TEVA/BARR, Commission Decision of 19 December 2008, Regulation (EC) No 139/2004 Merger Procedure-Article 6(1)(b) in conjunction with Art 6(2), EUR-lex document number: 32008M5295, Date: 19/12/2008, p. 1-83. [cited as: EU Commission Decision, *TEVA/BARR*, 2008], **282**

Case No COMP/M.5253 – SANOFI-AVENTIS/ZENTIVA, Commission Decision of 4 February 2009, Regulation (EC) No 139/2004 Merger Procedure-Article 6(2) in conjunction with Art 6(2), EUR-lex document number: 32009M5253 Date: 04/02/2009, p. 1-131. [cited as: EU Commission Decision, *SANOFI-AVENTIS/ZENTIVA*, 2009], **282**

Case No COMP/M.5476 – PFIZER/WYETH, Commission Decision of 17 July 2009, Regulation (EC) No 139/2004 Merger Procedure – Article 6(1)(b) in conjunction with Article 6(2), EUR-lex document number: 32009M5476, Date: 17/07/2009, p. 1-174. [cited as: EU Commission Decision, *PFIZER/WYETH*, 2009], **282**

Case AT.39595 – Continental/United/Lufthansa/Air Canada, Commission Decision of 23 May 2013, relating to proceedings pursuant to Article 101(3) of the Treaty on the Functioning of European Union, C(2013) 2836 final, Brussels, 23.5.2013, p. 1-36. [cited as: EU Commission Decision, *Continental/United/Lufthansa/Air Canada*, 2013], **263**

Case AT.39226 – Lundbeck, Commission Decision of 19 June 2013, relating to a proceeding under Article 101 of the Treaty on the Functioning of the European Union and Article 53 of the EEA Agreement, C(2013) 3803 final, Brussels,

Table of Cases

19.6.2013, p. 1-464. [cited as: EU Commission Decision, *Lundbeck*, 2013], **225, 266, 274, 285, 309-311, 315-320, 322-329, 332, 334-336, 340, 341, 345, 382**

Case AT.39685 – Fentanyl, Commission Decision of 10 December 2013, relating to a proceeding under Article 101 of the Treaty on the Functioning of the European Union C(2013) 8870 final, Brussels, 10.12.2013, p. 1-147. [cited as: EU Commission Decision, *Fentanyl*, 2013], **312, 313**

Case AT.39398 – Visa MIF, Commission Decision of 26 February 2014, relating to a proceeding under Article 101 of the Treaty on the Functioning of the European Union and Article 53 of the EEA Agreement, C(2014) 1199 final, Brussels 26.02.2014, p. 1-27. [cited as: EU Commission Decision, *Visa MIF*, 2014], **252**

CASE AT.39985 – MOTOROLA – ENFORCEMENT OF GPRS STANDARD ESSENTIAL PATENTS, ANTITRUST PROCEDURE, Commission Decision of 29 April 2014, Regulation 1/2003, in conjunction with Article 7, C(2014) 2892 final, Brussels, 29.4.2014 [cited as: EU Commission Decision, *MOTOROLA*, 2014], **295**

CASE AT.39939 – SAMSUNG – Enforcement of UMTS standard essential patents, Commission Decision of 29 April 2014, relating to proceedings under Article 102 of the Treaty on the Functioning of the European Union and Article 54 of the EEA Agreement, C(2014) 2891 final Brussels, 29.4.2014, p. 1-26. [cited as: EU Commission Decision, *SAMSUNG*, 2014], **294**

CASE AT.39612 – Perindopril (Servier), Commission Decision of 9 July 2014, relating to a proceeding under Article 101 and Article 102 of the Treaty on the Functioning of the European Union, C(2014) 4955 final, Brussels, 9.7.2014, p. 1-805. [cited as: EU Commission Decision, *Servier*, 2014], **225, 229, 254, 261, 274, 285, 286, 309-311, 340, 342-366, 384-386**

Case No COMP/M.7275 – *NOVARTIS/ GLAXOSMITHKLINE ONCOLOGY BUSINESS*, Commission Decision of 28 January 2015, Regulation (EC) No 139/2004 Merger Procedure-Article 6(1)(b) in conjunction with Art 6(2), C(2015) 538 final, Brussels, 28.01.2015, p. 1-27. [cited as: EU Commission Decision, *NOVARTIS/ GLAXOSMITHKLINE*, 2015], **282, 373**

2 Speeches

Speech of Alexander Italianer, Director-General for Competition, European Commission, "Competitor agreements under EU competition law," September 26, 2013, New York, U.S.A., Fordham Competition Law Institute. Available at: http://ec.europa.eu/competition/speeches/text/sp2013_07_en.pdf (last accessed on March 31, 2018). [cited as: ITALIANER, Competitor agreements, 2013], **263**

3 Staff Working Docs, Guidances, Papers & Policy Briefs

European Commission, Notice of 18 December 1978 concerning its assessment of certain subcontracting agreements in relation to Article 85 (1) of the EEC Treaty, OJ C 1, 3.1.1979, p. 2-3. [cited as: EU Commission, *Article 85 EEC: Subcontracting Agreements Notice*, 1979], **249**

European Commission, *Commission Notice on the definition of relevant market for the purposes of Community competition law*, OJ C 372, 9.12.1997, p. 5-13. [cited as: EU Commission, *Notice on the definition of relevant market*, 1997], **279, 280, 284–286, 288**

European Commission, *White Paper on Modernisation of the Rules Implementing Articles 85 and 86 of the EC Treaty*, Commission Programme No 99/027, OJ C 132/1, Brussels, 28.04.1999, pp. 1-47. [cited as: EU Commission, *White Paper Articles 85 & 86 EC Treaty*, 1999], **255**

European Commission, *Notice on agreements of minor importance which do not appreciably restrict competition under Article 81(1) of the Treaty establishing the European Community (de minimis)*, OJ C 368/13, 22.12.2001, p. 13-15. [cited as: EU Commission, *De Minimis Notice*, 2001], **258–260**

European Commission, *DG Competition discussion paper on the application of Article 82 of the Treaty to exclusionary abuses*, Brussels, December 2005, pp. 1-75. Available at: http://ec.europa.eu/competition/antitrust/art82/discpaper2005.pdf. (last accessed on March 31, 2018) [cited as: EU Commission, *Discussion Paper Article 82*, 2005], **280, 300**

European Commission, *EudraLex – Pharmaceutical Legislation Notice to applicants and regulatory guidelines medicinal products for human use*, Volume 2 A, Chapter 2, Mutual Recognition, (February 2007), pp. 1-49. Available at: http://ec.europa.eu/health/documents/eudralex/vol-2/index_en.htm. (last accessed on March 31, 2018) [cited as: EU Commission, *Pharma Legislation Notice: Chapter 2*, 2007], **227**

European Commission Staff Working Paper, *Accompanying the Report on the functioning of Regulation No. 1/2003*, COM(2009) 206 final, Brussels, 29.4.2009, pp. 1-96. [cited as: EU Commission, *Staff Working Paper Regulation No. 1/2003*, 2009], **238, 262**

European Commission, Communication, *Guidance on the Commission's enforcement priorities in applying Article 82 of the EC Treaty to abusive exclusionary conduct by dominant undertakings*, OJ C 45/7, 24.2.2009, p. 7-20. [cited as: EU Commission, *Guidance in applying Article 82*, 2009], **280, 287–291, 300**

European Commission, DG Health and Consumers, *Handling of Duplicate Marketing Authorisation Applications*, Ref. Ares 2011)1044649, 03.10.2011, pp. 1-11. Available at: https://ec.europa.eu/health/sites/health/files/files/latest_news/2011_09_duplicates_note_upd_01.pdf (last accessed on March 31, 2018). [cited as: EU Commission, *Duplicate Marketing Authorisation Applications*, 2011], **226**

European Commission, DG Competition, *Competition Policy Brief: Standard Essential Patents*, Issue 8, June 2014, pp. 1-5. Available at: http://ec.europa.eu/competition/publications/cpb/2014/008_en.pdf (last accessed on March 31, 2018) [cited as: EU Commission, *Competition Policy Brief: SEPs*, 2014], **293**

European Commission, Staff Working Document, *Guidance on restrictions of competition "by object" for the purpose of defining which agreements may benefit from the De Minimis Notice*, Brussels, 25.6.2014, SWD(2014) 198 final, pp. 6-7. [cited as: EU Commission, *Guidance on restrictions by object*, 2014], **252, 260**

Table of Cases

European Commission, *Notice on agreements of minor importance which do not appreciably restrict competition under Article 101(1) of the Treaty on the Functioning of the European Union (De Minimis Notice)*, OJ C 291/1, 30.8.2014, p. 1-4. [cited as: EU Commission, *De Minimis Notice*, 2014], **252, 259, 260**

European Commission, Staff Working Document, *Enhancing competition enforcement by the Member States' competition authorities: institutional and procedural issues*, accompanying the Communication from the Commission, SWD (2014 231 final), Brussels, 9.7.2014, pp. 1-29. Available at: http://ec.europa.eu/competition/consultations/2015_effective_enforcers/index_en.html. (last accessed on March 31, 2018) [cited as: EU Commission, *Enhancing NCA enforcement*, 2014], **236**

European Commission, DG Competition, *Competition Policy Brief: The Damages Directive: Towards a More Effective Enforcement of the EU Competition Rules*, Issue 2015-1, (January 2015). Available at: http://ec.europa.eu/competition/publications/cpb/2015/001_en.pdf (last accessed on March 31, 2018) [cited as: EU Commission, *Competition Policy Brief: Damages Directive*, 2015], **240**

4 Communications, Guidelines, Memos, FAQs

European Commission, Notice, *Guidelines on the applicability of Article 81 of the EC Treaty to horizontal cooperation agreements*, OJ C 3, 6.1.2001, p. 2-30. [cited as: EU Commission, *Article 81 EC: horizontal cooperation agreements*, 2001], **265**

European Commission, Notice, *Guidelines on the application of Article 81(3) of the Treaty*, OJ C 101, 27.4.2004, pp. 97-118. [cited as: EU Commission, *Article 81(3) Guidelines*, 2004], **237, 238, 248, 251, 254, 261, 263, 264, 274, 310**

European Commission, Notice, *Guidelines on the effect on trade concept contained in Articles 81 and 82 of the Treaty*, OJ C 101/81, 27.4.2004, p. 81-96. [cited as: EU Commission, *Guidelines: effect on trade in Articles 81 & 82*, 2004], **256, 257, 260, 277, 291**

European Commission, Notice, Guidelines on the application of Article 81 of the EC Treaty to technology transfer agreements, OJ C 101, 27.4.2004, p. 2-42, [cited as: EU Commission, *Article 81: Technology Transfer Agreements*, 2004], **271**

European Commission, Notice, *Guidelines on Vertical Restraints*, SEC/2010/0411 final, Brussels, 10.5.2010, p. 1-71. [cited as: EU Commission, *Guidelines on Vertical Restraints*, 2010], **249, 251, 263**

European Commission, *FAQs, Commission Adopts Revised Competition Rules on Horizontal Co-operation Agreements*, MEMO/10/676, Brussels, 14 December 2010. Available at: http://europa.eu/rapid/press-release_MEMO-10-676_en.htm?locale=en. (last accessed on March 31, 2018) [cited as: EU Commission, *FAQs: Horizontal Co-operation Agreements*, 2010], **266, 267**

European Commission, Public Consultation, *Revised Rules for the Assessment of Horizontal Cooperation Agreements under EU Competition Law*, from 04.05.2010 to 25.06.2010. Available at: http://ec.europa.eu/competition/consultations/2010_horizontals/. (last accessed on March 31, 2018) [cited as: EU Commission, *Public Consultation on Horizontal Cooperation Agreements*, 2010], **266**

European Commission, Communication, *Guidelines on the applicability of Article 101 of the Treaty on the Functioning of the European Union to horizontal co-operation agreements*, OJ C 11/1, 14.1.2011, p. 1–72. [cited as: EU Commission, *101 TFEU Guidelines*, 2011], **245, 254, 265–267, 350, 363**

European Commission, *Samsung – Enforcement of ETSI Standards Essential Patents (SEPs)*, Brussels, MEMO/12/1021, 21 December 2012. Available at: http://europa.eu/rapid/press-release_MEMO-12-1021_en.htm. (last accessed on March 31, 2018) [cited as: EU Commission, *Samsung Memo*, 2012], **294**

European Commission, *FAQs, Antitrust decisions on standard essential patents (SEPs) – Motorola Mobility and Samsung Electronics*, MEMO/14/322, Brussels, 29 April 2014. Available at: http://europa.eu/rapid/press-release_MEMO-14-322_en.htm (last accessed on March 31, 2018) [cited as: EU Commission, *SEPs Motorola Samsung Memo*, 2014], **295**

European Commission, Communication, *Ten Years of Antitrust Enforcement under Regulation 1/2003: Achievements and Future Perspectives*, COM(2014) 453 Final, Brussels, 9.7.2014, pp. 1-12. [cited as: EU Commission, *Communication: Ten Years Regulation 1/2003*, 2014], **238**

European Commission, *FAQs, Antitrust: Commission adopts revised competition regime for technology transfer agreements – frequently asked questions*, Brussels, 21 March 2014. Available at: http://europa.eu/rapid/press-release_MEMO-14-208_en.htm (last accessed on March 31, 2018) [cited as: EU Commission, *FAQs: Revised TTBER*, 2014], **270, 272**

European Commission, Communication, *Guidelines on the application of Article 101 of the Treaty on the Functioning of the European Union to technology transfer agreements*, OJ C 89/3, 28.3.2014, p. 3-50. [cited as: EU Commission, *Technology Transfer Agreements Guidelines*, 2014], **246, 271, 272, 274, 275**

European Commission, *FAQs, Antitrust: Commission adopts revised safe harbours for minor agreements ("De Minimis Notice") and provides guidance on "by object" restrictions of competition*, MEMO/14/440, Brussels 25.06.2014, pp. 1-3. Available at: http://europa.eu/rapid/press-release_MEMO-14-440_en.htm. (last accessed on March 31, 2018) [cited as: EU Commission, *FAQs: Revised De Minimis Notice*, 2014], **258**

5 Press Releases

European Commission, Press Release, *TetraPak I*, IP-88-497, Brussels 1988. Available at: http://europa.eu/rapid/press-release_IP-88-497_en.htm. (last accessed on March 31, 2018) [cited as: EU Commission Press Release, *Tetra Pak I*, 1988], **292**

European Commission, Press Release, *Competition: Commission fines AstraZeneca €60 million for misusing patent system to delay market entry of competing generic drugs*, IP/05/737, Brussels, 15 June 2000. Available at: http://europa.eu/rapid/press-release_IP-05-737_en.htm?locale=en. (last accessed on March 31, 2018) [cited as: EU Press Release, *AstraZeneca*, 2000], **296**

Table of Cases

European Commission Press Release, *Antitrust: Commission Launches Sector Inquiry into Pharmaceuticals with Unannounced Inspections*, IP/08/49, January 16, 2008. Available at: http://europa.eu/rapid/press-release_IP-08-49_en.htm?locale = en. (last accessed on March 31, 2018) [cited as: EU Commission Press Release, *Pharma Sector Inquiry, 2008*], **304**

European Commission, Press Release, *Commission Adopts Revised Competition Rules on Horizontal Co-operation Agreements*, IP/10/1702, Brussels, 14 December 2010. Available at: http://europa.eu/rapid/press-release_IP-10-1702_en.htm. (last accessed on March 31, 2018) [cited as: EU Commission Press Release, *Horizontal Co-operation Agreements, 2010*], **266, 267**

European Commission Press Release, *Antitrust: Commission opens investigation against pharmaceutical companies Cephalon and Teva*, IP/11/511, April 28, 2011. Available at: http://europa.eu/rapid/press-release_IP-11-511_en.htm?locale = en. (last accessed on March 31, 2018) [cited as: EU Commission Press Release, *Cephalon and Teva, 2011*], **313**

European Commission Press Release, *Mergers: Commission approves the acquisition of Cephalon by Teva, subject to conditions*, IP/11/1193, October 14, 2011. Available at: http://europa.eu/rapid/press-release_IP-11-1193_en.htm. (last accessed on March 31, 2018) [cited as: EU Commission Press Release, *Cephalon's Acquisition, 2011*], **314**

European Commission, Press Release, *Antitrust: Commission sends Statement of Objections to Samsung on potential misuse of mobile phone standard-essential patents*, IP/12/1448, Brussels, 21 December 2012. Available at: http://europa.eu/rapid/press-release_IP-12-1448_en.htm. (last accessed on March 31, 2018) [cited as: EU Commission Press Release, *Samsung SEPs, 2012*], **294**

European Commission, Press Release, *Antitrust: Commission fines Lundbeck and other pharma companies for delaying market entry of generic medicines*, IP/13/563, Brussels, June 19, 2013. Available at: http://europa.eu/rapid/press-release_IP-13-563_en.htm?locale = en. (last accessed on March 31, 2018) [cited as: EU Commission Press Release, *Lundbeck, 2013*], **315**

European Commission, Press Release, *Justice for Growth: Commission fills legal gaps for Unitary Patent Protection*, IP/13/750, Brussels, July 29, 2013. Available at: http://europa.eu/rapid/press-release_IP-13-750_en.htm (last accessed on March 31, 2018) [cited as: EU Commission Press Release, *Unitary Patent Protection, 2013*], **36, 222**

European Commission Press Release, *Antitrust: Commission fines Johnson & Johnson and Novartis €16 million for delaying market entry of generic pain-killer fentanyl*, IP/13/1233, Brussels, December 10, 2013. Available at: http://europa.eu/rapid/press-release_IP-13-1233_en.htm. (last accessed on March 31, 2018) [cited as: EU Commission Press Release, *Johnson & Johnson and Novartis, 2013*], **312**

European Commission, Press Release, *Antitrust: Commission finds that Motorola Mobility Infringed EU competition rules by misusing standard essential patents*, IP/14/489, Brussels, 29 April 2014. Available at: http://europa.eu/rapid/press-release_IP-14-489_en.htm. (last accessed on March 31, 2018) [cited as: EU Commission Press Release, *Motorola Mobility, 2014*], **295**

European Commission, Press Release, *Antitrust: Commission accepts legally binding commitments by Samsung Electronics on standard essential patent injunctions*, IP/14/490, Brussels, 29 April 2014. Available at: http://europa.eu/rapid/press-release_IP-14-490_en.htm. (last accessed on March 31, 2018) [cited as: EU Commission Press Release, *Samsung Commitments*, 2014], **294**

European Commission Press Release, *Antitrust: Commission fines Servier and five generic companies for curbing entry of cheaper versions of cardiovascular medicine*, IP/14/799, Brussels, July 9, 2014. Available at: http://europa.eu/rapid/press-release_IP-14-799_en.htm. (last accessed on March 31, 2018) [cited as: EU Commission Press Release, *Servier*, 2014], **342, 344**

European Commission Press Release, *Antitrust: Commission opens formal investigation into Aspen Pharma's pricing practices for cancer medicines*, IP/17/1323, Brussels, May 15, 2017. Available at: http://europa.eu/rapid/press-release_IP-17-1323_en.htm. (last accessed on March 31, 2018) [cited as: EU Commission, Press Release, *Aspen Pharma*, 2017], **308**

European Commission Press Release, *Antitrust: Commission sends Statement of Objections to Teva on "pay-for-delay" pharma agreement*, IP/17/2063, Brussels, July 17, 2017. Available at: http://europa.eu/rapid/press-release_IP-17-2063_en.htm (last accessed on March 31, 2018) [cited as: EU Commission Press Release, *Modafinil*, 2017], **313, 314**

6 Reports & Best Practices

European Commission, *Practical methods to assess efficiency gains in the context of Article 81(3) of the EC Treaty*, Final report, May 6, 2005, pp. 1-168. [cited as: EU Commission, *Efficiency Gains: Article 81(3)*, 2005], **262**

European Commission, *Pharmaceutical Sector Inquiry Final Report*, July 8, 2009, pp. 1-533. [cited as: EU Commission, *Pharma Sector Inquiry*, 2009], **12-19, 25-30, 34, 36, 225-230, 297, 304, 309, 310, 369**

European Commission DG Competition, *Best practices for the submission of economic evidence and data collection in cases concerning the application of Articles 101 and 102 TFEU and in Merger cases*, 2010, pp. 1-20. Available at: http://ec.europa.eu/competition/consultations/2010_best_practices/best_practice_submissions.pdf. (last accessed on March 31, 2018) [cited as: EU Commission, *Mergers: Best Practices*, 2010], **262**

European Commission, Economic Policy Committee (AWG), *Joint Report on Health Systems*, Occasional Papers 74, December 2010, p. 1-191. Available at: http://ec.europa.eu/economy_finance/publications/occasional_paper/2010/pdf/ocp74_en.pdf. (last accessed on March 31, 2018) [cited as: EU Commission, AWG, *Health Systems*, 2010], **307**

Executive Agency for Health and Consumers (EAHC), European Commission, *EU Pharmaceutical Expenditure Forecast*, Final Report, November 26, 2012, full pp. 1-107. Available at: https://ec.europa.eu/health/systems_performance_assessment/docs/creativ_ceutical_eu_pharmaceutical_expenditure_forecast.pdf. (last accessed on March 31, 2018) [cited as: EU Commission, *Pharmaceutical Expenditure Forecast*, 2012], **27**

European Commission, *The 2015 Ageing Report: Economic and budgetary projections for the 28 EU Member States (2013-2060)*, European Economy 3/2015, pp. 1-424. Available at: http://ec.europa.eu/economy_finance/publications/european_economy/2015/pdf/ee3_en.pdf (last accessed on March 31, 2018) [cited as: EU Commission, *2015 Ageing Report*], **308**

European Commission, European Semester Thematic Fiche: Health and Health Systems, 2017, pp. 1-14. Available at: https://ec.europa.eu/info/sites/info/files/european-semester_thematic-factsheet_health-systems_en_0.pdf (last accessed on March 31, 2018). [cited as: EU Commission, *Health Systems*, 2017], **307, 308**

European Commission, *8th Report on the Monitoring of Patent Settlements (period January – December 2016)*, published on Mar. 9, 2018, pp. 1-15. Available at: http://ec.europa.eu/competition/sectors/pharmaceuticals/inquiry/ (last accessed on March 31, 2018) [cited as: EU Commission, *8th Patent Settlements Report*, 2018], **31, 304, 305, 307**

OECD, European Commission, *Health at a Glance: Europe 2016 – State of Health in the EU Cycle*, December 2016, pp. 1-199. Available at: http://www.oecd.org/health/health-at-a-glance-europe-23056088.htm (last accessed on March 31, 2018) [cited as: OECD, EU Commission, State of Health, 2016], **307**

PENTHEROUDAKIS Chryssoula, BARON Justus A., "Licensing Terms of Standard Essential Patents: A Comprehensive Analysis of Cases," EU Commission, JRC Science for Policy Report, (2017), EUR 28302 EN; doi:10.2791/32230, pp. 1-179. [cited as: PENTHEROUDAKIS, BARON, *Standard Essential Patents Report*, 2017], **294**

7 Guidances, Studies & Inventories

European Commission, *Inventory of Union and Member State incentives to support research into, and the development and availability of, orphan medicinal products*, SWD(2015) 13 FINAL, State of Play 2015, pp. 1-44. Available at: http://ec.europa.eu/health/human-use/orphan-medicines/developments/index_en.htm. (last accessed on March 31, 2018) [cited as: EU Commission, *Orphan Drugs Incentives Inventory*, 2015], **232**

European Commission, DG Health & Consumers, Pharmaceutical Committee, *Study on off-label use*, March 26, 2014, pp. 1-4. Available at: ec.europa.eu/health/files/committee/72meeting/pharm655.pdf. Last accessed on March 31, 2018) [cited as: EU Commission, *Off-label Use Study*, 2014], **373**

European Commission, DG Health and Food Safety Health systems, medical products and innovation, *Study on enhanced cross-country coordination in the area of pharmaceutical product pricing*, February 24, 2016. Available at: https://ec.europa.eu/health/sites/health/files/systems_performance_assessment/docs/pharmaproductpricing_frep_en.pdf Last accessed on March 31, 2018) [cited as: EU Commission, *Pharma Product Pricing Study*, 2016], **230**

European Commission, STAMP Commission Expert Group, *Repurposing of Established Medicines/ Active Substances*, June 28, 2016. Available at: http://ec.europa.eu/

health/files/committee/stamp/2016-06_stamp5/3_repurposing_of_established_medicines_reflection_paper.pdf; (last accessed on March 31, 2018) [cited as: EU Commission, STAMP, *Repurposing Medicines*, 2016], **373**

8 EU Commission Website

European Commission, *Directive on Antitrust Damages Actions*. Available at: http://ec.europa.eu/competition/antitrust/actionsdamages/directive_en.html (last accessed on March 31, 2018) [cited as: EU Commission Website, *Antitrust Damages Directive*], **240**

European Commission Website, *European Competition Network*. Available at: http://ec.europa.eu/competition/ecn/competition_authorities.html (last accessed on March 31, 2018) [cited as: EU Commission Website, *European Competition Network*], **235, 236**

European Commission, DG Health and Food Safety, *Orphan Medicinal Products*. Available at: http://ec.europa.eu/health/human-use/orphan-medicines/index_en.htm (last accessed on March 31, 2018) [cited as: EU Commission Website, *Orphan Medicinal Products*], **232**

European Commission, DG Health and Food Safety, *The Centralised Procedure*. Available at: http://ec.europa.eu/health/authorisation-procedures-centralised_en.htm (last accessed on March 31, 2018) [cited as: EU Commission Website, *Centralised Procedure*], **227**

European Commission, DG Health and Food Safety, *The EU Pharmacovigilance System*. Available at: http://ec.europa.eu/health/human-use/pharmacovigilance/index_en.htm#geninf; (last accessed on March 31, 2018) [cited as: EU Commission Website, *EU Pharmacovigilance*], **224**

European Commission Website, *Research and Innovation Funding 2014-2020*. Available at: https://ec.europa.eu/research/fp7/index_en.cfm (last accessed on March 31, 2018) [EU Commission Website, *Research and Innovation Funding 2014-2020*], **16**

C Other Agencies and Organisations

1 Press Releases

1.1 United Kingdom

Office of Fair Trading, Press Release, *OFT Issue Decision in Reckitt Benckiser Case*, April 13, 2011. Available at: http://webarchive.nationalarchives.gov.uk/20140402142426/http://www.oft.gov.uk/news-and-updates/press/2011/53-11. (last accessed on March 31, 2018) [cited as: Office of Fair Trading, Press Release, *Reckitt Benckiser*, 2011], **366, 367**

Competition and Markets Authority (CMA), Press Release, *CMA fines Pfizer and Flynn £90 million for drug price hike to NHS*, December 7, 2016. Available at: https://www.gov.uk/government/news/cma-fines-pfizer-and-flynn-90-million-for-drug-price-hike-to-nhs. (last accessed on March 31, 2018) [cited as: CMA, Press Release, *Pfizer and Flynn*, 2016], **308**

1.2 France

Autorité de la Concurrence, Communiqué de Presse, *L'Autorité de la concurrence sanctionne Sanofi-Aventis à hauteur de 40,6 million d'euros pour avoir mis en place une stratégie de dénigrement à l'encontre des génériques de Plavix®, l'un des médicaments les plus vendus dans le monde*, Mai 14, 2013. Available (also in English) at: http://www.autoritedelaconcurrence.fr/user/standard.php?id_rub =482&id_article=2090. Last accessed on March 31, 2018) [cited: Autorité de la Concurrence, Press Release, *Sanofi-Aventis*, 2013], **367**

Autorité de la Concurrence, Communiqué de Presse, *L'Autorité de la concurrence sanctionne à hauteur de 15,3 million d'euros le laboratoire pharmaceutique Schering-Plough pour avoir entravé l'arrivée du générique de son médicament princeps Subutex*, décembre 19, 2013. Available (also in English) at: http://www.autoritedelaconcurrence.fr/user/standard.php?id_rub=482&id_article=2283. Last accessed on March 31, 2018) [cited: Autorité de la Concurrence, Press Release, *Schering-Plough*, 2013], **367**

1.3 Italy

Autorità Garante della Concorrenza et del Mercato (Italian Competition Authority), Press Release A431 – Pharmaceuticals: Pfizer sanctioned with 10.6 million euro fine for abuse of dominant position, January 17, 2012. Available at: http://www.agcm.it/en/newsroom/press-releases/1986-pfizer-sanctioned-with-106-million-euro-fine-for-abuse-of-dominant-position.html. Last accessed on March 31, 2018) **[cited:** Autorità Garante della Concorrenza, Press Release, *Pfizer*, 2012], **307**

Autorità Garante della Concorrenza et del Mercato (Italian Competition Authority), Press Release, *I760 – Pharmaceuticals and Antitrust: the Italian Competition Authority fines Roche and Novartis over eur 180 million for cartelizing the sales of two major ophthalmic drugs, Avastin and Lucentis*, March 5, 2014. Available at: http://www.agcm.it/en/newsroom/press-releases/2106-i760-pharmaceuticals-and-antitrust-the-italian-competition-authority-fines-roche-and-novartis-over-eur-180-million-for-cartelizing-the-sales-of-two-major-ophthalmic-drugs-avastin-and-lucentis.html Last accessed on March 31, 2018) [cited: Autorità Garante della Concorrenza, Press Release, *Roche/Novartis*, 2014], **404**

Autorità Garante della Concorrenza et del Mercato (Italian Competition Authority), Press Release, *A480 – Price increases for cancer drugs up to 1500%: the ICA imposes a 5 million Euro fine on the multinational Aspen*, October 14, 2016. Available at: http://www.agcm.it/en/newsroom/press-releases/2339-a480-price-increases-for-cancer-drugs-up-to-1500-the-ica-imposes-a-5-million-euro-fine-on-the-multinational-aspen.html. Last accessed on March 31, 2018) [cited: Autorità Garante della Concorrenza, Press Release, *Aspen*, 2016], **308**

2 Questions & Answers

European Medicines Agency Website, *Q&A Presubmission Guidance*. Available at: http://www.ema.europa.eu/ema/index.jsp?curl=pages/regulation/q_and_a/q_and_a_detail_000021.jsp&mid=WC0b01ac0580022711 (last accessed on March 31, 2018) [cited as: EMA Website, *Q&A Presubmission*], **226**

3 Guidelines & Recommendations

European Medicines Agency, *Guideline on the processing of renewals in the centralised procedure*, EMA/CHMP/2990/00 Rev. 4, 22 June 2012, pp. 1-17. Available at: http://ec.europa.eu/health/files/eudralex/vol-2/2012-06_gpr.pdf (last accessed on March 31, 2018) [cited as: EMA, *Guideline: Centralised Procedure Renewals*, 2012], **227**

European Medicines Agency Website, *Guidelines on Good Pharmacovigilance Practices*. Available at: http://www.ema.europa.eu/ema/index.jsp?curl=pages/regulation/document_listing/document_listing_000345.jsp&mid=WC0b01ac058058f32c. (last accessed on March 31, 2018) [cited as: EMA Website, *Guidelines on Good Pharmacovigilance Practices*], **224**

European Competition Network, *Recommendation on Investigative Powers, Enforcement Measures and Sanctions in the Context of Inspections and Requests for Information*, December 2013, pp. 1-14. Available at: http://ec.europa.eu/competition/ecn/documents.html. (last accessed on March 31, 2018) [cited as: ECN, *Inspections and Information Requests*, 2013], **236**

4 Reports

EFPIA, *The Pharmaceutical Industry in Figures – Key Data 2017*, pp. 1-28. Available at: https://www.efpia.eu/media/219735/efpia-pharmafigures2017_statisticbroch_v04-final.pdf. (last accessed on March 31, 2018) [cited as: EFPIA, *Pharma Key Data*, 2017], **12**

EFPIA, *The Pharmaceutical Industry in Figures – Key Data 2016*, pp. 1-15. Available at: https://www.efpia.eu/media/25055/the-pharmaceutical-industry-in-figures-june-2016.pdf. (last accessed on March 31, 2018) [cited as: EFPIA, *Pharma Key Data*, 2016], **13**

European Union Committee of Experts for Rare Diseases, 2014 *Report on the State of the Art of Rare Diseases Activities in Europe – Part I: Overview of Rare Disease Activities in Europe*, July 2014, pp. 1-68. Available at: http://www.eucerd.eu/?page_id=163 (last accessed on March 31, 2018) [cited as: EUCERD, *Rare Diseases Report*, 2014], **232**

European Medicines Agency, *2015 Report to the European Commission on the Application of the Paediatric Regulation*, pp. 1-75. Available at: http://ec.europa.eu/health/human-use/paediatric-medicines/index_en.htm. (last accessed on March 31, 2018) [cited as: EMA, *Paediatric Regulation Report*, 2015], **233**

Table of Cases

European Medicines Agency, *Human Medicines Highlights 2016*, p. 1. Available at: http://www.ema.europa.eu/ema/index.jsp?curl=pages/audience/alp_audiencetype_000004.jsp&mid=.(last accessed on March 31, 2018) [cited as: EMA, *Human Medicines Highlights*, 2016], **17**

European Observatory of Counterfeiting and Piracy, *Evidence and Right of Information in Intellectual Property Rights*, 2011, pp. 1-145. Available at: http://ec.europa.eu/internal_market/iprenforcement/docs/evidence_en.pdf. (last accessed on March 31, 2018) [cited as: European Observatory of Counterfeiting and Piracy, *Evidence and Right of Information*, 2011], **340**

European Observatory of Counterfeiting and Piracy, *Injunctions in Intellectual Property Rights*, 2011, pp. 1-118. Available at: http://ec.europa.eu/internal_market/iprenforcement/docs/injunctions_en.pdf. (last accessed on March 31, 2018) [cited as: European Observatory of Counterfeiting and Piracy, *Injunctions*, 2011], **340**

European Observatory on Infringements of Intellectual Property Rights, *Private Costs of Enforcement of IPRs*, March 2017, pp. 1-26. Available at: https://euipo.europa.eu/tunnel-web/secure/webdav/guest/document_library/observatory/documents/div/Private%20Costs%20of%20Enforcement%20of%20IPR%20-%20FORMATTED.pdf. (last accessed on March 31, 2018) [cited as: European Observatory of Intellectual Property Rights, *Private Costs of Enforcement of IPRs*, 2017], **34**

5 Websites

European Competition Network, *Model Leniency Program*, as revised in November 2012, pp. 1-19. Available at: http://ec.europa.eu/competition/ecn/documents.html. (last accessed on March 31, 2018) [cited as: ECN, *Model Leniency Program*, 2012], **235, 236**

Gov.UK, Competition and Markets Authority case, *Reckitt Benckiser: alleged abuse of a dominant position, 2008-2011.* Related Documents available at: https://www.gov.uk/cma-cases/reckitt-benckiser-alleged-abuse-of-a-dominant-position. (last accessed on March 31, 2018) [cited as: Gov.UK Website, *Reckitt Benckiser*, 2008-2011], **299**

European Patent Office Website, *Member States of the European Patent Office*. Last Updated September 7, 2015. Available at: https://www.epo.org/about-us/organisation/member-states.html. (last accessed on March 31, 2018) [cited as: EPO Website, *Member States*, 2015], **221**

European Pharmaceutical Market Research Association Website, *EphMRA Classifications (ATC and NFC)*. Available at: http://www.ephmra.org/Classification (last accessed on March 31, 2018) [cited as: EphMRA Website, *Classifications*], **282**

6 Statements, Indicators & Notes

Muscolo Gabriella, Commissioner of the Italian Competition Authority, Statement by Italy, *Seventh United Nations Conference to review the UN Set on Competition*

Policy, Roundtable on: Role of Competition in the Pharmaceutical Sector and its Benefits for Consumers, Geneva, 6-10 July 2015, pp. 1-15. Available at: http://unctad.org/meetings/en/Presentation/CCPB_7RC2015_RTPharma_Italy_en.pdf (last accessed on March 31, 2018) [cited as: Muscolo, ICA Statement: Pharma Competition, 2015], **370**

OECD, *Roundtable on Market Definition – Note by the European Union*, DAF/COMP/WD(2012)28, 31 May, 2012, pp. 1-9. Available at: http://ec.europa.eu/competition/international/multilateral/2012_jun_market_definition_en.pdf (last accessed on March 31, 2018) [cited as: OECD Roundtable, *Note by the European Union*, 2012], **280**

OECD, *Health at a Glance 2015: OECD Indicators*, November 2015, pp. 1-220. Available at: http://dx.doi.org/10.1787/health_glance-2015-en (last accessed on March 31, 2018) [cited as: OECD, *Health at a Glance 2015*], **17**

D European Member States

1 European Member States National Court Decisions

1.1 France

Arrêt n° 890 du 18 octobre 2016 (15-10.384) – Cour de cassation – Chambre commerciale, financière et économique – ECLI:FR:CCASS:2016:CO00890. Available at: https://www.courdecassation.fr/publications_26/arrets_publies_2986/chambre_commerciale_financiere_economique_3172/2016_7408/octobre_7799/890_18_35358.html. (last accessed on March 31, 2018), **368**

Arrêt n° 33 du 11 janvier 2017 (15-17.134) – Cour de cassation – Chambre commerciale, financière et économique, ECLI:FR:CCASS:2017:CO00033. Available at: https://www.courdecassation.fr/publications_26/arrets_publies_2986/chambre_commerciale_financiere_economique_3172/2017_7954/janvier_7955/33_11_35890.html. (last accessed on March 31, 2018), **369**

Arrêt n° 50 du 26 mars 2015, 2014/03330 – Cour d'appel de Paris – Pôle 5 – Chambre 5-7. Available at: http://www.autoritedelaconcurrence.fr/doc/ca_subutex_13d21.pdf. (last accessed on March 31, 2018), **369**

1.2 Italy

Il Consiglio di Stato, *Autorità Garante della Concorrenza e del Mercato c. Pfizer et al.*, N. 00116/2014REG.PROV.COLL., 15/1/2014. Available at: http://www.quotidianosanita.it/allegati/allegato4345250.pdf (last accessed on March 31, 2018), **372**

Il Consiglio di Stato, *F. Hoffmann-La Roche Ltd e Novartis Ag contro Autorità Garante della Concorrenza e del Mercato*, N. 00966/2016 REG.PROV.COLL., 11/03/2016. Available at: http://www.amministrazioneincammino.luiss.it/app/uploads/2016/04/cds_966_2016.pdf. (last accessed on March 31, 2018), **374**

Table of Cases

Tribunale Amministrativo Regionale per il Lazio, *Pfizer et al. c. Autorità' Garante della Concorrenza e del Mercato*, N. 09968/2011 REG.RIC., 3/9/2012. Available at: https://dottoratoblog.files.wordpress.com/2016/01/tar-lazio-pfizer_ratiopharm-copia.pdf. (last accessed on March 31, 2018), **371**

Tribunale Amministrativo Regionale per il Lazio, *Novartis e Roche contro Autorità Garante della Concorrenza e del Mercato*, N. 12168/2014 REG.PROV.COLL, 2/12/2014. Available at: https://www.giustizia-amministrativa.it/cdsintra/cdsintra/AmministrazionePortale/DocumentViewer/index.html?ddocname = UOXPTSFKKCFFCNJWOYADFYV42Y&q = Novartis (last accessed on March 31, 2018), **374**

Tribunale Amministrativo Regionale per il Lazio, *Aspen Pharma Trading Limited et al. c. Autorità Garante della Concorrenza e del Mercato*, N. 08945/2017 REG.RIC., 26/7/2017. Available at: https://www.giustizia-amministrativa.it/cdsintra/wcm/idc/groups/public/documents/document/mday/ntm4/~edisp/5e2rmfwdi3oqyig55npxxhkhmu.html (last accessed on March 31, 2018), **308**

2 National Competition Authorities' Decisions

2.1 United Kingdom

Office of Fair Trading, Decision No. CA98/02/2011, *Abuse of a dominant position by Reckitt Benckiser Healthcare (UK) Limited and Reckitt Benckiser Group plc*, April 12, 2011, pp. 9-13, 23-27. Non-confidential version of the decision available at: https://www.gov.uk/cma-cases/reckitt-benckiser-alleged-abuse-of-a-dominant-position. (last accessed on March 31, 2018) [cited as: Office of Fair Trading, Decision No. CA98/02/2011 *Reckitt Benckiser*, 2011], **366, 367**

2.2 France

Autorité de la Concurrence, *Décision n° 13-D-11 du 14 mai 2013 relative à des pratiques mises en oeuvre dans le secteur pharmaceutique*. Available at: http://www.autoritedelaconcurrence.fr/user/avisdec.php?numero = 13D11. (last accessed on March 31, 2018) [cited as: Autorité de la Concurrence, *Décision Sanofi/Aventis*, 2013], **367**

Autorité de la Concurrence, *Décision n° 13-D-21 du 18 décembre 2013 relative à des pratiques mises en oeuvre sur le marché français de la buprénorphine haut dosage commercialisée en ville*. Available at: http://www.autoritedelaconcurrence.fr/pdf/avis/13d21.pdf. (last accessed on March 31, 2018) [cited as: Autorité de la Concurrence, *Décision Schering-Plough*, 2013], **368**

2.3 Italy

Autorità Garante della Concorrenza et del Mercato, decision A431 of 11 January 2012, *Pfizer/Pharmacia*, (only in Italian). Available at: http://www.agcm.it/component/joomdoc/allegati-news/A431_chiusura.pdf/download.html. (last accessed on March 31, 2018) [cited as: Autorità Garante della Concorrenza, decision *Pfizer/Pharmacia*, 2012], **370**

3 Intellectual Property Authorities Decisions

Decision of the UK Intellectual Property Office, BL O/117/16 of 12 January 2016, *Merck Sharp & Dohme Corporation*, by Dr. L Cullen. Available at: https://www.ipo.gov.uk/p-challenge-decision-results/p-challenge-decision-results-bl?BL_Number=O/117/16 (last accessed on March 31, 2018) [cited as: UK Intellectual Property Office, *Merck Sharp & Dohme Corporation*, 2016], **370**

III International and Private Sources

A Reports

AIPLA, Summary of the 2015 Report of the Economic Survey, June 2015. Available at: http://www.aipla.org/about/newsroom/PR/Pages/150728PressRelease.aspx (Last accessed on March 31, 2018). [cited as: AIPLA, Report Summary 2015], **34**

EPO, *Patent Litigation in Europe: An overview of national law and practice in the EPC contracting States*, 4th ed., 2016, pp. 1-138. Available at: https://www.epo.org/learning-events/materials/litigation.html(Last accessed on March 31, 2018). [cited as: EPO, Patent Litigation Overview, 2016], **34**

EvaluatePharma, *World Preview 2018: Embracing the Patent Cliff*, 5th ed., 2012, pp. 1-38. Available at: download.bioon.com.cn/view/upload/201207/04104656_3288.pdf. (last accessed on March 31, 2018). [cited as: EvaluatePharma, *World Preview 2012*], **18,**

EvaluatePharma, *World Preview 2017, Outlook to 2022*, 10th ed., June 2017, pp. 1-41. Available at: https://www.efpia.eu/media/219735/efpia-pharmafigures2017_statisticbroch_v04-final.pdf. (last accessed on March 31, 2018). [cited as: EvaluatePharma, *World Preview 2017*], **17–19**

EvaluatePharma, *World Preview 2016, Outlook to 2022*, 9th ed., September 2016, pp. 1-48. Available at: http://www.evaluategroup.com/public/reports/EvaluatePharma-World-Preview-2016.aspx (Last accessed on March 31, 2018). [cited as: EvaluatePharma, *World Preview 2016*], **17, 18**

EvaluatePharma, *Orphan Drug Report*, 4th ed., February 2017, pp. 1-26. Available at: http://www.evaluategroup.com/public/Reports/EvaluatePharma-Orphan-Drug-Report-2017.aspx (Last accessed on March 31, 2018). [cited as: EvaluatePharma, *Orphan Drug Report* 2017], **70**

Deloitte LLP Centre for Health Solutions, *Measuring the Return from Pharmaceutical Innovation 2015: Transforming R&D Returns in Uncertain Times*, 2015, pp. 1-40. Available at: https://www2.deloitte.com/uk/en/pages/life-sciences-and-healthcare/articles/measuring-return-from-pharmaceutical-innovation.html (Last accessed on March 31, 2018). [cited as: Deloitte LLP, *R&D Returns* 2015], **19**

Table of Cases

Novartis, Annual Report 2017, pp. 1-280. Available at: https://www.novartis.com/investors/novartis-annual-report/novartis-annual-report-2017 (last accessed on March 31, 2018). [cited as: Novartis, *Annual Report* 2017], **13**

Pfizer, Financial Report 2016, pp. 1-142. Available at: https://investors.pfizer.com/financials/annual-reports/default.aspx (last accessed on March 31, 2018). [cited as: Pfizer, *Financial Report* 2016], **13**

WEDA Marjolein, HOEBERT Joëlle, VERVLOET Marcia, MOLTÓ PUIGMARTI Carolina, DAMEN Nikky, MARCHANGE Sascha, LANGEDIJK Joris, LISMAN John, VAN DIJK Liset, *Study on Off-label Use of Medicinal Products in the European Union*, February 2017, pp. 1-193. Available at: http://ec.europa.eu/health/sites/health/files/files/documents/2017_02_28_final_study_report_on_off-label_use_.pdf. Last accessed on March 31, 2018). [cited as: WEDA ET AL., *Study on Off-label Use in the EU*, 2017], **372, 373**

WHO, Report of the Commission on Macroeconomics and Health, *Macroeconomics and Health: Investing in Health for Economic Development*, December 20, 2001, pp. 1-200. Available at: whqlibdoc.who.int/publications/2001/924154550x.pdf (last accessed on March 31, 2018). [cited as: WHO, *Investing in Health*, 2001], **22**

B Websites

Federal Patent Court Website, *About the Court*. Available at: https://www.bundespatentgericht.ch/en/das-gericht/aufgaben-zustaendigkeiten/ (last accessed on March 31, 2018), **32**

Innovative Medicines Initiative Website, *Introducing IMI*. Available at: http://www.imi.europa.eu/content/mission. (last accessed on March 31, 2018), **16**

OECD.Stat Website, *Pharmaceutical Market: Generic Market*, 2016, Available at: http://stats.oecd.org/index.aspx?DataSetCode=HEALTH_STAT (last accessed on March 31, 2018), **29**

UPC Website, *Provisional Application*. Available at: https://www.unified-patent-court.org/news/upc-provisional-application (last accessed on March 31, 2018), **36**

Unified Patent Court Website, *About the UPC*. Available at: https://www.unified-patent-court.org/. (last accessed on March 31, 2018), **36**

Tables of Statutes & Legislation

I U.S. Statutes

A Statutes at Large

Act to Establish the Department of Justice, ch. 150, 16 Stat. 162 (1870), **50**
Biologics Price Competition and Innovation Act, amending 42 U.S.C. Public Health Service Act, Public Law No. 78-410, 58 Stat. 682, Chapter 373 (1944). [cited as: BPCI Act], **205**
Drug Price Competition and Patent Term Restoration Act, Pub. L. No. 98-417, 98 Stat. 1585 (1984). [cited as: Hatch-Waxman Act], **52, 61**
Food and Drug Administration Modernization Act, Public Law 105-115, 111 U.S. 2296, amending the Federal Food, Drug and Cosmetic Act, Title 21 U.S.C. 301: Food and Drugs. [cited as: FD&C Act], **70**
Food and Drug Administration Amendments Act of 2007 (FDAAA), 121 Stat. 823, Public Law 110-85, (September 27, 2007) [cited as: FDAAA], **200**
Medicare Prescription Drug, Improvement, and Modernization Act of 2003, Pub. L. No. 108-173, 117 Stat. 2066, 108th Congress, (2003), codified at 21 U.S.C. § 355(j)(5)(D). [cited as: MMA], **71**
Miller-Tydings Act, 50 Stat. 693 (1937), repealed by the Consumer Goods Pricing Act, 89 Stat. 801, amending 15 U.S.C. § 1, 45(a). [cited as: Miller-Tydings Act], **85**
Orphan Drug Act, Public Law 97-414, 96 Stat. 2049, "An Act to amend the Federal Food, Drug, and Cosmetic Act to facilitate the development of drugs for rare diseases and conditions, and for other purposes," Jan. 4, 1983, amending 21 U.S.C. Chapter 9 §§ 301 et seq., 360aa. [cited as: Orphan Drug Act], **69**
Patient Protection and Affordable Care Act, H.R. 3590, Public Law No: 111-148, 24 Stat. 119 through 124 Stat. 1025, 111th Congress, (2009-2010). [cited as PPACA], **205**
Preserve Access to Affordable Generics Act, S. 316, 110th Cong. (2007), **78**
Preserve Access to Affordable Generics Act, S. 369, 111th Cong. (2009), **78**
Preserve Access to Affordable Generics Act, S. 27, 112th Cong. (2011), **78**
Preserve Access to Affordable Generics Act, S. 214, 113th Cong. (2013), **78**
Protecting Consumers Access to Generic Drugs Act of 2013, H.R. 3709, 113th Cong., (2013-2014), **196**
Public Health Service Act, 58 Stat. 682, Chapter 373; 42 U.S.C., Chapter 6A, **66**

Tables of Statutes & Legislation

Public Health Service Act (PHS Act), Public Law No. 78-410, 58 Stat. 682, Chapter 373 (1944), **205**
Rule 16 of Federal Rules of Civil Procedure [cited as: FED. R. CIV. P. 16], **31, 32**
S.812 – Greater Access to Affordable Pharmaceuticals Act of 2002, 107th Congress (2001-2002), **71**
S. 754 – Drug Competition Act of 2002, 107th Congress, Section 3, (2001-2002), **75**
21 C.F.R. § 312.21, **51**
21 C.F.R. § 314.53, **74**
21 C.F.R. § 314.95, **59**
21 C.F.R. § 314.101, **55**
21 C.F.R. § 314.107, **91**
21 C.F.R. § 314.127, **57**
21 C.F.R. § 314.108, **67, 68**
21 C.F.R. § 316.20, **69**
21 C.F.R. 316.31, **69**
28 C.F.R., Chapter I, Department of Justice (2015), **50**
26 Stat. 209, 15 U.S.C. §§ 1–7 (Sherman Act), **82–86, 89, 92, 101, 103, 104, 106, 113, 132, 143, 146, 152, 155–156, 158, 187, 193, 207, 208, 210, 212, 234, 263, 385**

B U.S. Code

15 U.S.C. §§ 1-2, **83, 143, 155**
15 U.S.C. §§ 12-27, **386**
15 U.S.C. §§ 41-58, **48, 78, 135, 137**
21 U.S.C. § 301, **70**
21 U.S.C. Chapter 9 §§ 301 et seq, **69**
21 U.S.C. § 355, **51, 54–57, 59–61, 63–65, 68, 71–74, 79, 87, 119, 123, 142, 203**
21 U.S.C. § 360, **69**
35 U.S.C. § 102, **112, 116**
35 U.S.C. § 154, **47, 48**
35 U.S.C. § 156, **66, 67**
35 U.S.C. § 271, **53, 58, 74, 196, 197**
35 U.S.C. § 282, **48, 108**
35 U.S.C. § 284, **197**
42 U.S.C. § 262, **205**
308 U.S. 645 et seq. (1938), **31**

II European Union Legislation

A Primary Law

Consolidated version of the Treaty on the Functioning of the European Union, 2016/C 202/1, p. 47-200, Brussels, 7.6.2016, **225, 245, 246, 252, 264–267, 269, 270, 293, 294, 312**

Tables of Statutes & Legislation

Consolidated version of the Treaty on European Union, 2016/C 202/1, p. 13-46, Brussels, 7.6.2016, **239**

Charter of Fundamental Rights of the European Union, OJ C 326, 26.10.2012, p. 391–407, **236, 239**

B   Secondary Law

1   Regulations

EEC Council, Regulation No 17: First Regulation implementing Articles 85 and 86 of the Treaty, Official Journal 013, 21/02/1962, p. 0204-0211, **262**

Regulation No 19/65/EEC of 2 March of the Council on application of Article 85 (3) of the Treaty to certain categories of agreements and concerted practices, OJ 36, 6.3.1965, p. 533-535, **264**

Regulation (EEC) No 2821/71 of the Council of 20 December 1971 on application of Article 85 (3) of the Treaty to categories of agreements, decisions and concerted practices, OJ L 285/46, 29.12.1971, p. 46-48, **264**

Regulation (EEC) No 2349/84 of 23 July 1984 on the application of Article 85 (3) of the Treaty to certain categories of patent licensing agreements, OJ L 113/34, 26.4.1985, p. 34-34, **293**

Council Regulation (EEC) No 1534/91 of 31 May 1991 on the application of Article 85 (3) of the Treaty to certain categories of agreements, decisions and concerted practices in the insurance sector, OJ L 143/1, 7.6.1991, p. 1-3, **264**

Council Regulation (EEC) No 1768/92 of 18 June 1992, concerning the creation of a supplementary protection certificate for medicinal products, OJ L 182/1, 2.7.1992, pp. 1-5, **231**

Commission Regulation (EC) No 240/96 of 31 January 1996 on the application of Article 85 (3) of the Treaty to certain categories of technology transfer agreements, OJ L 31, 9.2.1996, p. 2-13, **293**

Council Regulation (EC) No 1215/1999 of 10 June 1999 amending Regulation No 19/65/EEC on the application of Article 81(3) of the Treaty to certain categories of agreements and concerted practices OJ L 148/1, 15.6.1999, p. 1-4, **264**

Regulation (EC) No 141/2000 of the European Parliament and of the Council of 16 December 1999 on orphan medicinal products, OJ L 18, 22.1.2000, p. 1-5, **232**

Commission Regulation (EC) No 2659/2000 of 29 November 2000 on the application of Article 81(3) of the Treaty to categories of research and development agreements, OJ L 304, 5.12.2000, p. 7-12, **265, 267**

Council Regulation (EC) No 1/2003 of 16 December 2002 on the implementation of the rules on competition laid down in Articles 81 and 82 of the Treaty, OJ L 1/1, 4.1.2003, pp. 1-25, **237**

Regulation (EC) No 726/2004 of the European Parliament and of the Council of 31 March 2004 laying down Community procedures for the authorisation and supervision of medicinal products for human and veterinary use and establishing a European Medicines Agency, OJ L 136/1, 30.04.2004, pp. 1-33, **225, 226**

Commission Regulation (EC) No 772/2004 of 27 April 2004 on the application of Article 81(3) of the Treaty to categories of technology transfer agreements, OJ L 123, 27.4.2004, p. 11-17, **271, 293**

Regulation (EC) No 1901/2006 of the European Parliament and of the Council of 12 December 2006 on medicinal products for paediatric use and amending Regulation (EEC) No 1768/92, OJ L 378/1, 27.12.2006, p. 1-19, **233**

Regulation (EC) No 1902/2006 of the European Parliament and of the Council of 20 December 2006 amending Regulation 1901/2006 on medicinal products for paediatric use, OJ L 378/20, 27.12.2006, p. 20-21, **233**

Council Regulation (EC) No 169/2009 of 26 February 2009 applying rules of competition to transport by rail, road and inland waterway, OJ L 61/1, 5.3.2009, p. 1-5, **265**

Council Regulation (EC) No 246/2009 of 26 February 2009 on the application of Article 81(3) of the Treaty to certain categories of agreements, decisions and concerted practices between liner shipping companies (consortia), OJ L 79/1, 25.3.2009, p. 1-4, **265**

Regulation (EC) No 469/2009 of the European Parliament and of the Council of 6 May 2009, concerning the supplementary protection certificate for medicinal products OJ L 152/1, 16.6.2009, pp. 1-10, **231**

Council Regulation (EC) No 487/2009 of 25 May 2009 on the application of Article 81(3) of the Treaty to certain categories of agreements and concerted practices in the air transport sector, OJ L 148/1, 11.6.2009, p. 1-4, **265**

Commission Regulation (EU) No 267/2010 of 24 March 2010 on the application of Article 101(3) of the Treaty on the Functioning of the European Union to certain categories of agreements, decisions and concerted practices in the insurance sector, OJ L 83/1, 30.3.2010, p. 1-7, **264**

Commission Regulation (EU) No 330/2010 of 20 April 2010 on the application of Article 101(3) of the Treaty on the Functioning of the European Union to categories of vertical agreements and concerted practices, OJ L 102/1, 23.4.2010, p. 1-7, **264, 266**

Commission Regulation (EU) No 461/2010 of 27 May 2010 on the application of Article 101(3) of the Treaty on the Functioning of the European Union to categories of vertical agreements and concerted practices in the motor vehicle sector, OJ L 129/52, 28.5.2010, p. 52-57, **264**

Commission Regulation (EU) No 1217/2010 of 14 December 2010, on the application of Article 101(3) of the Treaty on the Functioning of the European Union to certain categories of research and development agreements, OJ L 335/36, 18.12.2010, p. 36-42, **264–268, 270**

Commission Regulation (EU) No 1218/2010 of 14 December 2010, on the application of Article 101(3) of the Treaty on the Functioning of the European Union to certain categories of specialisation agreements, OJ L 335/47, 18.12.2010, p. 43-47, **264, 265, 269, 270**

Regulation (EU) No 1235/2010 of the European Parliament and of the Council of 15 December 2010, OJ L 348/1, p. 1-16, **224**

Regulation 1027/2012 of the European Parliament and of the Council of 25 October 2012, amending Regulation (EC) No 726/2004 as regards pharmacovigilance, OJ L 316/38, 14.11.2012, p. 38-40, **224**

Regulation (EU) No 1257/2012 of the European Parliament and of the Council of 17 December 2012 implementing enhanced cooperation in the area of the creation of unitary patent protection, OJ L 361, 31.12.2012, p. 1-8, **36, 222**

Council Regulation (EU) No 1260/2012 of 17 December 2012 implementing enhanced cooperation in the area of the creation of unitary patent protection with regard to the applicable translation arrangements, OJ L 361, 31.12.2012, p. 89-92, **36, 222**

Commission Regulation (EU) No 316/2014 of 21 March 2014 on the application of Article 101(3) of the Treaty on the Functioning of the European Union to categories of technology transfer agreements, OJ L 93/17, 28.3.2014, p. 17-23, **264, 265, 270-274, 293**

2 Directives

Directive 2001/20/EC of the European Parliament and of the Council of 4 April 2001, on the approximation of the laws, regulations and administrative provisions of the Member States, relating to the implementation of good clinical practice in the conduct of clinical trials on medicinal products for human use, OJ L 121/34, 1.5.2001, p. 34-44, **233**

Directive 2001/82/EC of the European Parliament and of the Council of 6 November 2001 on the Community code relating to veterinary medicinal products, OJ L 311/1, 28.11.2001, p. 1-66, **233**

Directive 2001/83/EC of the European Parliament and of the Council of 6 November 2001 on the Community code relating to medicinal products for human use, OJ L 311/67, 28.11.2001, p. 67-128, **233**

Directive No. 2004/27/EC of the European Parliament and of the Council of 31 March 2004 amending Directive No. 2001/83/EC on the Community code relating to medicinal products for human use, OJ L 136/34, 30.04.2004, p. 34-57, **297**

Directive 2010/84/EU of the European Parliament and of the Council of 15 December 2010, OJ L 348/74, 31.12.2010, p. 74-99, **224**

Directive 2012/26/EU of the European Parliament and of the Council of 25 October 2012 amending Directive 2001/83/EC as regards pharmacovigilance, OJ L 299/1, 27.10.2012, p. 1-4, **224**

Directive 2014/104/EU of the European Parliament and of the Council of 26 November 2014 on certain rules governing actions for damages under national law for infringements of the competition law provisions of the Member States and of the European Union, OJ L 349/1, 5.12.2014, p. 1-19, **240**

3 Decisions by the Council of the European Union

2011/167/EU: Council Decision of 10 March 2011 authorising enhanced cooperation in the area of the creation of unitary patent protection, OJ L 76, 22.3.2011, p. 53-55, **222**

Tables of Statutes & Legislation

4 National Legislation of European Member States

4.1 Italy

L. n. 79/2014, Conversione in legge, con modificazioni, del decreto-legge 20 marzo 2014, n. 36. Available at: http://www.federalismi.it/nv14/articolo-documento.cfm?Artid = 25047&content = Conversione + in + legge, + con + modificazioni, + del + decreto-legge + 20 + marzo + 2014, + n. + 36&content_author = (last accessed on March 31, 2018), **374**

4.2 United Kingdom

Competition Act of 1998, **235**

III International Conventions, Agreements & Other

Agreement on Trade Related Aspects of Intellectual Property Rights, Including Trade in Counterfeit Goods, Annex 1C of the Marrakesh Agreement Establishing the World Trade Organization, signed in Marrakesh, Morocco on 15 April 1994. [cited as TRIPS Agreement], **220, 319**

Agreement on a Unified Patent Court, OJ C 175, 20.6.2013, p. 1–40, **36, 222, 229**

Convention on the Grant of European Patents (European Patent Convention), 16th Edition, June 2016. Available at: http://www.epo.org/law-practice/legal-texts/epc.html (last accessed on March 31, 2018). [cited as: European Patent Convention], **221, 369**

European Convention for the Protection of Human Rights and Fundamental Freedoms, as amended by Protocols Nos. 11 and 14, Rome, 4.XI.1950, **236**

A Other states

1 Switzerland

1.1 Legislation

Swiss Civil Procedure Code of December 19, 2018, RO 2010 1739, **32**
Federal Act on the Federal Patent Court of March 20, 2009, RO 2010 513, **32**

1.2 Reports

Federal Patent Court, *Annual Report 2016*, Feb. 2, 2017, pp. 1-18. Available at: https://www.bundespatentgericht.ch/en/das-gericht/annual-reports/. (last accessed on March 31, 2018) [cited as: Federal Patent Court, *Annual Report* 2016], **32, 33**

Federal Patent Court, *Annual Report 2015*, Feb. 10, 2016, pp. 1-15. Available at: https://www.bundespatentgericht.ch/en/das-gericht/annual-reports/. (last accessed on March 31, 2018) [cited as: Federal Patent Court, *Annual Report* 2015], **28, 32**

Index

A

Abbreviated New Drug Application (ANDA), 54–65, 67, 68, 72–79, 87–89, 91, 93, 100, 119, 122–124, 142, 147, 149, 164, 172, 177, 179–181, 194, 196, 200, 206, 207, 213, 233
Abuse of dominance, 234, 256, 275, 276, 290–299, 301, 358–364, 366, 369–372, 376
Acquisition, 3, 208, 292–293, 342–348, 356, 360–363, 365, 386
Actavis, 78, 134, 335–341
Adversity, 2, 33, 75–79, 310–311, 322, 381
Ancillary, 84, 150, 271, 375
ANDA. *See* Abbreviated New Drug Application (ANDA)
AndroGel, 142–144, 147, 167, 168
Andrx Pharmaceuticals, 63, 87, 101, 102, 138
Annulment, 224, 364–365
Antitrust immunity, 82, 100, 105, 107, 110–118, 127, 146–147, 163, 174, 214, 376, 378, 379, 383
Appreciable, 254, 257–260, 278, 290, 311, 364
Article 101 TFEU, 219, 220, 240–277, 287, 293, 301, 303, 304, 310, 313, 314, 320, 322, 326, 332, 337, 344, 347, 363, 372, 374, 375, 378

Article 102 TFEU, 155, 219, 220, 234, 239, 275–301, 304, 308, 321, 342, 344, 358–367, 376, 385, 386
Artificial differentiation, 372–375
AstraZeneca, 208, 280, 283, 285, 296–299, 371
Authorised generic (AG), 19, 167, 168, 176–181, 183, 187, 189–193, 196, 213, 341, 345, 348–349, 354, 367, 384
Avastin, 372–375

B

Barrier to entry, 24, 153, 247, 286, 288–289, 292, 304
Beef Industry, 330–331
Benefits of settlements, 7, 9, 11, 30–38, 127, 145
Biosimilar, 28, 204–205, 224, 228, 229
Block Exemption Regulation, 219, 252, 258, 263–275, 293, 301, 358
Bolar exemption, 79, 228–300
Burden of proof, 47, 108, 119, 129, 131, 133, 151, 155, 191, 239, 264, 273, 316, 317, 340, 378

C

Cartes Bancaires, 252–253, 328–330, 349
Circuit split, 81, 130, 132
Citalopram, 314, 315, 318–320, 323, 334

Index

CJEU. *See* Court of Justice of the European Union (CJEU)
Clinical trial, 21, 29, 51, 53, 55–57, 69, 226, 228, 233
Collusion, 75, 97, 330, 333
Compound patent, 2, 62, 63, 103, 220, 313, 319, 359, 360
Consumer harm, 98, 173, 190, 277, 300, 361, 364
Consumer welfare, 24, 25, 39, 40, 96, 114, 128, 173–174, 209, 210, 261, 337
Court of Justice of the European Union (CJEU), 237, 240, 241, 243, 244, 247, 252–253, 255–258, 262, 278, 279, 284, 287, 292, 295–296, 299, 300, 314, 328–329, 331, 338–341, 349, 365, 366, 370, 371, 374–375

D

De minimis, 258–260, 299
Decentralised procedure, 226
Disparaging, 207, 366–369
Dissenting opinion, 117, 126, 141, 170–173, 190
Distribution, 3, 84, 109, 142, 166, 195, 199–202, 211, 215, 238, 241, 261, 266, 268, 269, 271, 272, 283–285, 304, 312, 345, 348, 353, 354, 356, 357, 359, 381, 382, 384
Divisional patent, 366–372
DoJ. *See* US Department of Justice (DoJ)
Dominance, 219, 256, 275–299, 303, 358–365, 369–372
Doryx, 210–212
Drug development, 13–15, 56
Drug entry to the market, 2, 45, 51–52, 217, 219

E

Entry of pharmaceuticals, 8, 45, 219, 224–234

EPC. *See* European Patent Convention (EPC)
EPO. *See* European Patent Office (EPO)
European Commission (EC), 4, 8, 219, 226, 237, 248, 277, 296, 300, 303, 308, 311, 312, 314–316, 318, 324, 342, 345, 375, 384
European Patent Convention (EPC), 220–224, 231, 300
European Patent Office (EPO), 220–224, 318, 340, 349, 352, 369–371
Evergreening, 18, 21, 62–63, 206, 344, 385
Exception, 17, 20, 34, 43, 48, 53, 65, 78, 101, 110, 113, 138, 163, 171, 223, 235, 241, 260–263, 266, 268, 293, 299, 333, 352, 353, 356, 359, 368, 388
Exclusivity, 19, 21, 25, 26, 46, 47, 54, 55, 57, 59–61, 63–65, 67–73, 75–79, 87, 89, 91, 92, 94, 98, 103, 122–124, 130, 136, 142, 149, 177, 178, 180, 181, 183, 187, 188, 190–192, 195, 196, 202, 209, 213, 224, 227–229, 231–234, 300, 319, 351, 384

F

FDA. *See* Food and Drug Administration (FDA)
Federal Food, Drug, and Cosmetic Act (FD&C Act), 52, 66, 70
Federal Trade Commission (FTC), 8, 38, 45, 48–50, 53, 71, 73, 78, 79, 82, 93, 95, 104, 105, 110, 120, 127, 129–137, 139, 314, 337
Fentanyl, 312–314
Food and Drug Administration (FDA), 16, 17, 27, 44–46, 51, 53–57, 59–64, 66–75, 78, 80, 87–89, 92–94, 135, 142, 149, 176, 182, 194, 200, 201, 203–207, 211, 213, 231

Forgiveness of damages, 141, 195–199, 215
FTC. *See* Federal Trade Commission (FTC)
FTC v. *Actavis*, 4, 8, 41, 49, 78, 79, 81, 82, 87, 95, 124, 130, 134, 138–215, 303, 317, 321, 322, 325–327, 336–338, 376, 378, 379, 383, 384
FTC v. *Endo*, 213
FTC v. *Watson*, 76, 95, 100, 102, 105, 122, 123, 125, 130, 134, 142–146, 148, 149,

G

Greater Access to Affordable Pharmaceuticals Act (GAAP), 71
Generic entry, 1–4, 6–8, 11, 19, 25–30, 39, 40, 45, 53, 56, 58, 59, 64, 72, 75–77, 79, 80, 89–91, 100–102, 115, 120, 127, 131–134, 136, 138, 140, 141, 143, 144, 155, 160, 163–169, 174, 176, 177, 179–181, 183, 189, 191, 193–195, 200, 202, 203, 206, 209, 211, 213–215, 230, 283, 296, 300, 301, 303–389
Generic penetration, 26–29, 309
Generic substitution, 26, 27, 29, 46, 160, 178, 200, 203–211, 213, 296, 309, 310, 344, 351, 366–368, 385
Geographic market, 86, 151, 256, 284–286, 359
Government-funded, 15–16
Grey zone, 381

H

Hard product switch, 208–210, 344, 366–367, 385
Hatch-Waxman Act, 2, 3, 7, 25, 41, 43, 45, 52–67, 71, 75, 77–80, 90, 98, 121–123, 136, 137, 141, 148–149, 172, , 175, 177, 178, 201, 202, 204, 228, 233, 301, 310, 378

Health expenditures, 43, 307–311, 377
Horizontal, 84–86, 92–94, 135–136, 140, 174, 240, 251, 254, 258–260, 265–266, 272, 275, 303

I

In re *Aggrenox*, 162, 166, 167, 176, 186, 189, 190, 193
In re *Cardizem*, 86, 87, 96, 99
In re *Cipro*, 65, 73, 76, 77, 98, 100, 102, 103, 106, 108, 109, 121–124, 126, 127, 136, 146, 150, 155, 161, 164, 166, 167, 169, 173, 174, 191
In re *Effexor*, 183, 184, 189, 193, 198, 199
In re *K-Dur*, 81, 82, 129, 132, 151
In re *Lamictal*, 186–188
In re *Lipitor*, 176, 183–186, 193, 197–199
In re *Loestrin*, 148, 166, 172, 180, 182, 184–186
In re *Nexium*, 161, 162, 178, 186, 189
In re *Niaspan*, 166, 167, 176, 186, 189, 192, 197
In re *Schering-Plough*, 76, 93, 129, 135, 138, 165
In re *Tamoxifen*, 64, 65, 73, 76, 77, 101–104, 106, 109, 110, 112, 117–128, 136, 146, 149
Innovation, 6, 7, 9, 11–25, 29, 36, 38–40, 52, 69, 79, 82, 95–98, 107, 113, 117, 125, 127–128, 139, 172, 174, 210, 212, 226, 232, 254, 266, 274, 299, 300, 370, 377, 379

J

Judicial preference, 121–128, 138
Jury trial, 35
Justification, 83, 86, 93, 97, 129, 133, 140, 147, 149–151, 154, 163–170, 175, 191, 215, 263, 299–300, 331–335, 337, 338, 356–358, 380, 387

Index

K

King Drug, 123, 191

L

Licensing, 3, 16, 102, 110, 135–137, 139, 145, 150, 163, 181, 193, 194, 256, 267, 269–272, 274, 293–296, 312, 341, 345, 355, 358, 369, 372, 374–376, 382–384

Litigation costs, 1, 33, 34, 39, 95, 121, 133, 154, 155, 161, 163–166, 168, 169, 173, 174, 184, 198, 334, 337, 338, 356, 357, 380–382, 387

Lucentis, 372–375

Lundbeck, 8, 140, 217, 252, 265, 285, 303, 311, 312, 314–342, 345, 346, 349, 350, 365, 376, 378, 379

M

Market definition, 159, 161–162, 279–286, 288, 301, 350

Market power, 22, 64, 67, 83, 91, 121, 145, 147, 153, 155–162, 208, 215, 254, 259, 260, 266, 271, 275, 276, 280, 281, 286–290, 293, 342, 350, 358, 363

Market share, 26, 27, 41, 87, 91–92, 153, 157, 159, 161, 197, 206, 257, 259, 260, 268, 269, 271, 284, 286–290, 309, 312, 348, 349, 351, 360, 367, 368, 370, 384

Marketing authorisation, 13, 30, 219, 224–229, 231–233, 285, 296, 297, 300, 301, 318, 340, 342, 354–356, 372–375

Medicare Prescription Drug, Improvement and Modernization Act (MMA), 62, 64, 71–75, 79, 179, 194, 202

Modafinil, 312–314

Monopoly, 2, 3, 12, 26, 29, 30, 39, 40, 53, 64, 76, 91–92, 94, 98, 99, 104, 109, 110, 114, 115, 117, 120, 122–124, 126, 135, 137, 139, 143, 145, 147, 148, 150, 158, 163, 171–173, 181, 185, 189–195, 202, 211–213, 215, 276, 280, 287, 292, 308, 309, 321, 331, 356, 358, 359, 363, 365, 378, 379, 384, 386, 388

Mutual recognition, 225–227, 300

Mylan Pharmaceuticals Inc. v. Warner Chilcott, 204, 207, 208, 210–212, 385

N

Naked restraint, 82–84, 93, 96, 133

Naming and shaming, 275, 368–369

National Competition Enforcement Authorities (NCAs), 235–236, 270

NDAs. *See* New Drug Applications (NDAs)

New Chemical Entity Exclusivity, 54, 55, 67–68

New Clinical Studies Exclusivity, 55, 57, 68–69

New Drug Applications (NDAs), 45, 46, 51, 52, 54, 55, 59, 61, 62, 66, 68, 70, 74, 142, 176

New Molecular Entities (NMEs), 17, 43, 44, 54

New York v. Actavis PLC, 207–210, 212, 385

No-authorized generic (No-AG) Commitment, 3, 139, 141, 166, 176–194, 213–215, 382, 384

Non-cash payment, 141, 175–194, 198, 215

Non-challenge, 273, 275, 304, 348, 351–353, 355, 357, 363, 387

Non-compete, 304, 341, 348, 351–354, 356–358

Index

Non-infringement, 37, 38, 58, 60, 64, 74, 111, 112, 119–121, 133, 142, 147, 190, 193, 199, 225, 310, 311, 316, 317, 324, 337, 339, 347, 352, 379, 384
Novartis, 13, 312, 313, 372–375

O

Off-label use, 69, 70, 372–374
180-day exclusivity, 25, 57, 59–61, 63–65, 72–73, 75–79, 88, 89, 91, 94, 98, 103–105, 122–124, 136, 149, 164, 177, 178, 180, 181, 187, 190, 192, 195, 196, 214, 234, 384
Opana ER, 213, 214
Opposition procedure, 223, 224
Orange Book, 46, 56, 58, 61, 74–75, 203, 204, 206
Orphan drug, 44, 55, 69–71, 232, 300

P

PAAG. See Preserve Access to Affordable Generic Act (PAAG)
Paediatric exclusivity, 70, 71, 233
Paragraph IV ANDA, 52, 58–65, 67, 68, 72, 73, 75–77, 87–89, 91, 119, 122–124, 147, 149, 164, 172, 179, 180, 194, 196, 207, 213
Patent cliff, 11, 12, 18–19, 209, 212
Patent grant, 48, 107, 109, 112, 116, 118, 219–224, 318, 321, 379
Patent infringement, 1–3, 6, 15, 30, 31, 33–38, 40, 49, 58, 60, 61, 64, 65, 71, 74, 75, 77–79, 82, 87–90, 94, 96, 97, 99, 100, 104, 105, 107, 109, 111, 114–122, 126, 127, 129, 131, 133–135, 138–140, 142–145, 149, 150, 164, 166, 167, 169–172, 174, 190, 194, 196, 206, 228, 234, 294, 316–318, 326, 333, 334, 336, 338–341, 345, 378–380, 382
Patent invalidation, 2, 3, 33, 36–38, 40, 47, 48, 58, 73, 76, 87, 100, 105, 110–112, 117, 119–121, 124, 142, 147, 154, 169, 170, 172, 190, 193, 199, 224, 310, 311, 316, 339, 353, 384
Patent term, 23, 52, 66–67, 119, 144, 164, 231, 233, 300, 322, 345, 387
Patentability, 20, 222–223, 304, 305
Pay-for-delay, 1, 49, 63, 78, 98, 127, 146, 151, 164, 166, 175, 179, 185, 190, 194, 252, 274, 312, 314, 337, 342, 375
Per se illegal, 3–4, 8, 41, 81–100, 106, 129, 130, 140, 150, 154, 158, 249, 263, 277
Perindopril, 342, 344, 347–356, 358–365
Pfizer, 13, 197, 198, 284, 308, 370–372
Pfizer/Pharmacia, 284
Plavix, 367, 368
Poison-pill clause, 77, 141, 195–196, 215
Potential competition, 24, 246–247, 254, 279, 317–318, 337, 347, 350, 361, 386
Preserve Access to Affordable Generic Act (PAAG), 78, 79, 165
Presumption of patent validity, 104, 107–110, 118, 137, 315–316, 338, 378
Price fixing, 84, 85, 106, 110, 251, 263, 269
Pricing, 16, 39, 178, 219, 229–230, 280, 281, 285, 292, 308, 309, 372
Prima facie, 47, 81, 82, 87, 90–92, 133, 134, 137–138, 140, 153, 155, 225, 277
Probabilistic, 116
Product reformulation, 3, 19, 202–214, 385
Product switch, 3, 207–214, 297, 344, 366–367, 385
Product-hopping, 18, 19, 140, 195, 202–215, 234, 296, 297, 366, 376, 385
Promotion, 3, 30, 126, 139, 143, 166, 167, 203, 213, 214, 313, 375, 381, 382, 385

Public interest, 31, 40, 69, 105, 126–127, 149–150, 274, 295, 300, 315, 321, 379

Q

Quick-look, 4, 8, 41, 82, 128, 134–139, 141, 150–152, 154

R

R&D. *See* Research and Development (R&D)
R&D expenditures, 12–14
R&D performance, 11, 16–19
Reasonableness, 117, 141, 152, 154, 215, 255, 337, 377, 380, 389
Reckitt Benckiser, 366–369
Reimbursement, 12, 29, 120, 165, 219, 229–231, 280, 285, 309, 367, 368, 372, 381
Relevant market, 25, 39, 69, 121, 135, 137, 155–162, 208, 211, 212, 215, 238, 246, 253, 254, 256, 257, 259, 261, 269, 278–283, 286, 287, 291, 292, 303, 309, 329, 350–351, 359–361, 365, 366, 368, 370, 371, 374
REMS. *See* Risk Evaluation and Mitigation Strategies (REMS)
Research and Development (R&D), 7, 11–41, 52, 66, 69, 78, 98, 114, 127, 228, 230, 264, 266–268, 273, 319
Restricted drug distribution, 3, 142, 199–202, 215
Restriction by object, 249–253, 263, 322, 324–325, 328, 331, 336, 338, 345, 349, 365, 374–375
Restriction by effect, 219, 254, 301
Reverse payment, 1–8, 41, 49, 72, 75, 77–141, 143, 144, 146–156, 158–166, 168–170, 172–175, 180–188, 191, 192, 194, 195, 198, 199, 213–215, 217, 219, 220, 234, 235, 247, 249, 265, 275, 301, 303, 310, 311, 315, 316, 320–329, 332–340, 343, 344, 347, 350, 356, 358–360, 365, 375, 377–379, 381–383, 386–388
Risk asymmetry, 332
Risk Evaluation and Mitigation Strategies (REMS), 200–202
Roche, 372–374
Roche/Novartis, 372–375
Rule of reason, 4, 8, 41, 78, 81–86, 96, 97, 100, 106, 116, 128–130, 138–141, 148, 150–155, 161, 163, 170, 172, 183, 188, 191, 192, 198, 208, 210, 214, 215, 234, 249, 255–256, 337, 381, 384

S

SANOFI-AVENTIS/ZENTIVA, 282, 283
SANOFI/SYNTHELABO, 283
Scope of the patent test, 4, 8, 41, 81, 82, 99–131, 134, 137, 138, 140, 141, 143–151, 153, 158, 168, 170, 171, 174, 214, 318–322, 337, 339, 350, 376–379
Second generation, 19, 344
Secondary patent, 2, 62, 100, 118, 135, 220
Section 505(b)(2) applications, 54–55
Section viii Statement, 57
Sector inquiry, 303–307, 311
SEP. *See* Standard Essential Patent (SEP)
Servier, 252, 265, 285, 286, 303, 311, 312, 341–366, 376, 384, 386
Sham, 62–63, 99, 101, 104–105, 120, 171, 202, 210, 304
Sherman Act, 82, 83, 85, 89, 92, 101, 103, 104, 113, 132, 143, 152, 155–156, 158, 187, 207, 212, 234, 263, 385

Side deal, 3, 130, 166–168, 185, 213, 215, 305, 312, 341, 345–349, 376, 381–383, 386, 387
Size of the payment, 102, 119–121, 129, 147, 161, 164–166, 172, 175
Social cost, 7, 9, 11, 23, 31, 38–40, 96, 114
Soft product switch, 207–214, 385
SPCs. *See* Supplementary Protection Certificates (SPCs)
SSNIP test, 279–280, 285
Standard Essential Patent (SEP), 294–296
Supplementary Protection Certificates (SPCs), 219, 221, 228, 231, 233, 270, 275, 296, 319, 370
Supreme Court, 4, 8, 58, 78, 81, 82, 85, 86, 95, 99, 106, 110, 113, 121, 124–126, 130, 132, 134, 137, 138, 140–142, 145–164, 166, 168–170, 172–174, 183, 185–188, 191, 198, 201, 208, 214, 215, 303, 317, 322, 326, 327, 336–338, 340, 369, 378–381

T

Technology acquisition, 342–344, 362
Technology transfer, 265, 270–275, 357–359, 361
Technology Transfer Block Exemption Regulation (TTBER), 270–274, 358
Temporal market, 286
Teva, 167, 168, 183, 187–188, 190, 192, 193, 208, 312–315, 343, 348, 349, 352, 354, 356
TEVA/BARR, 282, 283
30-month stay, 57, 60–63, 78, 80, 88, 124, 149, 194, 202, 206

Treaty on the Functioning of the European Union (TFEU), 155, 219, 220, 234–301, 303, 304, 308, 310, 312–314, 317, 320–323, 326, 327, 329, 331–338, 341, 342, 344–345, 347, 356–367, 372, 374–376, 378, 385, 386
Three-step test, 101
Transfer of value, 183, 184, 188, 314, 320, 323, 325, 327, 328, 356
Truncated, 95, 97, 128–130, 132, 138
TTBER. *See* Technology Transfer Block Exemption Regulation (TTBER)

U

US Department of Justice (DoJ), 45, 50, 82, 95, 126, 127, 129–134, 141
Uncertainty, 3–4, 31, 33, 35–38, 79, 112, 117, 124, 125, 134, 139, 165, 166, 169, 182, 228, 247–248, 327–331, 337, 339, 341, 349, 371, 373, 375, 379, 380
United States Patent and Trademark Office (USPTO), 35, 47–48, 109, 111, 112, 142

V

Valley Drug, 99, 101, 102, 105, 106, 117
Vertical, 84–86, 95, 240, 251, 258, 264, 266, 272

W

Watson, 105, 142, 143, 213

X

Xalatan, 370, 371

INTERNATIONAL COMPETITION LAW SERIES

1. Ignacio De Leon, *Latin American Competition Law and Policy: A Policy in Search of Identity*, 2001 (ISBN 90-411-1542-0).
2. Wim Dejonghe & Wouter Van de Voorde (eds), *M & A in Belgium*, 2001 (ISBN 90-411-1594-3).
3. Yang-Ching Chao, Gee San, Changfa Lo & Jiming Ho (eds), *International and Comparative Competition Law and Policies*, 2001 (ISBN 90-411-1643-5).
4. Martin Mendelsohn & Stephen Rose, *Guide to the EC Block Exemption for Vertical Agreements*, 2002 (ISBN 90-411-9813-X).
5. Clifford A. Jones & Mitsuo Matsushita (eds), *Competition Policy in the Global Trading System: Perspectives from the EU, Japan and the USA*, 2002 (ISBN 90-411-1758-X).
6. Christian Koenig, Andreas Bartosch, Jens-Daniel Braun & Marion Romes (eds), *EC Competition and Telecommunications Law*. Second Edition, 2009 (ISBN 978-90-411-2564-4).
7. Jürgen Basedow (ed.), *Limits and Control of Competition with a View to International Harmonization*, 2002 (ISBN 90-411-1967-1).
8. Maureen Brunt, Economic Essays on Australian and New Zealand Competition Law, 2003 (ISBN 90-411-1991-4).
9. Ky P. Ewing, Jr., *Competition Rules for the 21st Century: Principles from America's Experience*, Second Edition, 2006 (ISBN 90-411-2477-2).
10. Joseph Wilson, *Globalization and the Limits of National Merger Control Laws*, 2003 (ISBN 90-411-1996-5).
11. Peter Verloop & Valérie Landes (eds), *Merger Control in Europe: EU, Member States and Accession States*, Fourth Edition, 2003 (ISBN 90-411-2056-4).
12. Themistoklis K. Giannakopoulos, *Safeguarding Companies' Rights in Competition and Anti-dumping/Anti-subsidies Proceedings*, Second Edition, 2011 (ISBN 978-90-411-3404-2).
13. Marjorie Holmes & Lesley Davey (eds), *A Practical Guide to National Competition Rules across Europe*, Second Edition, 2007 (ISBN 978-90-411-2607-8).
14. Sigrid Stroux, *US and EU Oligopoly Control*, 2004 (ISBN 90-411-2296-6).
15. Tzong-Leh Hwang and Chiyuan Chen (eds), *The Future Development of Competition Framework*, 2004 (ISBN 90-411-2305-9).

16. Phedon Nicolaides, Mihalis Kekelekis and Maria Kleis, *State Aid Policy in the European Community: Principles and Practice*, Second Edition, 2008 (ISBN 978-90-411-2754-9).
17. Doris Hildebrand, *Economic Analyses of Vertical Agreements: A Self- Assessment*, 2005 (ISBN 90-411-2328-8).
18. Frauke Henning-Bodewig, *Unfair Competition Law: European Union and Member States*, 2005 (ISBN 90-411-2329-6).
19. Duarte Brito & Margarida Catalão-Lopes, *Mergers and Acquisitions: The Industrial Organization Perspective*, 2006 (ISBN 90-411-2451-9).
20. Nikos Th. Nikolinakos, *EU Competition Law and Regulation in the Converging Telecommunications, Media and IT Sectors*, 2006 (ISBN 90-411- 2469-1).
21. Mihalis Kekelekis, *The EC Merger Control Regulation: Rights of Defence. A Critical Analysis of DG COMP Practice and Community Courts' Jurisprudence*, 2006 (ISBN 90-411-2553-1).
22. Mark R. Joelson, *An International Antitrust Primer: A Guide to the Operation of United States, European Union and Other Key Competition Laws in the Global Economy*, Third Edition, 2006 (ISBN 90-411-2468-3).
23. Themistoklis K. Giannakopoulos, *A Concise Guide to the EU Anti-dumping/Anti-subsidies Procedures*, 2006 (ISBN 90-411-2464-0).
24. George Cumming, Brad Spitz & Ruth Janal, *Civil Procedure Used for Enforcement of EC Competition Law by the English, French and German Civil Courts*, 2007 (ISBN 978-90-411-2471-5).
25. Jürgen Basedow (ed.), *Private Enforcement of EC Competition Law*, 2007 (ISBN 978-90-411-2613-9).
26. Jung Wook Cho, *Innovation and Competition in the Digital Network Economy: A Legal and Economic Assessment on Multi-tying Practices and Network Effects*, 2007 (ISBN 978-90-411-2574-3).
27. Akira Inoue, *Japanese Antitrust Law Manual: Law, Cases and Interpretation of the Japanese Antimonopoly Act*, 2007 (ISBN 978-90-411-2627-6).
28. René Barents, *Directory of EC Case Law on Competition*, 2007 (ISBN 978-90-411-2656 6).
29. Paul F. Nemitz (ed.), *The Effective Application of EU State Aid Procedures: The Role of National Law and Practice*, 2007 (ISBN 978-90-411-2657-3).
30. Jurian Langer, *Tying and Bundling as a Leveraging Concern under EC Competition Law*, 2007 (ISBN 978-90-411-2575-0).
31. Abel M. Mateus & Teresa Moreira (eds), *Competition Law and Economics – Advances in Competition Policy and Antitrust Enforcement*, 2007 (ISBN 978-90-411-2632-0).
32. Alberto Santa Maria, *Competition and State Aid: An Analysis of the EC Practice*, 2007 (ISBN 978-90-411-2617-7).
33. Barry J. Rodger (ed.), *Article 234 and Competition Law: An Analysis*, 2007 (ISBN 978-90-411-2605-4).

34. Alla Pozdnakova, *Liner Shipping and EU Competition Law*, 2008 (ISBN 978-90-411-2717-4).
35. Milena Stoyanova, *Competition Problems in Liberalized Telecommunications: Regulatory Solutions to Promote Effective Competition*, 2008 (ISBN 978-90-411-2736-5).
36. *EC State Aid Law/Le Droit des Aides d'Etat dans la CE. Liber Amicorum Francisco Santaolalla Gadea*, 2008 (ISBN 978-90-411-2774-7).
37. René Barents, *Directory of EC Case Law on State Aids*, 2008 (ISBN 978-90-411-2732-7).
38. Ignacio De Leon, *An Institutional Assessment of Antitrust Policy: The Latin American Experience*, 2009 (ISBN 978-90-411-2478-4).
39. Doris Hildebrand, *The Role of Economic Analysis in EU Competition Law: TheEuropean School*, Fourth Edition, 2016 (ISBN 978-90-411-6245-8).
40. Eugène Buttigieg, *Competition Law: Safeguarding the Consumer Interest. A Comparative Analysis of US Antitrust Law and EC Competition Law*, 2009 (ISBN 978-90-411-3119-5).
41. Ioannis Lianos & Ioannis Kokkoris (eds), *The Reform of EC Competition Law: New Challenges*, 2010 (ISBN 978-90-411-2692-4).
42. George Cumming & Mirjam Freudenthal, *Civil Procedure in EU Competition Cases before the English and Dutch Courts*, 2010 (ISBN 978-90-411-3192-8).
43. A.E. Rodriguez & Ashok Menon, *The Limits of Competition Policy: The Shortcomings of Antitrust in Developing and Reforming Economies*, 2010 (ISBN 978-90-411-3177-5).
44. Mika Oinonen, *Does EU Merger Control Discriminate against Small Market Companies? Diagnosing the Argument with Conclusions*, 2010 (ISBN 978-90-411-3261-1).
45. Eirik Østerud, *Identifying Exclusionary Abuses by Dominant Undertakings under EU Competition Law: The Spectrum of Tests*, 2010 (ISBN 978-90-411-3271-0).
46. Marco Botta, *Merger Control Regimes in Emerging Economies: A Case Study on Brazil and Argentina*, 2011 (ISBN 978-90-411-3402-8).
47. Jürgen Basedow & Wolfgang Wurmnest (eds), *Structure and Effects in EU Competition Law: Studies on Exclusionary Conduct and State Aid*, 2011 (ISBN 978-90-411-3174-4).
48. George Cumming (ed.), *Merger Decisions and the Rules of Procedure of the European Community Courts*, 2012 (ISBN 978-90-411-3671-8).
49. Eduardo Molan Gaban & Juliana Oliveira Domingues (eds), *Antitrust Law in Brazil: Fighting Cartels*, 2012 (ISBN 978-90-411-3670-1).
50. Giandonato Caggiano, Gabriella Muscolo & Marina Tavassi (eds), *Competition Law and Intellectual Property: A European Perspective*, 2012 (ISBN 978-90-411-3447-9).
51. Ben Van Rompuy, *Economic Efficiency: The Sole Concern of Modern Antitrust Policy? Non-efficiency Considerations under Article 101 TFEU*, 2012 (ISBN 978-90-411-3870-5).

52. Liyang Hou, *Competition Law and Regulation of the EU Electronic Communications Sector: A Comparative Legal Approach*, 2012 (ISBN 978-90-411-4047-0).
53. Barry Rodger, *Landmark Cases in Competition Law: Around the World in Fourteen Stories*, 2012 (ISBN 978-90-411-3843-9).
54. Andreas Scordamaglia-Tousis, *EU Cartel Enforcement: Reconciling Effective Public Enforcement with Fundamental Rights*, 2013 (ISBN 978-90-411-4758-5).
55. Bernardo Cortese (ed.), *EU Competition Law: Between Public and Private Enforcement*, 2014 (ISBN 978-90-411-4677-9).
56. Barry Rodger (ed.), *Competition Law: Comparative Private Enforcement and Collective Redress across the EU*, 2014 (ISBN 978-90-411-4559-8).
57. Nada Ina Pauer, *The Single Economic Entity Doctrine and Corporate Group Responsibility in European Antitrust Law*, 2014 (ISBN 978-90-411-5262-6).
58. Urška Petrovčič, *Competition Law and Standard Essential Patents: A Transatlantic Perspective*, 2014 (ISBN 978-90-411-4960-2).
59. David Telyas, *The Interface between Competition Law, Patents and Technical Standards*, 2014 (ISBN 978-90-411-5418-7).
60. Katerina Maniadaki, *EU Competition Law, Regulation and the Internet: The Case of Net Neutrality*, 2014 (ISBN 978-90-411-4140-8).
61. Horacio Vedia Jerez, *Competition Law Enforcement and Compliance across the World: A Comparative Review*, 2015 (ISBN 978-90-411-5815-4).
62. Kadir Ba, *The Substantive Appraisal of Joint Ventures under the EU Merger Control Regime*, 2015 (ISBN 978-90-411-5816-1).
63. Alberto Santa Maria, *Competition and State Aid: An Analysis of the EU Practice*, Second Edition, 2015 (ISBN 978-90-411-5818-5).
64. Lúcio Tomé Feteira, *The Interplay between European and National Competition Law after Regulation 1/2003: "United (Should) We Stand?"*, 2016 (ISBN 978-90-411-5663-1).
65. Giovanni Pitruzzella & Gabriella Muscolo (eds), *Competition and Patent Law in the Pharmaceutical Sector: An International Perspective*, 2016 (ISBN 978-90-411-5927-4).
66. Małgorzata Cyndecka, *The Market Economy Investor Test in EU State Aid Law: Applicability and Application*, 2016 (ISBN 978-90-411-6102-4).
67. Damiano Canapa, *Trademarks and Brands in Merger Control: An Analysis of the European and Swiss Legal Orders*, 2016 (ISBN 978-90-411-6717-0).
68. Inge Graef, *EU Competition Law, Data Protection and Online Platforms: Data as Essential Facility*, 2016 (ISBN 978-90-411-8324-8).
69. Anders Jessen, *Exclusionary Abuse after the* Post Danmark I *Case: The Role of the Effects-Based Approach under Article 102 TFEU*, 2017 (ISBN 978-90-411-8996-7).
70. Baskaran Balasingham, *The EU Leniency Policy: Reconciling Effectiveness and Fairness*, 2017 (ISBN 978-90-411-8479-5).
71. Eugene Stuart & Iana Roginska-Green, *Sixty Years of EU State Aid Law and Policy: Analysis and Assessment*, 2018 (ISBN 978-90-411-8869-4).

72. Anna Renata Pisarkiewicz, *Margin Squeeze in the Electronic Communications Sector: Critical Analysis of the Decisional Practice and Case Law,* 2018 (ISBN 978-90-411-6246-5).
73. Ploykaew Porananond, *Competition Law in the ASEAN Countries: Regional Law and National Systems,* 2018 (ISBN 978-90-411-9102-1).
74. Corinne Ruechardt, *EU State Aid Control of Infrastructure Funding,* 2018 (ISBN 978-90-411-9099-4).
75. Amalia Athanasiadou, *Patent Settlements in the Pharmaceutical Industry under US Antitrust and EU Competition Law,* 2018 (ISBN 978-94-035-0113-0).